# THE LITERATURE OF
# THE JEWISH PEOPLE

EMIL SCHÜRER

# THE LITERATURE OF
# THE JEWISH PEOPLE
## IN THE TIME OF JESUS

*Edited with an Introduction by*
*Nahum N. Glatzer*

SCHOCKEN BOOKS · NEW YORK

First SCHOCKEN edition 1972

Copyright © 1972 by Schocken Books Inc.
Library of Congress Catalog Card No. 72–80038
*Translated by Rev. Peter Christie and Sophia Taylor*
Manufactured in the United States of America

# CONTENTS

# PUBLISHER'S NOTE

In 1961 Schocken Books published a new edition in one volume of Emil Schürer's political history of Palestine, from 175 B.C. to A.D. 135, i.e., The "First Division" of the original *The Jewish People in the Time of Jesus Christ* in the authorized English translation. The success of this edition prompted us to publish Schürer's volume III (§32, 33, 34) of the "Second Division," comprising the Jewish literature of the period. The text is unabridged. Added are an introduction and a bibliography on the Apocrypha, 1900–1970. Some misprints have been corrected. The translator's spelling of names (influenced by Schürer's German spelling) has been retained.

# INTRODUCTION

*I*

Emil Schürer (1844–1910), outstanding German academic
teacher, author of numerous studies, and editor of the prestigi-
ous *Theologische Literaturzeitung,* is best known for his monu-
mental *History of the Jewish People in the Time of Jesus
Christ.* This *History* was the first attempt to present a political,
religious, and literary history of Judaism in the centuries preceding the rise of Christianity and up to the Bar Kokhba
rebellion. A revised (second) edition of a text originally published in 1874 appeared in 1886 (vol. II) and 1890 (vol. I);
a still further revised and expanded (three volumes) edition in
1898–1902, and again in 1907–11. An authorized English translation (in five volumes) by John Macpherson (vols. I–II) and
Sophia Taylor and Peter Christie (vols. III–V) appeared in
Edinburgh in 1886–90, based on the second German edition of
the work. The last of the eleven reissues of the translation came
out in 1924. The *History* was divided into two "divisions," the
first comprising volumes I and II of the English edition ("Political History of Palestine"), the second consisting of volumes
III–V ("Internal Conditions, and of the Jewish People"). In
his work, Schürer applied modern methods of historic research,
a commitment that did not, however, free him from religious
bias.

## II

The pages that follow proffer information on some of the major revisions and additions Schürer made in the later editions of his German text. In addition, he enriched his extensive bibliographies and briefly discussed new insights by other scholars. References to revisions are followed by a brief account of post-Schürer research, wherever applicable.

In the section on *Jesus the Son of Sirach* (*Ben Sira*) (pp. 23–30), Schürer added a comment on the wisdom teacher's piety, to wit: It is vital, sound piety that molds his practical sagacity. True wisdom comes from God. The divine order is manifested in creation; the same wise order is continued in God's rule of the world (39:12–35). Happy is the man who trusts in Him; such a man is steadfast in suffering (2:1–18), courageous, and devoid of fear in all circumstances (31:13–20). Thus fear of the Lord is the highest rung of wisdom.

Though this piety is magnanimous, Schürer opines, it bears the specifically Israelitish features. Wisdom dwells in the people of Israel (24:8 ff.) and is expressed in the Law of Moses (24:23 ff.). Therefore the emphasis on observance (2:16) and knowledge of the Law (35:24–36:6), therefore the high position of the scribe (38:24–39:11). The temple cult, too, is significant (45:6–22). With fervor Ben Sira describes at length the high-priestly service of Simon (50).

Schürer ascribes this interest in the legitimate high priesthood to the incipient Hellenism in Judaea. Belonging to the men of tradition, Ben Sira laments the neglect of the Law by the godless (41:8). Though the priestly aristocracy is becoming increasingly hellenized, Ben Sira nevertheless hopes for the victory of the legitimate heirs of Zadok.

The unexpected discovery (in 1896 and shortly after) of fragments of a Hebrew text of the book in the Cairo *genizah* [1] was viewed as a most significant event for Judaic scholarship.

Following S. Schechter, Schürer offers a description of the leaves, the editions, and the scholarly discussions about the issue of originality of the Hebrew text. He did not venture beyond the technical aspects of the Hebrew *Ben Sira* and avoided a literary evaluation.

C. C. Torrey questioned the belief, common at the time, that the fragments are surviving portions of the original Hebrew text. The "second rate" Hebrew suggested to him rather an attempt of a reconstruction based mainly on the Syriac version.[2] The *Ben Sira* research has been given a solid foundation by the critical and thoroughly annotated edition of the Hebrew fragments by M. Z. Segal. In the introduction Segal analyzes our fragments and the Hebrew versions on which both the Greek and the Syriac translations are based. He finds that all texts were corrupt, including the one that was used by Sira's grandson, who produced the first Greek translation.[3] Despite the difficulties presented by this circumstance, Segal succeeded in creating a highly workable tool for all further investigation of this apocryphon.

Following the chapter on *The Book of Tobit* (pp. 37–44) Schürer inserted one on the Story of Ahikar; the relevant texts became sufficiently known only in 1898. Schürer relates briefly the adventures of Ahikar, a minister of Sennacherib, who is saved from various calamities by his wisdom and his recitation of wise sayings. The scholar's main concern is, naturally, with the problem of the book's origin. Of the three choices—Jewish, Christian, heathen—Schürer decides in favor of a Jewish origin, though older, pagan (Babylonian?) materials may have served as a basis. In agreement with many scholars, Schürer assumes that the work was composed in the pre-Maccabaean era, that it is older than *The Book of Tobit,* whose author most probably made use of the Story of Ahikar. In discussing the relationship between Ahikar and the Aesop literature, Schürer bases himself on the extensive study of Rudolf Smend.[4] An older version of the Story of Ahikar and Ahikar's proverbs was known to the Jews at Elephantine about 400 B.C., as proved by quotations and references in the Elephantine papyri.[5] The journey of the Ahikar proverbs through centuries and many lands is of particular fascination to the historian of literature and of religion, and to the folklorist.[6]

After Schürer, the Aramaic text of Ahikar was examined by Cowley,[7] who regards that text either as a translation from the Persian or produced "under Persian influence"; the original work, he thinks, was written in Babylonian about the middle of the sixth century B.C. Others prefer to consider the Ahikar story as a remnant of Persian popular literature.[8]

In reviewing his chapter on *The Book of Enoch* (pp. 54–73), Schürer took cognizance of the discovery (in 1886–87) of an extensive Greek fragment of an eighth-century manuscript at Akhmim in upper Egypt which contains, among other texts, the first 32 chapters of *Enoch;* the find, first presented by M. Bouriant and others (1892), enriched immensely our knowledge of the *Enoch* complex. The pre-Christian origin of *Enoch* (especially of the section of chapters 83–90) is affirmed by an increasing group of scholars. Torrey dates the book in the first decade of the last century B.C.,[9] O. Eissfeldt in about 170 B.C., i.e., preceding *The Book of Daniel.*[10]

Commenting on the section of chapters 1–36, Schürer points to its eschatology, which indicates the relatively ancient age of the section. Despite its fanciful details, the eschatology remains in the framework of Old Testament prophetic hope for the future: the events take place on this earth, not in the beyond. But some notions do presuppose a belief in a beyond (chapter 22), which prompts Schürer to suggest that the section lacks unity and its parts show marks of later revisions. The work as a whole is a mosaic, and an attribution to one single author is questionable.

The discovery of the extensive Greek fragment made certain

that the original was Semitic: Hebrew or Aramaic; Schürer assumes an Aramaic original. Torrey endeavored to prove that the book was composed in Aramaic.[11]

Though a Slavic *Enoch* was published for some time, it was only due to the notice of G. N. Bonwetsch [12] that scholarship started to pay attention to this text, which is based on a Greek *Vorlage*. It is an independent composition, though derived from the Ethiopic *Enoch*. The main body of the book is of Jewish origin, says Schürer; however, it is most probable that the text was amended by a Christian; the ethical sayings could be either Jewish or Christian. The work, a late addition to the *Enoch* literature, must have been composed at the latest before the end of the first or the beginning of the second Christian century, at which time the Church stopped admitting Jewish treatises to the group of devotional writings.

Continued research on *The Assumptio Mosis* prompted Schürer to change his opinion on the author's party leanings (pp. 79 f.). The author could not have been a Zealot. He is silent concerning the Maccabaean uprising, counsels strict observance of the Law, and recommends trust in the divine intervention in time of trouble.[13] Hence he must have been a "religious quietist," recalling, as Charles says (in his Introduction to *The Assumptio Mosis*),[14] "the Chasid of the early Maccabean times and upholding the traditions of quietude and resignation." Moreover, the author's eschatology points in the direction of "quietism": the salvation of Israel shall not come with the establishment of an earthly kingdom but in the community of the pious' enjoyment of heavenly bliss. The question of whether Hebrew was the original language of the work, Schürer leaves unresolved.

In the post-Schürer period, C. C. Torrey dated the work in the first years of the present era and determined the original language by the interpretation of the cryptic name Taxo in 9:1. Whereas Schürer considered Taxo simply a corruption of the text (p. 77, note 22), Torrey found Taxo to refer to Mattathias : the numerical value of the letters in Taxo corresponds to "the Hasmonaean" in Aramaic, but not in Hebrew. He also conjectured that the "seven sons" (9:1) represent the seven Hasmonaean rulers, from Judas to Antigonus.[15]

In his discussion of *The Apocalypse of Baruch*, Schürer was satisfied to state (p. 91) that the existing Syrian text has been taken from the Greek, as other scholars (Langen, Dillmann) have maintained. Later, Schürer tended to assume a Hebrew or Aramaic original, in partial agreement with Charles and especially with Wellhausen,[16] who postulated a Hebrew original. On the other hand, Schürer rejects Charles's contention that the work is composed of six different parts, each reflecting a different religious and eschatological viewpoint. Keeping in mind that apocalyptic writers worked with not always uniform traditional materials, such a contention is unnecessary.

Schürer (pp. 99–108) gave an extensive analysis of the attempts to interpret the eagle vision (11:1–12:39) in *The Fourth Book of Ezra*. After the publication of the studies on the subject by Carl Clemen [17] and J. Wellhausen,[18] he tended to the view that the six pairs of principal wings refer to the emperors from Caesar to Nero, and the four pairs of subordinate wings to the emperors Galba, Otho, Vitelius, and Nerva. But it should be realized that the details of the vision underwent change and revision so that a precise identification is no longer possible.

As to the issue of the original text of the apocalypse, Schürer, as did others, assumed that the no-longer-extant Greek version was the original and that this version must have been the *Vorlage* for the many secondary versions, such as the Syriac and the Latin. Wellhausen, followed by Gunkel, demonstrated that the Greek version was based on a Hebrew (or Aramaic) original. Bruno Violet postulated a Hebrew original,[19] as did G. H. Box [20] and A. Kaminka.[21] Léon Gry argued for an Aramaic original.[22] Torrey, too, decided in favor of Aramaic rather than Hebrew.[23] Eissfeldt states that all translations go back in the last resort to a Hebrew original.[24]

The chapter on *The Fourth Book of Ezra* is followed in later editions of Schürer's text by a chapter *The Apocalypse of Abraham*. This apocalypse was known since 1863 in a Slavic translation; the German translation by G. N. Bonwetsch [25] made the work more widely accessible. The divine names used throughout and the emphasis on the people of Israel mark the apocalypse as a Jewish piece; however, there are traces of Christian interpolations. God is presented as ingathering His suffering people from among the nations and as punishing by fire the nations that tormented Israel. The relative antiquity of the work is attested by its having been preserved by the Church.

Epiphanius mentions an *Apocalypse of Abraham* that was in use by the gnostic Sethians; this seems to have been a heretic piece of writing, hardly identical with our apocalypse. Origen, too, knew of an apocryphal Abraham book.

Distinct from our apocalypse is *The Testament of Abraham*, published by M. R. James (Cambridge, 1892). The work relates Abraham's refusal to accept the divine command to die and his visit to heaven whence he surveys the entire universe; finally, God takes Abraham's soul. Schürer sees no reason to assume a Jewish origin, while Louis Ginzberg does not doubt it.[26]

The new edition by Charles of *The Testaments of the Twelve Patriarchs* [27] gave Schürer new insights into the genesis and history of the text. Charles postulates a Hebrew original, or even two Hebrew recensions which became the basis for the two types of Greek textual tradition. Schürer is more cautious and assumes the probability of a Hebrew *or* Aramaic original. He assigns the date of the composition of the original to the period before the destruction of the Temple. Torrey considers the first years of the present era as more probable.[28]

Schürer takes notice of the Hebrew testament of Naphtali

published by M. Gaster,[29] but doubts whether this text is directly related to the assumed Hebrew original of our Greek testaments. Interesting, too, are the Aramaic and Greek fragments of the testament of Levi that turned up in the Cairo *genizah*.[30] Both in content and in their tendency, the fragments come close to the text of our *Testaments*. Schürer accepts Charles's opinion that both the Aramaic and the Greek texts are translations from the Hebrew.

Torrey emphasizes the popularity of the *Testaments* in the Christian Church, evident in the amount of interpolation and expansion the text has received. For a time critics tended to consider the work a Christian composition, but more careful study showed that the Christian material is secondary.[31]

Regarding *The Book of Jubilees,* Schürer first placed the work "with tolerable probability" in the first century A.D. (p. 139). Further research, or simply a more exact reading of the text, convinced him that the work must have been composed in the time between John Hyrcanus (135–104 B.C.), alluded to in the story of the subjection of the Edomites by the sons of Jacob (38:10–14), and Herod the Great (40–4 B.C.); 38:14 would be out of place if at the time of composition an Idumaean were King of Jerusalem. The reference to the priestly aristocracy (31:15) also points to the period of the Hasmonaean rule: the priestly class is still the bearer of the Law and the possessor of the sacred writings (45:16); the priests are not yet replaced by the nonpriestly scholars. Further indication of the pre-Herodian origin of the book is the opposition to the Pharisaic calendar (6:32–38) and the tenet of the soul's afterlife without resurrection (23:31). Also, halakhic details represent an earlier tradition than that recorded by Philo, Josephus, and the Mishnah.

In the post-Schürer period, S. Zeitlin's reading of *Jubilees* convinced him of the book's opposition to many of the Pentateuchal laws and of the fact that it does not betray any trace of the controversies between the Pharisees and the Sadducees. He therefore advanced the theory that the book was composed sometime in the fifth pre-Christian century, i.e., in the early post-exilic age.[32] W. F. Albright, motivated by Zeitlin's argument, placed the composition in the early third and possibly even the late fourth pre-Christian century.[33] Its importance lies in illustrating "the advance of Jewish theological ideas at the beginning of the Greek period, before Hellenism had begun to make inroads into Jewish thought." [34]

To the chapter "The Lost Legendary Works" (pp. 146–51) Schürer appended a short chapter on the apocryphal *Testament of Job*. This piece, preserved in a Greek version, was first published in 1833. But not until M. R. James issued his edition [35] and K. Kohler his edition and translation into English [36] did the scholarly world take notice of the work. In it, Job is presented as a saintly sufferer who accepts his fate with utter submissiveness to God. The friends' faith falters, but Job holds out in his trust in divine help. In the end he is miraculously restored. While Friedrich Spitta maintained Jewish authorship and Kohler pleaded for an Essene origin, Schürer declared this *Testament* to be a Christian work. Greater attention to the aggadic parallels would have convinced Schürer that the work must be viewed in the context of a Judaic legendary tradition of "Job the saint." It seems to me that that was a tradition which counteracted the group of writings, such as *The Testament of Abraham,* that presented Abraham as the exemplary saint.

In his chapter "Philo the Jewish Philosopher," Schürer, in concert with both some ancient and modern writers (including H. Graetz and I. M. Jost), denied Philo's authorship of *De vita contemplativa*. The view that the Therapeutae resemble Christian monks seemed sufficient reason for this denial (p. 358). Later, Schürer revised this opinion and tended to accept Paul Wendland's conviction of the treatise's genuineness.[37] Wendland's analysis is based mainly on the close similarity in style and thought in other works of Philo.

The treatise *De incorruptibilitate mundi* ("The Eternity of
the World") Schürer regarded with suspicion (p. 359). With
the appearance of the Philo studies of Jakob Bernays,[38] Schürer
thought the inauthenticity of the treatise proven, for in it the
author maintains the eternity of the world, a view foreign to
Philo. More recent scholarship, however, demands that a distinction be made between the earlier part up to the first sentence
of §20, where the author speaks himself, and the rest, where he
describes the arguments used by the advocates of the opinion
that the cosmos is uncreated.[39]

### III

While Schürer was working on his *History,* Emil Kautzsch,
aided by Hermann Gunkel, Rudolf Kittel, Paul Wendland, and
others, prepared his *Die Apokryphen und Pseudepigraphen des
Alten Testaments* (Tübingen, 1900).[40] This edition offered German translations of all texts available at the time, historical and
critical introductions, and copious notes. Shortly before World
War I appeared R. H. Charles's *The Apocrypha and Pseudepigrapha of the Old Testament* (2 vols., Oxford, 1913), to
which men like G. H. Box, A. E. Cowley, W. O. E. Oesterley,
and J. Rendel Harris contributed their best scholarship.[41] Modern methods of textual criticism and historical analysis were
used throughout. The motivating force behind the study of
apocryphal material and other writings of the Second Commonwealth period was the desire for a better—i.e., historical—
understanding of the New Testament and of Christian begin-
nings. Schürer's work, too, was inspired by such interest. Jewish
interest in Second Commonwealth nonrabbinic literature, dor-
mant for centuries, was awakened by the introduction of the
historical method into Judaic research, pride in a chapter in
Jewish history rich in literary production, and a mood of scholarly inquiry generated by the rebuilding of the Land of Israel.

An attempt to render the Apocrypha into Hebrew was made by Abraham Kahane (aided by men like Menahem Stein and T. H. Gaster).[42] The most complete collection, briefly annotated, is the German *Altjüdisches Schrifttum ausserhalb der Bibel,* edited by Paul Riessler (Heidelberg, 1966), a revised edition of a work first issued in 1928. The collection goes beyond the usual limits; it includes; e.g., the "Eighteen Benedictions" and some of Philo's treatises.

When Schürer wrote the history of that literature, there was already copious research available on individual works or particular problems. On the other hand, his work set an example for other presentations, e.g., for C. C. Torrey's *The Apocryphal Literature: A Brief Introduction* (New Haven, 1945); Robert H. Pfeiffer's *Introduction to the Apocrypha,* which is included in his *History of New Testament Times* (New York, 1949); or Bruce M. Metzger's *An Introduction to the Apocrypha* (New York, 1957). Otto Eissfeldt's *The Old Testament: An Introduction* (New York and Evanston, 1965), based on the third edition of the German work (1964), contains a section on the Apocrypha, Pseudepigrapha (a vague term), and on some Qumran writings.

One of the advantages of studying Schürer's account is that the student gains an insight into the scholar's laboratory and an impression of the infinite care accorded a detail under examination. Further, the student realizes that we have here not a series of unconnected, individual pieces but a semblance of a literature, or rather of two bodies of writings, the Palestinian-Jewish literature (§32) and the Graeco-Jewish literature (§33) with their subdivisions, such as historiography, poetry, wisdom, prophecy, apologetics, legend, propaganda.

Naturally, scholarly work in our period continued in full force after Schürer's death. Today's student has easy access to exquisite editions (with English translation and notes) of the works of Philo,[43] Josephus,[44] and some Apocrypha.[45]

Septuagint research has been the object of the Academy of

Science at Göttingen and its director, Alfred Rahlfs, and was advanced in this country by J. A. Montgomery, M. L. Margolis, and H. M. Orlinsky. Philo studies were pursued by Émile Bréhier,[46] Isaak Heinemann,[47] Erwin R. Goodenough,[48] and H. A. Wolfson.[49] *Hellenistic Civilization and the Jews* is the work of V. Tcherikover;[50] Saul Lieberman wrote *Greek in Jewish Palestine*[51] and *Hellenism in Jewish Palestine*.[52] Elias Bickerman contributed richly to our understanding of the period preceding the Maccabaean uprising and of the rebellion itself;[53] S. Zeitlin, in numerous monographs, examined the literary and historical problems of our period, and in *The Rise and Fall of the Judaean State*[54] portrays the period (332 B.C.–A.D. 66) as a whole. Joseph Klausner wrote a broadly conceived five-volume *History of the Second Commonwealth*[55] in which he regularly referred to religious, intellectual, and literary issues. Important insights were (and are being) contributed by Joseph Bonsirven, Louis Finkelstein, A. Momigliano, and Gershom Scholem; the latter teaches us to understand the mystical element in the history of Judaism, including the period under discussion.[56] *Theologisches Wörterbuch zum Neuen Testament,* started by Gerhard Kittel, later continued by Gerhard Friedrich with the cooperation of many scholars,[57] contains much material of immediate relevance.

While we acknowledge the enormous advance of research in the so-called "intertestamental," or early post-canonical, period, we are aware of what is still to be done. Texts have to be edited, dates of composition further clarified, literary influences established. We do not know who the Sadducees were; we do not understand the exact nature of Jewish Hellenism and the extent of its influence. We are still accustomed to viewing the literary phenomena of the period under the aspect of political or religious parties, and tend to overlook the fact that "Judaism was a living organism and must have expressed itself in almost innumerable moods and facets with constantly interweaving pat-

terns of thought." [58] The task of presenting this "living organism" of thought and faith and hope, a synthesis of the
various modes, awaits a future historian.

NAHUM N. GLATZER

*Brandeis University*
*June 1972*

# NOTES

1. A. Cowley and A. Neubauer, *The Original Hebrew of a Portion of Ecclesiasticus* (Oxford, 1897) ; S. Schechter and C. Taylor, *The Wisdom of Ben Sira* (Cambridge, 1899).

2. *The Apocryphal Literature* (New Haven, 1945), p. 97.

3. M. Z. Segal, *Sefer ben Sira ha-Shalem* (Jerusalem, 1953), pp. 53–66.

4. *Alter und Herkunft des Achikar-Romans und sein Verhältnis zu Aesop. Zeitschrift für die alttestamentliche Wissenschaft,* Beihefte XIII (1908).

5. See A. Cowley, *Aramaic Papyri of the Fifth Century B.C.* (Oxford, 1923), pp. 204–48.

6. F. C. Conybeare, S. Rendel Harris, and Agnes Smith Lewis offer a rich collection of texts in *The Story of Ahikar from the Syriac, Arabic, Armenian, Ethiopic, Greek and Slavonic Versions* (London, 1898).

7. *Op. cit.,* pp. 206 f.

8. A. Christensen, *Die Iranier* (Munich, 1933), p. 297.

9. *The Apocryphal Literature,* p. 114.

10. *The Old Testament: An Introduction* (New York, 1965), p. 619.

11. "Notes on the Greek Texts of Enoch," *Journal of the American Oriental Society,* LXII (1942), pp. 52–60.

12. *Das slavische Henochbuch* (Göttingen, 1896).

13. See *Assumptio Mosis,* chapter IX.

14. *Apocrypha and Pseudepigrapha,* II, p. 411.

15. " 'Taxo' in the Assumption of Moses," *Journal of Biblical Literature,* LXII (1943) ; see also LXIV (1945).

16. *Skizzen und Vorarbeiten,* VI (1899), p. 234.

17. *Theologische Studien und Kritiken,* 1898.

18. "Zur apokalyptischen Literatur," *Skizzen und Vorarbeiten,* VI (1899).

19. *Die Esra Apokalypse, zweiter Teil* (Leipzig, 1913).

20. *The Ezra-Apocalypse* (London, 1912).

21. "Beiträge zur Erklärung der Esra-Apocalypse," *Monatsschrift für Geschichte und Wissenschaft des Judentums,* LXXVI–LXXVII (1932–33).

22. *Les dires prophétiques d'Esdras* (Paris, 1938).

23. *Journal of Biblical Literature,* LXI (1942), pp. 72 ff.

24. *The Old Testament,* p. 627.

25. *Die Apokalypse Abrahams,* G. N. Bonwetsch, ed., in *Studien zur Geschichte der Theologie und Kirche* (Leipzig, 1897).

26. *The Jewish Encyclopedia,* I, p. 95.

27. *The Greek Versions of the Testaments of the Twelve Patriarchs Edited from Nine Mss, together with the Variants of the Armenian and Slavonic Versions and Some Hebrew Fragments* (Oxford, 1908).

28. *The Apocryphal Literature,* p. 131.

29. "The Hebrew Text of One of the Testaments of the Twelve Patriarchs," *Proceedings of the Society of Biblical Archaeology,* XVI (1894).

30. Published in *Jewish Quarterly Review,* XII (1900) and XIX (1907).

31. *The Apocryphal Literature,* p. 131.

32. *The Book of Jubilees, Its Character and Its Significance* (Philadelphia, 1939), pp. 8–16; and "The Apocrypha," *Jewish Quarterly Review,* XXXVII (1947), pp. 226–31.

33. *From Stone Age to Christianity* (Baltimore, 1940), p. 266.

34. *Op. cit.,* p. 267.

35. "Apocrypha Anecdota II," in J. A. Robinson, ed., *Texts and Studies* (Cambridge, 1897).

36. In *Semitic Studies in Memory of Dr. Alexander Kohut* (Berlin, 1897).

37. *Die Therapeuten und die Philonische Schrift vom beschaulichen Leben* (Leipzig, 1896).

38. Especially *Über die unter Philons Werken stehende Schrift über die Unzerstörbarkeit des Weltalls* (Berlin, 1882).

39. *Philo,* F. H. Colson, trans. Loeb Classical Library (Cambridge, Mass., and London, 1954), vol. IX, pp. 173 f.

40. Reprinted 1921 and 1962.

41. This was reissued in 1963 unchanged, without taking into consideration new materials and progress in scholarship in the course of half a century.

42. *Ha-Sefarim ha-Hitzoniim* (2 vols., Tel Aviv, 1936–37; 2d ed., 1956).

43. *Philo,* F. H. Colson and G. H. Whitaker, trans., with an index by J. W. Earp. Loeb Classical Library, 10 vols. (Cambridge, Mass., and London, 1929–62). Philo Supplement I and II, R. Marcus, ed., 1953.

44. *Josephus,* H. St. J. Thackeray, R. Marcus, A. Wikgren,

and L. H. Feldman, trans. Loeb Classical Library, 9 vols. (Cambridge, Mass., and London, 1926–65).

45. Dropsie College Edition, Jewish Apocryphal Literature. (New York, 1950 et seq.).

46. *Les Idées philosophiques et religieuses de Philon d'Alexandrie* (2d ed., Paris, 1925).

47. *Philons griechische und jüdische Bildung* (Breslau, 1932).

48. *By Light, Light: The Mystic Gospel of Hellenistic Judaism* (New Haven, 1935).

49. *Philo: Foundations of Religious Philosophy in Judaism, Christianity, and Islam* (2 vols., Cambridge, Mass., 1947).

50. Philadelphia, 1959.

51. Philadelphia, 1942.

52. New York, 1950.

53. *Der Gott der Makkabäer* (Berlin, 1937), and *From Ezra to the Last of the Maccabees* (New York, 1962).

54. Two vols., Philadelphia, 1962 and 1967.

55. *Historia shel ha-Bayit ha-Sheni* (Jerusalem, 1952).

56. See *Jewish Gnosticism, Merkabah Mysticism, and Talmudic Tradition* (New York, 1960).

57. Nine vols., Stuttgart, 1933–71, and nearing completion.

58. J. C. Raylaarsdam, "Intertestamental Studies since Charles's Apocrypha and Pseudepigrapha." In *The Study of the Bible Today and Tomorrow*, H. R. Willoughby, ed. (Chicago, 1947), p. 48.

# THE LITERATURE OF
# THE JEWISH PEOPLE

## § 32. THE PALESTINIAN JEWISH LITERATURE.

### *Preliminary Observations.*

UNQUESTIONABLE as it is on the one hand that zeal for the law of God and the hope of a better future constituted the two distinctive marks of the Judaism of the period now under consideration, still it must not be forgotten on the other that those interests sought to express themselves in a great variety of forms, and that, in the sphere of the spiritual life, there were yet other aims that claimed to rank along with them, though having no immediate connection with them. How far this was the case may be seen from a glance at the *Jewish literature* of our period. *The aspect which that literature presents is of so diversified a character* that it is difficult to combine all the different elements into one connected whole. And if this be true of the literature of Palestinian Judaism alone, it becomes much more so if we take into account the literature of Hellenistic Judaism as well. In that case there will be seen to stretch before us a field of so extensive and varied a character that it is scarcely any longer possible to make out the internal connection between all the various products of this literature.

In this strangely varied mass *two leading groups* may in the first instance be distinguished, the Palestinian and the Hellenistic. We select those designations for want of better; and to correspond with them we also divide our subject into two leading sections. But, at the same time, it must be distinctly borne in mind *that the line of demarcation between those two groups is of a somewhat fluctuating and indefinite character, and that the designations applied to them are to be*

*taken very much cum grano salis.* By the Palestinian Jewish
literature we mean that which, in all essential (but only
essential) respects, represents the standpoint of Pharisaic
Judaism as it had developed itself in Palestine; while by the
Hellenistic Jewish literature again we mean that which, either
as regards form or matter, bears traces, to any noticeable
extent, of Hellenistic influences. The products belonging to
the first-mentioned group were for the most part composed
in Hebrew; but the fact of their having been so composed
must not be regarded as a decisive criterion, and that for the
simple reason that, in numerous instances, it is no longer
possible to make out whether it was Hebrew or Greek that
was the original language, but further because, in the case of
several compositions, the circumstance of their being written in
Greek is a thing purely external and accidental. And hence
it is that we also include in this group several writings that
possibly, nay probably, were composed in Greek at the very
first, while reserving for the other group only those that show
pretty evident traces of Hellenistic influence either in the
form or the matter. But the line of demarcation between
the two cannot be sharply defined, there being in fact some
writings that have almost as much title to be included in the
one group as in the other. And just as the distinction we
have adopted is not intended to imply that those belonging
to the one group were written in Hebrew and those belonging
to the other in Greek, so as little do we intend it to be
understood by our use of the term "Palestinian" that all the
compositions included under this designation were written
in Palestine. For there was Palestinian Judaism outside of
Palestine, just as conversely there was Hellenistic Judaism
within it.

In the period now under consideration, literary efforts as
such were essentially foreign to "*Palestinian*" Judaism.
One might almost venture to say that it had no literature at
all. For the few literary productions of which it could boast
had, for the most part, a purely practical aim, and had but a

very slender connection with each other. *It is precisely from these writings themselves that we can see how true it is that zeal for the law and for the faith of the fathers eclipsed every other interest. When any one took to writing he did so as a rule for the purpose of, in one form or another, exhorting his readers to keep firm hold of those precious blessings,* or of indirectly helping to increase and strengthen a spirit of faithful devotion to the law. Literary pursuits as such, and the cultivation of literature in the interests of culture generally, were things quite unknown to genuine Judaism. Its "culture" consisted in the knowledge and observance of the law.

Looked at from this standpoint, it was a somewhat extraordinary thing to find that, in the palmy days of the Hasmonaean dynasty, works of *native history* had been composed (*the First Book of Maccabees, the Chronicles of Hyrcanus*). This presupposed the existence of a patriotic self-consciousness, for which native history as such was a thing of some value. Later on, after the Hasmonaean dynasty had been overthrown, we no longer meet with any further traces of Jewish historiography such as those now referred to; and so for his information with regard to this period Josephus had to depend on other than Jewish sources. We already begin to notice indications of an intimate connection with the aims of legal Judaism in those *Psalms* that were composed during this period in imitation of the older models (*the Maccabaean Psalms, the Psalter of Solomon*). The whole of those compositions were written with a view to religious edification, and therefore—for at that time religion meant simply a firm adherence to the law—more or less with the view of fostering and quickening a spirit of faithful devotion to the law. In our period, what is known as *gnomic wisdom* exercised a direct influence in the way of promoting the spirit in question. For notwithstanding the very diversified character of the wisdom of life exhibited in the proverbs of Jesus the son of Sirach, their alpha and omega is simply this: fear God and keep His commandments. Then in the maxims of the scribes of the

time of the Mishna, and which have been collected in the
*Pirke Aboth*, we hear from beginning to end and in every
variety of tone the exhortation to a strict observance of the
law.    But there was a species of literature of a totally
different character that also served precisely the same end,
viz. the *hortatory narrative* (*Judith, Tobit*).    When, in compositions of this class, we have brought before us, in a
somewhat imaginative fashion, the doings and the fortunes of
persons who had been distinguished for their heroic faith or
their exemplary piety, and who had at the same time been
sustained by the divine help, the object of the story is not to
entertain the reader, but to inculcate the truth that the fear
of God is the highest wisdom, and that a fear of God in the
sense of legal Pharisaic Judaism.    But in our period a more
favourite kind of literature still than the hortatory narrative
was the genuine *prophetic exhortation, i.e.* exhortations based
upon alleged special revelations with regard to the future
destinies of the people.    It was a favourite practice to put
such revelations in the mouths of the recognised authorities of the olden time, with the view of thereby giving
peculiar weight to the exhortations and the consolations based
upon them.    The object therefore of those *pseudepigraphic
prophetic compositions* (*Daniel, Enoch, The Ascension of Moses,
The Apocalypse of Baruch, The Apocalypse of Ezra, The Testaments of the Twelve Patriarchs and others*) was always of an
eminently practical kind, viz. consolation amid the sufferings
of the present, and encouragement to maintain a stedfast
adherence to the law by pointing to the certainty of future
rewards and punishments.    None of those literary productions
could be said to have had any direct connection with the
professional labours of the scribes.    No doubt they served to
promote a spirit of faithful devotion to the law, but they had
no concern with the law and the Holy Scriptures as such; we
should rather regard them as free literary productions of a
very diversified character, and composed for the most part in
imitation of the older models.    In the period now in question.

the labours of the scribes, labours which concerned themselves
with the text of the Holy Scriptures and with the work of
forming new adaptations of that text either on its legal or its
historical and dogmatic side, were as yet chiefly of an oral
kind. This holds true above all with regard to the process of
*adaptation as applied to the law.* It was not till toward the
close of our period, in the time of R. Akiba, that the results of
these learned adaptations of the law began to be committed to
writing (see Div. ii. vol. i. p. 376).[1] On the other hand however there undoubtedly existed as early as our period *literary
adaptations or reconstructions of sacred history* framed in the
spirit of scribism. The Book of Chronicles may be taken as a
case in point, inasmuch as it treats the earlier history of Israel
in such a way as to make it accord with the ideals of later
Judaism (see Div. ii. vol. i. p. 339). But we have a classical
example of the Haggadic Midrash in the *Book of Jubilees,*
which in any case falls within the period with which we are
here dealing. It reconstructs the history of the canonical
Book of Genesis entirely after the fashion of the Rabbinical
Midrash. Other literary productions, which in all probability
fall no less within our period, select certain episodes or
personages from sacred history around which they seek to
shed a halo of glory by means of fictitious legends (the Books
of Adam, the History of Jannes and Jambres, and others).
It would appear however that, at first, Hellenistic did more in
this way than Rabbinical Judaism. For this latter the palmy

---

[1] Epiphanius no doubt repeatedly mentions a *Mishna of the Hasmonaeans*
(*Haer.* xxxiii. 9 : δευτέρωσις . . . τῶν υἱῶν 'Ασαμωναίου, also *Haer.* xv., and
similarly *Haer.* xlii. p. 332, ed. Petav.). But the notice in question is of so
confused a character that it does not admit of being used for historical
purposes. There is also some degree of obscurity about the statement in
the *Megillath Taanith* to the effect that on the 14th of Tammuz " *the Book
of the Decrees* " (ספר גזירתא) had been abolished (Derenbourg, *Histoire de
la Palestine,* pp. 103, 443, 445 ; Grätz, *Gesch. der Juden,* 3rd ed. iii. 606).
According to the ordinary view a Sadducean penal code is supposed to be
meant. At all events we have no undoubted evidence to show that,
previous to the time of Akiba, the Pharisaic legal traditions had been
committed to writing.

days of haggadean fiction did not begin till the Talmudic age.
The object of those modifications or embellishments of sacred
history was now no longer of so directly practical a character
as it had been in the case of the majority of the writings
previously mentioned. They owed their origin in the first
instance to the universal interest that was taken in the sacred
history generally, to the desire to have as exact and complete
and accurate an acquaintance with it as possible, in connection
with which however the tendency to embellish it also began
at once to assert itself. And yet this tendency again had now
in like manner an ulterior practical aim. In thus throwing
around the sacred history as bright a halo as possible, the
object was to show to what an extent Israel had from time to
time been enjoying the miraculous protection of its God, but
above all how, by their exemplary conduct and wonderful
exploits, the holy patriarchs had proved themselves to be true
men of God.

Thus we see then that it was objects chiefly of a practical
kind that the literary efforts of Palestinian Judaism sought
to serve. This was at least true of the department of
history, with the consideration of which we will now enter
upon our present subject.

### I. HISTORIOGRAPHY.

### 1. *The First Book of Maccabees.*

Short notices of the Maccabaean rising, and of the brothers
Judas, Jonathan and Simon Maccabaeus, who played so
prominent a part in it, must have been committed to writing
shortly after the events themselves. For it is simply
impossible that any writer living two generations after could
have been so well informed with regard to those events as we
find the author of the First Book of Maccabees to be unless he
had been able to avail himself of existing written sources.[2]

[2] We have probably an allusion to those sources in 1 Macc. ix. 22: καὶ
τὰ περισσὰ τῶν λόγων Ἰούδα καὶ τῶν πολέμων καὶ τῶν ἀνδραγαθιῶν ὧν

Those *sources of the First Book of Maccabees* — though we know nothing further of their origin and nature—are therefore entitled to foremost mention in any complete list of the historical literature of our period.

Our *First Book of Maccabees* itself gives a connected, minute and graphic narrative of the events that led to the Maccabaean rising, then of the course of the rising itself, particularly of the exploits and fortunes of Judas Maccabaeus. It then proceeds to give the further history of the patriotic enterprises of the Jews, under the leadership of Jonathan, the brother of Judas, and of the institution of the Hasmonaean high priest-hood and the founding of Jewish independence by the former. Then lastly we have an account of Simon, Jonathan's brother and successor who, by establishing the combined office of priest and prince and making it hereditary in the family of the Hasmonaeans on the one hand, and by the complete emancipation of the Jewish people from Syrian supremacy on the other, completed on both its sides the work undertaken by Jonathan. The narrative is brought down to the death of Simon, so that altogether it embraces a period of forty years (175–135 B.C.). The *standpoint* of the author is that of orthodox, rigidly legal Judaism. But yet it is somewhat remarkable that the successes with which the Maccabaean enterprises were crowned are almost nowhere attributed to any immediate supernatural intervention on the part of God, but are represented throughout as the result of the military skill and political wisdom of the Maccabaean princes. Of course those princes always act with an unshaken trust in the powerful protection and help of God. It would therefore be a mistake to suppose that the author is not animated by a

---

ἐποίησε καὶ τῆς μεγαλωσύνης αὐτοῦ οὐ κατεγράφη, πολλὰ γὰρ ἦν σφόδρα. After οὐ κατεγράφη, we may suppose either "in this book" or "in the existing literature" to be understood. Probably the latter sense should be preferred, see Grimm, *Exeget. Handbuch zu* 1 *Makk.* p. 22 sq. The use of written sources in the First Book of Maccabees is also admitted for example by Nöldeke (*Die alttestamentliche Literatur,* p. 67) and Mendelssohn (*Acta societatis phil. Lips.,* ed. Ritschelius, vol. v. 1875, p. 99).

religious spirit. But still his way of putting things is at the
same time rather different from that of the earlier historical
works of the Old Testament. His *style* is the plain narrative
style, being similar to that adopted in Old Testament historiography. The author has at his disposal such a fund of details
that it is impossible to entertain any doubt as to the
*credibility* of his narrative as a whole. His book is one of
the most valuable sources we possess for the history of the
Jewish people. Nor is its value in this respect in any way
affected by the fact that the author shows himself to be very
imperfectly informed with regard to the state of things among
foreign nations. We see in this only the simple standpoint
of the observer who, following his sources, confines his view
exclusively to the circle of Jewish affairs. Again, the freedom
with which numbers are dealt with and discourses put in the
mouths of leading personages can scarcely be regarded as
telling against the author. In matters of this sort ancient
historians generally were never particularly scrupulous. It
is a singularly fortunate circumstance that the dates of *all
the more important events are duly fixed in accordance with a
definite era, namely the Seleucidian era of the year* 312 B.C.
(on the question as to whether in the present instance this
era was made to date from the usual starting-point or from
another somewhat different from it, see § 3). As regards
the *date of composition*, it is admitted on all hands that this
work must have been written previous to the Roman conquest, and therefore previous to the year 63 B.C. For as
yet the Romans are known to the author merely as friends
and protectors of the Jewish people in contrast to the
Syrian kings. On the other hand, he is already acquainted
with a chronicle referring to the history of John Hyrcanus,
so that he must have written, at the soonest, toward the
close of that prince's reign, probably not till after its close.
According to this the work would be composed during the
first decades of the first century before Christ. It was
written *originally in Hebrew* (or Aramaic), as may be confidently

inferred from its grammatical peculiarities, and as is further confirmed by the testimony of Origen and Jerome. The Hebrew (or Aramaic) title Σαρβὴθ Σαβαναιέλ, handed down by Origen, still continues to be as much as ever an unsolved enigma. The work has come down to us only in the form of a *Greek translation,* which was probably in existence as early as the time of Josephus. That it is still extant is due to the circumstance of its having been incorporated with the Greek Bible and, as forming part of this latter, read in the Christian Church.

At the close of his account of the Hebrew canon Origen adds (as quoted in Euseb. *Hist. eccl.* vi. 25. 2) : ῎Εξω δὲ τούτων ἰστὶ τὰ Μακκαβαϊκὰ, ἅπερ ἐπιγέγραπται Σαρβὴθ Σαβαναιέλ. Consequently he was acquainted with the First Book of Maccabees (for unquestionably it is it that is meant) in its Hebrew form, but as not belonging to the Hebrew canon. Jerome, *Pro-logus galeatus* to the Books of Samuel (*Opp.* ed. Vallarsi, ix. 459 sq.) : Machabaeorum primum librum Hebraicum reperi. Secundus Graecus est, quod ex ipsa quoque φράσει probari potest. An endless variety of hypotheses have been advanced with the view of explaining the meaning of the title mentioned by Origen (see Fabricius-Harles, *Biblioth. graec.* iii. 745 ; Grimm, *Exeget. Handbuch* to 1 *Macc.* p. xvii. ; Keil, *Commentar über die Bücher der Makkabäer*, p. 22 ; Curtiss, *The Name Machabee*, 1876, p. 30 ; and the general literature mentioned below). But nearly all of them are based upon the reading Σαρβὴθ Σαρβανεέλ so generally adopted since Stephanus, whereas, according to the testimony of the manuscripts, the only reading that can claim to be recognised is Σαρβὴθ Σαβαναιέλ (so also Josephus the Christian, *Hypomnest.* c. xxv. in Fabricius' *Codex pseudepigr. Vet. Test.* vol. ii. p. 48 of Appendix).

The *acquaintance of Josephus* with the *First Book of Maccabees* is generally regarded as beyond a doubt; his acquaintance, on the other hand, with our Greek text has been questioned. In his German translation of 1 Maccabees (1778), Michaelis has propounded the view that Josephus made use of the Hebrew text. His arguments however are not of a cogent nature. The conjecture has recently been hazarded by Destinon (*Die Quellen des Flavius Josephus,* 1882, pp. 60–91) that Josephus (or rather, as Destinon thinks, the anonymous writer whose work Josephus has merely remodelled) had an older redaction of 1 Maccabees before him which, on the one hand, was, in regard to many points, rather fuller than our book, while, on the other, it wanted as yet the whole of the last section, chaps. xiv.–xvi., which is to be regarded as a subsequent addition. But the first point cannot be sufficiently substantiated ; for the extra matters found in Josephus were either drawn from other sources or had their origin in the historian's own imagination. As for the other question again, whether Josephus was acquainted with the concluding section of the book, it is one that of course deserves consideration in view of the singular brevity with which the historian disposes of the reign of Simon. As favouring the view that Josephus was acquainted with our Greek text, see Grimm, *Exeget. Handbuch to* 1 *Macc.* p. xxviii. Bloch, *Die Quellen des Flavius Josephus,* 1879, pp. 80–90. In *the Christian Church* our book has been read from the very first. See Tertullian, *Adv. Judaeos,* c. iv.: Nam et temporibus Maccabaeorum sabbatis pugnando fortiter fecerunt, etc. (comp. 1 Macc. ii. 41 sqq.). Hippolytus, in narrating the history of the Maccabean rising in his *Comment. in Daniel,* c. xxxi.–xxxii. (*Opp.* ed. Lagarde, p. 163), adheres closely to our book, quoting 1 Macc. ii. 33 sqq. almost word for word. Origen (besides the passage in Euseb. *Hist. eccl.* vi. 25. 2, already mentioned), particularly *Comment. in epist. ad Rom.* book viii. chap. i. (in Lommatzsch, vii. 193) : Sicut Mathathias, de quo in primo libro Machabaeorum scriptum est quia "zelatus est in lege Dei," etc. (1 Macc. ii. 24). Observe the designation of our book as the *First Book of Maccabees,* precisely as in the case of Jerome in the passage already quoted and in that of Eusebius, *Demonstr. evang.* viii. 2. 72, ed. Gaisford. Cyprian quotes several passages from the book in his *Testimonia,* and always with the formula, *in Machabaeis* (*Testimon.* iii. 4, 15, 53). For the further history of the book in the Christian Church, see the various works and dissertations on the history of the Old Testament canon, also Jahn's *Einleitung in die göttl. Bücher des Alten Bundes,* 2nd ed. Part ii. § 3 and 4 (1803), 1st and 2nd supplements, and likewise my article "Apokryphen des A. T.," in Herzog's *Real-Enc.* 2nd ed. i. 485–489. As is well known, it has been the practice in the Protestant Church to follow Jerome in applying the designation "Apocrypha" to such books as are not included in the Hebrew canon, and it so happens that our book is one of them.

From the history of the book just given, it will be seen that the Greek text has been transmitted to us only through the manuscripts of the Greek Bible. The Books of Maccabees being omitted in Codex *Vaticanus,* 1209, the most important *manuscripts* here are the Codex *Sinaiticus* (quoted in Fritzsche's edition of the Apocrypha as x.), and the Codex *Alexandrinus* (known in Fritzsche, as in Holmes and Parsons before him, as No. iii.) ; next to these comes a Codex *Venetus* (known in the critical apparatuses as No. 23). All the other manuscripts are minusculi. For more precise information on this point, see my article "Apocrypha," in Herzog's *Real-Enc.* 2nd ed. i. pp. 489–491. The text of our book, in common with that of the so-called Apocrypha generally, is to be found in the majority of the *editions of the Septuagint.* The received text is borrowed from the Sixtine edition (*Vetus Testamentum juxta Septuaginta ex auctoritate Sixti v. Pont. Max. editum,* Romae 1587). The most copious critical apparatus we have is to be found in the *Vetus Testamentum Graecum,* edd. Holmes et Parsons, 5 vols. Oxonii, 1798–1827 (the whole of the Apocrypha are given together in the fifth volume). We have a handy portable edition in the shape of the *Vetus Testamentum Graece juxta LXX. interpretes,* ed. Tischendorf, 2 vols. Leipz. 1850 (6th ed. 1880). Tischendorf as well as Holmes and Parsons follow the Sixtine text. Among the *separate editions of the Apocrypha* we may mention the *Libri Vet. Test. Ap cryphi, textum graecum recognovit, Augusti,* Lips. 1804, and the *Libri Vet. Test. apocryphi graece, accurate recognitos*, ed. Apel, Lips. 1837. The latest and best of such editions, although even it fails as yet to satisfy every requirement, is the *Libri apocryphi Veteris Testamenti graece, recensuit et cum eommentario critico,* edidit Fritzsche, Lips. 1871 (Fritzsche gives a recension of his own based upon the materials furnished by Holmes and Parsons, and upon the recently acquired Codex Sinaiticus as well as the fragments in the Codex Ephraemi). So far as some of the books are concerned, Fritzsche had not as yet collated them with the most important of the manuscripts, the Codex Vaticanus, there being no complete collation in Holmes and Parsons. It is true no doubt that this manuscript had been already made use of for the Sixtine edition, so that so far it helped to shape the received text. But the text of the Vaticanus could not be said to be known to any trustworthy extent till the issue of the new Roman edition (*Bibliorum Sacrorum Graecus Codex Vaticanus,* edd. Vercellone et Cozza, 6 vols. Rome 1868–1881 ; comp. *Theol. Litztg.* 1882, p. 121). The edition of Mai (*Vetus et Novum Testamentum ex antiquissimo codice Vaticano,* 5 vols. Rome 1857) is unreliable. Nestle has added to the latest edition of Tischendorf's Septuagint, a collation based upon the edition of Vercellone and Cozza (also published separately under the title, *Veteris Testamenti codices Vaticanus et Sinaiticus cum textu recepto collati ab E. Nestle,* Lips. 1880).[3] For more on the editions, see Herzog's *Real-Enc.* 2nd ed. vol. i. 494 sq.

Of the *early translations* the following are of interest in connection with the history of the transmission of the text : (1) The Latin of which there are two, (*a*) the one that was incorporated with the Vulgate, and (*b*) another which, as far as chap. xiii., has been preserved in a *Codex Sangermanensis,* both being given in Sabatier, *Bibliorum sacrorum Latinae versiones antiquae,* vol. ii. Remis 1743. (2) The Syriac in the Peshito (separate edition, *Libri Vet. Test. apocryphi Syriace,* ed. Lagarde, Lips. 1861). In the great Peshito manuscript of Milan reproduced in photo-lithograph by Ceriani (*Translatio Syra Pescitto Veteris Testamenti ex codice Ambrosiano,* ed. Ceriani, 2 vols. Milan 1876–1883), we have, as far as chap. xiv., a Syriac translation which deviates from the printed received text ; see Ceriani's prolegomena ; and Nestle, *Theol. Literaturztg.* 1884, col. 28. For more on the early translations, see Herzog's *Real-Enc.* i. 491–494. Also the texts in the London *Polyglot,* vol. iv.

*Exegetical Aids.* (1) *Special lexicon:* Wahl, *Clavis librorum Veteris Testamenti apocryphorum philologica,* Lips. 1853. (2) *Modern versions:* the German translations of De Wette (*Die heil. Schrift des A. und N. T.'s übersetzt,* 4th ed. 1858) and of Holtzmann (in Bunsen's *Bibelwerk für die Gemeinde,* vol. vii. Leipzig 1869), the latter with short notes. Versions in other modern languages : Dijserinck, *De apocriefe boeken des ouden verbonds,*

---

[3] The above observations on the Codex Vaticanus are made merely with the view of indicating on what side Fritzsche's edition of the Apocrypha generally stands in need of revision and greater completeness. The *First Book of Maccabees* is precisely that portion of the Apocrypha to which those observations do not apply for the simple reason that it is not found in that codex.

*uit het grieksch opnieuw vertaald en met opschriften en eenige aanteekeningen voorzien*, Haarlem 1874.    Reuss, *La Bible, traduction nouvelle avec introductions et commentaires, Ancien Testament*, VIᵉ partie, *Philosophie religieuse et morale des Hebreux*, Paris 1879 (containing among others Sirach, Wisdom, Tobit, the appendices to Daniel, Baruch, the Prayer of Manasseh) ; VIIᵉ partie of the same work, *Literature politique et polemique*, Paris 1879 (containing among others, the Books of Maccabees, Judith, Bel and the Dragon, Epistle of Jeremiah).    Bissell, *The Apocrypha of the Old Testament with historical introductions, a revised translation, and notes critical and explanatory*, New York 1880.    On Luther's translation, see Grimm, *Luthers Uebersetzung der ATl. Apokr.* (*Stud. u. Krit.* 1883, pp. 375–400).    (3) *Commentaries:* J. D. Michaelis, *Deutsche Uebersetzung des ersten Buchs der Maccabäer mit Anmerkungen*, 1778.    Grimm, *Das erste Buch der Maccabäer erklärt* (*Exegetisches Handbuch zu den Apokryphen des A. T.'s*, 3 parts), Leipzig 1853 (by far the most sterling work on the subject which we possess).    Keil, *Commentar über die Bücher der Maccabäer*, Leipzig 1875.    For additional exegetical literature, see Grimm, p. xxxiv. sq.    Fürst, *Bibliotheca Judaica*, ii. 317 sq., and Herzog's *Real-Enc.* vol. i. 496.

*Works of critical inquiry :* Frölich, *Annales compendiarii regum et rerum Syriae*, Viennae 1744.    E. F. Wernsdorf, *De fontibus historiae Syriae in libris Maccabaeorum prolusio*, Lips. 1746.    Frölich, *De fontibus historiae Syriae in libris Maccabaeorum prolusio Lipsiae edita in examen vocata*, Viennae 1746.    Gottl. Wernsdorf, *Commentatio historico-critica de fide historica librorum Maccabaicorum*, Wratislav. 1747.    (Khell), *Auctoritas utriusque libri Maccabaici canonico-historica adserta*, Viennae 1749.    Rosenthal, *Das erste Maccabäerbuch*, Leipzig 1867.    Schnedermann, *Ueber das Judenthum der beiden ersten Maccabäerbücher* (*Zeitschr. für kirchl. Wissensch. und kirchl. Leben*, 1884, pp. 78-100).    Critical material is also to be found in the early and the more recent polemical treatises on the value of the Apocrypha by Rainold, Keerl, Stier, Hengstenberg, Vincenzi, and others ; see Herzog's *Real-Enc.* i. p. 489.

For the *circumstances under which* our book and the Apocrypha generally were written, see Jahn, *Einleitung in die göttl. Bücher des A. B.*, 2nd ed., second part, 3rd and 4th secs., Wien 1803.    Eichhorn, *Einleitung in die apokryphischen Schriften des A. T.*, Leipzig 1795.    Bertholdt, *Historisch-kritische Einl. in die sämtl. kanon. und apokr. Schriften des A. und N. T.'s*, 6 vols., Erlangen 1812–1819.    Welte, *Specielle Einleitung in die deuterokanonischen Bücher des A. T.'s*, Freiburg 1844 (also under the title, *Einl. in die heil. Schriften des A. T.'s von Herbst*, 2 parts, 3 divisions).    Scholz, *Einleitung in die heil. Schriften des A. und N. T.'s*, 3 vols., Köln 1845-1848.    Nöldeke, *Die Alttestamentliche Literatur in einer Reihe von Aufsätzen dargestellt*, Leipzig 1868.    De Wette, *Lehrbuch der hist.-krit. Einleitung in die kanonischen und apokryphischen Bücher des A. T.'s*, 8th ed., bearb. von Schrader, Berlin 1869.    Reusch, *Lehrb. der Einl. in das A. T.*, 4th ed., Freiburg 1870.    Keil, *Lehrb. der hist.-krit. Einleitung in die kanon. und apokryph. Schriften des A. T.'s*, 3rd ed., 1873.    Kaulen, *Einleitung in die heil. Schrift A. und N. T.'s*, 2 divisions, 1st part, *Besondere Einl. in das A. T.*, Freiburg 1881.    Kleinert, *Abriss der Einleitung zum A. T. in Tabel-*

*lenform*, Berlin 1878. Reuss, *Geschichte der heil. Schriften Alten Testaments*, Braunschweig 1881. Geiger, *Urschrift und Uebersetzungen der Bibel*, 1857, p. 200 sqq. Ewald, *Gesch. des Volkes Israel*, iv. 602 sqq. Fritzsche in: Schenkel's *Bibellex.* iv. 89 sqq.

## 2. The History of John Hyrcanus.

We have probably a work similar to that of the First Book of Maccabees in *the History of John Hyrcanus*, to which reference is made at the close of the former, where it is said, 1 Macc. xvi. 23, 24: καὶ τὰ λοιπὰ τῶν λόγων Ἰωάννου καὶ τῶν πολέμων αὐτοῦ καὶ τῶν ἀνδραγαθιῶν αὐτοῦ ὧν ἠνδραγάθησε, καὶ τῆς οἰκοδομῆς τῶν τειχέων ὧν ᾠκοδόμησε, καὶ τῶν πράξεων αὐτοῦ, ἰδοὺ ταῦτα γέγραπται ἐπὶ βιβλίῳ ἡμερῶν ἀρχιερωσύνης αὐτοῦ, ἀφ' οὗ ἐγενήθη ἀρχιερεὺς μετὰ τὸν πατέρα αὐτοῦ. Apart from this notice we have no further information regarding this work. As the reign of John Hyrcanus did not possess the same interest for subsequent generations as the epoch in which Jewish independence was established through the achievements of the Maccabees, the book would have but a limited circulation, and could not fail soon to be lost altogether. It is evident that Josephus knew nothing of it in his time, for the supposition that he made use of it in his *Antiquities* [4] is more than improbable. What few notices he has regarding the reign of John Hyrcanus at all are either borrowed, in so far as they refer to external political history, from Greek historians, or, in so far as they refer to internal affairs, are of a purely legendary character. No trace can be detected of the use of any contemporary Jewish source. Considering then at how early a period the history of Hyrcanus dropped out of sight, it is inconceivable that it should still have existed in manuscript in the sixteenth century as, following Sixtus Senensis, many have assumed.

In his *Bibliotheca sancta* (Venetiis 1566) Sixtus Senensis gives an account at p. 61 sq. of *a Fourth Book of Maccabees* which he saw in the library of Santes Pagninus at Lyons, and which began as follows: Καὶ

---

[4] So Bloch, *Die Quellen des Flavius Josephus* (1879), pp. 90–94.

μετὰ τὸ ἀποκτανθῆναι τὸν Σίμωνα ἐγενήθη Ἰωάννης υἱὸς αὐτοῦ ἀρχιερεὺς ἀντ
αὐτοῦ. Judging from the enumeration of the contents as given by Sixtus,
this book simply narrates *the history of John Hyrcanus*, and that precisely
as in Josephus (the same facts and in the same order). With regard to
this he himself observes: *Historiae* series et narratio eadem fere est quae
apud Josephum libro Antiquitatum decimo tertio; sed *stylus, hebraicis
idiotismis abundans*, longe dispar. Consequently he ventures to conjecture
that it may have been a Greek translation of the history of Hyrcanus
mentioned at the end of the First Book of Maccabees. Many modern
writers have concurred in this conjecture, and hence their regret that the
manuscript should have perished soon after, when the library just mentioned
was destroyed by fire (see Fabricius-Harles, *Biblioth. graeca*, iii. 748. Grimm,
*Exeget. Handbuch*, note on 1 Macc. xvi. 24). But, in view of the enumeration of the contents given by Sixtus, it seems to me there can hardly be
a doubt that the book was simply a reproduction of Josephus, the style
being changed perhaps for a purpose.

### 3. *Josephus' History of the Jewish War.*

In post-Hasmonaean times the fondness for writing histories
seems to have died away. At least we nowhere come across
any hint to the effect that the writing of anything like
connected historical narratives had been undertaken by any
one.[5] It was not till the important events of the war, extending from the year 66 to 70 B.C., that the occasion for such
histories once more presented itself. The Jewish priest
Joseph, son of Matthias, better known under the name of
Flavius Josephus, wrote *the history of this war*, of which he
himself had personal knowledge, whether as a passive observer
or as playing an active part in it. He composed the work in
his own vernacular, therefore in the *Aramaic tongue*, and
intended it chiefly for the benefit of the ἄνω βάρβαροι, *i.e.*
the Jews of Mesopotamia and Babylon. Of this work we
know nothing beyond what he himself mentions in his Greek

---

[5] We know of but two classes of historical documents of any kind
belonging to that period: (1) *Family registers*, the preservation and continuation of which were matters of consequence for religious reasons (on
these registers see vol. i. pp. 210 and 212). (2) The *Calendar of Fasts*,
*Megillath Taanith, i.e.* a list of the days on which, owing to some happy
event being commemorated, there was to be *no* fasting (for details, see
§ 3). But neither class of writings, although historical *documents*, can be
said to belong to the category of historical *literature*.

version of the history of the Jewish war, *Bell. Jud. prooem.* 1, where he says : προυθέμην ἐγὼ τοῖς κατὰ τὴν ʿΡωμαίων ἡγεμονίαν, ʿΕλλάδι γλώσσῃ μεταβαλών, ἃ τοῖς ἄνω βαρβάροις τῇ πατρίῳ συντάξας ἀνέπεμψα πρότερον, ἀφηγήσασθαι. The Greek version of this work, in common with the extant works of Josephus generally, belongs to the department of Hellenistico-Jewish literature, and will therefore fall to be mentioned in the next section.

## II. THE PSALMODIC LITERATURE.

### 1. *The Psalms of the Maccabaean Age.*

It had been already observed by Calvin with reference to the 44th Psalm that : Querimoniae quas continet, proprie conveniunt in miserum illud et calamitosum tempus, quo grassata est saevissima tyrannis Antiochi. Ever since, the question, whether psalms belonging to the Maccabaean age are also to be found in our canon, has been mooted and more and more answered in the affirmative. It was Hitzig, Lengerke, and Olshausen above all, that referred a large number of the psalms to the time of the Maccabaean struggles and to a still later period (embracing the reign of the Hasmonaean princes down to the second century B.C.). Others have limited the number of Maccabaean psalms to only a very few. But the fact that we have psalms belonging to Maccabaean times in the canon at all is being more and more recognised. Nor is it possible to allege any plausible reason for thinking otherwise. For the assertion, that that was an age but little calculated to develope religious fervour or poetical genius is a mere *petitio principii*, while as little can be said in favour of the other assertion, that at that time the canon had been already closed. For this is just a point about which we simply know nothing whatever unless we ought rather to say that the Book of Daniel alone is sufficient proof to the contrary. If therefore

the possibility of the existence of psalms belonging to
Maccabaean times be beyond question, then it can only be
shown from the contents of the different psalms themselves
how far that possibility is also a reality.  Accordingly there is
a wide consensus of opinion in favour of the view that
the 44th, 77th, 79th, and 83rd Psalms above all contain
within themselves the most powerful reasons possible for
ascribing their origin to the Maccabaean age.  It was only
then that it could be rightly and fairly asserted, as is done
in Ps. xliv., that the people had faithfully adhered to the
covenant made with Jehovah and had not deviated from it,
and that it was just for this very reason, therefore for their
religion, that they were being persecuted (Ps. xliv. 18, 19,
23).  It is only to such a time as that that we could well
refer the complaints that the " houses of God " (מוֹעֲדֵי־אֵל), *i.e.*
the synagogues, had been burnt in the land, and that there is
no longer any prophet there (Ps. lxxiv. 8, 9).  There is no age
except the Maccabaean to which all that could so well apply
which, in Ps. lxxix., is said about the desecration, but not the
destruction of the temple, and the laying waste of Jerusalem,
and in Ps. lxxxiii. on the persecution of Israel.  But, if these
four psalms had their origin in Maccabaean times, then there
are many more of a kindred nature that must be referred to
the same period.  The real point at issue then can only be
not " whether " there are any such psalms at all, but only
" how many of them " there are.  And this will always
remain a disputed point, for there are but few of the psalms
that bear such evident traces of the date and circumstances of
their origin as those just mentioned.  Meanwhile let it suffice
to have pointed out the fact that the holy Church of the
Maccabaean time has given proof of its creative powers in the
department of sacred lyrics as well, through those new psalms
in which it pours out its wail of distress before God and cries
for protection and help from the Almighty.

For the *literature* of this question, see the various introductions to the
Old Testament, for example De Wette-Schrader, *Einleit. in die kanon. und*

*apokr. Bücher des A. T.'s* (1869), § 334; Kleinert, *Abriss der Einl. zum A. T.* (1878) p. 45.

The following authorities have expressed themselves *in favour of the view that there are Maccabaean psalms* in our canon : Rüdinger (1580). Venema (1762–67). E. G. Bengel, *Dissertatio ad introductiones in librum Psalmorum supplementa quaedam exhibens*, Tübing. 1806. Hitzig, *Begriff der Kritik, am A. T. praktisch erörtert*, Heidelb. 1831. Idem, *Die Psalmen*, 2 vols. Heidelb. 1835, 1836. Idem, *Ueber die Zeitdauer der hebräischen Psalmenpoesie (Züricher Monatschr.* 1856, pp. 436–452). Hesse, *De psalmis Maccabaicis*, Vratisl. 1837. Lengerke, *Die fünf Bücher der Psalmen*, 2 vols. Königsberg 1847. Olshausen, *Die Psalmen erklärt*, Leipzig 1853 (being the fourteenth number of the Exegetical Handbook to the Old Testament). De Jong, *Disquisitio de Psalmis Maccabaicis*, Lugd. Bat. 1857. Steiner, art. "Psalmen," in Schenkel's *Bibellex.* vol. v. pp. 1–9. Reuss, *Gesch. der heil. Schriften Alten Testaments* (1881), § 481. Comp. further, Reuss, *La Bible Ancien Testament*, 5th part, Paris 1875. Giesebrecht, *Ueber die Abfassungszeit der Psalmen* (Stade's *Zeitsch. für die alttestamentl. Wissensch.* vol. i. 1881, pp. 276–332). Delitzsch in the more recent editions of his commentary on the psalms also admits the existence of several Maccabaean psalms.

The following authorities again take *an opposite view:* Gesenius in No. 81 of the supplements to the *Allgemeinen Literaturzeitung*, 1816. Hassler, *Comment. crit. de psalmis Maccab.* 2 vols. Ulm 1827–1832. Ewald, *Jahrb. der bibl. Wissensch.* vi. 1854, pp. 20–32, viii. 1857, p. 165 sqq. Dillmann, *Jahrbb. für deutsche Theol.* 1858, p. 460 sqq. Hupfeld, *Die Psalmen, übersetzt und ausgelegt*, 4 vols. Gotha 1855–1862. Ehrt, *Abfassungszeit und Abschluss des Psalters zur Prüfung der Frage nach Makkabäerpsalmen historisch-kritisch untersucht*, Leipzig 1869. Wanner, *Etude critique sur les Psaumes*, 44, 74, 79 *et* 83 *considérés par plusieurs théologiens comme provenant de l'époque des Maccabés*, Lusanne 1876 (comp. the reviews in the *Revue de théologie et de philosophie*, 1877, p. 399 sq.).

## 2. *The Psalms of Solomon.*

In the list of books as given in several copies of the Christian canon of the Old Testament the ψαλμοὶ Σολομῶντος are also included, and that, in some instances, under the category of ἀντιλεγόμενα along with the Books of Maccabees, the Wisdom of Solomon, Jesus the Son of Sirach, Judith, Tobit, etc. (as in the case of the so-called Stichometria of Nicephorus and in the *Synopsis Athanasii*), and in others under the category of ἀπόκρυφα along with Enoch, the Patriarchs, Apocalypses of Moses and Ezra, etc. (as in the case of an anonymous list of the canon still extant in various manuscripts). From its first-mentioned position we can see that, in the Christian Church, this book was in many quarters regarded as canonical. It is included under the category of ἀντιλεγόμενα, simply because, not being in the Hebrew canon, it was not acknowledged to be canonical by those who made that the standard. Besides this there are still in existence several Greek manuscripts of the Bible in which the *Psalms of Solomon* find a place precisely in accordance with the lists just mentioned; and it is just possible that, if the manuscripts of the Septuagint were carefully searched, there might be found to be still more of them than are already known to us. These psalms amount to *eighteen* in number. They were first printed from an Augsburg manuscript by de la Cerda (1626), and subsequently by Fabricius (1713), while, in our own time, an edition, collated with a Vienna manuscript, has been published by Hilgenfeld, whose text is also followed in the editions of Geiger, Fritzsche, and Pick.

The ascribing of these psalms to Solomon is simply due to the later transcribers. The work itself does not lay the slightest claim to such authorship; on the contrary, it betrays very distinct traces of the date of its composition. That certainly was not, as Ewald, Grimm, Oehler, Dillmann (at one time), Weiffenbach, and Anger would have us believe, the time of Antiochus Epiphanes, nor, as Movers, Delitzsch, and Keim suppose, the time of Herod, but, as is now universally admitted, — for example, by Langen, Hilgenfeld, Nöldeke, Geiger, Carriere, Wellhausen, Reuss, Dillmann (now), —the period shortly after the conquest of Jerusalem by Pompey. That the psalms were composed at that time may be regarded as absolutely certain from the various explicit indications of this in the *second, eighth,* and *seventeenth* psalms. The contemporary state of things which these psalms presuppose is somewhat as follows: A family to which the promise of ruling over Israel had not been given seized the reins of government by force (xvii. 6). They did not give God the glory, but of themselves assumed the king's crown, and took

possession of the throne of David (xvii. 7, 8). In their
time the whole of Israel fell into sin. The king despised
the law, the judge was unfaithful to truth, and the people
lived in sin (xvii. 21, 22). But God overthrew those princes
by raising up against them a man from a strange land, and
who was not of the race of Israel (xvii. 8, 9). From the
ends of the earth God brought one who could strike with a
mighty blow, who declared war against Jerusalem and all its
territory. The princes of the land in their blindness went
out to meet him with joy, and said to him : " Thy approach
has been longed for, come hither, enter in peace." They
opened the gates to him, so that he entered like a father into
the house of his sons (viii. 15–20). But after he had securely
established himself in the city he also seized the battlements,
and threw down the walls of Jerusalem with the battering-
ram (viii. 21, ii. 1). Jerusalem was trodden under foot by
the heathen (ii. 20); nay the strange peoples ascended the
altar of God itself (ii. 2). All the leading men and every
wise man in the council were put to death ; and the blood of
the inhabitants of Jerusalem was poured out like unclean
water (viii. 23). The inhabitants of the land were carried
away captive into the *West*, and its princes insulted (xvii.
13, 14, ii. 6, viii. 24). But at last the dragon that had
conquered Jerusalem (ii. 29) was itself put to death on the
mountains of Egypt by the sea-shore. But his body was
allowed to lie unburied (ii. 30, 31). It can scarcely require
any further commentary to prove that we are here dealing
with the time of the conquest of Jerusalem by Pompey, and
that it is to it alone that the circumstances presupposed can
be said to apply. The princes who had been so arrogant as
to assume the rule over Jerusalem and take possession of the
throne of David, are the *Hasmonaeans*, who, ever since Aristobulus I., had taken the title of king. The last of the princes
of this house, Alexander Jannaeus and Aristobulus II., openly
favoured the Sadducean party, so that in the eyes of our
author, with his Pharisaic leanings, they appeared in the light

of sinful and lawless men. The " man of the strange land,"
and " of powerful blows," whom God summons from the end of
the earth, is no other than *Pompey*. The princes who go out to
meet him are Aristobulus II. and Hyrcanus II. The supporters
of this latter opened the gates of the city to Pompey, who
then proceeded to take by storm (ἐν κριῷ, ii. 1) the other
portion of the town in which those belonging to Aristobulus's
party had entrenched themselves. All the rest that follows,
the contemptuous treading of the temple by the conquerors,
the mowing down of the inhabitants, the execution of the
leading men among them,[6] the carrying away of the captives
to the West, and of the princes to be mocked (εἰς ἐμπαιγμόν,
xvii. 14, *i.e.* for the triumphal procession in Rome), corresponds
with what actually took place. But it is above all the
circumstance of the captives being carried away to the West
(xvii. 14) that proves that the taking of Jerusalem by Pompey
is alone to be thought of. For the only other case besides
this that might possibly be in view is the conquest of Jerusalem by Titus, but to this none of the other circumstances
are found to apply.[7] But if there could be any doubt before,
it utterly vanishes when finally we are told that the conqueror
was killed on the coast of Egypt, on the sea-shore (ἐπὶ
κυμάτων), and that his body was left lying without being buried
(ii. 31). For this is precisely what actually took place in
the case of Pompey (in the year 48 B.C.). Consequently the
second psalm was undoubtedly composed soon after this event,
while the eighth and seventeenth, as well as most of the others,
may be assumed to have been written between the years
63–48. There exists no reason whatever for coming down so
late as to the time of Herod. For " the man from the strange
land," who, according to xvii. 9, rose up against the Hasmonaean

---

[6] Ps. viii. 23 : ἀπώλεσεν ἄρχοντας αὐτῶν καὶ πάντα σοφὸν ἐν βουλῇ, compare
with Joseph. *Antt.* xiv. 4. 4 (*Bell. Jud.* i. 7. 6) : τοὺς αἰτίους τοῦ πολέμου τῷ
πελέκει διεχρήσατο.

[7] There is above all the circumstance that nowhere in our psalms is there
any mention whatever of a *destruction* of the city and the temple.

princes, is, as the context makes it impossible to doubt, the
same personage who, according to xvii. 14, carries away the
captives to the West, and therefore not Herod, as Movers,
Delitzsch, and Keim would have us suppose, but Pompey.

The spirit which the psalms breathe is entirely that of
Pharisaic Judaism. They are pervaded by an earnest moral
tone and a sincere piety. But the righteousness which they
preach and the dearth of which they deplore is, all through,
the righteousness that consists in complying with all the
Pharisaic prescriptions, the δικαιοσύνη προσταγμάτων (xiv. 1).
The fate of man after death is represented as depending
simply upon his works. It is left entirely in his own option
whether he is to decide in favour of righteousness or unrighteousness (comp. especially ix. 7). If he does the former he
will rise again to eternal life (iii. 16); if the latter, eternal
perdition will be his doom (xiii. 9 sqq., xiv. 2 sqq., xv.) As
a contrast to the unlawful rule of the Hasmonaeans, which
had been put an end to by Pompey, the author cherishes the
confident expectation of that Messianic king of the house of
David who is one day to lead Israel to the promised glory
(xvii. 1, 5, 23–51, xviii. 6–10. Comp. further vii. 9, xi.).

The view previously held by Grätz, that our psalms are of
Christian origin, seems to have been abandoned by that writer
himself,[8] and, in any case, does not call for serious refutation.
But neither have we any right to assume that they contain
even Christian interpolations. For the sinlessness and holi-
ness which the author ascribes to the Messiah expected by
him (xvii. 41, 46), is not sinlessness in the sense of Christian
dogmatics, but simply rigid legalism in the Pharisaic sense.

Despite Hilgenfeld's view to the contrary, it is almost
universally allowed that the psalms were originally composed
in Hebrew. And undoubtedly not without good reason. For
the diction of the psalms is so decidedly Hebrew in its
character that it is impossible to suppose that they were

[8] The remark here referred to (*Gesch. der Juden*, vol. iii. 2nd ed. p. 439)
is not repeated in the 3rd ed. vol. iii. p. 621.

written originally in Greek. And for this reason it is no less certain that they were not written in Alexandria, but in Palestine. It may not be amiss to mention further the correspondence, to some extent a verbal one, between *Psalm* xi. and the fifth chapter of *Baruch*. If we are correct in supposing that the psalms were written originally in Hebrew, then the imitation must be regarded as being on the part of Baruch.

*The place assigned to our psalms in the Christian canon:* I. Among the ἀντιλεγόμενα: (1) in the Stichometria of Nicephorus as given in Credner, *Zur Geschichte des Kanons* (1847), p. 120, *Nicephori opuscula*, ed. de Boor (Lips. 1880), p. 134. (2) In the *Synopsis Athanasii*, as given in Credner, *Zur Gesch. des Kanons*, p. 144. II. Among the ἀπόκρυφα in an anonymous list of canonical books which has been printed (1) from a certain Codex Coislinianus as given in Montfaucon's *Bibliotheca Coisliniana*, Paris 1715, p. 194; (2) from a Parisian manuscript as given in Cotelier's *Patrum apost. Opp.* vol. i. 1698, p. 196; (3) from a certain Codex Baroccianus at Oxford, and as given in Hody's *De Bibliorum textibus*, 1705, p. 649, col. 44; (4) from a Vatican codex as given in Pitra's *Juris ecclesiastici Graecorum historia et monumenta*, vol. i. 1864, p. 100 (on the relation of those four texts to each other, see No. V. below, the chapter on the lost Apocalypses). III. In his scholia to the decrees of the Council of Laodicea, Zonoras observes in connection with the 59th canon (Beveregius, *Pandectae canonum*, Oxon. 1672, vol. i. p. 481): ἐκτὸς τῶν ρ′ ψαλμῶν τοῦ Δαβὶδ εὑρίσκονται καί τινες ἕτεροι λεγόμενοι τοῦ Σολομῶντος εἶναι καὶ ἄλλων τινῶν, οὓς καὶ ἰδιωτικοὺς ὠνόμασαν οἱ πατέρες καὶ μὴ λέγεσθαι ἐν τῇ ἐκκλησίᾳ διετάξαντο. Similarly Balsamon (in Beveregius, i. 480). IV. In the Codex Alexandrinus of the Greek Bible the Psalms of Solomon, as is shown by the list of contents prefixed to the codex, found a place in the Appendix to the New Testament after the Epistles of Clement (see Credner, *Gesch. des neutestamentl. Kanons*, 1860, p. 238 sq.). In the Vienna manuscript, on the other hand, where the Psalms are still extant, they come in between the Wisdom of Solomon and Jesus the Son of Sirach.

Up to the present time the *manuscripts* that have been found are five in number: (1) The manuscript from which the *editio princeps* of de la Cerda was printed; it was brought from Constantinople in the year 1615, was in the possession of David Höschel, and then found its way to the Augsburg library (Fabricius, *Cod. pseudepigr.* i. 973, 914 sq.), but it has now disappeared. (2) A Vienna codex (*cod. gr. theol.* 7), Haupt's collation of which Hilgenfeld made use of in his edition of the Psalms. (3) A Copenhagen manuscript, an account of which is given by Graux in the *Revue Critique*, 1877, No. 46, pp. 291–293. (4) A Moscow manuscript and (5) a Parisian one, both of which were discovered and collated by Gebhardt (see *Theol. Literaturzeitung*, 1877, p. 627 sq.). The three last-mentioned MSS. have not yet been made use of in any edition of our Psalms.

*Editions:* (1) De la Cerda, *Adversaria sacra*, Lyons 1626, Appendix.
(2) Fabricius, *Codex pseudepigraphus Veteris Testamenti*, vol. i. 1713, pp.
914-999. (3) Hilgenfeld, *Zeitschrift für wissenschaftl. Theologie*, 1868, pp.
134-168. Idem, *Messias Judaeorum*, Lips. 1869, pp. 1-33. (4) Eduard
Ephräm Geiger, *Der Psalter Salomo's herausgegeben und erklärt*, Augsburg
1871. (5) Fritzsche, *Libri apocryphi Veteris Testamenti graece*, Lips. 1871,
pp. 569-589. (6) Pick, *Presbyterian Review*, 1883, Oct. pp. 775-812. A
new edition was prepared by Gebhardt for the "*Texte und Untersuchungen*," edited by himself and Harnack.

*German translations* with explanatory notes have been published by
Geiger as above. Hilgenfeld, *Die Psalmen Salomo's deutsch übersetzt una
aufs Neue untersucht* (*Zeitschr. für wissenschaftl. Theologie*, 1871, pp. 383-
418). Wellhausen, *Die Pharisäer und die Sadducäer* (1874), pp. 131-164.
There is an *English translation* by Pick as above.

*On the circumstances under which our Psalms were written:* I. Ewald,
*Geschichte des Volkes Israel*, iv. 392 sq. (subsequently Ewald hit upon the
idea of dating the Psalms back to the time of Ptolemy Lagus; see the
reviews of the writing of Geiger and Carriere in the *Göttinger gel. Anzeigen*,
1871, pp. 841-850, and 1873, pp. 237-240). Grimm, *Exeget. Handbuch zu
1 Makk.* p. 27. Oehler, art. "Messias," in Herzog's *Real-Enc.* 1st ed.
ix. 426 sq. Dillmann, art. "Pseudepigraphen," in Herzog's *Real-Enc.* 1st
ed. xii. 305 sq. Weiffenbach, *Quae Jesu in regno coelesti dignitas sit
synopticorum sententia exponitur* (Gissae, 1868), p. 49 sq. Anger, *Vorlesungen
über die Geschichte der messianischen Idee* (1873), p. 81 sq. II. Movers in
Wetzer und Welte's *Kirchenlex.* 1st ed. i. 340. Delitzsch, *Commentar über
den Psalter*, 1st ed. ii. 381 sq. Keim, *Geschichte Jesu von Nazara*, i. 243.
III. Langen, *Das Judenthum in Palästina* (1866), pp. 64-70. Hilgenfeld,
*Zeitschr.* 1868, *Messias Judaeorum proleg.*, *Zeitschr.* 1871. Nöldeke, *Die
alttestamentl. Literatur* (1868), p. 141 sq. Hausrath, *Neutestamentl. Zeitgesch.*
2nd ed. i. pp. 157 sq., 168. Geiger in his edition of our Psalms. Fritzsche,
*prolegom.* to his edition. Wittichen, *Die Idee des Reiches Gottes* (1872),
pp. 155-160. Carriere, *De psalterio Salomonis*, Argentorati 1870. Wellhausen, *Die Pharisäer und die Sadducäer*, p. 112 sqq. Stähelin, *Jahrb. für
deutsche Theol.* 1874, p. 203. Drummond, *The Jewish Messiah* (1877), pp.
133-142. Kaulen in Wetzer und Welte's *Kirchenlex.* 2nd ed. i. 1060 sq.
Lucius, *Der Essenismus* (1881), pp. 119-121. Reuss, *Gesch. der heil.
Schriften A. T.'s*, § 526. Dillmann in Herzog's *Real-Enc.* 2nd ed. vol.
xii. 1883, p. 346. Pick, *The Psalter of Solomon* (*Presbyterian Review*, 1883,
Oct. pp. 775-812).

## III. THE GNOMIC WISDOM.

### 1. *Jesus the Son of Sirach.*

There is nothing that shows so clearly the practical character
of the Palestinian Jewish literature of our period, as the fact

that even in the *merely theoretical speculations* of the time there was always an eye to the practical aims and tasks of life. A theoretical philosophy strictly so called was a thing entirely foreign to genuine Judaism. Whatever it did happen to produce in the way of "*philosophy*" (= *wisdom*, חָכְמָה) either had practical religious problems as its theme (Job, Ecclesiastes), or was of a directly practical nature, being: *directions based upon a thoughtful study of human things for so regulating our life as to ensure our being truly happy*. The form in which those contemplations and instructions were presented was that of the מָשָׁל, *the apothegm*, which contained a single thought expressed in concise and comprehensive terms, and in a form more or less poetical, and in which there was nothing of the nature of discussion or argument. A collection of aphorisms of this sort had already found a place among the canonical writings of the Old Testament in the shape of the so-called proverbs of Solomon. We have a collection of a similar character in the book known as *Jesus the Son of Sirach*, and which we now proceed to consider. This book takes that older collection as its model, not only as regards the form, but the matter as well, though it contributes a large number of new and original thoughts. The fundamental thought of the author is that of *wisdom*. For him the highest and most perfect wisdom resides only in God, who has established and who continues to govern all things in accordance with His marvellous knowledge and understanding. On the part of man, therefore, true wisdom consists in his trusting and obeying God. The fear of God is the beginning and end of all wisdom. Hence it is that the author, living as he did at a time when the fear of God and the observance of the law were already regarded as one and the same thing, inculcates above all the duty of adhering faithfully to the law and keeping the commandments. But besides this he also points out in the next place how the truly wise man is to comport himself in the manifold relationships of practical life. And accordingly his book contains an inexhaustible fund of rules

for the regulation of one's conduct in joy and sorrow, in prosperity and adversity, in sickness and in health, in struggle
and temptation, in social life, in intercourse with friends and
enemies, with high and low, rich and poor, with the good and
the wicked, the wise and the foolish, in trade, business and
one's ordinary calling, above all, in one's own house and family
in connection with the training of children, the treatment of
men-servants and maid-servants, and the way in which a man
ought to behave toward his own wife and the fair sex generally.
For all those manifold relationships the most precise directions
are furnished, directions that are prompted by a spirit of
moral earnestness which only now and then degenerates into
mere worldly prudence. The counsels of the author are the
mature fruit of a profound and comprehensive study of human
things and of a wide experience of life. In entering as they
do into such a multiplicity of details, they at the same time
furnish us with a lively picture of the manners and customs
and of the culture generally of his time and his people.
How far the thoughts expressed, as well as the form in which
they are expressed, were the author's own, and how far he
only collected what was already in current and popular use
it is of course impossible in any particular instance to determine. To a certain extent he may have done both. But in
any case he was not a mere collector or compiler, the characteristic personality of the author stands out far too distinctly
and prominently for that. Notwithstanding the diversified
character of the apothegms, they are all the outcome of one
connected view of life and the world.

At the close of the book, chap. L. 27, the author calls
himself Ἰησοῦς υἱὸς Σιρὰχ ὁ Ἱεροσολυμίτης. Many manuscripts insert Ἐλεάζαρ after Σιράχ; but this, despite the
strong testimony in its favour, must be regarded as a gloss
(see Fritzsche's edition and commentary). The name Σιράχ is
equivalent to the Hebrew סִירָא, "a coat of mail" (the accent
being on the final syllable as in ἀκελδαμάχ, Acts i. 19). The
singular mistake of Syncellus (*Chron.* ed. Dindorf, i. 525),

who alleges that he was a high priest, can only have arisen
from the fact that in the chronicle of Eusebius, which
Syncellus makes use of, our Jesus the Son of Sirach is
mentioned after the high priest, Simon the son of Onias II.,
though not as a high priest, but only as the author of the
book now under consideration (Euseb. *Chron. ad Ol.* 137–38,
ed. Schoene, ii. 122). Again, the notion that he was an
ordinary priest is also entirely without foundation, notwithstanding the fact that it has found expression in the text of
the *cod. Sinaiticus*, L. 27. The *time* at which he lived may
be determined with tolerable precision. His *grandson*, who
translated the book into Greek, states in the prologue prefixed
to it that he (the grandson) came to Egypt ἐν τῷ ὀγδόῳ καὶ
τριακοστῷ ἔτει ἐπὶ τοῦ Εὐεργέτου βασιλέως. By the "thirty-
eighth year" he, of course, does not mean that of his own
age, but the thirty-eighth year of the reign of Euergetes.
Now seeing that of the two Ptolemys who bore this surname,
the one reigned only twenty-five years, it is only the second
that can be intended, and whose full name was Ptolemaeus
VII. Physcon Euergetes II. This latter in the first instance
shared the throne along with his brother (from the year 170
onwards), and subsequently reigned alone (from the year 145
onwards). But he was in the habit of reckoning the years of
his reign from the former of those dates. Consequently that
thirty-eighth year in which the grandson of Jesus the son of
Sirach came to Egypt would be the year 132 B.C. That
being the case, his grandfather may be supposed to have
lived and to have written his book somewhere between 190
and 170 B.C. This further accords with the fact that in the
book (l. 1–26) he pays a respectful tribute to the memory
of the high priest, Simon the son of Onias, by whom we
are to understand, not Simon I. (in the beginning of the third
century, see Joseph. *Antt.* xii. 2. 4), but Simon II. (in the
beginning of the second century, see Joseph. *Antt.* xii. 4. 10).
Jesus the son of Sirach passes an encomium upon the
meritorious character of this personage, who had just passed

away from the world, and the thought of whom was still so fresh in his memory.

The book has come down to us only in the form of the Greek translation which, according to the prologue, was executed by the author's grandson. We further learn from this prologue what is also confirmed by the character of the diction, that the work was originally *composed in Hebrew*, by which we are to understand Hebrew strictly so called and not Aramaic (see Fritzsche, *Exeget. Handbuch*, p. 18). The Hebrew text was still in existence in the time of Jerome, who tells us that he had seen it, see *Praef. in vers. libr. Salom.* (Vallarsi, ix. 1293 sq.) : Fertur et πανάρετος Jesu filii Sirach liber et alius ψευδεπίγραφος, qui Sapientia Salomonis inscribitur. Quorum priorem Hebraicum reperi, non Ecclesiasticum, ut apud Latinos, sed Parabolas praenotatum, cui juncti erant Ecclesiastes et Canticum Canticorum, ut similitudinem Salomonis non solum librorum numero, sed etiam materiarum genere coaequaret.

The fact that a Hebrew text was still extant in the time of Jerome is evidence of itself that the book was also prized within the circle of Rabbinical Judaism. Not only so, but quotations from it are repeatedly met with in Talmudic literature. But it was prized far more highly still within the Christian Church. It is frequently quoted as γραφή by the Greek and the Latin Fathers alike, and that too in the form in which it has come down to us in the manuscripts of the Bible. The restricting of the Christian canon to precisely the same number of books as was in the Hebrew Bible was, in the early Church and that of the Middle Ages, almost always a pure matter of theory, and was only practically recognised and acted upon for the first time in the Protestant Church.

On the quotations from בן סירא in Talmudic literature, see Wolf, *Bibliotheca Hebraea*, i. 257 sqq. Zunz, *Die gottesdienstlichen Vorträge der Juden*, p. 101 sqq. Delitzsch, *Zur Geschichte der jüdischen Poesie*, pp. 20 sq., 204 sq. Dukes, *Rabbinische Blumenlese*, p. 67 sqq. Fritzsche, *Exeget. Handbuch*, p. xxxvii. Joel, *Blicke in die Religionsgeschichte* (1880), p. 71 sqq. Strack in Herzog's *Real-Enc.* 2nd ed. vii. 430 sq. We must beware of confounding with those quotations the very late and apocryphal *Alphabet of Ben Sira*, a collection of 44 (2 × 22) sayings arranged in alphabetical order. On this see Wolf, *Bibliotheca Hebraea*, i. 260 sqq., iii. 156 sq.  Fabricius-Harles, *Biblioth. graec.* iii. 726 sq.  Steinschneider, *Catalogus librorum Hebraeorum in bibliotheca Bodleiana* (1852–1860), col. 203–205.  Fürst, *Biblioth. Judaica*, iii. 341.  Modern edition, *Alphabetum Siracidis utrumque*, ed. Stein-schneider, Berlin 1858.

*On the title of our book*, see in particular the passage from Jerome quoted above.  In the manuscripts it runs thus: Σοφία Ἰησοῦ υἱοῦ Σιράχ.  In the Greek Church the designation ἡ πανάρετος σοφία, which according to Euseb., *Hist. eccl.* iv. 22. 8, was in the first instance usually applied to the proverbs of Solomon, came to be extended to our book as well.  So for the first time Eusebius, *Chron.* ed. Schoene, ii. 422 (where the conformity on the part of Syncellus and Jerome with the Armenian text serves to show that the expression is peculiar to Eusebius himself).  *Demonstr. evang.* viii. 2. 71, ed. Gaisford: Σίμων, καθ᾽ ὅν Ἰησοῦς ὁ τοῦ Σιράχ ἐγνωρίζετο, ὅ τὴν καλουμένην πανάρετον Σοφίαν συντάξας.  This designation does not occur as yet in con-nection with any of the numerous quotations in Clement and Origen.  In the Latin Church *Ecclesiasticus* came to be adopted as the regular title of the book (Cyprian, *Testimon.* ii. 1, iii. 1, 35, 51, 95, 96, 97, 109, 110, 111).  Comp. the Latin translation of Origen, *In Numer. homil.* xviii. 3 (ed. Lom-matzsch, x. 221) : In libro qui apud nos quidem inter Salomonis volumina haberi solet et Ecclesiasticus dici, apud Graecos vero sapientia Jesu filii Sirach appellatur.

*The use of the book in the Christian Church* begins with the New Testa-ment itself.  In the Epistle of James, above all, there are unmistakeable reminiscences of it.  See in general, Bleek, *Stud. u. Krit.* 1853, pp. 337 sq., 344–348.  Werner, *Theol. Quartalschr.* 1872, p. 265 sqq.  The express quotations begin with Clement of Alexandria, who quotes our book times without number, and on most occasions using either the formula ἡ γραφὴ λέγει, φησίν and such like (thirteen times: *Paedag.* i. 8. 62, 8. 68, ii. 2. 34, 5. 46, 8. 69, 8. 76, 10. 98, 10. 99, iii. 3. 17, 3. 23, 4. 29, 11. 58, 11. 83), or ἡ σοφία λέγει, φησίν and such like (nine times: *Paedeg.* i. 8. 69, 8. 72, 9. 75, ii. 1. 8, 2. 24, 7. 54, 7. 58, 7. 59; *Strom.* v. 3. 18) ; or further, quoting passages now and again as the words of the παιδαγωγός (*Paedag.* ii. 10. 99, 101. 109).  He speaks of the book as the σοφία Ἰησοῦ only twice (*Strom.* i. 4. 27, 10. 47).  On one occasion he appears to call Solomon the author (*Strom.* ii. 5. 24) ; the quotation however is somewhat uncertain.  In one instance again an expression in our σοφία is described as Sophoclean (*Paedag.* ii. 2. 24).  It is very much the same with regard to the quotations in Origen, only here it is impossible in many instances to make out the exact formulae made use of, seeing that the majority of Origen's writings are extant only in Latin translations.  Like Clement he also appears to have quoted the book most frequently as γραφή.  In the Latin text Solomon is several times spoken of as the author (*In Numer. homil.* xviii. 3 = Lommatzsch, x. 221 ; *In Josuam homil.* xi. 2 = Lommatzsch, xi. 108; *In Samuel. homil.* i. 13 = Lommatzsch, xi. 311).  But that this cannot be taken as representing the opinion of Origen himself is proved by the following passage in *contra Cels.* vi. 7 (ed. Lommatzsch, xix. 312) : παραδείξωμεν ἀπὸ τῶν ἱερῶν γραμμάτων, ὅτι προτρέπει καὶ ὁ θεῖος λόγος ἡμᾶς ἐπὶ διαλεκτικήν· ὅπου μὲν Σολομῶντος λέγοντος . . . . ὅπου δὲ τοῦ τὸ σύγγραμμα τὴν σοφίαν [l. τῆς σοφίας] ἡμῖν καταλιπόντος 'Ἰησοῦ υἱοῦ Σειράχ Φάσκοντος. Cyprian uniformly quotes our book as being a work of Solomon's quite as much as any of the rest of his writings (*Testimon.* ii. 1, iii. 6. 12, 35, 51, 53, 95, 96, 97, 109, 113; *Ad Fortunatum*, chap. ix. ; *De opere et eleemosynis*, chap. v. ; *Epist.* iii. 2). Similarly other Latin writers. See especially the passage quoted above from the Latin version of Origen, *In Numer. homil.* xviii. 3 (Lommatzsch, x. 221), and also Jerome who, in his *Comment. in Daniel.* chap. ix. (*Opp.* ed. Vallarsi, v. 686), reproduces the passage from Euseb. *Demonstr. evang.* viii. 2. 71, as follows : Simon, quo regente populum Jesus filius Sirach scripsit librum, qui Graece πανάρετος, appellatur et plerisque Salomonis falso dicitur. On the further history of the use of the book in this way, comp. the works and dissertations devoted to the history of the Old Testament canon, also Jahn's *Einleitung in die göttl. Bücher des A. B.* 2nd ed. vol. ii. § 3 and 4 (1803), 1st and 2nd appendices, as well as my article in Herzog's *Real-Enc.* i. 485–489.

The most important *manuscripts* are : (1) The *Vaticanus*, 1209, *i.e.* the famous Vatican manuscript of the Bible, which however, if we except the eclectic use made of it in the Sixtine edition, has not as yet been made available for the criticism of the text in connection with any edition of our book, not even that of Fritzsche (comp. p. 10). (2) The *Sinaiticus*, in Fritzsche's edition marked No. x. (3) The *Alexandrinus*, in Fritzsche, as in Holmes and Parsons before him, marked No. iii. (4) The fragments of the *Codex Ephraemi*, in Fritzsche = C. (5) A *Venetian* codex, in Fritzsche, who, following Holmes and Parsons, marks it No. xxiii. For further information regarding these manuscripts, see Herzog's *Real-Enc.* 2nd ed. i.489-491.

On the *editions*, see p. 10, and Herzog's *Real-Enc.* i. 494 sq. Separate edition : *Liber Jesu Siracidae Graece, ad fidem codicum et versionum emendatus et perpetua annotatione illustratus a C. G. Bretschneider*, Ratisb. 1806. For further separate editions, see Herzog's *Real-Enc.* i. 495.

Of the *early translations* the following may be specially mentioned : (1) The *old Latin* one which Jerome did *not* revise (*praef. in edit. librorum Salmonis juxta Sept. interpretes* [Vallarsi, x. 436] : Porro in eo libro qui a plerisque Sapientia Salomonis inscribitur et in Ecclesiastico, quem esse Jesu filii Sirach nullus ignorat, calamo temperavi, tantummodo canonicas scripturas vobis emendare desiderans). It found its way into the Vulgate, and hence it came to be printed in all subsequent editions of this latter. The variations of four manuscripts (for Jesus the Son of Sirach as well as for the Wisdom of Solomon) are given by Sabatier in his *Bibliorum sacrorum versiones antiquae*, vol. ii. Remis 1743. The text of the Codex *Amiatinus* has been published (for those two books also) by Lagarde in his *Mittthelunᵧen*, 1884. (2) The two *Syrian* versions : (*a*) The Peschito or the Syrian received text, on the editions of which comp. p. 11 ; (*b*) the *Syrus hexaplaris* which, for our book as well as for the Wisdom of

Solomon, was edited for the first time from a Milan manuscript by Cerini,
*Codex Syro-Hexaplaris, Ambrosianus photolithographice editus*, Mediol.
1874 (forming vol. vii. of the *Monum. Sacra et prof.*). For more on the
early versions, see Herzog's *Real-Enc.* i. 491–494. Also texts in the London
*Polyglot*, vol. iv.

For the *exegetical aids* generally, see p. 11. *Commentaries:* Bret-
schneider in the separate edition previously mentioned. Fritzsche, *Die
Weisheit Jesus Sirach's erklärt und übersetzt (Exegetisches Handbuch zu den
Apokryphen*, 5 Thl.), Leipzig 1859. For the earlier literature, see Fabricius,
*Biblioth. graec.* ed. Harles, iii. 718 sqq. Fürst, *Biblioth. Judaica*, iii. 341 sq.
Fritzsche, p. xl. Herzog's *Real-Enc.* i. 496.

*Special disquisitions:* Gfrörer, *Philo*, vol. ii. (1831) pp. 18–52. Dähne,
*Geschichtl. Darstellung der jüdisch-alexandrinischen Religionsphilosophie*,
vol. ii. (1834) pp. 126–150. Winer, *De utriusque Siracidae aetate*, Erlang.
1832. Comp. also Winer's *Realwörtb.*, art. "Jesus Sirach." Zunz, *Die
gottesdienstl. Vorträge der Juden* (1832), pp. 100–105. Ewald, "Ueber das
griech. Spruchbuch Jesus' Sohnes Sirach's" (*Jahrbb. der bibl. Wissensch.* vol. iii.
1851, pp. 125–140). Bruch, *Weisheitslehre der Hebräer*, 1851, pp. 266–319.
Geiger, *Zeitschr. der deutschen morgenländ Gesellsch.* xii. 1858, pp. 536–543.
Ewald, *Gesch. des Volkes Israel*, iv. 340 sqq. Horowitz, *Das Buch Jesus
Sirach*, Breslau 1865. Fritzsche in Schenkel's *Bibellex.* iii. 252 sqq. Grätz,
*Monatsschr. für Gesch. und Wissensch. des Judenth.* 1872, pp. 49 sqq., 97 sqq.
Merguet, *Die Glaubens- und Sittenlehre des Buches Jesus Sirach*, Königsberg
1874. Seligmann, *Das Buch der Weisheit des Jesus Sirach (Josua ben Sira)
in seinem Verhältniss zu den salomonischen Sprüchen und seiner historischen
Bedeutung*, Breslau 1883. The various introductions of Jahn, Eichhorn,
Bertholdt, Welte, Scholz, Nöldeke, De Wette-Schrader, Reusch, Keil,
Kaulen, Kleinert, Reuss (see p. 12).

## 2. *The Pirke Aboth.*

Nor did the gnomic wisdom become extinct in the period
following that of Jesus the son of Sirach. Jesus Christ
Himself indeed frequently clothed His teaching in this
aphoristic form. But besides the work we have just been
considering, there is still extant, and that in Hebrew, a
collection of such proverbial sayings as we have referred to
above, and which, so far at least as its substratum is concerned, belongs to our period, we mean the so-called *Pirke
Aboth* (פִּרְקֵי אָבוֹת, *sayings of the fathers*), known also under
the abbreviated form of *Aboth.* This collection was inserted
among the tractates of the Mishna (among those of the fourth

division), though strictly speaking it is quite out of place there. For while the rest of the Mishna is simply a codification of Jewish law, our tractate contains a collection of aphorisms after the manner of Jesus the son of Sirach. The only difference is that the Pirke Aboth is not the work of a single individual like that book, but a collection of sayings by some sixty learned doctors, who are mentioned by name. The majority of these latter are also otherwise known as distinguished doctors of the law. As a rule each doctor is represented in the work by a couple or more of his characteristic maxims, such as he had been in the habit of inculcating upon his disciples and contemporaries as rules of life well worthy of special consideration. Many of those maxims are of a purely utilitarian character, but the most of them are related in some way or other to the domain of religion; and it is extremely significant as regards the characteristic tendency of this later age that here the importance and necessity of the study of the law are inculcated with quite a special emphasis (comp. the specimens given at Div. ii. vol. ii. p. 44). The authorities whose utterances were collected in this fashion belong for the most part to the age of the Mishna, *i.e.* to the period extending from the year 70 to 170 A.D. Besides these a few, but only a few, of the authorities belonging to earlier times are also taken notice of. The tractate consists of five chapters. In many editions a sixth chapter is added, but it is of much later origin.

Our tractate is given in every edition of the Mishna (on this see § iii. above). In the edition of the Mishna published under Jost's supervision by Lewent in Berlin 1832–1834, there is an excellent German translation printed in the Hebrew character. There is also a Latin version in Surenhusius, *Mishna*, etc. vol. iv. 1702, pp. 409–484. Of the numerous *separate editions* (some of them accompanied with translations) the following may be specially mentioned: P. Ewald, *Pirke Aboth oder Sprüche der Vater*, ᴜ. 'ersetzt und erklärt, Erlangen 1825. Cahn, *Pirke Aboth, sprachlich und sachlich erläutert, erster Perek* (all that has been published), Berlin 1875. Taylor, *Sayings of the Jewish Fathers*, comprising *Pirke Aboth* and *Pereq R. Meir* in Hebrew and English, with critical and illustrative notes, etc., Cambridge 1877 (where the text is given exactly in accordance with a

Cambridge manuscript, *University Addit.* 470. 1).   Strack, פרקי אבות
*Die Sprüche der Väter, ein ethischer Mischna-Traktat, mit kurzer Einleitung,*
*Anmerkungen und einem Wortregister,* 1882 (where additional literature is to
be found in the introduction).

## IV. HORTATORY NARRATIVE.

### 1. *The Book of Judith.*

The hortatory narrative was a peculiar species of literature
which was frequently cultivated during our period.   Stories
of a purely fictitious character were composed which the author
no doubt intended to be regarded as founded on fact, though
at the same time the object in view was not so much to impart
historical information, as to use these stories as a vehicle for
conveying moral and religious lessons and exhortations.   From
the incidents narrated—and which are taken from the history
of the Jewish people, or from the life of certain individuals—
the readers are expected to learn the truth that the fear of God
is after all the highest wisdom, for God always delivers His
children in some wonderful way in the end, although for a little
He may bring them into circumstances of trouble and danger.

The history of Judith is a narrative of this description.
The following is an outline of the story.   Nebuchadnezzar,
the king of Assyria (*sic !*), calls upon the peoples of Asia
Minor, and among them the inhabitants of Palestine, to
furnish him with troops to help him in the war he was waging
against Arphaxad the king of Media.   As those who received
this summons did not think proper to comply with it,
Nebuchadnezzar, as soon as he had vanquished Arphaxad,
sent his general, Holofernes, with a large force against the
nations of the West, with the view of chastising them for
their disobedience.   Holofernes executes his orders, devastates
the various countries one after another, and demolishes their
sanctuaries in order that Nebuchadnezzar alone might receive
the worship due to God (i.–iii.).   When he got as far as the

plain of Esdrelon, the Jews, who had just returned from the captivity, and had newly re-established their worship (*sic !* in Nebuchadnezzar's time), prepare to offer resistance. By order of Joakim, the high priest, they intercept Holofernes on his way to Jerusalem at Fort Betylua ($B\epsilon\tau\nu\lambda o\acute{\nu}\alpha$; Latin, Bethulia), opposite the plain of Esdrelon (iv.–vi.).[9] Now when Holofernes was besieging Betylua, and the distress within the town had reached a climax, a wealthy, beautiful, and pious widow called Judith resolved to save her people by an act of daring (vii.–ix.). Richly attired, and having no one with her but a bondwoman, she betakes herself to the enemy's camp, and there, under the pretext of wishing to show him how to get to Jerusalem, she contrives to obtain an interview with Holofernes. This latter reposes confidence in her, and is charmed with her beauty. After spending three days in the camp she is called upon to be present at a banquet, at the conclusion of which she is left alone with Holofernes in his tent. But the general is so intoxicated with wine that Judith now finds an opportunity for carrying out her design. She accordingly takes Holofernes's own sword and cuts off his head with it. She then manages to get away from the camp without being observed, while the slave brings away the head of Holofernes in a bag. Having thus accomplished her object,

---

[9] The town of $B\epsilon\tau\nu\lambda o\acute{\nu}\alpha$ (Bethulia) is mentioned nowhere else (except by Christian pilgrims who, on the ground of our story, point sometimes to one place and sometimes to another, as the spot where it stood). That the town actually existed however is hardly to be doubted, for it is scarcely likely that the author would also have to invent an artificial geography to suit his story. On the probable site of the place, see Robinson's *Palestine*, iii. pp. 337 sq. Idem, *Modern Biblical Researches*, p. 443. Fritzsche in Schenkel's *Bibellex.* i. 431. Guérin, *Samarie*, i. pp. 344–350. The Palestine pilgrim Theodosius (ed. Gildemeister, 1882) speaks in § xx. of Betulia, *ubi Olofernes mortuus est*, as being in the extreme south of Palestine, twelve miles south of Raphia. There no doubt a place of this name must have existed (see Wesseling, *Vetera Romanorum itineraria*, p. 719. Kuhn, *Die städtische und bürgerliche Verfassung des römischen Reichs*, ii. 367 sq. Gildemeister's notes to Theodosius). But this cannot have been the locality in question, for our Betylua must have been much farther north, viz. in Samaria.

she returns to Betylua, where she is welcomed with great rejoicings (x.–xiii.). When the enemy discovered what had been done they fled in all directions, and were without difficulty mown down by the Jews. But Judith was extolled by all Israel as their deliverer (xiv.–xvi.).

As our book happens to have found a place in the Christian Bible, not only Catholic but also many Protestant theologians have felt it to be their duty to defend the historical character of the narrative (as was still done, on the Protestant side, above all by O. Wolff, 1861). But the historical blunders are so gross, and the hortatory purpose so obvious, that one cannot venture to assume even a nucleus of fact. The book is a piece of fiction composed with the view of encouraging the people to offer a brave resistance to the enemies of their religion and their liberties. The standpoint of the author is already entirely that of Pharisaic legalism. It is precisely the scrupulous care with which she observes the laws regarding purifications and meats that is so much admired in Judith, while it is plainly enough intimated that it was just for this reason that she had had God upon her side. But the story points to a time when danger threatened not only the people themselves, but their religion as well. For Holofernes demands that Nebuchadnezzar should be worshipped instead of God. This is suggestive of Daniel and the Maccabaean age. Consequently the origin of the book may with great probability be referred to this period (so also Fritzsche, for example, and Ewald, Hilgenfeld 1861, Nöldeke). Seeing that the author appears to be quite as deeply interested in political as in religious liberty, probably we ought to understand him as referring, not to the earlier days of the insurrection, but to a somewhat later period. It would hardly be advisable to come so far down as the Roman age, for the political background (the high priest as supreme head of the Jewish common-wealth, the Hellenistic cities as independent towns, and subject to the suzerain only to the extent of having to furnish troops in time of war) corresponds far more with the Greek than the Roman period. It is entirely out of the question to refer the composition of the book to the time of Trajan (so Hitzig, Grätz, and above all Volkmar, who finds in it a disguised account of Trajan's campaigns); for the story of Judith was already known to Clement of Rome (toward the end of the first century of our era).

Jerome had the book before him in a Chaldee text (see below). How far this agreed with or differed from our Greek text we are not in a position to say exactly, for we have no means of knowing to what extent Jerome followed the Chaldee text when he was preparing the Latin one. In any case, judging from internal grounds, it is tolerably certain— and moreover almost universally acknowledged—that our Greek text is a translation of a Hebrew (or Aramaic) original (see Movers in the article mentioned below, and Fritzsche, *Handb.* p. 115 sq.).

In the time of Origen the book was not in use *among the* (Palestinian) *Jews,* nor was any Hebrew text of it known to exist, for in *Epist. ad African.* chap. xiii. he says: Ἑβραῖοι τῷ Τωβίᾳ οὐ χρῶνται οὐδὲ τῇ Ἰουδήθ· οὐδὲ γὰρ ἔχουσιν αὐτὰ ἐν ἀποκρύφοις ἑβραϊστί· ὡς ἀπ᾽ αὐτῶν μαθόντες ἐγνώκαμεν. It may therefore be conjectured that the Hebrew original was lost at an early period, and that the Chaldee text, with which Jerome was acquainted, was a later version based upon the Greek one. For yet later Jewish versions, see Zunz, *Die gottesdienstl. Vorträge der Juden,* p. 124 sq. Lipsius, "Jüdische Quellen zur Judithsage" (*Zeitschr. für wissenschaftl. Theol.* 1867, pp. 337–366).

*Use in the Christian Church:* Clement of Rome, chap. lv.: Ἰουδὶθ ἡ μακαρία. Tertullian, *De monogam,* chap. xvii.: Nec Joannes aliqui Christi spado, nec Judith filia Merari nec tot alia exempla sanctorum (!). Clement of Alexandria, *Strom.* ii. 7. 35, iv. 19. 118 (Judith being expressly mentioned in the latter passage). Origen, *Fragm. ex libro sexto Stromatum,* in Jerome, *adv. Rufin.* Book I. (Lommatzsch, xvii. 69 sq.): Homo autem, cui incumbit necessitas mentiendi, diligenter attendat, ut sic utatur interdum mendacio, quomodo condimento atque medicamine; ut servet mensuram ejus, ne excedat terminos, quibus usa est Judith contra Holophernem et vicit eum prudenti simulatione verborum. Further quotations in Origen are to be found: *Comm. in Joann.* vol. ii. chap. xvi. (Lommatzsch, xi. 279). In *Lib. Judicum homil.* ix. 1 (Lommatzsch, xi. 279); *De Oratione,* chap. xiii. (Lommatzsch, xvii. 134); *De Oratione,* chap. xxix. (Lommatzsch, xvii. 246). For the further history of the use, see the history of the canon.

*The Greek text* exists in *three different recensions:* (1) The original text, which is that given in the majority of manuscripts, and among others also in the Codex Vaticanus (marked in the critical apparatuses as No. ii.), Alexandrinus (No. iii.) and Sinaiticus (No. x.). (2) A revised text, viz. that of Codex 58 (according to numbering of the manuscripts in Holmes and Parsons). It is on this text also that the Latin and Syriac versions are based. (3) Another recension, though akin to the one just mentioned, is to be found in Codices 19 and 108. *On the editions*, see p. 10.

Of the *early versions* the following call for special mention in the case of our book as well: (1) The *Latin*, and that (*a*) the *Vetus Latinus* (previous to Jerome), for which Sabatier collated five manuscripts, in which the deviations from each other are found to be so great as entirely to corroborate what Jerome says about the *multorum codicum varietas vitiosissima* in his day (Sabatier, *Bibliorum sacrorum Latinae versiones antiquae*, vol. i. Remis 1743, pp. 744–790). On the relation of the texts to one another and to the Greek text, see Fritzsche's *Commentar*, p. 118 sqq. (*b*) Jerome's translation (=Vulgata), on the origin of which he himself says in the preface (*Opp.* ed. Vallarsi, x. 21 sq.): Apud Hebraeos liber Judith inter apocrypha (al. hagiographa) legitur . . . Chaldaeo tamen sermone conscriptus inter historias computatur. Sed quia hunc librum Synodus Nicaena in numero sanctarum scripturarum legitur computasse, acquievi postulationi vestrae, immo exactioni, et sepositis occupationibus, quibus vehementer arctabar, huic unam lucubratiunculam dedi, magis sensum e sensu quam ex verbo verbum transferens. Multorum codicum varietatem vitiosissimam amputavi : sola ea, quae intelligentia integra in verbis Chaldaeis invenire potui, Latinis expressi. According to this, his own confession, the work is a free rendering and one too that was executed somewhat hurriedly. It was based upon the old Latin version. Comp. Fritzsche's *Commentar*, p. 121 sq. For the criticism of the text, see Thielmann, *Beiträge zur Textkritik der Vulgata, insbesondere des Buches Judith*, a school program, Speier 1883. (2) *The Syriac Version*, on which and its editions see p. 11. The London Polyglot gives, in addition to the Greek text, only the Latin Vulgate and the Syriac version.

For *the exegetical aids* generally, see p. 11. Commentaries : Fritzsche, *Die Bücher Tobi und Judith erklärt* (*Exegetisches Handbuch zu den Apokryphen*, 2 vols.), Leipzig 1853. O. Wolff, *Das Buch Judith als geschichtliche Urkunde vertheidigt und erklärt*, Leipzig 1861. The older literature in Fabricius, *Biblioth. graec.* ed. Harles, iii. 736–738. Fürst, *Biblioth. Judaica*, ii. 51 (under "Jehudit"). Volkmar, *Handb. der Einl. in die Apokryphen*, i. 1 (1860), pp. 3–5. Herzog's *Real-Enc.* 2nd ed. i. 496.

*Special disquisitions:* Montfaucon, *La vérité de l'histoire de Judith*, Paris 1690. Movers, "Ueber die Ursprache der deuterokanonischen Bücher des A. T." (*Zeitschr. für Philos. und kathol. Theol.*, Part 13, 1835, p. 31 sqq. [on Judith exclusively]). Schoenhaupt, *Etudes historiques et critiques sur le livre de Judith*, Strasb. 1839. Reuss, art. "Judith," in Ersch and Gruber's *Allg. Enc.* § ii. vol. xxviii. (1851) p. 98 sqq. Nickes, *De libro Judithae*, Vratislav. 1854. *Journal of Sacred Literature and Biblical Record*, vol. iii. 1856, pp. 342–363, vol. xii. 1861, pp. 421–440. Volkmar, " Die Composition des Buches Judith " (*Theol. Jahrbb.* 1857, pp. 441–498). Hilgenfeld, *Zeitschr. für wissenschaftl. Theol.* 1858, pp. 270–281. R. A.

Lipsius, *ibid.* 1859, pp. 39–121. Hitzig, *ibid.* 1860, pp. 240–250. Volkmar, *Handbuch der Einleitung in die Apokryphen*, Part 1, Div. 1, Judith, 1860. Hilgenfeld, *Zeitschr. f. wissensch. Theol.* 1861, pp. 335–385. K. H. A. Lipsius, "Sprachliches zum Buche Judith" (*Zeitschr. f. wissensch. Theol.* 1862, pp. 103–105). Ewald, *Gesch. des Volkes Israel*, vol. iv. (3rd ed. 1864) p. 618 sq. Grätz, *Gesch. der Juden*, vol. iv. (2nd ed. 1866) note 14, p. 439 sqq. R. A. Lipsius, "Judische Quellen zur Judithsage" (*Zeitschr. f. wissenschaftl. Theol.* 1867, pp. 337–366). Fritzsche in Schenkel's *Bibellex.* iii. 445 sqq. The introductions of Jahn, Eichhorn, Bertholdt, Welte, Scholz, Nöldeke, De Wette-Schrader, Reusch, Keil, Kaulen, Kleinert, Reuss (see p. 12).

## 2. *The Book of Tobit.*

The Book of Tobit is a work of a similar character to that of Judith, only it does not move in the domain of political history, but in that of biography, though like it it addresses its exhortations not to the people at large, but to the individual reader. Tobit, the son of Tobiel, of the tribe of Naphtali, who, in the days of Shalmaneser king of Assyria, had been taken captive to Nineveh, relates how, both before and after going into captivity, even under the succeeding kings Sennacherib and Esarhaddon, he, and his wife Anna, and his son Tobias, had always lived in strict accordance with the requirements of the law. Besides this he had been particularly in the habit of interring the bodies of such of his countrymen as had been put to death by the Assyrians and allowed to lie unburied. One day, after performing a kind service of this sort, he lay down to sleep in the open air (in order that, defiled as he was by contact with a dead body, he might not communicate the defilement to his house), when some sparrow's dung fell upon his eyes, in consequence of which he lost his sight (i.–iii. 6). At the same time there was living in Ecbatana in Media a pious Jewess called Sarah, the daughter of Raguel, who already had had seven husbands, but all of whom had been put to death on the marriage night by the evil spirit Asmodeus (iii. 7–17). Meanwhile the aged Tobit remembered, in the midst of his distress, that on one occasion he had left ten talents of silver at Rages in Media, in charge

of one Gabael a member of his own tribe. Consequently
when he saw that his end was approaching he sent his son
Tobias to Rages with instructions to get the money, which he
was to retain as his patrimony. Tobias sets out, taking with
him a fellow-traveller, this latter however being, in reality, no
other than the angel Raphael (iv.–v.). On his way Tobias
bathes in the Tigris and, while doing so, he catches a fish.
At the angel's behest he takes out the fish's heart, liver and
gall, and carries them away with him. Having now reached
Ecbatana they take up their quarters at the house of Raguel.
This latter recognises in Tobias one of her own relations and
gives him her daughter Sarah to be his wife. As soon as the
new-married couple had entered the bride-chamber, Tobias,
acting on the instructions of the angel, raises a smoke by
burning the heart and the liver of the fish, which had the
effect of expelling the demon Asmodeus, who was bent on
disposing of him too precisely as he had disposed of the
former husbands of Sarah. Thus the fourteen days of marriage
festivity were allowed to pass by without disturbance
or interruption, the angel having meanwhile taken the
opportunity to go to Rages to get the money from Gabael
(vi.–ix.). After the marriage celebrations were over Tobias
returns to Nineveh to his parents accompanied by Sarah his
wife, and there he contrives to cure his father's blindness by
anointing his eyes with the gall of the fish (x.–xii.). Full of
gratitude to God, Tobit chants a song of praise, and continues
to live for nearly a hundred years longer. Tobias also lives
to the age of 127 years (xiii.–xiv.).

The plot of the story is well contrived, there is great
variety of details, and the various threads joined on at different
points in the narrative are skilfully interwoven with each
other. Consequently as a literary product our book is
decidedly superior to that of Judith. But the religious
standpoint is exactly the same. Here too, as in Judith, the
whole stress is laid upon the strict observance of the law, of
which the practice of deeds of kindness also forms a part.

And in connection with this, we at the same time get some
instructive glimpses of the superstition of the time. As the
whole story centres in the dispersion, it would seem from this
that the author wrote mainly for the *Jews of the dispersion.*
By holding up those patterns of excellence before the eyes of
his readers he hopes to produce such an impression upon the
minds of those of his countrymen scattered among the Gentiles
as may lead them to adhere no less faithfully to the law, and
to observe it in an equally strict and conscientious manner.
In consequence of the purpose of the book being as here
described, it is impossible to determine whether it had its
origin in Palestine or in the dispersion.

The date of the composition of the work can only be fixed
within tolerably wide limits. Comparatively speaking, it may
be regarded as most certain of all that the book was written
*previous to the building of the temple of Herod.* No doubt Hitzig
thought (*Zeitschr. für wissenschaftl. Theol.* 1860, p. 250 sqq.)
that we were bound to assume that it was written after the
destruction of the temple by Titus, because among the predictions at the close of the book it is above all foretold that
the temple will be rebuilt again with great magnificence
(xiii. 16 f., xiv. 4, 5). But on more careful consideration we
will find it probable that the author wrote when the temple
of Zerubbabel was still standing. He places himself at the
standpoint of the Assyrian age, and from this he predicts first
of all the destruction of the temple by the Chaldaeans, and
then its reconstruction, where however he distinguishes between
two things: (1) the restoration of an unpretending structure
till the lapse of a definite period; and (2) the rebuilding with
extraordinary magnificence and splendour that is to take place
at the expiry of this period (xiv. 5 : καὶ οἰκοδομήσουσι τὸν
οἶκον, οὐχ οἷος ὁ πρότερος, ἕως πληρωθῶσι καιροὶ τοῦ αἰῶνος·
καὶ μετὰ ταῦτα ἐπιστρέψουσιν ἐκ τῶν αἰχμαλωσιῶν καὶ
οἰκοδομήσουσιν Ἱερουσαλὴμ ἐντίμως· καὶ ὁ οἶκος τοῦ θεοῦ ἐν
αὐτῇ οἰκοδομηθήσεται εἰς πάσας τὰς γενεὰς τοῦ αἰῶνος οἰκο-
δομῇ ἐνδόξῳ, καθὼς ἐλάλησαν περὶ αὐτῆς οἱ προφῆται).

The *historical structure* with which the author is acquainted
is therefore more unpretending than the former one, the temple
of Solomon (οὐχ οἷος ὁ πρότερος). For surely he could
hardly have expressed himself as he does if he was already
acquainted with the temple of Herod. If this latter then
forms the *terminus ad quem* for the composition of our book,
the safest course would be to say that it was written *in the
course of the last two centuries before Christ*. For we are
precluded by the whole spirit of the book from going farther
back.

In preparing his Latin version of our book Jerome made
use of a *Chaldee text* precisely as in the case of the Book of
Judith (see below). Such a text is *still extant* in the shape
of a manuscript that only at a comparatively recent date found
its way into the Bodleian library at Oxford, from which
Neubauer took his edition (*The Book of Tobit, a Chaldee text*,
etc., ed. by Neubauer, Oxford 1878). Both texts, the Latin
of Jerome and the Chaldee one, are marked by a singular
peculiarity common to themselves, and to themselves alone.
The peculiarity in question is this, that while, according to
the Greek text and the other versions, Tobit in the first
section (i. 1—iii. 6) tells his story in the *first* person, and only
changes to the *third* after Sarah makes her appearance in the
narrative, Jerome and the author of the Chaldee text, on the
other hand, make use of the third person from beginning to
end. From this it is highly probable that Jerome had before
him, if not exactly our Chaldee text, at all events one very
much akin to it (that our Chaldee text is only the reproduction of an older one is probable for other reasons, see
below). But the peculiarity just referred to also serves to
prove at the same time that our Chaldee text is *not* based
upon the Greek one. For the inserting of the third person
all through is clearly an afterthought, while the transition
from the first to the third correctly represents the original
text. *But there is no ground whatever for supposing that our
Greek text is a version based upon a Semitic original*. For the

two Hebrew texts, which were printed in the sixteenth
century, are also later products (see below). On the other
hand, there are numerous peculiarities of diction (for example
the phrase καλὸς καὶ ἀγαθός, vii. 7) which serve to confirm
the view that the Greek must have been the original text.[10]

It would appear, from what Origen asserts, that in his time our book was
not in use among *the* (Palestinian) *Jews*, and that a Hebrew text was
unheard of (Origen, *Epist. ad African.* chap. xiii. ; for the terms of the
passage, see p. 35. Idem, *De oratione*, chap. xiv. = Lommatzsch, xvii.
143 : τῇ δὲ τοῦ Τωβὴτ βίβλῳ ἀντιλέγουσιν οἱ ἐκ περιτομῆς ὡς μὴ ἐνδιαθήκῳ).
But that it came to be received with favour not long after is proved by
the existing Semitic manuscripts, with one of which Jerome was already
acquainted.

Its use in *the Christian Church* is already evidenced by the apostolic
Fathers. Comp. 2 Clem. xvi. 4 = Tobit xii. 8 (on which see Harnack's
notes to 2 Clem.). *Epist. Polycarp.* x. 2 = Tobit iv. 10. According to
Irenaeus, i. 30. 11, the Ophites included Tobias among the Old Testament
prophets. Clement of Alexandria repeatedly quotes the book as γραφή
(*Strom.* ii. 23. 139, vi. 12. 102). Hippolytus in his commentary on the
story of Susannah brings in the story of Tobit by way of parallel (Hippolyt.
ed. Lagarde, p. 151). Origen in his *Epist. ad African.* refers at some
length to the story of Tobias, and adds quite in a general way : χρῶνται τῷ
Τωβίᾳ αἱ ἐκκλησίαι. Consequently he in like manner frequently quotes it
as γραφή (*Comment. in epist. ad Rom.* book viii. chap. xi. *fin.* = Lommatzsch, vii. 272 ; *De oratione*, chap. xi. = Lommatzsch, xvii. 124 ; comp.
besides, *De oratione*, chaps. xiv. and xxxi. = Lommatzsch, xvii. 143, 284 ;
*contra Cels.* v. 19 = Lommatzsch, xix. 196). Cyprian makes frequent use
of the book (*Testimon.* iii. 1, 6, 62 ; *Ad Fortunatum*, chap. xi. ; *De opere et
eleemosynis*, chaps. v. and xx.). For more on this subject, see the works on
the history of the Canon ; also Jahn's *Einleit. in die göttl. Bücher des Alten
Bundes*, 2nd ed. vol. ii. § 3 and 4 (1803), 1st and 2nd appendices.

Of *the Greek text* there are *three recensions* in existence : (1) The one
found in the majority of manuscripts, and among others also in *Codex
Vaticanus* (No. ii.) and *Alexandrinus* (No. iii.). To it the Syrian version
adheres as far as chap. vii. 9. (2) The text of the *Codex Sinaiticus* (No. x.),
which deviates very much from the ordinary text. To it again the old
Latin version adheres, though not entirely yet chiefly. (3) The text of
*Codices* 44, 106 and 107 (according to the numbering of Holmes
and Parsons), which is akin to that of the *Codex Sinaiticus*. However,
this latter appears to have been adhered to by the manuscripts just
mentioned only from vi. 9 to xiii. 8, while in all that precedes and follows
they conform to the ordinary recension. This text again is that on which,

---

[10] Comp. also Fritzsche's *Commentar*, p. 8. Nöldeke, *Monatsberichte de
Berliner Akademie*, 1879, p. 61.

from vii. 10 onwards, the Syrian version is based. Whether the ordinary text or that of the *Codex Sinaiticus* is the original one it is difficult to determine, for the claims of both admit of being well supported. Fritzsche (*Proleg.* to his edition), and Nöldeke (*Monatsberichte der Berliner Akademie*), 1879, p. 45 sqq., decide in favour of the ordinary text, while Reusch (in his separate edition; comp. also *Theol. Literaturzeitung*, 1878, p. 333 sq.) upholds the claims of the *Codex Sinaiticus*. In Fritzsche's edition of the Apocrypha the whole three texts are printed alongside of each other. The text of the *Codex Sinaiticus* has been published separately by Reusch (*Libellus Tobit e codice Sinaitico editus et recensitus*, Bonnae 1870). Comp. further on the editions, p. 10.

Of the *early versions* we may mention: (1) The *Latin*, and that (*a*) the *old Latin one*, the text of which shows very considerable variations in the four manuscripts collated by Sabatier, though it substantially agrees with that of the *Codex Sinaiticus* (Sabatier, *Bibliorum sacrorum Latinae versiones antiquae*, vol. i.). Sabatier's four manuscripts represent two recensions, the one of which is contained in three of them, and the other in the remaining one (*Vat.* 7).[11] Fragments of a third recension are furnished by the quotations given in the *Speculum Augustini* (on which see Reusch, *Das Buch Tobias*, 1857, p. xxvi.), edited by Mai. The text of a certain *Codex Ambrosianus* has not yet been inspected. Ceriani contemplates preparing an edition of it for the *Monum. sacra et profana*, but so far as I am aware it has not as yet appeared. The same may be said of a Münich codex, which Ziegler purposes editing (Neubauer, *The Book of Tobit*, p. 10, note 6). See in general, Ilgen, *Die Geschichte Tobi's*, p. 183 sqq. Fritzsche, *Handb.* p. 11 sq. Reusch, *Das Buch Tobias*, p. 25 sqq. Sengelmann, *Das Buch Tobit*, pp. 49-56. (*b*) Jerome's version (= *Vulgata*), which was executed in circumstances similar to those under which that of Judith was prepared, see *Praef. in vers. libri Tob.* (Vallarsi, x. 1 sq.): Exigitis, ut librum Chaldaeo sermone conscriptum ad Latinum stilum traham, librum utique Tobiae, quem Hebraei de catalogo divinarum scripturarum secantes his quae apocrypha [al. hagiographa] memorant manciparunt. Feci satis desiderio vestro . . . . Et quia vicina est Chaldaeorum lingua sermoni Hebraico, utriusque linguae peritissimum loquacem reperiens, unius diei laborem arripui, et quidquid ille mihi Hebraicis verbis expressit, hoc ego accito notario sermonibus Latinis exposui. A comparison of this version with the old Latin one will show that Jerome based his translation upon this latter, giving a somewhat free rendering of it, however much he may, at the same time, have kept the Chaldee text in view. Comp. Ilgen, p. cxliv. sqq. Fritzsche, p. xii. sq. Reusch, p. xxxii. Sengelmann, pp. 56-61. We have no further means of verification notwithstanding the recovery of the Chaldee text, for this latter is itself simply a reproduction, with greater or less accuracy, of the original one. (2) The *Syriac* text which has come down to

---

[11] The text of *Vaticanus* 7 has (according to Reusch, *Libellus Tobit*, 1870, p. 4) been more carefully edited by Bianchini, *Vindiciae canonicarum scripturarum*, Romae 1740, p. cccl., than by Sabatier. On this text comp. also Bickell, *Zeitschr. für kathol. Theol.* 1878, p. 218.

**us** (printed for the first time in the *London Polyglot*, vol. iv.) is composed of the fragments of two different versions, one of which (as far as vii. 9) followed the ordinary Greek text, while the other (from vii. 10 onwards) followed the text of Codices 44, 106, 107. See Ilgen, pp. cxxxvii. sq., clxix. sqq. Reusch, p. xx. sq. Sengelmann, p. 47 sq. On the editions, see p. 11. The Book of Tobit is not given in the large Peschito manuscript of Milan.

(3) The *Chaldee* text (see p. 40 above), edited by Neubauer, agrees substantially with the Greek recension of the *Codex Sinaiticus* on which it was probably based. But the text as we now have it is in all likelihood only an abridged and modified form of an older Chaldee text. See, besides Neubauer's edition, Bickell, *Zeitschr. für kathol. Theol.* 1878, pp. 216–222, and especially Nöldeke, *Monatsberichte der Berliner Akademie*, 1879, pp. 45–69.

(4) Lastly, we have further to mention *two Hebrew versions* which have been frequently printed since the sixteenth century, namely : (*a*) The so-called *Hebraeus Fagii*, a Hebrew version based upon the ordinary Greek text published first of all at Constantinople in 1517, and then by Fagius in 1542. On this see Ilgen, p. cxxxviii. sqq. Fritzsche, p. 9 sq. Reusch, p. xlvii. Sengelmann, p. 63 sq. (*b*) The Codex *Hebraeus Münsteri*, a free Hebrew version which (according to Neubauer, p. 12) was published first at Constantinople in 1516, and then by Sebastian Münster in 1542. Until the discovery of the Chaldee text it was supposed that the old Latin version was based upon it (so Ilgen, p. ccxvii. sqq. ; Fritzsche, p. 14 ; Reusch, p. xlvii. sq. ; Sengelmann, p. 61 sqq.). After seeing the Chaldee text, we cannot but regard it as certain that the Codex *Hebraeus Münsteri* is based upon *it*, though not on that text as it has come down to us, but on an older form of it. See especially Nöldeke as above; also Bickell as above. As in the Greek text, so also in this older form, the first person was made use of in the first three chapters, and this has also been retained in the Codex *Heb. Münst.* Neubauer has published an excellent edition of this codex based upon a collation of two manuscripts, and accompanied with an English translation (*The Book of Tobit, a Chaldee text*, etc., ed. by Neubauer, Oxford 1878). Both the Hebrew texts along with a Latin translation have also found a place in the *London Polyglot*, vol. iv. On the earlier editions, comp. Wolf, *Bibliotheca Hebraea*, i. 391 sqq., ii. 413 sq., iii. 275, iv. 154. Fabricius-Harles, *Biblioth. graec.* iii. 738 sq. Steinschneider, *Catalogus librorum Hebraeorum in Bibliotheca Bodleiana* (1852–1860), cols. 200–202. Fürst, *Biblioth. Judaica*, iii. 425.

For the *exegetical aids* generally, see p. 11, above. Commentaries: Ilgen, *Die Geschichte Tobi's nach drei verschieden Originalen, dem Griechischen dem Lateinischen des Hieronymus und einem Syrischen übersetzt und mit Anmerkungen exegetischen und kritischen Inhalts auch einer Einleitung versehen*, Jena 1800. Fritzsche, *Die Bücher Tobi und Judith erklärt (Exeget. Handb. zu den Apokryphen*, vol. ii.), Leipzig 1853. Reusch, *Das Buch Tobias übersetzt und erklärt*, Freiburg 1857. Sengelmann, *Das Buch Tobit erklärt*, Münster 1877. For the older literature, consult Fabricius-Harles, iii. 738 sq. Fürst, *Bibl. Jud.* iii. 425 sq. Fritzsche, p. 20. Herzog's *Real-Enc.* 2nd ed. i. 496.

*Special disquisitions:* [Eichhorn], "Ueber das Buch Tobias" (*Allgem. Biblioth. der bibl. Literatur*, ii. 410 sqq.). Reusch, "Der Dämon Asmodäus im B. Tobias" (*Theol. Quartalschr.* 1856, pp. 422–445). Idem, Review of Sengelmann, in the *Theol. Quartalschr.* 1858, pp. 318–332. *Journal of Sacred Literature and Biblical Record*, iv. 1857, pp. 59–71, vi. 1858, pp. 373–382. Hitzig, *Zeitschr. für wissenschaftl. Theol.* 1860, pp. 250–261. Hilgenfeld, *ibid.* 1862, pp. 181–198. Ewald, *Gesch. des Volkes Israel*, vol. iv. (3rd ed.) p. 269 sqq. Grätz, *Gesch. der Juden*, vol. iv. (2nd ed.) p. 466 sq. note 17. Kohut, "Etwas über die Moral und die Abfassungszeit d. B. Tobias" (Geiger's *Jüdische Zeitschr. für Wissenschaft u. Leben*, x. 1872, pp. 49–73 ; also in a separate form). Fritzsche in Schenkel's *Bibellex.* v. 540 sqq. Renan, *L'église chrétienne* (1879), pp. 554–561. Grätz, *Monatsschr. f. Gesch. und Wissensch. des Judenth.* 1879, pp. 145 sqq., 385 sqq., 433 sqq., 509 sqq. Grimm, *Zeitschr. f. wissenschaftl. Theol.* 1881, pp. 33–56. Preiss, *Zeitschr. f. wissenschaftl. Theol.* 1885, pp. 24–51. The introductions of Jahn, Eichhorn, Bertholdt, Welte, Scholz, Nöldeke, De Wette-Schrader, Reusch, Keil, Kaulen, Kleinert, Reuss (see p. 12).

## V. PSEUDEPIGRAPHIC PROPHECIES.

The whole of the literary products hitherto mentioned were fashioned more or less after the models of the older and by that time the canonical literature, to which moreover they made the closest approximation both in point of spirit and matter. We have now a new species of literature, and one that, in our period, was more popular and influential than any other, namely, the *pseudepigraphic prophecies.* The old prophets, in their teachings and exhortations, addressed themselves directly to the people, and that first and foremost through their oral utterances and then, but only as subordinate to these, by means of written discourse as well. But now when men felt themselves impelled at any time by their religious enthusiasm to try to influence their contemporaries through their teaching and exhortations, instead of directly addressing them in person like the prophets of old, they did so by a writing purporting to be the work of some one or other of the great names of the past, in the hope that in this way the effect would be all the surer and all the more powerful. We may venture to regard the predilection shown for the kind of medium here in question as evidence of the somewhat degenerate character of the age. It shows that there were natures of a highly religious cast who nevertheless had no longer the courage to confront their contemporaries with the proud claim to have their words listened to as the words of God Himself, but who rather seemed to think it necessary to conceal themselves under the guise of some one or other of the acknowledged authorities of the olden time. And so for this reason all the writings of a prophetic character that make their appearance in our period are *pseudepigraphic*. They are given to the world bearing the name of an *Enoch*, a *Moses*, a *Baruch*, an *Ezra*, or of the *twelve patriarchs*, but we do not know who the real author is of any one of them. Then the standpoint of the pseudonymous author to whom the work is ascribed is, as a rule, skilfully maintained throughout. The writings are composed in such a way as to make it appear as though they had actually been intended for the contemporaries of the respective personages whose names they bear. But what is addressed to those assumed contemporaries is in reality of such a nature that it concerns rather more the contemporaries of the real author himself. From his artificially assumed standpoint the writer looks on into the future and predicts, often with considerable detail, the future history of Israel and the world, but always taking care to see that predictions stop short at his (the real author's) own time, and so to arrange matters as to make it appear that this was also to be the time of judgment and of the dawn of redemption alike, and all this for the purpose of serving as a warning to sinners on the one hand and to comfort and encourage the godly on the other. The fact that the alleged predictions are seen to have been already fulfilled in the previous history of Israel and the world, serves at the same time to inspire confidence in the prophet so that there will now be a readier disposition to believe him when he predicts what (from the standpoint of the real contemporaries) still lies in the future.

The *contents* of those pseudepigraphic prophecies are of a very varied description. As in the older prophetic writings, so also in these two things were as a rule combined with each other, viz. *instruction* and *exhortation*. Prominence is given sometimes to the one and sometimes to the other, to the former for example in the Book of Enoch, to the latter in the Testaments of the Twelve Patriarchs. But in no case is one or other of them found to be entirely absent. The exhortation is uniformly based upon the previous instruction, while the religious instruction thus imparted always aims at stimulating the reader to a behaviour of a corresponding nature. But the character of the writings varied very much according as one or other of those elements happened to predominate in them. At one time they give one more the impression of moral sermons (as for example the Testaments of the Twelve Patriarchs), at another they are more concerned with the unveiling of divine mysteries (as in the case of the Book of Enoch). Yet however much they may thus differ from one another, they all belong, so far as their essential character is concerned, to one and the same category. The revelations given in them, in due keeping with their hortatory purpose, have reference first of all to the history of the Jewish people and of mankind in general, but they also concern themselves, though only in a more subordinate way, with certain theological problems, such as the question regarding the connection between sin and calamity on the one hand and righteousness and prosperity on the other. But besides this they also seek to enlighten the reader with regard to the mysteries of nature, the supernatural and heavenly background of the operations of the natural world. On all those matters, which are more or less remotely connected with the religious life, they claim to give authentic information.

The *form* in which those communications are clothed is that of *apocalypse*. They claim throughout to be supernatural revelations given to mankind by the mouth of those men of God in whose names the various writings appear. The peculiarity of this later "apocalyptic" medium as distinguished from the older genuine prophecy is this, that it imparts its revelations not in clear and plain language, but in a mysterious *enigmatical form*. The thing intended to be communicated is veiled under parables and symbols, the meaning of which can only be guessed at. However, the extent to which this veiling is carried is not always the same. At one time it only goes the length of the author's abstaining from mentioning the *names* of persons that are otherwise plainly enough indicated, while at another again the whole thing is symbolical from begininng to end. Persons are represented under the symbolism of animals, events in the history of the human race under that of the operations of nature. And if, as sometimes happens, the interpretation is added, this latter again is only a less obscure form of the enigma and not a solution of it.

The majority of those writings were *occasioned* by times of trouble and distress, or by the depressed circumstances of the people generally. It is the contradiction that is found to exist between the ideal and the actual, between the promises which God has given to His people and the existing bondage and persecution which they had to endure at the hands of Gentile powers,—it was this contradiction I say that impelled their authors to write those works. And where no present trouble or persecution actually existed, the motive for writing may be looked for in the pessimistic view of things which they were cherishing at the time. The existing state of matters, the present condition of the chosen people, was felt to be a glaring contradiction to its true destiny. Such a state of things could not last, an entire revolution must of necessity take place and that ere long. Such is the conviction to which expression is given in the whole of the writings now in question. They therefore owe their origin, on the one hand, to a pessimistic view of the present and, on the other, to an intense faith in the glorious future of the people. And the *object* at which their authors aim is to awaken and quicken the same faith in others as well. They insist that there must be no such thing as doubting, but rather a clinging with all stedfastness to the belief that God will conduct His people safely through all the afflictions which He has been sending upon them in order to test and purify them, and bring them at length to greatness and glory. This belief must meanwhile comfort and encourage the people in the midst of their present sufferings. But inasmuch as the revolution in question is represented as being near at hand, the wicked are meant at the same time to take warning from this and repent so long as there is an opportunity to do so. For the coming judgment will be a right stern one, bringing salvation to the godly and perdition to the wicked. The actual *effect* of those enthusiastic predictions appears to have been both powerful and lasting. Through them the Messianic hope was quickened, through them the people were confirmed in the belief that they were called not to serve but to rule. But it is for this very reason that this apocalyptic literature has played so important a part in developing the political sentiments of the people. If we find that, from the date of the tax imposed by Quirinius, whereby Judaea was placed directly under Roman administration, revolutionary tendencies among the people grew stronger and stronger year by year till they led at last to the great insurrection of the year 66, then there cannot be a doubt that this process was essentially promoted if not exclusively caused by the apocalyptic literature.

The standpoint of the whole of those writings is essentially that of orthodox Judaism. They exhort to a God-fearing behaviour in accordance with the regulative principles of the law, and deplore the tendency to disregard the law that was manifesting itself here and there. But, at the same time, it is not the official Judaism of the Pharisaic scribes to which expression is give here. The principal stress is laid not on what the people have *to do*, but on what they have *to expect*. In regard to the former of these, viz. conduct, matters are treated more in their general aspect, without any special stress being laid exactly upon scholastic correctness in details. We should further add that neither are these writings without numerous individual peculiarities, as is only to be expected in the case of the products, such as these are, of an intense religious enthusiasm. However, we cannot feel warranted in specifying the particular circle from which any one of those writings may be supposed to have emanated. The *Essenes* above all have been thought of in this connection.[12] But what points of contact there are, are far too slender to admit of our speaking even of one of the writings in question as an Essenian product. The most we can say is, that they are not the product of the school, but of a free religious individuality.

## 1. *The Book of Daniel.*

The oldest and most original of the kind of writings now under consideration—and the one that at the same time served as a model for those of a later date—is the canonical Book of Daniel. The unknown author of this apocalypse originated with creative energy those modes of representation of which the subsequent authors of similar works knew how to avail themselves. The book is the *direct product of the Maccabaean struggles,* in the very heart of which it came into existence. With the conflict actually raging around him, the author aims at encouraging and comforting his co-religionists by assuring them of speedy deliverance.

The book is divided into two parts. *The first part* (i.–vi.) *contains a series of hortatory narratives; the second* (vii.–xii.) *a series of prophetic visions.* Chap. i. rehearses how young Daniel and his three companions were brought up at the court of Nebuchadnezzar king of Babylon. We are told how, in order to avoid defiling themselves by partaking of Gentile food, the four young men refused to eat of the meat provided for them by the king, and preferred pulse and water instead.

[12] So Hilgenfeld in his book entitled *Die jüdische Apokalyptik* (1857), p. 253 sqq. ; and, to a certain extent, also Lucius, *Der Essenismus* (1881), p. 109 sqq.

Notwithstanding this, as we further learn, they seemed to thrive better than the other young men who partook of the royal fare. The hortatory object of this narrative is obvious at a glance. In chap. ii. Nebuchadnezzar the king dreams a dream, and calls upon the magi not only to interpret it, but also to tell him what the dream itself was. Not one however of the magi of the country is found able to do this. Daniel alone shows himself capable of performing such a feat, and for this he is abundantly rewarded by the king, and appointed to the office of chief of all the magi of Babylon. In the course of the interpretation of the dream it is intimated that the kingdom of Nebuchadnezzar would be succeeded by yet three other kingdoms, the last of which (the Greek one) would be "split up" (into that of the Ptolemies on the one hand, and that of the Seleucidae on the other) and crushed to pieces by the hand of God. In chap. iii. Nebuchadnezzar causes a golden image to be set up and orders it to be worshipped. For refusing to comply with this order Daniel's three companions are cast into a fiery furnace, but when it is found that they were not in the least injured by the flames, Nebuchadnezzar sees his own folly and promotes the three young men to positions of high distinction. In chap. iv. Nebuchadnezzar publishes an edict in which he confesses how, as a punishment for his impious presumption, he was smitten with insanity; and how, after he had duly given God the glory, he is restored once more to his former greatness. In chap. v. Belshazzar king of Babylon and son of Nebuchadnezzar makes a great feast, at which the vessels which his father had taken from the temple at Jerusalem are made use of as drinking-cups. To punish Belshazzar for this he loses both his kingdom and his life together that very night. In chap. vi. Darius king of the Medes, and the conqueror and successor of Belshazzar, in order to punish Daniel for praying to his own God in defiance of the king's prohibition, causes him to be cast into a den of lions, where however he does not sustain the slightest injury. The result of this is that

Darius comes to see his own folly, and issues a decree to the effect that Daniel's God is to be worshipped throughout the whole kingdom. It is no less obvious that a hortatory purpose pervades the last four of those narratives (iii.–vi.) as well, while, at the same time, the contemporary historical background is also plainly discernible. By the three kings we are in every instance to understand Antiochus Epiphanes as being the person meant, who, with impious arrogance, assumed such lofty airs (iv.), who carried off the sacred vessels from the temple at Jerusalem (v.), who forbade the Jews to worship their own God (vi.), and commanded them to pay divine honour to the gods of the Gentiles (iii.). We are shown how, as a judgment for his misdeeds, he is given over to destruction, and how, on the other hand, the Jews whom he persecuted are miraculously delivered. While therefore all those narratives are meant to stimulate to unfailing stedfastness the faithful people whom Antiochus was persecuting, we are introduced in the *second part* of the book (vii.–xii.) to a series of visions in which, from the standpoint of the Chaldaean period, the future development of the events of the world is foretold. The whole of the visions agree in this, that the monarchy which they foretell as being the last is the Greek one, which ultimately resolves itself into the godless rule of Antiochus Epiphanes, who, though not mentioned by name, is plainly enough indicated. We have above all in the last vision (from x. to xii.) a prediction of a highly detailed character, in which are foretold the history of the kingdoms of the Ptolemies and the Seleucidae respectively (for it is these that are meant by the kingdom of the south and the kingdom of the north), and their manifold relations to one another. Here the most remarkable thing is that the prediction becomes more and more minute and detailed the nearer it approaches to the time of Antiochus Epiphanes. Precisely the history of this monarch is here related with the utmost minuteness, without his name being once mentioned (xi. 21 sqq.). It is still the suppression of the Jewish worship, the desecration of the temple, and the erection of the heathen altar for sacrifice, as well as the commencement of the Maccabaean insurrection (xi. 32–35), that are predicted. But at this point the predictions suddenly stop, and the author now cherishes the expectation that, immediately after the struggles connected with the rising in question, the consummation will come and the kingdom of God begin to appear. Nor is it merely in the eleventh chapter that the predictions stop at this period, but in no other part of the book does the horizon of the author ever stretch beyond it, not even in the visions of the four monarchies (ii. and vii.). For the fourth is not the Roman Empire, but the Greek monarchy, as any one who candidly considers the matter will readily admit (the first being the Babylonian, the second that of the Medes, the third the Persian, and the fourth the Greek). In presence of these facts it is admitted by all the expositors of the present day—by all, that is, who are not hampered by dogmatic predilections—that our book was composed at the time of the Maccabaean rising, or, to speak more precisely, between 167 and 165 B.C., that is to say before the re-consecrating of the temple, for as yet this latter event lies beyond the horizon of the author. It is only as viewed in the light of this period that the book can be said to have either sense or meaning. From beginning to end it is framed with the view of exercising a practical influence precisely in such a time as this. With its various narratives and revelations it seeks, on the one hand, to encourage the hosts of faithful Israelites to maintain a stedfast adherence to the law, and, on the other, to console them with the certain prospect of immediate deliverance. It is even at this very moment—such is the author's thought—when the distress is at its height, that the deliverance is also nearest at hand. The days of the Gentile monarchies are drawing to a close. The last and, at the same time, the most godless and criminal of them all, is on the point of being annihilated through the impending miraculous breaking in on the part of God upon the current of the

world's history, whereupon the sovereignty of the world will
be committed to the "saints of the Most High," the faithful
Israelites.   They will inherit the kingdom and possess it for
ever and ever.    That is what those who are just now so
sorely oppressed and persecuted are to bear in mind for their
comfort and encouragement.

The book was composed partly in Hebrew and partly in
Aramaic (Chaldee), the Aramaic portion being that extending
from ii. 4 to vii. 28.   And so from this we can see that it was
just then that the Aramaic came to be the prevailing dialect
of Palestine, while the Hebrew fell more and more into
desuetude.   In the course of two centuries after this, viz. in
the time of Jesus Christ, we find that the process, which at
this point is thus beginning, has been already fully completed
(see Div. ii. vol. i. p. 9).

The high *estimation* in which from the first this book was held by
believing Israelites is best shown by the fact that it always continued to
*retain its place in the canon.*   Even that somewhat older work, the Wisdom
of Jesus the Son of Sirach, was ultimately excluded from the Hebrew canon,
and that, although in point of form and contents it approximates more
closely to the early Hebrew literature than the Book of Daniel.   Obviously
the reason of both those facts is this, that the work of Jesus the son of
Sirach was published under the author's real name, whereas the Book of
Daniel appeared under the name of one of the older authorities.   It is in
fact the only literary product of its time that retained a place in the canon,
with the exception of a number of psalms which happened to have been
previously embodied in the Psalter.   We already find evidence of *acquaintance with our book* in the oldest of the Sibyls (*Orac. Sibyll.* iii. 396–400,
only a few decades later than Daniel) ; further in 1 Macc. ii. 59, 60, and
Baruch i. 15–18.

The *exegetical and critical literature* of the Book of Daniel is enumerated
in De Wette-Schrader's *Einleitung in die kanon. und apokr. Bücher des
A. T.* (1869), p. 485 sq.   Kleinert, *Abriss der Einleitung zum A. T.* (1878),
pp. 59–61.   Reuss, *Gesch. der heil. Schriften Alten Testaments* (1881),
§ 464.   Graf, art. "Daniel," in Schenkel's *Bibellex.* i. 564.

Perhaps we may be allowed in passing to offer here a small contribution
toward the exposition of chap. ix. 24–27.   In that passage the author
endeavours to explain the seventy years of Jeremiah (Jer. xxv. 11, 12), by
taking them to mean seventy *weeks of years* ($70 \times 7$)   And this number
again he proceeds to break up into $7 + 62 + 1$.   Then, as the context makes
it well-nigh impossible to doubt, he reckons the first seven weeks of years
(therefore 49 years) as the period that would elapse between the *destruc-*

*tion of Jerusalem* and the accession of Cyrus, which pretty nearly coincides with the actual number of years embraced in that period (588–537 B.C.). The subsequent sixty-two weeks of years he reckons, and that with rather more nicety than before, as being the period extending from the time of Cyrus to his (the author's) own day : till " an anointed one shall be cut off," by which we have probably to understand the murder of the high priest Onias III. in the year 171. But the number of years between 537 and 171 is only 366, whereas 62 weeks of years would be equal to 434. Consequently the author has miscalculated to the extent of 70 years. Some have supposed that this is impossible, and have therefore tried in various ways to evade the only interpretation of which the context will permit. But that such an error as this is actually possible is proved most conclusively by the circumstance that Josephus, for example, likewise falls into an error of a similar kind, as may be seen from the three following passages : (1) *Bell. Jud.* vi. 4. 8, where he gives 639 as the number of years that elapsed between the second year of Cyrus's reign till the destruction of Jerusalem by Titus (70 A.D.). In that case the second year of Cyrus's reign would have to be the year 569 B.C. (2) *Antt.* xx. 10, where he makes out that there was a period of 414 years between the return from the captivity (in the first year of Cyrus's reign) and the time of Antiochus V. Eupator (164–162). (3) *Antt.* xiii. 11. 1, where he calculates that 481 years elapsed between the return from the captivity (in the first year of the reign of Cyrus) and the time of Aristobulus (105–104). Consequently according to (1) the accession of Cyrus must have taken place in the year 570 B.C., according to (2) somewhere about 578 B.C., and according to (3) in 586 B.C., whereas in point of fact it took place in 537 B.C. *Josephus therefore has miscalculated to the extent of from forty to fifty years too many.* A somewhat nearer approach to the numbers of Daniel is made by the Jewish Hellenist Demetrius, who reckons that 573 years elapsed between the carrying away of the ten tribes into captivity and the time of Ptolemy IV. (222 B.C.), and so, *precisely like Daniel, putting it at some seventy years too many* (see the passage as given in Clement of Alexand. *Strom.* i. 21. 141 ; for more about Demetrius, see § 33 below). Therefore, in estimating the length of the period in question at some seventy years too much, Daniel is obviously following some current view on the matter. Just at the time now under consideration there was as yet an absence of the necessary means for determining the correct chronology. In Daniel's case, however, the error is all the less to be wondered at, that his estimating the length of the period referred to at sixty-two year weeks was simply a consequence of his interpretation of Jeremiah's prophecy.

## 2. *The Book of Enoch.*

*Enoch* (in common with Elijah) occupies this singular position among the Old Testament men of God, that when removed from the earth he was carried directly to heaven.

A man of this stamp could not but appear peculiarly well fitted to serve as a medium through which to communicate to the world revelations regarding the divine mysteries, seeing that he had even been deemed worthy of immediate intercourse with God. Accordingly at a somewhat early period, probably as far back as the second century before Christ, an apocalyptic writing appeared purporting to have been composed by Enoch, which work was subsequently issued in an enlarged and revised form. This Book of Enoch was already known to the author of the Book of " Jubilees " and of the " Testaments of the Twelve Patriarchs," and was afterwards a great favourite in the Christian Church. As is well known, it is quoted in the Epistle of Jude (14, 15), while many of the Fathers use it without hesitation as the genuine production of Enoch, and as containing authentic divine revelations, although it has never been officially recognised by the Church as canonical. We still find the Byzantine chronicler, George Syncellus (about 800 A.D.), quoting two long passages from it (Syncell. *Chron.* ed. Dindorf, i. 20–23 and 42–47). But after that the book disappeared, and was looked upon as lost till, in the course of last century, the discovery was made that an *Ethiopic version of it was still extant* in the Abyssinian Church. In the year 1773, Bruce the English traveller brought three manuscripts of it to Europe. But it was not till the year 1821 that the whole work was given to the world through the English translation of Laurence. A German translation was issued by Hoffmann which, from chap. i. to lv. (1833), was based upon the English version of Laurence, and from chap. lvi. to the end (1838) on the Ethiopic version collated with a new manuscript. The Ethiopic text was published first by Laurence in 1838, and subsequently by Dillmann in 1851, after having collated it with five manuscripts. Dillmann likewise issued (1853) a new German translation, in which there were material emendations, and on which all disquisitions connected with this book have been based ever since. It seemed as though there were reason to hope that more light would be thrown upon this book when a small fragment of it in Greek (extending from ver. 42 to ver. 49 of chap. lxxxix.), taken from a *Codex Vaticanus* (*cod. gr.* 1809), written in tachygraphic characters, was published in facsimile by Mai (*Patrum Nova Biblioth.* vol. ii.), and deciphered by Gildmeister (*Zeitschr. der DMG.* 1855, pp. 621–624). For, from what was stated by Mai, one was led to suppose that there was still far more in the codex than had yet been published. But, alas! a fresh examination by Gebhardt revealed the fact that the deciphered fragment was all of the Book of Enoch that it contained (Merx' *Archiv*, vol. ii. p. 243).

But in order to be able to form something like a clear idea of the origin and character of this remarkable book, it will be necessary to present to the reader a brief outline of its contents.

Chap. i. 1: Title. Enoch's benediction on the elect and the righteous. Chaps. i.–v.: Introduction. Enoch rehearses the fact that he saw a vision in heaven, which was shown him by the angels who communicated to him the history of all the future generations of men, telling him that the wicked would be sentenced to everlasting damnation, while the righteous would obtain eternal life. Chaps. vi.–xi. contain an account of the fall of the angels, based upon the sixth chapter of Genesis, though in a much more elaborate form. God ordains the kind of punishment to which the fallen angels are to be condemned, and appoints the mode in which the earth is to be purged of their evil-doing and wickedness. The angels are entrusted with the task of executing both those behests. In chaps. xii.–xvi. Enoch, who mingles among the angels in heaven, is commissioned by these latter to betake himself to the earth for the purpose of announcing to the fallen angels the impending judgment (here Enoch resumes the use of the first person). When he has fulfilled his commission the fallen angels prevail upon him to intercede with God in their behalf. But God refuses to entertain the intercession of Enoch, who in a new and imposing vision receives a fresh commission to go and announce once more their approaching destruction. In xvii.–xxxvi. Enoch relates (in the first person) how he was carried over mountains, water and rivers, and shown everywhere the secret divine origin of all the objects and operations of nature. He also tells how he was shown the ends of the earth, and the place to which the evil angels were banished; and the abode of departed spirits, of the just as well as the unjust; and the tree of life which is in store for the elect righteous; and the place of punishment for the condemned; and the tree of knowledge of which Adam and Eve had eaten. Chaps. xxxvii. to lxxi. record "the second vision of wisdom which Enoch the son of Jared saw," consisting of *three allegories.* Chaps. xxxviii. to xliv. contain the first allegory. Enoch sees in a vision the dwellings of the righteous and the resting-places of the saints. He also sees the myriads upon myriads who stand before the majesty of the Lord of spirits, and the four archangels Michael, Raphael, Gabriel, and Phanuel. He is further permitted to look upon the mysteries of heaven, to see the places where the winds are kept, and the receptacles for the sun and moon, and lastly to behold the lightning and the stars of heaven, all of which have their own special names, and which names they respectively answer to. Chaps. xlv. to lvii. contain the second allegory. Enoch is favoured with information regarding the "Chosen One," the "Son of man," *i.e.* regarding the Messiah, His nature and mission, how He is to judge the world and establish His kingdom. Chaps. lviii. to lxix. contain the third allegory, treating of the blessedness of the righteous and the elect; of the mysteries of the thunder and lightning; of the day on which the Chosen One, the Son of man, is to sit in judgment upon the world. Here several portions are inserted which interrupt the continuity and plainly show that they are interpolations by another hand. Chaps. lxx.–lxxi. contain the conclusion of the allegories. In chaps. lxxii.–lxxxii. we have "the book concerning the revolutions of the lights of heaven," or *the astronomical book.* Here Enoch favours us with all sorts of astronomical information which he himself had obtained from the angel Uriel. Chaps. lxxxiii. to xc. contain *two visions*. (*a*) In lxxxiii. to lxxxiv. Enoch sees in a dreadful vision the destruction (by the flood) which is awaiting the sinful world, and prays God not to annihilate the whole human family. (*b*) In lxxxv. to xc. we have the vision of the cattle, sheep, wild beasts and shepherds; under the symbolism of which the whole history of Israel is predicted down to the commencement of the Messianic era. As this historical vision is the only part of the book which enables us with anything like approximate certainty to determine the date of its composition, we will devote more special attention to its contents at a subsequent stage. In chap. xci. we have Enoch's exhortation to his children to lead a righteous life (by way of conclusion to what goes before). Chap. xcii. forms the introduction to the next section. In xciii. and xciv. 12-17, Enoch enlightens us " out of the books " regarding the *world-weeks*. In the first week Enoch lives, in the second Noah, in the third Abrabam, in the fourth Moses, in the fifth the temple is built, at the end of the sixth it is destroyed again, in the seventh an apostate generation arises, and at the end of those weeks the righteous are instructed in the mysteries of heaven; in the eighth righteousness receives a sword, and sinners are given into the hands of the righteous, and a house is built for the great King; in the ninth the judgment is revealed; in the tenth and in the seventh part of it the final judgment will take place. Chaps. xciv. to cv. contain woes upon the wicked and the ungodly, the announcement of their certain destruction, and an exhortation to cherish joyful expectations addressed to the righteous (very diffuse and full of mere repetitions). In chaps. cvi. and cvii. we have a narrative of the birth of Noah and what took place at it. The wonderful appearance of this personage gives Enoch occasion to predict the flood. Chap. cviii. contains " a further writing by Enoch," in which he tells hows he had got certain information from an angel regarding the fire of hell to which the souls of the wicked and the blaspheming are to be consigned, as well as regarding the blessings that are in store for the humble and the righteous.

As may be seen from this outline of its contents, this book purports to be a series of revelations with which Enoch was favoured in the course of his peregrinations through heaven and earth, and of his sojourn among the heavenly spirits. These revelations he committed to writing for the benefit of mankind and transmitted them to posterity. The contents are of an extremely varied character. They embrace the laws of nature no less than the organization and history of the kingdom of God. To impart information regarding the whole of those matters is the purpose and object of this mysterious book. The work furnishes but few data that can be turned to account in the way of enabling us to make out the circumstances under which it was composed. Consequently the views that have been expressed relative to this are of a widely divergent order. Still a certain consensus of opinion has grown up with regard to at least a few leading points. In the first place we may say that the view of J. Chr. K. von Hofmann, Weisse, and Philippi, to the effect that the *entire* book is the work of a *Christian* author (Hofmann holding that the interpolations are but of a trifling character) is confined pretty much to those writers themselves.[13] In the case of the whole three of them the entertaining of such a view is essentially due to dogmatic reasons, while, in the case of Hofmann and Philippi in particular, it is to be attributed to a desire to get rid of the fact that our book is quoted in the Epistle of Jude (for they would have us believe that conversely it was that passage in the Book of Jude that first suggested the writing of the book now under consideration). But speaking generally, it may be affirmed that there is scarcely any modern scholar who holds that the whole work was composed by one and the same author. Even Dillmann,

[13] Lücke, who at one time (1st ed.) was also disposed to favour this view, decidedly abandoned it afterwards.

who in his translation and exposition still continued to assume a substantial unity of authorship (the interpolations being only trifling, although tolerably numerous), has—in spite of Wittichen's almost entire concurrence in it—long ago abandoned this view. He is now at one with almost all the critics in holding that the book consists of several pieces, and all of them entirely different from one another. On this assumption it is almost universally admitted that the *so-called* "*allegories*," chaps. xxxvii.–lxxi., *are above all to be ascribed to a separate author* (so for example Krieger, Lücke, 2nd ed., Ewald, Dillmann latterly, Köstlin, Hilgenfeld, Langen, Sieffert, Reuss, Volkmar). Likewise in the case of the other leading sections of the book (i.–xxxvi. and lxxii.–cviii.), interpolations more or less numerous are almost universally acknowledged to exist, although there is considerable diversity of opinion as to where in each instance they begin and end. Again, there is, comparatively speaking, a high degree of unanimity with regard to the date of the composition of each of those leading sections, above all, of the one containing the visions (lxxxiii.–xc.). Volkmar alone has found his predilection for the time of Barcocheba too much for him in this instance as well, preferring, as he does, to regard the portions in question as having been written by one of Akiba's disciples. All the others are agreed in holding that they belong to the second century B.C., either limiting the date to the earlier years of the Maccabaean period (so Krieger, Lücke, 2nd ed., Langen), or finding it further on, viz. in the days of John Hyrcanus (so Ewald, Dillmann, Köstlin, Sieffert, Reuss, likewise Wittichen), or even so late as the time of Alexander Jannaeus (so Hilgenfeld). But it is with respect to that section which, as regards its contents, is the most important of any, viz. the allegories, chaps. xxxvi.–lxxi., that opinion fluctuates most of all. Here Hilgenfeld and Volkmar agree with Hofmann, Weisse, and Philippi thus far, that in common with these latter they ascribe the section in question to a Christian author (Hilgenfeld to a Gnostic writer). All other critics refer it to some pre-Christian period, Langen to the earlier days of the Maccabaean age in common with the rest of the book, Ewald to somewhere about 144 B.C., Köstlin, Sieffert, and Dillmann (Herzog's *Real-Enc.* 2nd ed. xii. 351 sq.) to some date previous to 64 B.C., Krieger and Lücke to the early part of Herod's reign, while Reuss refrains from suggesting any date at all.

Such unanimity as has thus far been secured may serve at the same time to give us an idea how far we can here hope to obtain results of a trustworthy character. If there is one thing more certain than another it is this, that the *book is not all the production of one and the same author.* Not only is the section containing the allegories, chaps. xxxvii.–lxxi., undoubtedly a perfectly independent portion of the book, but all the rest of the work is composed of very heterogeneous elements, and obviously interspersed with a great number of longer or shorter interpolations. Confining ourselves to the leading portions of the work, the following groups may be distinguished :—

1. The *original writing, i.e.* the leading portion consisting of i.–xxxvi., lxxii.–cv., but with the restriction just referred to. The only clue we get to the date of its composition is that furnished by the *historical vision* in chaps. lxxxv.–xc. Here we have a representation of the entire history of the theocracy from Adam down to the author's own day, and that under the symbolism of cattle and sheep. In a vision presented to him in a dream, Enoch saw how a white ox (Adam) once sprung out of the earth ; and then a white cow (Eve) ; and along with this latter yet other cattle, a black ox (Cain) and a red one (Abel). The black ox gored the red one, which thereupon vanished from the earth. But the black ox begat many other black cattle. Thereupon the cow just referred to (Eve) gave birth to a white ox (Seth), from which sprung a great many other white cattle. But stars (angels) fell from heaven, and after having had intercourse with the cows of the black cattle (the daughters of Cain), they begat elephants, camels, and asses (the giants). And so in this way the history **is**

proceeded with, the theocratic line being always represented
by the white cattle. From Jacob onwards white sheep are
substituted for the white cattle. The symbolic character of
the representation is patent all through, while it presents
hardly any difficulty in the way of interpretation till we
come to the point where the sheep are attacked by wild
animals, *i.e.* till the hostile powers of Assyria and Babylon
come upon the stage. For in lxxxix. 55 it is narrated how
the Lord of the sheep delivered them into the hand of the
lions and tigers and wolves and jackals, and into the hand of
the foxes, and all manner of wild beasts; and how the
wild beasts began to tear the sheep to pieces. And the Lord
forsook their house (Jerusalem) and their tower (the temple),
lxxxix. 56, *i.e.* He withdrew His gracious presence from them
(for there is no question of the destruction of these till a
much later stage). And He appointed *seventy shepherds* to
feed the sheep, and charged them to allow as many to be
torn to pieces by the wild beasts as He would order them, but
not more (lxxxix. 59, 60). And he summoned "another"
and commanded him to write down the number of sheep
destroyed by the shepherds (lxxxix. 61 – 64). And the
shepherds fed them " each his time," and delivered the sheep
into the hand of the lions and tigers. And these latter
burnt down that tower (the temple) and destroyed that house
(Jerusalem, lxxxix. 65, 66). And the shepherds delivered to
the wild beasts far more sheep than they had been ordered to
do (lxxxix. 68–71). And when the shepherds had fed the
flock *twelve* hours, three of those sheep came back and began
to rebuild the house (Jerusalem) and the tower (the temple),
chap. lxxxix. 72, 73. But the sheep were so blinded as to
mingle with the beasts of the field; and the shepherds did
not rescue them from the hand of the beasts (lxxxix. 74, 75).
But when *five-and-thirty* [14] shepherds had fed them, all the

---

[14] Dillmann reads thirty-six, which is not supported by manuscript
authority. The manuscripts read thirty-seven. But, from what follows,
there can hardly be a doubt that thirty-five is the correct reading.

fowls of the air, the eagles, the hawks, the kites and the
ravens came and began to prey upon those sheep and to peck
out their eyes and to devour their flesh (xc. 1, 2). And
again when *three-and-twenty* shepherds had tended the flock
and *eight-and-fifty* times in all were completed (xc. 5), then
little lambs were born of the white sheep, and they began to
cry to the sheep; but these pay no heed to them (xc. 6, 7).
And the ravens swooped down upon the lambs and seized one
of them, and tore and devoured the sheep, till horns grew
upon the lambs, and, above all, a large horn shot out to which
all the young ones betake themselves (xc. 8–10). And the
eagles and the hawks and the kites still continue to tear the
sheep to pieces. And the ravens sought to break to pieces
the horn of that young sheep and struggled with it; and it
strove with them. And the Lord came to the help of that
young one; and all the beasts flee and fall before him (xc.
11–15). Here the narrative breaks off. For what follows
seems for the author to lie in the future. It is only further
remarked that *the twelve last shepherds* had destroyed more
than those who had preceded them (xc. 17).

In their endeavours to interpret this narrative, so clear and
perspicuous in all the leading points, the expositors seem
almost to have vied with each other in trying who would
misunderstand it most. Strangely enough, all the earlier
expositors down to Lücke inclusive have taken the first thirty-
seven shepherds to mean the native kings of the kingdoms of
Israel and Judah! It is true no doubt that in the present
day all are agreed that the seventy shepherds are intended to
represent the period during which Israel was subjected to the
sway of the Gentile powers. But it is a strange misappre-
hension, into which almost all the expositors have been
betrayed, when they suppose that the seventy shepherds are
intended to represent a corresponding number of Gentile
rulers. The whole narrative leaves no room whatever to
doubt, *that the shepherds are rather to be understood as angels*
who are entrusted with the duty of seeing that only as many

of the sheep are torn to pieces as God intends and no more.
So far as I am aware, up till the publication of the first
edition of the present work, Von Hofmann was the only
writer who recognised this (*Schriftbeweis*, i. 422).[15] It is, as
it is impossible to doubt, the wild beasts and the birds of
prey that represent the Gentile rulers. Consequently the
shepherds must have some other meaning altogether. But
they certainly cannot be taken as representing human beings,
for throughout the entire vision these latter are, without
exception, represented under the symbolism of animals,
whereas the angels appear even in chap. lxxxvii. under that
of men. And that the shepherds are as matter of fact
intended to represent angels is still further confirmed by what
follows: (1) Before they commence to tend the flock they *all*
appear before God *at one and the same time*, and from Him
receive their commission to feed the flock one after the other
(lxxix. 59). How could this apply to Gentile rulers? Or
are we to think of them as in a pre-existent state? (2) At
the judgment they are classed along with the fallen angels
(xc. 20 sqq.). (3) The angel that is summoned to write down
the number of sheep that are destroyed is in lxxxix. 61 briefly
spoken of as " another," which would surely justify us in assuming that the shepherds mentioned immediately before belong
to precisely the same category as this " other." (4) Nor can
the shepherds be identified with the Gentile rulers for this
further reason, that according to lxxxix. 75 they are also
entrusted with the duty of protecting the sheep from the
wild beasts. Consequently they are evidently an impartial
power placed over the sheep and the wild beasts alike, or
they are meant to be so at least.[16] The thought in the
author's mind then is this, that from the moment that in

---

[15] Since then this view has been endorsed by Kesselring (*Lit. Centralbl.*
1874, p. 133), Drummond (*The Jewish Messiah*, p. 40 sqq.) and Wieseler
(*Zeitschr. der deutschen morgenländ. Gesellsch.* 1882, p. 186).

[16] Even in the later Jewish Haggadah we meet with the idea that
seventy angels were set over the Gentile world, that is to say one over each

accordance with the divine purpose Israel was assailed and subjugated by the Gentile powers, God appointed angels whose duty it was to see that these powers executed upon Israel the judgment with which He intended them to be visited ; and not only so, but also to see that they did not oppress and persecute Israel unduly. But the watchers neglect their duty ; they allow the wild beasts to destroy a greater number than they ought to have done, and, as is predicted toward the conclusion, they are for this to be cast into hell-fire along with the fallen angels.

It would lead to too great a digression were we to do more in the way of refuting the misapprehensions here in question. We must content ourselves with briefly stating what—following Dillmann and Ewald above all—we conceive to be the correct interpretation. The numbers in the text serve to show that the author divides the time of the duration of the Gentile supremacy into *four periods* arranged thus : $12 + 23 + 23 + 12$, which are simply intended to denote in a general way two shorter periods (at the beginning) and two longer ones (in the middle). For every calculation pretending to chronological exactness must be radically erroneous, whether, with Hilgenfeld, we take year - weeks or, with Volkmar, take decades as our basis. Nor can there be any doubt as to where the different periods are intended to begin and end. The *first* begins with the time when the Gentile powers (consequently that of Assyria in the first instance) began to turn against Israel, and extends to the time of the return of the exiles in the reign of Cyrus, the only difficulty here being as to who are meant by the three returning sheep (lxxxix. 72). Probably the author here alludes to Zerubbabel, Ezra, and Nehemiah, the less prominent colleague of Zerubbabel, viz. Joshua, being left out of account. The *second* period extends

of the seventy Gentile nations. See *Targum of Jonathan* on Deut. xxxii. 8. *Pirke de-Rabbi Eliezer*, chap. xxiv. Wagenseil's note on *Sota* vii. 5 (in Surenhusius's *Mishna*, iii. 263 sq.). Schegg, *Evangelium nach Lukas übers. und erklärt*, ii. 69. Also the expositors generally on Luke x. 1.

from Cyrus to Alexander the Great. For the substitution of
the birds of prey for the wild beasts (xc. 2) plainly marks the
transition from the Persians to the Greeks. The *third*
extends from Alexander the Great to Antiochus Epiphanes.
Nothing but stubborn prejudice can prevent any one from seeing that, by the symbolism of the lambs (xc. 6), the Maccabees
are to be understood. Lastly, the *fourth* period extends from
the commencement of the Maccabaean age on to the author's
own day. That, everything considered, this latter coincides
with the time of the Hasmonaean princes it is impossible to
doubt. And it is very likely that, by the great horn which
is mentioned last, it is John Hyrcanus that is referred to.
Only we feel bound to agree with Gebhardt, who, owing to
the uncertain character of the Ethiopic text, warns us against
being too detailed in our interpretation. But (seeing that
from the beginning of the Maccabaean age onwards the times
of twelve shepherds had elapsed) this may be regarded as
certain, *that the author wrote some time in the last third of
the second century* B.C. If we compare the $12 + 23 + 23 + 12$
times, that are put down to represent the four periods, with
the actual duration of those periods, we will find that, for the
eye of the author looking backwards, the length of the time
is foreshortened. He represents the third period (333–175
B.C.) as being of precisely the same length as the second,
whereas in point of fact this latter was considerably longer
(537–333 B.C.). And for his eye the first period dwindles
down still more. All this is exactly what we might expect
in the case of one who is looking back upon the events of the
past.

If we were to be allowed to assume that the author of
the historical vision is, in the main, the author of chaps.
i.–xxxvi., lxxii.–cv. as well, then the date of the composition
of the whole of those sections would thereby be determined
at the same time.

2. *The allegories,* chaps. xxxvii.–lxxi. (with the exception
of the Noachian portions). Even on a hasty perusal one

cannot fail to notice that the allegories form one distinct whole, and that they are different from the remaining portions of the book. In fact there cannot be the slightest doubt but that they are the production of a different author. The use of the names of God, the angelology, the eschatology, and the doctrine of the Messiah differ essentially from those of the rest of the book (comp. especially Köstlin, pp. 265–268). And as little can there be any room to doubt that they are of a *later date* than the original work. For the favourite notion of Ewald, that they rank first in point of time, has been sufficiently refuted by Köstlin (pp. 269–273). Among the peculiarities of the allegories we notice this in particular, that a decided prominence is given in them to the Messianic hope and the person of the Messiah, whereas, in the other parts of the book, those are matters that are touched on once or twice at the most. This again is connected with a further peculiarity to which Köstlin in particular has directed attention, namely, that here, instead of its being the wicked and the ungodly in general who appear in contrast to the pious, as is the case in the rest of the book, it is rather the Gentile rulers, the kings and the powerful ones of the earth (chaps. xxxviii. 4, 5, xlvi. 7, 8, xlviii. 8–10, liii. 5, liv. 2, lv. 4, lxii. 1, 3, 6, 9–11, lxiii. 1–12). This circumstance serves to explain why it is that precisely in these allegories such decided prominence is given to the Messianic hope. But when, it may now be asked, were they composed? The only passage which furnishes any clue to the date is chap. lvi., where it is predicted that, in the closing period, the Parthians and Medes would come from the east and invade the Holy Land, but that they would encounter obstacles at the holy city, when they would turn upon and destroy each other (lvi. 5–7). When Köstlin would have us infer from this passage that the writing here in question must have been composed previous to the year 64 B.C., as otherwise we should have expected that the Romans would have been mentioned as well, we may reply that such an expectation is absolutely groundless and unwarrantable. It would be much nearer the truth to conclude, with Lücke, that this passage presupposes what had already taken place, viz. the Parthian invasion of Palestine (40–38 B.C.), the recollection of which would have some influence in shaping the author's eschatological hopes, so that, according to this, the allegories would be composed *at the very soonest in the time of Herod*. On the other hand, the prediction to the effect that the Parthian power would collapse outside the walls of Jerusalem, presupposes that the city was still standing, as otherwise it would surely have been necessary first of all to predict its restoration. But the main question now is this, are the allegories of pre- or of post-Christian origin ? An answer to this question is all the more desirable, that it is precisely in these that we find so many points of contact with the Christology and eschatology of the Gospels. But unfortunately it is extremely difficult to arrive at any positive decision. However, this much at least ought to be admitted, that the view of the Messiah presented in the part of the book at present under consideration is perfectly explicable on Jewish grounds, and that, to account for such view, it is not necessary to assume that it was due to Christian influences. Nothing of a specifically Christian character is to be met with in any part of this section. But, supposing the reverse to have been the case, it is, to say the least of it, quite incredible that a Jew would have been likely to have borrowed it, and so there would be nothing for it but to pronounce at once in favour of a *Christian* origin. And this is what has actually been done by all those who cannot see their way to admit the pre-Christian origin of the writing (Hofmann, Weisse, Hilgenfeld, Volkmar, Philippi). But no sooner is such a view seriously entertained than the difficulties begin to accumulate. An anonymous Christian author would scarcely have been so reserved as to avoid making any allusion to the historical personality of Jesus. Surely if the writer had any object in view at all it would be to win converts to the faith. But how could he hope to accomplish this object, if he always spoke merely of the coming of the Messiah in glory, merely of "the Chosen One" as the Judge of the world, without making the slightest reference to the fact that, in the first place, He would have to appear in His estate of humiliation? Surely any one who candidly weighs the arguments on the one side and on the other must feel constrained to admit that the pre-Christian origin is decidedly more probable than the Christian one. Further, the objection based upon the circumstance that, according to Matt. xvi. 13–16, John xii. 34, the expression "Son of man" was not as yet a current designation for the Messiah in the time of Christ, whereas it is of frequent occurrence in this sense in the allegories, is without force. For we are by no means at liberty to infer from those passages that the expression "Son of man" was not at that time currently in use as a Messianic title. In the case of the passage in John this inference is based simply upon false exegesis (see, on the other hand, Meyer for example). The passage in Matthew again is disposed of by the circumstance that, in its original form as preserved in Mark viii. 27 = Luke ix. 18, the expression "Son of man" does not occur at all.

3. *The Noachian portions.* The investigations of Dillmann, Ewald, and Köstlin have already sufficiently proved that the passages liv. 7–lv. 2, lx. 65–lxix. 25 break the sequence, and were only inserted among the allegories at a later period. And if further proof were needed, we have it in the fact that in chap. lxviii. 1, "The Book of the Allegories of Enoch" is expressly quoted. Those portions have been called Noachian, partly because they treat of Noah and his time, and partly because they purport to have been written by him. Probably chaps. cvi., cvii. should also be included among them. Chap. cviii. is an independent addition inserted at a later period. It is utterly impossible to say at what dates those various interpolations were made.

The whole Book of Enoch, which was gradually put together in the way we have just stated, undoubtedly owes its origin to Palestine (comp. Dillmann, *Einleitung*, p. 51). But as our present Ethiopic version is taken from the Greek, it becomes a question whether this latter was the original or whether it was in turn a translation from the Hebrew or Aramaic. Certainly the numerous Hebrew names of the angels point to this latter as probable, to say nothing of the fact that, in the Hasmonaean age, Greek was hardly ever used for literary purposes. Consequently it has been almost universally assumed that the original was composed in Hebrew or Aramaic.[17] The only exceptions are Volkmar (*Zeitschr. der DMG.* 1860, p. 131) and Philippi (p. 126), who feel compelled to adopt the view that Greek was the language of the original.

For the Enoch-legend generally, comp. (next to Gen. v. 18–24) Jesus the Son of Sirach xliv. 16, xlix. 14 ; Heb. xi. 5 ; Irenaeus, v. 5. 1 ; Tertullian, *De anima*, chap. l. ; Hippolyt. *De Christo et Antichristo*, chaps. xliii.-xlvii. ; *Evang. Nicodemi* (=*Acta Pilati*), chap. xxv. ; *Historia Josephi* (*apocr.*), chaps. xxx.–xxxii. Thilo, *Codex apocr. Nov. Test.* p. 756 sqq. Rud. Hofmann, *Das Leben Jesu nach den Apokryphen*, p. 459 sqq. Winer, *Realwörtb.* art. "Henoch." Hamburger, *Real-Encycl. für Bibel und Talmud*, Part ii. art. "Henochsage." The Bible dictionaries generally. The expositors on Revelation xi. For a great number of earlier dissertations, consult Fabricius, *Cod. pseudepigr. Vet. Test.* i. 222 sq.

*To an acquaintance with our book* is perhaps to be traced so early a notice as that of a Jewish or Samaritan Hellenist (probably not Eupolemus, but some person unknown, see § xxxiii.) which has been transmitted to us by Alexander Polyhistor, and after him by Eusebius, to the effect that Enoch was the inventor of astrology (Euseb. *Praep. evang.* ix. 17. 8, ed. Gaisford : τοῦτον εὑρηκέναι πρῶτον τὴν ἀστρολογίαν). In the Book of Jubilees not only is our book largely drawn upon, but expressly mentioned (see Ewald's *Jahrbb. der bibl. Wissensch.* ii. 240 sq., iii. 18 sq., 90 sq. Rönsch, *Das Buch der Jubiläen*, p. 403 sqq.). In the following nine passages in the *Test. XII. Patr.* express reference is made to Enoch's prophetical writings : Simeon v. ; Levi x. 14, 16 ; Judah xviii. ; Zebulon iii. ; Dan v. ; Naphtali iv. ; Benjamin ix. Further, the mention of the ἐγρήγορες (watchers= angels) in Reuben v., Naphtali iii., may also be said to point to Enoch.

*Christian testimonies: Epist. of Jude*, 14 : ἐπροφήτευσεν δὲ καὶ τούτοις ἕβδομος ἀπὸ Ἀδὰμ Ἐνὼχ λέγων κ.τ.λ. *Epist. of Barnabas* iv. : τὸ τέλειον σκάνδαλον ἤγγικεν περὶ οὗ γέγραπται, ὡς Ἐνὼχ λέγει. *Ibid.* xvi. : λέγει γὰρ ἡ γραφή (then follows a quotation from the Book of Enoch). Irenaeus

---

[17] For the view that the original was in Hebrew, see in particular Hallévi, *Journal Asiatique*, 1867, April–May, pp. 352–395.

iv. 16. 2 : Sed et Enoch sine circumcisione placens Deo, cum esset homo, Dei legatione ad angelos fungebatur et translatus est et conservatur usque nunc testis justi judicii Dei. Tertullian, *De cultu feminarum*, i. 3 : Scio scripturam Enoch, quae hunc ordinem angelis dedit, non recipi a quibusdam, quia nec in armarium Judaicum admittitur. Opinor, non putaverunt illam ante cataclysmum editam post eum casum orbis omnium rerum abolitorem salvam esse potuisse. . . . Tertullian then goes on to point out how this was still quite possible, after which he proceeds as follows : Sed cum Enoch eadem scriptura etiam de domino praedicarit, a nobis quidem nihil omnino rejiciendum est, quod pertineat ad nos. Et legimus omnem scripturam aedificationi habilem divinitus inspirari. A Judaeis potest jam videri propterea rejecta, sicut et cetera fere quae Christum sonant. . . . Eo accedit, quod Enoch apud Judam apostolum testimonium possidet. Comp. besides the whole of the introduction to chap. ii., the subject of which is taken from Enoch. Idem, *De cultu feminarum*, ii. 10 : (iidem angeli) damnati a deo sunt, ut Enoch refert. Idem, *De idololatr.* iv.: Antecesserat Enoch praedicens, etc. Idem, *De idololatr.* xv.: Haec igitur ab initio praevidens spiritus sanctus (!) etiam ostia in superstitionem ventura praececinit per antiquissimum propheten Enoch. Clemens Alex. *Eclogae prophet.* chap. ii. (Dindorf, iii. 456): "Εὐλογημένος εἶ ὁ βλέπων ἀβύσσους, καθήμενος ἐπὶ Χερουβίμ" ὁ Δανιὴλ λέγει ὁμοδοξῶν τῷ Ἐνὼχ τῷ εἰρηκότι "καὶ εἶδον τὰς ὕλας πάσας." Idem, *Eclogae prophet.* chap. liii. (Dindorf, iii. 474): ἤδη δὲ καὶ Ἐνὼχ φησιν τοὺς παραβάντας ἀγγέλους διδάξαι τοὺς ἀνθρώπους ἀστρονομίαν καὶ μαντικὴν καὶ τὰς ἄλλας τέχνας. Celsus, in Origen, *Contra Cels.* v. 52, endeavours to show that Christians would contradict themselves were they to maintain that Christ was the only ἄγγελος sent down into the world by God. As evidence of this he quotes the following words: ἐλθεῖν γὰρ καὶ ἄλλους λέγουσι πολλάκις καὶ ὁμοῦ γε ἑξήκοντα ἢ ἑβδομήκοντα· οὓς δὴ γενέσθαι κακοὺς καὶ κολάζεσθαι δεσμοῖς ὑποβληθέντας ἐν γῇ· ὅθεν καὶ τὰς θερμὰς πηγὰς εἶναι τὰ ἐκείνων δάκρυα κ.τ.λ. In commenting on this passage Origen (*Contra Cels.* v. 54, 55) remarks that it is taken from the Book of Enoch. He thinks however that Celsus did not read it there himself, but heard it from somebody or other, for he does not mention the author's name. Origen, *Contra Cels.* v. 54: ἐν ταῖς ἐκκλησίαις οὐ πάνυ φέρεται ὡς θεῖα τὰ ἐπιγεγραμμένα τοῦ Ἐνὼχ βιβλία (observe the plural). Idem, *De principiis*, i. 3. 3 : Sed et in Enoch libro his similia describuntur. Idem, *De principiis*, iv. 35 : Sed et in libro suo Enoch ita ait : "Ambulavi usque ad imperfectum " . . . scriptum namque est in eodem libello dicente Enoch : "Universas materias perspexi." Idem, *In Numer. homil.* xxviii. 2 (de la Rue, ii. 384=Lommatzsch, x. 366): De quibus quidem nominibus plurima in libellis, qui appellantur Enoch, secreta continentur et arcana : sed quia libelli isti non videntur apud Hebraeos in auctoritate haberi, interim nunc ea, quae ibi nominantur, ad exemplum vocare differamus. Idem, *In Joannem*, vol. vi. chap. xxv. (de la Rue, iv. 142 = Lommatzsch, i. 241): ὡς ἐν τῷ Ἐνὼχ γέγραπται, εἴ τῳ φίλον παραδέχεσθαι ὡς ἅγιον τὸ βιβλίον. Anatolius in Eusebius, *Hist. eccl.* vii. 32. 19: Τοῦ δὲ τὸν πρῶτον παρ' Ἑβραίοις μῆνα περὶ ἰσημερίαν εἶναι, παραστατικὰ καὶ τὰ ἐν τῷ Ἐνὼχ μαθήματα. Jerome, *De viris illustr.*

chap. iv.: Judas frater Jacobi parvam, quae de septem catholicis est,
epistolam reliquit. Et quia de libro Enoch, qui apocryphus est, in ea
assumit testimonia a plerisque rejicitur, etc. Idem, *Comment. in Epist. ad
Titum*, i. 12 (Vallarsi, vii. 1. 708): Qui autem putant totum librum debere
sequi eum, qui libri parte usus sit, videntur mihi et apocryphum Enochi,
de quo apostolus Judas in epistola sua testimonium posuit, inter ecclesiae
scripturas recipere. In the so-called stichometry of Nicephorus and in the
*Synopsis Athanasii*, the Book of Enoch is classed with the Apocrypha
(Credner, *Zur Geschichte des Kanons*, pp. 121, 145). So also in the anonymous list of the canonical books which has been edited by Montfaucon,
Cotelier, Hody, and Pitra respectively (see v. 7 below). *Constit. apostol.*
vi. 16: καὶ ἐν τοῖς παλαιοῖς δέ τινες συνέγραψαν βιβλία ἀπόκρυφα Μωσέως
καὶ 'Ενώχ καὶ 'Αδὰμ 'Ησαΐου τε καὶ Δαβὶδ καὶ 'Ηλία καὶ τῶν τριῶν
πατριαρχῶν, Φθοροποιὰ καὶ τῆς ἀληθείας ἐχθρά. For yet other *testimonia
patrum*, consult Fabricius, *Codex pseudepigr. Vet. Test.* i. 160–223, ii.
55–61. Philippi, *Das Buch Henoch*, p. 102 sqq. Also the two large fragments from Syncellus in Dillmann, *Das Buch Henoch*, pp. 82–86.

*Editions of the Ethiopic text:* Laurence, *Libri Enoch versio Aethiopica*,
Oxoniae 1838. Dillmann, *Liber Henoch Aethiopice, ad quinque codicum
fidem editus, cum variis lectionibus*, Lipsiae 1851.

*Versions:* (1) English ones: Laurence, *The Book of Enoch, an apocryphal
production supposed to have been lost for ages, but discovered at the close
of the last century in Abyssinia, now first translated from an Ethiopic MS.
in the Bodleian Library*, Oxford 1821. Schodde, *The Book of Enoch,
translated with Introduction and Notes*, Andover 1882. (2) German ones:
Hoffmann (Andreas Gottlieb), *Das Buch Henoch in vollständiger Uebersetzung mit fortlaufendem Commentar, ausführlicher Einleitung und erläu-
ternden Excursen*, 2 vols. Jena 1833–1838. Dillmann, *Das Buch Henoch,
übersetzt und erklärt*, Leipzig 1853.

*Critical inquiries:* Laurence in his English translation. Hoffmann
(Andr. Gottl.), art. "Henoch," in Ersch and Gruber's *Encycl.* § 2, vol. v.
(1829) pp. 399–409. Idem, in his German translation. Gfrörer, *Das
Jahrhundert des Heils* (also under the title, *Gesch. des Urchristenthums*,
vol. i.–ii. 1838), i. 93–109. Wieseler, *Die 70 Wochen und die 63 Jahr-
wochen des Propheten Daniel*, 1839, p. 162 sqq. Krieger (Lützelberger),
*Beiträge zur Kritik und Exegese*, Nürnberg 1845. Lücke, *Einleitung in die
Offenbarung des Johannes* (2nd ed. 1852), pp. 89–144; comp. 1171–1173.
Hofmann (J. Chr. K.), "Ueber die Entstehungszeit des Buch Henoch"
(*Zeitschr. der deutschen morgenländ. Gesellsch.* vol. vi. 1852, pp. 87–91).
Idem, *Schriftbeweis* (2nd ed.), i. 420–423. Idem, *Die heil. Schrift N. T.'s
zusammenhängend untersucht*, vii. 2, p. 205 sqq. Dillmann in his German
translation. Idem, in Herzog's *Real-Enc.* 1st ed. xii. 308–310. Idem,
*Zeitschr. DMG.* 1861, pp. 126–131. Idem, in Schenkel's *Bibellex.* iii.
(1871) pp. 10–13. Idem, in Herzog's *Real-Enc.* 2nd ed. xii. (1883)
pp. 350–352. Ewald, "Abhandlung über des äthiopischen Buches Henôkh
Entstehung, Sinn und Zusammensetzung" (*Abhandlungen der königl. Gesellsch.
der Wissensch.* zu Göttingen, vol. vi. 1853–1855, Historico-philosoph. section,
pp. 107–178. Also separate reprint). Idem, *Gesch. des Volkes Israel*, 3rd

ed. iv. 451 sqq. Weisse, *Die Evangelienfrage* (1856), pp. 214–224. Köstlin, "Ueber die Entstehung des Buchs Henoch" (*Theol. Jahrbücher* 1856, pp. 240–279, 370–386). Hilgenfeld, *Die jüdische Apokalyptik* (1857), pp. 91–184. Idem, *Zeitschr. für wissenschaftl. Theol.* vol. iii. 1860, pp. 319–334; iv. 1861, pp. 212–222; v. 1862, pp. 216–221; xv. 1872, pp. 584–587. Volkmar, "Beiträge zur Erklärung des Buches Henoch nach dem äthiopischen Text" (*Zeitschr. der DMG.*, vol. xiv. 1860, pp. 87–134, 296). Idem, in *Der Zeitschr. für wissensch. Theol.* vol. iv. 1861, pp. 111–136, 422 sqq.; v. 1862, p. 46 sqq. Idem, *Eine Neutestamentliche Entdeckung und deren Bestreitung, oder die Geschichts-Vision des Buches Henoch im Zusammenhang*, Zürich 1862. Geiger, *Jüdische Zeitschr. für Wissensch. und Leben*, for year 1864–65, pp. 196–204. Langen, *Das Judenthum in Palästina* (1866), pp. 35–64. Sieffert, *Nonnulla ad apocryphi libri Henochi originem et compositionem nec non ad opiniones de regno Messiano eo prolatas pertinentia*, Regimonti Pr. 1867 (the *same work* under the title, *De apocryphi libri Henochi origine et argumento*, Regimonti Pr. s. a.). Hallévi, "Recherches sur la langue de la redaction primitive du livre d'Enoch" (*Journal asiatique*, 1867, April–May, pp. 352–395). Philippi, *Das Buch Henoch, sein Zeitalter und sein Verhältniss zum Judasbriefe*, Stuttg. 1868. Wittichen, *Die Idee des Menschen* (1868), pp. 63–71. Idem, *Die Idee des Reiches Gottes* (1872), pp. 118–133, 145–148, 149 sq. Gebhardt, "Die 70 Hirten des Buches Henoch und ihre Deutungen mit besonderer Rücksicht auf die Barkochba-Hypothese" (Merx' *Archiv für wissenschaftl. Erforschung des A. T.* vol. ii. part 2, 1872, pp. 163–246). Tideman, "De apocalypse van Henoch en het Essenisme" (*Theol. Tijdschrift*, 1875, pp. 261–296). Drummond, *The Jewish Messiah* (1877), pp. 17–73. Lipsius, art. "Enoch," in Smith and Wace's *Dictionary of Christian Biography*, vol. ii. (1880) pp. 124–128. Reuss, *Gesch. der heil. Schriften A. T.'s*, § 498–500. Wieseler, "Zur Abfassungszeit des Buchs Henoch" (*Zeitschr. der DMG.* 1882, pp. 185–193).

## 3. *The Assumptio Mosis.*

It had long been known from a passage in Origen (*De princip.* iii. 2. 1) that the legend referred to in the Epistle of Jude (ver. 9) regarding a dispute between the archangel Michael and Satan about the body of Moses, was taken from an apocryphal book entitled the *Ascensio Mosis.* Some little information regarding this Ἀνάληψις Μωυσέως had also been gleaned from quotations found in the Fathers and subsequent writers (see below). But it was not till somewhat recently that a large portion of this work in *an old Latin version* was discovered in the Ambrosian Library at Milan by Ceriani, and published by him (1861) in the first part of his *Monumenta.*

It is true the fragment bears no title, but its identity with
the old 'Ανάληψις Μωυσέως is evident from the following
quotation (*Acta Synodi Nicaenae*, ii. 18, in Fabricius, i. 845):
Μέλλων ὁ προφήτης Μωυσῆς ἐξιέναι τοῦ βίου, ὡς γέγραπται
ἐν βίβλῳ 'Αναλήψεως Μωυσέως, προσκαλεσάμενος 'Ιησοῦν
υἱὸν Ναυῆ καὶ διαλεγόμενος πρὸς αὐτὸν ἔφη· Καὶ προεθεά-
σατό με ὁ θεὸς πρὸ καταβολῆς κόσμου εἶναί με τῆς διαθήκης
αὐτοῦ μεσίτην. These same words also occur in Ceriani's
fragment, i. 14: Itaque excogitavit et invenit me, qui ab
initio orbis terrarum praeparatus sum, ut sim arbiter testamenti illius. Since its publication by Ceriani this writing
has been edited by Hilgenfeld (*Clementis Romani Epist.* 1866,
2nd ed. 1876), Volkmar (Latin and German, 1867), Schmidt
and Merx (Merx' *Archiv*, 1868), and Fritzsche (*Libri apocr.*
1871). A rendering back into the Greek from which the
Latin version had been taken was executed by Hilgenfeld
(*Zeitschr.* 1868, and *Messias Judaeorum*, 1869).

The following is an outline of the contents of the writing
(and here we adopt Hilgenfeld's division of the chapters,
which is also adhered to by Schmidt-Merx and Fritzsche, and
departed from by Volkmar alone):—

Chap. i. 1–9. The introduction, in which we are given to
understand that what follows was an *address which Moses gave
to Joshua* when he appointed him to be his successor at
Ammon beyond Jordan. In i. 10–17 Moses discloses to
Joshua the fact that the course of his life has come to an end,
and that he is on the point of departing to his fathers. By
way of legacy he hands over to Joshua certain books of
prophecies which he is requested to preserve in a place
appointed by God for the purpose. In chap. ii. Moses reveals
to Joshua in brief outline the future history of Israel, from the
entrance into Palestine down to the destruction of the kingdoms of Israel and Judah. In chap. iii. it is stated that a king
(Nebuchadnezzar) will come from the east and destroy the
city and the temple with fire, and carry away the inhabitants
into his own domains. The captives will then remember that

all this had been already foretold by Moses.  Chap. iv. In
answer to the prayers of a man who is over them (Daniel),
God will again take pity upon them and raise up a king
(Cyrus), who will allow them to return to their native land.
A few fragments of the tribes will return and will rebuild
the holy place, and will remain stedfast in their allegiance
to the Lord, only sad and sighing because they cannot sacrifice
to the God of their fathers.[18]   Chap. v. And judgment will
overtake their kings (their Gentile rulers).   But they themselves (the Jews) will be divided in regard to the truth.[19]
And the altar will be defiled by men who are not (true)
priests, but slaves born of slaves.   And their scribes (magistri
[et] doctores eorum) will be partial and will pervert justice.
And their land will be full of unrighteousness.   Chap. vi.
Then kings will arise among them, and priests of the Most
High God will be appointed, who will nevertheless commit
wickedness even in the very holy of holies itself (plainly allud-
ing to the Hasmonaeans).   And these will be succeeded by
an insolent monarch not belonging to the family of the priests,
an arrogant and ungodly man.   And he will deal with those
who have preceded him as they deserve.   He will cut off
their proud ones with the sword, and bury their bodies in
secret places so that nobody will know where they have been
laid.[20]   He will put to death old and young alike, and will
not spare.   Then there will be great dread of him among
them throughout the land, and he will sit in judgment upon
them, as did the Egyptians, for *four-and-thirty years* (all
which obviously points to Herod the Great).   And he will

[18] The author seems to think that the sacrificial worship of the second
temple could not be regarded as true worship owing to their being under
Gentile supremacy, and because the conducting of the worship was in the
hands of priests friendly to the Greeks.

[19] Hilgenfeld has correctly held that the words " Et ipsi dividentur ad
veritatem " are to be regarded as beginning a new sentence.   Schmidt and
Merx have given a happy reproduction of the Greek text in the words Καὶ
αὐτοὶ διαμεοισθήσονται πρὸς τὴν ἀλήθειαν (comp. Luke xi. 17).

[20] Comp. Joseph. *Antt.* xv. 10. 4 : πολλοὶ δὲ καὶ φανερῶς καὶ λεληθότως
εἰς τὸ φρούρια ἀναγόμενοι, τὴν Ὑρκανίαν, ἐκεῖ διεφθείροντο.

beget sons who will reign, though for shorter periods, as his successors. Cohorts of soldiers will come into their land, and a powerful monarch of the West (Quintilius Varus), who will conquer them and take them captive, and destroy a part of their temple with fire, while some of them he will crucify around their city.[21] Chap. vii. After this will come the end of the times. Their course will have run after the expiry of yet four hours . . . (then follow several lines in the manuscript that are hardly legible). And there will reign among them wicked and ungodly men, who say that they are righteous. They are deceitful men, who will live only to please themselves, dissemblers in all their concerns, and at every hour of the day lovers of feasts, mere gluttons . . . (here again follows a hiatus). They devour the possessions of the poor, and declare that they do this out of pity. Their hands and their minds indulge in impurity, and their mouth utters high-sounding things; and further, they say, " touch me not lest thou defile me." . . . Chap. viii. Vengeance and wrath will come upon them, such as has never been among them from the beginning till the time when he will raise up to them the king of kings (Antiochus Epiphanes), who will crucify those who profess circumcision, and will cause them to get their children uncircumcised again, and to carry about the impure idols in public, and to contemn the word. Chap. ix. Then, in obedience to the command of that king, there will appear a man of the tribe of Levi, whose name will be *taxo,* who will have seven sons, to whom he will say: Behold, my sons, vengeance has once more come upon the people, a cruel vengeance without one touch of pity. For what nation

---

[21] According to Fritzsche's amended form of it, the passage runs thus: Et producet natos (qui su)ccedentes sibi [=ei] breviora tempora dominarent [*cod.* donarent]. In partes eorum cohortes [*cod.* mortis] venient et occidentis rex potens, qui expugnabit eos, et ducet captivos, et partem aedis ipsorum igni incendet, aliquos crucifiget circa coloniam eorum. Comp. with regard to the burning of the temple, Joseph. *Antt.* xvii. 10. 2; and, for the crucifixions, *Antt.* xvii. 10. 10. What is in view therefore is the war of Varus in the year 4 B.C.

of the ungodly has ever had to endure anything equal to what has befallen us ? Now listen, my sons, and let us do this: Let us fast three days, and on the fourth let us go into a cave which is in the field and die there rather than transgress the commandments of our Lord, the God of our fathers.[22] Chap. x. And then will His kingdom appear throughout His whole creation. Then will the devil have an end, and sorrow will disappear along with him. For the Heavenly One will rise up from His throne. And the earth will tremble, the sun will withhold its light, and the horns of the moon will be broken. For God the Most High will appear and He will punish the Gentiles. Then wilt thou be happy, O Israel, and God will exalt thee. And now, Joshua (and here Moses turns again to address his successor), keep these words and this book. As for me, I am going to the resting-place of my fathers. Chap. xi. then goes on to relate how, after this address was ended, Joshua turned to Moses and lamented over the prospect of his departure, and regretted that, in consequence of his own weakness and incompetency, he would not be equal to the great task that had been imposed upon him. Thereupon chap. xii. proceeds to tell how Moses

---

[22] It is usually assumed that chaps. viii.–ix. have direct reference to the closing period. But this appears to be only indirectly the case. For the author represents Moses as prophesying that, in the closing period, there will be a state of matters the like of which will never have been before except once, viz. in the time of Antiochus Epiphanes. It is the description of this period of persecution under Antiochus that is also pursued in chap. ix., in which we accordingly meet with a legend similar to that in 2 Macc. vii. The object of the hiding in the cave is not merely to escape persecution, but also to find a place where the law can be observed without hindrance ; comp. in particular 2 Macc. vi. 11 and the Rabbinical legends regarding Simon ben Jochai (Grätz, *Gesch. der Juden*, iv. 470 sqq.) ; also in general, Lucius, *Der Essenismus*, p. 128. There has been an unnecessary amount of puzzling of the brains over the enigmatical term *taxo*. It is undoubtedly to be looked upon as a corruption of the text. But one is at a loss to conceive how Hilgenfeld could ever suppose that under it there lay a reference to the Messiah. That would surely be a strange Messiah who could find nothing better to do than creep into a hole and there await the approach of death. Yet, according to Philippi, this latter is to be under-stood as referring to Christ and His disciples (pp. 177–180).

exhorted Joshua not to under-estimate his ability and not to despair of the future of his people, seeing that, however much they might be punished for their sins, they could never be utterly destroyed.

Here the manuscript ends. But all that has gone before leads us to expect, what the fragments tend to confirm, that in the subsequent portion of the book it had gone on to give an account of how Moses was taken away from the earth, the scene from which the whole work obtained the title of the Ἀνάληψις Μωυσέως. It is also in this concluding part of the work that the dispute between the archangel Michael and Satan about the body of Moses must have occurred, which dispute, as is well known, is also mentioned in verse 9 of the Epistle of Jude.

Opinion is very much divided regarding the date of the composition of this book. Ewald, Wieseler, Drummond and Dillmann refer it to the first decade after the death of Herod; Hilgenfeld calculates that it may have been written in the course of the year 44–45 A.D.; Schmidt and Merx say some time between 54 and 64 A.D.; Fritzsche and Lucius trace it to the sixth decade of the first century A.D.; Langen thinks it must have been shortly after the destruction of Jerusalem by Titus (chap. viii. being erroneously interpreted as referring to this event); Hausrath prefers the reign of Domitian; Philippi, the second century of our era (the latter fixing on this date solely with the object of his being able to ascribe the authorship to a *Christian,* and of reversing the relation in which our book and ver. 9 of the Epistle of Jude stand to each other; see in particular, pp. 177, 182); while Volkmar (in accordance with his well-known predilection for the time of Barcocheba) thinks the date would be some time in the course of the year 137–138 A.D. Almost the whole of the critics just mentioned base their calculation upon the well-nigh illegible fragments of numbers in chap. vii. But surely one may fairly question the propriety of trying to found anything whatever upon lines so mutilated as those are; and if we had no other data but these to help us to fix the date in question, we would have nothing for it but to abandon the attempt altogether. Still I cannot help thinking that there are two such data at our disposal. (1) Toward the end of chap. vi. it is plainly stated that the sons of Herod are to reign for a shorter period (*breviora tempora*) than their father. Now it is well known that Philip and Antipas reigned longer than their father; and one cannot help seeing the embarrassment to which those words have led in the case of all those critics who refer the composition of our book to a latish date. They are capable of being explained solely on the assumption that the work was written toward the commencement of the reign of the last-mentioned princes. (2) It is as good as universally admitted that the concluding sentences of chap. vi. refer to the war of Varus in the year 4 B.C.[23] When therefore chap. vii. goes on to say: Ex quo facto finientur tempora, surely there can hardly be room for any other inference than this, that the author wrote subsequent to the war of Varus. In that case the enigmatical numbers that follow in this same chapter cannot be supposed to be a continuation of the narrative, but are to be regarded as a calculation added by way of supplement after the narrative has been brought down to the date at which the author was writing. Only, considering how mutilated those numbers are, every attempt to explain them must prove a failure. Consequently the view of Ewald, Wieseler, Drummond and Dillmann with regard to the date of the composition of our book is substantially correct.

Some light is thrown upon the author's *party leanings*, partly by chap. vii. and partly by chap. x. The *homines pestilentiosi* against whom he inveighs in chap. vii. are by no means the Herodian princes (so Hilgenfeld), nor the Sadducees

---

[23] So Hilgenfeld, Volkmar, Schmidt-Merx, Wieseler, Dillmann and others, also Langen, *Theol. Literaturbl.* 1871, No. 3, Sp. 90 (where he retracts his previous absolutely untenable reference of the passage to Pompey ; see *Judenth. in Paläst.* p. 109).

(so Volkmar, p. 105; Geiger, p. 45 sq.; Lucius, p. 116 sqq.), nor the Sadducees and Pharisees (so Wieseler, p. 642 sq., who refers vv. 3, 4 to the former and vv. 6–10 to the latter); but the Pharisees and the Pharisees alone, to whom every word is unmistakably applicable (so Ewald, *Gesch.* v. 81; Schmidt-Merx, p. 121; Philippi, p. 176). Our author then was *inimical to the Pharisees,* though, at the same time, he was neither an Essene, for as such he would not have jeered, as he does in chap. vii., at the Pharisaical purifications (Joseph. *Bell. Jud.* ii. 8. 10), nor a Sadducee, for, according to chap. x., he looks forward with the most fervent longings for the advent of the kingdom of God, and that too a kingdom accompanied with outward pomp and circumstance. Wieseler is perhaps nearest the truth in seeking him among the Zealots who, notwithstanding their kinship to the Pharisees, had still an intense dislike to them, because they looked upon them as being too dogmatic and formal as regards the law and too undecided with respect to their politics. That the book was written in Palestine may, to say the least of it, be accepted as the most obvious and natural supposition. Hilgenfeld and Hausrath have suggested Rome, without however alleging any ground for doing so. On the assumption that it was composed in Palestine, it becomes further probable that it was written originally in Hebrew or Aramaic. But we are not in a position positively to assert this. Only this much is certain, that our old Latin version was taken from the Greek.

*Of the legend regarding the death of Moses* extensive and varied use has been made in Jewish literature. Besides our book there fall to be mentioned: Philo (*Vita Mosis*), Josephus (*Antt.* iv. *fin.*), *Midrash Tanchuma debarum* (translated into German by Wünsche, 1882), and a *Midrash* which treats specially of the departure of Moses (פטירת משה, *Petirath Moshe*). This latter has been frequently published in two recensions, among others by Gilb. Gaulminus, Paris 1629, with a Latin translation; then this Latin translation was published by itself by John Alb. Fabricius, Hamburg 1714, and by Gfrörer, *Prophetae veteres pseudepigraphi,* Stuttg. 1840 (see Wolf, *Bibliotheca Hebraea,* ii. 1278 sq., 1395. Zunz, *Die gottesdienstlichen Vorträge der Juden,* p. 146. Steinschneider, *Catal. librorum Hebraeorum in Biblioth. Bodl.* p. 630 sq.). For one of these two recensions see also

Jellinek, *Beth ha-Midrash*, vol. i. 1853. Also a third, which Jellinek regards as the oldest, in his *Beth ha-Midrash*, vol. vi. 1877. Comp. in general on these legends: Bernard's edition of Josephus, note on *Antt.* iv. *fin.* Fabricius, *Cod. pseudepigr. Vet. Test.* i. 839 sqq. Beer, *Leben Moses nach Auffassung der jüdischen Sage*, Leipzig 1863. Benedetti, *Vita e morte di Mosé, leggende ebr. tradotte, illustrate e comparate*, Pisa 1879 (on which see *Magazin für die Wissensch. des Judenth.* 1881, pp. 57 - 60). Leop. v. Ranke, *Weltgeschichte*, vol. iii. 2nd part (1883), pp. 12–33.

Care must be taken not to confound our *Assumptio Mosis* with the Christian *Apocalypse of Mosis* in Greek which has been edited by Tischendorf (*Apocalypses apocryphae*, Lips. 1866) ; similarly, from a Milanese manuscript, by Ceriani, *Monumenta sacra et profana*, v. 1. This work belongs to the class of Adamic books, for it records the history of the life and death of Adam as it had been revealed to Moses. On this comp. Tischendorf, *Stud. u. Krit.* 1851, p. 432 sqq. Le Hir, *Etudes Bibliques* (1869), ii. pp. 110–120. Rönsch, *Das Buch der Jubiläen*, p. 470 sqq. According to Euthalius and others, Gal. vi. 15 (οὔτε περιτομή τι ἐστιν οὔτε ἀκροβυστία, ἀλλά καινή κτίσις) found a place in an *Apocryphum Mosis*, where, of course, it could only have been borrowed from the Epistle to the Galatians (Euthalius in Zaccagni's *Collectanea monumentorum veterum*, 1698, p. 561 = Gallandi, *Biblioth. Patr.* x. 260. Similarly Syncellus, ed. Dindorf, i. 48, and an anonymous list of the quotations in the New Testament given in Montfaucon, *Bibliotheca Bibliothecarum*, i. 195 = *Diarium Italicum*, p. 212, and in Cotelier, *Patr. apost.*, note on *Const apost.* vi. 16). Now, seeing that Euthalius also makes use of precisely the same formula of reference (Μωυσέως ἀποκρύφου) as in the case of verse 9 of the Epistle of Jude (Zaccagni, p. 485), we may perhaps venture to assume that he had before him a Christian version of the *Assumptio Mosis*, in which Gal. vi. 15 had been inserted. Syncellus and the author of the anonymous list just referred to have clearly drawn upon Euthalius. *Gnostic Books of Moses* are mentioned as being in use among the Sethites by Epiphan. *Haer.* xxxix. 5. For *Apocrypha Mosis* generally, see *Const. apost.* vi. 16. Fabricius, *Cod. pseudepigr. Vet. Test.* i. 825–849, ii. 111–130. Lücke, *Einleitung in die Offenbarung Johannis*, pp. 232–235. Dillmann, art. "Pseudepigraphen" in Herzog's *Real-Enc.* 2nd ed. xii. 352 sqq. (Nos. 4, 18, 26, 29, 35).

Use of the *Assumptio Mosis in the Christian Church:* Epistle of Jude, ver. 9. Clement of Alexandria, *Adumbrat. in epist. Judae* (in Zahn's *Supplementum Clementinum*, 1884, p. 84): Hic confirmat assumptionem Moysi. Other legends in Clement of Alexandria regarding the death and ascension of Moses, have in all probability been borrowed no less from our writing (*Strom.* i. 23. 153, vi. 15. 132. Comp. Zahn, p. 96 sq.). Origen, *De principiis*, iii. 2. 1 : Et primo quidem in Genesi serpens Evam seduxisse describitur, de quo in Adscensione Mosis, cujus libelli meminit in epistola sua apostolus Judas, Michael archangelus cum diabolo disputans de corpore Mosis ait a diabolo inspiratum serpentem causam exstitisse praevaricationis Adae et Evae. Idem, *In Josuam homil.* ii. 1 (ed. Lommatzsch, xi. 22) : Denique et in libello quodam, licet in canone non habeatur, mysterii tamen

hujus figura describitur. Refertur enim, quia duo Moses videbantur:
unus vivus in spiritu, alius mortuus in corpore. Didymus Alex., *In
epist. Judae enarratio* (in Gallandi, *Biblioth. Patr.* vi. 307), finds in Jude,
ver. 9, evidence in favour of the view that even the devil is not evil by
nature or *substantialiter*, and alleges that the adversarii hujus contempla-
tionis praescribunt praesenti epistolae et Moyseos assumptioni propter eum
locum ubi significatur verbum Archangeli de corpore Moyseos ad diabolum
factum. *Acta Synodi Nicaen.* ii. 20 (in Fabricius, i. 844): 'Εν βιβλίῳ δὲ
'Αναλήψεως Μωυσέως Μιχαὴλ ὁ ἀρχάγγελος διαλεγόμενος τῷ διαβόλῳ λέγει
κ.τ.λ. For another passage from these same Acts, see p. 74 above.
Evodii epist. ad Augustin. (*Augustin. epist.* cclix. in Fabricius, i. 845 sq.):
Quanquam et in apocryphis et in secretis ipsius Moysi, quae scriptura caret
auctoritate, tunc cum ascenderet in montem ut moreretur vi corporis,
efficitur ut aliud esset quod terrae mandaretur, aliud quod angelo comitanti
sociaretur. Sed non satis urget me apocryphorum praeferre sententiam
illis superioribus rebus definitis. For additional passages, and chiefly from
Greek scholia, see Rönsch, *Zeitschr. für wissenschaftl. Theol.* 1869, pp.
216–220. Hilgenfeld, *Clementis Romani epist.* 2nd ed. pp. 127–129. In
the lists of the apocryphal books we find a Διαθήκη Μωυσέως and an
'Ανάληψις Μωυσέως (the one immediately after the other in the stichometry
of Nicephorus, and in the "Synopsis Athanasii" as given in Credner's *Zur
Geschichte des Kanons*, pp. 121, 145 ; as also in the anonymous list edited
by Pitra and others, see v. 7 below). Now, seeing that the writing that
has come down to us is in point of fact a "Testament (will) of Moses,"
though, as we have already seen, it is quoted in the Acts of the Council of
Nicaea under the title 'Ανάληψις Μωυσέως, it may be assumed that both
these designations were the titles of two separate divisions of one and the
same work, the first of which has been preserved, whereas the quotations
in the Fathers almost all belong to the second.

*Editions* of the Latin text : Ceriani, *Monumenta sacra et prof.* vol. i. fasc.
i. (Milan 1861), pp. 55–64. Hilgenfeld, *Clementis Romani epistulae* (likewise under the title *Novum Testam. extra canonem receptum*, fasc. i.), 1st
ed. 1866, pp. 93–115, 2nd ed. 1876, pp. 107–135. Volkmar, *Mose Prophetie
und Himmelfahrt, eine Quelle für das Neue Testament, zum erstenmale
deutsch herausgegeben im Zusammenhang der Apokrypha und der Chris-
tologie überhaupt*, Leipzig 1867. Schmidt (Moriz) and Merx, "Die
Assumptio Mosis mit Einleitung und erklärenden Anmerkungen herausgegeben" (Merx' *Archiv für wissenschaftl. Erforschung des A. T.'s*, vol. i.
Part ii. 1868, pp. 111–152). Fritzsche, *Libri apocryphi Vet. Test. graece*
(Lips. 1871), pp. 700–730 ; comp. *Prolegom.* pp. 32–36. A rendering back
into the Greek was attempted by Hilgenfeld, for which see *Zeitschr. für
wissensch. Theol.* 1868, pp. 273–309, 356, and his *Messias Judaeorum*, 1869,
pp. 435–468 ; comp. *Prolegom.* pp. 70–76.

For contributions toward the *criticism* and *exposition* of our book, see,
besides the editions just mentioned, Ewald, *Göttinger gelehrte Anz.* 1862,
St. 1. Idem, *Gesch. des Volkes Israel*, vol. v. (3rd ed. 1867), pp. 73–82.
Langen, *Das Judenthum in Palästina* (1866), pp. 102–111. Idem, in
Reusch's *Theolog. Literaturbl.* 1871, No. 3. Hilgenfeld, *Zeitschr. für*

*wissensch. Theol.* 1867, pp. 217–223. *Ibid.* Haupt, p. 448. Rönsch,
*Zeitschr. f. wiss. Theol.* vol. xi. 1868, pp. 76–108, 466–468 ; xii. 1869, pp.
213–228 ; xiv. 1871, pp. 89–92 ; xvii. 1874, pp. 542–562 ; xxviii. 1885, pp.
102–104. Philippi, *Das Buch Henoch* (1868), pp. 166–191. Colani,
"L'Assomption de Moïse" (*Revue de Théologie*, 1868, 2nd part). Carriere,
*Note sur le Taxo de l'Assomption de Moïse* (*ibid.* 1868, 2nd part). Wieseler,
"Die jüngst aufgefundene Aufnahme Moses nach Ursprung und Inhalt
untersucht" (*Jahrbb. für deutsche Theol.* 1868, pp. 622–648). Idem,
" Θασσί und Taxo" (*Zeitschr. der deutschen morgenländ. Gesellsch.* 1882, p.
193 sq.). Geiger's *Jüdische Zeitschr. für Wissensch. und Leben*, 1868, pp.
41–47. Heidenheim, "Beiträge zum bessern Verständniss der *Ascensio
Mosis*" (*Vierteljahrschr. für deutsch. und Englisch - theol. Forschung und
Kritik*, vol. iv. (Part I. 1869). Hausrath, *Neutestamentl. Zeitgesch.* 2nd ed.
iv. pp. 76–80 (1st ed. iii. 278–282). Stähelin, *Jahrbb. für deutsche Theol.*
1874, pp. 216–218. Drummond, *The Jewish Messiah* (1877), pp. 74–84.
Lucius, *Der Essenismus* (1881), pp. 111–119, 127 sq. Reuss, *Gesch. der
heil. Schriften A. T.'s*, § 572. Dillmann, art. "Pseudepigraphen " in Herzog's
*Real - Enc.* 2nd ed. xii. 352 sq. Deane, " The Assumption of Moses"
(*Monthly Interpreter*, March 1885, pp. 321–348).

### 4. *The Apocalypse of Baruch.*

The large Peshito manuscript of Milan (*Cod. Ambros. B.
21, inf.*) also contains a *Revelation of Baruch*, regarding which
we have no further information of a trustworthy kind. Only
a small fraction of it, viz. the epistle addressed to the nine
and a half tribes in the captivity, inserted at the close (chaps.
lxxviii.–lxxxvi.), has been otherwise transmitted to us and
already printed in the Paris and London Polyglots. But
beyond this there is hardly any other trace of it to be met
with (see below). The book was first introduced to public
notice through a Latin version prepared and edited by
Ceriani (1866). This scholar subsequently published the
Syrian text itself (in ordinary type in 1871, and in a photo-
lithographed fac-simile in 1883). Fritzsche, after making a
few emendations upon it, embodied Ceriani's Latin version in
his edition of the Apocrypha (1871). The book purports to
be a writing composed by Baruch in which he recounts (using
the first person throughout) what happened to him immediately before and after the destruction of Jerusalem, and
what revelations were made to him. The contents are substantially as follows :—*First section,* chaps. i.–v. : In the five

and twentieth year of the reign of Jeconiah [a complete confounding of dates by which the author means to indicate
the time of the destruction of Jerusalem] God intimates to
Baruch the impending ruin of Jerusalem and the kingdom of
Judah.    Chaps. vi.–viii.: On the following day the Chaldean
army appears before the walls of the city.    However it is not
the Chaldeans but four angels that destroy it.    No sooner is
this done than the Chaldeans enter the city and carry away
its inhabitants into captivity.    Chaps. ix.–xii.: While Jeremiah
accompanies these latter, Baruch, in obedience to the command of God, remains behind among the ruins.    *Second section*,
chaps. xiii.–xv.: After he had fasted seven days, God informs
him that one day judgment would overtake the Gentiles as
well and that in his own time; and He calms his apprehensions generally about the prosperity of the ungodly and the
calamities of the righteous.    Chaps. xvi.–xx.: Baruch brings
forward yet further grounds of perplexity, but God discourages
his doing so, and ultimately orders him to prepare, by another
seven days' fasting, for receiving a revelation of the order of
the times.    *Third section*, xxi.–xxvi.: After fasting and praying
to God, he is first of all censured by God for his doubts and
pusillanimity, and then, in answer to his question as to when
the judgment of the ungodly would take place and how long
it would last, God communicates to him the following (chaps.
xxvii.–xxviii.): The time of the tribulation will be divided
into twelve parts, and each part will bring with it its own
special disaster.    But the measure of that time will be two
parts, weeks of seven weeks (duae partes hebdomades septem
hebdomadarum).    Chaps. xxviii.–xxx.: To the further question
of Baruch whether the tribulation would be confined to only
*one* part of the earth or extend to the whole of it, God
answers that it will of course affect the whole earth.    But
after that the Messiah will appear and times of joy and glory
begin to dawn.    Chaps. xxxi.–xxxiv.: After receiving those
revelations Baruch summons a meeting of the elders of the
people in the valley of Kidron, when he announces to them

that : post modicum tempus concutietur aedificatio Sion, ut aedificetur iterum. Verum non permanebit ipsa illa aedificatio, sed iterum post tempus eradicabitur, et permanebit desolata usque ad tempus. Et postea oportet renovari in gloria, et coronabitur in perpetuum. *Fourth section,* chaps. xxxv.– xxxviii. : Hereupon, Baruch, as he sits lamenting upon the ruins of the Holy of holies, falls asleep and in a dream is favoured with a new revelation. He sees a large forest surrounded by mountains and rocks. Over against it grew a vine, and from under the vine flowed a spring which developed into large streams that made channels for themselves under- neath the forest and the mountains till these latter fell in and were swept away. Only a single cedar was left, but at last it too was uprooted. Thereupon the vine and the spring came and ordered the cedar to betake itself to where the rest of the forest had already gone. And the cedar was burnt up, but the vine continued to grow and everything around it flourished. Chaps. xxxviii.–xl. : In answer to Baruch's request God inter- prets the dream to him as follows : Behold the kingdom that destroys Zion will itself be overthrown and subjugated by another that will succeed it. And this in its turn will be overthrown and a third will arise. And then this also will be swept away and a fourth will arise, more terrible than all that have preceded it. And when the time for its overthrow has come then Mine Anointed will appear, who is like a spring and a vine, and He will annihilate the armies of that kingdom. And that cedar means the last remaining general (*dux,* prince ?) in it who will be condemned and put to death by Mine Anointed. And the reign of Mine Anointed will endure for ever. Chaps. xli.–xliii. : Baruch receives a com- mission to exhort the people and at the same time to pre- pare himself, by renewed fasting, for fresh revelations. Chaps. xliv.–xlvi. : Baruch exhorts the elders of the people. *Fifth section,* chaps. xlvii.–xlviii. 24 : He fasts seven days and prays to God. Chap. xlviii. 25–50 : The new revelations have reference, in the first instance, to the tribulations of the last time generally. Chaps. xlix.-lii.: When, upon this, Baruch expresses a desire to learn something more about the nature of the new resurrection bodies of the righteous his wish is complied with; not only so, but he is enlightened with regard to the future blessedness of the righteous and the misery of the ungodly generally. *Sixth section,* chap. liii.: In a new vision Baruch sees a huge cloud rising from the sea and covering the whole earth and discharging first black water and then clear, then black again and then clear, and so on twelve times in succession. At last there came black waters and after them bright lightning, which latter brought healing to the whole earth, and ultimately there came twelve streams and subjected themselves to this lightning. Chaps. liv.-lv.: In answer to his prayer Baruch receives through the angel Ramiel the following interpretation of the vision: Chaps. lvi.-lvii.: The huge cloud means the present world. The *first,* the *dark* water means the sin of Adam, whereby he brought death and ruin into the world. The *second,* the *clear* water means Abraham and his descendants, who, although not in possession of the written law, nevertheless complied with its requirements. The *third,* the *dark* water represents the subsequent generations of sinful humanity, particularly the Egyptians. The *fourth,* the *clear* water means the appearing of Moses, Aaron, Joshua, and Caleb, and the giving of the law, and God's revelations to Moses. The *fifth,* the *dark* water represents the works of the Amorites and the magicians, in which Israel also participated. The *sixth,* the *clear* water represents the time of David and Solomon. The *seventh,* the *dark* water means the revolt of Jeroboam and the sins of his successors and the overthrow of the kingdom of the ten tribes. The *eighth,* the *clear* water means the integrity of Hezekiah and his deliverance from Sennacherib. The *ninth,* the *dark* water means the universal ungodliness in the days of Manasseh and the announcing of the destruction of Jerusalem. The *tenth,* the *clear* water denotes the reign of the good king Josiah. The *eleventh,* the *dark* water represents the present tribulation (*i.e.* in Baruch's own time), the destruction of Jerusalem, and the Babylonian captivity. Chap. lxviii.: But the *twelfth*, the *clear* water means that the people of Israel will again experience times of joy, that Jerusalem will be rebuilt, that the offering of sacrifices will be resumed, and that the priests will return to their duties. Chaps. lxix.–lxxi.: But the *last dark* water which is yet to come, and which proves worse than all that went before, means this: that tribulation and confusion will come upon the whole earth. A few will rule over the many, the poor will become rich and the rich will become poor, knaves will be exalted above heroes, wise men will keep silence and fools will speak. And in obedience to God's command the nations which He has prepared for the purpose will come and war with such of the leaders as are still left (cum ducibus, qui reliqui fuerint tunc). And it will come to pass that he who escapes from the war will perish by the earthquake, and he who escapes from the earthquake will perish by fire, and he who escapes the fire will perish with hunger. And he who escapes the whole of those evils will be given into the hands of Mine Anointed. Chaps. lxxii.–lxxiv.: But this dreadful dark water will at length be followed by yet more *clear water.* This means that the time of Mine Anointed will come and that He will judge the nations and sit for ever upon the throne of His kingdom. And all tribulation will come to an end, and peace and joy will reign upon the earth. Chaps. lxxv.–lxxvi.: Baruch thanks God for the revelation with which he had been favoured, and then God directs him to wait for forty days and then go to the top of a certain mountain where all the different regions of the earth would pass before his view. After this he is to be removed from the world. *Seventh section*, chap. lxxvii.: Baruch delivers a hortatory address to the people, and at the request of the latter he, on the 21st day of the eighth month, also composes two hortatory addresses to be sent to their brethren in the captivity, one to the nine and a half tribes and the other to the remaining two and a half. Chaps. lxxviii.–lxxxvi.:

The import of the first of the two addresses is as follows :
Baruch in the first place reminds his readers that the judgment of God which has overtaken them is a just judgment,
he then tells them of the destruction of Jerusalem by
Nebuchadnezzar and the carrying away of the inhabitants
into captivity, and intimates to them the judgment of God
that is awaiting their oppressors and then their own ultimate
deliverance.   In conclusion, he founds upon this an exhortation to continue steadfast in their devotion to God and His
law.   Chap. lxxxvii.: He sends this epistle to the nine and
a half tribes in captivity through the medium of an eagle.

At this point the book, as we now possess it, breaks off.
But originally it must have contained somewhat more, for
from lxxvii. 19 there is reason to infer that the epistle
addressed to the nine and a half tribes was followed by a
similar one addressed to the other two and a half tribes.  And
from chap. lxxvi. it is to be presumed that the book would
proceed to tell how Baruch was shown all the countries of the
world from the top of a mountain and was thereafter taken
away from the earth.

As regards the date of the composition of our apocalypse
this much at least may be affirmed with certainty, that it was
not written till after the destruction of Jerusalem by Titus.
For in chap. xxxii. 2–4, Baruch announces to the assembled
people that (after its first destruction by Nebuchadnezzar)
Jerusalem is to be rebuilt again.   *But that this building
will not continue to stand, but that it will in like manner be
destroyed again.*   And then the city will lie waste for a long
period, until the glorious time when it will be rebuilt and
crowned for ever.   But, with the exception of this passage,
there is not another that throws any light upon the date of the
composition of our book.   For nothing bearing upon this is to
be gathered from the obscure passage in which we are informed
that the time of tribulation is to last " two parts, weeks of
seven weeks " (xxviii. 2: duae partes hebdomades septem
hebdomadarum), for the meaning of these words is as uncer-

tain as it is obscure. Consequently the calculations which Ewald, Hilgenfeld, Wieseler, and Dillmann above all have tried to found upon this passage have no certain basis on which to rest. Possibly one would be much more likely to find some clue to the date in question in *the affinity which this work bears to the Fourth Book of Ezra.* For the points of contact between both those books in regard to thought and expression alike are (as Langen has pointed out, pp. 6–8) so numerous that we must of necessity assume either that they were written by one and the same author, or that the one borrowed from the other. It is now almost universally believed that it may be proved with a greater or less degree of certainty that our book has drawn upon the Fourth Book of Ezra (so Ewald, Langen, Hilgenfeld, Hausrath, Stähelin, Renan, Drummond, Dillmann). It appears to me however that as yet no decisive arguments have been advanced in support of this view. In the case of Langen, who was the first to go thoroughly into this question, and who has done much to influence subsequent opinion on the matter, his main argument was that the Book of Baruch corrected, as he supposed, the somewhat crude notions of Ezra respecting the doctrine of original sin. In order that the reader may be in a more favourable position for estimating the value of this argument, we will here subjoin in parallel columns what each of the two books says on this point:—

| EZRA: | BARUCH: |
|---|---|
| iii. 7 : Et huic (Adamo) mandasti diligere viam tuam, et praeteriviteam; et statim instituisti in eum mortem et in nationibus ejus. | xvii. 3 : (Adam) mortem attulit et abscidit annos eorum, qui ab eo geniti fuerunt. |
| iii. 21–22 : Cor enim malignum bajulans primus, Adam transgressus et victus est; sed et omnes, qui de eo nati sunt. Et facta est permanens infirmitas. | xxiii. 4 : Quando peccavit Adam et decreta fuit mors contra eos, qui gignerentur, etc. |
| | xlviii. 42 : O quid fecisti Adam omnibus, qui a te geniti sunt! |
| iv. 30 : Quoniam granum seminis mali seminatum est in corde Adam ab initio, et quantum impietatis generavit usque nunc, et generat usque dum veniat area! | liv. 15, 19 · Si enim Adam prior peccavit, et attulit mortem super omnes immaturam; sed etiam illi qui ex eo nati sunt, unusquisque ex eis praeparavit animae suae tormentum futurum : et iterum unusquisque ex |

vii. 48 : O tu quid fecisti Adam ?
Si enim tu peccasti, non est factus
solius tuus casus, sed et nostrum, qui
ex te advenimus.

eis elegit sibi gloriam futuram . . .
Non est ergo Adam causa, nisi animae
suae tantum ; nos vero unusquisque
fuit animae suae Adam.

Now Langen supposes that the last of the passages quoted
from Baruch (liv. 19 : Non est ergo Adam causa, nisi animae
suae tantum ; nos vero unusquisque fuit animae suae Adam)
is above all intended to modify the somewhat harsh view of
Ezra. But one can easily see that the utterances of Baruch
on other occasions are quite as blunt as those of Ezra.
And, on the other hand, there are passages to be met with in
Ezra in which the author emphasizes quite as strongly as
Baruch liv. 19, though in different terms, the thought that
every man is to blame for his own ruin. To take only a single
example, compare viii. 55–61. Here then we have not even
an actual difference of view, far less a correction of the one
writer on the part of the other. Further, such other reasons
as have been advanced in favour of the priority of Ezra and
the dependent character of Baruch are merely considerations
of an extremely general kind which may be met with,
considerations equally well calculated to prove quite the
reverse. Some are inclined to think that in the case of the
author of the Fourth Book of Ezra "there is more of a des-
pairing frame of mind, that his striving after light and his
desire to have his apprehensions quieted are deeper, more
urgent, and of a more overmastering character, that, because
the impressions produced by the dreadful events are rather
fresher in his mind, his narrative is also, for this very reason
and in spite of its verbosity, the more impressive of the two,
and so on " (so Dillmann). My own opinion is that it is quite
the converse of this, and that it would be nearer the truth to
say that it is precisely in the case of Baruch that this problem
is uppermost, viz. How is the calamity of Israel and the
impunity of its oppressors possible and conceivable ? while in
the case of Ezra, though this problem concerns him too, still
there is a question that almost lies yet nearer his heart, viz.

Why is it that so many perish and so few are saved ? The subordination of the former of these questions to the other, which is a purely theological one, appears to me rather to indicate that Ezra is of a later date than Baruch. Not only so, but it is decidedly of a more finished character, and is distinguished by greater maturity of thought and a greater degree of lucidity than the last-mentioned book. But this is a point in regard to which it is scarcely possible to arrive at a definite conclusion. And hence we are equally unable to say whether our book was written shortly after the destruction of Jerusalem (so Hilgenfeld, Fritzsche, Drummond), or during the reign of Domitian (so Ewald), or in the time of Trajan (so Langen, Wieseler, Renan, Dillmann). Undoubtedly the most probable supposition of all is that it was composed not long after the destruction of the holy city, when the question " How could God permit such a disaster ? " was still a burning one. It is older at all events than the time of *Papias*, whose chimerical fancies about the millennial kingdom (Irenaeus, v. 33. 3) are borrowed from our Apocalypse (xxix. 5).[24] The existing Syrian text has been taken from the Greek (see Langen, p. 8 sq.; Kneucker, p. 192 sq.; Dillmann, p. 358).

With the exception of the passage in Papias just mentioned, no certain trace of the *use of our book* in the Christian Church is anywhere to be met with. There is every reason to believe that it had been pushed into the background by the kindred Ezra-apocalypse. Still the fact of its finding a place in the *Peshito manuscript* of Milan serves to show that it was still in use at a later period at least in the Syrian Church. In the lists of the apocrypha given in the Stichometry of Nicephorus and the "Synopsis Athanasii" (in Credner, *Zur Geschichte des Kanons*, pp. 121, 145) there are added at the close: Βαρούχ, Ἀββακούμ, Ἐζεκιήλ καὶ Δανιήλ ψευδεπίγραφα. But it is

---

[24] In his edition of Irenaeus (ii. 417), Harvey attempts to show that the text of Papias presupposes a *Syrian original* on which it is based, for he thinks that a certain anomaly occurring in his text may be most easily accounted for by the hypothesis of such an original. If this were correct, it would be of considerable interest as regards the matter now in hand. The anomaly in question admits however of being otherwise explained. See Gebhardt and Harnack's edition of the *Epistle of Barnabas* (2nd ed. 1878), p. 87.

extremely uncertain whether, by the first-mentioned book, it is our apocalypse that is meant, for besides the Baruch of the Greek Bible, and which
in the lists just referred to is included among the canonical books, there
were also *other apocryphal writings bearing this name.* (1) There are considerable fragments of a *gnostic* Book of Baruch given in the *Philosophumena*
v. 26–27 (comp. v. 24).   (2) A *Christian* Book of Baruch, which is akin to
our apocalypse and has borrowed largely from it, has been published in
Ethiopic by Dillmann under the title "Reliqua verborum Baruchi" (in
Dillmann's *Chrestomathia aethiopica*, Lips. 1866), as it had been previously
in Greek in a Greek *Menaeus* (Venetiis 1609), and recently again by
Ceriani under the title "Paralipomena Jeremiae" (*Monumenta sacra et
profana*, vol. v. 1, Mediol. 1868), and finally in a German version by
Prätorius (*Zeitschr. für wissensch. Theol.* 1872, pp. 230–247), and by König
(*Stud. u. Krit.* 1877, pp. 318–338).   On this book comp. also Ewald, *Gesch.
des Volkes Israel*, vii. 183.   Fritzsche, *Libri apocr. prolegom.* p. 32.
Sachsse, *Zeitschr. für wissensch. Theol.* 1874, p. 268 sq.   Kneucker, *Das
Buch Baruch*, p. 196 sq.   Dillmann in Herzog's *Real-Enc.* 2nd ed. xii.
358 sq.   (3) In the *Altercatio Simonis Judaei et Theophili Christiani*, lately
published by Harnack, there occurs the following passage from a Book of
Baruch (Gebhardt and Harnack, *Texte und Untersuchungen*, vol. i. part 3,
1883, p. 25): Prope finem libri sui de nativitate ejus [scil. Christi] et de
habitu vestis et de passione ejus et de resurrectione ejus prophetavit dicens:
Hic unctus meus, electus meus, *vulvae incontaminatae jaculatus*, natus et
passus dicitur.   Judging from the Christology implied in this passage,
the Baruch here in question can only have been composed at the soonest
in the fourth century of our era (see Harnack, p. 46).   Further, in
Cyprian's *Testim.* iii. 29, we find that in *one* manuscript there has been
inserted a quotation from some Book of Baruch or other, which quotation,
however, we have no means of verifying.   (4) Tichonrawow contemplates
editing an Apocalypse of Baruch in the *old Slavonic* version (see *Theol.
Literaturztg.* 1877, p. 658).   Whether it has as yet appeared, and what its
relation to other Books of Baruch with which we are already acquainted,
I am unable to say.

*The epistle to the nine and a half tribes in the captivity*, which forms
the conclusion of our apocalypse, has been already printed in the Paris
Polyglot, vol. ix., in the London Polyglot, vol. iv., in Lagarde's edition of the
Syrian version of the apocrypha (*Libri Vet. Test. apocryphi syriace*, ed.
de Lagarde, Lips. 1861), also in Latin in Fabricius, *Codex pseudepigr. Vet.
Test.* ii. 145–155.   Also in an English and French version; see Fritzsche's
*Exeget. Handbuch zu den Apokryphen*, i. 175 sq., and *Libri Apocr.* p. xxxi.
Kneucker, *Das Buch Baruch*, p. 190 sq.

Ceriani's Latin version of our apocalypse appeared in the *Monumenta
sacra et profana*, vol. i. fasc. 2 (Mediol. 1866), pp. 73–98.   For this see
also Fritzsche, *Libri apocryphi Vet. Test. graece* (Lips. 1871), pp. 654–699.
The Syrian text was edited by Ceriani in the *Monumenta sacra et profana*,
vol. v. fasc. 2 (Mediol. 1871), pp. 113–180.   This latter was also included
in the photo-lithographed fac-simile of the whole manuscript, published
under the title *Translatio Syra Pescitto Veteris Testamenti ex codice*

*Ambrosiano sec. fere VI. photolithographice edita curante et adnotante Antonio Maria Ceriani,* 2 vols. in 4 parts, Milan 1876-1883 (the Apocalypse of Baruch being in the last part). Comp. *Theol. Literaturzeitung,* 1876, p. 329; 1878, p. 228; 1881, col. 4; 1884, col. 27.

*Critical inquiries:* Langen, *De apocalypsi Baruch anno superiori primum edita commentatio,* Friburgi in Brisgovia, 1867 (xxiv. p. 4). Ewald, *Göttinger gel. Anzeigen,* 1867, p. 1706 sqq. Idem, *Gesch. des Volkes Israel,* vii. 83–87. Hilgenfeld, *Zeitschr. für wissensch. Theol.* 1869, pp. 437–440. Idem, *Messias Judaeorum,* p. lxiii. sq. Wieseler, *Theol. Stud. u. Krit.* 1870, p. 288 (in his article on the Fourth Book of Ezra). Fritzsche, *Libri apocr. Prolegom.* pp. 30–32. Hausrath, *Neutestamentl. Zeitgesch.* 2nd ed. iv. 88 sq. (1st ed. iii. 290). Stähelin, *Jahrbb. für deutsche Theol.* 1874, p. 211 sqq. Renan, "L'Apocalypse de Baruch" (*Journal des Savants,* April 1877, pp. 222–231). Idem, *Les évangiles,* 1877, pp. 517–530. Drummond, *The Jewish Messiah,* 1877, pp. 117–132. Kneucker, *Das Buch Baruch,* 1879, pp. 190–198. Kaulen in Wetzer and Welte's *Kirchenlex.* 2nd ed. i. 1058 sq. (art. "Apokryphen-Literatur"). Dillmann in Herzog's *Real-Enc.* 2nd ed. xii. 356–358 (art. "Pseudepigraphen"). Deane, "The Apocalypse of Baruch," i. (*Monthly Interpreter,* April 1885, pp. 451–461).

## 5. *The Fourth Book of Ezra.*

Of all the Jewish apocalypses none has been so widely circulated in the early Church and in the Church of the Middle Ages as the so-called Fourth Book of Ezra. By Greek and Latin Fathers it is used as a genuine prophetical work (see below). The fact of there being Syrian, Ethiopic, Arabic, and Armenian versions of the book is evidence of the extent to which it was circulated in the East. Then the circumstance that a Latin version has come down to us in a large number of Bible manscripts is calculated to show the favour with which, in like manner, it was still regarded by the Church of Rome in the Middle Ages. It was for this reason no doubt that it was also added as an appendix to the authorized Roman Vulgate. Not only so, it even found its way into German versions of the Protestant Bible (see more below). The whole of the five versions which we possess are taken, some of them directly, others indirectly, from a Greek text (now no longer extant), which, moreover, is to be regarded as the original one.

The text of the Latin Vulgate consists of sixteen chapters. But, as is generally admitted, the two first and the two last of

these, which do not appear in the Oriental versions, are later
additions by a Christian hand. Accordingly in its original
form the book would only embrace the portion between chaps.
iii. and xiv. inclusive. The contents of the original work are
divided into *seven visions*, with which, as he himself informs
us, Ezra had been favoured. *First vision* (iii. 1–v. 20):
In the thirtieth year after the destruction of the city (Jerusalem) Ezra is in Babylon, and in his prayer to God he complains of the calamities of Israel on the one hand, and of the
prosperity of the Gentile nations on the other (iii. 1–36).
The angel Uriel comes, and, in the first place, reproves him
for his complaints (iv. 1–21), and then proceeds to remind him
that wickedness has its appointed time (iv. 22–32), just as
the dead have an appointed time during which they require
to stay in the nether world (iv. 33–43). But the most of the
distress is already past, and its end will be announced by
means of definite signs (iv. 44–v. 13). Ezra is so exhausted
by the revelation that has been imparted to him that he
requires to be strengthened by the angel. By fasting for
seven days he prepares himself for a new revelation (v. 14–20).
*Second vision* (v. 21–vi. 34): Ezra renews his complaints,
and is once more rebuked by the angel (v. 21–40). This
latter points out to him that in the history of mankind one
thing must come after another, and that the beginning and
the end cannot come at one and the same time. Ezra is
reminded, however, that he may nevertheless see that the
end is already approaching. It will be brought about by
God Himself, the Creator of the world (v. 41–vi. 6). The
signs of the end are more fully enumerated than in the
previous vision (vi. 7–29). Uriel here takes leave of Ezra,
with the promise of further revelations (vi. 30–34). *Third
vision* (vi. 35–ix. 25): Ezra complains again, and is again
rebuked by the angel (vi. 35–vii. 25). Upon this he is
favoured with the following revelation :—Whenever the signs
(enumerated in the preceding visions) begin to appear, then
those delivered from the calamities in question will see won-

derful things : For my Son, the Anointed One, will appear
with His retinue, and He will diffuse joy among those that
are spared, and that for four hundred years. And at the
expiry of those years, my Son, the Anointed One, will die, He
and all who have the breath of life. For the space of seven
days, corresponding to the seven creative days, there will not
be a single human being upon the earth. Then the dead will
rise ; and the Most High will come and sit upon the judg-
ment-seat, and proceed with the judgment (vii. 26–35).[25]
And the place of torment will be revealed, and over against
it the place of rest. And the length of the day of judgment
will be a year-week (vi. 1–17 = Bensly, vv. 36–44). Only
a few men will be saved. The majority will be consigned to
perdition (vi. 18–48 = Bensly, vv. 45–74). Moreover, the
ungodly do not enter at death into habitations of rest, but
when they die are at once consigned to sevenfold torment, of
which this also forms a part, that they find it no longer possible to repent, and that they foresee their future condemnation.
But the righteous, on the other hand, enter into rest, and
experience sevenfold joy, of which, among other things, this
forms a part, that they foresee their ultimate blessedness
(vi. 49–76 = Bensly, 75–101). But on the day of judgment
each receives what he has deserved ; and no one, by interced-
ing for him, can alter the fate of another (vi. 77–83 = Bensly,
102–105).[26] Ezra's objection, that surely the Scriptures
speak of the righteous having often interceded in behalf of the
ungodly, is dismissed with the remark on the part of the angel,
that what might avail for this world will not do so for eternity

[25] What follows (vi. 1–83) is not found in the majority of the manuscripts
of the Latin version, and can only have been borrowed at some former period
from the Oriental manuscripts and inserted here. Fritzsche gives the fragment according to the Syriac version, though retaining the numbering of
the chapters and verses usually followed in the Ethiopic one. Since 1875
and 1877 we have been made acquainted with the Latin text through two
manuscripts (see below). I give above both the numbering of the verses
adopted by Fritzsche and that followed by Bensly in his edition of the
Latin text.

[26] At this point the Latin Vulgate text comes in again.

as well (vii. 36–45). When Ezra is deploring that the whole ruin of the human race has been brought about by Adam, the angel refers him to the impiety of men through which they have become the authors of their own ruin (vii. 46–69). Then follow further explanations, having reference to the circumstance that of the many that are created so very few are saved (viii. 1–62). Finally, the signs of the last time are unfolded to Ezra anew (viii. 63–ix. 13), and his anxiety at the thought of so many being lost is once more set at rest (ix. 14–25). *Fourth vision* (ix. 26–x. 60): While Ezra is again indulging his complaints, he sees a woman on his right hand weeping, and who, in answer to his questions, tells him that after thirty years of barrenness she gave birth to a son, brought him up with great difficulty, and then procured a wife for him, but that just as he was entering the bride-chamber he fell and was killed (ix. 26–x. 4). Ezra chides her for bewailing the mere loss of a son, when she ought rather to be weeping over the destruction of Jerusalem and the ruin of so many men (x. 5–24). Then all at once her face is lifted up, she utters a cry, the earth quakes, and instead of the woman there appears a strongly built city. At this sight Ezra is so perplexed that he cries to the angel Uriel, who at once appears and gives him the following explanation of what he had just seen: The woman is Zion. The thirty years of barrenness are the 3000 years during which no sacrifices had as yet been offered on Zion. The birth of the son represents the building of the temple by Solomon, and the instituting of sacrificial worship on Zion. The death of the son refers to the destruction of Jerusalem. But the newly built city was shown to Ezra in the vision with the view of comforting him, and of saving him from despair (x. 25–60). *Fifth vision* (xi. 1–xii. 51): In a dream Ezra sees an eagle rise out of the sea, having *twelve wings* and *three heads*. And out of the wings grew *eight subordinate wings*, which became small and feeble winglets. But the heads were resting, and the centre one was larger than the others. And the eagle flew and ruled over the land. And from within its body there issued a voice which ordered the wings to rule one after another. And the twelve wings ruled, one after the other (the second more than twice as long as any of the others, xi. 17), and then vanished, and similarly two of the winglets, so that at last only the three heads and the six winglets were left. Two of those winglets separated themselves from the rest, and placed themselves under the head on the right-hand side. The other four wanted to rule, but two of them soon vanished and the two were consumed by the heads. And the middle head ruled over the whole earth and then vanished. And the two other heads also ruled. But the one on the right-hand side devoured the one on the left (xi. 1–35). Then Ezra sees a lion, and hears how, with a human voice, it describes the eagle just referred to as being the fourth of those animals to which God has in succession committed the empire of the world. And the lion announces to the eagle its impending destruction (xi. 36–46). Thereupon the only remaining head also vanished. And the two winglets which had joined themselves to it began to rule.[37] But their rule was of a feeble character. And the whole body of the eagle was consumed with fire (xii. 1–3). The meaning of the vision which Ezra rehearses is as follows. The eagle represents the last of Daniel's kingdoms. The twelve wings are twelve kings who are to rule over it, one after another. The second will begin to reign, and will reign longer than the others. The voice which issues from the body of the eagle means that in the course of the duration of that kingdom (*inter tempus regni illius,* as we ought to read with the Syriac and the other Oriental versions) evil disorders will arise; and it will be involved in great trouble, only it will not fall, but regain its power. But the eight subordinate wings represent eight kings, whose respective times will be of short duration. Two of these will

---

[37] Here the correct text is that presented by the Oriental versions. See Hilgenfeld and Fritzsche (in answer to Volkmar, who adheres to the corrupt LA. of the Latin version).

perish when the intermediate time approaches (*appropin-quante tempore medio, i.e.* that interregnum to which reference had just been made). Four of them will be reserved for the time when the end is approaching, and two for the time of the end itself. But the meaning of the three heads is as follows. At the time of the end the Most High will raise up three kings,[28] who will rule over the earth. And they will cause impiety to reach a climax, and will bring about the end. The one (=the middle head) will die in his bed, but in the midst of torment. Of the remaining two one will be cut off by the sword of the other, while the latter will himself fall by the sword at the time of the end. Finally, the two subordinate wings, which joined the head on the right, represent the two remaining kings of the closing period, whose reign will be feeble and full of disorder (xii. 4–30). But the lion which announces to the eagle its impending destruction represents the Messiah, whom the Most High has reserved for the end. He will arraign them (the kings?) while yet alive before His tribunal, and convict them of their wickedness, and then destroy them. But the people of God He will cause to rejoice (during 400 years, as was foretold in the third vision) till the day of judgment comes (xii. 31–34). After receiving those revelations Ezra is commissioned to write what he had seen in a book, and preserve it in a secret place (xii. 35–51).— *Sixth vision* (xiii. 1–58): Once more he sees in a dream a man rising up out of the sea. And an innumerable company of men gathered themselves together for the purpose of warring against that man. And when they marched out against him, he emitted a fiery breath and flames from his mouth, so that they were all burnt up. Thereupon other men advanced toward him, some of them joyfully, others in sadness, and some again in fetters (xiii. 1–13). In answer to Ezra's request this vision is explained to him as follows. The man who rises out of the sea is he by whom God will redeem His whole creation. He will annihilate his enemies, not with the spear

[28] So the Oriental versions. The Latin has *tria regna.*

or implements of war, but by means of the law, which is like unto fire. But the peaceful crowd that advances towards him is the ten tribes returning from the captivity (xiii. 14–58).— *Seventh vision* (xiv. 1–50): Ezra is commissioned by God to instruct the people and set his house in order and withdraw from mortal things, for he is about to be taken from the earth. Moreover, he is to take to himself five men who, during a period of forty days, are to write down what they are told to write. And Ezra did so. And the men wrote what they did not understand. Thereupon Ezra was carried away and conveyed to the place appointed for such as he (xiv. 1–50).

For anything at all decisive with regard to the *date of the composition* of this remarkable book, we are chiefly indebted to the interpretation of the vision of the eagle. For the data furnished by the other passages that have been brought to bear upon this point are of too uncertain a character to be of much service. For example in chap. vi. 9 it is stated that the present world is to end with the rule of Edom, while the world to come is to begin with the supremacy of Israel (finis enim hujus saeculi Esau, et principium sequentis Jacob). But it is open to question whether by Edom it is the Herodians (so Hilgenfeld, Volkmar) or whether it is the Romans (so Oehler in Herzog's *Real-Enc.* 1st ed. vol. ix. p. 430, 2nd ed. vol. ix. p. 660; Ewald, *Excursus*, p. 198; Langen, p. 125 sq.) that are meant. The latter is no doubt the correct view of the matter.[29] But even if the former were to be preferred, very little after all would be gained considering the long period embraced by the Herodian dynasty (down till the year 100 of our era). Then as for the calculation of the

[29] In Rabbinical literature Edom is quite a common designation for Rome; see Buxtorf's *Lexicon Chaldaicum*, col. 29 sqq. Otho, *Lex Rabb.* under "Roma." Levy, *Neuhebr. Wörterb.* i. 29. Grünbaum, *Zeitschr. der DMG* xxxi. pp. 305–309. Weber, *System der altsynag. paläst. Theol.* p. 348 and elsewhere. This designation occurs so early as in the *Sifre* (see Weber, p. 60). Comp. further Jerome's *Comment. ad Jesaj.* xxi. 11, 12 (*Opp.* ed. Vallarsi, iv. 217): Quidam Hebraeorum pro Duma Romam legunt, volentes prophetiam contra regnum Romanum dirigi, frivola persuasione qua semper in Idumaeae nomine Romanos existimant demonstrari.

world-periods as given in chap. xiv. **11, 12** (Duodecim enim
partibus divisum est saeculum, et transierunt ejus decimam et
dimidium decimae partis, superant autem ejus duae post
medium decimae partis). The mere fact of the reading
fluctuating so much here (in the Syriac and Armenian
versions the passage does not occur at all) should of itself
have been enough to deter any one from attempting any
calculation whatever of these world-periods. It will be seen
then that, apart from the general purport of the book, it is the
*vision of the eagle* alone that can be said to furnish a clue to
the date of its composition. In the interpretation of this
vision the *following points*, which naturally present themselves
on a general survey of the contents, are *to be kept steadily in
view*: the twelve principal wings, the eight subordinate ones,
and the three heads represent twenty-three sovereigns or rulers
who reign one after the other, and that in the following order.
First we have the twelve principal wings and two of the
subordinate ones. Then comes a time of disorder. At the
expiry of this period four subordinate wings have their turn,
and after them the three heads. During the reign of the
third head the Messiah appears, upon which follows the overthrow of the third head and the short feeble reign of the two
remaining subordinate wings. We thus see that, from the
author's standpoint, both the overthrow of the third head and
the reign of the last two subordinate wings were still in the
future; from which it follows that he must have written
during the reign of the third head, and that the reign of the
two last subordinate wings is not matter of history, but exists
only in the author's imagination. Further, the following
points are to be specially noted: (1) The second principal
wing reigns more than twice as long as any of the rest
(xi. 17). (2) Many of the wings, particularly of the subordinate wings, come upon the scene without actually getting
the length of reigning, and therefore represent mere pretenders
and usurpers. (3) All the rulers belong to *one and the same*
kingdom, and are, or at least aim at being, the rulers of the

whole of that kingdom. (4) The first dies a natural death (xii. 26), the second is murdered by the third (xi. 35, xii. 28). Now, with the help of this exegetical result, let us test the various *interpretations that have been attempted*, and which we may divide into three leading groups, according as the eagle has been supposed to refer either (1) to Rome under the monarchy and the republic, or (2) to the Greek rule, or (3) to Rome under the emperors.

1. Laurence, van der Vlis and Lücke (2nd ed.) understand the vision of the eagle as referring to the history of Rome from the time of Romulus till that of Caesar. Those three writers are all agreed in this, that the three heads represent *Sulla, Pompey* and *Caesar*, and that our book was composed in the time of Caesar (Lücke), or shortly after his assassination (van der Vlis), or a little later still (Laurence). No doubt the interpretation 12 + 8 wings is beset with considerable difficulty, but this is supposed to be got over by falling back upon those persons who at a later period aspired to the throne, and upon the party leaders in the time of the civil wars. But even if this were not a somewhat doubtful proceeding, there are still two considerations that could not fail to prove fatal to this view : first, the fact that for a Jewish apocalyptic writer the whole period previous to the time of Pompey would have simply no interest whatever ; and then this other fact, that if Rome is to be thought of at all, the reference can only be to a time when she was mistress of the world. For the whole of the wings and heads are intended to represent rulers who exercised or at all events aspired to exercise sway over the entire world.

2. Hilgenfeld supposes the vision to have reference to the Greek rule. It is true that previously (*Apokalyptik*, pp. 217–221) he took the 12 + 8 wings to mean the *Ptolemies*. The twelve wings and the first two of the subordinate wings he made out to be the following :—(1) Alexander the Great, (2) Ptolemy I. Lagi, (3–8) Ptolemy II. to Ptolemy VII., (9) Cleopatra I., (10-14) Ptolemy VIII. Lathyrus to Ptolemy

XII. Auletes. The other six subordinate wings were supposed to refer to the offshoots from the Ptolemaic dynasty down to Cleopatra the younger († 30 B.C.). Then some time after (*Zeitschr.* 1860, pp. 335–358) he substituted the *Seleucidae* for the Ptolemies, and reckoned the kings from Alexander the Great on to the descendants of Seleucus. But still he always adhered strictly to the view, that the three heads were to be taken as referring to *Caesar*, *Antony* and *Octavian*, and that the book must have been composed immediately after Antony's death in the year 30 B.C. (*Zeitschr.* 1867, p. 285 : "exactly 30 years before Christ"). Although this interpretation enables us more easily to find room for the twenty kings than the foregoing one, still it can hardly be said to be a bit more tenable. One great objection to it above all is this, that while it supposes the twenty wings to refer to Greek rulers, it regards the three heads, on the other hand, as referring to *Roman* rulers, whereas the text obviously requires us to regard the whole as rulers of one and the same kirgdom. But Hilgenfeld's interpretation is incompatible above all with the statement that the second wing was to rule twice as long as any of the others (xi. 17). For this will suit neither the case of Ptolemy I. nor that of Seleucus I. Nicator. Hilgenfeld too has fully realized the awkwardness of this passage, and while at one time he was disposed to look upon it as an interpolation, he has more recently had recourse to the expedient of supposing that, in the statement in question, the author had in view only the first six wings, namely those on the right side, on which assumption he finds that the notice exactly suits the case of Seleucus I. (*Zeitschr.* 1867, p. 286 sq., 1870, p. 310 sq.). But the text does not in the least degree sanction such a limitation as this (nemo post te tenebit tempus tuum, sed nec dimidium ejus). There is a further contradiction of the text in the referring of the first head to *Caesar*, who, as is well known, was assassinated, whereas, according to chap. xii. 26, the ruler in question was to die *super lectum*. *But let us say generally that every interpretation is to be regarded as untenable which proceeds on the assumption that the book was written earlier than the destruction of Jerusalem by Titus.* One of the principal objects of the book is just this, to comfort the people on the occasion of the destruction in question. Ezra over and over again prays to have an explanation of the mystery of Jerusalem's lying low in the dust while the Gentile nations exult in triumph. It is with regard to this that, through the medium of a divine revelation, he obtains instruction and comfort. Now to write a work of this nature could hardly be supposed to have any meaning or object whatsoever except at a time when Jerusalem was actually lying in ruins. No doubt it is the first destruction of the city (by Nebuchadnezzar) that is in view. But as it is of course impossible that the book can have been written in the decades immediately following this event (if for nothing but chap. xi. 39, xii. 11, where Daniel is presupposed), the only course open to us is to come down to a date subsequent to the destruction by Titus, and to assume that the author intended that first destruction by Nebuchadnezzar to be regarded as, so to speak, a type of the second, and that the consolations purporting to have been communicated to Ezra were in reality meant for that generation in whose minds the recollection of the destruction of the year 70 was still fresh; although for the pseudo-Ezra this event was perhaps more a thing of the past than it was for the pseudo-Baruch. Then a distinct allusion to the destruction of the city by the Romans may also be found in the words which the lion addresses to the eagle (xi. 42): Destruxisti habitationes eorum qui fructificabant et humiliasti muros eorum qui te non nocuerunt. Consequently there cannot be a doubt that—

3. Corrodi, Lücke (1st ed.), Gfrörer, Dillmann, Volkmar, Ewald, Langen, Wieseler, Keil, Hausrath, Renan, Drummond, Reuss, Gutschmid, Le Hir are correct in holding that the eagle is to be understood as representing imperial Rome. They are all at one in this, that the line of rulers should begin with *Caesar*, and that, by the second wing, the duration of

whose reign was more than twice as long as that of any of the others (xi. 17), it is *Augustus* that is meant. This point may in fact be regarded as settled. For the placing of Cæsar as the first in the line of Roman emperors is also to be met with elsewhere (Joseph. *Antt.* xviii. 2. 2, 6. 10 ; *Orac. Sibyll.* v. 10–15. Comp. Volkmar, p. 344). Moreover the length of time during which Augustus reigned is estimated, as a rule, at 56 years, counting from his first consulate in the year 711 A.U.C. = 43 B.C. (see Volkmar, p. 344 ; Gutschmid, *Zeitschr.* 1860, p. 37). According to this calculation the actual duration of the reign of Augustus is found to have been more than twice longer than that of all the other Roman emperors belonging to the first three centuries.

But there is one point in regard to which there is an essential difference between Gutschmid and Le Hir on the one hand and all the other writers mentioned above on the other. For while Corrodi (i. 208) and the others understand the three heads as referring to the three Flavian emperors (Vespasian, Titus, and Domitian), and accordingly regard the book as having been written during the last decades of the first century of our era, Gutschmid interprets as follows :— He takes the twelve principal wings to represent : (1) Caesar, (2) Augustus, (3) Tiberius, (4) Caligula, (5) Claudius, (6) Nero, (7) Vespasian, (8) Domitian, (9) Trajan, (10) Hadrian, (11) Antoninus Pius, (12) Marcus Aurelius. The first two of the subordinate wings he supposes to refer to Titus and Nerva, and the four immediately following them to : (1) Commodus, (2) Pertinax, (3) Didius Julianus, and (4) Pescennius Niger. The three heads again he takes to represent, *Septimius Severus* (193–211 A.D.) with his two sons *Caracalla* and *Geta.* Geta was murdered by Caracalla, but this latter also fell by the sword (217 A.D.). The last two of the subordinate wings he supposes to be intended for Macrinus and his son Diadumenianus, who were assassinated in the year 218 A.D. He thinks therefore that the vision of the eagle must have been written immediately before, in the month of June 218

(*Zeitschr.* 1860, p. 48).   Moreover Gutschmid regards the
vision of the eagle as a later interpolation, while he thinks—
and here he is more in accord with Hilgenfeld—that the main
body of the book must have been written in the year 31 B.C.
Le Hir, in *his* interpretation of the vision now in question,
coincides with Gutschmid in almost every particular (*Etudes
Bibliques*, i. pp. 184–192).   The only point in which they
differ is this, that Le Hir, founding upon the list of emperors
given by Clement of Alexandria, counts the reign of Marcus
Aurelius and Commodus as simply one, thus including the
latter among those represented by the principal wings, while,
to make up for this, he inserts Clodius Albinus after
Pescennius Niger among those represented by the subordinate
wings.   Nor does he think that the entire book was written
in the year 218 A.D., but is of opinion that there was in the
first instance a Jewish original, and subsequently a Christian
revision and modification of this latter.   He holds that the
former, which is already made use of in the Epistle of
Barnabas, was written in the last quarter of the first century
of our era, while the Christian revision, in which the vision
of the eagle was inserted, would be composed in the year
218 A.D. (*Etudes Bibliques*, i. p. 207 sq.).

The tempting thing about this interpretation is, that it
enables us actually to specify all the rulers represented by
the 12 + 8 wings, which, if we suppose the Flavian period to
be in view, it is impossible to do.   But, for all that, it is
unquestionably erroneous.   It is precluded above all by the
circumstance that the book is already quoted by Clement of
Alexandria.   Consequently it must have been in existence
toward the close of the second century.   No doubt Gutschmid
and Le Hir are disposed to fall back upon the hypothesis of
interpolation or of revision and modification.   But the book
itself furnishes neither occasion nor justification for such a
hypothesis.   The vision of the eagle fits in admirably, and
could scarcely be omitted without completely mutilating the
work.   The hypothesis of interpolation is therefore gratuitous

in the extreme, to say nothing of the fact that it is incompatible with many points of detail. For example Galba, Otho and Vitellius are completely left out of account. Commodus is classed by Gutschmid with those who are represented by the subordinate wings, while Le Hir counts his reign and that of Marcus Aurelius as constituting simply one reign, all which is extremely forced. But the most awkward thing of all is, that the two subordinate wings, Titus and Nerva, did not reign, as the text however requires us to suppose (xii. 21), appropinquante tempore medio, *i.e.* shortly before the interregnum, before the period of disorder, but in the heart of the peaceful rule of the principal wings.[30]

Consequently if we are to adopt the ordinary interpretation we will have to stop at the Flavian period. There can be no mistaking the fact that all that is said with regard to *the three heads* will apply admirably to the three Flavian emperors, Vespasian, Titus and Domitian. Those who had brought about the destruction of the holy city really constituted for the Jew the acme of power and ungodliness. Vespasian died, as we are told xii. 26, super lectum et tamen cum tormentis (comp. Sueton. *Vesp.* xxiv. Dio Cass. lxvi. 17). It is true Titus was not murdered by Domitian as is presupposed in chaps. xi. 35, xii. 28. Yet it was currently believed that this was the case, and certainly Domitian's demeanour at the time of his brother's death gave ample occasion for such a belief (Sueton. *Domitian II.* Dio Cass. lxvi. 26 ; *Orac. Sibyll.* xii. 120–123. Aurelius Victor, *Caesar*, x. and xi., states explicitly that Titus had been poisoned by Domitian). This likewise corresponds with the actual fact that several of the subordinate wings, *i.e.* of the usurpers, had been disposed of with the help of the other two heads. But after all, the finding of a place for the whole 12 + 8 wings is not a matter of insuperable difficulty. The twelve principal wings may be regarded as representing say the following rulers:—(1) Caesar, (2) Augustus, (3) Tiberius, (4) Caligula, (5) Claudius, (6) Nero, (7) Galba,

[30] In answer to Gutschmid, see also Volkmar, p. 389 sq.

(8) Otho, (9) Vitellius, to whom may be added the three usurpers: (10) Vindex, (11) Nymphidius, (12) Piso. But what is to be made of the eight subordinate wings? To dispose of them Volkmar and Ewald have had recourse to expedients of the most singular kind. Volkmar, who is followed by Renan, makes out the number of rulers to be not 12 + 8, but, by taking the wings as pairs, only 6 + 4. The six rulers he takes to be the Julian emperors from Caesar to Nero; the four again he takes to be: Galba, Otho, Vitellius, and Nerva. So Volkmar and Renan, and that although we are plainly told in chap. xii. 14 that: Regnabunt autem in ea reges duodecim, unus post unum; and in ver. 20 of the same chapter find the words: exsurgent enim in ipso octo reges. Ewald again goes the length of thinking that not only the eight subordinate wings, but also the three heads, are to be regarded as included among the twelve principal wings, and consequently that the three groups of rulers are to be identified, and that we should reckon only twelve rulers altogether (counting from Caesar to Domitian). The most obvious exegetical principles should have been sufficient to prevent any such attempts at explanation as we have here. Nor can Langen be said to have altogether eschewed this arbitrary style of criticism when he inclines, as he does, to take the numbers merely as round numbers, and to regard the twelve principal wings as intended to represent the six Julian emperors. For the text undoubtedly requires us to assume that there were 12 + 8 rulers, or at all events pretenders. No less untenable is the view of Gfrörer (i. 90 sq.), who refers the eight subordinate wings partly to Herod and some of his descendants, partly to Jewish (!!) agitators, as John of Gischala and Simon Bar-Giora; or that of Wieseler, who thinks that the whole eight subordinate wings are meant to represent the Herodian dynasty alone. In point of fact however the only distinction between the subordinate and the principal wings is this, that in the case of the former the reign is short and feeble (xii. 20), or they fail ever to get the

length of reigning at all (xi. 25-27). As for the rest they
are, quite as much as the principal wings, rulers of the entire
empire, or at all events aspire to be so. Consequently it is
impossible to suppose that it is vassal princes that are represented by those subordinate wings ; rather must we hold, with
Corrodi (*Gesch. des Chiliasmus*, i. 207), that it is "governors,
rival candidates for the throne, and rebels," or with Dillmann
(Herzog's *Real-Enc.* 1st ed. vol. xii. p. 312), that it is
"Roman generals and pretenders" that are in view. Of
course we have had to avail ourselves of the better known
among the usurpers in order to complete the number twelve.
But it would appear that the author reckons along with them
all those Roman generals who, during the period of disorder
(68–70), had at any time put forward claims to the throne.
And of these surely it would not be difficult to make out six.
For it is only a question of six, seeing that, as has been already
noticed, the last two of the subordinate wings do not represent
actual historical personages.

If the view which represents the three heads as referring
to the Flavian emperors be correct, it should not be difficult
to determine the date of the composition of our book. We
have already seen that the author wrote during the reign of
the third head, inasmuch as he is already acquainted with
the manner in which the second was put to death, while on
the other hand he is looking forward to the overthrow of the
third after the Messiah has made His appearance. Consequently the composition of the book is not, with Corrodi and
Ewald, to be referred to so early a date as the time of Titus,
nor again, with Volkmar, Langen, Hausrath and Renan, to
one so late as the time of Nerva, but, with Gfrörer, Dillmann,
Wieseler and Reuss, to the reign of Domitian (81–96 A.D.).

The designation *Fourth Book of Ezra*, under which our work is known,
is current only in the Latin Church, and is to be traced to the fact that the
canonical books Ezra and Nehemiah were reckoned as First and Second Ezra
respectively, while the Ezra of the Greek Bible was regarded as Third Ezra
(so Jerome, *Praef. in version. libr. Ezrae*, *Opp.* ed. Vallarsi, ix. 1524 : Nec

quemquam moveat, quod unus a nobis editus liber est; nec apocryphorum tertii et quarti somniis delectetur). This mode of designating those different books has also been retained in the official Roman Vulgate, where Third and Fourth Ezra are inserted at the end of the New Testament. In the manuscript of Amiens, from which Bensly edited the Latin fragment, the canonical books Ezra and Nehemiah taken together are regarded as First Ezra, the so-called Third Ezra is counted as Second Ezra, while Fourth Ezra is divided into three books, chaps. i.–ii. being counted as Third Ezra, chaps. iii.–xiv. as Fourth Ezra, and chaps. xv., xvi. as Fifth Ezra (Bensly, *The Missing Fragment*, p. 6). Similarly, though with greater complication still, in the *Codex Sangermanensis* and the manuscripts derived from it (Bensly, p. 85 sq.). The earliest designation seems to have been Ἔσδρας ὁ προφήτης (Clemens Alex. *Strom.* iii. 16. 100) or Ἔσδρα ἀποκά-λυψις, for it is doubtless our Fourth Book of Ezra that is meant by the apocryphal work bearing that name which occurs in the list of the Apocrypha edited by Montfaucon, Cotelier, Hody and Pitra (see p. 126). For more on the different titles, see Volkmar, *Das vierte Buch Esra*, p. 3. Hilgenfeld, *Messias Judaeorum*, pp. xviii.–xxi.

*Use and high repute of the book in the Christian Church.*—It is probable that it is this work that is referred to in the following passage in the Epistle of Barnabas, chap. xii. : Ὁμοίως πάλιν περὶ τοῦ σταυροῦ ὁρίζει ἐν ἄλλῳ προφήτῃ λέγοντι· Καὶ πότε ταῦτα συντελεσθήσεται; λέγει κύριος· Ὅταν ξύλον κλιθῇ καὶ ἀναστῇ, καὶ ὅταν ἐκ ξύλου αἷμα στάξῃ. Comp. Fourth Ezra, iv. 33: Quomodo et quando haec? . . . v. 5: Si de ligno sanguis stillabit. It is true that here the first half of the quotation is wanting, but for all that Le Moyne and Fabricius (*Cod. pseudepigr.* ii. 184) were undoubtedly correct in tracing it to Fourth Ezra. Comp. further, Cotelier, Hilgenfeld and Harnack in their editions of the Epistle of Barnabas; Hilgenfeld, *Die apostol. Väter*, p. 47. It is also extremely probable that we are indebted to Fourth Ezra for the legend to the effect that, when *the Holy Scriptures* had perished on the occasion of the destruction of Jerusalem by Nebuchad-nezzar, *Ezra completely restored them again by means of a miracle*. So Irenaeus, iii. 21. 2. Tertullian, *De cultu femin.* i. 3. Clemens Alex. *Strom.* i. 22. 149. Comp. Fourth Ezra xiv. 18–22 and 37–47. Fabricius, *Codex pseudepigr.* i. 1156–1160. Hilgenfeld, *Messias Judaeorum*, p. 107. Strack in Herzog's *Real-Enc.* 2nd ed. vol. vii. 414 sq. (art. "Kanon des A. T.'s").

The *first express quotation* occurs in Clemens Alex. *Strom.* iii. 16. 100: Διὰ τί γὰρ οὐκ ἐγένετο ἡ μήτρα τῆς μητρός μου τάφος, ἵνα μὴ ἴδω τὸν μόχθον τοῦ Ἰακὼβ καὶ τὸν κόπον τοῦ γένους Ἰσραήλ; Ἔσδρας ὁ προφήτης λέγει. Comp. 4 Ezra v. 35. Our book is repeatedly used and quoted as prophetical, above all by Ambrose. See the passages in Fabricius, *Cod. pseudepigr.* ii. pp. 183, 185 sqq. Hilgenfeld, *Messias Judaeorum*, p. xxii. sq. Le Hir, *Etudes Bibliques*, i. 142. Bensly, *The Missing Fragment*, pp. 74–76. It is also quoted as *propheta Esdras* in the so-called *Opus imperfectum in Matthaeum* printed among Chrysostom's works (ed. Montfaucon, vol. vi.), *Homil.* xxxiv. *s. fin.* Jerome, who maintains a critical attitude toward the Apocrypha generally, is the only one who expresses himself unfavourably. See the passage quoted above from the *Praef. in version. libr. Ezrae*, and especially *Adv. Vigilantium*, chap. vi. (*Opp.* ed. Vallarsi, ii. 393): Tu vigilans dormis et dormiens scribis et proponis mihi librum apocryphum. qui sub nomine Esdrae a te et similibus tui legitur, ubi scriptum est, quod post mortem nullus pro aliis audeat deprecari, quem ego librum numquam legi. Quid enim necesse est in manus sumere, quod ecclesia non recepit. But although our book continued to be excluded from the canon, it nevertheless enjoyed a wide circulation, especially in the Middle Ages. Bensly has proved by actual verification that it finds a place in *more than* sixty Latin manuscripts of the Bible (Bensly, *The Missing Fragment*, pp. 42, 82 sqq.), and this without taking into account scarcely any of the Italian libraries. As we have already mentioned, it appears in the official Vulgate as an appendix. It also finds a place in not a few *German editions of the Bible*, Lutheran and Reformed as well as Catholic (for the evidence in regard to this, see Gildemeister, *Esdrae liber quartus arabice*, 1877, p. 42). On the history of the use, comp. further, Fabricius, *Codex pseudepigr.* ii. 174–192. Idem, *Cod. apocryph. Nov. Test.* i. 936–938. Volkmar, *Das vierte Buch Ezra*, p. 273 sq. Hilgenfeld, *Messias Judaeorum*, pp. xviii.–xxiv., lxix. sq.

Care must be taken not to confound the Fourth Book of Ezra with the Christian work entitled the *Apocalypse of Ezra* which Tischendorf has edited (*Apocalypses apocryphae*, Lips. 1866, pp. 24–33). On this comp. Tischendorf, *Stud. u. Krit.* 1851, p. 423 sqq. Idem, *Prolegom.* to his edition, pp. 12–14. Le Hir, *Etudes Bibliques* (Paris 1869), ii. 120–122. By the "Εσδρα ἀποκάλυψις, which occurs in the list of the Apocrypha edited by Montfaucon, Pitra and others, it is possibly the Fourth Book of Ezra that is meant (see p. 126). On the Ezra-Apocrypha, comp. also Fabricius, *Cod. pseudepigr.* i. 1162. On the later *additions to the Fourth Book of Ezra* (chaps. i.–ii. and xv. xvi.), which in the manuscripts appear as yet as separate Books of Ezra, and which came for the first time to be blended with the main work in the printed text, see Dillmann in Herzog's *Real-Enc.* 2nd ed. vol. xii. 356, and Bensly, *The Missing Fragment*, pp. 35–40.

The *texts* of the Fourth Book of Ezra *that have come down to us* are the following :—

(1.) The old *Latin version*, which is the most literal, and therefore the most important of all. The vulgar text, as it had long been printed, was extremely inaccurate. In the edition of Fabricius (*Codex pseudepigraphus Vet. Test.* vol. ii. 1723, pp. 173–307) the Arabic version, which was given to the public through Ockley's English translation in 1711, was collated throughout with the Latin text. Sabatier was the first to lay the foundation for the critical restoration of the text by his publication of the variants of the important *Codex Sangermanensis* (Sabatier, *Bibliorum sacrorum Latinae versiones antiquae*, vol. iii. 1743, pp. 1038, 1069–1084). Numerous emendations based upon the *Codex Sangermanensis*, and the Ethiopic version published by Laurence in 1820, were proposed by Van der Vlis (*Disputatio critica de Ezrae libro apocrypho vulgo quarto dicto*, Amstelod. 1839). The first critical edition was published by Volkmar (*Handbuch der Einleitung in die Apocryphen*, second part : *Das vierte Buch Ezra*, Tüb. 1863). In this edition Sabatier's collation of the *Cod. Sangermanensis* and a Zürich manuscript collated by Volkmar himself were made use of. These manuscripts however were not collated with sufficient care, as the subsequent editions of Hilgenfeld (*Messias Judaeorum*, Lips. 1869) and Fritzsche (*Libri apocryphi Vet. Test. graece*, Lips. 1871) have shown. Both these writers give the Latin text according to three different manuscripts: (*a*) the *Cod. Sangermanensis saec.* ix., collated anew for Hilgenfeld's edition by Zotenberg; (*b*) the *Cod. Turicensis saec.* xiii., also collated anew for Hilgenfeld's edition by Fritzsche; (*c*) a *Cod. Dresdensis saec.* xv., collated by Hilgenfeld. *In the whole of those editions a considerable fragment is wanting between chaps.* vii. 35 *and* vii. 36, which could only be supplied from the Oriental versions. This fragment was first discovered, so far as the Latin text is concerned, by Bensly in a manuscript at Amiens (formerly at Corbie near Amiens) in the year 1875 (Bensly, *The Missing Fragment of the Latin Translation of the Fourth Book of Ezra, discovered and edited with an Introduction and Notes*, Cambridge 1875. Comp. *Theol. Literaturztg.* 1876, p. 43 sq.). After this it was also published by Hilgenfeld (*Zeitschr. für wissensch. Theol.* 1876, pp. 421–435). Two years after this again the same fragment was edited from a *Madrid* manuscript (formerly in Alcalá de Henares) by Wood, and from among the remains of John Palmer the Orientalist († 1840), who had transcribed it as early as the year 1826 (*Journal of Philology*, vol. vii. 1877, pp. 264–278). Besides the manuscripts hitherto mentioned, Bensly (pp. 42, 82 sqq.) has verified some *sixty others of the Latin text*.[31] Those of them in which there is the large hiatus in chap. vii., and this holds true of probably the whole of them, at all events of the *Turicensis* and the *Dresdensis*, as also of the printed vulgar text, are of no value, for the hiatus in the *Cod. Sangermanensis* was due to the cutting out of a leaf, so that all the manuscripts and texts in which precisely the same hiatus occurs must have followed that codex (as from a letter addressed to Bensly, Gildemeister appears to have already noted in the year 1865). Consequently in the case of any future edition consideration will be due, in the first instance, only to: (*a*) the *Cod. Sangermanensis* (now in Paris), dating from the year 822 A.D. (Bensly, p. 5); (*b*) the Amiens manuscript, also belonging to the ninth century, and independent of the *Cod. Sanger.*; and (*c*) the Madrid manuscript. At the same time we may observe that *the Latin manuscripts of the Bible in the majority of the Italian libraries have not yet been examined in connection with our book.*

(2.) Next to the Latin the best and most trustworthy version is the Syriac, which has been transmitted to us in the large Peshito manuscript of Milan (*Cod. Ambros.* B. 21, Inf.). It was published for the first time by Ceriani first of all in a Latin version (Ceriani, *Monumenta sacra et profana*, vol. i. fasc. 2, Mediol. 1866, pp. 99–124), then in the Syriac text itself (Ceriani, *Mon. sac. et prof.* vol. v. fasc. 1, Mediol. 1868, pp. 4–111). This latter is also given in the photo-lithographed facsimile of the whole manuscript (*Translatio Syra Pescitto Veteris Testamenti ex cod. Ambr. photolithographice*, ed. Ceriani, 2 vols. in 4 parts, Milan 1876–1883 ; comp. vol.

---

[31] On two Parisian and two Berlin manuscripts, see Gildemeister, *Esdrae liber quartus Arabice*, 1877, p. 44 *fin.*

iii. p. 92). Hilgenfeld has embodied Ceriani's Latin version in his *Messias Judaeorum* (Lips. 1869).

(3.) The Ethiopic version, which is also of importance for the reconstruction of the original text. It had been previously published by Laurence, accompanied with a Latin and English version, but only from a *single* manuscript, and not quite free from errors (Laurence, *Primi Ezrae libri, qui apud Vulgatam appellatur quartus, versio Aethiopica, nunc primo in medium prolata et Latine Angliceque reddita*, Oxoniae et Londoni 1820). Numerous corrections have been made by van der Vlis (*Disputatio critica de Ezrae libro apocrypho vulgo quarto dicto*, Amst. 1839). A collection of the variants in the other manuscripts has been furnished by Dillmann in the appendix to Ewald's dissertation in the *Abhandlungen der Göttinger Gesellsch. der Wissensch.* vol. xi. 1862 - 1863. Then, in the last place, Prätorius, availing himself of Dillmann's collection of variants, and also collating with a Berlin manuscript, has made various emendations in the Latin version which Hilgenfeld has embodied in his *Messias Judaeorum* (Lips. 1869). A critical edition is still a desideratum. Among the Ethiopic manuscripts of the so-called Magdala collection, which some years ago were forwarded to the British Museum at the close of the war between the English and King John of Abyssinia, there happen to be no fewer than eight of our book (see Wright's catalogue in the *Zeitschr. der DMG.* 1870, p. 599 sqq., Nos. 5, 10, 11, 13, 23, 24, 25, 27. Bensly, *The Missing Fragment*, p. 2, note 3).

(4.) The two Arabic versions are of but secondary importance, owing to the great freedom in which their authors often indulge. (*a*) One of them, which is in a manuscript in the Bodleian Library at Oxford, was in the first instance published only in an English version by Ockley (in Whitson's *Primitive Christianity revived*, vol. iv. London 1711). Ewald was the first to publish the Arabic text (*Transactions of the Göttingen Gesellsch. der Wissensch.* vol. xi. 1862–1863). Emendations upon Ockley's version and Ewald's text were furnished by Steiner (*Zeitschr. für wissensch. Theol.* 1868, pp. 426–433), with whose assistance Hilgenfeld also composed a Latin rendering for his *Messias Judaeorum* (Lips. 1869). The Arabic version here in question is also found in a Codex Vaticanus, which, though merely a transcript of the one in the Bodleian library, is nevertheless of some value in so far as it was copied before the leaf, which is at present wanting in the Bodleian codex, went amissing (Bensly, *The Missing Fragment*, p. 77 sq. Gildemeister, *Esdrae liber quartus*, p. 3 ; this latter supplies at pp. 6–8 the text of this fragment, which is omitted in Ewald's edition). (*b*) An *extract* from another Arabic version is likewise found in a Bodleian codex, from which it has been edited by Ewald (as above). A German version of this extract was furnished by Steiner (*Zeitschr. f. wissensch. Theol.* 1868, pp. 396–425). On the extract itself, comp. further, Ewald, *Transactions of the Göttingen Gesellsch. der Wissensch.* 1863, pp. 163–180. *The complete text* of this version was published by Gildemeister in Arabic and Latin from a Codex Vaticanus (*Esdrae liber quartus arabice, e codice Vaticano nunc primum edidit*, Bonnae 1877).

(5.) The Armenian version, which is still freer than the Arabic one, and is of but little service for the restoration of the original text. It was published as early as the year 1805 in the edition of the Armenian Bible issued under the superintendence of the Mechitarists, but Ceriani was the first to rescue it from oblivion, while Ewald again furnished specimens of it in a German rendering (*Transactions of the Göttingen Gesellsch der Wissensch.* 1865, pp. 504–516). A Latin version, prepared by Petermann and based upon a collation of four manuscripts, is given in Hilgenfeld's *Messias Judaeorum* (Lips. 1869). In the older editions of the Armenian Bible (the first dating as far back as 1666) there is an Armenian version of our book which was prepared by the first editor, Uscanus himself, and taken from the Vulgate (see Scholtz, *Einl. in die heiligen Schriften*, vol. i. 1845, p. 501. Gildemeister, *Esdrae liber quartus arabice*, p. 43. This may be made use of for the purpose of correcting Bensly, p. 2, note 2).

*German versions* of our book have been published by Volkmar (*Das vierte Buch Esra*, 1863) and Ewald (*Transactions of the Göttingen Gesellsch. der Wissensch.* vol. xi. 1862, 1863), while Hilgenfeld attempted a rendering back into the Greek (*Messias Judaeorum*, Lips. 1869).

*Critical inquiries.* For the earlier literature, see Fabricius, *Codex pseudepigr.* ii. 174 sqq. Lücke, *Einl.* p. 187 sqq. Volkmar, *Das vierte Buch Esra* (1863), pp. 273–275, 374 sqq. Hilgenfeld, *Messias Judaeorum*, p. liv. sqq. Corrodi (also spelt Corodi), *Kritische Geschichte des Chiliasmus*, vol. i. (1781) pp. 179–230. Gfrörer, *Das Jahrhundert des Heils* (also under the title, *Geschichte des Urchristenthums*, vols. i., ii.), 1838, i. 69–93. Lücke, *Versuch einer vollständigen Einleitung in die Offenbarung des Johannes* (2nd ed. 1852), pp. 144–212. Bleek, *Stud. u. Krit.* 1854, pp. 982–990 (review of Lücke's *Einl.*). Noack, *Der Ursprung des Christenthums*, vol. i. (1857) pp. 341–363. Hilgenfeld, *Die jüdische Apokalyptik* (1857), pp. 185–242. Idem, *Die Propheten Esra und Daniel*, 1863. Idem, *Zeitschr. für wissensch. Theologie*, vol. i. 1858, pp. 250–270; iii. 1860, pp. 335–358; vi. 1863, pp. 229–292, 457 sq.; x. 1867, pp. 87–91, 263–295; xiii. 1870, pp. 308–319; xix. 1876, pp. 421–435. Gutschmid, "Die Apokalypse des Esra und ihre späteren Bearbeitungen" (*Zeitschr. für wissensch. Theol.* 1860, pp. 1–81). Dillmann in Herzog's *Real - Enc.* 1st ed. vol. xii. 1860, pp. 310–312; 2nd ed. vol. xii. 1883, pp. 353–356 (art. "Pseudepigraphen"). Volkmar, *Handbuch der Einleitung in die Apokryphen*, second part: *Das vierte Buch Esra*, Tüb. 1863. At a previous date by the same author, *Das vierte Buch Esra und apokalyptische Geheimnisse überhaupt*, Zürich 1858. "Einige Bemerkungen über Apokalyptik" (*Zeitschr. für wissensch. Theol.* 1861, pp. 83–92). Ewald, "Das vierte Esrabuch nach seinem Zeitalter, seinen arabischen Uebersetzungen und einer neuen Wiederherstellung" (*Transactions of the Royal Gesellsch. der Wissensch. of Göttingen*, vol. xi. 1862–1863, histor.-philol. section, pp. 133–230. Also as a separate reprint). Idem, *Gesch. des Volkes Israel*, vol. vii. 3rd ed. 1868, pp. 69–83. Ceriani, "Sul Das vierte Ezrabuch del Dottor Enrico Ewald" (*Estratto dalle Memorie del R. Instituto Lombardo di scienze e lettere*), Millano 1865. Langen, *Das Judenthum in Palästina*, 1866, pp. 112–139. Le Hir, "Du IV.e livre d'Esdras" (*Etudes Bibliques*, 2 vols. Paris 1869, i. 139–250). Wieseler, "Das vierte Buch Esra nach Inhalt und Alter untersucht" (*Stud.*

*u. Krit.* 1870, pp. 263–304). Keil, *Lehrb. der histor.-krit. Einleitung in die kanon. und apokr. Schriften des A. T.* 3rd ed. 1873, pp. 758–764. Hausrath, *Neutestamentl. Zeitgesch.* 2nd ed. iv. 80–88 (1st ed. iii. 282–289). Renan, "L'apocalypse de l'an 97" (*Revue des deux Mondes*, 1875, March, pp. 127–144). Idem, *Les évangiles*, 1877, pp. 348–373. Drummond, *The Jewish Messiah*, 1877, pp. 84–117. Reuss, *Gesch. der heiligen Schriften Alten Testaments* (1881), sec. 597.


### 6. *The Testaments of the Twelve Patriarchs.*

In the pseudepigraphic prophecies which we have hitherto been considering, revelations and predictions—and therefore the apocalyptic element—chiefly predominated.   But just as these revelations themselves had practical objects as their ultimate aim, such objects as the strengthening and comforting of the faithful, so alongside of them there was also another class of works in which the exhortations and encouragements were more directly expressed.   We have a pseudepigraphic prophecy of this description in *The Testaments of the Twelve Patriarchs,* which is chiefly composed of such direct exhortations.   This somewhat extensive work has come down to us in its entirety *in the Greek text,* which was published for the first time by Grabe (1698), although, from the beginning of the sixteenth century, a good many printed copies of a Latin version prepared in the thirteenth by Robert Grossetest, Bishop of Lincoln, had been in circulation.

The book, as we now have it, contains a great many direct allusions to the incarnation of God in Christ, for which reason almost all modern critics look upon it as the production of a *Christian* author.   But it is extremely doubtful whether this is a correct view of the matter, and whether we ought not rather to assume that the work in its original form is of Jewish authorship, and that the passages that are of a Christian character were interpolated at some later date.   As is indicated by the title itself, the book consists of the spiritual " testaments " which the twelve sons of Jacob left behind them for their descendants.   *In each of those testaments three different elements may be distinguished.*   (1) The patriarch in each instance rehearses in the first place *the history of his own life,* in the course of which he either charges himself with sins he has committed (as is done by the majority of them), or on the other hand boasts of his virtues. The biographical notices follow the lines of the Biblical narrative, although, after the fashion of the Haggadean Midrash, they are enriched with a large number of fresh details. (2) The patriarch then proceeds to address to his descendants a number of *appropriate exhortations* based upon the preceding autobiographical sketch, urging them to beware of the sin that had been the cause of such deep distress to their ancestor, and in the event of his being able to boast of something redounding to his credit, recommending them to imitate his virtuous behaviour. The subject on which the exhortations turn is, as a rule, one that happens to have a very intimate connection with the biographical notices, the patriarch's descendants being warned precisely against that sin or, it may be, to imitate that virtue which had been exemplified in his own life. (3) But besides this, we also find toward the end of each of the testaments (with the exception perhaps of that of Gad, where this point is only briefly hinted at) certain *predictions* regarding the future of the particular tribe in question, the patriarch for example predicting that his descendants would one day apostatize from God or, what sometimes appears to amount to the same thing, sever their connection with the tribes of Levi and Judah, and thereby involve themselves in misery, and especially the evils of captivity and dispersion. This prediction is frequently accompanied with an exhortation to adhere to the tribes of Levi and Judah. On the other hand, these predictions are interspersed with a large number of very direct references to redemption through Christ.

The circles of thought in these "testaments" are of a very heterogeneous character. On the one hand, they contain a great deal that it seems impossible to explain except on the assumption that they were composed by a Jewish author. The history of the patriarchs is amplified precisely in the style

of the Haggadean Midrash.    The author assumes that salvation is in store only for the children of Shem, while those of
Ham are doomed to destruction (Simeon vi.).    He manifests
a lively interest in the Jewish tribes as such; he deplores
their apostasy and dispersion; he exhorts them to cleave to
the tribes of Levi and Judah as being those which God has
specially called to be the leaders of the others; [32] he cherishes
the hope of their ultimate conversion and deliverance.    It is
true, no doubt, that in his positive injunctions he nowhere
inculcates the observance of the ceremonial law, such injunctions being more of a moral character throughout nearly the
entire book, and consisting for example of warnings against the
sins of envy, avarice, anger, lying, incontinency, exhortations
to the love of one's neighbour, compassion, integrity, and such
like.    But at the same time he does not fail to speak of the
priestly sacrificial worship, and that even with many details
introduced into it not met with in the Old Testament itself, as
being an institution of divine appointment. [33]    On the other hand
again we also meet with numerous passages which can only
have been written by a Christian, passages which teach the
Christian doctrine of the universal character of salvation as
well as that of redemption through the incarnation of God,
nay in one instance there is a distinct reference to the

---

[32] Reuben vi. : Τῷ γὰρ Λευὶ ἔδωκε Κύριος τὴν ἀρχὴν καὶ τῷ Ἰούδᾳ.
Judah xxi. : Καὶ νῦν, τέκνα, ἀγαπήσατε τὸν Λευί, ἵνα διαμείνητε· καὶ μὴ
ἐπαίρεσθε ἐπ' αὐτόν, ἵνα μὴ ἐξολοθρευθῆτε. Ἐμοὶ γὰρ ἔδωκε Κύριος τὴν βασιλείαν, κἀκείνῳ τὴν ἱερατείαν, καὶ ὑπέταξε τὴν βασιλείαν τῇ ἱερωσύνῃ. Issachar
v. fin. : Καὶ ὁ Λευὶ καὶ ὁ Ἰούδας ἐδοξάσθη παρὰ Κυρίου ἐν υἱοῖς Ἰακώβ. Καὶ
γὰρ Κύριος ἐκλήρωσεν ἐν αὐτοῖς, καὶ τῷ μὲν ἔδωκε τὴν ἱερατείαν, τῷ δὲ τὴν βασιλείαν. Dan v. : Οἶδα γὰρ ὅτι ἐν ἐσχάταις ἡμέραις ἀποστήσεσθε τοῦ Κυρίου,
καὶ προσωχθιεῖτε τὸν Λευὶ καὶ πρὸς Ἰούδαν ἀντιτάξεσθε. Naphtali v. (in a
parable) : Καὶ ὁ Λευὶ ἐκράτησε τὸν ἥλιον, καὶ ὁ Ἰούδας Φθάσας ἐπίασε τὴν
σελήνην. Ibid. viii. : Καὶ ὑμεῖς οὖν ἐντείλασθε τοῖς τέκνοις ὑμῶν, ἵνα ἑνοῦνται
τῷ Λευὶ καὶ τῷ Ἰούδᾳ.

[33] Levi ix.  Note for example the prescription : Καὶ πρὸ τοῦ εἰσελθεῖν εἰς
τὰ ἅγια λούευ· καὶ ἐν τῷ θύειν, νίπτου (with which comp. vol. i. p. 278);
further, the prescription in the same passage to the effect that no wood
was to be used for the altar of burnt-offering but that of trees which
were always in leaf (comp. Book of Jubilees, chap. xxi., in Ewald's Jahrbb.
iii. 19).

Apostle Paul (Benjamin xi.). The Christology upon which those passages proceed is of a decidedly patripassian character.[34]

Grabe, who was the first to edit the Greek text, already endeavoured to account for those incongruities by the hypothesis, that the book was written by a Jew, but had been subsequently interpolated by a Christian. All modern critics however (since Nitzsch) have entirely dismissed this hypothesis, and the only point on which there is a difference of opinion amongst them is as to whether the author occupied the standpoint of a *Jewish* or a *Gentile* Christian. The former is the prevailing view; the latter was propounded by Ritschl in the first edition of his *Entstehung der altkatholischen Kirche*, was subsequently adopted by Vorstman and Hilgenfeld, but was ultimately abandoned again by Ritschl himself. At the same time there was no doubt a feeling on the part of many that it would be impossible to solve the difficulty without having recourse to the interpolation hypothesis. Kayser above all tried to demonstrate the existence of a tolerably large number of such interpolations. But even in his case the matter is dealt with only incidentally, to enable him to maintain the view as to the Jewish-Christian character of the writing. It was reserved for Schnapp to enter in a systematic manner into the question as to whether the whole work had not been reconstructed from beginning to end. He endeavoured to show, that to the book in its original form belonged only the parts mentioned under Nos. 1 and 2 above, *i.e.* merely the biographical narratives and their accompanying exhortations. But he seeks to prove that all those portions in which the future fortunes of the tribes are predicted, with

---

[34] Simeon vi. : Κύριος ὁ Θεὸς μέγας τοῦ Ἰσραήλ, φαινόμενος, ἐπὶ γῆς ὡς ἄνθρωπος. *Ibid.*: Θεὸς σῶμα λαβὼν καὶ συνεσθίων ἀνθρώποις ἔσωσεν ἀνθρώπους. Issachar vii. : ἔχοντες μεθ᾽ ἑαυτῶν τὸν Θεὸν τοῦ οὐρανοῦ, συμπορευόμενον τοῖς ἀνθρώποις ἐν ἁπλότητι καρδίας. Zebulon ix. *fin.* : ὄψεσθε Θεὸν ἐν σχήματι ἀνθρώπου. Dan v. *fin.* : Κύριος ἔσται ἐμμέσῳ αὐτῆς, τοῖς ἀνθρώποις συναναστρεφόμενος. Naphtali viii. : ὀφθήσεται Θεὸς κατοικῶν ἐν ἀνθρώποις ἐπὶ τῆς γῆς. Asher vii. : ἕως οὗ ὁ ὕψιστος ἐπισκέψηται τὴν γῆν, καὶ αὐτὸς ἐλθὼν ὡς ἄνθρωπος μετὰ ἀνθρώπων ἐσθίων καὶ πίνων. Benjamin x. : παραγενόμενον Θεὸν ἐν σαρκὶ ἐλευθερωτὴν οὐκ ἐπίστευσαν.

some other things of a kindred nature (visions in particular), are to be regarded as later interpolations, though he distinguishes at the same time between Jewish and Christian interpolations. He thinks that the bulk of these interpolations would be made by a Jewish hand, but that into these again numerous references to the redemption through Christ had been afterwards inserted by a Christian hand. He considers therefore that the original work itself must also have been of Jewish origin. It appears to me that the latter part of this hypothesis, in so far, that is, as the Christian revision is concerned, has at all events hit the mark. It would be vain to attempt to reduce the heterogeneous utterances in our Testaments to a common Jewish-Christian standpoint, all of them that bear a specifically Christian stamp being without exception of a Gentile-Christian and universalist character. The salvation is destined εἰς πάντα τὰ ἔθνη. The Christology is the patripassian Christology that so largely prevailed in many quarters in the Christian Church during the second and third centuries. There is nothing here that can be said to indicate a "Jewish-Christian" standpoint. Again it is impossible to reconcile with the Christian passages in question that series of utterances characterized above which can only have emanated from a Jewish author. How is it ever to be supposed that a Christian, ay, or even a Jewish-Christian, author should think of characterizing the tribes of *Levi* and *Judah* as those to whom God had committed the guidance of Israel. Then what could we conceive such an author to mean by exhorting the rest of the tribes to join themselves to the two just mentioned and to submit themselves to their authority ? Why, it was precisely the tribes of Levi and Judah, *i.e.* the official Judaism of Palestine, that distinguished themselves above all the others in the way of rejecting the gospel. We can hardly imagine therefore that even a Jewish-Christian author would be likely to represent them as occupying the leading position above referred to. Nor does he so represent them as one who is merely taking a

theoretical survey of history, and as though he meant to
censure the defection from the tribes of Levi and Judah
merely as a thing of the past. But he also urges a loyal
adherence to those tribes as a present duty. Nor can we
here suppose that Levi is intended to represent the Christian
clergy. For what in that case would Judah be supposed to
represent? [34a] Then there is the further circumstance, that
many of the Christian passages obviously disturb the connection and thus proclaim themselves to be interpolations at the
very outset. What is more, the much canvassed passage
regarding Paul in the Testament of Benjamin (xi.) is wanting in
the case of two independent testimonies among the manuscripts
and versions as at present known to us, namely in the Roman
manuscript and the Armenian version.[35] From all this it
may be regarded as tolerably certain, that *all the Christian
passages are to be ascribed to some interpolator* who, with a
Jewish original before him, introduced modifications here and
there to adapt it to the purposes and needs of the Christian
Church. This assumption will also enable us to explain
how it comes to be stated in our Testaments that Christ was
a descendant of the tribes of Levi and Judah alike.[36] How it

---

[34a] That the various utterances regarding the tribes of Levi and Judah
are of a strictly Jewish character, may be further seen from others of a
precisely similar nature in the Book of Jubilees, chap. xxxi. (Ewald's
*Jahrbücher*, iii. 39 sq.).

[35] See Sinker, *Testamenta XII. Patriarcharum*, Appendix (1879), pp. 27
and 59 ; and Harnack's notice in *Theol. Literaturztg.* 1879, p. 515. The
Roman manuscript has the original text in still another passage (perhaps in
more?), where the others show that passage to have undergone a Christian
revision. Simeon vii. according to the Roman MS. runs thus: Καὶ νῦν,
τεκνία μου, ἐπακούσατε τοῦ Λευὶ καὶ τοῦ Ἰούδα, as without doubt it was
originally written, whereas the Cambridge MS. reads: Καὶ νῦν, τεκνία μου,
ὑπακούετε Λευὶ καὶ ἐν Ἰούδᾳ λυτρωθήσεσθε.

[36] Simeon vii. : Ἀναστήσει γὰρ Κύριος ἐκ τοῦ Λευὶ ὡς ἀρχιερέα καὶ ἐκ τοῦ
Ἰούδα ὡς βασιλέα, Θεὸν καὶ ἄνθρωπον. Levi ii. : διὰ σοῦ καὶ Ἰούδα ὀφθή-
ιεται Κύριος ἐν ἀνθρώποις. Dan v. : Καὶ ἀνατελεῖ ὑμῖν ἐκ τῆς φυλῆς Ἰούδα
καὶ Λευὶ τὸ σωτήριον Κυρίου. Gad viii. : ὅπως τιμήσωσιν Ἰούδαν καὶ τὸν Λευί·
ὅτι ἐξ αὐτῶν ἀνατελεῖ Κύριος σωτῆρα τῷ Ἰσραήλ. Joseph xix. : τιμᾶτε τὸν
Ἰούδαν καὶ τὸν Λευί· ὅτι ἐξ αὐτῶν ἀνατελεῖ ὑμῖν ὁ ἀμνὸς τοῦ Θεοῦ, χάριτι
σώζων πάντα τὰ ἔθνη.

would ever occur to a Christian author himself to emphasize this point so much, even supposing Mary to have belonged to the tribe of Levi, it is difficult to see, for in the primitive Christian tradition it was only upon the descent from Judah that stress was laid. But the matter becomes perfectly intelligible when we assume that the author had a text before him in which *Levi* and *Judah* were held up as the chosen and model tribes. For finding this in his text he proceeds to justify it from his Christian standpoint by representing Christ as descended from thé tribe of Levi in His capacity as priest, and from that of Judah in His capacity as king, it being left an open question whether he assumes the Levitical descent of Mary or has in view only some spiritual connection on the part of Christ with both those tribes in virtue of His twofold office of priest and king.[37] It is further worthy of note that, deviating from his Jewish original, the Christian interpolator as a rule puts the tribe of Judah first. How long or short those Christian interpolations may have been it is not always possible to determine with any degree of certainty. It is probable however that they were on a larger scale than Schnapp is inclined to suppose.

It is rather more difficult to answer this other question, namely, whether this Jewish original itself was not the production of several authors. The grounds on which Schnapp bases his attempt to distinguish and eliminate the prophetic portions of the book are not quite so cogent in the case of Christian passages. At the same time, there is no denying that in most instances those predictions start up in the book

[37] This latter view is favoured by Simeon vii.; at the same time it is possible that, on the strength of Luke i. 36 ('Ελισάβετ ἡ συγγενίς σου), the author has assumed the Levitical descent of Mary, as many of the Fathers have also done (on which see Spitta, *Der Brief des Julius Africanus an Aristides*, 1877, p. 44 sqq.). But in any case it is certain that, previous to the author of the Testaments, no writer within the Church had ever directly maintained or in any way emphasized the Levitical descent of Jesus. For Hilgenfeld and, following him, Spitta, have contrived to elicit something of this from the words of Clemens Romanus, chap. xxxii., only by an exegesis of a very singular kind.

with a remarkable suddenness. The Testaments seem to have been intended, in the first instance, to serve as a kind of moral sermon. They concern themselves, as a rule, with some special sin or other of which the patriarch had been guilty and against which he warns his descendants. When we find then that all of a sudden, and in quite a general way, there comes in some prediction about the falling away of the tribes, and that without any further notice being taken of the special sin that had been previously treated of, it becomes evident at once that the connection is thereby interrupted and disturbed, all the more that the terms with which the Testaments conclude are such as imply that they had been preceded by exhortations, and exhortations alone. Comp. above all Simeon v.–vii.; Levi xiv.–xix.ᵃ; Judah xxi.–xxv.; Dan v. In any case we can have no difficulty in detecting in the Testaments a good many interpolations of considerable length, even apart from those passages that are of a specifically Christian kind; take for example the two visions in the Testament of Levi ii.–v. and viii., which only interrupt the connection. Then in the biographical portion of the Testament of Joseph we find two perfectly parallel narratives coming the one immediately after the other (chaps. i.–x.ᵃ and x.ᵇ–xviii.), of which only one can be supposed to be the original one. Again in the course of what is said with regard to the tribe of Levi we come across this glaring contradiction, that while on the one hand it is recommended to the other tribes as their leader, it is represented on the other as having itself fallen away, nay as having been instrumental in seducing the rest into apostasy (Levi xiv.; Dan v.). Both those classes of statements cannot possibly have emanated from one and the same person. We may therefore say that in any case the Testaments have undergone repeated revision and remodification. But this much however may be held as certain, that the great bulk of the book is of Jewish origin. *The foremost place in it is assigned to these moral sermons*, which remind us partly of Jesus the Son of Sirach, and partly of Philo, and which must have emanated from some author to whom moral conduct was a matter of deeper interest than the ceremonial law.    Along with these we have prophetic passages composed by the same or some other author, in which the falling away from Levi and Judah is represented as being the cause of all evil, while the members of the nation, scattered throughout the whole world, are recommended to enter into close relationship with these tribes, therefore with the leading circles of Palestine. On the *date of the composition* of our book it is impossible to express anything like a definite opinion.    As it is probable that the Christian revision was already known to Irenaeus, the Jewish original cannot have been composed later than the first century of our era, though, on the other hand, we can scarcely venture to refer it to an earlier date, seeing that the author probably made use of the Book of Jubilees (see below). In several passages the destruction of Jerusalem and the temple is presupposed (Levi xv.; Dan v. *fin.*).    But it is extremely doubtful whether these are to be regarded as belonging to the work in its original shape.    Possibly they were subsequently inserted by some Christian hand.

On the *references in our book to earlier writings*, see Sinker, *Testamenta XII. Patriarcharum* (1869), pp. 34–48; Dillmann in Ewald's *Jahrb. der bibl. Wissensch.* iii. 91–94; Rönsch, *Das Buch der Jubiläen* (1874), pp. 325 sqq., 415 sqq.    References to the predictions of Enoch are of very frequent occurrence (Simeon v.; Levi x., xiv., xvi.; Judah xviii.; Zebulon iii.; Dan v.; Naphtali iv.; Benjamin ix.).    These passages all belong to the prophetic sections, though in the majority of instances they are not actual quotations, but free allusions to alleged predictions of Enoch, with the view of explaining how the patriarchs obtained their information with regard to the future.    Surely from this it is perfectly obvious that the author must have already been acquainted with one or more of the various books bearing the name of Enoch.    In the biographical portions therefore, in those sections which undoubtedly belong to the original work, there are numerous coincidences with the Book of Jubilees.    But neither are these absent from those portions which, according to Schnapp, are supposed to belong to the author of the Jewish revision.    See in general Dillmann and Rönsch, as above.

In *patristic literature* the notion of the descent of Christ from the tribes of Levi and Judah is met with as early as the time of Irenaeus, which notion is probably to be traced to our book ; see Irenaeus, *Fragm.* xvii. (ed. Harvey, ii. 487): 'Εξ ὧν ὁ Χριστὸς προετυπώθη καὶ ἐπεγνώσθη καὶ ἐγεννήθη·

ἐν μὲν γὰρ τῷ Ἰωσὴφ προετυπώθη· ἐκ δὲ τοῦ Λευὶ καὶ τοῦ Ἰούδα τὸ κατὰ σάρκα ὡς βασιλεὺς καὶ ἱερεὺς ἐγεννήθη· διὰ δὲ τοῦ Συμεὼν ἐν τῷ ναῷ ἐπεγνώσθη κ.τ.λ. The passages in Tertullian, *Adv. Marcion.* v. 1, *Scorpiace* xiii., which since Grabe's time (*Spicileg.* i. 132) have usually been traced to the Testament of Benjamin xi., are simply based on Gen. xlix. 27; similarly *Hippolyt.* ed. Lagarde, p. 140, fragm. 50. It is not unlikely that the passage about Paul in Benjamin xi. would be inserted in the text of the Testament at a very late period, and that on the strength of the patristic interpretation of Gen. xlix. 27; comp. p. 119. The Testaments are expressly quoted by Origen, *In Josuam homil.* xv. 6 (ed. de la Rue, ii. 435; Lommatzsch, xi. 143): Sed et in aliquo quodam libello, qui appellatur testamentum duodecim patriarcharum, quamvis non habeatur in canone, talem tamen quendam sensum invenimus, quod per singulos peccantes singuli satanae intelligi debeant (comp. Reuben iii.). It is doubtful whether Procopius Gazaeus may be supposed to have our book in view in his *Comment. in Gen.* xxxviii. (see the passage in Sinker's *Test. XII. Patr.* p. 4). In the Stichometry of Nicephorus the Πατριάρχαι are included among the ἀπόκρυφα along with Enoch, the Assumptio Mosis and such like (Credner, *Zur Gesch. des Kanon*s, p. 121); similarly in the *Synopsis Athanasii* (Credner, p. 145) and in the anonymous list of canonical books edited by Montfaucon, Pitra and others (on which see p. 126 below). In the *Constitut. apostol.* vi. 16, mention is made of an apocryphal work entitled οἱ τρεῖς πατριάρχαι, which must be different from the book now in question, unless there has been some mistake with regard to the number.

*Four manuscripts* of the Greek text are extant: (1) A Cambridge one belonging to the tenth century; (2) an Oxford one belonging to the fourteenth (on both of which see Sinker's *Test. XII. Patr.* pp. vi.-xi.); (3) a manuscript in the Vatican Library belonging to the thirteenth century; and (4) one in the cloister of St. John in Patmos belonging to the sixteenth (on both of which again see Sinker, *Appendix*, 1879, pp. 1-7). In addition to these we should also mention, as independent testimonies, (1) the as yet unprinted *Armenian* version, eight manuscripts of which have been verified by Sinker, and the oldest of which dates from the year 1220 A.D. (Sinker, *Appendix*, pp. 23-27, and p. vii. sq.); and (2) the *Old Slavonic* version, which was published by Tichonrawow in his *Painjatniki otretschennoi russkoi literatury* (2 vols. Petersburg 1863), but which has not yet been submitted to critical investigation.

As yet no trace has been discovered of any early Latin version. But coming down to the thirteenth century we find the *Latin version* of Robert Grossetest, Bishop of Lincoln, and which, as Sinker has shown, is based upon the Cambridge manuscript (see Grabe's *Spicileg.* i. 144; Sinker, *Appendix*, p. 8). This version has come down to us through numerous manuscripts (Sinker's *Test.* pp. xi.-xv., Appendix, p. 9), and, since the beginning of the sixteenth century, it has not only been frequently printed (at first without place or date being given, though probably about 1510-1520, see Sinker, *Appendix*, p. 10; on the later impressions consult Sinker, *Test.* p. xvi. sq.), but likewise translated into almost every modern language —English, French, German, Dutch, Danish, Icelandic, Bohemian, while these translations again were also frequently printed in the sixteenth and seventeenth centuries (Sinker, *Appendix*, pp. 11–23).

The first *edition* of the Greek text was prepared by Grabe, who based it upon the Cambridge manuscript, collating it at the same time with the Oxford one. This edition also contained Grossetest's Latin version, for which two manuscripts belonging to the Bodleian Library were made use of (Grabe, *Spicilegium Patrum*, vol. i. Oxon. 1698, 2nd ed. 1714 ; on the use of the manuscripts, see p. 336 sq.). Grabe's text has been reproduced by Fabricius (*Codex pseudepigraphus Vet. Test.* vol. i. Hamburg 1713), Gallandi (*Bibliotheca veterum patrum*, vol. i. Venetiis 1788), and Migne (*Patrolog. graec.* vol. ii.). A careful edition of the Cambridge manuscript, accompanied with the variants of the Oxford one, has been printed by Sinker (*Testamenta XII. Patriarcharum, ad fidem codicis Cantabrigiensis edita, accedunt lectiones cod. Oxoniensis*, Cambridge 1869). Some time after this same scholar published in an Appendix a collation of the Vatican and the Patmos manuscripts (*Testamenta XII. Patriarcharum: Appendix containing a collation of the Roman and Patmos MSS. and bibliographical notes*, Cambridge 1879).

*Special disquisitions:* Grabe in his edition (*Spicileg.* i. 129–144 and 335–374). Corrodi, *Kritische Geschichte des Chiliasmus*, ii. 101–110. K. J. Nitzsch, *Commentatio critica de Testamentis XII. Patriarcharum, libro V. T. pseudepigrapho*, Wittenberg 1810. Wieseler, *Die 70 Wochen und die 63 Jahrwochen des Propheten Daniel* (1839), p. 226 sqq. Lücke, *Einl. in die Offenbarung Johannis* (2nd ed. 1852), pp. 334–337. Dorner, *Entwicklungsgesch. der Lehre von der Person Christi*, i. 254–264. Reuss, *Gesch. der heil. Schriften Neuen Testaments*, § 257. Ritschl, *Die Entstehung der alt-kathol. Kirche* (2nd ed. 1857), pp. 172–177. Kayser, "Die Test. der XII. Patr.," in the *Beiträge zu den theologischen Wissenschaften*, edited by Reuss and Cunitz, 3 vols. (1851) pp. 107–140. Vorstman, *Disquisitio de Testamentorum Patriarcharum XII. origine et pretio*, Rotterd. 1857. Hilgenfeld, *Zeitschr. für wissenschaftl. Theol.* 1858, p. 395 sqq.; 1871, p. 302 sqq. Van Hengel, " De Testamenten der twaalf Patriarchen op nieuw ter sprake gebragt " (*Godgeleerde Bijdragen*, 1860). Ewald, *Gesch. des Volkes Israel*, vii. 363–369. Langen, *Das Judenthum in Palästina* (1866), pp. 140–157. Sinker in his edition. Geiger, *Jüdische Zeitschr. für Wissensch. und Leben*, 1869, pp. 116–135 ; 1871, pp. 123–125. Friedr. Nitzsch, *Grundriss der christl. Dogmengeschichte*, vol. i. 1870, pp. 109–111. Renan, *L'église chrétienne* (1879), pp. 268–271. An article in *The Presbyterian Review* for January 1880 (mentioned by Bissell, *The Apocrypha*, p. 671). Dillmann, art. "Pseudepigraphen," in Herzog's *Real-Enc.* 2nd ed. vol. xii. p. 361 sq. Schnapp, *Die Testamente der zwölf Patriarchen untersucht*, Halle 1884 (and notice of this work in the *Theolog. Literaturzeitung*, 1885, p. 203).

## 7. *The Lost Pseudepigraphic Prophecies.*

Besides the pseudepigraphic prophecies that have come down to us, many others of a similar description were in

circulation in the early Church, as we learn partly from the
lists of the canon and partly from quotations found in the
Fathers.    In the case of most of them it is of course no
longer possible to determine with any certainty whether they
were of Jewish or of Christian origin.    But, considering that
in the earliest days of the Christian Church this was a
species of literary activity that flourished chiefly among the
heretical sects, and that it was not till a somewhat later period
that it began to be cultivated in Catholic circles as well, it
may be assumed with some degree of probability that *those
Old Testament pseudepigraphic writings which are mentioned in
terms of high respect by the earliest of the Fathers, down say to
Origen inclusive, are to be regarded generally as being of Jewish
and not of Christian origin.*    With the criterion thus obtained
we may combine still another.    We happen to have several
*lists of the canon* in which the Old Testament Apocrypha
are enumerated with great completeness.    Now, among the
writings thus enumerated, occur those which have come down
to us (Enoch, the Twelve Patriarchs, the Assumptio Mosis, the
Psalms of Solomon), and which are undoubtedly of Jewish
origin.    This then must surely be regarded as sufficiently
justifying the conjecture that the others would also be of
similar origin.    The lists in question are the following:—

1. The so-called *Stichometry of Nicephorus, i.e.* a list of the
canonical and apocryphal books of the Old and New Testaments along with the number of verses in each book, and
which list is given as an appendix to the *Chronographia
compendiaria* of Nicephorus Constantinopolitanus (about
800 A.D.), though it is, without doubt, of a considerably
earlier origin (printed in the appendix to Dindorf's edition of
George Syncellus, further in a critically amended text given
by Credner in two programmes for the University of Giessen
1832–1838, and also reproduced in Credner's *Zur Geschichte
des Kanons*, 1847, pp. 117–122, but best of all in de Boor's
*Nicephori opuscula*, Lips. 1880).    Here the list of the Old
Testament ἀπόκρυφα runs thus (ed. de Boor, p. 134 sq.):—

α′ Ἐνὼχ στίχων ͵δω′ (4800).

β′ Πατριάρχαι στίχων ͵ερ′ (5100).

γ′ Προσευχὴ Ἰωσὴφ στίχων ͵αρ′ (1100).

δ′ Διαθήκη Μωϋσέως στίχων ͵αρ′ (1100).

ε′ Ἀνάληψις Μωϋσέως στίχων ͵αυ′ (1400).

ϛ′ Ἀβραὰμ στίχων τ′ (300).

ζ′ Ἐλὰδ (sic) καὶ Μωδὰδ στίχων ν′ (400).

η′ Ἠλία προφήτου στίχων τιϛ′ (316).

θ′ Σοφονίου προφήτου στίχων χ′ (600).

ι′ Ζαχαρίου πατρὸς Ἰωάννου στίχων φ′ (500).

ια′ Βαρούχ, Ἀμβακούμ, Ἰεζεκιὴλ καὶ Δανιὴλ ψευδεπίγραφα.

2. The so-called *Synopsis Athanasii*, which simply reproduces from the *Stichometry of Nicephorus* the section containing the Apocrypha, without giving however the number of the verses (Credner, *Zur Geschichte des Kanons*, p. 145).

3. Akin to this latter is an *anonymous list* which was published: (*a*) from a *Codex Coislinianus* belonging to the tenth century by Montfaucon, *Bibliotheca Coisliniana*, Paris 1715, p. 194; (*b*) from a *Cod. Paris. Regius* by Cotelier, *Patrum Apost. Opp.* vol. i. 1698, p. 196; (*c*) from a *Cod. Baroccianus* by Hody, *De Bibliorum textibus*, 1705, p. 649, col. 44 (those three manuscripts are based upon each other in the order just given and as may be seen from a more careful comparing of them with the text); and lastly, (*d*) from a *Codex Vaticanus* by Pitra, *Juris ecclesiastici Graecorum historia et monumenta*, vol. i. Romae 1864, p. 100. As appears from the numbering, there is an omission in the three first-mentioned manuscripts (No. 8 being left out). According to Pitra, the complete list of the ἀπόκρυφα is as follows:—

α′ Ἀδάμ.

β′ Ἐνώχ.

γ′ Λάμεχ.

δ′ Πατριάρχαι.

ε′ Ἰωσὴφ προσευχή.

ς΄ Ἐλδὰμ καὶ Μοδάμ (al. Ἐλδὰδ καὶ Μωδάδ).

ζ΄ Διαθήκη Μωσέως.

η΄ Ἡ ἀνάληψις Μωσέως.

θ΄ Ψαλμοὶ Σολομῶντος.

ι΄ Ἡλίου ἀποκάλυψις.

ια΄ Ἡσαίου ὅρασις.

ιβ΄ Σοφονίου ἀποκάλυψις.

ιγ΄ Ζαχαρίου ἀποκάλυψις.

ιδ΄ Ἔσδρα ἀποκάλυψις.

ιε΄ Ἰακώβοι ἱστορία.

ις΄ Πέτρου ἀποκάλυψις, and so on (these being followed by other New Testament Apocrypha).

This list is in the main identical with that of the *Stichometry of Nicephorus*. With a single exception (No. 6, Ἀβραάμ), the whole of the first ten numbers of the *Stichometry* are reproduced in it. But besides this these nine numbers have this in common with each other, that they are probably all of them *prophetic pseudepigraphs*, *i.e.* writings purporting to have been composed by the various men of God whose names they bear, or at all events containing a record of revelations with which those men are alleged to have been favoured, a circumstance which probably accounts for their comparatively wide circulation throughout the Church. The last of the nine here in question shows by its title, Ζαχαρίου πατρὸς Ἰωάννου, that it belongs to the Christian Apocrypha. With regard to the others, four of them have already been considered by us (Enoch, the Patriarchs, the Testament and the Ascension of Moses; on the two latter, see p. 81), while the remaining four (Joseph's Prayer, Eldad and Modad, Elias, Zephaniah) are all quoted with deference either by Origen or by some still older Fathers, and may therefore be regarded, with a certain degree of probability, as *Jewish* products. Consequently they fall to be more fully considered by us here.

1. Joseph's Prayer (Προσευχὴ Ἰωσήφ). For the infor-

mation we possess regarding this production we are indebted
above all to repeated quotations from it found in Origen.
This Father speaks of it as "a writing not to be despised"
(οὐκ εὐκαταφρόνητον γραφήν), and expressly states that it was
*in use among the Jews* (παρ' Ἑβραίοις).   In the passages
quoted it is Jacob who figures all through, describing himself
as the first-born of all living beings, nay as the head of all the
angels themselves.   He informs us that when he was coming
from Mesopotamia he met Uriel who wrestled with him, and
claimed to be the foremost of the angels.   But he says that
he corrected him, and told him that he, Uriel, was only the
eighth in rank after himself.   In another passage Jacob states
that he had had an opportunity of inspecting the heavenly
records, and that there he read the future destinies of men.

Origen, *In Joann.* vol. ii. chap. xxv. (*Opp.* ed. de la Rue, iv. 84 ; Lommatzsch, i. 147): Εἰ δέ τις προσίεται καὶ τῶν παρ' Ἑβραίοις φερομένων
ἀποκρύφων τὴν ἐπιγραφομένην Ἰωσὴφ προσευχήν, ἄντικρυς τοῦτο τὸ δόγμα καὶ
σαφῶς εἰρημένον ἐκεῖθεν λήψεται . . . Φησὶ γοῦν ὁ Ἰακώβ· "Ὁ γὰρ λαλῶν
πρὸς ὑμᾶς, ἐγὼ Ἰακὼβ καὶ Ἰσραήλ, ἄγγελος θεοῦ εἰμι ἐγὼ καὶ πνεῦμα ἀρχικόν·
καὶ Ἀβραὰμ καὶ Ἰσαὰκ προεκτίσθησαν πρὸ παντὸς ἔργου· ἐγὼ δὲ Ἰακώβ, ὁ
κληθεὶς ὑπὸ ἀνθρώπων Ἰακώβ, τὸ δὲ ὄνομά μου Ἰσραήλ, ὁ κληθεὶς ὑπὸ θεοῦ
Ἰσραήλ, ἀνὴρ ὁρῶν θεόν, ὅτι ἐγὼ πρωτόγονος παντὸς ζῴου ζωουμένου ὑπὸ
θεοῦ." Καὶ ἐπιφέρει· "Ἐγὼ δὲ ὅτε ἠρχόμην ἀπὸ Μεσοποταμίας τῆς Συρίας,
ἐξῆλθεν Οὐριὴλ ὁ ἄγγελος τοῦ θεοῦ, καὶ εἶπεν, ὅτι κατέβην ἐπὶ τὴν γῆν καὶ
κατεσκήνωσα ἐν ἀνθρώποις· καὶ ὅτι ἐκλήθην ὀνόματι Ἰακώβ, ἐζήλωσε καὶ
ἐμαχέσατό μοι, καὶ ἐπάλαιε πρὸς μὲ λέγων· προτερήσειν ἐπάνω τοῦ ὀνόματός
μου τὸ ὄνομα αὐτοῦ καὶ τοῦ πρὸ [*l.* πρὸ τοῦ] παντὸς ἀγγέλου. Καὶ εἶπα
αὐτῷ τὸ ὄνομα αὐτοῦ, καὶ πόσος ἐστὶν ἐν υἱοῖς θεοῦ· οὐχὶ σὺ Οὐριὴλ ὄγδοος
ἐμοῦ, κἀγὼ Ἰσραὴλ ἀρχάγγελος δυνάμεως κυρίου καὶ ἀρχιχιλίαρχός εἰμι ἐν
υἱοῖς θεοῦ; οὐχὶ ἐγὼ Ἰσραὴλ ὁ ἐν προσώπῳ θεοῦ λειτουργὸς πρῶτος, καὶ
ἐπεκαλεσάμην ἐν ὀνόματι ἀσβέστῳ τὸν θεόν μου."

Origen, *ibid.* (Lommatzsch, i. 148): Ἐπὶ πλεῖον δὲ παρεξέβημεν παρα-
λαβόντες τὸν περὶ Ἰακὼβ λόγον, καὶ μαρτυράμενοι ἡμῖν οὐκ εὐκαταφρόνητον
γραφήν.

Origen, *Fragm. comment. in Genes.*[38] vol. iii. chap. ix. toward the end (ed.
de la Rue, ii. 15 ; Lommatzsch, viii. 30 sq. = Euseb. *Praep. evang.* vi. 11. 64,
ed. Gaisford): Διόπερ ἐν τῇ προσευχῇ τοῦ Ἰωσὴφ δύναται οὕτω νοεῖσθαι τὸ
λεγόμενον ὑπὸ τοῦ Ἰακώβ· "Ἀνέγνων γὰρ ἐν ταῖς πλαξὶ τοῦ οὐρανοῦ, ὅσα
συμβήσεται ὑμῖν καὶ τοῖς υἱοῖς ὑμῶν." Comp. also *ibid.* chap. xii. toward the

---

[38] The large fragment from the third book of the Commentary on Genesis
is to be found in the *Philocalia,* chap. xxiii. (*Origenis Opp.* ed. Lommatzsch,
vol. xxv.), and the most of it also in Eusebius, *Praep. evang.* vi. 11.

end of the chapter (ed. de la Rue, ii. 19; Lommatzsch, viii. 38), where the
contents of the somewhat lengthened fragment first quoted are given in an
abridged form.

Fabricius, *Codex pseudepigr. Vet. Test.* i. 761–771. Dillmann, art.
"Pseudepigraphen," in Herzog's *Real-Enc.* 2nd ed. xii. 362.

2. The book entitled *Eldad and Modad.* This was a
writing that was circulated under the name of two Israelites
called אֶלְדָּד and מֵידָד (Sept. Ἐλδὰδ καὶ Μωδάδ), who according to Num. xi. 26–29 uttered certain predictions in the
camp during the march through the wilderness. Besides
being mentioned in the lists of the Apocrypha, this book is
also quoted in the Shepherd of Hermas, and that as a genuine
prophetical work. According to the *Targum of Jonathan* on
Num. xi. 26–29, the predictions of the two personages here
in question had reference chiefly to Magog's final attack upon
the congregation of Israel. But whether this may be regarded
as indicating what the theme of our book is likely to have
been is extremely doubtful.

Hermas, *Pastor, Vis.* ii. 3: Ἐγγὺς κύριος τοῖς ἐπιστρεφομένοις, ὡς γέγραπται ἐν τῷ Ἐλδὰδ καὶ Μωδάτ, τοῖς προφητεύσασιν ἐν τῇ ἐρήμῳ τῷ λαῷ.

The Targum of Jonathan on the Pentateuch is given in the fourth volume
of the London Polyglot along with a Latin translation. Comp. also Beer,
"Eldad und Medad im Pseudojonathan" (*Monatsschr. für Gesch. und
Wissensch. des Judenth.* 1857, pp. 346–350). Weber, *System der altsyna-
gogalen palästinischen Theologie,* 1880, p. 370.

Fabricius, *Codex pseudepigr. Vet. Test.* i. 801–804. Dillmann, art.
"Pseudepigraphen," in Herzog's *Real-Enc.* 2nd ed. xii. 363. Cotelier,
Hilgenfeld and Harnack in their editions of the Shepherd of Hermas, notes
on Vision ii. 3.

3. The *Apocalypse of Elijah.* The prophet Elijah has this
in common with Enoch, that like him he was taken up to
heaven without dying. Consequently in the legends of the
saints he is often associated with Enoch (for the literature
of this, see Enoch, p. 70), and like this latter could not
fail to be regarded as a peculiarly suitable medium through
which to communicate heavenly revelations. A writing bearing his name is mentioned in the *Constitut. apostol.* vi. 16,
and in the patristic quotations simply as an Apocryphum.
According to the more exact titles as given in the lists of the

Apocrypha (Ἠλία προφήτου in Nicephorus, Ἠλίου ἀποκάλυψις in the anonymous list) and in Jerome (see below), this
book was a somewhat short apocalyptic work consisting,
according to the Stichometry of Nicephorus, of 316 verses.
It is often mentioned by Origen and subsequent ecclesiastical
writers as being the source of a quotation made by Paul, and
which cannot be traced to any part of the Old Testament
(1 Cor. ii. 9: καθὼς γέγραπται· ἃ ὀφθαλμὸς οὐκ εἶδεν καὶ
οὖς οὐκ ἤκουσεν καὶ ἐπὶ καρδίαν ἀνθρώπου οὐκ ἀνέβη κ.τ.λ.).
No doubt Jerome strongly protests against the notion that
Paul is here quoting an apocryphal work. But the thing is
not at all incredible, for do we not find that the Book of
Enoch has also been undoubtedly quoted by the author of the
Epistle of Jude ? If that be so, then this circumstance serves
at the same time to prove the early existence and Jewish
origin of the Apocalypse of Elijah. This same passage that
is quoted in First Corinthians is likewise quoted by Clemens
Romanus, chap. xxxiv. fin. Now as non-canonical quotations
occur elsewhere in Clement, it is just possible that he, in like
manner, has made use of the Apocalypse of Elijah. At the
same time it is more likely that he has borrowed the quotation
from the First Epistle to the Corinthians. According to
Epiphanius, the passage Eph. v. 14 (ἔγειρε ὁ καθεύδων καὶ
ἀνάστα ἐκ τῶν νεκρῶν καὶ ἐπιφαύσει σοι ὁ Χριστός) was also
taken from our Apocryphum. But seeing that Origen makes
no mention of this in his collations of passages of this sort,
that statement is of a very questionable character, and probably rests upon some confusion or other. According to
Euthalius, Eph. v. 14 was taken from an apocryphal work
that bore the name of Jeremiah.

Origen, *Comment. ad Matth.* xxvii. 9 (de la Rue, iii. 916; Lommatzsch, v.
29): Et apostolus scripturas quasdam secretorum profert, sicut dicit alicubi:
"quod oculus non vidit, nec auris audivit" (1 Cor. ii. 9); in nullo enim
regulari libro hoc positum invenitur, nisi in secretis Eliae prophetae. Comp.
further, *Comment. ad Matt.* xxiii. 37 (de la Rue, iii. 848; Lommatzsch, iv. 237
sqq.), where, in connection with the saying of Christ that Jerusalem killed
*the prophets*, Origen observes that the Old Testament records only a single

instance of a prophet being put to death in Jerusalem, and then proceeds
to add : Propterea videndum, ne forte oporteat ex libris secretioribus, *qui
apud Judaeos feruntur*, ostendere verbum Christi, et non solum Christi, sed
etiam discipulorum ejus (for example such further statements as Heb. xi.
37) . . . Fertur ergo in scripturis non manifestis serratum esse Jesaiam,
et Zachariam occisum, et Ezechielem. Arbitror autem circuisse in melotis
[ἐν μηλωταῖς, Heb. xi. 37], in pellibus caprinis Eliam, qui in solitudine et in
montibus vagabatur. And so among the other passages that go to prove
that apocryphal books are sometimes referred to in the New Testament we
should also include 1 Cor. ii. 9. Lastly, Origen goes on to observe : Oportet
ergo caute considerare, ut nec omnia secreta, quae feruntur in nomine
sanctorum, suscipiamus propter *Judaeos*, qui forte ad destructionem veritatis scripturarum nostrarum quaedam finxerunt, confirmantes dogmata
falsa, nec omnia abjiciamus, quae pertinent ad demonstrationem scripturarum nostrarum. The whole connection here plainly shows that it is
exclusively *Jewish* Apocrypha that Origen has in view.

Euthalius in his learned statistical work on the Epistles of Paul (458 A.D.)
likewise traces 1 Cor. ii. 9 to the Apocalypse of Elijah (Zaccagni, *Collectanea
monumentorum veterum*, Romae 1698, p. 556=Gallandi, *Biblioth. patrum*,
x. 258). In this he is followed by Syncellus, ed. Dindorf, i. 48, and an
anonymous list of quotations in Paul's Epistles, which is given (*a*) by
Montfaucon (*Diarium Italicum*, p. 212 sq., and *Bibliotheca Bibliothecarum*,
i. 195) from a *Codex Basilianus*, and (*b*) by Cotelier (in his edition of the
Apostolic Fathers, note on *Constitut. apost.* vi. 16) from two Parisian
manuscripts.

Jerome, *Epist.* 57 *ad Pammachium*, chap. ix. (*Opp.* ed. Vallarsi, i. 314) :
Pergamus ad apostolum Paulum. Scribit ad Corinthios : Si enim cogno-
vissent Dominum gloriae, etc. (1 Cor. ii. 8–9). . . . Solent in hoc loco
apocryphorum quidam deliramenta sectari et dicere, quod de apocalypsi Eliae
testimonium sumtum sit, etc. (Jerome then traces the quotation to Isa.
lxiv. 3). Idem, *Comment. in Jesaiam*, lxiv. 3 [*al.* lxiv. 4] (Vallarsi, iv. 761) :
Paraphrasim hujus testimonii quasi Hebraeus ex Hebraeis assumit apostolus
Paulus de authenticis libris in epistola quam scribit ad Corinthios (1 Cor.
ii. 9), non verbum ex verbo reddens, quod facere omnino contemnit, sed
sensuum exprimens veritatem, quibus utitur ad id quod voluerit roborandum.
Unde apocryphorum deliramenta conticeant, quae ex occasione hujus testimonii ingeruntur ecclesiis Christi. . . . Ascensio enim Isaiae et *Apocalypsis
Eliae* hoc habent testimonium.

Clemens Rom. chap. xxxiv. *fin.*: λέγει γάρ· Ὀφθαλμὸς οὐκ εἶδεν καὶ οὖς
οὐκ ἤκουσεν καὶ ἐπὶ καρδίαν ἀνθρώπου οὐκ ἀνέβη ὅσα ἡτοίμασεν τοῖς ὑπομένουσιν
αὐτόν (in St. Paul: τοῖς ἀγαπῶσιν αὐτόν). Comp. the note on this in
Gebhardt and Harnack's edition. The passage is also frequently quoted
elsewhere in patristic literature, and was a special favourite with the
Gnostics ; see Hilgenfeld, *Die apostol. Väter*, p. 102 ; Ritschl, *Die Entstehung der altkathol. Kirche*, p. 267 sq.

Epiphanius, *Haer..* xlii. p. 372, ed. Petav. (Dindorf, ii. 388) : " Διὸ λέγει,
ἔγειρε ὁ καθεύδων καὶ ἀνάστα ἐκ τῶν νεκρῶν, καὶ ἐπιφαύσει σοι ὁ Χριστός "
(Eph. v. 14). Πόθεν τῷ ἀποστόλῳ τὸ " διὸ καὶ λέγει," ἀλλὰ ἀπὸ τῆς παλαιᾶς

δῆλον διαθήκη, ; τοῦτο δὲ ἐμφέρεται παρὰ τῷ 'Ηλίᾳ. Hippolytus, *De Christo et Antichr.*, chap. lxv., quotes the same passage (Eph. v. 14) with the formula ὁ προφήτης λέγει, and with a slight deviation in regard to the terms (ἐξεγέρθητι instead of ἀνάστα). It also occurs with the same deviation and with the formula ἡ γραφὴ λέγει in an utterance of the Naasenes quoted by Hippolytus (*Philosophum.* v. 7, p. 146, ed. Duncker). But both those quotations are undoubtedly to be traced simply to the Epistle to the Ephesians (Hilgenfeld, *Nov. Test. extra canonem receptum*, 2nd ed. iv. 74, thinks, though without any distinct ground for doing so, that they may have been taken from the Apocalypse of Peter). According to Euthalius, Eph. v. 14 formed part of an Apocryphum that bore the name of *Jeremiah* (Zaccagni, *Collectanea monumentorum veterum*, p. 561 = Gallandi, *Biblioth. patr.* x. 260). Similarly Syncellus, ed. Dindorf, i. 48, and the above-mentioned anonymous list of Paul's quotations from the Scriptures, which simply reproduces Euthalius. We may safely venture to assume that this Apocryphum bearing the name of Jeremiah was itself of Christian origin.

The work by the Hellenist Eupolemus, περὶ τῆς 'Ηλίου προφητείας (Euseb. *Praep. evang.* ix. 30), has nothing to do with our Apocryphum. On this see sec. 33. Isr. Levi endeavours to make out the probable existence of a *Hebrew Apocalypse of Elijah* on the strength of two Talmudic passages (*Sanhedrin* 97b; *Joma* 19b), where certain utterances of Elijah regarding questions of Messianic dogma happen to be quoted (*Revue des études juives*, vol. i. 1880, p. 108 sqq.). On a passage of this sort from post-Talmudic times, see Jellinek, *Bet-ha-Midrash*, vol. iii.

Fabricius, *Cod. pseudepigr. Vet. Test.* i. 1070–1086. Lücke, *Einleitung in die Offenbarung des Johannes*, 2nd ed. p. 235 sq. Bleek, *Stud. u. Krit.* 1853, p. 330 sq. Dillmann in Herzog's *Real-Enc.* 2nd ed. xii. 359. The commentaries on 1 Cor. ii. 9 and Eph. v. 14.

4. *The Apocalypse of Zephaniah.* Apart from the Stichometry of Nicephorus and the anonymous list of the Apocrypha (see p. 126), all we know of this writing is from a quotation in Clement of Alexandria.

Clemens Alex. *Strom.* v. 11. 77 : 'Αρ' οὐχ ὅμοια ταῦτα τοῖς ὑπὸ Σοφονία λεχθεῖσι τοῦ προφήτου ; " καὶ ἀνέλαβέν με πνεῦμα καὶ ἀνήνεγκέν με εἰς οὐρανὸν πέμπτον καὶ ἐθεώρουν ἀγγέλους καλουμένους κυρίους, καὶ τὸ διάδημα αὐτῶν ἐπικείμενον ἐν πνεύματι ἁγίῳ καὶ ἦν ἑκάστου αὐτῶν ὁ θρόνος ἑπταπλασίων φωτὸς ἡλίου ἀνατέλλοντος, οἰκοῦντας ἐν ναοῖς σωτηρίας καὶ ὑμνοῦντας θεὸν ἄρρητον ὕψιστον."

Fabricius, *Cod. pseudepigr. Vet. Test.* i. 1140 sq. Dillmann in Herzog's *Real-Enc.* xii. 360.

The Apocalypses we have just been considering are far from exhausting the number of them that were in circulation in the early Church. At the end of the Stichometry of Nicephorus mention is made of ψευδεπίγραφα of Baruch

Habakkuk, Ezekiel, and Daniel. As we have already stated, Euthalius was acquainted with an Apocryphum bearing the name of Jeremiah. Jerome mentions a Hebrew Apocryphum bearing this prophet's name in which Matt. xxvii. 9 occurred.[39] But as regards all these and many others besides, it is extremely doubtful, for various reasons, and chiefly from their appearing somewhat late in the Christian Church, whether they are of Jewish origin. It is obvious that the four last-mentioned pseudepigraphs are to be regarded as an addition at some subsequent period to the original Stichometry of Nicephorus.

## VI. THE SACRED LEGENDS.

The authors of the pseudepigraphic prophecies had chiefly in view the practical aim of imparting greater weight to the lessons and exhortations which they desired to address to their contemporaries by ascribing them to the sacred authorities whose names they bear. Not only however did they represent the holy men of God themselves as speaking to posterity, but it was not uncommon at the same time to enrich the accounts we have *regarding those personages* with new material, partly for the purpose of giving to the present generation a clearer view of the sacred narrative generally by the addition of copious details, and partly by surrounding these saints of the olden time with a halo of glory, to hold them up more and more unreservedly as shining models for Israel to imitate (comp. in general, Div. ii. vol. i. p. 339 et seq.). Now there were two ways in which the things here in question, viz. the amplifying and embellishing of the sacred story and adapting it to purposes of edification, could be effected, either by *a continual modifying of the text of the Biblical narrative,* or by *singling*

---

[39] Jerome, *ad Matth.* xxvii. 9 (Vallarsi, vii. 1, 228) : Legi nuper in quodam Hebraico volumine, quod Nazaraenae sectae mihi Hebraeus obtulit, Jeremiae apocryphum, in quo haec ad verbum scripta reperi.

*out certain personages in it and making them the heroes of ficti-
tious legends.*   At first it was the former of these courses that
was chiefly followed, though afterwards the latter came more
and more to be adopted as well.   A classical example of each
of those two modes of enriching the sacred story has come
down to us from a comparatively early period, from somewhere
about the time of Christ.   The so-called *Book of Jubilees* is
an instance of the way in which the text was modified, while in
the *Martyrdom of Isaiah* we have a specimen of the fictitious
legend.   Other writings of this description are either known
to us merely from quotations or have come down to us only
in the shape of Christian versions of them.   But a large
amount of material of this sort is also to be found in writings
the principal objects of which are different from those mentioned above.   Legendary amplifications of the sacred narrative
are also to be met with in almost all of the pseudepigraphic
prophecies.   This, as appears from what has been already
said, is true above all of the Testaments of the Twelve Patriarchs into which the biographical element enters so largely.
And so for this reason it has also very many points of contact
with the first of the two principal works which we will now
proceed to consider.

## 1. *The Book of Jubilees.*

Didymus Alexandrinus, Epiphanius, and Jerome quote an
apocryphal book under the title τὰ Ἰωβηλαῖα or ἡ λεπτὴ
Γένεσις, from which they borrow various details connected
with the history of the patriarchs.   Then copious extracts
from this same work are given by the Byzantine chroniclers
Syncellus, Cedrenus, Zonoras, Glycas, from the beginning of
the ninth down to the twelfth century.   But at this latter
point the book disappears, and for a long time it was looked
upon as lost, till it turned up again in the present century in
the Abyssinian Church, where it was found in an Ethiopic
version.   It was published for the first time by Dillmann in

a German translation (Ewald's *Jahrbücher*, ii.–iii. 1850–1851), and afterwards in the Ethiopic text (1859). Besides this Ethiopic version, a large fragment of the work is likewise extant in an old Latin version which in like manner was not discovered till modern times, the author of the discovery being Ceriani, who found it in a manuscript in the Ambrosian Library at Milan, and afterwards published it among the *Monumenta sacra et profana* (vol. i. fasc. 1, 1861). This Latin fragment was also subsequently edited by Rönsch, accompanied with a Latin rendering by Dillmann of the corresponding portion in the Ethiopic version, as well as a commentary and several excursuses full of valuable matter (1874).

The contents of the book are substantially the same as those of our canonical Genesis, for which reason it is also generally styled "*the smaller Genesis,*" not because it is of smaller dimensions (on the contrary, it is larger than the other), but because it is inferior in point of authority to the canonical book. It stands to this latter very much in the same relation as a *Haggadean commentary* to the text of the Bible. At the same time it is as far as possible from being an actual exposition of the text, which in fact the Haggadean Midrash never pretends to be, but simply *a free reproduction of the early Biblical history from the creation of the world down to the institution of the Passover* (Ex. xii.), *and that from the standpoint and in the spirit of later Judaism.* The whole is made to assume the form of a revelation imparted to Moses on Mount Sinai by an "angel of the presence." The object of the author in selecting this form was to secure at once for the new matters which he has to communicate the same authority as was already accorded to the text of the Bible. In his reproduction he has paid special attention to the matter of chronology, the due fixing of this being without doubt one of the leading objects for which his book was written. He takes as the basis of reckoning the *jubilee-period* of 49 years, which again resolves itself into seven year-weeks of seven years each, and then, in fixing the date of any event, he determines the exact month of the exact year of the exact year-week of the exact jubilee-period in which it occurred. From this it is not difficult to see why the whole book was called τὰ Ἰωβηλαῖα, "the Jubilees." As the author was interested in chronology generally, so he lays a peculiar stress upon the observance of the *annual festivals*, and endeavours to prove with regard to each of the leading feasts that it had been instituted in the very earliest times; so for example with regard to Pentecost or the feast of Weeks (Ewald's *Jahrbb.* ii. 245, iii. 8), the feast of Tabernacles (*Ibid.* iii. 11), the great Day of Atonement (iii. 46), and the feast of the Passover (iii. 68 sq.). This also serves to explain why it is that he happens to finish with the institution of the Passover (Ex. xii.).

As the author seeks to reproduce the history of primitive times *in the spirit of his own day*, he deals with the Biblical text in a very free fashion. Many things that did not happen to interest him, or that he considered objectionable, were either omitted or altered, while others were still further amplified by the addition of numerous particulars of one kind or another. He is always by way of showing exactly where the founders of the primitive families or races got their wives from; he explains how far Gen. ii. 17 had been literally fulfilled (comp. Justin, *Dial. c. Tryph.* chap. lxxxi.), with whose help Noah brought the animals into the ark, how the Hamitic family of the Canaanites and the Japhetic one of the Medes found their way within the sphere of the Semitic family, why Rebecca had such a decided preference for Jacob,[40] and so on. He is acquainted with the names of the wives of the whole of the patriarchs from Adam down to the twelve sons of Jacob, he knows the name of the particular peak of Mount Ararat on which Noah's ark rested, and many other things of a similar kind.[41] All those embellishments and amplifications

[40] Dillmann in Ewald's *Jahrbb.* vol. iii. p. 78 sq.
[41] *Ibid.* p. 80.

are entirely in the spirit of later Judaism. A peculiarly characteristic feature is the circumstance that the patriarchs are represented as paragons of moral excellence to even a greater extent than in the Biblical narrative itself, and as being already in the habit of observing the whole of the Mosaic ritual, of offering sacrifices and firstlings, and of celebrating the annual festivals, the new moons, and the Sabbaths. It is further characteristic, that everywhere the *hierarchia coelestis* is represented as forming the background of this world's history. The angels, good and evil alike, are regularly interfering with the course of human affairs, and inciting men to good and evil actions. We learn that the angels observed the law in heaven long before it was promulgated upon earth. For from the very beginning that law stood inscribed upon the heavenly tablets, and it was only by degrees that it was copied from these and communicated to men. It appears moreover that the whole of the divine teachings had not been openly published to the people of Israel, many of them having been communicated to the patriarchs only in secret books which were transmitted by them to later generations.

Notwithstanding its many salient features of a characteristic nature, it is still difficult to say amid what circles the book had its origin. Jellinek regards it as an Essenian work of an anti-Pharisaic tendency. But although a good many things in it, such as its highly developed angelology, its secret books, its doctrine of the continued existence of the soul without any resurrection of the body (iii. 24), seem to favour the hypothesis of an Essenian origin, yet there are others that but the more decisively preclude such a hypothesis. It says nothing about those washings and purifications that formed so important a feature of Essenism. It is true the author strongly reprobates the eating of blood, still he by no means expresses his disapproval of animal sacrifices as was so emphatically done by the Essenes. Still less are we to think of a Samaritan origin as Beer is disposed to do, for this hypothesis again is precluded by the fact that the author speaks of the garden of Eden, the mount of the east, Mount Sinai, and Mount Zion as being "the four places of God upon earth" (ii. 241, 251), and thus excludes Gerizim from the number. Again, Frankel's view, that the book was written by a Hellenistic Jew belonging to Egypt, is no less untenable. For, as will be seen immediately, the language in which it was originally composed was not Greek but Hebrew. There cannot be a doubt that the greater number of the peculiarities by which this book is characterized are such as it has in common with the prevailing Pharisaism of the time. And one might refer it to this without further ado were it not that several difficulties stand in the way, such as its opposition to the mode of reckoning adopted in the Pharisaic calendar (ii. 246), and its doctrine of a continued existence of the soul apart from any resurrection (ii. 24). But it would be absolutely erroneous again if, in consequence of these facts, and because of the decided prominence given to the tribe of Levi (iii. 39 sq.), we were to suppose that a Sadducee was the author of our work, for its elaborate angelology and its doctrine of immortality are of themselves sufficient to render such a supposition impossible. The truth of the matter would rather seem to be this, that the author, while of course *representing in all essential respects the standpoint of the dominant Pharisaism of his time*, gives expression to his own personal views only in connection with one or two particulars here and there (so also for example Dillmann, Rönsch, Drummond).

That the book had its origin in Palestine is already evidenced by the fact that it was *written originally in Hebrew*. For although the Ethiopic and the Latin versions have been taken from the Greek, this does not alter the fact that the original was composed in Hebrew, as is evident from explicit statements to this effect made by Jerome. The *date of the composition* of our work may be determined, if not within very narrow limits, yet with an approximate degree of certainty. For we find, on the one hand, that our author undoubtedly makes use of, nay that he actually quotes the Book of Enoch. Then it is extremely probable, on the other, that the author of the *Testaments of the Twelve Patriarchs* had our book before him when he wrote. In addition to this there is the further circumstance that we nowhere find any reference whatever to the destruction of Jerusalem; on the contrary, it is assumed throughout to be still standing as the central place of worship (comp. above all, iii. 42, 69). From all this we may venture, with tolerable probability, to refer the composition of our work to the first century of our era.

On the various *titles* of the book, see Rönsch, *Das Buch der Jubiläen*, pp. 461–482. Besides those mentioned above, we also find in Syncellus and Cedrenus the title ἀποκάλυψις Μωυσέως (Syncellus, ed. Dindorf, i. 5 and 49; Cedrenus, ed. Bekker, i. 9).

The Ethiopic and Latin versions are both based upon a *Greek text*, on the former of which see Dillmann in Ewald's *Jahrbb.* iii. 88 sq., and on the latter, Rönsch, *Zeitschr. für wissenchaftl. Theol.* 1871, pp. 86–89. Idem, *Das Buch der Jubiläen*, pp. 439–444. But, according to Jerome, we must assume that the original text was in Hebrew. It may be conjectured that the Greek version would be prepared only at a comparatively late date, say in the third century A.D., which would serve to explain how it happened that the book did not come into use in the Christian Church till the fourth century A.D.

It is obvious that in our work a liberal use is made of the Book of Enoch, nay in one passage (Ewald's *Jahrbb.* ii. 240) it is said of Enoch that: "He wrote in a book the signs of heaven in the order of their months, in order that the children of men might know the seasons of the years according to the order of the various months. . . . He saw in his dream the past and the future, what was going to happen to the sons of the children of men in their generations one after another down to the day of judgment. All this he saw and knew and wrote it down as a testimony, and left it on the earth as a testimony for all the sons of the children of men and for their generations." This and all that is said elsewhere regarding Enoch agrees entirely with the contents of our Book of Enoch. See in general, Dillmann in Ewald's *Jahrbb.* iii. 90 sq. Rönsch, *Das Buch der Jubiläen*, pp. 403–412.

On the allusions to our book in the Testaments of the Twelve Patriarchs, see p. 122. The *quotations* found in the Fathers and the Byzantine writers are collected by Fabricius in his *Codex pseudepigr. Vet. Test.* i. 849–864, ii. 120 sq. Rönsch, *Zeitschr. für wissensch. Theol.* 1871, p. 69 sq. Idem, *Das Buch der Jubiläen*, pp. 250–382.

Didymus Alex., *In epist. canonicas enarrationes*, ad 1 *John* iii. 12 (Gallandi, *Biblioth. patr.* vi. 300): Nam et in libro qui leprogenesis [*l.*

leptogenesis] appellatur, ita legitur, quia Cain lapide aut ligno percusserit Abel (to which quotation Langen has drawn attention in the *Bonner Theol. Literaturbl.* 1874, p. 270).

Epiphanius, *Haer.* xxxix. 6 : 'Ως δὲ ἐν τοῖς 'Ιωβηλαίοις εὑρίσκεται, τῇ καὶ λεπτῇ Γενέσει καλουμένῃ, καὶ τὰ ὀνόματα τῶν γυναικῶν τοῦ τε Καὶν καὶ τοῦ Σὴθ ἡ βίβλος περιέχει κ.τ.λ.

Jerome, *Epist.* 78 *ad Fabiolam, Mansio* 18 (Vallarsi, i. 483), speaking of the name of a place called *Ressa* (רִפָּה, Num. xxxiii. 21), observes : Hoc verbum quantum memoria suggerit nusquam alibi in scripturis sanctis apud Hebraeos invenisse me novi absque libro apocrypho qui a Graecis λεπτή id est parva Genesis appellatur ; ibi in aedificatione turris pro stadio ponitur, in quo exercentur pugiles et athletae et cursorum velocitas comprobatur. *Ibid. Mansio* 24 (Vallarsi, i. 485), speaking again of the name of a place called *Thare* (תָּרַח, Num. xxxiii. 27), observes : Hoc eodem vocabulo et iisdem literis scriptum invenio patrem Abraham, qui in supradicto apocrypho Geneseos volumine, abactis corvis, qui hominum frumenta vastabant, abactoris vel depulsoris sortitus est nomen.

In the *Decretum Gelasii* we find included among the Apocrypha a work entitled *Liber de filiabus Adae Leptogenesis* (see Credner, *Zur Gesch. des Kanons,* p. 218. Rönsch, pp. 270 sq., 477 sq.). It may be conjectured that here we have an erroneous combination of two titles belonging to two separate works. However, we can see from this as well as from the circumstance of their being a Latin version of it, that the book was also *known in the West.* On the indications of its having been made use of by occidental writers, see Rönsch, pp. 322–382 *passim.*

Syncellus, ed. Dindorf, i. 5 : ὡς ἐν λεπτῇ Φέρεται Γενέσει, ἣν καὶ Μωϋσέως εἶναί Φασί τινες ἀποκάλυψιν. i. 7 : ἐκ τῆς λεπτῆς Γενέσεως. i. 13 : ἐκ τῶν λεπτῶν Γενέσεως. i. 49 : ἐν τῇ Μωϋσέως λεγομένη ἀποκαλύψει. i. 183 : ἡ λεπτὴ Γένεσίς Φησιν. i. 185 : ὡς ἐν λεπτῇ κεῖται Γενέσει. i. 192 : ὥς Φησιν ἡ λεπτὴ Γένεσις. i. 203 : ἐν λεπτῇ Γενέσει Φέρεται.

Cedrenus, ed. Bekker, i. 6 : καὶ ἀπὸ τῆς λεπτῆς Γενέσεως. i. 9 : ὡς ἐν λεπτῇ Φέρεται Γενέσει, ἣν καὶ Μωσέως εἶναί Φασί τινες ἀποκάλυψιν. i. 16 : ὡς ἡ λεπτὴ Μωσέως Γένεσίς Φησιν. i. 48 : ὡς ἐπὶ τῇ λεπτῇ κεῖται Γενέσει. i. 53 : ἐν τῇ λεπτῇ Γενέσει κεῖται. i. 85 : ἐν τῇ λεπτῇ Γενέσει κεῖται.

Zonoras, ed. Pinder (given in common with the two foregoing in the Bonn edition of the *Corpus scriptorum historiae Byzantinae*), vol. i. p. 18 : ἐν τῇ λεπτῇ Γενέσει.

Glycas, ed. Bekker (also given in the Bonn collection), p. 198 : ἡ λεγομένη λεπτὴ Γένεσις. P. 206 : ἡ δὲ λεπτὴ Γένεσις λέγει. P. 392 : ἡ δὲ λεγομένη λεπτὴ Γένεσις, οὐκ οἶδ' ὅθεν συγγραφεῖσα καὶ ὅπως, Φησίν.

The *literature* of our book is enumerated and considered at some length by Rönsch in *Das Buch der Jubiläen,* pp. 422–439.

*Texts : Kufâlê sive Liber Jubilaeorum, aethiopice ad duorum libror. manuscr. fidem primum,* ed. Dillmann, Kiel 1859. Dillmann, *Das Buch der Jubiläen oder die kleine Genesis, aus dem Aethiopischen übersetzt* (Ewald's *Jahrbb. der bibl. Wissensch.* vol. ii. 1850, pp. 230–256 ; vol. iii. 1851, pp. 1–96). Ceriani, *Monumenta sacra et profana,* vol. i. fasc. 1 (1861), pp. 15–54. Rönsch, *Das Buch der Jubiläen oder die kleine Genesis, unter*

*Beifügungen des revidirten Textes der in der Ambrosiana aufgefundenen lateinischen Fragmente, etc. etc., erläutert untersucht und herausgegeben,* Leipzig 1874. *Special disquisitions:* Treuenfels, *Die kleine Genesis* (Fürst's *Literaturbl. des Orients,* 1846, Nos. 1–6; comp. vol. for 1851, No. 15), which was written before the Ethiopic text was discovered. Jellinek, *Ueber das Buch der Jubiläen und das Noach-Buch,* Leipzig 1855 (reprinted from part 3 of the *Bet ha-Midrasch*). Beer, *Das Buch der Jubiläen und sein Verhältniss zu den Midraschim,* Leipzig 1856. Idem, *Noch ein Wort über das Buch der Jubiläen,* Leipzig 1857. Frankel, *Monatsschr. für Gesch. und Wissensch. des Judenthums,* 1856, pp. 311–316, 380–400. Dillmann, *Zeitschr. der deutschen morgenländ. Gesellsch.* xi. 1857, pp. 161–163. Krüger, "Die Chronologie im Buch der Jubiläen" (*Zeitschr. der DMG.* vol. xii. 1858, pp. 279–299). Langen, *Das Judenthum in Palästina* (1866), pp. 84–102. Rubin, *Das Buch der Jubiläen oder die kleine Genesis in's Hebräische übersetzt, mit einer Einleitung und mit Noten versehen,* Wien, Beck's *Univ.-Buchhandlung,* 1870. Ginsburg, art. "Jubilees, Book of," in Kitto's *Cyclopaedia of Biblical Literature.* Rönsch, *Zeitschr. für wissensch. Theol.* 1871, pp. 60–98. Idem, *Das Buch der Jubiläen,* Leipzig 1874. Hilgenfeld, *Zeitschr. für wissensch. Theol.* 1874, pp. 435–441. Drummond, *The Jewish Messiah* (1877), pp. 143–147. Reuss, *Gesch. der heil. Schriften A.T.'s,* § 571. Dillmann, *Beiträge aus dem Buch der Jubiläen zur Kritik des Pentateuch-Textes* (*Transactions of the Berlin Academy,* 1883, pp. 323–340). Idem, in Herzog's *Real-Enc.* 2nd ed. xii. 364 sq.


## 2. *The Martyrdom of Isaiah.*

An apocryphal work containing an account of the martyrdom of Isaiah is repeatedly mentioned by Origen. He simply calls it an ἀπόκρυφον, tells us nothing of its contents beyond the statement that Isaiah had been sawn asunder, and plainly describes it as a *Jewish* production. Again in the *Constitutiones apostol.* reference is made merely in a general way to an Apocryphum Ἡσαΐου. On the other hand, in the list of the canon edited by Montfaucon, Pitra, and others there is a more precise mention of a Ἡσαΐου ὅρασις (see p. 127). Epiphanius knows of ɩɩɴ ἀναβατικὸν Ἡσαΐου, which was in use among the Archontics and the Hieracites. Jerome speaks of an *Ascensio Isaiae.* It is extremely probable that these references are not all to one and the same work, that, on the contrary, Origen had in view a purely Jewish production, while the others referred to a Christian version of it, or to

some Christian work quite independent of it. For there
exists a Christian Apocryphum on Isaiah which, at all events,
is made up of a variety of elements, though the oldest of
them may be pretty clearly seen to be a Jewish *history of the
martyrdom of Isaiah*. This Apocryphum, like so many others,
has come down to us in its entirety only in an Ethiopic
version, and was published for the first time by Laurence
(1819). The second half of it is likewise extant in an old
Latin version, which was printed at Venice in 1522, but had
long disappeared until it was brought to light again by
Gieseler (1832). This whole material, accompanied with
valuable disquisitions and elucidations, has been embodied in
Dillmann's edition (*Ascensio Isaiae*, Lips. 1877). Lastly,
Gebhardt published (1878) a Greek text, which however does
not profess to be the original book, but an adaptation of it in
the shape of a Christian legend of the saints.

The contents of the whole work, as given in the Ethiopic
text, are as follows: *First part:* the martyrdom (chaps.
i.–v.). Isaiah intimates to Hezekiah the future impiety of
his son Manasseh (chap. i.). After Hezekiah's death,
Manasseh, as had been foretold, abandons himself entirely to
the service of Satan, in consequence of which Isaiah and those
of his way of thinking retire into solitude (chap. ii.). Thereupon a certain person called Balkirah complains to King
Manasseh that Isaiah had been uttering prophecies against
the king and the people (chap. iii. 1–12). As for Balkirah,
he had been incited to this hostility to Isaiah by Satan
(Berial), who was angry at the former because he had predicted the coming redemption by Christ. Here the writer
takes occasion to recount the whole history of Jesus and His
Church as it had been foretold by Isaiah, and that from
Christ's incarnation down to the Neronic persecution (chap.
iv. 2) and the last judgment (iii. 13–iv. *fin.*). In deference
to the clamours for the punishment of the prophet, Manasseh
orders him to be sawn asunder, a martyr death which he
bears with singular firmness (chap. v.). *Second part:* the

vision (chaps. vi.–xi.). In the twentieth year of Hezekiah's reign Isaiah sees the following vision, which he communicates to King Hezekiah and to Josab his own (the prophet's) son (chap. vi.). An angel conducts the prophet first of all through the firmament and throughout the whole six lower heavens, and shows him all that was to be seen in each of them (chaps. vii. viii.). At last they reach the seventh heaven, where Isaiah sees all the righteous that have died from Adam downwards, and then he sees God the Lord Himself (chap. ix.). After having heard God the Father giving to his Son Jesus Christ His commission to descend into the world, Isaiah comes back again to the firmament accompanied by the angel (chap. x.). Here there is revealed to him the future birth of Jesus Christ and the history of His life upon earth down to His crucifixion and resurrection, whereupon the angel returns to the seventh heaven, while Isaiah goes back to his earthly body (chap. xi.).

This outline of the contents of our book will suffice to show that here we have to do with two elements of a totally distinct and dissimilar nature. There is no connection whatever between the vision and the martyrdom. Not only so, the vision is with singular awkwardness made to follow the martyrdom which, in the order of time, it should of course have preceded. Nor does the martyrdom again form one connected whole. Above all is the whole passage iii. 13 – v. 1, which interrupts and disturbs the connection, obviously to be regarded as a later interpolation, as is also the kindred passage in the second part, xi. 2–22. And lastly, the introduction again has only an apparent connection with what follows. On closer examination we find reason to suspect that in all probability that introduction was inserted at some subsequent period. On the strength of these facts Dillmann has propounded the following hypotheses regarding the origin of our book. In the first place we are to distinguish two elements that are independent of each other. (1) The account of the martyrdom of Isaiah, chaps. ii. 1–iii. 12, and v. 2–14, which is of Jewish origin; and (2) the vision of Isaiah, chaps. vi.–xi. (exclusive of xi. 2–22), which is of Christian origin. Then we are to regard these two elements (3) as having been amalgamated by a Christian who at the same time composed and inserted the introduction (chap. i.). Lastly, when the work had assumed this shape, another Christian would afterwards insert the two sections (chaps. iii. 13–v. 1, and xi. 2–22). These conjectures may at least be regarded as extremely probable. They are borne out not only by the internal indications already referred to, but by external testimony as well. In the free version of the whole book edited by Gebhardt no trace is to be met with of sections iii. 13–v. 1 and xi. 2–22. Besides this latter section (xi. 2–22) does not occur in the Latin version, which, as has been previously observed, embraces only chaps. vi.-xi. It is evident therefore that the sections in question must be later interpolations. But the circumstance that the vision and the vision alone is all that has come down to us in the Latin version, goes to confirm the assumption that this vision of itself originally formed an independent whole. By the ὄρασις, the ἀναβατικόν, ascensio Isaiae mentioned by the Fathers, we have therefore to understand merely that visionary journey of Isaiah through the seven heavens which had been composed by some Christian or another. In the case of Origen however it is the Jewish account of the martyrdom of Isaiah (chaps. ii. 1–iii. 12 and v. 2–14) that is in view. This latter is simply a legendary story composed for the purpose of glorifying the prophet. It contains nothing of an apocalyptic character, and consequently does not belong to the category of prophetic pseudepigraphs, but to that of legendary works.

The story of the *sawing asunder of Isaiah* is mentioned by writers of so early a date as Justin Martyr, *Dial. c. Tryph.* chap. cxx. ; Tertullian, *De patientia*, chap. xiv. ; *Scorpiace*, chap. viii. (comp. Div. ii. vol. i. p. 345). It is probably this too that the author of the Epistle to the Hebrews has in view in chap. xi. 37. In so far as it is probable that the reference here is to our book, so far have we at the same time a clue to the date of the composition of that Epistle.

Origen, *Epist. ad Africanum*, chap. ix. (de la Rue, i. 19 sq. ; Lommatzsch,

xvii. 51). With the view of proving that the Jewish authorities had sup-
pressed everything that represented them in an unfavourable light, some
specimens of which have nevertheless come down to us in apocryphal
writings (ὧν τινα σώζεται ἐν ἀποκρύφοις), Origen proceeds as follows : Καὶ
τούτου παράδειγμα δώσομεν τὰ περὶ τὸν Ἡσαΐαν ἱστορούμενα, καὶ ὑπὸ τῆς
πρὸς Ἑβραίους ἐπιστολῆς μαρτυρούμενα, ἐν οὐδενὶ τῶν φανερῶν βιβλίων γεγραμ-
μένα (here follows the quotation Heb. xi. 37). . . . Σαφὲς δ᾽ ὅτι αἱ παρα-
δόσεις λέγουσι πεπρίσθαι Ἡσαΐαν τὸν προφήτην· καὶ ἔν τινι ἀποκρύφῳ τοῦτο
φέρεται· ὅπερ τάχα ἐπίτηδες ὑπὸ Ἰουδαίων ῥεραδιούργηται, λέξεις τινὰς τὰς
μὴ πρεπούσας παρεμβεβληκτόων τῇ γραφῇ, ἵν᾽ ἡ ὅλη ἀπιστηθῇ.

Origen, *Ad Matth.* xiii. 57 (de la Rue, iii. 465 ; Lommatzsch, iii. 49): Καὶ
Ἡσαΐας δὲ πεπρίσθαι ὑπὸ τοῦ λαοῦ ἱστόρηται· εἰ δέ τις οὐ προσίεται τὴν ἱστορίαν
διὰ τὸ ἐν τῷ ἀποκρύφῳ Ἡσαΐα αὐτὴν φέρεσθαι, πιστευσάτω τοῖς ἐν τῇ πρὸς
Ἑβραίους οὕτω γεγραμμένοις (Heb. xi. 37).

Origen, *Ad Matth.* xxiii. 37 (de la Rue, iii. 848 ; Lommatzsch, iv. 237 sq.) :
Propterea videndum, ne forte oporteat ex libris secretioribus, qui apud
Judaeos feruntur, ostendere verbum Christi et non solum Christi, sed etiam
discipulorum ejus. . . . Fertur ergo in scripturis non manifestis serratum
esse Jesaiam, etc.

Origen, *In Jesaiam homil.* i. 5 (de la Rue, 108 ; Lommatzsch, xiii. 245 sq.) :
Ajunt [Judaei] ideo Isaiam esse sectum a populo quasi legem praevari-
cantem et extra scripturas annuntiantem. Scriptura enim dicit: "nemo
videbit faciem meam et vivet." Iste vero ait: "vidi Dominum Sabaoth."
Moses, ajunt, non vidit et tu vidisti ? Et propter hoc eum secuerunt et
condemnaverunt eum ut impium. And this is precisely as the affair is
represented in our book, chap. iii. 8 sqq.

Epiphanius, *Haer.* xl. 2 (speaking of the Archontics): λαμβάνουσι δὲ
λάβας ἀπὸ τοῦ ἀναβατικοῦ Ἡσαΐα, ἔτι δὲ καὶ ἄλλων τινῶν ἀποκρύφων.
Idem, *Haer.* lxvii. 3 : βούλεται δὲ [scil. Hierakas] τὴν τελείαν αὐτοῦ σύστασιν
ποιεῖσθαι ἀπὸ τοῦ ἀναβατικοῦ Ἡσαΐου, δῆθεν ὡς ἐν τῷ ἀναβατικῷ
λεγομένῳ ἔλεγεν ἐκεῖσε (here follows a quotation which substantially coincides with a passage in chap. ix. of our book).

Jerome, *Comm. in Isaiam,* chap. lxiv. 3 [*al.* lxiv. 4] (Vallarsi, iv. 761) :
Ascensio enim Isaiae et apocalypsis Eliae hoc habent testimonium, namely,
the passage 1 Cor. ii. 9. With regard to the *Apocalypsis Eliae,* see p. 129.
The passage actually occurs in the *Latin* text of the *Ascensio Isaiae.* It is
wanting, however, in the Ethiopic, and so is obviously an interpolation.

Jerome, *Comm. in Isaiam,* chap. lvii. *fin.* (Vallarsi, iv. 666): Judaei . . .
arbitrantur . . . Isaiam de sua prophetare morte quod serrandus sit a
Manasse serra lignea, quae apud eos certissima traditio est.

On the patristic quotations, comp. also Fabricius, *Codex pseudepigr. Vet.
Test.* i. 1086–1100.

The *Ethiopic text* was published by Laurence, accompanied with a Latin
and English version (*Ascensio Isaiae vatis, opusculum pseudepigraphum,
cum versione Latina Anglicanaque publici juris factum,* Oxoniae 1819). Mai
(*Scriptorum veterum nova collectio,* vol. iii. 2, 1828, p. 238 sq.) published
two fragments of an old Latin version, viz. chaps. ii. 14–iii. 13 and vii. 1–19,
without being aware that they formed part of our Apocryphum. After

Niebuhr had discovered the source from which they came they were fully discussed by Nitzsch (*Stud. u. Krit.* 1830, p. 209 sqq.). The old Latin version of the *Visio* (chaps. vi.–xi. of the Ethiopic text), which had been printed at Venice in 1522, and had then disappeared for a long time, was found again and reprinted by Gieseler in a Göttingen program (*Vetus translatio latina visionis Jesaiae*, etc., Götting. 1832). The Latin version of Laurence, accompanied with the old Latin texts, was also reprinted by Gfrörer, *Prophetae veteres pseudepigraphi*, Stuttg. 1840. A German version of those texts was published by Jolowicz (*Die Himmelfahrt und Vision des Propheten Jesaja, aus dem Aethopischen* [or as it should rather have been? *aus Laurence' lateinischer Uebersetzung*] *und Lateinischen in's Deutsche übersetzt*, Leipzig 1854). A critical edition of the Ethiopic text, along with an amended translation, and containing also the old Latin versions, was issued by Dillmann (*Ascensio Isaiae, Aethiopice et Latine cum prolegomenis, adnotationibus criticis et exegeticis, additis versionum Latinarum reliquiis edita*, Lips. 1877). Gebhardt published a Greek text, in which we have a free version of the whole book, framed in the style of the later Christian legends of the saints (*Zeitschr. für wissenschaftl. Theologie*, 1878, pp. 330–353).

*Special disquisitions:* Gesenius, *Commentar über den Jesaja*, vol. i. 1821, p. 45 sqq. Nitzsch, *Stud. u. Krit.* 1830, pp. 209–246. Gieseler, *Göttinger Progr.* 1832 (see above). Gfrörer, *Das Jahrhundert des Heils*, 1838, i. p. 65 sqq. A. G. Hoffmann, art. "Jesajas," in Ersch and Gruber's *Allg. Encycl.* sec. ii. vol. xv. (1838) pp. 387–390. Lücke, *Einleitung in die Offenbarung des Johannes*, 2nd ed. 1852, pp. 274–302. Bleek, *Stud. u. Krit.* 1854, pp. 994–998. Reuss, *Gesch. der heil. Schriften Neuen Testaments*, sec. 274. Ewald, *Gesch. des Volkes Israel*, vii. 369–373. Langen, *Das Judenthum in Palästina* (1866), pp. 157–167. Dillmann in his edition (1877). Idem, in Herzog's *Real-Enc.* 2nd ed. vol. xii. 359 sq. Renan, *L'église chrétienne* 1879), p. 528 sq.

### 3. *The Lost Legendary Works.*

In a manner similar to that which we have just seen exemplified in the case of Isaiah, pretty nearly the whole of the prominent personages belonging to the hallowed days of old were laid hold of by the legendary spirit for the purpose of throwing around them a halo of glory. The plain narratives of Holy Scripture were far too simple and unadorned to satisfy the tastes and the needs of later times. A desire was manifested to know more about those men, above all to know something regarding them of a more piquant and edifying character than was furnished by the canonical records. Accordingly we find that it is the lives of the three great heroes, Adam the progenitor of the human race, Abraham the father of Israel, and Moses the great lawgiver, that have been most elaborately embellished by fictitious legends. And there are many other men of God besides whose lives have been subjected to a similar treatment (comp. in general vol. i. Div. ii. p. 341 et seq.). Then *Christians* have laid hold of the existing *Jewish* legends, and elaborated them with equal, nay if possible with greater zeal. Consequently, as in the case of the Apocalypses so also here, we often find it impossible to distinguish with any certainty between what is Jewish and what is Christian. The foundations of the legends themselves are in most cases undoubtedly Jewish. But it is not improbable that the earliest *writings* of this class are also to be ascribed to Jewish authors. This holds true above all of the three great founders of new epochs, Adam, Abraham and Moses, to whom therefore we will here confine ourselves.

1. *Books of Adam.* A variety of tolerably voluminous *Christian* works on the life of Adam have come down to us, an Ethiopic one, a Syriac one, another in Syriac and Arabic, one in Greek, and another in Latin. Although the whole of these are unquestionably of Christian origin, and although there is not one of them that can be regarded as based upon a Jewish original, still it is probable that they have drawn upon Jewish material. A *Jewish Book of Adam* is mentioned in the Talmud. The *Constitutiones apostol.* vi. 16 mention an apocryphal Ἀδάμ along with the Apocrypha bearing the names of Moses, Enoch and Isaiah. Again, in the list of the Apocrypha published by Montfaucon, Pitra and others, Ἀδάμ finds a place among the rest of the Jewish Apocrypha (see p. 126). Indeed at an early period there already existed Gnostic ἀποκαλύψεις τοῦ Ἀδάμ (Epiphanius, *Haer.* xxvi. 8). In the *Decretum Gelasii* there occurs a Liber, qui appellatur Poenitentia Adae (Credner, *Zur Gesch. des Kanons,* p. 219).

Editions of the Christian books of Adam: (1) Dillmann published a German translation of an *Ethiopic* Book of Adam (Ewald's *Jabrbb. der bibl. Wissensch.* vol. v. 1853, pp. 1–144). The Ethiopic text was published

by Trumpp (*Transactions of the Akademie der Wissensch. of Münich*,
philosopho-philol. department, vol. xv. 1879–1881), and an English version
by Malan (*Book of Adam and Eve, also called the Conflict of Adam and
Eve with Satan, translated from the Ethiopic*, London 1882).  (2) Akin to
the above and, if we are to believe Dillmann, possessing a greater claim to
originality, is a *Syriac* work, entitled "the treasure hole" (*i.e.* the hole in
which the treasures of Paradise were kept), which as yet is known only
through a German version published by Bezold (*Die Schatzhöhle, aus dem
syr. Texte dreier unedirter Handschriften in's Deutsche übersetzt*, Leipzig
1883).  (3) Another *Syriac* and *Arabic* work entitled, "The Testament of
Adam," has been published by Renan, in the Syriac text accompanied with
a French translation (*Journal asiatique*, fifth series, vol. ii. 1853, pp. 427–71).
(4) Tischendorf published a *Greek* Book of Adam under the title *Apocalypsis Mosis* (*Apocalypses apocryphae*, Lips. 1866), and which was also
published by Ceriani (*Monum. sacra et prof.* v. 1).  On this comp. p. 81.
(5) Nearly allied to this Greek work, in fact to some extent identical
with it, is the Latin *Vita Adae et Evae*, published by Wilh. Meyer
(*Transactions of the Münich Academy*, philos.-philol. department, vol. xiv.
1878).

Comp. in general Fabricius, *Codex pseudepigr. Vet. Test.* i. 1–94, ii. 1–43.
Zunz, *Die gottesdienstlichen Vorträge der Juden*, 1832, p. 128 sq. (the
Rabbinical quotations here).  Dukes in Fürst's *Literaturbl. des Orients*,
1849, coll. 76–78.  Comp. also *ibid.* 1850, pp. 705 sqq., 732 sqq.  Lücke,
*Einl. in die Offenbarung des Johannes*, 2nd ed. p. 232.  Hort, art. "Adam,
Books of," in Smith and Wace's *Dictionary of Christian Biography*, vol. i.
1877, pp. 34–39.  Renan, *L'église chrétienne* (1879), p. 529 sq.  Dillmann
in Herzog's *Real-Enc.* 2nd ed. xii. 366 sq.

2. *Abraham.*  A short apocryphal book of Ἀβραάμ (consisting of 300 verses) occurs in the Stichometry of Nicephorus
and the *Synopsis Athanasii* (see p. 125).  And as in these
lists it is found in the very heart of the Jewish Apocrypha,
it is of course a different book from that of the ἀποκάλυψις
Ἀβραάμ which was in use among the Sethites (Epiphanius,
*Haer.* xxxix. 5).  On the other hand, it is no doubt the
former of these that Origen has in view in the case of those
statements regarding Abraham which he borrows from a
certain apocryphal work.

Origen, *In Lucam homil.* xxxv. *init.* (de la Rue, iii. 973 ; Lommatzsch,
v. 217) : Legimus, si tamen cui placet hujuscemodi scripturam recipere,
justitiae et iniquitatis angelos super Abrahami salute et interitu disceptantes
dum utraeque turmae suo eum voluunt coetui vendicare.

Comp. also Lücke, *Einl. in die Offenb. Joh.* p. 232 ; and for the Abra-
hamic legend generally, see vol. i. Div. ii. p. 343 ; and Fabricius, *Cod.*

*pseudepigr.* i. pp. 341–428, ii. p. 81 sq. B. Beer, *Leben Abrahams nach Auffassung der jüdischen Sage*, Leipzig 1859.

3. *Moses and his time.* The apocryphal literature regarding Moses himself has been already considered at p. 80. But among the books referring both to himself and his time there is still another work to be mentioned, the theme of which was a single episode in the lawgiver's life, we mean the Book of *Jannes and Jambres*, the two Egyptian magicians who, according to Ex. vii. 8 sqq., wrought miracles before Pharaoh equal to those of Moses and Aaron, but were nevertheless beaten in the end. The names are not mentioned in the Old Testament, but they occur at a comparatively early date in the legends, and they were known not only in Jewish, but in Gentile and Christian circles as well, as the names of the two famous Egyptian magicians in question. The orthography fluctuates exceedingly. In the Greek texts the prevailing spelling is Ἰαννῆς καὶ Ἰαμβρῆς, as in the Targum of Jonathan it is יניס וימבריס. In the Talmud, on the other hand, we find יוחני וממרא (Jochane and Mamre), while in the Latin texts the names are almost uniformly spelt Jannes (or Jamnes) et Mambres. What the original spelling was it is difficult to determine. In any case the names appear to be of Semitic origin (see Steiner in Schenkel's *Bibellex.* iii. 189; Riehm's *Wörterb.* p. 665 sq.; Orelli in Herzog's *Real-Enc.* vi. 478 sq.). The book written about the magicians in question is mentioned by Origen, and in the *Decretum Gelasii*. As the name of Jannes was known even to so early a writer as Pliny, and as it is probable that those anonymous personages owed their name and individuality first of all to the apocryphal book itself, we may perhaps venture to refer the date of the composition of this work to pre-Christian times.

For the *Rabbinical passages* referring to Jannes and Jambres, see Buxtorf's *Lex. Chald.* col. 945–947. Schoettgen, *Horae hebr.* note on 2 Tim. iii. 8. Wetstein, *Nov. Test.* note on same passage. Levy, *Chald. Wörterb.* i. 337. Idem, *Neuhebr. Wörterb.* ii. 226. The form יוחני וממרא is found in *Menachoth* lxxxv.[a]; יניס וימבריס in the *Targum of Jonathan* on Ex. i. 15.

vii. 11; Num. xxii. 22; and also יונוס ויומברוס (Jonos and Jombros) in the *Tanchuma* and *Sohar*.

Of *heathen writers* Pliny and Apuleius are acquainted with Jannes, while the neo-Platonist Numenius knows both Jannes and Jambres. (1) Pliny, *Hist. Nat.* xxx. 1. 11: Est et alia magices factio a Mose et Janne et Lotape ac Judaeis pendens, sed multis milibus annorum post Zoroastren. (2) Apuleius, *Apolog.* (or *De magia*) chap. xc. ed. Hildebrand: Ego ille sim Carinondas vel Damigeron vel is Moses vel Jannes vel Apollonius vel ipse Dardanus, vel quicumque alius post Zoroastren et Hostanen inter magos celebratus est. (3) Numenius in Eusebius, *Praep. evang.* ix. 8: Τὰ δ' ἑξῆς Ἰαννῆς καὶ Ἰαμβρῆς Αἰγύπτιοι ἱερογραμματεῖς, ἄνδρες οὐδένος ἥττους μαγεῦσαι κριθέντες εἶναι, ἐπὶ Ἰουδαίων ἐξελαυνομένων ἐξ Αἰγύπτου. Μουσαίῳ γοῦν τῷ Ἰουδαίων ἐξηγησαμένῳ, ἀνδρὶ γενομένῳ θεῷ εὔξασθαι δυνατωτάτῳ, οἱ παραστῆναι ἀξιωθέντες ὑπὸ τοῦ πλήθους τοῦ τῶν Αἰγυπτίων οὗτοι ἦσαν, τῶν τε συμφορῶν ἃς ὁ Μουσαῖος ἐπῆγε τῇ Αἰγύπτῳ, τὰς νεανικωτάτας αὐτῶν ἐπιλύεσθαι ὤφθησαν δυνατοί. In view of this passage Origen, *Contra Celsum,* iv. 51, says with regard to Numenius that: Ἐκτίθεται καὶ τὴν περὶ Μωϋσέως καὶ Ἰαννοῦ καὶ Ἰαμβροῦ ἱστορίαν. Owing to the circumstance that the term Μουσαῖος, which is here used for Moses, is precisely the same as that employed by the Hellenist Artapan, Freudenthal (*Alexander Polyhistor.* 1875, p. 173) is disposed to think that the story is borrowed from Artapan, and that he is the author of the legend. But this argument however cannot be regarded as conclusive. Then the names of the magicians, which in all probability are Semitic, seem rather to point to a Palestinian origin.

Then passing within the pale of *Christianity* the passage that first claims attention is 2 Tim. iii. 8: ὃν τρόπον δὲ Ἰαννῆς καὶ Ἰαμβρῆς ἀντέστησαν Μωϋσεῖ. Further, among Greek authors we may mention *Evang. Nicodemi* (=*Acta Pilati*), chap. v.; *Constitut. apostol.* viii. 1, and subsequent Fathers; but above all the hagiologist Palladius, who relates in his *Historia Lausiaca* (written about 420 A.D., see Fabricius-Harles, *Bibl. graec.* x. 98 sqq.) that Macarius visited the κηποτάφιον, which Jannes and Jambres had erected for themselves, and that he had an interview with the demons that had their abode there (see the passage in Fabricius, *Cod. pseudepigr.* ii. 106–111). *Latin* writers: The Latin text of the *Evang. Nicodemi* (=*Gesta Pilati*), chap. v.; *Abdiae hist. apostol.* vi. 15 (in Fabricius, *Cod. apocr. Nov. Test.* i. 622). Cyprian, *De unitate ecclesiae,* chap. xvi. The Latin translator of Origen in the passages to be quoted below. The *Decretum Gelasii* (in Credner, *Zur Gesch. des Kanon's,* p. 220) and subsequent Fathers. The Latin writers as well as the Western authorities for the text of 2 Tim. iii. 8 (Cod. *FG* and the text of the Itala) read Jannes (or Jamnes) et Mambres almost uniformly. See the various readings in connection with 2 Tim. iii. 8 in the critical editions of the New Testament; also Thilo, *Cod. apocr. Nov. Test.* p. 553, and the earlier literature given there. As the Talmud adopts the spelling ממרא, Westcott and Hort are warranted in observing, as they do in the note on 2 Tim. iii. 8 in their edition of the New Testament, that "the Western text probably derived Μαμβρῆς from a Palestinian source."

The Book of Jannes and Jambres (or Mambres) is mentioned: (1) By

Origen, *Ad Matth.* xxvii. 9 (de la Rue, iii. 916; Lommatzsch, v. 29): Quod ait, "sicut Jannes et Mambres restiterunt Mosi" non invenitur in publicis scripturis, sed in libro secreto, qui suprascribitur : Jannes et Mambres liber. (2) Again Origen, *Ad Matth.* xxiii. 37 (de la Rue, iii. 848; Lommatzsch, iv. 239), quotes 2 Tim. iii. 8: "sicut Jannes et Mambres restiterunt Mosi sic et isti resistunt veritati," as evidence that apocryphal writings are sometimes referred to in the New Testament. Nec enim scimus in libris canonizatis historiam de Janne et Mambre resistentibus Mosi. (3) It is also mentioned in the *Decretum Gelasii* (in Credner, *Zur Gesch. des Kanon's*, p. 220) : Liber, qui appellatur Poenitentia Jamnis et Mambre, apocryphus.

Comp. in general: Fabricius, *Codex pseudepigr. Vet. Test.* i. 813–825, ii. 105–111. Suicer, *Thesaurus*, under 'Ιαννῆς. Wolf, *Curae philol. in Nov. Test.* note on 2 Tim. iii. 8; and the commentaries generally on this passage. J. G. Michaelis, *De Janne et Jambre famosis Aegyptiorum magis*, Hal. 1747 The lexicons to the New Testament and the Bible Dictionaries of Winer, Schenkel, and Riehm. Rud. Hofmann, *Das Leben Jesu nach den Apokryphen* (1851), p. 352 sq. Orelli in Herzog's *Real-Enc.* 2nd ed. vi. 478 sq. Dillmann, *ibid.* xii. 365. Holtzmann, *Die Pastoralbriefe* (1880), p. 140 sq. Heath in *Palestine Exploration Fund, Quarterly Statement* 1881, pp. 311–317.

Whatever other works based on Biblical legends were in use in the early Church are either entirely unknown to us (such for example as the Book of Λάμεχ, quoted in the list of the Apocrypha edited by Montfaucon and Pitra, see p. 126), or they may, without hesitation, be regarded as Christian productions, as for instance the history of Noria the wife of Noah (Epiph. *Haer.* xxvi. 1), or the ἀναβαθμοὶ 'Ιακώβου (Epiph. *Haer.* xxx. 16), or the history of Asenath the wife of Joseph (according to Gen. xli. 45), which are still extant in various texts. What the Jewish substratum may have been in those instances it is impossible to make out with any degree of certainty, although there can scarcely be a doubt that Jewish *Books of Noah* for example were once to be met with. For further information regarding this whole literature, consult Fabricius, *Cod. pseudepigr.*, and Dillmann, art. "Pseudepigraphen," in Herzog's *Real-Enc.*

## VII. BOOKS OF MAGIC AND MAGICAL SPELLS.

By way of appendix to the above we may here mention further a class of literary productions which lie on the extreme confines of *Jewish* literature, and which serve to show that the superstition that had sprung from the soil of the heathen nature - religions also continued to flourish with no little vigour among the people of Israel: we refer to the books of magic and magic spells.  In the ancient world these represented the popular *arts of healing*.  As even in our own day Christians are often met with who prefer the quack doctor to the skilled physician, so in the ancient world, at least in that part of it that was under the influence of the East, there was often a tendency to have recourse to the *magician* and the *exorcist* rather than to the regular doctor in every sort of ailment.  It is interesting in this connection to hear for example what Celsus says about the Egyptians (in Origen, *Contra Cels.* viii. 58): " That some (higher) being or other controls things of even the most trifling nature, may be learnt from what is alleged by the Egyptians, who tell us that thirty-six (or as others affirm, a good many more) demons or divinities of the air have allotted among themselves the human body, which is supposed to be divided into a corresponding number of parts, and that each has taken one of these parts under his own peculiar charge.  And they know the names of the demons in their native tongue, such as Chnumen and Chachumen and Knat and Sikat and Biu and Eru and Erebui and Ramanor and Reinanoor, or whatever else they may be called.  By invoking these they cure the ailments of the different members of the body."  What Celsus here alleges with respect to the Egyptians is confirmed *mutatis mutandis* by hundreds of testimonies in regard to the rest of the ancient world as well.  Magic and exorcism, and that above all for curative purposes, were uncommonly popular and prevalent throughout the entire Roman Empire.  Nor did the *Jewish people* form an exception.  We know from the Old and New Testaments as well as from Josephus how extensively the various forms of magic prevailed also among them.  In later times *Solomon* was regarded as being above all the author of this art (on the strength of 1 Kings v. 12, 13).  Josephus informs us that this monarch composed and bequeathed to posterity certain incantations by means of which demons could be restrained and so effectually expelled that they would never re-enter the man again. By way of showing the efficacy of those incantations he tells a very amusing story about a Jew of the name of Eleazar who, on one occasion and in presence of Vespasian and his sons and several Roman officers, drew out a demon through the demoniac's nose by holding a magic ring under this organ and, repeating at the same time the incantations of Solomon, forbade him ever to enter again. At length, to prove that the demon was actually expelled, he ordered this latter to overturn a vessel of water that was near at hand, which order was at once complied with (Joseph. *Antt.* viii. 2. 5). From the way in which Josephus speaks of the Solomonic incantations we feel constrained to assume that they must have been *embodied in special books*. Origen distinctly alleges as much. Those books survived, although only after having undergone a variety of adaptations, till far on into the Middle Ages. We still hear of one of the name of Aaron being at the court of Manuel Comnenus, and who was in possession of a βίβλον Σολο-μώντειον by means of which whole legions of demons could be exorcised. This literature also found its way into *Christian circles*. The *Decretum Gelasii* knows of a *Contradictio Salomonis*, while a Christian *Testamentum Salomonis* is still extant. And it is through popular Christian works of this sort, that the knowledge of the efficacy of Solomon's magic spells has come down to more modern times and found its way into Goethe's *Faust* (the exorcising of the poodle : "Für solche halbe Höllenbrut Ist Salomonis Schlüssel gut ").

Official Judaism did not of course quite approve of those books of magic, although the Babylonian Talmud itself is full of superstition. According to a tradition, which is found both in the Mishna and in certain Byzantine writers (Suidas, Glycas), we learn that the pious king Hezekiah ordered the suppression of Solomon's "Book of Cures," because the people trusted it so much that they neglected to pray to God.

On the subject of magic in *the ancient world generally*, an abundant store of material is to be found in Georgii's art. "Magia," in Pauly's *Real-Encyc. der class. Alterthumswissensch.* iv. 1377–1418. On the same *among the Jews*, see the article "Zauberei," in the Bible dictionaries of Winer, Schenkel, and Riehm. On this subject in Talmudic Judaism again, see Brecher, *Das Transcendentale, Magie und magische Heilarten im Talmud*, Wien 1850. Joel, *Der Aberglaube und die Stellung des Judenthums zu demselben*, 1st part, Breslau 1881.

On Solomon, see Fabricius, *Codex pseudepigr. Vet. Test.* i. 1032–1063. The *Crypta ubi Salomon daemones torquebat* were still seen at Jerusalem by the pilgrim of Bordeaux in the fourth century A.D. (Tobler, *Palaestinae descriptiones*, 1869, p. 3).

Joseph. *Antt.* viii. 2. 5: 'Επῳδάς τε συνταξάμενος αἷς παρηγορεῖται τὰ νοσήματα, τρόπους ἐξορκώσεων κατέλιπεν, οἷς ἐνδούμενα τὰ δαιμόνια ὡς μηκέτ' ἐπανελθεῖν ἐκδιώκουσι κ.τ.λ. (here follows the story about Eleazar, referred to above).

Origen, *Ad. Matth.* xxvi. 63 (de la Rue, iii. 910 ; Lommatzsch, v. 7) : Quaeret aliquis, si convenit vel daemones adjurare ; et qui respicit ad multos, qui talia facere ausi sunt, dicet non sine ratione fieri hoc. Qui autem adspicit Jesum imperantem daemonibus, sed etiam potestatem dantem discipulis suis super omnia daemonia, et ut infirmitates sanarent, dicet quoniam non est secundum potestatem datam a Salvatore, adjurare daemonia ; Judaicum est enim. Hoc etsi aliquando a nostris tale aliquid, fiat, simile fit ei, quod a Salomone scriptis adjurationibus solent daemones adjurari. Sed ipsi, qui utuntur adjurationibus illis, aliquoties nec idoneis constitutis libris utuntur ; quibusdam autem et de Hebraeo acceptis adjurant daemonia.

On the βίβλον Σολομώντειον of Aaron in the time of Manuel Comnenus, see the passage from Nicetas Choniates quoted in Fabricus, *Cod. pseudepigr.* i. 1037 sq.

*Decretum Gelasii* (in Credner, *Zur Gesch. des Kanons*, p. 224), § 61 : Scriptura quae appellatur Contradictio Salomonis, apocr. *Ibid.* § 62 : Philacteria omnia quae non angelorum, ut illi confingunt, sed daemonum magis conscripta sunt nominibus apocr.

The Christian *Testamentum Salomonis* was published by Fleck, *Wissenschaftl. Reise durch Deutschland, Italien*, etc. vol. ii. 3 (1837), pp. 111–140. Also in Fürst's *Orient*, vols. v. and vii. A German translation was contributed by Bornemann (*Zeitschr. für die histor. Theol.* 1844, iii. pp. 9–56). Comp. also Bornemann, *Conjectanea in Salomonis Testamentum* (*Biblische Studien von Geistlichen des Königr. Sachsen*, second year 1843, pp. 45–60, for fourth year 1846, pp. 28–69). With regard to the date of its composition, comp. the passage from Leontius as given in Fabricius, *Cod. pseudepigr.* i. 1063 sq. In how strange a manner Jewish-Christian and heathen elements were all mixed up with each other may be seen for

example from two Greek manuscripts containing magical treatises which
were published by Parthey (*Transactions of the Berlin Academy*, 1865).

Mishna, *Pesachim* iv. 9: "Hezekiah concealed the book of cures (נגנ ספר
רפיאות), and the learned approved of this." Comp. the commentary of
Maimonides on this in Surenhusius's *Mishna* ii. 150, where it is expressly
stated that the tradition had in view Solomon's Book of Cures. Suidas
(Lex. under Έζεκίας): Ἦν Σολομῶνι βίβλος ἰαμάτων πάθους παντός, ἐγκεκο-
λαμμένη τῇ τοῦ ναοῦ φλιᾷ. Ταύτην ἐξεκόλαψεν Έζεκίας, οὐ προσέχοντος τοῦ
λαοῦ τῷ θεῷ διὰ τὸ τὰς θεραπείας τῶν παθῶν ἐνθένδε τοὺς πάσχοντας αὐτοὺς
κομίζεσθαι, περιορῶντας αἰτεῖν τὸν θεόν. Glycas in Fabricius, *Cod. pseudepigr.*
i. 1042 sq.

## § 33. THE GRAECO-JEWISH LITERATURE.

### *Preliminary Remarks.*

STILL more varied than the Palestinian-Jewish is the Graeco-Jewish literature. Scriptural and Rabbinic Judaism on the one hand, Greek philosophers, poets and historians on the other, form the factors, through whose co-operation a literature of the most motley and varied character sprang up upon the soil of the Jewish Dispersion; a literature many-sided with respect not only to its forms, but also to the standpoints taken up by its authors and the objects they pursued.

Hellenistic Judaism and its literature partake of the general intellectual and literary character of the period, viz. of that *Alexandrino-Roman epoch of Greek literature,* during which the latter left the soil of Greek nationality and became a universal literature.[1] For the nations of the Mediterranean region did not merely assimilate Greek culture, but also contributed on their part to the literary productivity of the age. In all lands authors made their appearance, whose Greek education prepared them to participate in every kind of literary effort, and whose co-operation imparted to Greek literature a cosmopolitan character; cosmopolitan in the twofold respect of origin and effect. The tide of the mental acquisitions of the East now flowed in increasingly upon Greek literature. Religion and philosophy received thence fresh impulses, poets and historians fresh material. And on the other hand the effect aimed at

[1] On its characteristics, comp. Dähne, *Geschichtliche Darstellung der jüd.-alexandr. Religionsphilosophie,* i. 1–15. Bernhardy, *Grundriss der griechischen Literatur,* vol. i. (4th edit. 1876) pp. 498–577. Volkmann, art. "Alexandriner," in Pauly's *Real-Enc.* i. 1 (2nd edit.), pp. 743–753 (where other literature is also given). Nicolai, *Griech. Literaturgeschichte,* vol. ii. (1876) p. 80 sq.

was also cosmopolitan, for they, who now took pen in hand, wrote not only for the little nation of the Greeks, but for the educated classes throughout the world.

In this literary productivity Hellenized Jews also took a part. And what has just been said applies to them above all others, viz. that they introduced a new element into Greek literature. The religious knowledge of Israel, which had hitherto been the possession of only a small circle, now brought its influence to bear in the department of Greek literature. The religious faith of Israel, its history and its great and sacred past, were depicted in the forms and with the means furnished by the literary culture of the Greeks, and thus made accessible to the whole world. Such Jews wrote not only for their compatriots and co-religionists, but for the purpose of making known to all mankind the illustrious history of Israel and its pre-eminent religious enlightenment.

*The connection between their own national culture and that of the Greeks* was of course, in the case of the Jews as well as of other Orientals, no merely external one. Judaism and Hellenism now really entered upon a process of mutual internal amalgamation.[2] Judaism, which in its unyielding Pharisaic phase appears so rigidly exclusive, proved itself uncommonly pliable and accommodating upon the soil of Hellenism, and allowed a far-reaching influence to the ascendant Greek spirit. The Hellenistic Jews were as unwilling as others to let themselves be deprived of that common possession of the entire educated world, the great poets, philosophers and historians of Greece. They too derived from the living spring of the Greek classics that human culture, which seemed to the ancient world the supreme good. Under its influence however Judaism imperceptibly underwent a change. It stripped itself of its particularistic character. It discovered that there were true

---

[2] On Hellenistic Judaism in general, comp. Dähne, *Geschichtliche Darstellung*, i. 15 sqq. Lutterbeck, *Die neutestamentlichen Lehrbegriffe*, i. 99–120. Herzfeld, *Gesch. des Volkes Jisrael*, iii. 425–579. Ewald, *Gesch. des Volkes Israel*, iv. 303 sqq. Siegfried, *Philo*, etc. pp. 1–27. The same, " Der jüdische Hellenismus" (*Zeitschr. für wissensch. Theol.* 1875, pp. 465–489).

and Divine thoughts in the literature of the heathen world and appropriated them, it embraced all men as brethren, and desired to lead all, who were still walking in darkness, to the knowledge of the truth.

But while the Jews were thus, like other Orientals, becoming Greeks, it was at the same time seen that Judaism was something very different from the heathen religions. Its internal *power of resistance* was incomparably greater than theirs. While the other Oriental religions were merged in the general religious medley of the times, Judaism maintained itself essentially inviolate. It adhered strictly and firmly to the unity of the Godhead and the repudiation of all images in worship, and maintained the belief that God's dealings with mankind tend to a blissful end. Judaism by thus firmly adhering, in presence of the pressure exercised by Hellenism, to that which formed its essence, proved the pre-eminence of its religious strength.

The consciousness of this pre-eminence impresses its character upon the Graeco-Jewish literature. It pursues for the most part the *practical aim* of not only strengthening its co-religionists and making them acquainted with their great past, but also of convincing its non-Jewish readers of the folly of heathenism and of persuading them of the greatness of Israel's history and of the futility of all attacks upon that nation. Great part of it is therefore in the most comprehensive sense apologetic. In the predominance of the practical aim it is akin to the Palestinian. For as the latter has chiefly in view the strengthening and reviving of fidelity to the law, the Graeco-Jewish literature at least for the most part pursues the object of inspiring the non-Jewish world with respect for the people and the religion of Israel, nay if possible of bringing them to embrace the latter.

The *chief seat* of Hellenistic Judaism, and consequently of Graeco-Jewish literature, was Alexandria, the capital of the Ptolemies, which through their exertions had been raised to the first rank as a place of scholarship in the Hellenistic period.

The means of culture afforded by the age were here at disposal in a profusion not to be found elsewhere; while at the same time Jews were nowhere else found living together in so great numbers out of Palestine. Hence there was an inward necessity that Hellenic Judaism should here reach its utmost prosperity, and its literature be here chiefly cultivated. But it would be a mistake to suppose that such pursuits were cultivated *only* in Alexandria. They were indeed by no means specifically " Alexandrine," but the common possession of Hellenistic, that is extra-Palestinian Judaism in general. Nay even in Palestine they found advocates, although the Maccabean movement opposed a strong barrier to the encroachments of this tendency.[3]

The diversity both in literary form and theological standpoint of the works now to be discussed is chiefly dependent on their greater adherence, now to scriptural types, now to Greek models. Between the two extremes here mentioned however are found a great variety of productions, which it is difficult to subject to definite classification. The following groups may perhaps be most fitly distinguished.

### I. TRANSLATIONS OF THE HOLY SCRIPTURES.

#### 1. *The Septuagint.*

The foundation of all Judaeo-Hellenistic culture is the ancient anonymous Greek translation of the Scriptures, known by the name of the *Septuagint* (οἱ ἑβδομήκοντα, septuaginta interpretes), and preserved entire by the tradition of the Christian Church; Hellenistic Judaism is as inconceivable without it as the evangelical Church of Germany without Luther's translation of the Bible.[4]

[3] Comp. on Hellenistic Judaism in Palestine, especially Freudenthal, *Alexander Polyhistor* (1875), pp. 127–129.

[4] The name " Septuagint " referred in the first place to the translation of the Pentateuch, but was afterwards transferred to the other books also.

The single name must not mislead us to the notion, that we have here to deal with a single work *not only the work of different authors, but the work also of different times* being subsequently comprised under this name. The oldest part is the translation of *the Pentateuch,* of the origin of which the so-called Epistle of Aristeas gives a detailed narrative. King Ptolemy II. Philadelphus (283–247 B.C.) was induced by his librarian Demetrius Phalereus to have the laws of the Jews also translated into Greek for his library. At his request the Jewish high priest Eleasar sent him seventy-two able men, six out of each tribe, by whose labours the whole was finished in seventy-two days (for particulars, see No. VII.). The historical nature of this account, embellished as it is by a multitude of graphic details, is now generally given up. The only question is whether the foundation of the fictitious embellishment may not perhaps be some historical tradition, the essence of which was, that the translation of the Jewish law into Greek was projected by Ptolemy Philadelphus at the instance of Demetrius Phalereus.[5] This would in itself be very possible. For the learned and literary zeal of the Ptolemies and especially of Ptolemy Philadelphus would certainly make it conceivable, that he should wish to incorporate the law of the Jews also in his library. In favour of this view may also be cited the circumstance, that the Jewish philosopher Aristobulus, in the time of Ptolemy VI. Philometor, relates just what we have designated as the possible essence of the tradition, without betraying any acquaintance with the fictitious embellishments of the Epistle of Aristeas, which seems to show that he was following some tradition quite independent of the said Epistle.[6] It is how-

[5] So *e.g.* Wellhausen in his revision of Bleek's *Einleitung in das Alte Testament* (4th ed. 1878), p. 571 sqq.

[6] The passage from Aristobulus is given in Euseb. *Praep. evang.* xiii. 12, 1–2 (ed. Gaisford). Aristobulus is here speaking of the fact, that Plato was already acquainted with the Jewish legislation. To show the possibility of this he asserts, that its virtual contents had been translated into Greek before Demetrius Phalereus. Then he continues : ʹΗ δʹ ὅλη ἑρμηνεία

ever suspicious, that according to a very trustworthy account, Demetrius Phalereus did not live at the court of Ptolemy at all, but had already been banished by him from Alexandria immediately after the death of Ptolemy Lagos.[7] Thus the supposed essence of the tradition also falls, and there remains merely a bare possibility that the Septuagint translation of the Pentateuch owes its origin to the literary efforts of Ptolemy Philadephus. It is also as possible, that it was called forth by the exigencies of the Jews themselves. For Jews, who had at heart the maintenance of an acquaintance with the law even among the Dispersion, observing that the knowledge of the sacred language was more and more decreasing, and that the Jews of the Dispersion were appropriating Greek as their mother tongue, might feel themselves induced to translate the law into Greek for the purpose of preserving the knowledge of it among Greek Jews also. This translation, having been in the first place undertaken as a private labour, gradually obtained official validity also. But obscure as is the origin of the translation, it may be safely admitted, on internal grounds, that its *locality was Alexandria* and its date the third century before Christ, for the Hellenist Demetrius, who wrote in the time of Ptolemy IV. (222–205), certainly made use of it (see below, No. III.).

The preceding remarks apply only to the translation of the Pentateuch, to which alone the Aristeas legend refers. But after the sacred Thorah had once been made accessible to Hellenistic Jews, the need of possessing the rest of the Scriptures in the Greek tongue was gradually experienced. Hence translations first of the *prophets* and afterwards of the *Hagiographa* followed. These too chiefly originated in Egypt.

---

τῶν διὰ τοῦ νόμου πάντων ἐπὶ τοῦ προσαγορευθέντος Φιλαδέλφου βασιλέως, σοῦ δὲ προγόνου, προσενεγκαμένου μείζονα Φιλοτιμίαν, Δημητρίου τοῦ Φαληρέως πραγματευσαμένου τὰ περὶ τούτων.

[7] The authority for this is Hermippus Callimachus, who lived under Ptolemy III. and IV. See the passage from Diogenes Laert. v. 78, in Müller, *Fragm. hist. graec.* iii. 47, and in the same work, p. 48, the discussions on the credibility of the information.

Some of the Hagiographa, such as the Book of Daniel and some of the psalms, not having been composed till the era of the Maccabees, the Greek translations of these more recent Hagiographa cannot have been made earlier than about the middle of the second century before Christ. It seems however that in fact the translations into Greek of the bulk of the Hagiographa together with the prophets were at about this time already in existence. Sirach the grandson of Jesus, who came to Egypt in the year 132, excuses the defects of his translation by the fact, that what is said in Hebrew does not retain the same meaning when translated into another language, which is, he says, the case not only in his work, but also in the Law and the Prophets and the other Scriptures (Wisdom, Prolog.: οὐ γὰρ ἰσοδυναμεῖ αὐτὰ ἐν ἑαυτοῖς ἑβραϊστὶ λεγόμενα καὶ ὅταν μεταχθῇ εἰς ἑτέραν γλῶσσαν· οὐ μόνον δὲ ταῦτα, ἀλλὰ καὶ αὐτὸς ὁ νόμος καὶ αἱ προφητεῖαι καὶ τὰ λοιπὰ τῶν βιβλίων οὐ μικρὰν ἔχει τὴν διαφορὰν ἐν ἑαυτοῖς λεγόμενα). Hence he evidently was already acquainted with a translation of the Prophets and the "other Scriptures." The Septuagint translation of Chronicles was certainly known to Eupolemus, who wrote about the middle of the second century before Christ (see below, paragraph 3, and Freudenthal, *Alexander Polyhistor*, p. 119); that of the Book of Job to the historian Aristeas, whose date it must be admitted is not exactly known, but who, being quoted by Alexander Polyhistor, must have lived at latest in the first half of the first century before Christ (see below, No. III., and Freudenthal, *Alexander Polyhistor*, p. 139).[8]

After what has been said no further proof of all these translations being of Jewish origin is needed. The character of the translation differs widely in the different books, being now tolerably free, now helplessly verbal, but chiefly the latter. As yet a precise investigation has been made only

---

[8] Grätz insists, on utterly insufficient grounds, on transposing the translation of Job to the first century after Christ (*Monatsschr. für Gesch. und Wissensch. des Judenthums*, 1877, pp. 83–91).

of individual books. A special difficulty in such investigation lies in the fact, that it is often necessary to reconstruct
the Hebrew text, which must have been in the hands of the
translators. In one point however all these works are alike,
viz. in the barbarous Greek produced under the influence of
the Hebrew originals. *Quite a new language, swarming with
such strong Hebraisms that a Greek could not understand it,* is
here created. Not to mention the imitation of Hebrew
constructions, many Greek words, which correspond to *one*
meaning of a Hebrew word, are without further ceremony
made equivalent to the *whole extent* of the meanings comprised in the Hebrew word, and thus significations are forced
upon words, which they do not at all possess in Greek (*e.g.* the
words δόξα, εἰρήνη and many others). How far colloquial
intercourse with Hellenized Jews may have anticipated the
labours of the translators cannot be determined. It is
probable that an alternative action here took place. Much
which the translators ventured upon was already found by
them in colloquial language. But then the reaction upon the
development of Judaic Greek exercised by a translation, which
came into general use, would at the least be quite as great.

For the translations in question were not only combined
into a whole, but were also *universally accepted by the Jews of
the Dispersion as their text of Scripture.* The oldest Hellenists,
Demetrius and Eupolemus, in their compilations of Scripture
history rely solely upon the Septuagint; Philo throughout
assumes it, Josephus does so for the most part. With Philo
the text of the Septuagint is so far a sacred text, that he
argues from its casual details, nay, not only did this translation universally penetrate into private use, but it was also used
as Holy Scripture in the synagogue service (see vol. ii. Div. ii.
p. 285). It was then transferred from the hands of the Jews
to the Christian Church and regarded by it as the authentic
text of Scripture. But the very circumstance of the Christian
Church taking possession of this translation and deriving
thence its polemical weapons in its conflict with the Jews,

gradually co-operated in bringing the Septuagint into discredit with them and in giving rise to new Jewish translations, especially that of Aquila, which in the time of Origen stood in higher respect with the Jews than did the Septuagint.

*The text* of the Septuagint has come down to us solely by the tradition of the Christian Church. In its history the learned labours of Origen, which finally—and not without his own fault—led to a base corruption of the text, are epoch-making. Origen, on account of the uncertainty of the Septuagint text, and its great deviations from the Hebrew, prepared a large edition of the Bible, in which were written, in six adjacent columns: (1) The Hebrew text in Hebrew characters; (2) the Hebrew text in Greek characters; (3) the translation of Aquila; (4) that of Symmachus; (5) the Septuagint; (6) the translation of Theodotion, and indeed in this order (see Hieronymus, *Comment. in Tit.* iii. 9 [*Opp.* ed. Vallarsi, vii. 1. 734]; Epiphan. *de mensuris et ponderibus*, § 19, and the other evidences in Field, *Origenis hexaplorum quae supersunt prolegom.* p. 50). This was to lay a sure foundation for learned Scripture exegesis, and especially for learned controversy against the Jews, who often reproached Christians with their ignorance of the genuine text of Scripture (see on the motive and object of his undertaking, Origen, *Comment. in Matth.* vol. xv. c. xiv.; *epist. ad African.* § 5). The work, affording a sixfold Scripture text, was called *the Hexapla*. Origen also prepared another edition without the two Hebrew columns, which was called *the Tetrapla* (Euseb. *Hist. eccl.* vi. 16). On the other hand it was also called *Octapla*, because in certain books of the Old Testament two anonymous Greek translations were added to the above-named six texts (Epiphan. *de mensuris et ponderibus*, § 19 ; Euseb. *Hist. eccl.* vi. 16. Comp. on the whole work the Prolegomena in Field, *Origenis Hexaplorum quae supersunt*, 2 vols. Oxonii 1875, and the Introductions to the Old Test. of *e.g.* De Wette-Schrader, § 56 ; Bleek-Wellhausen, § 282). The fatal circumstance was, that Origen was not content with placing the text of the Septuagint in juxtaposition with the others, but, to facilitate its use, *noted in the Septuagint text itself the deviations from the Hebrew* by (*a*) furnishing such words, sentences, or paragraphs as were missing in the Hebrew with an obelus (the sign of erasure), and (*b*) *by interpolating, with the addition of an asterisk, from other translations, and mostly from Theodotion*, those found in the Hebrew and missing in the Septuagint (see his own remarks in his *Comment. in Matth* vol. xv. c. xiv. [Lommatzsch, iii. 357] : καί τινα μὲν ὠβελίσαμεν ἐν τῷ ἑβραϊκῷ μὴ κείμενα, οὐ τολμήσαντες αὐτὰ πάντη περιελεῖν· τινὰ δὲ μετ᾽ ἀστερίσκων προσεθήκαμεν. Hieronymus, *Praef. in vers. Paralipom.* [ed. Vallarsi, ix. 1407 sq.]: sed, quod majoris, audaciae est, in editione Septuaginta Theodotionis editionem miscuit, asteriscis designans quae minus ante fuerant, et virgulis, quae ex superfluo videbantur apposita). He often proceeded also in a similar manner with inaccurate translations of the LXX. " by adding with an asterisk, behind the obelized reading of the LXX., the parallel passages corresponding with the Hebrew from another version" (Bleek-Wellhausen, p. 586). This text then, especially copied from the Hexapla, and often showing very careless dealing with the critical marks, being disseminated since Eusebius (see Field, *Proleg.* p. 99), a mass of such "hexaplarian" readings was introduced into the traditional text of the Septuagint; the common text (κοινὴ ἔκδοσις) being corrected by this hexaplarian one. The exclusion of hexaplarian additions is therefore the chief task of Septuagint criticism; and this is still approximately attainable for most of the books of the Old Testament, the critical notes of Origen being still extant, partly in certain Greek manuscripts, partly in the Syriac translation of the hexaplarian Septuagint text (see Bleek-Wellhausen, *Einl. in das A. T.* pp. 593, 588 sqq.). The inserted matter has been very completely collected in Field, *Origenis Hexaplorum quae supersunt, sive veterum interpretum Graecorum in totum Vetus Testamentum fragmenta*, 2 vols. Oxonii 1875. By the separation however from the hexaplarian text of the Septuagint of the passages marked with an asterisk, the original text is by no means obtained. The MSS. already varied very much in the time of Origen (see *Comment. in Matth.* vol. xv. c. xiv., ed. Lommatzsch, iii. 357). Origen first compiled from them a text for himself, and then quietly altered, according to the Hebrew, many particulars in it, which could not be made known by obelus or asterisk (Field, p. 60 sqq.). Hence such a proceeding will only obtain the *Recension of Origen*.

Others besides Origen have occupied themselves with learned labours upon the text of the Septuagint. We know especially of two other recensions, those of Hesychius and Lucianus; the former of these was disseminated in Egypt, the latter from Antioch to Constantinople (Hieronymus, *praef. in vers. Paralipom.*, ed Vallarsi, ix. 1405 sq.: Alexandria et Egypta in Septuaginta suis Hesychium laudat auctorem. Constantinopolis usque Antiochiam Luciani Martyris exemplaria probat. Mediae inter has provinciae Palestinos codices legunt, quos ab Origine elaboratos Eusebius et Pamphilus vulgaverunt; totusque orbis hac inter se trifaria varietate compugnat). Hesychius is perhaps identical with the Egyptian bishop of this name, who suffered martyrdom in the persecution of Maximinus, 312 (Euseb. *Hist. eccl.* viii. 13. 7). No particulars are known concerning the nature of his recension. Lucianus was the noted presbyter of Antioch, who also suffered martyrdom in the persecution of Maximinus, 312 (Euseb. *Hist. eccl.* viii. 13. 2, ix. 6. 3). His recension was an emendation of the Septuagint according to the Hebrew with the help of other Greek translations (Suidas, *Lex. s.v.*: Λουκιανὸς ὁ μάρτυς· αὐτὸς ἀπάσας [*scil.* τὰς ἱερὰς βίβλους] ἀναλαβὼν ἐκ τῆς Ἑβραΐδος αὐτὰς ἐπανενεώσατο γλώττης, ἣν καὶ αὐτὴν ἠκριβωκὼς ἐς τὰ μάλιστα ἦν). Comp. Field, *Proleg.* cap. ix. Harnack in Herzog's *Real-Enc.* 2nd ed. viii. 767 sqq. on "Hesychius and Lucianus." Also the Introductions to the Old Testament, *e.g.* De Wette-Schrader, § 57 ; Bleek-Wellhausen, § 283. According to the recent investigations of Field and Lagarde (see *Theol. Litztg.* 1876, p. 605), the recension of Lucianus is still preserved in several MSS. Lagarde has edited the text according to these (one volume has as yet appeared, *Librorum Veteris Testamenti canonicorum pars* 1 *graece edita*, Götting. 1883).

The labours however of Hesychius and Lucianus have but contributed to further confusion in the text of the Septuagint. For the text of the κοινή is now not only mixed up with the Hexapla text, but also with those of Hesychius and Lucianus, and the former having been, even in the text of Origen, very uncertain, there is no longer any prospect of a certain recovery of the *original* text of the Septuagint. It is true that being still acquainted with the chief recensions, we are in a position safely to pronounce judgment as to which of the MSS. is comparatively freest from the peculiarities of these recensions, and therefore represents with the greatest comparative purity the original text. The *old Latin texts* also furnish important assistance.

Among those Greek *manuscripts,* which contain the whole Old Testament or at least a great part of it, the *Vaticanus* (1209) is acknowledged to hold the first rank with respect to the purity of the text. Its text has been ostensibly published by Mai (*Vetus et Novum Testamentum ex antiquissimo codice Vaticano,* 5 vols. Rome 1857). His edition is however very untrustworthy. More accurate is the new Roman *édition de luxe* in facsimile type (*Bibliorum Sacrorum Graecus codex Vaticanus,* edd. Vercellone and Cozza, 6 vols. Rom 1868–1881, price of each vol. £6 ; comp. also *Theol. Litztg.* 1882, p. 121). Next to the Vaticanus must be mentioned the *Sinaiticus,* discovered by Tischendorf in the year 1859, of which about half of the Old Testament has been preserved. *Edition de luxe, Bibliorum Codex Sinaiticus Petropolitanus,* ed. Tischendorf, 4 vols. Petersburg 1862. Tischendorf had previously discovered a smaller portion of this manuscript, and published it under the title of Frederico-Augustanus (*Codex Frederico-Augustanus,* ed. Tischen-

dorf, Lips. 1846).—The Alexandrinus, which is already much
infected by hexaplarian readings, ranks third among these great
Bible manuscripts. It forms the foundation of Grabe's edition
of the Septuagint. The *Vetus Testamentum Graecum e Codice
MS. Alexandrino, cura Henrici Herveii Baber*, 3 vols. London
1812–1826, gives the text of the MS. itself. Recently an
edition has been prepared in photo-lithographic facsimile, of
which the portion comprising the New Testament has been
first issued (*Facsimile of the Codex Alexandrinus, New Testament
and Clementine Epistles, published by order of the Trustees*,
London 1879; comp. *Theol. Litztg.* 1880, p. 230).—The Old
Testament appeared in 3 vols. 1881 sqq. Comp. also on
the manuscripts the Prolegomena of the editions, especially
Holmes - Parsons and Tischendorf. The publications of
Tischendorf (*Monumenta sacra inedita*) and Ceriani (*Monumenta
sacra et profana*) contain much material.

Bibliographical information concerning the numerous editions
of the Septuagint will be found in Le Long, *Bibliotheca sacra*,
ed. Masch. vol. ii. 2, 1781, pp. 262–304. Fabricius, *Bibliotheca
graeca*, ed. Harles, iii. 673 sqq. Rosenmüller, *Handbuch für die
Literatur der bibl. Kritik und Exegese*, vol. ii. 1798, pp. 279–322.
Winer, *Handbuch der Theol. Literatur*, i. 47 sq. Frankel,
*Vorstudien zu der Septuaginta*, 1841, pp. 242–252. Tischendorf, Prolegomena to his edition. De Wette-Schrader, *Einleitung
in das A. T.* § 58. All the editions fall back upon the following
four chief editions: (1) The Complutensian Polyglot, 6 vols.
*in Complutensi universitate*, 1514–1517. (2) The Aldina, *Sacrae
Scripturae Veteris Novaeque omnia*, Venice 1518. (3) The
Roman or Sixtine edition, *Vetus Testamentum juxta Septuaginta
ex auctoritate Sixti V. Pont. Max. editum*, Rome 1587. The
text of this edition is relatively the best among the printed
texts, conforming as it does frequently, though by no means
entirely, to the Vaticanus, 1209. Since the majority of the
more recent editions reproduce this Sixtine text, the printed
common text is a relatively good one. (4) Grabe's edition,
*Septuaginta Interpretum*, vols. i.–iv. ed. Grabe, Oxonii 1707–1720.
It chiefly follows the Codex Alexandrinus. Of recent editions
the most important is *Vetus Testamentum Graecum*, edd. Holmes
and Parsons, 5 vols. Oxonii 1798–1827. The text is reproduced
from the Sixtine edition, but accompanied by an unusually
copious collection of manuscript various readings. Though
what is offered is not quite trustworthy, and rather confuses than
instructs by its copiousness, still this edition has the merit of
having for the first time brought forward the material furnished
by the MSS. in general (comp. Bleek and Wellhausen, *Einl. in
das A. T.* p. 592 sq.). The manual edition of Tischendorf, *Vetus
Testamentum Graece juxta LXX. interpretes*, 2 vols. Lips. 1850,

2nd ed. 1880, also gives the Sixtine text with only unimportant corrections. Nestle has added to the sixth edition a collation of the Vaticanus and Sinaiticus, as well as of the Alexandrinus already collated by Tischendorf (*Veteris Testamenti Graeci codices Vaticanus et Sinaiticus cum textu recepto collati ab E. Nestle*, Lips. 1880).

The literature on the Septuagint is almost unbounded (comp. Fabricius-Harles, *Biblioth. gr.* iii. 658 sqq. Rosenmüller, *Handb. für die Literatur der bibl. Kritik und Exegese*, ii. 395 sqq. De Wette-Schrader, *Einl. in das A. T.* § 51 sqq. Fritzsche in Herzog's *Real-Enc.* 2 vols. i. 280 sqq.). The chief work of earlier date is: Hody, *De bibliorum textibus originalibus, versionibus Graecis et Latina vulgata*, Oxon. 1705. Of recent times may be mentioned: (1) On single books, Thiersch, *De Pentateuchi versione Alexandrina*, Erlang. 1841. Hollenberg, *Der Charakter der alexandrinischen Uebersetzung des Buches Josua und ihr textkritischer Werth*, Moers 1876 (Gymnasialprogr.). Wichelhaus, *De Jeremiae versione Alexandrina*, Halis 1847. Vollers, *Das Dodekapropheten der Alexandriner*, 1st half, Berlin 1880. The same in Stade's *Zeitschr. für die alttestamentl. Wissensch.* vol. iii. 1883, pp. 219–272, vol. iv. 1884, pp. 1–20. Lagarde, *Anmerkungen zur griechischen Uebersetzung der Proverbien*, Leipzig 1863. Bickell, *De indole ac ratione versionis Alex. in interpretando libro Jobi*, Marb. 1863. (2) On the whole: Frankel, *Vorstudien zu der Septuaginta*, Leipzig 1841. Herzfeld, *Gesch. des Volkes Jisrael*, iii. 465 sqq., 534–556. Ewald, *Gesch. des Volkes Israel*, iv. 322 sqq. Gfrörer, *Philo*, ii. 8–18. Dähne, *Geschichtliche Darstellung der jüd.-alex. Religions-Philosophie*, ii. 1–72. Fritzsche, art. " Alexandrinische Uebersetzung des A. T.," in Herzog's *Real-Enc.* 2nd ed. i. 280–290. The Introductions to the Old Testament of Eichhorn, Bertholdt, Hävernick, Keil and others, especially De Wette, *Lehrbuch der hist.-krit. Einl. in die kanon und apokr. Bücher des A. T.* viii., edited by Schrader (1869), § 51–58. Bleek, *Einleitung in das Alte Testament*, 4th ed., superintended by Wellhausen (1878), pp. 571–598. Reuss, *Gesch. der heil. Schriften Alten Testaments* (1881), § 436–439.

## 2. *Aquila and Theodotion.*

The Septuagint translation was indisputably regarded as the sacred text of the Scriptures by Hellenistic Jews down to the beginning of the second century after Christ. The period of its ascendancy is at the same time that of the prime of Hellenistic Judaism. Subsequently to the second century the latter entered upon a slow but continuous course of retrogression, which—to leave out of consideration the limits prescribed to the encroachments of Judaism by political legislation—was mainly brought about by the co-operation of two factors, viz. the increased power of Rabbinic Judaism and the victorious advance of Christianity. A significant symptom in this movement was *the new Greek translations of the Bible, the object of which was to place in the hand of Greek-speaking Jews a text in conformity with the authorized Hebrew one.* It is true, that on the one hand the undertaking of such translations was a proof of the still existing strength and importance of Hellenistic Judaism. On the other hand however they show, that Hebrew authority had now attained acceptance and acknowledgment in a far stricter sense than formerly in the region of Hellenistic Judaism. The Jews of the Dispersion were renouncing their own culture and placing themselves under the guardianship of the Rabbins. These translations are at the same time a monument in the history of the struggle between Judaism and Christianity. They were to place in the hands of the Jews a polemical weapon in their contest with Christian theologians, who were making the most of the very uncertain Septuagint text in their own cause (comp. especially Justin, *Dial. c. Tryph.* c. 68, *s. fin.*, 71 and elsewhere).

Of the three Greek translations of the Bible, which Origen placed in his Hexapla of the Septuagint (Aquila, Symmachus and Theodotion, see above, p. 164) only Aquila and Theodotion will here engage our notice; for Symmachus was, according to Euseb. *Hist. eccl.* vi. 17, an Ebionite and therefore a Christian. Of Theodotion too it is not certain whether he was a Jew. Aquila on the contrary is unanimously designated as such, and indeed as a proselyte.

According to Irenaeus, who is the first to mention Aquila, he was a Jewish proselyte of Pontus. The statement with respect to his native land is, by reason of its striking parallel with Acts xviii. 2, somewhat suspicious, though Epiphanius more precisely names Sinope in Pontus as his home. On the

other hand it seems certain—notwithstanding his thorough
knowledge of Hebrew—that Aquila was a proselyte.　For he
is designated as such (עֲקִילָס הַגֵּר) not only by all the Fathers,
but also in the Jerusalem Talmud and in Rabbinic literature
in general.　Of the fables related of him by Epiphanius—
that he was a relation (πενθερίδης) of the Emperor Hadrian,
that he at first turned Christian, then was excluded from the
Christian Church on account of his inclination to astrology
and became a Jew—thus much is credible, that he lived in
the time of Hadrian.　Rabbinical tradition also places him in
the time of R. Elieser, R. Joshua and R. Akiba, and thus in the
first decades of the second century after Christ.　The aim of
his translation was to imitate the Hebrew text as exactly as
possible, so that he not only ventured upon the bold formation
of a multitude of new words, for the purpose of obtaining
Greek terms, which should exactly correspond with Hebrew
ones, but he slavishly rendered Hebrew particles by Greek
particles, even when their meaning did not allow it (for proof
of this see Field and others).　A noted example ridiculed by
Jerome is, that in the very first sentence of Genesis he rendered
the sign of the accusative אֵת by σύν (σὺν τὸν οὐρανὸν καὶ
σὺν τὴν γῆν).　This attention to the most trifling detail may
perhaps be referred to the influence of Akiba, whose pupil
Aquila is said to have been.　Jerome often mentions a *prima*
and *secunda editio* of Aquila.　And the numerous passages in
which two different translations are referred to Aquila
(collected in Field), confirm the existence of two different
editions of the work.　On account of its close accordance
with the Hebrew text the work was at its first appearance
favoured by R. Elieser and R. Joshua the eminent Rabbinical
authorities, and was, as testified by Origen and also indirectly
confirmed by Justinian's 146th *Novella*, soon much preferred
to the LXX. by Hellenistic Jews.　About a dozen passages
are quoted from it in Rabbinic literature.　The work as a
whole perished with Rabbinic Judaism.　For what remains
of it we are indebted to its admission into Origen's Hexapla.

Numerous notices of Aquila's translation are preserved from
the latter work, some by quotations in Eusebius, Jerome and
other Fathers, who still made use of the original Hexapla in
the library of Pamphilus at Caesarea (Hieron. *comment. in Tit.*
iii. 9, ed. Vallarsi, vii. 1. 734), some in marginal notes in the
MSS. of the Hexaplarian Septuagint text.

Irenaeus, iii. 21. 1 (in Greek in Eusebius, *H. E.* v. 8. 10): ἀλλ'
οὐχ ὡς ἔνιοί φασι τῶν νῦν τολμώντων μεθερμηνεύειν τὴν γραφήν· "ἰδοὺ ἡ
νεᾶνις ἐν γαστρὶ ἔξει καὶ τέξεται υἱόν," ὡς Θεοδοτίων ἡρμήνευσεν ὁ Ἐφέσιος
καὶ Ἀκύλας ὁ Ποντικὸς, ἀμφότεροι Ἰουδαῖοι προσήλυτοι. Eusebius,
*Demonstr. evang.* vii. 1. 32, ed. Gaisford (p. 316, ed. Paris):
προσήλυτος δὲ ὁ Ἀκύλας ἦν, οὐ φύσει Ἰουδαῖος. Epiphanius, *De
mensuris et ponderibus*, § 14, 15.

Hieronymus, *Epist.* 57 *ad Pammachium*, c. 11 (*Opp.* ed.
Vallarsi, i. 316): Aquila autem proselytus et contentiosus
interpres, qui non solum verba sed etymologias quoque verborum
transferre conatus est, jure projicitur a nobis. Quis enim pro
frumento et vino et oleo possit vel legere vel intelligere χεῦμα,
ὀπωρισμόν, σιλπνότητα, quod nos possumus dicere fusionem poma-
tionem et splendentiam. Aut quia Hebraei non solum habent
ἄρθρα sed et πρόαρθρα, ille κακοζήλως et syllabas interpretatur et
literas dicitque σὺν τὸν οὐρανὸν καὶ σὺν τὴν γῆν, quod Graeca et
Latina lingua omnino non recipit. Jerome generally gives a
very favourable opinion of the accuracy and trustworthiness of
Aquila. See *Epist.* 32 *ad Marcellam* (Vallarsi, i. 152), *Comm.
in Jesaj.* xlix. 5, 6 (Vallarsi, iv. 564), *Comm. in Hoseam* ii.
16, 17 (Vallarsi, vi. 656). See the passages of Jerome in which
he mentions the *prima* and *secunda editio* of Aquila, in Field,
*Origenis Hexaplae quae supersunt, proleg.* p. xxv. sq.

Talmud jer. *Megilla* i. 11, fol. 71ᶜ: תירגם עקילם הגר התורה
לפני ר' אליעזר ולנפי ר' יהושע וקילסו אותו ואמרו לו יפיפית מבני אדם,
"Aquila the proselyte translated the Thorah in the time of R.
Elieser and R. Joshua; and they praised him and said to him,
'Thou art the fairest among the children of men'" (Ps. xlv. 3,
with an allusion to the translation of the Thorah into the
Japhetic). Jer. *Kiddushin* i. 1, fol. 59ᵃ: תירגם עקילם הגר לפני ר'
עקיבה, "Aquila the proselyte translated in the time of Akiba,"
etc. Hieronymus, *Comment. in Jes.* viii. 11 sqq. (Vallarsi, iv.
122 sq.): Akibas quem magistrum Aquilae proselyti autumant.
(Comp. vol. i. Div. ii. p. 376.) A collection of Rabbinical passages, in which the translation of Aquila is quoted, is already
given by Asariah de Rossi, *Meor Enajim*, c. 45 ; comp. also Wolf,
*Biblioth. Hebraea*, i. 958–960, iii. 890–894; Zunz, *Die gottesdienstlichen Vorträge der Juden*, p. 82 sq.; and most exhaust-

ively by Anger, *De Akila*, pp. 12–25. The name of Aquila is in Rabbinical literature often distorted into אונקלוס (Onkelos) ; so also *e.g.* in all the passages of the Tosefta, see Zuckermandel's edition, Index, *s.v.* אונקלס.

Origenes, *epist. ad African.* c. 2 : 'Ἀκύλας . . . φιλοτιμότερον πεπιστευμένος παρὰ 'Ιουδαίοις ἡρμηνευκέναι τὴν γραφήν· ᾧ μάλιστα εἰώθασιν οἱ ἀγνοοῦντες τὴν 'Εβραίων διάλεκτον χρῆσθαι, ὡς πάντων μᾶλλον ἐπιτετευγμένῳ. It is mentioned in Justinian's *Novella* 146, that it was disputed among the Jews themselves, whether the Scriptures were to be read in Hebrew or Greek in the synagogue service. Justinian directs that the latter shall not be hindered, and, as a Christian emperor, recommends in the first place the use of the Septuagint, but permits also the use of Aquila's translation (which was thus manifestly preferred by the Jews).

The fragments are very completely collected in Field, *Origenis Hexaplorum quae supersunt*, 2 vols. Oxonii 1875. The chief work formerly was Montfaucon, *Hexaplorum Origenis quae supersunt*, 2 vols. Paris 1713. Freudenthal regards the Septuagint translation of Ecclesiastes as the work of Aquila, see *Alexander Polyhistor*, p. 65, note.

The Literature : Hody, *De bibliorum textibus* (1705), pp. 573–578. Montfaucon, *Hexapl. Orig., praelim.* pp. 46–51. Fabricius, *Biolioth. graec.* ed. Harles, iii. 690–692. Anger, *De Onkelo, Chaldaico quem ferunt Pentateuchi paraphraste et quid ei rationis intercedat cum Akila, Graeco Veteris Testamenti interprete*, Part I.: *De Akila*, Lips. 1845. Field, *Proleg.* pp. xvi.–xxvii. Arnold, art. "Bibelübersetzungen," in Herzog's *Real-Enc.* 1st ed. ii. 187 sq. Ewald, *Gesch. des Volkes Israel*, vii. 386–390. Herzfeld, *Gesch. des Volkes Jisrael*, iii. 62–64. Grätz, *Gesch. der Juden*, iv. 2nd ed. p. 437 sqq. Lagarde, *Clementina* (1865), p. 12 sqq. Joel, *Blicke in die Religionsgeschichte* (1880), p. 43 sqq. *Die Einleitungen in's Alte Testament von Eichhorn* (4th ed.), i. 521–531 ; Bertholdt, ii. 534–537 ; Herbst, i. 155–157 ; Keil (3rd ed.), p. 557 sq.; De Wette-Schrader, § 55; Bleek-Wellhausen, § 281.

It might appear questionable whether Theodotion, who as well as Symmachus is as a rule called an Ebionite by Jerome, should be named here at all. But Jerome elsewhere calls him a Jew, and in a passage, in which he expresses himself most precisely, states the former as only the opinion of some. The other opinion, viz. that Theodotion was a Jew, and indeed a Jewish proselyte, is evidenced by Irenaeus and also by Epiphanius, whose fictions (that Theodotion was at first a

Marcionite and then went over to Judaism) are not deserving
of credit.    According to Irenaeus, Theodotion was a native of
Ephesus.    Epiphanius makes him a Marcionite and a native
of Pontus.    With regard to his date Epiphanius, who places
him under Commodus (A.D. 180–192), is generally credited.
But the statements of Epiphanius are here untrustworthy.
Nor must the circumstance, that Origen places Theodotion in
the last place in his Hexapla, mislead us to the notion of his
being the most recent of these translators of Scripture.[9]    He
is at all events a predecessor of Irenaeus and very probably
not more recent than Aquila, for *the use of his translation in
the Shepherd of Hermas* has lately been raised to almost a
certainty.    The work of Theodotion pursues in general the
same object as that of Aquila, viz. that of furnishing a translation, which should render the Hebrew text more accurately
than is done by the LXX.    Theodotion however bases his
work upon the LXX., correcting the latter according to the
Hebrew, so that it can only be called a thorough revision of
this translation with which it is however in very close
accordance.    One peculiarity of his work is, that he tran-
scribes Hebrew words into Greek without translating them even
more frequently than Aquila and Symmachus (Field gives a list
of all the known cases, *Proleg.* p. 40 sq.).    We have no evidence
of the use of this translation among the Jews.    *His translation
of Daniel*, having been received by the Christian Church and
having therefore supplanted the original Septuagint translation
of Daniel in the Septuagint manuscripts, *has come down to us
complete* (the latter is preserved in only *one* MS., a *codex
Chisianus*).[10]    For the rest numerous fragments of Theodotion
have been preserved in the same manner as those of Aquila.

[9] The order in the Hexapla is arranged simply from the view-point of
matter.    Origen gives first the Hebrew text, then Aquila and Symmachus
as most closely conforming to the Hebrew text, then the LXX. and after
this Theodotion, because his work was properly but a revision of the LXX.

[10] In Theodotion's version of Daniel, *the apocryphal additions are also
retained*.    From this Jerome translated them (see *Opp.* ed. Vallarsi, ix
1376. 1399).

Hieronymus, *De viris illustr.* c. liv. (Vallarsi, ii. 893): Aquilae scilicet Pontici proselyti et *Theodotionis Hebionei* et Symmachi ejusdem dogmatis. Idem, *Comment. in Habak.* iii. 11–13 (Vallarsi, vi. 656): Theodotio autem vere quasi pauper et *Ebionita* sed et Symmachus ejusdem dogmatis pauperem sensum secuti Judaice transtulerunt. . . . Isti *Semichristiani* Judaice transtulerunt, et Judaeus Aquila interpretatus est ut Christianus. Idem, *praef. in vers. Iob* (Vallarsi, ix. 1100): Judaeus Aquila, Symmachus et Theodotio *judaizantes haeretici.* Elsewhere however Jerome calls Theodotion simply a Jew, see *Epist.* 112 *ad Augustin.* c. 19 (Vallarsi, i. 752): *hominis Judaei atque blasphemi.* Jerome expresses himself most precisely in the *praef. comment. in Daniel* (Vallarsi, v. 619 sq.): Illud quoque lectorem admoneo, Danielem non juxta LXX. interpretes sed juxta Theodotionem ecclesias legere, qui utique post adventum Christi *incredulus fuit, licet eum quidam dicant Ebionitam,* qui altero genere Judaeus est.

Irenaeus, iii. 21. 1 (= Euseb. *H. E.* v. 8. 10); see the passage above, p. 171. Epiphanius, *De mensuris et ponderibus,* § 17, 18.

As for the chronology, the circumstance which is chiefly decisive is, that Theodotion was certainly the predecessor of Irenaeus. For the latter not only expressly mentions him, but also makes use of his translation of Daniel (see Zahn, art. "Irenaeus," in Herzog's *Real-Enc.* 2nd ed. vii. 131). The relation of Justin Martyr to Theodotion is doubtful. The text of the long portion, which he quotes from Daniel, *Dial. c. Tryph.* c. xxxi., agrees indeed in many minutiae with Theodotion in opposition to the Septuagint of the *cod. Chisianus,* and yet the use of the former cannot be inferred, because the agreement with the latter preponderates. See Credner, *Beiträge zur Einl. in die biblischen Schriften,* vol. ii. (1838) pp. 253–274. In the Shepherd of Hermas, *Vis.* iv. 2. 4, however use is freely made of Daniel vi. 23, and that in a form which strikingly agrees with Theodotion in opposition to the LXX. (see Hort in John Hopkins' *University Circular,* December 1884, and Harnack, *Theol. Litztg.* 1885, p. 146). Hence it can scarcely be doubted that he preceded Hermas. *But perhaps he was also a predecessor of Aquila,* for after the acceptance of Aquila's translation by the Hellenistic Jews, forming as it does the first halting-place on the way to the formation of a Greek translation of the Bible in strict conformity with the Hebrew, his would have been tolerably superfluous. This assumption will also explain his disappearance from Jewish tradition. It is also worthy of remark, *that Irenaeus names him before Aquila.* Finally, it may also be mentioned, that in the *Revelation of St. John* sentences and expressions from Daniel are used in a form

which accords more with Theodotion than the Septuagint (ix.
20, x. 5, xiii. 7, xx. 4. Comp. Salmon, *Introduction to the
Study of the Books of the Old Testament*, 1885, pp. 654–668 ;
and in accordance with it Harnack, *Theol. Litztg.* 1885, p. 267).
It must however be confessed, that the accordances are not of
a kind to allow us to infer with certainty an acquaintance with
Theodotion's work on the part of the writer of the Apocalypse.

On the relation of Theodotion to the Septuagint, Jerome says
in his *Comment. in Ecclesiastes*, ii. (Vallarsi, iii. 396): Septuaginta vero et Theodotio sicut in pluribus locis ita et in hoc
quoque concordant (*i.e.* in opposition to Aquila and Symmachus).

*The acceptance of Theodotion's version of Daniel by the
Christian Church* in place of the Septuagint is repeatedly
testified by Jerome, see *Contra Rufin.* ii. 33 (Vallarsi, ii. 527);
*praef. comment. in Daniel* (Vallarsi, v. 619 sq.); *praef. in
version. Daniel* (Vallarsi, ix. 1361 sq.).

The Literature : Hody, *De bibliorum textibus* (1705), pp.
579–585. Montfaucon, *Hexapl. Orig. praelim.* pp. 56, 57.
Fabricius, *Bibliotheca graec.*, ed. Harles, iii. 692–695. Field,
*Orig. Hexapl. proleg.* pp. xxxviii.–xlii.. Arnold, art. " Bibelübersetzungen," in Herzog's *Real-Enc.* 1st ed. ii. 188. Fürst in the
*Literaturbl. des Orients*, 1848, p. 793. Credner, as above. Zahn,
as above. *Supernatural Religion* (complete edition, 1879), ii.
210 sq. The Introductions to the Old Testament of Eichhorn,
Bertholdt, Herbst, Keil, De Wette - Schrader, Bleek - Well-
hausen and others. The older literature in Fürst, *Biblioth.
Judaica*, iii. 420–422.

## II. REVISION AND COMPLETION OF SCRIPTURE LITERATURE.

The work of Aquila and its favourable reception on the
part of the Hellenistic Jews prove, that from about the
second century after Christ, Hellenistic Judaism also kept
strictly to the text and canon of the Palestinians. This is
confirmed by the expressions of Origen in his Epistle to
Julius Africanus. He here speaks of such component parts
of the canon as are missing in the Hebrew, especially of the
additions to Daniel and Esther, and the Books of Tobit and
Judith, as if they had never belonged to the Jewish canon.
He regards them as the exclusive possession of Christians and

says plainly that they are rejected by the Jews, without
making any distinction between Greek and Hebrew Jews
(*Epist. ad African.* c. 2, 3, and 13). Hence the canon of
the Palestinians was at that time absolutely valid among the
Jews of the Dispersion also. This was not the case in earlier
times. The Jews of the Dispersion indeed always possessed
on the whole the same Scriptures as those of Palestine. But
*in Palestine the canon attained a settled form about the second
century before Christ.* Later works, even when they appeared
under the name of sacred authorities and found approbation,
were no longer incorporated therein. *Among the Hellenistic
Jews, on the contrary, the boundaries still fluctuated for some
centuries.* A whole multitude of works, originating in the
last two centuries before or even in the first after Christ,
were united by them to the collection of the Holy Scriptures,
and among them some also which, being originally written in
Hebrew and originating in Palestine, did not become the
property of Hellenistic Judaism till they had been translated
into Greek. We have certainly no direct evidence of this
fact. But the fact that the Christian canon of the Old
Testament was from the beginning of wider and more
vacillating extent than the Hebrew, can only be explained by
the circumstance, that the Christian Church received the
canon in just this form from the hands of Hellenistic Judaism.
Hence the latter, at the time of the founding of the Christian
Church, had in its collection of Holy Scriptures those books,
which are in the Protestant Church designated, according to
the precedent of Jerome, as "apocryphal," because they are
absent from the Hebrew canon. One thing however must not
be forgotten, that on the whole no settled boundary existed.

It is in accordance with this long maintained freedom in
dealing with the canon, that the *Hellenistic Jews allowed
themselves a liberty of procedure with single works longer than
the Palestinians did.* In the same manner as Palestinian
Judaism had *formerly* acted with respect to its literature, did
Hellenistic Judaism during our period also, freely handle and

enrich by additions works already canonical in Palestine. This treatment had as a rule the same motives and objects as the legendary embellishment of more ancient sacred history. The only difference was, that in the case of books already canonical, the legend was placed beside the Scripture text, while in that of books not as yet received into the canon, it was interpolated in the text itself.

The majority of those books which, though admitted by the Hellenistic Jews into the collection of the Holy Scriptures, originally made no claim to be esteemed as such, has therefore been treated of by us elsewhere. We here group together only (1) the revisions and completions of such books as had in their more ancient forms become canonical in Palestine (Ezra, Esther, Daniel, the Prayer of Manasseh [an addition to 2 Chron. xxxiii.]), and (2) certain books, which from the first aspired to be regarded as Scripture, and which entered as such into the Hellenistic collection of the Scriptures (Baruch, the Epistle of Jeremiah).

## 1. *The Greek Ezra.*

Besides the Greek translation of the Hebrew canonical Book of Ezra, there is also a free Greek revision, differing from the canonical Ezra partly by transpositions, partly by interpolations. The exact relation between the two will appear from the following survey of the composition of the Greek Ezra :—

> Chap. i. = 2 Chron. xxxv.–xxxvi. : Restoration of the temple worship under Josiah (639–609), and history of the successors of Josiah down to the destruction of the temple (588).
>
> Chap. ii. 1–14 = Ezra i. : Cyrus in the first year of his reign (537) permits the return of the exiles and delivers up the sacred vessels.

Chap. ii. 15–25 = Ezra iv. 7–24 : In consequence of
a complaint against the Jews, Artaxerxes forbids
(465–425) the continuance of the rebuilding of
(the temple and) the walls of Jerusalem.

Chap. iii.–v. 6 : independent : Zerubbabel obtains the
favour of Darius (521–485) and receives from
him permission for the return of the exiles.

Chap. v. 7–70 = Ezra ii. 1–iv. 5 : A list of those
who returned with Zerubbabel, the operations of
Zerubbabel and the interruption of the building of
the temple in the time of Cyrus (536–529) till
the second year of Darius (520).

Chap. vi.–vii. = Ezra v.–vi. : Resumption and completion of the rebuilding of the temple in the
sixth year of Darius (516).

Chap. viii. – ix. 36 = Ezra vii. – x. : Return of Ezra
with a train of exiles in the seventh year of
Artaxerxes (458) ; commencement of Ezra's operations.

Chap. ix. 37–55 = Neh. vii. 73–viii. 13 : Public
reading of the law by Ezra

According to this survey the reviser of the canonical
Ezra took in hand the following changes : 1. The portion
chap. iv. 7–24 of the canonical Ezra is removed to an earlier
place.    2. The portion chaps. iii.–v. 6 of the Greek Ezra is
interpolated from an unknown source.    3. The book opens
with 2 Chron. xxxv.–xxxvi.    4. Neh. vii. 73–viii. 13 is
added at the close.    By the two first-named operations the
confusion partly begotten by the canonical Ezra is considerably increased.    For in this latter the portion chap. iv. 6–23
stands out of place.    It belongs to a much later period, and
treats not of the interruption of the rebuilding of the temple,
but of an interruption in the building of the walls.    The
editor of the Greek Ezra has indeed rescued this passage
from the connection in which it is incorrectly placed, but

only to transpose it to a position if possible still more erroneous, taking at the same time the liberty of adding to it by way of completion the interruption of the building of the temple. Not however contented with this, he has also interpolated the paragraph chaps. iii.–v. 6, which transposes us to the times of Darius, while subsequently (v. 7–70) the times of Cyrus are again spoken of. Thus then the history goes directly backwards ; first we have (ii. 15–25) Artaxerxes, then (iii.–v. 6) Darius, and lastly (v. 7–70) Cyrus. And in the last-named portion we are told in the most unembarrassed manner that Zerubbabel returned with the exiles in the time of Cyrus (comp. v. 8, 67–70), while previously it was expressly stated that Zerubbabel received permission for their return from the special favour of Darius. With respect to the documents which were in the hands of our compiler only two things remain to be noticed : 1. That he did not translate the canonical Ezra from the Hebrew (so Fritzsche and most others), but compiled from the Septuagint (so rightly Keil, *Einl.* 3rd ed. p. 704 sq.). 2. That he certainly discovered beforehand the portion chaps. iii.–v. 6, since it stands in direct opposition to the rest of the narrative. It seems to be a Greek original and not a translation from the Hebrew. The *object* of the whole compilation has been on the whole correctly expressed by Bertholdt (*Einl.* iii. 1011) : " He intended to compile from older works a history of the temple from the last epoch of the legal worship to its rebuilding and the restoration of the prescribed ritual therein." Evidently however he meant to give also still more concerning Nehemiah, for the abrupt conclusion could not possibly have been intentional. With respect to the date of the book, all that can be said is, that it was already used by Josephus (*Antt.* xi. 1–5).

Josephus in his account of the restoration of the theocracy (*Antt.* xi. 1–5) entirely conforms to the course of this Greek Ezra. For he brings what is contained in chaps. ii. 15–25 and iii.–v. 6 of this book into the same position and the same order, *i.e.* interpolates it between the first and second chapters of the canonical Ezra (*Antt.* xi. 2–3). In so doing however he does not proceed without historical criticism, for he simply changes Artaxerxes, who in the Greek Ezra is inserted in a quite impossible place, into Cambyses, so as to restore the correct order: Cyrus, Cambyses, Darius. He removes the further historical stumbling-block of the Greek Ezra, of Cyrus re-appearing after Darius, by doing away with Cyrus in this place and making the return of the exiles first take place under Darius. This indeed restores the correct order of the Persian kings, but a narrative is thus concocted, which differs still more widely from actual history than that of the Greek Ezra itself.

Apparently this book was generally and from the first used in the Christian Church also. Clemens Alex. *Strom.* i. 21. 124: 'Ἐνταῦθα Ζοροβάβελ σοφίᾳ νικήσας τοὺς ἀνταγωνιστὰς τυγχάνει παρὰ Δαρείου ὠνησάμενος ἀνανέωσιν Ἱερουσαλὴμ καὶ μετὰ "Εσδρα εἰς τὴν πατρῴαν γῆν ἀναζεύγνυσι (can only refer to chaps. iii. iv. of the Greek Ezra). Origenes, *Comment. in Johann.* vol. vi. c. 1 (Lommatzsch, i. 174): Καὶ κατὰ τοὺς "Εσδρα χρόνους, ὅτε νικᾷ ἡ ἀλήθεια τὸν οἶνον καὶ τὸν ἐχθρὸν βασιλέα καὶ τὰς γυναῖκας, ἀνοικοδομεῖται ὁ ναὸς τῷ θεῷ (comp. *Esra graec.* iv. 33 sqq.). Idem, *in Josuam homil.* ix. 10 (Lommatzsch, xi. 100): et nos dicamus, sicut in Esdra scriptum est, quia " a te domine est victoria et ego servus tuus, benedictus es deus veritatis " (*Esra graec.* iv. 59–60). *Cyprian epist.* lxxiv. 9 : Et apud Hesdram veritas vicit, sicut scriptum est: " Veritas manet et invalescit in aeternum et vivit et obtinet in saecula saeculorum," etc. (*Esra graec.* iv. 38–40). For numerous passages from later Fathers see Pohlmann, *Tüb. Theol. Quartalschrift*, 1859, p. 263 sqq. In the authorized editions of the Vulgate, the book is placed in the Appendix to the Bible *after* the New Testament.

The book is sometimes entitled the *first* Book of Ezra (so the Greek MSS. : "Εσδρας α'), sometimes the *third* Book of Ezra, the canonical Books of Ezra and Nehemiah being reckoned the first and second (so Jerome [*praef. in version. libr. Esrae*, ed. Vallarsi, ix. 1524: nec quemquam moveat, quod, unus a nobis editus liber est ; nec apocryphorum tertii et quarti somniis delectetur], and especially the authorized editions of the Vulgate).

Among the Greek *manuscripts* the *Vaticanus* (called No. 2 in Fritzsche's edition, as well as by Holmes and Parsons) and the *Alexandrinus* (No. 3) hold the first rank, the book not being contained in the Sinaiticus. On the editions, see above, pp. 10 and 11.

*Ancient translations:* 1. The old Latin preserved in two recensions, one of which is found in the manuscripts and

editions of the Vulgate, the other in the *cod. Colbertinus* 3703.
Both texts in Sabatier, *Bibliorum sacrorum Latinae versiones
antiquae*, vol. iii. (in the Appendix after the New Testament
corresponding to the position in the Vulgate).    On the relation
of both to one another, see Fritzsche, *Handb.* i. 10.    2. The
Syriac, on which comp. p. 11.    This book is not contained in
the large Milan Peshito manuscripts.

On the exegesis in general, see p. 11.    Commentary: Fritzsche,
*Exeget. Handbuch zu den Apokryphen*, Part i. Leipzig 1851.

Separate investigations: [Trendelenburg] "On the apocryphal
Esras" (Eichhorn's *Allg. Biblioth. der bibl. Literatur*, vol. i. 1787,
pp. 178–232). Dähne, *Geschichtl. Darstellung der jüd.-alex.
Religionsphilosophie*, vol. ii. (1834) pp. 116–125.    Herzfeld,
*Gesch. des Volkes Jisrael*, i. 320 sqq., iii. 72 sqq.    Treuenfels,
"Ueber das apokryphische Buch Esra" (Fürst's *Literaturbl. des
Orients*, 1850, Nos. 15–18, 40–49).    The same, "Entstehung des
Esra apocryphus" (Fürst's *Orient*, 1851, Nos. 7–10).    Pohlmann,
"Ueber das Ansehen des apokryphischen dritten Buchs Esras"
(*Tüb. Theol. Quartalschr.* 1859, pp. 257–275).    Ewald, *Gesch. des
Volkes Israel*, iv. 163–167.    Bissell, "The First Book of Esdras"
(*Bibliotheca sacra*, 1877, pp. 209–228 ; reprinted in Bissell,
*The Apocrypha of the Old Testament*, 1880, p. 62 sqq., Clark,
Edinburgh).    The Introductions of Eichhorn, Bertholdt, De
Wette-Schrader, Keil, Reuss (see above, p. 12).

## 2. *Additions to Esther.*

The canonical Book of Esther relates how a Jewish virgin,
a foster-daughter of Mordecai, was chosen for his wife by the
Persian king Ahasuerus (Xerxes); how Haman, the prime
minister of the king, published a decree in his name for the
extirpation of all the Jews, and was already making preparations to hang Mordecai; how Mordecai however, who had
formerly saved the king's life, was raised to great honour and
Haman hanged on the gibbet destined for Mordecai, whereupon Mordecai by an edict promulgated in the king's name
revoked the edict of Haman and gave permission to the Jews
to destroy their enemies; and finally, how the Jewish feast of
Purim was instituted for the commemoration of this wonderful
deliverance of the Jews.    A multitude of passages are interpolated in the Greek revision of the book, *e.g.* the edict

of Haman, a prayer of Mordecai and a prayer of Esther, the edict of Mordecai and the like.   In these portions the spirit of the narrative is maintained and they present nothing needing remark.   There is no reason for adopting the view of a Hebrew model (so *e.g.* Langen).   According to the superscription of the Greek edition it was the work of Lysimachus, the son of Ptolemy of Jerusalem, and was brought to Egypt in the fourth year of King Ptolemy and Cleopatra by the priest Dositheus and his son Ptolemy.   Since no less than four Ptolemies had a Cleopatra to wife, the information, even if it be regarded as trustworthy, is not of much chronological value.   It is certain only that Josephus was already acquainted with the Greek revision with the additions.

Josephus in his reproduction of its contents (*Antt.* xi. 6) has admitted also all the additions of the Greek revision.

Origenes, *Epist. ad African.* c. 3, mentions these additions and expressly names the most important ; assuming as self-evident the canonicity of the book in this form (the additions included).   He also mentions, *De oratione*, c. 13 (Lommatzsch, xvii. 134), the prayers of Mordecai and Esther inserted between chaps. iv. and v., and gives in the same work, c. 14 (Lommatzsch, xvii. 143), the first words of both prayers.

The Greek text is extant in two widely differing recensions : (1) the common, which is supported by the best manuscripts, the Vaticanus (No. 2), the Alexandrinus (No. 3) and the Sinaiticus (No. 10) ; and (2) a much retouched one in *codd.* 19, 93, 108 (or more precisely 19, 93[a] and 108[b], the last two manuscripts containing both the common and the touched-up texts).   Langen thought he could prove that Josephus already had access to the latter.   But Josephus chiefly coincides with the common text (comp. *e.g.* the portion, Esth. ii. 21–23=Joseph. *Antt.* xi. 6. 4, which is entirely expunged from the revised text , the name of the eunuch Achrathaios, Esth. iv. 5 = Joseph. *Antt.* xi. 6. 4, which is also absent in the revised text and other matters).   It has also been rendered very probable by recent investigations, that the revised text is derived from Lucianus (see above, p. 165).   If then one or two instances of contact between Josephus and the revised text are really not accidental, this would only prove that the words in question were formerly found in the common text also.   Fritzsche published both texts, at first separately ('Εσθήρ, *duplicem libri textum*, ed. O. F. Fritzsche, Zurich 1848), then in his edition of the *Libri apocryphi Vet. Test. graece* (1871). Comp. on the editions, p. 10 above.

*Ancient translations.* 1. *The Latin.* (*a*) The old Latin according to a *cod. Corbeiensis* with the various readings of two other manuscripts in Sabatier, *Bibliorum sacrorum Latinae versiones antiquae,* vol. i. The beginning of the book, according to the same translation, is also found in *Bibliotheca Casinensis,* vol. i. (1873), *Florileg.* pp. 287–289. On the character of the translation, see Fritzsche, *Exeget. Handb.* i. 74 sq. (*b*) The translation of Jerome, who, in his translation of the book from the Hebrew, gives also a free Latin version of the Greek additions, but places them all at the end, and marks them with the obelus (*Opp.* ed. Vallarsi, ix. 1581: Quae habentur in Hebraeo, plena fide expressi. Haec autem, quae sequuntur, scripta reperi in editione vulgata, quae Graecorum lingua et literis continetur . . . quod juxta consuetudinem nostram obelo ÷ id est veru praenotavimus). 2. The Syriac translation, see above, p. 11.

For the exegesis in general, see above, p. 11. Commentary: Fritzsche, *Exeget. Handbuch zu den Apokryphen,* Part i., Leipzig 1851. The other literature : Zunz, *Die gottesdienstlichen Vorträge der Juden* (1832), pp. 120–122. Langen, "Die beiden griechischen Texte des Buches Esther" (*Theol. Quartalschr.* 1860, pp. 244–272). The same, *Die deuterokanonischen Stücke des Buches Esther,* Freiburg 1862. The introductory works of von Jahn, Eichhorn, Bertholdt, Welte, Scholz, Nöldeke, De Wette-Schrader, Reusch, Keil, Kaulen, Kleinert, Reuss (see above, p. 12).

### 3. *Additions to Daniel.*

The Greek text of the Book of Daniel contains the following additions : (*a*) *The Prayer of Azariah and the Thanksgiving of the Three Children in the Furnace.* For when the three companions of Daniel were cast into the furnace (Dan. iii.), one of them, Azariah, who was also called Abed-Nego, first uttered a prayer for deliverance and, when this was heard, all three joined in a song of praise. The words of both are given. (*b*) *The History of Susannah.* A beautiful Jewess named Susannah, the wife of Jehoiakim, is, while bathing, surprised by two lustful Jewish elders, and then, when she cries for assistance, slanderously accused by them of having committed adultery with a youth. Upon the false witness of the elders Susannah is condemned to death, but saved by the wisdom of the youthful Daniel, who procures a fresh investigation, and by a skilful examination convicts the elders of perjury. (c) *The History of Bel and the Dragon.* Properly two independent narratives, both of which are intended to expose the worthlessness and imposture of idolatrous worship. In the one, we are told how King Cyrus (so Theodotion, the king's name not being mentioned in the Septuagint text) was convinced by a clever contrivance of Daniel, that the image of Bel did not itself consume the food laid before it. In the other, how Daniel having fed the Dragon, to whom divine honours were paid by the Babylonians, with cakes made of pitch, fat, and hair, and so killed it, was cast into the den of lions, and there miraculously fed by the prophet Habakkuk, and after seven days drawn out of the pit unhurt. Of these fragments only the first (the Prayer of Azariah and the Song of the Three Children) is properly speaking a completion of the canonical Book of Daniel, the two others having no internal connection with it. In the text of Theodotion *the History of Susannah stands at the commencement of that book, the History of Bel and the Dragon at its close.* This position is also evidenced by the Fathers (Hippolytus, Julius Africanus and Origen). Neither of the fragments gives occasion for assuming a Hebrew original. The History of Susannah is even very certainly a Greek original, as Julius Africanus and Porphyry already showed from the play upon the words σχῖνος and σχίζειν (vers. 54, 55), πρῖνος and πρίειν (vers. 58, 59) (African. *epist. ad Origen, Porphyr.* quoted by Jerome, *praef. comment. in Daniel,* ed. Vallarsi, 619).[11]

Specially copious material is in existence for the *history of the use and canonical validity of these fragments in the Christian Church.*

Justin Martyr mentions, *Apol.* i., Ananias, Azarias and Misael, the three companions of Daniel. But it is not clear from his

---

[11] The Catholic apologists from Origen (*Epist. ad African.* c. vi. and xii.) to Wiederholt (*Theol. Quartalschr.* 1869, pp. 290–321), have in vain endeavoured to do away with the proof furnished by this play upon words.

brief notice of them whether he was also acquainted with the additions.

Irenaeus and Tertullian quote both the History of Susannah and that of Bel and the Dragon. Irenaeus, iv. 26. 3: audient eas quae sunt a Daniele propheta voces, etc. (comp. Susanna, vers. 56 and 52, 53 according to Theodotion). Idem, iv. 5. 2: Quem (Deum) et Daniel propheta, cum dixisset ei Cyrus rex Persarum: "Quare non adoras Bel?" annuntiavit dicens: "Quoniam," etc. Tertullian, *De corona*, c. iv. (Susanna). Idem, *De idololatria*, c. xviii. (Bel and the Dragon); *de jejunio*, c. vii. *fin.* (the same).

Hippolytus in his commentary on Daniel deals also with the Greek additions. The explanation of the History of Susannah (*Opp.* ed. Lagarde, pp. 145–151) and a few notes on the Song of the Three Children (Lagarde, p. 186, fragm. 122, p. 201, fragm. 138) are extant. It is evident from the beginning of the notes on Susannah, that Hippolytus read this portion as the commencement of the Book of Daniel. See in general, Bardenhewer, *Des heiligen Hippolytus von Rom Commentar zum Buche Daniel,* Freiburg 1877; and Zahn, *Theol. Litztg.* 1877, p. 495 sqq.

Julius Africanus alone among the older Fathers disputes the canonicity of these fragments. In his *Epistola ad Origenem* (printed in the editions of Origen, *e.g.* in Lommatzsch, xvii. 17 sqq.) he calls Origen to account for appealing in a disputation to the History of Susannah, which is but a spurious addition to Daniel: Θαυμάζω δὲ, πῶς ἔλαθέ σε τὸ μέρος τοῦ βιβλίου τοῦτο κίβδηλον ὄν . . . ἥδε ἡ περικοπὴ σὺν ἄλλαις δύο ταῖς ἐπὶ τῷ τέλει τῷ παρὰ τῶν Ἰουδαίων εἰλημμένῳ Δανιὴλ οὐκ ἐμφέρεται. The last remark refers, as appears from the reply of Origen, to the two pieces of Bel and of the Dragon. Hence Africanus read these at the close and the History of Susannah at the beginning of the book.

Origen in his reply (*Epistola ad Africanum*) seeks to defend the genuineness and canonicity of these pieces with a great amount of scholarship.[12] In so doing he mentions, not only the History of Susannah and those of Bel and the Dragon, but also the Prayer of Azariah, and the Song of the Three Children, and indeed speaks of them as standing in the midst of the text of Daniel, remarking that *all three were found both in the LXX. and in the text of Theodotion* (*Epist. ad African.* c. ii.). In the tenth book of his *Stromata* he gives an exegesis of the

---

[12] Wetstein in his separate edition of the letters (*Julii Africani de historia Susannae epistola ad Origenem et Origenis ad illum responsio,* ed. J. R. Wetstenius, Basil. 1674) incorrectly denies that Origen really desired to prove the canonicity of these fragments. See on the contrary the *Monitum* in de la Rue and Lommatzsch.

History of Susannah and that of Bel, from which Jerome makes extracts in his commentary on Daniel, chaps. xiii.–xiv. (Hieron. *Opp.* ed. Vallarsi, v. 730–736 ; also in Orig. *Opp.* ed. Lommatzsch, xvii. 70–75). All the fragments are elsewhere frequently quoted by Origen, and that according to the text of Theodotion. (1) Susannah, *Comm. in Joann.* vol. xx. c. 5 (Lommatzsch, ii. 204) ; *ibid.* vol. xxviii. c. 4 (Lommatzsch, ii. 316); *Comm. in Matth.* series lat. c. 61 (Lommatzsch, iv. 347) ; *Comm. in Epist. ad. Rom.* lib. iv. c. 2 (Lommatzsch, vi. 249) ; *Fragm. in Genes.* vol. iii. c. iv. (Lommatzsch, viii. 13); *in Genes. homil.* xv. 2 (Lommatzsch, viii. 261) ; *in Josuam homil.* xxii. 6 (Lommatzsch, xi. 190); *Selecta in Psalmos*, Ps. xxxvi. (xxxvii.) *homil.* iv. 2 (Lommatzsch, xii. 210) ; in Ezekiel, *homil.* vi. 3 (Lommatzsch, xiv. 82) ; *Selecta in Ezek.* c. 6 (Lommatzsch, xiv. 196). Comp. especially with respect to canonicity *in Levit. homil.* i. 1 (Lommatzsch, ix. 173) against those who adhere to the literal and historical sense of Scripture : sed tempus est nos adversus improbos presbyteros uti sanctae Susannae vocibus, quas illi quidem repudiantes historiam Susannae de catalogo divinorum voluminum desecarunt. Nos autem et suscipimus et opportune contra ipsos proferimus dicentes, "Angustiae mihi undique." (2) Prayer of Azariah and Song of the Three Children : *Comm. in Matth.* vol. xiii. c. 2 (Lommatzsch, iii. 211); *Comm. in Matth.* series lat. c. 62 (Lommatzsch, iv. 352); *Comm. in Epist. ad Rom.* lib. i. c. 10 (Lommatzsch, vi. 37) ; *ibid.* lib. ii. c. 9 (Lommatzsch, vi. 108) ; *ibid.* lib. vii. c. 1 (Lommatzsch, vii. 87); *De Oratione*, c. xiii. and xiv. (Lommatzsch, xvii. 134, 143). (3) Bel and the Dragon : *Exhortatio ad martyrium*, c. 33 (Lommatzsch, xx. 278).

Cyprian, *de dominica oratione*, c. 8, adduces the Song of the Three Children as a standard example of publica et communis oratio. Comp. also *De Lapsis*, c. 31. He quotes the story of Bel, *ad Fortunatum*, c. 11 ; and *Epist.* lviii. 5.

The *Greek text* used by the Fathers since Irenaeus was that of Theodotion, which has also passed into the manuscripts and editions of the LXX. (see above, p. 173). The genuine Septuagint text of Daniel is preserved to us in only *one* manuscript, a *cod. Chisianus;* and after the previous labours of others (Bianchini and Vincentius, *de Regibus*, see *Theol. Litztg.* 1877, p. 565) has been published for the first time by Simon de Magistris (*Daniel secundum LXX. ex tetraplis Origenis nunc primum editus e singulari Chisiano codice*, Rom. 1772). On this edition, which is not free from errors, are based the more recent ones, and also that of Hahn (Δανιὴλ κατὰ τοὺς ἑβδομήκοντα, e cod. Chisiano ed. etc., H. A. Hahn, Lips. 1845). Still more incorrect is the text, in part formed from Holmes and Parsons'

Apparatus of Various Readings, which Tischendorf has added
to his edition of the Septuagint. It is to Cozza (*Sacrorum
Bibliorum vetustissima fragmenta Graeca et Latina*, ed. Cozza,
pars iii. Romae 1877; comp. the notice of Gebhardt, *Theol.
Litztg.*1877,p.565 sq.) that we are first indebted for a trustworthy
impression of the MSS. *The Syriac translation of the hexaplarian LXX. text*, of which Daniel and other books have been
preserved in a Milan manuscript, serves as a check and criticism
of the *cod. Chisianus*. The Book of Daniel from this translation has already been published by Bugati (*Daniel secundum
editionem LXX. interpretum ex Tetraplis desumtam, ex codice
Syro-Estranghelo Bibliothecae Ambrosianae Syriace edidit*, etc.,
Caj. Bugatus, Mediol. 1788). A photo-lithographic copy of the
whole manuscript has been published by Ceriani (*Codex Syro-
Hexaplaris Ambrosianus photolithographice editus*, Mediol. 1874,
as vol. vii. of the *Monum. sacra et prof.*). Fritzsche in his
edition of the Apocrypha, gives both the Greek texts (LXX.
and Theodotion) of Susannah, Bel and the Dragon, and the
Septuagint only, with the various readings of Theodotion, of
the Prayer of Azarias, and the Song of the Three Children,
in which Theodotion has made but few alterations. Comp.
on the editions of the Greek text (*i.e.* of Theodotion), p. 10
above.

*Ancient translations.* A *Vetus Latinus*, only fragmentary in
Sabatier, *Biblior. sacror. Latinae versiones antiquae*, vol. ii. The
Greek original is Theodotion. Jerome has likewise translated
the Greek additions from Theodotion and admitted them,
marked with the obelus, into his translation of Daniel from the
Hebrew. See his remarks, ed. Vallarsi, ix. 1376,1399. On the
editions of the Syriac common text, see above, p. 11. The
Syriac translation of the Story of Bel and the Dragon, from a
collection of Midrashim, is also found in Neubauer, *The Book of
Tobit*, 1878, pp. 39–43.

For the exegesis in general, see above, p. 11. Commentary:
Fritzsche, *Exeget. Handbuch zu den Apocryphen*, Pt. i. Leipzig
1851. The other literature: Zunz, *Die gottesdienstlichen Vorträge
der Juden* (1832), p. 122 sq. Delitzsch, *De Habacuci prophetae
vita atque aetate* (Lips. 1842), pp. 23 sqq., 105 sqq. Frankel,
*Monatsschr. f. Gesch. und Wissensch. des Judenth.* 1868, pp.
440–449 (on Susannah). Wiederholt, *Theol. Quartalschr.* 1869,
pp. 287 sqq., 377 sqq. (History of Susannah); 1871, p. 373 sqq.
(Prayer of Azarias and Song of the Three Children); 1872, p.
554 sqq. (Bel and the Dragon). Rohling, *Das Buch des Propheten
Daniel*,1876. Brüll, "Das apokryphische Susannabuch" (*Jahrbb.
für jüd. Gesch. und Literatur*,Pt. iii.1877, pp. 1–69; also separate).
The Introductions of Jahn, Eichhorn, Bertholdt, Welte, Scholz,

Nöldeke, De Wette-Schrader, Reusch, Keil, Kaulen, Kleinert, Reuss (see above, p. 12).

## 4. *The Prayer of Manasseh.*

In like manner as the prayers of Mordecai and Esther were interpolated as supplements to the Book of Esther, and the Prayer of Azariah and the Song of the Three Children to that of Daniel, so was a prayer of Manasseh, in which the king in his captivity humbly confesses his sin before God and prays for pardon, composed as a completion of 2 Chron. xxxiii. 12, 13. There was the more occasion for the composition of such a prayer, since it is stated in 2 Chron. xxxiii. 18, 19, that the Prayer of Manasseh is written in the history of the kings of Israel and in the Chronicle of Hosai. The prayer stands in most manuscripts in the appendix to the Psalms, where many other similar fragments are collected (so *e.g.* in the *cod. Alexandrinus*).

The Prayer is first *quoted* in the *Constitut. apostol.* ii. 22, where it is given in its literal entirety. For later Christian testimony to its canonicity, see Fabricius, *Biblioth. Graec.* ed. Harles, iii. 732 sq. In the authorized Romish Vulgate it is in the appendix to the Bible, after the New Testament (like 3 and 4 Ezra).

*The Latin translation,* which has passed into the Vulgate, is " of quite another kind from the usual old Latin, and is certainly of more recent origin" (Fritzsche, i. 159). Sabatier has compared three manuscripts for it (*Biblior. sacror. Lat. vers. ant.* iii. 1038 sq.).

The editions and the exegesis are the same as of the other Apocrypha. Commentary: Fritzsche, *Exeget. Handbuch zu den Apocryphen,* Pt. i. Leipzig 1851.

For other legends (Jewish and Christian) with respect to Manasseh, see Fabricius, *Cod. pseudepigr.* i. 1100–1102. Id. *Biblioth. gr.* ed. Harl. iii. 732 sq. Fritzsche, *Handb.* i. 158.

## 5. *The Book of Baruch.*

The Greek Book of Baruch properly belongs to the class of Pseudepigraphic prophets, and is distinguished among them by its very meritorious contents. We place it here as being, at least according to its second half, of Graeco-Jewish origin, and as having been admitted into the Greek Bible as a canonical book.

The whole claims to be the composition of Baruch, the confidential friend and companion of the prophet Jeremiah. Its contents are tolerably miscellaneous, and are divided into two halves, the second of which again comprises two sections. The first half (chaps. i. 1-iii. 8) begins with a superscription, in which what follows is described as a Book of Baruch, which he wrote in the fifth year after the destruction of Jerusalem by the Chaldeans (i. 1, 2). This book was read by Baruch before King Jeconiah and all the exiles in Babylon; and the reading produced such an impression, that it was resolved to send money to Jerusalem, that sacrifices and prayers might there be offered for King Nebuchadnezzar and his son Belshazzar. At the same time the Jews dwelling in Jerusalem were enjoined to read out in the temple on the feast days the writing therewith sent (i. 3–14). This writing, which is next given in full, is evidently identical with that read by Baruch, and therefore announced in the superscription.[13] It is *an ample confession of sin on the part of the exiles*, who recognise in the fearful fate which has overtaken themselves and the holy city, the righteous chastisement of God for their sins, and entreat Him again to show them favour. They confess especially that their disobedience to the King of Babylon was a rebellion against God Himself, because it was His will that Israel should obey the King of Babylon (ii. 21–24). The second half of the book (chaps. iii. 9–v. 9) contains *instruction and consolation for the humbled people*: (*a*) Instruction—Israel is humbled, because they have forsaken

---

[13] The writing announced in the superscription and read by Baruch cannot, as many critics suppose, be chap. iii. 7 sqq. For the effect of the reading is, that a sacrifice for Nebuchadnezzar and Belshazzar is resolved upon, and this can only refer to chap. ii. 21–24. The superscription i. 1, 2, too, is by no means in accordance with iii. 9 sqq., this latter section giving no kind of hint of its having been written by Baruch. Comp. Reuss, *Gesch. der heil. Schriften Alten Testaments*, § 510.

the source of wisdom. True wisdom is with God alone. To it must the people return (iii. 9–iv. 4). (*b*) Consolation— Jerusalem is not laid waste for ever, nor are the people to be always in captivity. They must take courage, for the scattered members shall again be assembled in the Holy Land (iv. 5–v. 9).

The second half is joined to the first without any intervening matter at chap. iii. 9. An internal connection only so far exists, that both halves presuppose the same historical situation, viz. the desolation of Jerusalem and the carrying away of the people into captivity. In other respects however they stand in no connection with each other, and it is hardly conceivable that they formed from the first part of the same whole. To this must be added, that the style and mode of expression widely differ, being in the first half Hebraistic, and in the second fluent and rhetorical Greek. Hence Fritzsche, Hitzig, Kneucker, Hilgenfeld and Reuss have correctly inferred, that the two halves are the works of different authors. Nay, one might feel inclined, with Hitzig, Kneucker and Hilgenfeld, to regard even the first half as no single work, but to look upon chap. i. 3–14 as a later interpolation. For it cannot be denied that the narrative of the reading of the Book of Baruch and of the effect produced thereby, comes in like an interruption between i. 1, 2 and i. 15–iii. 8. After the superscription i. 1, 2, the book itself is expected. A discrepancy of statement also ensues owing to the inserted narrative, the destruction of the temple being assumed by the book itself (i. 2, ii. 26), and the continuance of the sacrificial service by the narrative (i. 10–14). But lastly, all these inconsistencies are possible in one and the same author; and other matters, such especially as the like dependence on Daniel in i. 11, 12 and i. 15– ii. 20 favour identity of authorship.

Most of the older critics adopt the view of a Hebrew original for the whole; and Kneucker, in spite of his assumption of three different composers, firmly maintains it, nay,

tries with much care to reconstruct the Hebrew original.
There are however sufficient points of contact for this *in the
first half only*. The second half is evidently a Greek original.
Hence we are constrained, with Fritzsche, Hilgenfeld and
Reuss, to admit, concerning the origin of this book, that its
first half was originally composed in Hebrew, then translated
into Greek, and completed by the addition of the second
half.

In determining the *date of its composition*, its close dependence on the Book of Daniel is decisive. There are in it corre-
spondences with the latter, which make the employment of it
by the author of Baruch indubitable. Especially is there an
almost verbal agreement between Dan. ix. 7–10 and Baruch
i. 15–18. The juxtaposition too of Nebuchadnezzar and
Belshazzar is common to both books (Dan. v. 2 sqq. = Baruch
i. 11, 12). That so thoroughly original and creative a mind
however as the author of the Book of Daniel should have
copied from the Book of Baruch is certainly not to be
admitted. Thus we have already arrived at the Maccabaean
period, and most Protestant critics stop there (so *e.g.* Fritzsche,
Schrader, Keil). But the situation assumed in the Book of
Baruch by no means agrees with the Maccabaean era. The
Book of Baruch, and especially its first half, with which we are
first of all concerned, *presupposes* the destruction of Jerusalem
and the leading of the people into captivity (i. 2, ii. 23, 26).
In this catastrophe the people recognise a judgment of God
for their sins, and particularly for their rebellion against the
heathen authority, which God Himself had set over Israel
(ii. 21–24). The penitent people hasten therefore to order
sacrifices and prayers for their heathen rulers (i. 10, 11).
All this — as the destruction by the Chaldeans is out of
question—only suits the time *after the destruction of Jerusalem
by Titus*. This very catastrophe was moreover brought about
by the rebellion of the people against the heathen authorities.
And the special act of rebellion was, as Josephus expressly
states, the doing away with the daily sacrifice for the Roman

emperor (*Bell. Jud.* ii. 17. 2–4; comp. above, Div. ii. vol. i. p. 302 sq.). In this political revolution our author saw a rebellion against the will of God, and therefore in the fearful catastrophe, the righteous judgment of God upon it. And he sought, by all he relates of the exiles in the time of Baruch, to bring this view to bear upon his fellow-countrymen. It must therefore certainly be admitted, as by Hitzig and Kneucker, that this book was written after the year A.D. 70. For the quite non-historical juxtaposition of Nebuchadnezzar and Belshazzar, recalling the relation of Vespasian and Titus, also agrees with that date. The narrative that in the straits of war parents ate the flesh of their children (ii. 3) frequently recurs indeed in the description of the horrors of war, but is also found just in the description of the siege of A.D. 70 by Josephus (*Bell. Jud.* vi. 3. 4).

What has been said applies chiefly to only the first half of the book. But the second half also essentially assumes the same situation, viz. the desolation of Jerusalem and the leading of the people into captivity (iv. 10–16). Its object is to give instruction and consolation in view of these events. Hence its composition cannot well be placed much later than that of the first half. At all events this second half is later than the Salomonian Psalter. For Baruch v. agrees almost verbally with Psalt. Salom. xi.; and the dependence must, by reason of the psalm-like character and the probably primitive Hebrew of the Salomonian Psalter, be sought for on the side of the Book of Baruch.

The fact that it found acceptance in the Christian Church is not opposed to our conclusion as to the somewhat recent composition of the book. For exactly the same thing took place in the case of the Apocalypse of Baruch and the fourth Book of Ezra.

The existence of a Hebrew text of this book is disputed by Jerome, see *praef. comment. in Jerem.* (Vallarsi, iv. 834): Libellum autem Baruch, qui vulgo editioni Septuaginta copulatur nec habetur apud Hebraeos. Idem, *praef. in version.*

*Jerem.* (Vallarsi, ix. 783): Librum autem Baruch notarii ejus, qui apud Hebraeos nec legitur nec habetur. So too Epiphanius, *De mensuris et ponderibus,* § 5 : τῶν θρήνων αὐτοῦ καὶ τῶν ἐπιστολῶν Βαρούχ, εἰ καὶ οὐ κεῖνται ἐπιστολαὶ παρ' 'Εβραίοις. But both Jerome and Epiphanius for the most part try only to prove that the book was not in the Hebrew canon. Certainly they seem to have known of no Hebrew text at all, but that does not prove that none ever existed. For its existence may be cited the remark found three times in the Milan manuscript of the *Syrus hexaplaris* (on i. 17 and ii. 3), "this is not in the Hebrew" (see Ceriani's notes to his edition in the *Monum. sacra et prof.* i. 1, 1861).

Among the Jews (*i.e.* among the Hellenistic Jews ?) this book, together with the Lamentations of Jeremiah, was, according to the testimony of the *Apostolic Constitutions,* read at public worship on the 10th Gorpiaios (by which is certainly meant the 10th Ab, the day of the destruction of Jerusalem), *Const. apost.* v. 20 : καὶ γὰρ καὶ νῦν δεκάτη τοῦ μηνὸς Γορπιαίου συναθροιζόμενοι τοὺς θρήνους 'Ιερεμίου ἀναγινώσκουσιν . . . καὶ τὸν Βαρούχ. In the Syriac text of the *Const. apost.* the Book of Baruch, it is true, is not named. See Bunsen, *Analecta Ante-Nicaena,* ii. 187. On the date of the 10th Gorpiaios, comp. also Freudenthal, *Die Flavius Josephus beigelegte Schrift über die Herrschaft der Vernunft* (1869), p. 147 sq.

*On its use in the Christian Church,* see the copious proofs in Reusch, *Erklärung des Buch's Baruch* (1853), pp. 1–21 and 268 sqq. The book is very frequently quoted as a *work of the prophet Jeremiah,* because it was from early times combined with his book. *The passage concerning the appearance of God upon earth* (Bar. iii. 37: μετὰ τοῦτο ἐπὶ τῆς γῆς ὤφθη καὶ ἐν τοῖς ἀνθρώποις συνανεστράφη), which Kneucker rightly regards as a Christian gloss, was a favourite one with the Fathers. The oldest quotation is in Athenagoras, *Suppl.* c. 9, where Bar. iii. 35 is cited as the saying of a προφήτης. Irenaeus, iv. 20, refers to Bar. iii. 37. He also quotes (v. 35. 1) Bar. iv. 36 to v. *fin.* with the formula, significavit Jeremias propheta dicens. Clemens Alexandrinus, *Paedag.* i. 10. 91, 92, quotes various passages of this book as sayings of the prophet Jeremiah. In *Paedag.* ii. 3. 36 he quotes Bar. iii. 16 – 19 with the formula ἡ θεία που λέγει γραφή. Hippolytus mentions in his work *Contra Λoetum,* that Noetus and his followers appealed to Bar. iii. 35-37, among other passages, in proof of their patripassian Christology (*Hippol.* ed. Lagarde, p. 44). He then, to help himself out of difficulty, himself gives (ed. Lagarde, p. 47) a very sophistical interpretation of the passage. Hence the book is for Hippolytus as well as Noetus a standard

authority. Origenes, *in Jerem. homil.* vii. 3 (Lommatzsch, xv.
190): γέγραπται· "ἄκουε Ἰσραήλ κ.τ.λ." = Bar. iii. 9–13. Idem,
*Selecta in Jerem.* c. 31 (Lommatzsch, xv. 456): γέγραπται ἐν τῷ
Βαρούχ· "τί ὅτι ἐν γῇ κ.τ.λ."= Bar. iii. 10. Commodian. *Carmen
apologet.* (ed. Ludwig) vers. 367, 368 : Hieremias ait: Hic deus
est, etc.= Bar. iii. 35–37. Cyprian. *Testim.* ii. 6 : Item apud
Hieremiam prophetam : Hic deus noster, etc. = Bar. iii.
35–37. Material from later Fathers will be found in Reusch as
above quoted, to which need only be added *Altercatio Simonis
Judaei et Theophili Christiani*, ed. Harnack, p. 17 (in Gebhardt
and Harnack, *Texte und Untersuchungen*, vol. i. No. 3, 1883).

Among the *Greek manuscripts* the most important are : the
*Vaticanus* (which however, not having been collated for this
book by Holmes and Parsons, has also been paid no regard to
in Fritzsche's edition), the *Alexandrinus* (No. iii. in Holmes
and Parsons) and the *Marchalianus* (No. xii.). The Sinaiticus
does not contain the Book of Baruch. On the editions, see
above, p. 10.

*Ancient translations.* 1. The Latin which is extant in two
widely differing recensions : (*a*) that which has passed into the
Vulgate, and (*b*) one first published by Joseph Caro, Rome
1688. The latter according to three MSS. in Sabatier, *Biblior.
sacror. Latinae versiones antiquae*, vol. ii. p. 734 sqq. Also in
*Bibliotheca Casinensis*, vol. i. (1873), *Florileg.* pp. 284–287. On
the relation of the two to each other, see Fritzsche, *Handb.*
i. 175. Reusch, *Erklärung des Buchs Baruch*, p. 88 sq.
Kneucker, *Das Buch Baruch*, p. 157 sqq. 2. The two *Syriac
translations*, (*a*) the *Peshito* or the Syriac common text, comp.
above, p. 11. (*b*) The *Syrus hexaplaris*, contained for this
book in the Milan manuscript of the *Syrus hexaplaris*. The
Book of Baruch with the letter of Jeremiah of this MS. were
first published by Ceriani (*Monumenta sacra et profana*, vol. i.
fasc. i. 1861). Also in the photo-lithographic copy of the
entire manuscript, see above, p. 187. 3. A Coptic translation
published by Brugsch (*Zeitschr. für ägyptische Sprache und
Alterthumskunde*, 10–12th year, 1872–1874, comp. 1876, p. 148).

The exegesis in general, see above, p. 11. Commentaries :
Fritzsche, *Exeget. Handb. zu den Apokryphen*, Part i. Leipzig
1851. Reusch, *Erklärung des Buchs Baruch*, Freiburg 1853.
Ewald, *Die Propheten des Alten Bundes*, vol. iii. (2nd ed.
1868), pp. 251–298. Kneucker, *Das Buch Baruch, Geschichte
und Kritik, Uebersetzung und Erklärung*, Leipzig 1879. The
other literature : Hävernick, *De libro Baruchi apocrypho comm.
crit.* Regim. 1843. Hitzig, *Zeitschr. für wissenschaftl. Theol.*
1860, pp. 262–273. Ewald, *Gesch. des Volkes Israel*, vol. iv.
(1864) p. 265 sqq. Hilgenfeld, *Zeitschr. für wissensch. Theol.* vol.

v. 1862, pp. 199–203; xxii. 1879, pp. 437–454; xxiii. 1880, pp. 412–422. Kneucker, the same periodical, 1880, pp. 309–323. The Introductions of Jahne, Eichhorn, Bertholdt, Welte, Scholz, De Wette-Schrader, Reusch, Keil, Kaulen, Kleinert, Reuss (see above, p. 12).

### 6. *The Letter of Jeremiah.*

The letter of Jeremiah, which is said to have been written to the exiles destined to be led away to Babylon, is a *warning against idolatry*, turning upon the theme, that images of wood, silver and gold, are the weak, powerless and perishable creatures of man's hand, which can absolutely do neither good nor harm. The author seeks by these particulars to restrain his co-religionists in the Dispersion from all participation in heathen rites. This small fragment is certainly of Greek origin.

Many have seen in the passage 2 Macc. i. 1 sqq. *a reference to this letter*. But what is there said does not actually suit it. When Origen asserts, that the Lamentations and "the letter" also were combined in the Hebrew canon with the Book of Jeremiah (Euseb. *Hist. eccl.* vi. 25. 2: Ἰερεμίας σὺν θρήνοις καὶ τῇ ἐπιστολῇ ἐν ἑνί), this certainly rests upon an oversight. Origen only means to say, that the writings of Jeremiah were reckoned by the Jews as *one*, so that the number twenty-two is consequently that of the collected books of Holy Scripture. *Christian quotations:* Tertullian, *Scorpiace*, c. 8. Cyprian, *De dominica oratione*, c. 5, and later writers.

In the majority of editions and manuscripts, the letter is appended to the Book of Baruch (in the Vulgate as its sixth chapter). Hence what has been said of manuscripts, editions, ancient translations and exegesis with respect to that book applies almost throughout in this case.

### III. HISTORICAL LITERATURE.

The literary productions as yet discussed are in part compilations, in part imitations of older scriptural works. Hence there is but little specifically "Hellenistic" to be observed in them. The peculiarity of Judaeo-Hellenistic literature is apparent in an entirely different manner in

those works, which incline in form towards non-scriptural
Greek models and are thus found in the department of
historical, poetic and philosophic literature. And first for
the historical. Pharisaic Judaism as such had scarcely an
interest in history. It saw in history merely an instruction,
a warning, how God ought to be served. Hellenistic Judaism
was certainly in a far higher degree interested in history as
such. A knowledge of the history of the past formed part of
the culture of the times. And no people could lay claim to
be reckoned among the civilised nations, unless they could
point to an old and imposing history. Even nations hitherto
regarded as barbarian now compiled their histories and clad
them in Greek garments for the purpose of making them
accessible to the entire cultured world. The Hellenistic
Jews also took their part in such efforts. They too worked
up their sacred history for the instruction of both their own
fellow-countrymen and the non-Jewish world. The most
comprehensive work of the kind, with which we are acquainted,
is the great historical work of Josephus. He had however a
series of predecessors, who laboured some upon longer, some
upon shorter periods of Jewish history in various forms.
Of these some set to work in modest annalistic manner
(Demetrius), some with fantastic and legendary embellishments
*in majorem Judaeorum gloriam* (Eupolemus, Artapanus), while
some sought in a philosophical manner to represent the great
Jewish lawgiver as the greatest of philosophers, nay as the
father of all philosophy (Philo). But the Greek Jews
occupied themselves not only with the older Jewish history,
but also depicted—as Pharisaic Judaism had ceased to do—
important occurrences, which they had as contemporaries
experienced, for the purpose of transmitting them to posterity
(Jason of Cyrene, Philo, Josephus, Justus of Tiberias). Many
who carried on authorship as a vocation were active in both
departments. We therefore here place together historical
works of both kinds, viz. compilations of the older sacred
history and delineations of contemporary events.

The most ancient of these Judaeo-Hellenistic historians have
been only rescued from utter oblivion by Alexander Polyhistor.   This voluminous writer, who lived about the years
80–40 B.C. (according to the statements of Suidas, *Lex. s.v.*
᾽Αλέξανδρος, and Sueton. *De gramm.* c. 20, comp. Müller,
*Fragm.* iii. 206, and Unger, *Philologus*, 1884, p. 528 sqq.),
composed among other works one περὶ ᾽Ιουδαίων, in which he
strung together, apparently with scarcely any additions of his
own, extracts from foreign authors concerning the Jews.
Eusebius in his turn embodied in his *Praeparatio evangelica*
(ix. 17–39) a large portion of this collection of extracts.
And it is to this circumstance, that we are almost entirely
indebted for our acquaintance with the oldest Judaeo-
Hellenistic and Samaritan compilations of scriptural history
whether in poetic or prosaic form, with those of Demetrius,
Eupolemus, Artapanus, Aristeas, Kleodemus, Philo, Theodotus
and Ezekiel.   Besides Eusebius, Clemens Alexandrinus also
once quotes Alexander's work περὶ ᾽Ιουδαίων (*Strom.* i. 21.
130); and he undoubtedly makes use of it, even when he
quotes Demetrius, Philo, Eupolemus, Artapanus and Ezekiel,
from whom Alexander gives extracts (*Strom.* i. 21. 141,
23. 153–156).   The quotation also in Josephus, *Antt.*
i. 15, is certainly derived from the work περὶ ᾽Ιουδαίων, with
which Josephus elsewhere betrays his acquaintance (*contra
Apion.* i. 23, and various traces in the *Antiquities*).   But
this is all that is preserved of independent quotation from
Alexander's work.   The extracts in Eusebius are in chronological order.   They begin with fragments on the history
of Abraham from Eupolemus, Artapanus, Molon, Philo,
Kleodemus.   Then follow portions on the history of Jacob
from Demetrius and Theodotus, then others on Joseph from
Artapanus and Philo.   That this order is not first derived
from Eusebius, but was followed by Alexander Polyhistor,
is shown by the nature of the text.   For the single portions
are joined together by the connecting words of Alexander
himself.

This is moreover confirmed by a comparison of the quotations in Clemens Alexandrinus. For as in Eusebius so in Clemens Alexandrinus the extracts on the history of Moses follow each other in direct succession :—

Eupolemus = Euseb. ix. 26 = Clemens, *Str.* i. 23. 153.
Artapanus  = Euseb. ix. 27 = Clemens, *Str.* i. 23. 154.
Ezekiel    = Euseb. ix. 28 = Clemens, *Str.* i. 23. 155, 156.

Hence we see that this is the original order of Alexander Polyhistor. The genuineness of Alexander's work has of late been frequently disputed, especially by Rauch and Cruice. It is thought inconceivable, that a heathen author like Alexander should have had so special an interest in Jewish affairs ; it is also thought strange that he should call the Old Testament Scriptures ἱεραὶ βίβλοι (Euseb. ix. 24, 29. 15), and that he should here give such detailed accounts of Jewish history, while he elsewhere betrays the strangest ignorance of it. Its genuineness has been defended against these objections by Hulleman (p. 156 sq.), Müller (*Fragm.* iii. 209), and especially with convincing proofs by Freudenthal (pp. 174–184). The question is moreover one of minor importance, since it is tolerably indifferent whether these extracts were collected by Alexander or by some one else ; for in either case the extraordinary differences in form and contents existing in these fragments is a guarantee, that we have here to deal with extracts from works then actually existing and not with the single work of a forger. Only the determination of the date would be affected, if it could be really proved, that the collection was not the production of Alexander Polyhistor, inasmuch as the time of Alexander would then cease to be a limit. The fragments in themselves furnish no cause for relegating them to a later date. For the most recent of the authors, from whom the extracts are made, and whose date can be determined independently of Alexander, is Apollonius Molon (Euseb. ix. 19), a Greek orator of probably about 120–100 B.C. (see No. VI. below).

References to Jewish affairs are also found in other works
of Alexander Polyhistor. He quotes the Jewish Sibyl in his
Chaldaean ancient history (Euseb. *Chron.* ed. Schöne, i. 23.
Cyrill. *adv. Julian.* ed. Spanh. p. 9ᶜ. Syncell. ed. Dindorf, i. 81.
Comp. Joseph. *Antt.* i. 4. 3 ; Freudenthal, p. 25 sq.). In his
work on Italy is found the odd assertion, that the Jewish law
was derived from a female named Moso (Suidas, *Lex. s.v.*
'Αλέξανδρος. Müller, *Fragm.* n. 25) ; and to his work on Syria
belongs probably the information that Judaea received its
name from Juda and Idumaea, the children of Semiramis
(Steph. *Byz. s.v.* 'Ιουδαία. Müller, *Fragm.* n. 98–102). It is
just these strange statements which have given rise to the
denial of Alexander's authorship of the work περὶ 'Ιουδαίων—but
very incorrectly, for he simply copied what he found in his
authorities. Consequently, according to their nature, his information is now correct, now incorrect. It rests upon only a
somewhat wanton combination, when the pseudo - Justinian
*Cohort. ad Graec.* c. 9 ascribes also to Alexander a statement
concerning the date of Moses (see my article on "Julius
Africanus as the source of the pseudo-Justinian *Cohortatio ad
Graecos,*" in Brieger's *Zeitschr. für Kirchengesch.* vol. ii. 1878, p.
319 sqq.).

The *text* of the fragment περὶ 'Ιουδαίων is in Euseb. *Evangelicae
Praeparationis libri,* xv. ed. Gaisford, 4 vols. Oxford 1843.
Clementis Alex. *Opera,* ed. Dindorf, 4 vols. Oxford 1869.
Müller, *Fragmenta historicorum Graecorum,* vol. iii. pp. 211–230.
The prose fragments, partly according to a recent collation of
manuscripts, are best given in Freudenthal, *Alex. Polyhistor,* pp.
219–236. On the manuscripts and editions of Eusebius, see
Freudenthal, pp. 199–202.

Comp. in general : Rauch, *De Alexandri Polyhistoris vita
atque scriptis,* Heidelb. 1843, quoted by Müller and others as
"Rumpf." Cruice, *De Fl. Josephi in auctoribus contra Apionem
afferendis fide et auctoritate* (Paris 1844), pp. 20–30. Hulleman,
"De Corn. Alexandro Polyhistore" (*Miscellanea philologa et
paedagoga edd. gymnasiorum Batavorum doctores,* vol. i. 1849,
pp. 87–178). C. Müller, *Fragm. hist. graec.* iii. 206–244.
Vaillant, *De historicis qui ante Josephum Judaicas res scripsere,
nempe Aristea, Demetrio, Eupolemo, Hecataeo Abderita, Cleo-
demo, Artapano, Justo Tiberiensi, Cornelio Alexandro Polyhistore*
(Paris 1851, Didot), pp. 88–98 (a follower of Cruice). Creuzer,
*Theol. Stud. und Krit.* 1853, p. 76 sqq. Herzfeld, *Gesch. des
Volkes Jisrael,* iii. 570 sqq. Westermann in Pauly's *Real-Enc.
der class. Alterthums-wissensch.* i. 1 (2nd ed. 1864), p. 734 sq.
Freudenthal, *Alexander Polyhistor und die von ihm erhaltenen
Reste judaischer und samaritanischer Geschichtswerke,* Bresl.

1875. Reuss, *Gesch. der heiligen Schriften A. T.'s* (1881), § 520, 521. Unger, "Wann schrieb Alexander Polyhistor?" (*Philologus*, vol. xliii. 1884, pp. 528–531).

## 1. *Demetrius.*

In the same century in which Berosus composed the ancient history of the Chaldaeans, and Manetho that of the Egyptians, but about sixty years later, Demetrius, a Jewish Hellenist, compiled in a brief chronological form a history of Israel, his work being equally with theirs according to the sacred records. Clem. Alex. *Strom.* i. 21. 141 states its title to have been περὶ τῶν ἐν τῇ Ἰουδαίᾳ βασιλέων. And it can be scarcely a reason for doubting the correctness of this title, that the fragments deal almost all with only the most ancient period (so Freudenthal, p. 205 sq.). For Justus of Tiberias *e.g.* also treated of the time of Moses in his Chronicle of the Jewish kings. The first fragment in Euseb. *Praep. evang.* ix. 21 concerns the history of Jacob from his emigration to Mesopotamia till his death. At the close the genealogy of the tribe of Levi is carried on to the birth of Moses and Aaron. Chronology is made a special aim. Nay, the whole is far more a settlement of chronology than a history properly so called. The date of every single circumstance in the life of Laban, *e.g.* the birth of each of his twelve sons and such matters, is precisely determined. Of course many dates have to be assumed for which Scripture offers no support. A large portion of the chronological statements is obtained by combinations, and in some instances very complicated combinations of actual dates of Holy Scripture. A second fragment (Euseb. *Praep. evang.* ix. 29. 1–3) from the history of Moses is chiefly occupied in proving, that Zipporah the wife of Moses was descended from Abraham and Keturah. This fragment is also used in the *Chronicon paschale*, ed. Dindorf, i. 117, and is quoted from Eusebius in the *Chron. Anon.* in Cramer, *Anecdota*, Paris, ii. 256. In a third (Euseb. *Praep.*

*evang.* ix. 29. 15) the history of the bitter waters (Ex. xv.
22 sqq.) is related. Lastly, the chronological fragment preserved in Clem. Alex. *Strom.* i. 21. 141 gives precise statements
concerning the length of time from the carrying away into
captivity of the ten tribes and the tribes of Judah and Benjamin
to Ptolemy IV. It is just this fragment which gives us also
a key to the date of Demetrius. For it is evident that he chose
the time of Ptolemy IV. (222–205 B.C.) as a closing point for
his calculations, because he himself lived in the reign of that
monarch. Hence we obtain also an important standpoint for
determining the date of the LXX. For that Demetrius made
use of the Septuagint translation of the Pentateuch is acknowledged even by Hody, although such acknowledgment is
unfavourable to his tendency of pointing out the limited
diffusion obtained by the LXX. A glance at the contents of
the fragment renders it needless to prove that *its author was
a Jew.* It would certainly never have entered the mind of a
heathen to take such pains in calculating and completing the
Biblical chronology. Nevertheless Josephus took him for one
and confounded him with Demetrius Phalereus (*Contra Apion.*
i. 23 = Euseb. *Praep. evang.* ix. 42; comp. Müller, *Fragm.* ii.
369ª. Freudenthal, p. 170, note). Among moderns too, *e.g.*
Hody, is found the mistaken notion that he was a heathen.
The correct one is however already met with in Eusebius,
*Hist. eccl.* vi. 13. 7, and after him in Hieronymus, *De vir.
illustr.* c. 38 (ed. Vallarsi, ii. 879).

Clemens Alex. *Strom.* i. 21. 141: Δημήτριος δέ φησιν ἐν τῷ περὶ
τῶν ἐν τῇ Ἰουδαίᾳ βασιλέων τὴν Ἰούδα φυλὴν καὶ Βενιαμὶν καὶ Λευὶ μὴ
αἰχμαλωτισθῆναι ὑπὸ τοῦ Σεναχηρείμ, ἀλλ' εἶναι ἀπὸ τῆς αἰχμαλωσίας
ταύτης εἰς τὴν ἐσχάτην, ἣν ἐποιήσατο Ναβουχοδονόσορ ἐξ Ἱεροσολύμων, ἔτη
ἑκατὸν εἴκοσι ὀκτὼ μῆνας ἕξ. ἀφ' οὗ δὲ αἱ φυλαὶ αἱ δέκα ἐκ Σαμαρείας
αἰχμάλωτοι γεγόνασιν ἕως Πτολεμαίου τετάρτου [B.C. 222] ἔτη πεντακόσια ἑβδομήκοντα τρία μῆνας ἐννέα, ἀφ' οὗ δὲ ἐξ Ἱεροσολύμων ἔτη
τριακόσια τριάκοντα ὀκτὼ μῆνας τρεῖς. The text of this fragment is
in many instances corrupt. 1. It is impossible that Demetrius,
with his minute accuracy in scriptural chronology, could have
reckoned from 573–338, *i.e.* 235 years from the carrying away
of the ten tribes to the carrying away of the tribes of Benjamin

and Judah, when the interval amounts to about a hundred
years less. Hence the number 573 must either be reduced, or
that of 338 increased, by one hundred. The latter is undoubtedly correct, since it may be shown, that other ancient
chronologists have made the post-exilian period too long (see
above on Daniel, p. 54). If Demetrius therefore put down
about seventy years too much for this time, there is for just this
reason utterly no motive for doing away with this mistake by
altering "Ptolemy IV." into "Ptolemy VII." For even in the
accurate Demetrius such a mistake concerning the length of
the post-exilian period cannot seem surprising, since the scriptural figures here leave him in the lurch. 2. By abbreviation
of the text arose the absurdity that an αἰχμαλωτισθῆναι ὑπὸ τοῦ
Σεναχηρείμ is first denied, and then that this αἰχμαλωσία is
computed from. The thought of the original text undoubtedly
is, that the tribes of Judah and Benjamin were not made
captives, but only laid under contribution, by Sennacherib; and
that 120 years elapsed between this pillaging expedition of
Sennacherib and the carrying away of Judah and Benjamin.
With this computation it best agrees, that from the carrying
away of the ten tribes to that of Judah and Benjamin 573 –
438 = 135 years are reckoned. For the carrying away of the
ten tribes by Shalmanezer actually took place about seven or
eight years *before* Sennacherib's attack upon Judah (2 Kings
xviii. 9–13).

Comp. in general: Vigerus' *Anmerkungen* to his edition of the
*Praep. evang.* of Eusebius (1628). Huetius, *Demonstr. evang.*
(5th ed. Lips. 1703) Prop. iv. c. 2, § 22, 30. Hody, *De
biblior. textibus* (1705), p. 107. Valckenaer, *De Aristobulo*, p.
18. Dähne, *Geschichtl. Darstellung der jüd.-alex. Rel.-Phil.* ii.
220 sq. Cruice, *De Fl. Josephi fide* (1844), pp. 53–58. C.
Müller, *Fragm. hist. graec.* iii. 207 sqq. Vaillant, *De historicis
qui ante Josephum Judaicas res scripsere* (Paris 1851). pp.
45–52. Herzfeld, *Gesch. des Volkes Jisrael*, iii. 486–488, 575 sq.
M. Niebuhr, *Gesch. Assur's und Babel's* (1857), pp. 101–104.
Freudenthal, *Alexander Polyhistor* (1875), pp. 35–82, 205 sqq.,
219 sqq. Mendelssohn, *Anzeige Freudenthal's in der Jenaer,
Lit.-Ztg.* 1885, No. 6. Siegfried, *Zeitschr. f. wissenschaftl. Theol.*
1875, p. 475. Gutschmid, *Jahrbb. für Protestant. Theol.* 1875,
p. 744 sqq. Grätz, *Monatsschr. f. Gesch. u. Wissensch. d.
Judenth.* 1877, p. 68 sqq. Bloch, *Die Quellen des Fl. Josephus*
(1879), p. 56 sqq.

## 2. *Eupolemus.*

In place of the dry chronological computations of Demetrius, we find in Eupolemus a chequered narrative which freely handles the scriptural history and further embellishes it with all kinds of additions. Formerly *three* different works of this writer were spoken of: 1. Περὶ τῶν τῆς 'Ασσυρίας 'Ιουδαίων; 2. Περὶ τῆς 'Ηλίου προφητείας; and 3. Περὶ τῶν ἐν τῇ 'Ιουδαίᾳ βασιλέων (so Kuhlmey, p. 3). The first of these falls away, because in the fragment in Euseb. *Praep. evang.* ix. 17: Εὐπόλεμος δὲ ἐν τῷ περὶ 'Ιουδαίων τῆς 'Ασσυρίας φησὶ πάλιν Βαβυλῶνα πρῶτον μὲν κτισθῆναι ὑπὸ τῶν κ.τ.λ., the words τῆς 'Ασσυρίας certainly refer to what follows (Rauch, p. 21; Freudenthal, p. 207). The title περὶ τῶν ἐν τῇ 'Ιουδαίᾳ βασιλέων is certified by Clemens Alex. *Strom.* i. 23. 153. To this work also undoubtedly belongs the fragment referring to the history of David and Solomon in Euseb. *Praep. evang.* ix. 30–34, which Alexander Poly- histor asserts that he took from a work περὶ τῆς 'Ηλίου προφητείας (Freudenthal, p. 208). Thus we in truth obtain only one work instead of the supposed three. The first fragment (Euseb. *Praep. evang.* ix. 17) probably does not belong to Eupolemus at all (comp. hereon No. 6 below); a second almost verbally identical in Euseb. *Praep. evang.* ix. 26, and Clemens Alex. *Strom.* i. 23. 153, represents Moses as the "first sage," who transmitted to the Jews the art of alphabetical writing, which was then handed on by the Jews to the Phoenicians, and by the latter to the Hellenes. The *Chronicon paschale*, ed. Dindorf, i. 117, also has this frag- ment from Eusebius, and Cyrillus Alex. *adv. Julian.* ed. Spanh. p. 231[d], has it from Clement. The long passage in Euseb. *Praep. evang.* ix. 30–34 refers to the history of David and Solomon. It commences with a summary of chronology from Moses to David, then briefly relates the chief events of the history of David (Euseb. ix. 30), and then gives a corre-

spondence between Solomon and the kings Uaphres of Egypt
and Suron of Phoenicia about assistance in the building of the
temple (Euseb. ix. 31–34; comp. Clemens Alex. *Strom.* i.
21. 130; *Chron. pasch.* ed. Dind. i. 168); and lastly
describes in detail the building of the temple (Euseb. ix.
34). The correspondence with Suron = Hiram is taken from
2 Chron. ii. 2, 15, comp. 1 Kings v. 15–25; and that with
Uaphres freely imitated from this model. Probably the
fragment in Euseb. ix. 39, in which it is related how Jeremiah
foretold the captivity, and how his prediction was fulfilled by
the conquest of Jerusalem by Nebuchadnezzar, also belongs
to Eupolemus. The fragment is according to the reading of
the best manuscripts anonymous, but may on internal grounds
be ascribed to Eupolemus (Freudenthal, p. 208 sq.). A
chronological fragment in Clemens Alex. *Strom.* i. 2114. 1,
which computes in a summary manner the time from Adam
and Moses respectively to the fifth year of Demetrius, or the
twelfth of Ptolemy, gives us information concerning the *date
of Eupolemus.* For by this Demetrius we must probably
understand (see below) Demetrius I. Soter (162–150 B.C.),
and hence Eupolemus would have written in the year
158–157 B.C. or shortly afterwards. He may therefore be,
as many have supposed, identical with the Eupolemus
mentioned 1 Macc. viii. 17. In this case he would be a
Palestinian, which is certainly favoured also by the circumstance, that he seems, besides the translation of the LXX.,
of which the Book of Chronicles was certainly in his hands,
to have made use also of the original Hebrew text (Freudenthal, pp. 108, 119). Concerning his nationality, whether
Jew or heathen, opinions are, as also in the case of Demetrius,
divided; Josephus, *c. Apion.* i. 23 (= Euseb. *Praep. evang.* ix.
42), esteemed him a heathen, as do also Hody and Kuhlmey.
On the other hand, Eusebius, *Hist. eccl.* vi. 13. 7, and
Jerome, *De viris illustr.* c. 38, regard him as a Jew. And
this, as Freudenthal has recently shown, is undoubtedly
correct (pp. 83–85).

Clemens Alex. *Strom.* i. 21. 141 : ῎Ετι δὲ καὶ Εὐπόλεμος ἐν τῇ ὁμοίᾳ πραγματείᾳ τὰ πάντα ἔτη φησὶν ἀπὸ ᾿Αδὰμ ἄχρι τοῦ πέμπτου ἔτους Δημητρίου βασιλείας, Πτολεμαίου τὸ δωδέκατον βασιλεύοντος Αἰγύπτου, συνάγεσθαι ἔτη ͵ερμθ´. ἀφ᾿ οὗ δὲ χρόνου ἐξήγαγε Μωυσῆς τοὺς ᾿Ιουδαίους ἐξ Αἰγύπτου ἐπὶ τὴν προειρημένην προθεσμίαν συνάγεσθαι ἔτη δισχίλια πεντακόσια ὀγδοήκοντα. [ἀπὸ δὲ τοῦ χρόνου τούτου ἄχρι τῶν ἐν ῾Ρώμῃ ὑπάτων Γαΐου Δομετιανοῦ Κασιανοῦ συναθροίζεται ἔτη ἑκατὸν εἴκοσι]. In this fragment also the text is defective. Above all, it is certain that the number 2580 must be corrected to 1580, since Eupolemus could not have reckoned 2580 years from Moses to his own time. Then the synchronism of the fifth year of Demetrius with the twelfth of Ptolemy causes difficulties. For no twelfth year of any Ptolemy coincides with the fifth year of Demetrius II. (= 142–141 B.C.). The twelfth year indeed of Ptolemy VII. (= 159–158) concurs with the fifth year of Demetrius I. (= 158-157 B.C.). But Ptolemy VII. Physcon was at that time only ruler of Cyrenaica. He reigned in Egypt contemporaneously with his brother Ptolemy VI. Philometor, who however began his reign four years previously. We must therefore either regard, with Gutschmid, the whole statement concerning Ptolemy as a gloss or, which is more simple, alter the number. However this may be, the supposition that Demetrius I. Soter is intended is especially favoured by the circumstance, that at all events such was the view of Clemens Alex. For he reckons from the fifth year of Demetrius to the consulship of Cn. Domitius Calvinus and C. Asinius Pollio (these names being certainly hidden under the corrupted words Γαΐου Δομετιανοῦ Κασιανοῦ), *i.e.* to the year 40 B.C. in which Herod was named king (Joseph. *Antt.* xiv. 14. 5) 120 years, which of necessity reach back to Demetrius I., even if the reckoning is not quite accurate. Gutschmid has best restored the closing words by the complement Γναίου Δομετίου καὶ ᾿Ασινίου ὑπὸ Κασιανοῦ συναθροίζεται. Cassianus is mentioned as a chronologist by Clem. *Strom.* i. 21. 101.

Comp. in general: Huetius, *Demonstr. evang. Prop.* iv. c. ii. § 29. Hody, *De biblior. textib.* p. 106. Valckenaer, *De Aristobulo*, pp. 18, 24. Dähne, *Geschichtl. Darstellung*, ii. 221 sq. Kuhlmey, *Eupolemi fragmenta prolegomenis et commentario instructa*, Berol. 1840. Rauch, *De Alex. Polyh.* pp. 20–22. Cruice, *De Fl. Jos. fide*, pp. 58–61. C. Müller, *Fragm. hist. gr.* iii. 207 sqq. Vaillant, *De historicis*, etc., pp. 52–59. Herzfeld, *Gesch. des Volkes Jisrael*, iii. 481–483, 572–574. M. Niebuhr, *Gesch. Assur's*, pp. 353–356. Cobet in Λόγιος ῾Ερμῆς ἐκδ. ὑπὸ Κόντου, vol. i. (Leyden 1866) p. 168 sq. Ewald, *Gesch. d. V. Isr.* i. 76, vii. 91, 92. Freudenthal, *Alex. Polyh.* pp. 82 sqq., 105–130, 208 sqq., 225 sqq. Siegfried, *Zeitschr. f. wissenschaftl. Theol.* 1875,

p. 476 sqq. Gutschmid, *Jahrbb. f. prot. Theol.* 1875, p. 749 sqq. Grätz, *Monatsschr. f. Gesch. u. Wissensch. d. Judenth.* 1877, p. 61 sqq. Bloch, *Die Quellen des Fl. Josephus* (1879), p. 58 sqq.

### 3. *Artapanus.*

In his work περὶ Ἰουδαίων Artapanus is still farther removed than Eupolemus from the sober and unadorned style of Demetrius. The sacred history is quite methodically embellished, or to speak more correctly remodelled, by fantastic and tasteless additions — and this recasting is throughout in the interest of the tendency to a glorification of the Jewish people. One chief aim is directed towards proving, that the Egyptians were indebted to the Jews for all useful knowledge and institutions. Thus the very first fragment (Euseb. *Praep. evang.* ix. 18) relates that Abraham, when he journeyed into Egypt, instructed the king, Pharethothes, in astrology. A second (Euseb. ix. 23) narrates how Joseph, when raised by the king to be the chief governor of the country, provided for the better cultivation of the land. And finally, the long article concerning Moses (Euseb. ix. 27) gives detailed information of his being the real founder of all the culture and even of the worship of the gods in Egypt. For he it was whom the Greeks call Musaeus, the instructor of Orpheus, the author of a multitude of useful inventions and attainments, of navigation, architecture, military science, and philosophy. He also divided the country into thirty-six provinces, and commanded each province to worship God; he also instructed the priests in hieroglyphics. He introduced order into State affairs. Hence he was beloved by the Egyptians, who called him Hermas, διὰ τὴν τῶν ἱερῶν γραμμάτων ἑρμηνείαν. King Chenephres however sought, out of envy, to get rid of him. But none of the means he used succeeded. When Chenephres was dead, Moses received commandment from God to deliver His people from Egyptian bondage. The history of the exodus and of all that preceded it, especially of the miracles by which the permission to depart was extorted, is then related at length and in accordance with the Scripture narrative, but at the same time with many additions and embellishments. Single traits from this history are related, with express appeal to Artapanus, in Clemens Alex. *Strom.* i. 23. 154, in *Chron. pasch.* ed. Dindorf, i. 117, and in the *Chron. anonym.* in Cramer, *Anecdota*, Paris, ii. 176. Traces of the employment of this work may be pointed out especially in Josephus (see Freudenthal, pp. 169–171). The more plainly its Jewish authorship is manifested by the tendency of the whole work, the more strange does it appear, that Moses and the patriarchs should be exhibited as founders of the Egyptian worships. Jacob and his sons are represented as founding the sanctuaries at Athos and Heliopolis (23. 4). Moses directs each province to honour God ($\tau\grave{o}\nu$ $\Theta\epsilon\grave{o}\nu$ $\sigma\epsilon\phi\theta\acute{\eta}\sigma\epsilon\sigma\theta\alpha\iota$); he prescribes the consecration of the Ibis (27. 9) and of Apis (27. 12). In a word, the religion of Egypt is referred to Jewish authority. This fact has been explained by Freudenthal by the surely incorrect notion, that the author was indeed a Jew, but wanted to pass for a heathen, and indeed for an Egyptian priest (pp. 149 sq., 152 sq.). For nowhere does such an attempt come plainly forward. And with such a tendency, an entirely unknown name such as Artapanus would certainly never have been chosen as a shield. Nor does it at all explain the phenomena. For if the work had appeared under a heathen mask, we should surely expect, that it would have energetically denounced in the name of this acknowledged authority the abomination of idol-worship, as is actually done, *e.g.* in the case of the Sibyllist (iii. 20), and of pseudo-Aristeas (pp. 38, 14 sq., ed. Mor. Schmidt). Thus, under all circumstances, the strange fact remains, that a Jewish author has represented Moses as the founder of Egyptian rites. But however strange this may appear, it is explained by the tendency of the whole. Moses was the introducer of all culture, even of religious culture. This and nothing else is the meaning. Besides, it

must be considered, that the heathen worship is in reality
represented in a tolerably innocent light. For the sacred
animals are not so much worshipped, as on the contrary
"consecrated" for their utility—τῷ Θεῷ, as we cannot but
conclude. But even thus, we certainly have still to do with
a Jewish author, who cared more for the honour of the Jewish
name, than for the purity of divine worship. Perhaps too an
apologetic purpose co-operated in causing the Jews, who were
decried as despisers of the gods, to figure as founders of religious worship. Considering the marked pr ominence of Egyptian
references, there needs no other proof that the author was an
Egyptian. With regard to date, it can only be affirmed with
certainty of him and of those who follow, that they were
predecessors of Alexander Polyhistor.

Comp. in general: Huetius, *Demonstr. evang.* Prop. iv. c. ii.
§ 62. Valckenaer, *De Aristobulo*, p. 26. Dähne, *Geschichtl.
Darstellung*, ii. 200–203. Rauch, *De Alexandro Polyhistore*,
p. 22 sq. C. Müller, *Fragm.* iii. 207 sqq. Vaillant, *De historicis*,
etc., pp. 74–83. Herzfeld, *Gesch. des Volkes Jisrael*, iii. 483–486,
574. Cobet in the Λόγιος Ἐρμῆς, i. 170, 171. Ewald, ii. 129.
Freudenthal, *Alex. Polyh.* pp. 143–174, 215 sqq., 231 sqq.
Bloch, *Die Quellen des Josephus*, p. 60 sqq.


## 4. *Aristeas.*

A fragment from the work of one otherwise unknown,
Aristeas περὶ Ἰουδαίων, in which the history of Job is briefly
related in accordance with the Bible, is given in Euseb.
*Praep. ev.* ix. 25. The history itself presents nothing worthy
of remark, but the personal accounts both of Job and his
friends are supplemented on the ground of other scriptural
material. Thus it is said of Job, that he was formerly called
*Jobab*, Ἰώβ being evidently identical with Ἰωβάβ, Gen.
xxxvi. 33. Upon the ground of this identification Job is
then made a descendant of Esau, for Jobab was a son of
Serach (Gen. xxxvi. 33), and the latter a grandson of Esau
(Gen. xxxvi. 10, 13). According indeed to the extract of

Alexander Polyhistor, Aristeas is said to have related that
Esau himself "married Bassara and begot Job of her" (τὸν
Ἡσαυ γήμαντα Βασσάραν ἐν Ἐδὼμ γεννῆσαι Ἰώβ). Most
probably however this rests upon an inaccurate reference of
Alexander Polyhistor; for Aristeas, who was quoting from
the Bible, must certainly have called Jobab not the son, but
correctly the great-grandson of Esau. From Gen. xxxvi. 33
is also derived the name Bassara as the mother of Job (Ἰωβὰβ
υἱὸς Ζαρὰ ἐκ Βοσόῤῥας, where indeed Bosra is in reality
not the mother, but the native place of Jobab). Our author
already used the LXX. translation of the Book of Job. It
is moreover remarkable, that in the supplement to Job in
the Septuagint the personal accounts of Job are compiled
exactly after the manner of Aristeas. Freudenthal thinks it
certain that this supplement was derived from Aristeas.

Comp. in general: C. Müller, *Fragm.* iii. 207 sqq. Herzfeld,
*Gesch. des Volkes Jisrael*, iii. 488 sqq., 577-579. Ewald, vii. 92.
Freudenthal, *Alex. Polyhistor*, pp. 136-143, 231.

### 5. *Cleodemus or Malchus.*

The work of a certain Cleodemus or Malchus, of which unfortunately only a short notice is preserved, seems to have presented a classic example of that intermixture of native (Oriental)
and Greek traditions, which was popular throughout the region
of Hellenism. The notice in question is communicated by
Alexander Polyhistor, but is taken by Eusebius, *Praep. evang.*
ix. 20, not directly from the latter, but from Josephus, *Antt.*
i. 15, who on his part quotes literally from Alexander. The
author is here called Κλεόδημος ὁ προφήτης ὁ καὶ Μάλχος,
ὁ ἱστορῶν τὰ περὶ Ἰουδαίων καθὼς καὶ Μωϋσῆς ἱστόρησεν ὁ
νομοθέτης αὐτῶν. Both the Semitic name Malchus and the
contents of the work prove, that the author was no Greek,
but either a Jew or a Samaritan. Freudenthal prefers the
latter view chiefly on account of the intermixture of Greek
and Jewish traditions. But about 200-100 B.C. this is

quite as possible in a Jew as in a Samaritan. In the work
of this Malchus it is related, that Abraham had three sons
by Keturah, Ἀφέραν, Ἀσουρείμ, Ἰάφραν, from whom the
Assyrians, the town of Aphra and the land of Africa derive
their names. The orthography of the names (which I have
given according to Freudenthal) vacillates considerably. Hence
אַשּׁוּרִם, עֵיפָה and עֵפֶר, Gen. xxv. 3, 4, are evidently identical
with them. But while in Gen. xxv. Arab tribes are intended,
our author derives from them entirely different nations, which
were known to him. He then further relates, that the three
sons of Abraham departed with Heracles to Libya and Antaeus,
that Heracles married the daughter of Aphra, and of her
begat Diodorus, whose son again was Sophonas (or Sophax),
from whom the Sophaki derive their name. These last
traditions are also found in the Libyan (or Roman ?) history
of King Juba (Plutarch. Sertor. c. ix., also in Müller, *Fragm.
hist. gr.* iii. 471) ; only that the genealogical relation of
Diodorus and Sophax is reversed : Heracles begets Sophax
of Tinge, the widow of Antaeus, and Diodorus is the son of
Sophax.

Comp. in general : C. Müller, *Fragm.* iii. 207 sqq. Vaillant,
*De historicis*, etc., pp. 72–74. Herzfeld, *Gesch. des Volkes Jisrael*,
iii. 489, 575. Ewald, vii. 91. Freudenthal, *Alex. Polyh.*
pp. 130–136, 215, 230. Siegfried, *Zeitschr. f. wissensch. Theol.*
1875, p. 476 sq.

### 6. *An Anonymous Writer.*

Among the extracts of Alexander Polyhistor are found,
Euseb. *Praep. evang.* ix. 17 and 18, two, which to judge by
their contents are evidently identical, although the one is much
shorter than the other. The longer (Euseb. ix. 17) is given
as an extract from Eupolemus, who relates that Abraham
descended in the [thir]teenth generation from the race of
giants, who after the deluge built the tower of Babel, that he
himself emigrated from Chaldaea to Phoenicia and taught the
Phoenicians τροπὰς ἡλίου καὶ σελήνης καὶ τὰ ἄλλα πάντα.

He also proved of assistance to them in war. He then
departed by reason of a famine to Egypt, where he lived with
the priests in Heliopolis and taught them much, instructing
them in τὴν ἀστρολογίαν καὶ τὰ λοιπά. The real discoverer
however of astrology was Enoch, who received it from the
angels and imparted it to men. We are told the same
virtually, but more briefly, in the second extract, Euseb. ix. 18,
which Alexander Polyhistor derived from *an anonymous work*
(ἐν δὲ ἀδεσπότοις εὕρομεν). If this parallel narrative is itself
striking, it must also be added, that the longer extract can
scarcely be from Eupolemus. Eupolemus was a Jew, but in
the extract Gerizim is explained by ὄρος ὑψίστου. Also
according to Eupolemus Moses was the first sage (Euseb. ix.
26), while in the extract Abraham is already glorified as the
father of all science. Hence the supposition of Freudenthal,
that the original of both extracts was one and the same, viz.
*the anonymous work of a Samaritan*, and that the longer
extract of Alexander has been ascribed by an oversight to
Eupolemus, is one which commends itself. In this work
also, as remains to be mentioned, Greek traditions and
Scripture history are again blended.

Comp. in general : C. Müller, *Fragm.* iii. 207 sqq. Freudenthal, *Alex. Polyh.* pp. 82–103, 207 sq., 223 sqq. Siegfried,
*Zeitschr. für wissenschaftl. Theol.* 1875, p. 476.

### 7. *Jason of Cyrene and the Second Book of Maccabees.*

The authors from whom extracts were made by Alexander
Polyhistor compiled chiefly from the older Scripture history.
The work of Jason of Cyrene, on which our second Book of
Maccabees is based, is an example of the treatment of those
important epochs of later Jewish history, in which they had
themselves lived, by Hellenistic Jews. For this book is, as
the author himself informs us, only an abridgment (ἐπιτομή,
2 Macc. ii. 26, 28) from the larger work of a certain Jason
of Cyrene (2 Macc. ii. 23). The original work comprised five

volumes, which are in our second Book of Maccabees condensed into one (2 Macc. ii. 23). Thus the contents of the former seem to have been parallel with those of the latter. The abridgment handed down to us tells first of an unsuccessful attack upon the treasury of the temple, undertaken in the time of Seleucus IV. (B.C. 175) by his minister Heliodorus; it then relates the religious persecution of Antiochus Epiphanes and the apostasy of a portion of the Jews; and lastly recounts the Maccabaean rising and its progress down to the decisive victory of Judas over Nicanor (160 B.C.). Thus the book comprises a period of not much more than fifteen years, 175–160 B.C. The events related are for the most part the same as in the first Book of the Maccabees. But the narrative differs in many particulars, and in some parts even in the order of the events, from the account in the first book. The differences are of such a kind that an acquaintance with that book can hardly be assumed on the part of our author (Hitzig, *Gesch. des Volkes Israel*, ii. 415, holds the opposite view). At the same time there can be no doubt, that on the whole, the simple narrative of 1 Macc., based as it is on good native sources, deserves the preference over the rhetorical narrative of the second. On the other hand the latter offers a copiousness of independent detail, especially in the preliminary history of the Maccabaean rising, the historical truth of which there are no grounds for doubting. The view must therefore be accepted, that contemporary sources of information were at the disposal also of Jason of Cyrene, but that these were probably not in writing, but only the oral accounts of contemporaries, who narrated from memory the events of those fifteen years. If such narratives reached Jason not directly, but through a series of intermediaries, this would explain both the copiousness and the inaccuracy of the details.

If the view that Jason of Cyrene derived the history he relates from the lips of contemporaries is correct, he must have written not long after 160 B.C. At all events, unless we are willing to allow for the use of written documents also, we must not make the interval between the events and the date of the author too long, as otherwise an acquaintance with such numerous and yet relatively correct particulars would be no longer possible. Nor does the mythical character of many of the narratives (*e.g.* the martyrdom of Eleazar and the seven brethren, 2 Macc. vi.–vii.) tend against the view of so early an origin. For a period of a few decades—especially at a distance from the scene of the events—is more than sufficient for the formation of such myths. The unhistorical notice, xv. 37, that after the victory over Nicanor Jerusalem remained in the hands of the Hebrews, can indeed only have been written by one at a great distance from the events. But on the other hand this scarcely affects Jason but his epitomizer. Why the narrative breaks off at the victory over Nicanor is somewhat enigmatical. Perhaps this ending was not contemplated by Jason.

With respect to the date of the epitomizer it can only be said, that he is certainly *more ancient than Philo*, who seems to have been acquainted with this book. Both the original work and the epitome were without doubt *originally written in Greek*. For it is very characteristically distinguished by its rhetorical Greek style from the annalistic Hebrew style of the first Book of Maccabees. The second book is very unlike the first in another respect also; it aims directly at edification by the narrative of the heroic faith of the Maccabees, and of the marvellous events by which God preserved the continuance of the Jewish religion and worship.

*The two letters*, which are now placed before this book (2 Macc. i.–ii. 18), stand in no connection with it. They are letters of the Palestinian to the Egyptian Jews, in which the latter are summoned to the feast of the Dedication. They are evidently two originally independent pieces of writing, afterwards combined by a later hand, but not that of the epitomizer, with this second Book of Maccabees. Their purpose is to influence the Egyptian Jews with respect to the feast of the Dedication.

In Philo's work, *Quod omnis probus liber*, § 13 (Mang. ii. 459), is described the manner in which many tyrants have persecuted the pious and virtuous. The several features of this description so greatly recall that of Antiochus Epiphanes in the second Book of Maccabees, that an acquaintance with this book on the part of Philo can scarcely be doubted; comp. Lucius, *Der Essenismus* (1881), pp. 36–39. Josephus has indeed a few points in common with this book, which are absent from 1 Macc. (see Grimm, *Exeget. Handb. zu* 2 *Macc.* p. 13). It is nevertheless very improbable that he was acquainted with the second Book of Maccabees (see Grimm, p. 20). On the other hand the philosophical exhortation, known as the fourth Book of Maccabees, is entirely based upon it.

*Christian testimony* begins with Heb. xi. 35 ; for ἐτυμπανίσθησαν evidently refers to 2 Macc. vi. 19, 28 (ἐπὶ τὸ τύμπανον προσῆγε, ἐπὶ τὸ τύμπανον εὐθέως ἦλθε), while other allusions in Heb. xi. 35 sq. recall 2 Macc. vi.–vii. Comp. Bleek, *Stud. und Kritik*, 1853, p. 339, and Bleek's *Commentary* on Heb. xi. 35. The oldest quotation is Clemens Alex. *Strom.* v. 14. 97 : Ἀριστοβούλῳ . . . οὗ μέμνηται ὁ συνταξάμενος τὴν τῶν Μακκαβαϊκῶν ἐπιτομήν (comp. 2 Macc. i. 10). Hippolytus in his work, *de Christo et Antichristo*, c. 49 (Lagarde, p. 25), refers to this book in the words : καὶ ταῦτα μὲν . . . σεσήμανται ἐν τοῖς Μακκαβαϊκοῖς.

Origen appeals in many passages to this book in proof of important doctrines : 1. Of the doctrine of creation *ex nihilo* to 2 Macc. vii. 28 (ἐξ οὐκ ὄντων ἐποίησεν αὐτὰ ὁ Θεός): *Comment. in Joann.* vol. i. c. 18 (Lommatzsch, i. 37); *de principiis*, ii. 1. 5 (Lommatzsch, xxi. 142). 2. Of the doctrine of the intercession of saints to 2 Macc. xv. 14 (ὁ πολλὰ προσευχόμενος περὶ τοῦ λαοῦ καὶ τῆς ἁγίας πόλεως Ἰερεμίας): *Comment. in Joann.* vol. xiii. c. 57 (Lommatzsch, ii. 120); *in Cant. Cant.* lib. iii. (Lommatzsch, xv. 26); *de oratione*, c. 11 (Lommatzsch, xvii. 125). 3. He also makes special and very full mention of the history of Eleazar and the seven Maccabaean brothers (2 Macc. vi. 18–vii. *fin.*) as glorious examples of dauntless martyrdom in the *Exhortatio ad martyrium*, c. 22–27 (Lommatzsch, xx. 261–268); comp. also *Comment. in epist. ad Rom.* lib. iv. c. 10 (Lommatzsch, vi. 305). 4. Other quotations in Origen : *fragm. in Exod.* (Lommatzsch, viii. 302); *contra Cels.* viii. 46, *fin.* (Lommatzsch, xx. 176).

Cyprian also quotes the history of the Maccabaean martyrs, 2 Macc. vi.–vii. (*ad Fortunatum*, c. 11, and *Testim.* iii. 17). The Fathers in general have delighted in treating of these Maccabaean martyrs (often with the use of the so-called fourth Book of Maccabees); nay, they were at last transplanted among Christian saints. For material bearing on this, see Wetstein's

notes on Origen, *Exhort. ad martyr.* c. 23 (Lommatzsch, xx. 262),
and the *Vitae Sanctorum* (Lipomannus, Surius, Bollandist.,
Nilles' *Kalendarium manuale*, 1879 to August 1); some also in
Freudenthal, *Die Flavius Josephus beigelegte Schrift über die
Herrschaft der Vernunft* (1869), p. 29 sqq. Creuzer, *Stud. und
Krit.* 1853, p. 85 sq. Bähr, *Die christlichen Dichter und
Geschichtschreiber Roms* (2nd ed. 1872), p. 50 sqq.

*Its title as the second Book of the Maccabees* is first found in
Euseb. *Praep. evang.* viii. 9, *fin.:* 'Αριστόβουλος . . . οὗτος δ' αὐτὸς
ἐκεῖνος, οὗ καὶ ἡ δευτέρα τῶν Μακκαβαίων ἐν ἀρχῇ τῆς βίβλου
μνημονεύει. Hieronymus, *Prol. galeatus* to the Books of Samuel
(Vallarsi, ix. 459): Machabaeorum primum librum Hebraicum
reperi. *Secundus* Graecus est, quod ex ipsa quoque φράσει
probari potest.

With respect to *manuscripts, editions* and *ancient translations,*
what was said above, p. 10, in the case of the first Book of
Maccabees, applies in most instances to the second. We need
only remark : (1) that the second Book of Maccabees is not contained in the cod. Sinaiticus, and (2) that besides the old Latin
translation, which has passed into the Vulgate (and which alone
Sabatier, *Biblior. sacror. Lat. versiones antiquae*, vol. ii., knows),
there is another in a cod. Ambrosianus from which Peyron has
published it (*Ciceronis orationum pro Scauro, pro Tullio et in
Clodium fragmenta inedita*, 1824, p. 73 sqq.); the edition of the
same text promised for Ceriani's *Monumenta sacra et prof.* vol. i.
fasc. 3, has, as far as I know, not yet made its appearance.

The *exegetical and critical literature* also of this book is
almost entirely the same as that of the first Book of Maccabees
(see above, p. 11 sq.). In the *Exegetisches Handbuch zu den
Apokryphen* (Leipzig 1857) the fourth part compiled by Grimm
treats of the second, third and fourth Books of the Maccabees.
We mention besides: [H. Eberh. Glo. Paulus], " Ueber das
zweyte Buch der Maccabäer " (Eichhorn's *Allg. Biblioth. der
bibl. Literatur*, vol. i. 1787, pp. 233–241). Bertheau, *De secundo
libro Maccabaeorum*, Gotting. 1829. Herzfeld, *Gesch. des Volkes
Jisrael*, ii. 443–456. Patrizzi, *De consensu utriusque libri
Machabaeorum*, Romae 1856. Cigoi, *Historischchronologische
Schwierigkeiten im zweiten Makkabäerbuche*, Klagenfurt 1868.
Kasten, *Der historische Werth des zweiten Buches der Makkabäer*,
Stolp 1879 (Gymnasialprogr.).

*On the two letters* at the beginning of the book see (besides
the above-named literature): Valckenaer, *De Aristobulo*, pp.
38–44. Schlünkes, *Epistolae quae secundo Macc. libro* i. 1–9,
*legitur explicatio*, Colon. 1844. The same, *Difficiliorum locorum
epistolae quae 2 Macc.* i. 10–ii. 18, *legitur explicatio*, Colon. 1847.
Grätz, " Das Sendschreiben der Palästinenser an die ägyptisch-

judäischen Gemeinden wegen der Feier der Tempelweihe"
(*Monatsschr. für Gesch. und Wissensch. des Judenth.* 1877,
pp. 1–16, 49–60).

## 8. *The Third Book of Maccabees.*

The so - called third Book of Maccabees may here be
mentioned along with the second, as having at least the form
of an historical narrative of a supposed episode of later Jewish
history.    In truth it is a tolerably insipid piece of fiction
founded at most on an entirely unascertainable historical fact.
It relates how Ptolemy IV. Philopator, after his victory over
Antiochus the Great at Raphia, came to Jerusalem and
entertained the desire of entering also the interior of the
temple.    As he was not to be turned from his purpose by
any representations, the Jews in their distress cried to God,
who heard their prayer and struck Ptolemy, so that he fell
stunned to the ground (i.–ii. 24).    Ptolemy exasperated
returned to Egypt and meditated revenge.    He deprived the
Alexandrian Jews of their civic rights, and commanded that
all the Jews in Egypt, together with their wives and children,
should be brought in chains to Alexandria, where they were
confined in the racecourse.    Their number was so great, that
the clerks, who were to write down the names of each, had
not, after forty days' labour, come to the end, and were obliged
to leave off for want of writing materials (ii. 25–iv. *fin.*).
Ptolemy now commanded that five hundred elephants should
be intoxicated by wine and incense and incited against the
people in the racecourse.    When all preparations had been
made the execution was delayed till the next day, because
the king had slept till the time for his chief meal.    On the
second day too nothing was done, because the king had,
through the dispensation of God, suddenly forgotten everything, and was very angry to find that hostile designs were
entertained against his faithful servants the Jews.    On the
same day however he repeated at his repast the former

order for the extirpation of the Jews. When then on the third day matters at last seemed getting serious, and the king was already approaching the racecourse with his troops, two angels appeared from heaven at the prayer of the Jews and paralysed the troops of the king with terror. The elephants then rushed upon the troops of the king, trampled on and destroyed them (v.–vi. 21). The king was now much irritated against his counsellors and commanded the Jews to be liberated from their chains, nay, to be entertained for seven days at his expense. Then they celebrated their deliverance with feasting and rejoicing, and resolved to keep these days as festivals for ever. And the king issued a letter of protection in favour of the Jews to all governors in the provinces, and gave the Jews permission to put to death such of their fellow-countrymen as had apostatized from the faith. They made abundant use of this permission and returned joyfully home (vi. 22–vii. *fin.*).

This narrative is not only almost throughout a mere fiction, but it belongs, among productions of the kind, to those of the weakest sort. The author evidently revels in keeping up psychological impossibilities. The style also corresponds, being bombastic and involved. The only foundation for the author's fiction seems to have been an old legend which we still read in Josephus. For he relates (*contra Apion.* ii. 5) that Ptolemy VII. Physcon cast the Jews of Alexandria, who as adherents of Cleopatra were his political opponents, to intoxicated elephants, who however turned instead against the friends of the king, whereupon the king gave up his purpose and the Jews of Alexandria celebrated the day in remembrance of the event. According to this account the celebration of this festival, which is also mentioned in the third Book of Maccabees (vi. 36), seems at all events to be historical. And some unascertained fact may certainly be the foundation of the legend, the older form of which seems to have been in the hands of Josephus, since all is in his account simpler and more psychologically comprehensible, and he was evidently unacquainted with the third Book of Maccabees. When then the latter refers the history to Ptolemy IV. instead of VII., this is already a divergence from the older legend, and still more so are the other additions with which the author has enriched his narrative.

As to the *date of the author,* the utmost that can be ventured is a conjecture. The contents and tendency of the book seem to presuppose a persecution of the Alexandrian Jews, on account of which the author desires to comfort and encourage his co-religionists. This leads our thoughts to *the time of Caligula,* when such a persecution on a large scale took place for the first time. Hence Ewald, Hausrath, Reuss and others place the composition of the book in his reign. But then it would be strange, that the author does not make Ptolemy lay claim to divine honours, which was the chief stumbling-block in the case of Caligula. On the whole we should expect in it more special references to events under Caligula. Hence we can but approve of Grimm's reservation, though he has every inclination to agree with Ewald's hypothesis (*Exeget. Handb.* p. 218 sq.). In general, we may say, that the book originated at the earliest in the first century before Christ, at the latest in the first century after Christ; the former, because the author already knows the Greek additions to Daniel (vi. 6); the latter, because it would otherwise have found no acceptance with the Christian Church.

*The oldest Christian testimony* is the *Canones apost.* (in Cotelier, *Patr. apost.* 2nd ed. i. 453) canon 76 (*al.* 85): Μακκα- βαίων τρία. The stichometry of Nicephorus also reckons: Μακκαβαϊκὰ γ′ (in Credner, *Zur Gesch. des Kanons,* p. 119). In the *Synopsis Athanasii* stands instead Μακκαβαϊκὰ βιβλία δ′, Πτολεμαϊκά (Credner, p. 144), where, according to Credner's conjecture, καί is perhaps to be read instead of the number δ′, so that our third Book of Maccabees would have to be understood by Πτολεμαϊκά. For other testimony, see Eichhorn, *Einl. in die apokr. Schriften des A. T.* p. 288 sq. Grimm, *Handb.* p. 221 sq. *The book seems never to have been known in the Latin Church*, on which account it is absent from the Vulgate. On the other hand, it found approbation *in the Syrian Church*, as the existing old Syriac translation proves. The name "Book of Maccabees" has been very inaptly given to the book, merely because here also a persecution of Jews faithful to their religion is the subject.

The book is as a rule found in the *manuscripts* of the Septuagint, so especially in the cod. Alexandrinus. Hence it is also found in most *editions* of the Septuagint and in the separate editions of the Greek apocryphal books (see above, p. 10 sq.). Of ancient versions the old Syriac need only be mentioned here (see above, p. 11).

For the exegetical aids in general, see above, p. 11. Commentary: Grimm, "Das zweite, dritte und vierte Buch der Maccabäer" (*Exegetisches Handbuch zu den Apokryphen des A.T.'s*, Part 4), Leipzig 1857. Investigations: Eichhorn, *Einl. in die apokryphischen Schriften des A.T.'s*, pp. 278–290. Bertholdt, *Einl. in sammtliche kanon. und apokr. Schriften des A. u. N. T.* vol. iii. pp. 1082–1091. Ewald, *Gesch. des Volkes Israel*, iv. 611–614. De Wette-Schrader, *Einl. in das A.T.'s*, p. 572 sq. Keil, *Einl. in das A.T.* 3rd ed. p. 720 sq. Hausrath, *Neutestamentl. Zeitgesch.* 2nd ed. ii. 262–265. Reuss, *Gesch. der heil Schriften Alten Testaments*, § 574.

## 9. *Philo's Historical Works.*

Philo, the philosopher, must also be named here as a writer of works on Jewish history. Indeed he has left us narratives not only from the *more ancient* history, but also from that of *his own times*.

1. With respect to the former a large work, which has been preserved almost entire, viz. a comprehensive *delineation of the Mosaic legislation*, must first be mentioned. It is not indeed an historical narrative properly so called, but a systematic statement; still it is one so made, that Philo attempts therein to give a survey of the legislative labours of Moses himself, *i.e.* of the virtual contents of the Pentateuch. That he does not do this without being essentially influenced by his own philosophical views is a thing self-evident. But still his purpose is simply to give, in an objective historical manner, a survey of the Mosaic legislation. The several

parts of this work have come down to us in the manuscripts
and editions under special titles, as though they were separate
books.   It will be shown below, § 34, that the plan of the
whole work is as follows: (*a*) The first book refers to the
*creation of the world*.   For Moses treated of this in the
beginning of his work, to make it plain that his legislation
was according to the will of nature.   (*b*) The following books
treat of the lives of Enos, Enoch, Noah, Abraham, Isaac,
Jacob and Joseph, but so that the first three are only briefly
treated in the introduction to the life of Abraham, while the
last four have each a separate book devoted to them.   The
lives of Abraham and Joseph have been preserved.   The
histories of all these individuals is related, because by their
lives they exhibit the universal types of morality, "the living
unwritten laws."   (*c*) Next follows *the legislation proper, the
ten chief commandments*, first in one book and then in four
books, *the special laws* arranged according to the rubrics of the
ten commandments (particulars, § 34).   Thus a survey is
really taken of the actual contents of the Pentateuch.   The
tendency of the entire work is everywhere to hold up the
Jewish law as the wisest and most humane.   The ritual and
ceremonial laws are not passed by; but Philo always knows
how to realize their rational side, so that he who perfectly
observes them is not only the best, but also the most cultured
man, the true philosopher.   This also makes it clear that the
work, if not solely, was chiefly intended for *non-Jewish readers*.
The educated of all nations were to be brought by it to the
perception, that the Jewish was the most perfect law, the law
by which men were best trained to be good citizens and true
philosophers.

In a separate work, which does not, as has been usually
supposed, belong to this collective work, Philo has also written
*a life of Moses* himself.   In this also the manner and object
are the same as in the systematic work.   Moses is described
as the greatest and wisest of lawgivers, and as raised above all
others by mighty deeds and miraculous experiences.

2. Philo also described in a lengthy work the most important and the saddest episode of the Jewish history of his times, *the persecutions of the Jews under Caligula*. By way of introduction he spoke also in it of the persecutions brought about by Sejanus in the reign of Tiberius. The work, according to Eusebius, contained five books. The two which have come down to us (*in Flaccum* and *de legatione ad Cajum*) probably formed the third and fourth (particulars, § 34). Philo having been an eye-witness of the events he narrates, nay, as leader of a Jewish embassy to Caligula, a prominent sharer in them, his work is a first-class authority for the history of this period.

## 10. *Josephus.*

The best known historian of Jewish affairs in the Greek language is the Palestinian Josephus, properly Joseph, the son of Matthias, a priest of Jerusalem. Of his two chief works one is, the Ἰουδαϊκὴ Ἀρχαιολογία, a *comprehensive delineation of the entire Jewish history* from the beginning to his own times. It is the most extensive work on Jewish history in the Greek language with which we are acquainted, and has on that account so retained the lasting favour of Jewish, heathen and Christian readers, as to have been preserved entire in numerous manuscripts (particulars, see above, Div. i. vol. i. § 3). Notwithstanding its great difference from the philosophizing delineation of Philo, its tendency is similar. For it is the purpose of Josephus, not only to instruct his heathen readers, for whom it was in the first instance intended, in the history of his people, but also to inspire them with respect for the Jewish nation, both as having a history of hoar antiquity, and a long series of celebrities both in peace and war to point to, and as able to bear comparison in respect of laws and institutions with any nation (comp. especially *Antt.* xvi. 6. 8). The other chief work of Josephus, the *History of the Jewish War from* A.D. 66–73, gives the history more for its own sake. The events of these years are in themselves so important, that they seemed worthy of a detailed description. Perhaps it was written by command of Vespasian, from whom Josephus received an annual salary (*Vita*, 76), and to whom the work was delivered as soon as it was completed (*contra Apion.* i. 9 ; *Vita*, 65). If a tendency to boasting is detected in it, this refers rather to the individual Josephus and the Romans than to the Jewish nation.

## 11. *Justus of Tiberias.*

Justus of Tiberias, a contemporary and fellow-countryman of Josephus, was also his fellow-labourer. He too devoted himself to authorship after the destruction of his nation, but having been less successful therein than Josephus, his works were less read, and have therefore been lost. He has this in common with Josephus, that he too treated both of Jewish history as a whole and of the events of his own times, each in one work. His *History of the Jewish Kings*, from Moses to Agrippa II., was, according to the statement of Photius, who was still acquainted with it (*Biblioth. Cod.* 33), " very brief in expression, and passed over much that was necessary." As it was made use of by Julius Africanus in his *Chronicle*, it may well be supposed that its form was that of a chronicle, in which stress was chiefly laid upon the settling of the chronology.

In another work Justus seems to have presented, whether wholly or partly, the *History of the Jewish War* in a manner by which Josephus felt himself compromised, since in his *Vita* he enters into a very warm controversy against Justus.

## IV. EPIC POETRY AND THE DRAMA.

### 1. *Philo, the Epic Poet.*

The appropriation of Greek forms of literature on the part of the Hellenistic Jews did not stop at prose. *Even the epic*

*and dramatic poetry of the Greeks were transplanted to the soil
of Hellenistic Judaism,* the sacred history being sung under the
form of the Greek Epos, nay, represented in the form of the
Greek drama. For what is still preserved of this remarkable
literature, we are indebted to the extracts of Alexander
Polyhistor, which have been inserted by Eusebius in his
*Praeparatio evangelica* (see above, p. 197 sqq.).

Three small fragments from a Greek poem "On Jerusalem"
(Περὶ τὰ Ἱεροσόλυμα) by a certain Philo are given by
Eusebius (Euseb. *Praep. evang.* ix. 20, 24, 37). The subject
of the first is *Abraham,* of the second *Joseph,* of the third
*the springs and water - pipes of Jerusalem,* the abundance
of which is extolled. The first and third are taken from the
first book of the work quoted (ix. 20: Φίλων ἐν τῷ πρώτῳ
τῶν Περὶ τὰ Ἱεροσόλυμα; ix. 37: Φίλων ἐν τοῖς Περὶ
Ἱεροσολύμων . . . ἐν τῇ πρώτῃ); the second professedly
from the fourteenth (ix. 24: Φίλων ἐν τῇ ιδ΄ τῶν Περὶ
Ἱεροσόλυμα). But that Philo should have used fourteen
books to get as far as the history of Joseph is too improbable.
Hence we may suppose with Freudenthal, that possibly we
must read ἐν τῇ ιδ΄ instead of ἐν τῇ δ΄. The language of Philo
is that of the Greek epic, but his hexameters are written
with a true contempt of Greek prosody, and the diction is
pompous, and so involved as to be unintelligible

The Philo mentioned by Clemens Alex. *Strom.* i. 21. 141,
and by Josephus, *contra Apion.* i. 23 (= Euseb. *Praep. evang.*
ix. 42), and whom Josephus distinguishes from the more
recent philosopher by calling him Philo the elder (Φίλων ὁ
πρεσβύτερος), is certainly identical with our epic writer.
According to the notice of him in Clemens Alexandrinus, we
might indeed suppose, that some prose writer, who treated
Jewish history in like manner as Demetrius and Eupolemus
do, was spoken of (*Strom.* i. 21. 141: Φίλων δὲ καὶ αὐτὸς
ἀνέγραψε τοὺς βασιλεῖς τοὺς Ἰουδαίων διαφώνως τῷ Δημη-
τρίῳ). Josephus took him for a heathen, for he adduces him,
together with Demetrius and Eupolemus, as a proof, that many

heathen authors also had a tolerably accurate acquaintance with Jewish history. But the circumstance that both Clemens and Josephus, in the passages cited, place this Philo *in the same series* as Demetrius and Eupolemus (both have the order Demetrius, Philo, Eupolemus), proves, that both were drawing from the same source, and this can be no other than Alexander Polyhistor. Since then no other Philo than the epic writer occurs in the copious contributions from Alexander Polyhistor in Eusebius, there is no doubt that Clemens and Josephus mean the same. Consequently Philo, as the fragments in Eusebius give us reason to suppose, sang in such wise of the town of Jerusalem as to give at the same time a history of the Jewish kings.

As to the date of Philo this much only can be said, that he preceded Alexander Polyhistor. Hence he may be perhaps placed in the second century before Christ. There is no direct evidence that he was a Jew, but from the tenor of his poem it can scarcely be doubtful.

Comp. in general: Huetius, *Demonstr. ev. Prop.* iv. c. 2, § 33. Viger's *Anm. zu Euseb.* ix. 20. Philippson, *Ezechiel des jüdischen Trauerspieldichters Auszug aus Egypten und Philo des Aelteren Jerusalem*, 1830. Delitzsch, *Zur Gesch. der jüd. Poesie* (1836), pp. 24, 209. Dähne, *Geschichtl. Darstellung der jüd.-alex. Religions-Philosophie*, ii. 215, note. Cruice, *De Fl. Josephi fide* (1844), p. 61 sq. Müller, *Fragm. hist. graec.* iii. 207 sqq. Herzfeld, *Gesch. des Volkes Jisrael*, iii. 519, 575. Ewald, *Gesch. des Volkes Israel*, iv. 338, vii. 91. Freudenthal, *Alex. Polyhistor*, pp. 34, 100, 170.

## 2. *Theodotus.*

The poem of Theodotus on Sichem, a long portion from which is given partly by verbal quotation, partly by a statement of its contents, in Euseb. *Praep. evang.* ix. 22, seems to have been of the same kind as that of Philo on Jerusalem. The entire portion refers to the *history of the town of Sichem*. Its situation is first described, and then its seizure by the

Hebrews, in accordance with Gen. xxxiv.; how Jacob first
dwelt in Mesopotamia, there married and begat children, then
departed with them to the district of Sichem, and received a
portion of land from Emmor the king of Sichem; next, how
Sichem the son of Emmor ravished Dinah, Jacob's daughter,
whereupon Jacob declared himself ready to give Dinah to
Sichem to wife, on condition that all the Sichemites should
be circumcised; and lastly, how Simeon and Levi, two of
Jacob's sons, slew Emmor and Sichem and, in conjunction
with their brethren, destroyed the city of the Sichemites.
Jacob's sojourn in Mesopotamia not being mentioned till after
the description of the town of Sichem, and only as an introduction to the history of its seizure by the Hebrews which
follows, it is evident that the history of the town of Sichem is
the real theme of the poem; and since it is called a "holy city"
(ἱερὸν ἄστυ), it can scarcely be doubted that Theodotus was a
Samaritan. Hence the title Περὶ Ἰουδαίων given to the
poem in Eusebius can hardly be accurate. At the commencement of the extract it is said, that the town had its name
from Sikimios, a son of Hermes (ἀπὸ Σικιμίου τοῦ Ἑρμοῦ).
Theodotus thus seems like other Hellenists to have embellished
Jewish history with scraps from Greek mythology. The
diction, as well as the construction of the hexameters, is
better than Philo's. With respect to date, what was said of
Philo applies here also.

Comp. in general: Huetius, *Demonstr. ev.* iv. 2. 32. Fabricius-
Harles, *Biblioth. gr.* x. 516. Müller, *Fragm. hist. gr.* iii. 207 sqq.
Pauly's *Real-Enc. der class. Alterthumswissensch.*, art. "Theo-
dotus," Nr. 13. Herzfeld, *Gesch. des Volkes Jisrael,* iii. 520 sq.,
576 sq. Ewald, *Gesch. des Volkes Israel,* iv. 338, vii. 91.
Freudenthal, *Alex. Polyh.* p. 99 sq.

### 3. *Ezekiel, the Tragic Poet.*

The most remarkable phenomenon in the department of
Judaeo-Hellenistic poetry is the manufacture of scriptural
matter into Greek dramas. We know indeed of only one

such Jewish dramatist, Ezekiel; and it must be left uncertain
whether he had either successor or predecessor.   But at all
events he composed other dramas besides the one which is
known to us by extracts, being called "The poet of Jewish
tragedies" (Clemens Alex. *Strom.* i. 23. 155 : ὁ Ἐζεκίηλος ὁ
τῶν Ἰουδαϊκῶν τραγῳδιῶν ποιητής.   Euseb. *Praep. evang.* ix.
28 : Ἐζεκιῆλος ὁ τῶν τραγῳδιῶν ποιητής).   We know more
by extensive extracts in Eusebius and Clemens Alexandrinus
(after Alexander Polyhistor) of one of them, which was called
"*the Exodus,*" Ἐξαγωγή, and which depicted the history of
the departure of the Jews from Egypt (Clemens Alex. *Strom.*
i. 23. 155 : ἐν τῷ ἐπιγραφομένῳ δράματι "Ἐξαγωγή." Euseb.
*Praep. evang.* ix. 29. 14, ed. Gaisford : ἐν τῷ δράματι τῷ
ἐπιγραφομένῳ Ἐξαγωγή).   The moment chosen as the starting-
point of the action was apparently that when Moses fled to
Midian after slaying the Egyptian (Ex. ii.); for the first extract
transposes us to that period (Euseb. *Praep. evang.* ix. 28 =
Clemens Alex. *Strom.* i. 23. 155–156).   It is a long monologue
of Moses, in which he relates the history of his life down to that
juncture, and concludes with the words, that he is now in
consequence a wanderer in a foreign land.   He then sees the
seven daughters of Raguel approaching (Ex. ii. 16 sqq.) and
asks who they are, when Zipporah gives him the information.
The further progress of the action is only alluded to in the
extract, where we are told that the watering of the flock and
the marriage of Zipporah with Moses now takes place (Ex. ii.
16 sqq.).   In the second extract (Euseb. ix. 29. 4–6, ed.
Gaisford) Moses relates a dream to his father-in-law, which
the latter explains to mean, that Moses will attain to a high
official post, and will have the knowledge of things past,
present and future.   In another scene (Euseb. ix. 29. 7–11,
ed. Gaisford) it is represented, on the authority of Ex. iii.–iv.,
how God spoke to Moses from a burning bush and commissioned him to deliver the people of Israel from bondage.   As
God speaks invisibly from the bush, He is not made to
appear on the stage, but only His voice is heard.   The details

are pretty much in agreement with Ex. iii.–iv. In the
extract which follows (Euseb. ix. 29. 12–13, ed. Gaisford) God
gives (according to Ex. xi.–xii.) more exact directions concerning the departure and the celebration of the Passover.
It cannot be decided, whether this also belongs to the scene of
the bush. In a further scene (Euseb. ix. 29. 14, ed. Gaisford)
an Egyptian enters, who has escaped the catastrophe in the
Red Sea, and relates how the Israelites passed safely through
the waters and the Egyptian host perished in them. Finally,
in the last fragment (Euseb. ix. 29. 15–16) a messenger, in
whom we are to imagine one sent to reconnoitre for the
Israelites, announces to Moses the discovery of an excellent
place of encampment at Elim, with twelve springs of water
and seventy palm trees (Ex. xv. 27 = Num. xxxiii. 9). Then
the messenger relates how a marvellously strong bird, nearly
twice as large as an eagle, which all the other birds followed
as their king, appeared. The description of this bird is also
found, without mention of the name of Ezekiel, in Eustathius,
*Comm. in Hexaemeron*, ed. Leo Allatius (1629), p. 25 sq.

From these fragments it appears, that the action agrees
pretty closely with the scriptural narrative, though with many
embellishments of detail. The poetry of the author is very
prosaic. On the other hand a certain amount of skill in
dramatizing the material cannot be denied him. The diction
and versification (Iambic trimeters) are tolerably fluent. It
has been doubted—incorrectly it seems to me—whether this
drama was ever intended for representation. The aim of it
is certainly the same as that of the scriptural dramas of the
Middle Ages (the passion plays, etc.), viz. on the one hand
to make the people, in this way also, better acquainted with
sacred history, on the other and chiefly, to supplant as far as
possible profane and heathen pleasures by the supply of such
" wholesome food." Here perhaps, as in other productions of
Judaeo-Hellenistic literature, heathen readers and spectators
were calculated on.

That Ezekiel was a Jew is undoubtedly shown even by his

name. What was said of the dates of Philo and Theodotus applies in his case also.

Comp. in general: Huetius, *Demonstr. evang.* iv. 2. 24. Fabricius, *Biblioth. graec.* ed. Harles, ii. 305 sq., viii. 624 sq., 635, 636. Eichhorn, "De Judaeorum re scenica," in the *Commentationes Societ. Gotting. recentiores,* vol. ii. Gotting. 1813. Philippson, *Ezechiel des jüdischen Trauerspieldichters Auszug aus Egypten und Philo des Aelteren Jerusalem,* 1830. Delitzsch, *Zur Gesch. der jüdischen Poesie* (1836), pp. 28, 209, 211–219. Dähne, *Geschichtl. Darstellung der jüd.-alex. Religions-Philosophie,* ii. 199 sq. Fürst, *Biblioth. Jud.* i. 264. Frankel, *Ueber den Einfluss der palästinischen Exegese auf die alexandrinische Hermeneutik* (1851), pp. 113–119. Herzfeld, *Gesch. des Volkes Jisrael,* iii. 517–519. Ewald, *Gesch. des Volkes Israel,* ii. 127, iv. 338. Bähr in Pauly's *Real-Enc.* iii. 365. Dübner in the appendix to *Fragmenta Euripidis, iterum,* ed. F. G. Wagner (*accedunt indices locupletissimi, Christus patiens, Ezechieli et christianorum poetarum reliquiae dramaticae*), Paris, Didot 1846, pp. 7–10 and 1–7. Magnin, *Journal des Savants,* 1848, pp. 193–208 (Recension of Dübner's appendix to *Fragm. Eurip.* ed. Wagner). Dindorf, *Praefat.* to his edition of Euseb. *Opp.* vol. i. pp. 19–25. Bernhardy, *Grundriss der griechischen Litteratur,* ii. 2 (3rd ed. 1872), p. 76. Cobet in the Λογιος Ερμης, i. 457–459.

### V. PHILOSOPHY.

In the departments of history and poetry it was chiefly only the external form that was borrowed from the Greeks, but in that of philosophy a real internal blending of Jewish and Greek *thought,* a strong actual influencing of Jewish belief by the philosophy of the Greeks, took place. We perceive this the most plainly in Philo. He exhibits a completely double aspect; on one side he is a Jew, on the other a Greek philosopher (particulars, § 34). But we should be much mistaken if we took him for an isolated phenomenon in the history of his people and age. He is but a classic representative of a current flowing through centuries and necessarily implied by the nature of Hellenistic Judaism. To Greek *culture* belonged also an acquaintance with the great thinkers of the Greeks. The Hellenistic Jews, in appropriating the

former, thereby placed themselves also under the influence of
Greek philosophy. We have certain proofs of this since the
second century before Christ. But we may assume, that the
fact mentioned is in general as old as Hellenistic Judaism
itself. The Jew, whom Aristotle met in Asia Minor, was
already Ἑλληνικὸς οὐ τῇ διαλέκτῳ μόνον ἀλλὰ καὶ τῇ
ψυχῇ (see vol. ii. 225).

The Jewish feature of this Judaeo-Hellenistic philosophy
appears chiefly in the fact, that like the Palestinian חָכְמָה it
pursued essentially *practical aims*. Not logic or physics, but
ethic was in its sight the chief matter. This ethic was indeed
often founded upon the theoretic philosophy of the Greeks.
Still the latter is but a means to an end, the proper end of
Jewish philosophers, viz. the practical one of educating man
to true morality and piety.

Also in the choice made of the *literary form*, the Jewish
foundation is still apparent. The case here is exactly the
reverse of what it is in poetry. The contents exhibit a strong
Greek influence, but the literary form is derived from Palestine.
The author of the Wisdom of Solomon chooses the form of
*proverbs*, Philo gives his discussions in the manner of Rabbinic
*Midrash, i.e.* in prolix learned commentaries on the text of
the Pentateuch, from which the most heterogeneous philosophic ideas are developed by the help of allegorical exegesis.
The so-called fourth Book of the Maccabees is a hortatory
address, of which the synagogue sermon may perhaps be
regarded as the model. Only in a few smaller pieces does Philo
choose the form of inquiry and dialogue after Greek models.

In the *mixture of Jewish and Greek notions* in these
writers the proportions of course vary. In some the influence of Greek ideas is stronger, in others weaker. But
even those which are most saturated with Greek ideas are
essentially rooted in the soil of Judaism. For they not only
insist upon the unity of a supramundane God and the
control of Divine Providence, which punishes the wicked and
rewards the good, but they also firmly adhere to the belief

that the most perfect knowledge of things human and divine is given in the Mosaic revelation, so that Judaism is the way to true wisdom and virtue. And not only does the amount of Greek influence vary, but different Greek systems are preferred, now one, now another being more agreed with. Plato, Aristotle, the Stoics and Pythagoreans have all furnished material to the sphere of ideas of these Jewish philosophers. Especially in the Platonico-Pythagorean and in the Stoic teaching did Jewish thinkers find many elements capable of being assimilated with the Jewish faith. That the appropriation of these was always eclectic is self-evident. But here Jewish philosophy only participates in the fundamental characteristic of later Greek philosophy in general.

### 1. *The Wisdom of Solomon.*

We place the so-called "Wisdom of Solomon" first, not because it is certainly the oldest of the literary productions to be here discussed, but because it most closely resembles in form the ancient Palestinian *proverbial wisdom*. In like manner as Jesus the son of Sirach does the author praise true wisdom, which is to be found only with God, and is imparted to man by God alone. But the execution is quite different from that of Jesus Sirach. While the latter shows, how the truly wise man comports himself in the different circumstances of practical life, this book is properly only *a warning against the folly of ungodliness*, and especially of idolatry. Around this one theme do the contents of the whole book revolve, and consequently the proverbial form is not strictly adhered to, but often passes into that of connected discourse.

According to chap. ix. 7 sqq., Solomon himself is to be regarded as the speaker, and those addressed are the judges and kings of the earth (i. 1: οἱ κρίνοντες τὴν γῆν; vi. 1: βασιλεῖς, δικασταὶ περάτων γῆς). Thus it is properly an exhortation of Solomon to *his royal colleagues the heathen potentates.* He, the wisest of all kings, represents to them the folly of ungodliness, and the excellence of true wisdom. Its contents may be divided into three groups. It is first shown (chaps. i.–v.) that the wicked and ungodly, although for a period apparently prosperous, will not escape the judgments of God, but that the pious and just, after having been for a time tried by sufferings, attain to true happiness and immortality. In a second section (chaps. vi.–ix.) Solomon directs his royal colleagues to his own example. It is just because he has loved high and divine wisdom, and has united himself to her as his bride, that he has attained to glory and honour. Hence he still prays for such wisdom. The third section (chaps. x.–xix.) points out, by referring to the history of Israel, and especially to the different lots of the Israelites and the Egyptians, the blessing of godliness and the curse of ungodliness. A very long tirade on the folly of idolatry (chaps. xiii.–xv.) is here inserted.

The work being in its chief contents a warning against the folly of ungodliness, it can only be so far intended for Jewish readers, as ungodliness was to be found among them also. But we should be hardly mistaken, if we were to suppose, that the author had heathen readers, at least as much in view. The numerous allusions to Scripture history seem indeed to presuppose Jewish readers (so *e.g.* Grimm, *Exeget. Handb.* p. 27). But then what is the purpose of the garment chosen, according to which the kings and potentates of the earth are addressed ? Why the long-winded discourse on the folly of idolatry, for which there was no occasion with Jewish readers, who still deserved the name ? The contents recall in many respects the Sibylline oracles, which, going forth under a heathen authority, were certainly intended for heathen readers. As in these so in the book in question the folly of an ungodly life is set before its readers. At all events its warning and instruction are addressed to heathen-minded readers, whether these are by birth Jews or heathen, and chiefly indeed to the great and mighty of this world.

The special theological *standpoint* of the author agrees with

that of Palestinian proverbial wisdom, as we find it in the
Proverbs of Solomon and in Jesus the son of Sirach.  *Divine
Wisdom is the supreme good,* the source of all truth, virtue and
happiness with our author also.  But while, like the author of
the Book of Proverbs and Jesus Sirach, he starts from the
assertion, that this Wisdom is first of all present with God,
it becomes in his conception almost an independent person
beside God.  His utterances indeed do not seem to really
exceed what we already read in Prov. viii.–ix.  But what
is there more a poetic personification becomes with him a
philosophic theory.  Wisdom is according to him a breath
(ἀτμίς) of God's power, a pure effluence (ἀπόρρια) from the glory
of the Almighty, the brightness (ἀπαύγασμα) of the everlasting
light (vii. 25, 26).  It is most intrinsically united with God
(συμβίωσιν θεοῦ ἔχουσα), is initiated into the knowledge of
God (μύστις τῆς τοῦ θεοῦ ἐπιστήμης), and a chooser of His
works (αἱρέτις τῶν ἔργων αὐτοῦ), *i.e.* chooses among the works,
of which God has conceived the idea, which shall be carried
into execution (viii. 3, 4 : comp. Grimm on the passage), is
assessor on God's throne (ix. 4 : ἡ τῶν σῶν θρόνων πάρεδρος),
understands the works of God, and was present when He
created the world, knows what is well-pleasing in His eyes
and right according to His commandments (ix. 9).  Wisdom
is thus not only represented as the special possession of God,
but as an assistant of God, originating from His own nature.
Together therewith "the almighty word of God" (ὁ παντο-
δύναμός σου λόγος) is also personified in a manner which
approaches hypostatic union (xviii. 15 sq.).  Thus we have
here already the elements, from which the Philonian doctrine
of the λόγος ( = reason and word of God) as a hypostasis
mediating between God and the world is formed.  For
Wisdom occupies in our author a position similar to that of
Philo's Logos with respect to the world also.  She has a
spirit which is easily moving, all-overseeing, all-pervading
(vii. 22–24 : εὐκίνητον, πανεπίσκοπον, διήκει καὶ χωρεῖ διὰ
πάντων, etc.).  She works everything (viii. 5 : τὰ πάντα

ἐργαζομένη), rules all things (viii. 1 : διοικεῖ τὰ πάντα),
makes all things new (vii. 27 : τὰ πάντα καινίζει). "By
passing from generation to generation into holy souls, she
prepares friends of God and prophets" (vii. 27). It is she
who was manifested in the history of Israel, *e.g.* in the pillar
of fire and cloud, which led the Israelites through the wilderness (x. 17 and chap. x. in general). Hence Wisdom is in
a word the medium by which God works in the world. The
tendency of this whole speculation is evidently the same as
in Philo, viz. to secure, by the insertion of such an intermediary,
the absolute supramundane nature of God, who cannot be
conceived of as in direct contact with a sinful world. But it
must not be lost sight of, that it is by no means our author's
concern to dwell upon this thought. He desires, on the contrary, to exhibit Divine Wisdom as the supreme good. He
does not seek to show that Wisdom is different from God, but,
on the contrary, how near it is to Him. While then he is
moving in this sphere of thought, he merely takes up a view
already current among his associates.[14]

The *influence of Greek philosophy* is moreover shown in
the details of execution. The formulae, with which the rule
of wisdom in the world is described (vii. 24 : διήκει, χωρεῖ ;
viii. 1 : διοικεῖ), recall the Stoic doctrine of the world-spirit of
God as the wisdom of the world immanent in and pervading
it.[15] The enumeration also of the four cardinal virtues (viii. 7 :
σωφροσύνη, φρόνησις, δικαιοσύνη, ἀνδρεία) is to be referred to
Stoic influence (see Zeller as above). The psychology of the
author on the other hand is Platonico-dualistic. The soul of
man is pre-existent. If it is good, it enters an undefiled body
(viii. 20 : ἀγαθὸς ὢν ἦλθον εἰς σῶμα ἀμίαντον). The body

---

[14] Compare on this "doctrine of Wisdom" in general : Lücke, *Commentar über das Ev. Joh.* i. p. 257 sqq. Bruch, *Weisheitslehre der Hebräer,
ein Beitrag zur Gesch. der Philosophie*, Strassb. 1851. Oehler, *Grandzüge
der alttestamentl. Weisheit*, Tüb. 1855. Grimm, *Exeget. Handb. zu den
Apokr.* Pt. vi. p. 1 sq.

[15] Zeller, *Die Philosophie der Griechen*, iii. (3rd ed. 1881) p. 271.
Heinze, *Die Lehre vom Logos*, p. 192.

is only an " earthly tabernacle " for the νοῦς (ix. 15 : γεῶδες σκῆνος). After a short time the body must restore the soul like a loan and then fall to dust (xv. 8). In this anthropology the territory of the Jewish view is entirely forsaken. Instead of a resurrection of the body, we have here the Greek view of the immortality of the soul.

With respect to the author's *date*, it must be regarded as certain that he succeeds Jesus the son of Sirach, but *precedes Philo*. For his standpoint is a preliminary step to Philo's. This would not in itself prove a higher antiquity. But with the near affinity of the two, it is not conceivable, that our author would have remained unaffected by Philo if he had succeeded him. There is absolutely no foundation for the notion (as *e.g.* by Weisse) of Christian origin. That the author was an Alexandrian may, by reason of the great prominence of references to Egyptian matters, be regarded as certain. On the other hand it cannot be imagined, that Philo was himself the author of this book, as was believed by some even in the time of Jerome (Hieron. *praef. in vers. libr. Salom.* *Opp.* ed. Vallarsi, ix. 1293 sq. : " Nonnulli scriptorum veterum hunc esse Judaei Philonis affirmant ") ; and also by many moderns, as Luther, Joh. Gerhard, Calovius, and others (see Grimm, *Handb.* p. 21 sqq.). The authorship of Philo is entirely excluded by the difference of his sphere of thought.

The book has been used from the beginning *in the Christian Church.* Even in the *Pauline Epistles* such loud echoes are found as make St. Paul's acquaintanceship with the book probable (see Bleek, *Stud. und Krit.* 1853, pp. 340–344; on the other side, Grimm, *Exeget. Handb.* p. 35 sqq.). It is tolerably certain that it was known to Clemens Romanus (Clem. Rom. xxvii. 5 = *Sap. Sal.* xii. 12, and xi. 21 ; comp. also Clem. lx. 1 = *Sap.* vii. 17). In Tatian, *Oratio ad Graecos,* c. vii. *init.*, the same is said of Christ as is said (*Sap.* ii. 23) of God. Irenaeus, in his large work on heresy, nowhere quotes indeed *Sap. Sol.,* but borrows from it (iv. 38. 3) the saying : ἀφθαρσία δὲ ἐγγὺς εἶναι ποιεῖ θεοῦ (*Sap.* vi. 20). With reference to this Eusebius (*Hist. eccl.* v. 8. 8) says of Irenaeus : Καὶ ῥητοῖς δέ τισιν ἐκ τῆς Σολομῶνος σοφίας κέχρηται, μονονουχὶ φάσκων "Ορασις δὲ θεοῦ περιποιητικὴ ἀφθαρσίας, ἀφθαρσία δὲ ἐγγὺς εἶναι ποιεῖ θεοῦ. In the βιβλίον διαλέξεων διαφόρων,

which has not come down to us, Irenaeus, according to the
testimony of Eusebius, expressly quoted from the Book of
Wisdom (*Hist. eccl.* v. 26: τῆς λεγομένης σοφίας Σολομῶντος
μνημονεύει). *Canon Muratorianus*, lin. 69–71: "Sapientia ab
amicis Salomonis in honorem ipsius scripta." See also Hesse,
*Das muratorische Fragment* (1873), p. 239 sqq. Tertullian,
*adv. Valentinianos*, c. 2, refers to Wisd. i. 1 in the words: "ut
docet ipsa Sophia, non quidem Valentini sed Salomonis." Tertullian also made use of the Book of Wisdom. Clemens
Alexandrinus quotes it nine times, and frequently makes use of it
besides. The express quotations are introduced as either sayings
of Solomon (so *Strom.* vi. 11. 93, 14. 110, 14. 114, 15. 120–121),
or of the σοφία (*Paedag.* ii. 1. 7; *Strom.* ii. 2. 5, iv. 16. 103–104,
v. 14. 89), or with the formula εἴρηται (*Strom.* vi. 14. 113).
Hippolytus repeatedly quotes the book as a genuine προφητεία
Σολομῶν περὶ Χριστοῦ (*adv. Judaeos*, § 9 and 10 = Lagarde, p. 66 sq.),
especially the passage ii. 12–20, which is also frequently interpreted in a Messianic sense by moderns (see vol. ii. p. 139).

Origen is, after the author of the Muratorian Fragment, the
first to intimate a doubt with respect to the Solomonian authorship. He quotes it with the sceptical formula as ἡ ἐπιγεγραμμένη
τοῦ Σολομῶντος σοφία (*in Joann.* vol. xx. c. 4 = Lommatzsch,
ii. 202), ἡ σοφία ἡ ἐπιγεγραμμένη Σολομῶντος (*in Jerem. homil.*
viii. 1 = Lommatzsch, xv. 193), ὁ περὶ τῆς σοφίας εἰπὼν (*Selecta in
Jerem.* c. 29 = Lommatzsch, xv. 453), ἐν τῇ ἐπιγεγραμμένη
Σολομῶντος σοφίᾳ (*contra Cels.* v. 29 = Lommatzsch, xix. 216), "in
sapientia quae dicitur Salomonis, qui utique liber non ab
omnibus in auctoritate habetur" (*de principiis*, iv. 33 = Lommatzsch, xxi. 472 sq.). But he quotes it almost as frequently
simply as a work of Solomon. And that it is to him a
canonical book is especially shown by the entire section, *de
principiis*, i. 2. 5–13, where he uses the passage Wisd. vii. 25, 26
together with Col. i. 15 and Heb. i. 3 as fundamental passages
from which he develops his Christology. The whole section,
*de princ.* i. 2. 9–13, is nothing but an exegetical discussion of
Wisd. vii. 25, 26. On the whole, there are about forty
quotations from this book in Origen.

Cyprian uses the Book of Wisdom as in the fullest sense
canonical. He quotes it as Sapientia Salomonis (*Testim.* ii. 14,
iii. 16, 53, 58, 59, 66; *Ad Fortunatum*, c. 1), scriptura divina
(*De habitu virginum*, c. 10; *Epist.* vi. 2), scriptura sancta (*Ad
Demetrianum*, c. 24), or with the formulae as scriptum est (*De
zelo et livore*, c. 4; *Epist.* iv. 1, lv. 22), per Salomonem docet
spiritus sanctus, and the like (*De mortalitate*, c. 23; *Ad
Fortunatum*, c. 12). He quotes, two or three times, passages
from the Proverbs with the formula in Sapientia Salomonis

(*Testim.* iii. 1, 6, 16, 56) ; and once a passage from Wisdom with the formula in Ecclesiastico (*Testim.* iii. 112) ; but both from inadvertence, since he elsewhere decidedly distinguishes between Proverbs, Ecclesiasticus and Wisdom.

The *manuscripts, editions* and *ancient translations* (together with their editions) are the same for this book as for Ecclesiasticus (see above, p. 29), the two books being as a rule combined with each other. The *cod. Vaticanus* has been used for our book in Fritzsche's edition of the Apocrypha, but apparently only according to the data in Reusch (*Observ. crit.* 1861), which on their part rest upon the untrustworthy edition of the codex by Mai (see upon this, p. 11 above). Valuable contributions to the textual criticism are given in Reusch, *Observationes criticae in librum Sapientiae*, Frib. 1861. The separate edition (Reusch, *Liber Sapientiae graece*, Frib. 1858) gives the text of the Sixtine edition. An edition of the Greek text with the old Latin and the Authorized English translation : Deane, Σοφια Σαλωμων, *The Book of Wisdom, the Greek text, the Latin Vulgate and the Authorized English version, with an introduction, critical apparatus and a commentary*, Oxford 1881.

*The exegesis in general*, see above, p. 11. Commentaries: Bauermeister, *Commentarius in Sapientiam Salomonis*, Götting. 1828. Grimm, *Commentar über das Buch der Weisheit*, Leipzig 1837. J. A. Schmid, *Das Buch der Weisheit, übersetzt und erklärt*, 1858 (Cathol.). Grimm, *Das Buch der Weisheit erklärt* (*Exegetisches Handbuch zu den Apokryphen*, 6 pts.), Leipzig 1860 (not a new edition of the former work, but an entirely new one). Gutberlet, *Das Buch der Weisheit, übersetzt und erklärt*, 1874 (Cathol.). Deane in the above-named separate edition. The older literature in Fabricius, *Biblioth. graec.* ed. Harles, iii. 727–732. Fürst, *Biblioth. Jud.* iii. 219–221. Grimm, *Exeget. Handb.* p. 45 sq. Herzog's *Real-Enc.* 2nd ed. i. 496.

*Separate investigations :* Salthenius, *Diss. critico-theol. de auctore libri Sapientiae Philone potius Alexandrino quam seniore*, Regim. 1739. Bretschneider, *De libri Sapientiae parte priore c. i.–xi. e duobus libellis conflata.* Pts. i.–iii. Viteb. 1804. Winzer, *De philosophia morali in libro Sap. exposita*, Viteb. 1811. Grimm, *De Alexandrina Sapientiae libri indole perperam asserta*, Jen. 1833 (subsequently withdrawn by himself). Gfrörer, *Philo*, vol. ii. (1831) pp. 200–272. Dähne, *Geschichtl. Darstellung der jüd.-alex. Religionsphilosophie*, vol. ii. (1834) pp. 152–180. Bruch, *Weisheitslehre der Hebräer*, Strassb. 1851, pp. 322–378. Schmieder, *Ueber das B. der Weisheit*, 1853. Weisse, *Die Evangelienfrage* (1856), p. 202 sqq. Noach, *Psyche*, iii. 2, pp. 65–102. Nägelsbach in Herzog's *Real-Enc.* 1st ed. xvii. 622 sqq. Ewald, *Gesch. des Volkes Israel*, iv. 626 sqq.

The same, *Jahrbb. der bibl. Wissensch.* iii. 264 sq., ix. 234 sq., x. 219 sq., xi. 223 sqq. Zeller, *Die Philosophie der Griechen,* iii. 2 (3rd ed. 1881), pp. 271–274. Kübel, "Die ethischen Grundanschauungen der Weisheit Salomo's" (*Stud. und Krit.* 1865, pp. 690–722). Heinze, *Die Lehre vom Logos* (1872), pp. 192–202. Fritzsche in Schenkel's *Bibellex.* v. 647 sqq. Hausrath, *Neutestamentl. Zeitgesch.* 2nd ed. ii. 259 sqq. Grätz, *Gesch. der Juden,* vol. iii. (3rd ed. 1878) pp. 628–630 (note 3). Perez, *La Sapienza di Salomone, saggio storico-critico,* Firenze 1871. The same, *Sopra Filone Alessandrino e il suo libro detto,* "*La Sapienza di Salomone,*" Palermo 1883. The Introductions of Jahn, Eichhorn, Bertholdt, Welte, Scholz, Nöldeke, De Wette-Schrader, Reusch, Keil, Kaulen, Kleinert, Reuss (see above, p. 12).

## 2. *Aristobulus.*

The author of the Wisdom of Solomon is one whose views are still chiefly based upon the Palestinian Proverbial Wisdom, which in him is only peculiarly modified by the influence of Greek philosophy. The Alexandrian Aristobulus on the contrary is a Hellenistic philosopher in the proper sense. He is acquainted with, and expressly quotes the Greek philosophers Pythagoras, Socrates, Plato, and is at home with their views as a philosopher by profession.

The statements of the ancients do not indeed entirely agree as to his date. It may however pass for certain that he lived in the time of Ptolemy VI. Philometor, and therefore towards the middle of the second century before Christ (about 170 – 150 B.C.). He himself says, in one of his works addressed to a Ptolemy, that the Greek translation of the Pentateuch was made "under King Philadelphus, thy ancestor" (Euseb. *Praep. evang.* xiii. 12. 2, ed. Gaisford: ἐπὶ τοῦ προσαγορευθέντος Φιλαδέλφου βασιλέως, σοῦ δὲ προγόνου). Thus he at all events wrote under a descendant of Ptolemy II. Philadelphus. But both Clemens Alexandrinus and Eusebius in his *Chronicle* distinctly mention Philometor.[16] The same

---

[16] Clemens Alex. *Strom.* i. 22. 150 : Ἀριστόβουλος ἐν τῷ πρώτῳ τῶν πρὸς τὸν Φιλομήτορα. The reading here is guaranteed, for in Eusebius also, who

chronology is also presupposed, when Clemens Alexandrinus
and Eusebius identify this Aristobulus with the one who is
mentioned in the beginning of the second Book of Maccabees
(2 Macc. i. 10).[17]   In opposition to such evidence, it cannot
be taken into consideration, that Anatolius places him under
Ptolemy II. Philadelphus,[18] and that the only manuscript
of the *Stromata* of Clemens Alexandrinus has erroneously
Philadelphus instead of Philometor in one passage.[19]

According to Clem. Alex. *Strom.* v. 14. 97, this Aristobulus wrote βιβλία ἱκανά.   Probably Clemens does not mean
to say that he wrote several books, but that the one work
which he knew of his was an extensive one.   We are
indebted for further particulars to Clemens Alexandrinus
(*Strom.* i. 15. 72, i. 22. 150, v. 14. 97, vi. 3. 32), Anatolius
(in Euseb. *Hist. eccl.* vii. 32, 16–19, Anatolius was an older
contemporary of Eusebius) and Eusebius (*Praep. evang.* vii. 14,
viii. 10, xiii. 12).   Aristobulus is also briefly mentioned by
Origen (*contra Cels.* iv. 51).   The only two passages which
are verbally preserved are in Euseb. *Praep. evang.* viii. 10 and
xiii. 12.   For whatever other verbal quotations are found
(Clemens, *Strom.* i. 22. 150 = Euseb. *Praep.* ix. 6.   Clemens,
*Strom.* vi. 3. 32 = Euseb. *Praep.* vii. 14) are certainly contained
also in the text of these larger fragments.[20]   The passage,
which Cyrillus Alex. (*contra Julian.* p. 134, ed. Spanh.)

in the *Praep. evang.* ix. 6 gives this passage from Clemens, the manuscripts
all have Φιλομήτορα. Euseb. *Chron. ad Olymp.* 151 (ed. Schoene, ii. 124 sq.).
The Greek text, which is preserved in the *Chronicon paschale*, is as follows:
᾿Αριστόβουλος ᾿Ιουδαῖος περιπατητικὸς Φιλόσοφος ἐγνωρίζετο, ὃς Πτολεμαίῳ τῷ
Φιλομήτορι ἐξηγήσεις τῆς Μωϋσέως γραφῆς ἀνέθηκεν. So too the Armenian
and Jerome.   The 151st Olympiad=176–172 B.C.

[17] Clemens Alex. *Strom.* v. 14. 97.   Euseb. *Praep. evang.* viii. 9, *fin.*

[18] Anatolius in Euseb. *Hist. eccl.* vii. 32. 16.

[19] Clemens, *Strom.* v. 14. 97.   The *cod. Laurentianus, i.e.* the only manuscript in which the *Stromata* of Clemens has come down to us (for the
*Parisinus*, saec. 15, is only a copy from it), has here Φιλάδελφον.   Modern
editors have however correctly replaced it by Φιλομήτορα.

[20] Namely: (1) Clem. *Str.* i. 22. 450=Eus. *Pr.* ix. 6=Eus. *Pr.* xiii.
12. 1.   (2) Clem. *Strom.* vi. 3. 32 = Eus. *Pr.* viii. 10. 14.   (3) Eus. *Pr.* vii.
14 = Eus. *Pr.* xiii. 12. 10–11.

ascribes to Aristobulus, is derived from the third Book of
the *Indica* of Megasthenes, and has been only ascribed to
Aristobulus in consequence of a very inconsiderate use of
Clem. Al. *Strom.* i. 15. 72.

The work which was in the hands of these Fathers is
designated as *an explanation of the Mosaic laws.*[21] According
however to the fragments preserved, we must conceive of it
not as an actual commentary on the text, but as a *free reproduction of the contents of the Pentateuch,* in which the latter is
philosophically explained. Hence it is not Philo's allegorical
commentaries on single passages of the text, but his systematic
delineation of the Mosaic legislation, the characteristics
of which have been described p. 219 above, which is
analogous to it. Like Philo, Aristobulus already seems to
have given a connected representation of the contents of
the Pentateuch, for the purpose of showing to the cultured
heathen world, that the Mosaic law, if only correctly understood, already contained all that the best Greek philosophers
subsequently taught. The work was first of all intended
*for King Ptolemy Philometor himself,*[22] who is therefore
addressed in the text (Eus. *Pr.* viii. 10. 1 sqq., xiii. 12. 2).
Hence it is self - evident, that it is addressed simply to
heathen readers. His chief object was, as Clement says, to
show "that the peripatetic philosophy was dependent upon
the law of Moses and the other prophets" (*Strom.* v. 14. 97:
᾿Αριστοβούλῳ . . . βιβλία πεπόνηται ἱκανὰ, δι᾽ ὧν ἀποδείκ-
νυσι τὴν περιπατητικὴν φιλοσοφίαν ἔκ τε τοῦ κατὰ Μωυσέα

---

[21] Euseb. *Praep. evang.* vii. 13. 7, ed. Gaisford: τὴν τῶν ἱερῶν νόμων
ἑρμηνείαν. Euseb. *Chron. ad Olymp.* 151 (ed. Schoene, ii. 124 sq.):
ἐξηγήσεις τῆς Μωυσέως γραφῆς (this Greek wording, preserved by means of
the *Chron. paschale,* is confirmed by the Armenian [enarrationem librorum
Moysis] and by Jerome [*explanationem in Moysen commentarios*]). Anatolius in Euseb. *Hist. eccl.* vii. 32. 16: βίβλους ἐξηγητικὰς τοῦ Μωϋσέως
νόμου.

[22] Clemens Al. *Strom.* i. 22. 150=Eus. *Praep. evang.* ix. 6. 6: ἐν τῷ
πρώτῳ τῶν πρὸς τὸν Φιλομήτορα. Euseb. *Praep. evang.* viii. 9, *fin.*: ἐν τῷ
πρὸς Πτολλεμαῖον τὸν βασιλέα συγγράμματι. Euseb. *Praep. evang.* vii.
13, *fin.* Anatolius in Euseb. *Hist. eccl.* vii. 32. 16.

νόμου καὶ τῶν ἄλλων ἠρτῆσθαι προφητῶν). This is substantially confirmed by the fragments preserved, only instead of the peripatetic the Greek philosophy in general should rather be spoken of. For Aristobulus is not contented with exhibiting the intrinsic agreement of the Mosaic law with the philosophy of the Greeks, but roundly asserts *that the Greek philosophers, a Pythagoras, a Socrates, a Plato, derived their doctrines from Moses*, nay, that even the poets *Homer* and *Hesiod* borrowed much from him, for that the essential contents of the Pentateuch had been rendered into Greek long before the Greek translation of the Pentateuch made under Ptolemy Philadelphus.[23] This bold assertion, that Moses was the father of Greek philosophy and culture, was embraced also by later Jewish Hellenists. Especially do we again meet with it in Philo.

The fragments preserved give us at least an approximate notion of the execution in detail. A large portion of the passages are employed in settling the true sense of the Biblical anthropomorphisms. Thus *e.g.* the long passage in Euseb. *Pr. evang.* xiii. 12. 1–8, which, according to the parallel passage in Clemens Alex. *Strom.* i. 22. 150 = Euseb. *Pr.* ix. 6, is taken from the first book of Aristobulus' work, and evidently belonged to the explanation of the history of the Creation, shows, that nothing else is meant by the words "God said, and it was," than that everything came to pass by the operation (δυνάμει) of God, as indeed was taught by the Greek philosophers Orpheus and Aratus. The following passage (Eus. *Pr.* xiii. 12. 9–16), which also belonged to the explanation of the history of the Creation, treats of the seventh day as the day of rest, and explains its meaning by an appeal, among other things, to supposed verses of Hesiod, Homer, and Linus.[24] Another passage (Eus. *Pr.* viii. 10)

---

[23] See especially Euseb. *Praep. evang.* xiii. 12. 1 = Clemens, *Strom.* i. 22. 150 = Euseb. *Praep.* ix. 6. 6-8. Pythagoras, Socrates and Plato: Eus. *Pr.* xiii. 12. 4, ed. Gaisford. Homer and Hesiod: Eus. *Pr.* xiii. 12. 13.

[24] A small portion of this (Eus. *Pr.* xiii. 12. 10–11) is also found *Pr. evang.* vii. 14.

shows what we are to understand, when the hands, arms, face and feet of God, or a walking of God, are spoken of.[25] Lastly, the extract from Anatolius, given in Euseb. *Hist. eccl.* vii. 32. 17–18, is occupied with the Passover, which is celebrated, when both the sun and moon are in the equinox, viz. the sun in the vernal, and the moon opposite him in the autumnal equinox. Just this fragment shows, that Aristobulus by no means occupied himself with only philosophically explaining away the text of the Pentateuch, but that he really gave a description and explanation of the Mosaic law. While endeavouring however to settle its meaning, he often enters, as Origen especially intimates (*contra Cels.* iv. 51), into the region of allegorical interpretation.

The fragments give no further disclosure concerning the *philosophical standpoint* of Aristobulus. It may without any hesitation be assumed that he was an eclectic. The fragment on the meaning of the Sabbath "enters into a Pythagorean-like dilation on the power of the number seven." [26] Elsewhere Aristobulus appeals not only generally to Pythagoras, Socrates and Plato, but, when entering more into detail, to the peripatetic doctrine in particular.[27] That he the more closely adhered to the latter is vouched for by the Fathers, who unanimously call him a *peripatetic*.[28]

It is almost incomprehensible, that many more recent scholars (*e.g.* Richard Simon, Hody, Eichhorn, Kuenen, Grätz, Joel) should have disputed the genuineness of the whole work of Aristobulus. The picture, which we obtain from the fragments of the work that have come down to us, so entirely coincides with all that we elsewhere learn of the intellectual tendency of Hellenistic Judaism, that there is absolutely no occasion for any kind of doubt. The sole reason against the

[25] A small sentence from it is found in Eus. *Pr.* viii. 10. 14; also in Clem. Alex. *Strom.* vi. 3. 32.

[26] Zeller, *Die Philosophie der Griechen*, iii. 2. (3rd ed.) p. 264.

[27] Eus. *Pr. ev.* xiii. 12. 10–11=vii. 14.

[28] Clemens, *Strom.* i. 15. 72, v. 14. 97. Euseb. *Praep. evang.* viii. 9, *fin.*, ix. 6. 6. *Chron. ad Olymp.* 151 (ed. Schoene, ii. 124 sq.).

genuineness, which at all deserves mention, is the certainly
indisputable fact that Aristobulus cites supposed verses of
Orpheus, Hesiod, Homer, and Linus, which are certainly
forged by a Jew. It is thought, that such audacity is inconceivable in a work intended for King Ptolemy himself. The
assumption on which the argument starts is, that the verses
were forged by Aristobulus himself—an assumption not only
incapable of proof, but in the highest degree improbable. The
verses were probably derived from an older Jewish work (see
on this point No. VII.), and adopted by Aristobulus in all good
faith in their genuineness. Aristobulus only did what later
Christian apologists have also done, without thereby affording
a ground for doubting the genuineness of their works.

*The entire work of Aristobulus is said,* according to a marginal
note in the cod. Laurentianus of Clemens Alexandrinus'
*Stromata, to have been still extant towards the close of the Middle
Ages in a library at Patmos* (on *Strom.* i. 22. 150, a hand of the
fifteenth or sixteenth century remarks: 'Αριστοβούλου βίβλος αὕτη
ἡ πρὸς τὸν Φιλομήτορα ἐστίν εἰς τὴν Πάτμον, ἣν ἔγωγε οἶδα; see the note
in Dindorf's ed.). Whether this note is worthy of credence is
however very doubtful.

Compare in general: Richard Simon, *Histoire critique du
Vieux Testament,* pp. 189, 499. Hody, *De bibliorum textibus,*
p. 50 sqq. Fabricius, *Biblioth. graec.* ed. Harles, i. 164, iii. 469
sq. Eichhorn, *Allgem. Bibliothek der biblischen Literatur,* vol. v.
(1793) pp. 253–298. Valckenaer, *Diatribe de Aristobulo Judaeo,
philosopho peripatetico Alexandrino,* Lugd. Bat. 1806 (chief
work). Gabler's *Journal für auserlesene theolog. Literatur,*
vol. v. (1810) pp. 183–209 (advertisement of Valckenaer's work).
Winer in Ersch and Gruber's *Allgem. Encyclop.* § 1, vol. v.
(1820) p. 266. Lobeck, *Aglaophamus,* i. (1829) p. 448.
Gfrörer, *Philo,* ii. 711–21. Dähne, *Geschichtl. Darstellung der
jüd.-alex. Religionsphilosophie,* ii. 73–112. Fürst, *Biblioth. Jud.*
i. 53 sq. Herzfeld, *Gesch. des Volkes Jisrael,* iii. 473 sqq., 564 sqq.
Ewald, *Gesch. des Volkes Israel,* iv. 335 sqq. Teuffel in Pauly's
*Real-Enc.* i. 2 (2nd ed.), p. 1600. Cobet in the Λογιος Ἑρμης, i.
(1866) pp. 173–177, 521. Zeller, *Die Philosophie der Griechen,*
iii. 2 (3rd ed.), pp. 257–264. Ueberweg, *Grundriss,* 4th ed. i.
240 sqq. Binde, *Aristobulische Studien,* 2 pts. Glogau 1869–
1870 (Gymnasialprogr.). Heinze, *Die Lehre vom Logos* (1872),
pp. 185–192. Kuenen, *De godsdienst van Israël,* ii. (1870)
pp. 433–440. Freudenthal, *Alexander Polyhistor,* pp. 166–169.

Grätz, *Monatsschr. für Gesch. und Wissensch. des Judenth.* 1878, pp. 49–60, 97–109. Joel, *Blicke in die Religionsgeschichte zu Anfang des zweiten christlichen Jahrhunderts* (1880), pp. 77–100.

### 3. *Philo.*

Philo, the more recent fellow-countryman of Aristobulus by two centuries, represents the same tendency. His main effort also is to prove, that the views derived from Greek philosophers were genuinely Jewish. And this he does now for heathen, now for Jewish readers; for the former to inspire them with respect for Judaism, for the latter to educate them to such a Judaism as he himself represents. It may safely be assumed, that there were between Aristobulus and Philo other representatives of this tendency. For it presented itself in Philo with such assurance, and in such maturity of form, as would not be conceivable without historical connection. Nothing however of the supposed literary productions of such individuals has come down to us.

Since Philo, by reason of his eminent importance and the extent of his extant works, demands a separate delineation (§ 34), we will here only briefly mention those writings of his in which philosophical instruction and discussion form the main object. Among these are in the first place two of his principal works on the Pentateuch, viz.: (1) the Ζητήματα καὶ λύσεις, a short explanation of Genesis and Exodus in the form of questions and answers; and (2) the Νόμων ἱερῶν ἀλληγορίαι, the extensive allegorical commentaries on select passages of Genesis, in the form of Rabbinical Midrash. These form Philo's chief philosophical work properly so called, and constitute in extent about the half of Philo's still extant writings. (3) The work, Περὶ τοῦ πάντα σπουδαῖον εἶναι ἐλεύθερον (*Quod omnis probus liber*), properly only the second half of a work, whose first half, which is lost, dealt with the theme περὶ τοῦ δούλου εἶναι πάντα φαῦλον, was also occupied in the discussion of philosophical questions. (4) Περὶ προνοίας. (5) Ἀλέξανδρος ἢ περὶ τοῦ λόγον ἔχειν τὰ ἄλογα ζῷα. Particulars concerning

all these works will be found in § 34. The two last-named
are also of interest, because Philo in them chooses the form of
the Greek dialogue in discussing the theme.

### 4. *The Fourth Book of Maccabees.*

To philosophical literature belongs also the so-called fourth
Book of Maccabees. For the Judaism, which the author
recommends, is influenced by the Stoic philosophy.

In its *form* this piece of writing is a *discourse.* It directly
addresses its hearers or readers (i. 1, xviii. 1).[29] The contents
being of a religious and edifying kind, it might even be called
a *sermon,* and the choice of this form referred to the custom of
religious lectures in the synagogues. But when Freudenthal
(pp. 4–36) emphatically insists that we have here an actual
specimen of synagogue preaching, this is not only incapable
of proof, but also improbable, the theme discoursed on being
not a text of Holy Scripture, but a philosophic proposition.

The author had only Jews in view, whether as hearers or
readers (xviii. 1: ὦ τῶν Ἀβραμιαίων σπερμάτων ἀπόγονοι
παῖδες Ἰσραηλῖται). He desires to show them, that it is not
difficult to lead a pious life, if only they follow the precepts
of "pious reason." For "*pious reason is the absolute ruler of
the motives*" (i. 1: αὐτοδέσποτός ἐστι τῶν παθῶν ὁ εὐσεβὴς
λογισμός). This proposition is the proper theme of the discourse ; its meaning is first explained, and its truth afterwards
proved by facts from Jewish history, especially by the laudable
martyrdom of Eleazar, and the seven Maccabaean brothers. A
large portion of the contents is therefore devoted to a description of the martyrdom of these heroes of faith. In his grossly
realistic delineation of the several tortures, the author shows
even greater want of taste than the second Book of Maccabees,
and the psychology assumed is as contrary as possible to
nature. His authority seems to have been the second Book of

[29] I quote according to the division into chapters and verses of Fritzsche's
edition of the Apocrypha.

Maccabees. At least it cannot be proved that he drew, as Freudenthal (pp. 72–90) supposes, from the larger work of Jason of Cyrene (2 Macc. ii. 23).

The author's own *standpoint* is influenced by *Stoicism*. The fundamental idea of the whole discourse is that of Stoic morality, viz. the rule of reason over impulse. The setting up too of four cardinal virtues (φρόνησις, δικαιοσύνη, ἀνδρεία, σωφροσύνη) is derived from Stoicism. But this influence of Stoicism does not anywhere penetrate more deeply with the author. Even the fundamental idea is transformed in Jewish fashion. For the reason, to which he ascribes dominion over desire, is not human reason as such, but *pious* reason : ὁ εὐσεβὴς λογισμός (i. 1, vii. 16, xiii. 1, xv 20, xvi. 1, xviii. 2), *i.e.* reason *guiding itself according to the rule of the divine law* (comp. also i. 15 sq.). He also goes his own way in the description and division of the affections (see Freudenthal, p. 55 sqq.; Zeller, iii. 2. 276). But it would be doing him too much honour to designate him as an eclectic philosopher. He is but a dilettante *in philosophicis*, somewhat after the fashion of Josephus, who also knows how to give his Judaism a philosophic tinge. Of all Jewish philosophers known to us, our author stands relatively nearest to Pharisaism, for just what he extols in the Maccabaean brethren is their punctilious adherence to the ceremonial law. Two of his Jewish views in particular may be brought forward as worthy of notice—(1) his belief in the resurrection, the form of which is not that of the Pharisaic belief in that doctrine, but the form met with among other Jewish Hellenists, of a faith in an eternal and blessed life of pious souls in heaven (xiii. 16, xv. 2, xvii. 5, xviii. *fin.*) ;[30] and (2) the notion that the martyrdom of the righteous serves as an atonement for the

---

[30] For further particulars, see Grimm, *Exeget. Handb.* p. 289, and Freudenthal, pp. 67–71. Caution is however needed in the settlement of details, because the text seems to be not quite free from Christian interpolations. See Freudenthal, p. 165 sqq. Such an interpolation are the words εἰς τοὺς κόλπους αὐτῶν, which are wanting in the cod. Alex. and Sin. The thought however remains the same even without these words.

sins of the people (vi. 29 : καθάρσιον αὐτῶν ποίησον τὸ ἐμὸν αἷμα, καὶ ἀντίψυχον αὐτῶν λάβε τὴν ἐμὴν ψυχήν; xvii. 29 : ἀντίψυχον γεγονότας τῆς τοῦ ἔθνους ἁμαρτίας).³¹

*Josephus* is named by Eusebius and other Church writers as the *author* of this book. This view however has only the value of a hypothesis. For the book still appears in many manuscripts anonymously, and was therefore certainly at first issued without the name of the author. The entirely different style, and the circumstance, that Josephus in his *Antiquities* nowhere makes use of the second Book of Maccabees and thus seems not to know it, while the work in question is entirely based upon it, speak against his authorship., The first century after Christ is generally accepted as the *date of composition,* chiefly because the book must have been written before the destruction of Jerusalem. Though the latter cannot be proved, this view must be pretty nearly correct, since a more recent book would no longer have been accepted by the Christian Church.

Eusebius, speaking of the writings of Josephus, says concerning the *title* and *authorship, Hist. eccl.* iii. 10. 6 : Πεπόνηται δὲ καὶ ἄλλο οὐκ ἀγεννὲς σπούδασμα τῷ ἀνδρὶ περὶ αὐτοκράτορος λογισμοῦ, ὅ τινες Μακκαβαϊκὸν ἐπέγραψαν κ.τ.λ. Hieronymus, *De viris illustr.* c. 13 (Vallarsi, ii. 851) : "Alius quoque liber ejus, qui inscribitur περὶ αὐτοκράτορος λογισμοῦ valde elegans habetur, in quo et Machabaeorum sunt digesta martyria." The same, *contra Pelagianos,* ii. 6 (Vallarsi, ii. 749): "Unde et Josephus Machabaeorum scriptor historiae frangi et regi posse dixit perturbationes animi non eradicari ( = 4 Macc. iii. 5)." The article in Suidas, *Lex. s.v.* Ἰώσηπος, is taken from the Greek translation of Hieron. *de viris illustris,* c. 13. For other authors who attribute this book to Josephus, see Grimm, *Handb.* p. 293 sq. It is also frequently attributed to Josephus in the MSS. (Grimm as above. Freudenthal, p. 117 sqq.). Its title as the fourth Book of Maccabees (Μακκαβαίων δ') is found in Philostorgius and Syncellus, and in some Scripture MSS., and indeed in the latter without the mention of Josephus as its author (so esp. *cod. Alex.* and *Sin.*). For further particulars, see Freudenthal, pp. 117–120. On the use of the book in Christian ascetic literature, see above, p. 214.

³¹ Comp. Freudenthal, p. 68.

The *manuscripts*, in which our book has come down, are *some of them manuscripts of Scripture, some of Josephus*. The former are not numerous, since as a rule only three books of Maccabees were received as canonical (Freudenthal, pp. 118, 119). Still the two most important manuscripts for our book are Scripture MSS., viz. the *codex Alexandrinus* (No. iii. in Fritzsche) and *Sinaiticus* (No. x. in Fritzsche). On the editions of these manuscripts, see above, p. 166. More concerning them will be found in Fabricius-Harles, *Biblioth. graec.* v. 26 sq. Grimm, *Handb.* p. 294. Freudenthal, pp. 120–127, 169 sq., 173. Fritzsche, *Prolegom.* p. xxi. sq. Collations chiefly in Havercamp's edition of *Josephus*, ii. 1. 497 sqq., ii. 2. 157 sqq. A fragment in Tischéndorf, *Monumenta sacra inedita*, vol. vi. 1869. Various readings of a Florentine MS. (*Acquis. ser.* iii. No. 44) are given by Pitra, *Analecta sacra*, vol. ii. (1884) pp. 635–640.

The text is *printed* in accordance with the manuscripts, on the one hand in some editions of the Septuagint and in separate editions of the Apocrypha, on the other and chiefly in the *editions of Josephus*. Most of the editors have troubled themselves very little about the manuscripts. The first attempt at a recension of the text from the best authorities is made in Fritzsche's edition of the *Libri apocryphi Vet. Test. graece* (Lips. 1871). For more on the editions, see Grimm, *Handb.* p. 294 sq. Freudenthal, pp. 127–133.

Erasmus compiled a *Latin paraphrase* of this book (printed *e.g.* in Havercamp's *Josephus*, ii. 2. 148–156). Nothing reliable is as yet known of any *ancient Latin translation* on which it is based. See Grimm, p. 296. Freudenthal, p. 133 sqq. The old *Syriac translation* is published in Ceriani's photo-lithographic edition of the Milan Peshito manuscript (see above, p. 92).

Grimm has given a careful commentary on this book in his *Exeget. Handb. zu den Apokryphen*, 4 parts, Leipzig 1857. Freudenthal's *Die Flavius Josephus beigelegte Schrift Ueber die Herrschaft der Vernunft* (4 *Makkabäerbuch*), *eine Predigt aus dem ersten nachchristlichen Jahrhundert, untersucht*, Breslau 1869, is a complete monograph. A *German translation* is contained in the *Bibliothek der griechischen und römischen Schriftsteller über Judenthum und Juden in neuen Uebertragungen und Sammlungen*, 2 vols. Leipzig 1867.

Comp. in general: Gfrörer, *Philo*, ii. 173–200. Dähne, *Geshichtl. Darstellung der jüd.-alex. Religionsphilosophie*, ii. 190–199. Ewald, *Gesch. des Volkes Israel*, iv. 632 sqq. Langen, *Das Judenthum in Palästina* (1866), pp. 74–83. Geiger, *Jüdische Zeitschr. für Wissensch. und Leben*, 1869, pp. 113-116. Fritzsche in Schenkel's *Bibellex.* iv. 98–100. Keil, *Einl. in's*

*A. T.*, 3rd ed. (1873) p. 722 sqq. Grätz, *Monatsschr. für Gesch. und Wissensch. des Judenth.* 1877, p. 454 sqq. Reuss, *Gesch. der heil. Schriften A. T.'s,* § 570. Zeller, *Die Philosophie der Griechen,* iii. 2 (3rd ed. 1881), pp. 275–277.


### VI. APOLOGETICS.

The peculiarity of the Jewish people involved the circumstance that the Jews were felt to be, more than other Orientals, an anomaly in the framework of the Graeco-Roman world. Denying all authority to other religions, they were paid in the same coin, and their right of existence upon the soil of Hellenistic culture disputed. The town municipalities tried to get rid of such inconvenient fellow-citizens; the populace was always ready to lift up a hand against them, while by the educated they were despised and derided (see vol. ii. pp. 273–276, 291). Hellenistic Judaism thus found itself continually at war with the rest of the Hellenistic world; it had ever to draw the sword in its own defence. *Hence a large share of the entire Graeco-Jewish literature subserves apologetic purposes.* Especially does the historic and philosophic literature essentially pursue the design of showing that the Jewish nation was, by reason of the greatness of its history and the purity of its teaching, if not superior, at least equal to others. Besides these indirectly apologetic works, there were also some *which sought in a systematic manner to refute the reproaches with which Judaism was assailed.* These were called forth by the sometimes utterly absurd fables propagated by certain Greek literati concerning the Jews, and generally by the direct accusations brought against them in Greek and Latin literature. These accusations had their rise in Egypt (Joseph. *contra Apion.* i. 25). Alexandrian literati were the first to write against the Jews. From these turbid waters later writers, especially Tacitus, drew. In what follows we shall speak in the first place of literary opponents, and afterwards of the apologetic works and the points of dispute themselves (Attack and Defence).

## 1. *The Literary Opponents.*

**1.** *Manetho* (comp. Josephus, *contra Apion.* i. 26–31).
The Egyptian priest Manetho composed, in the time of
Ptolemy II. Philadelphus, therefore about 270–250 B.C., a
learned work on Egyptian history in the Greek language,
derived from the sacred records themselves (Joseph. *contra
Apion.* i. 14: γέγραφε Ἑλλάδι φωνῇ τὴν πάτριον ἱστορίαν,
ἔκ τε τῶν ἱερῶν, ὡς φησὶν αὐτός, μεταφράσας. *Ibid.* i. 26:
ὁ τὴν Αἰγυπτιακὴν ἱστορίαν ἐκ τῶν ἱερῶν γραμμάτων μεθερμηνεύειν ὑπεσχημένος). From these Αἰγυπτιακά of Manetho
Josephus gives in two places long fragments, which however,
as Josephus himself states, are of very different character.
The portions (from the second Book of the Αἰγυπτιακά) in
i. 14–16, which treat of the rule of the Hyksos in Egypt,
make, by the copiousness of their contents and the conciseness
of their form, the most favourable impression. Nothing in
them gives occasion for doubting that their contents are really
derived from the ancient records. Of quite another kind are
the portions in i. 26, 27. These do not indeed pretend to
be authentic history, but only give, according to Manetho's
own confession, *the legends current concerning the Jews* (i. 16:
ὁ Μανεθὼν οὐκ ἐκ τῶν παρ' Αἰγυπτίοις γραμμάτων, ἀλλ' ὡς
αὐτὸς ὡμολόγηκεν, ἐκ τῶν ἀδεσπότως μυθολογουμένων
προστέθεικεν. I. 26: μέχρι μὲν τούτων ἠκολούθησε ταῖς
ἀναγραφαῖς, ἔπειτα δὲ δοὺς ἐξουσίαν αὐτῷ διὰ τοῦ φάναι
γράψειν τὰ μυθευόμενα καὶ λεγόμενα περὶ τῶν Ἰουδαίων,
λόγους ἀπιθάνους παρενέβαλεν). It is here related, how King
Amenophis of Egypt assembled in one place all the lepers of
the country, 80,000 in number, and sent them to work in
the stone quarries east of the Nile. After they had laboured
there a long time they petitioned the king to assign to them
the town of Auaris, which had formerly been inhabited by
the Hyksos, as a place of residence. The king granted their
request. When however they had taken possession of the

town, they were attacked by the king and chose a priest of
Heliopolis named Osarsiph as their head, who gave them new
laws, in which they were especially commanded to worship
no gods and to kill the sacred animals. He also invoked the
aid of the Hyksos from Jerusalem as allies. With their
assistance the lepers now drove away King Amenophis and
ruled Egypt for thirteen years. The priest Osarsiph then
took the name of Moses. After the thirteen years the Hyksos
and the lepers were driven out of Egypt by King Amenophis.
This history concerning the origin of the Jews was therefore
read in his text of Manetho by Josephus. Whether it is
derived from Manetho himself is questionable. Many recent
investigators, *e.g.* Boeckh, Carl Müller, Kellner, regard it as a
later insertion.[32] The possibility of its being such cannot be
disputed, since this much read work already existed in various
recensions even in the time of Josephus.[33] This view does
not however appear to me to be probable in the case in
question. For if an enemy of the Jews had subsequently
inserted the passage, he would scarcely have been so truthful
as expressly to bring forward the fact, that he was not giving
a history accredited by ancient records, but only τὰ μυθευόμενα
καὶ λεγόμενα περὶ τῶν Ἰουδαίων. In these words we hear
the strict investigator, who indeed as an enemy of the Jews
cannot deny himself the reporting of these tales, but expressly
distinguishes them as legends from authentic history. At
any rate Josephus read the section in all the copies known
to him of Manetho; for he says nothing of any difference
in this respect.[34]

---

[32] Boeckh, *Manetho und die Hundssternperiode*, p. 302. Müller, *Fragm.
hist. graec.* ii. 514[b]. Kellner, *De fragmentis Manethonianis*, p. 52 sq.

[33] In the passage, i. 14, Josephus gives a long extract from Manetho, in
which the name *Hyksos* is explained by " Shepherd Kings." On this
Josephus remarks, that " *in another copy*" (ἐν ἄλλῳ ἀντιγράφῳ) another
explanation is given. Ἐν ἄλλη δέ τινι βίβλῳ (i. 14 near the end) must be
understood in the same sense, *i.e.* of another manuscript, not of another
part of Manetho's work.

[34] It must not be urged (as by Kellner) against the origin of the section
in question, that it is contradictory to the passage given, i. 14. Such a

The fragments of Manetho are best collected in Carl Müller, *Fragmenta historicorum Graecorum*, vol. ii. (1848) pp. 511–616. Comp. on Manetho in general: Böckh, *Manetho und die Hundssternperiode, ein Beitrag zur Geschichte der Pharaonen*, Berlin 1845. Bähr in Pauly's *Real-Enc.* iv. 1477 sqq. Nicolai, *Griechische Literaturgeschichte*, 2nd ed. vol. ii. (1876) pp. 198–200. Krall, "Die Composition und die Schicksale des Manethonischen Geschichtswerkes" (*Sitzungsberichte der Wiener Akademie, philos.-histor. Classe*, vol. xcv., yearly course 1879, pp. 123–226), treats, pp. 152–169, especially of the fragments in Josephus.

On the fragments in Josephus: Hengstenberg, *Die Bücher Moses und Aegypten*, with an appendix: *Manetho und die Hyksos*, Berlin 1841. Ewald, *Gesch. des Volkes Israel* (3rd ed.), ii. 110 sqq. Kellner, *De fragmentis Manethonianis, quae apud Josephum contra Apionem*, i. 14 and i. 26 sunt., Marburg 1859. J. G. Müller, *Des Flavius Josephus Schrift gegen den Apion* (Basel 1877), pp. 120 sqq., 185 sqq., 214 sqq.

2. *Apollonius Molon (or Molonis?)*. Among the literary opponents of Judaism Josephus frequently names one ᾽Απολλώνιος ὁ Μόλων (*contra Apion.* ii. 14, ii. 36), in a later passage ὁ Μόλων ᾽Απολλώνιος (comp. ii. 7: Apollonium Molonis), whose full name he also abridges so as to write either only ᾽Απολλώνιος (ii. 14 and ii. 37, twice) or only Μόλων (ii. 2, ed. Bekker, 226. 13; comp. ii. 33 and ii. 41: Μόλωνες). This adversary of the Jews in Josephus is undoubtedly identical with him, from whom Alexander Polyhistor gives a passage (in Euseb. *Praep. evang.* ix. 19: ὁ δὲ τὴν συσκευὴν τὴν κατὰ ᾽Ιουδαίων γράψας Μόλων).[35] An orator of the same name (Apollonius Molon) is elsewhere frequently mentioned as the teacher of Cicero and Caesar and as a writer on rhetoric.[36] It seems however that some discrepancies had already crept in concerning him among the ancients. For

contradiction only exists if the Hyksos are identified—as by Josephus—with the Jews, which is certainly a mistake.

[35] The form Μόλων is given by Gaisford according to the better manuscripts ; other editions have Μήλων.

[36] Quintilian, xii. 6. 7. Sueton. *Caesar*, 4. Quintilian, iii. 1. 16. Phoebammon in *Rhetores graeci*, ed. Walz, viii. 494 (here ᾽Απολλώνιος ὁ ἐπικληθεὶς Μόλων).

Strabo distinguishes two orators, an Apollonius and a Molon,
evidently by reason of a more accurate knowledge of the
matter. He mentions both (xiv. 2. 13, p. 655) as eminent
men, who lived in Rhodes, and remarks that both came from
Alabanda in Caria, but that Molon came to Rhodes subsequently to Apollonius, on which account Apollonius said to
him, " ὀψὲ μολών." Thus they were not only fellow-countrymen but contemporaries. Strabo also distinguishes them in
another passage, in which he is enumerating the eminent men
of Alabanda (xiv. 2. 26, p. 661). Cicero too mentions both,
and indeed so that he calls the one only Apollonius, and the
other, who was Cicero's tutor, only Molon.[37] Hence we must
certainly distinguish between the two. Apollonius however
was called by his full name, Ἀπολλώνιος ὁ τοῦ Μόλωνος
(Plutarch. Cicero 4, Caesar 3 ; Joseph. Apion. ii. 7) ; and he
seems, by placing his father's name beside his own, according
to a custom which may be pointed to elsewhere, to have
called himself Ἀπολλώνιος ὁ Μόλων.[37a] This gave rise to
his being frequently confounded with Molon. Cicero had
probably heard both, but his own teacher was Molon.
We are here concerned, not with the latter, but with his
older fellow-countryman Apollonius, who, according to
Cicero, was already a noted teacher 120 years before
Christ.[38]

There existed before the end of the second century before

---

[37] For proof, see Riese, *Molon or Apollonius Molon?* (*Rhein. Museum*,
1879, pp. 627–630), from which the above details concerning the distinct-
ness of the two men is taken.

[37a] Comp. *Quaestiones epicae*, 1837, p. 23, note (with appeal to Sturz, *Opp.*
p. 14). The supposition of Riese, that the name Apollonius Molon originated
in a misunderstanding of the title-superscription Ἀπολλωνίου τοῦ Μόλωνος,
is, according to what has been said, neither necessary nor probable.

[38] Cicero makes Scaevola say, *De orat.* i. 17. 75 : " Quae, cum *ego praetor*
Rhodum venissem et cum illo summo doctore istius disciplinae Apollonio ea
quae a Panaetio acceperam contulissem, irrisit ille quidem, ut solebat,
philosophiamque contempsit," etc. Scaevola was praetor about A.U.C.
633=121 B.C. (see Pauly's *Enc.* v. 183). Cicero also mentions this same
Apollonius, *De oratore*, i. 28. 126 (*Alabandensem Apollonium*) and i. 28. 130.
*De inventione*, i. 56. 109.

Christ, in Caria and Rhodes, sufficient occasion for the composition of a polemical work against the Jews by a living
orator. For we know that just here the Jews were already
numerously dispersed during the second century B.C.[39] The
work of Apollonius was, according to Alexander Polyhistor, a
συσκευὴ κατὰ Ἰουδαίων (Euseb. *Praep. evang.* ix. 19). Hence
it dealt not merely occasionally, like Manetho's Αἰγυπτιακά,
but exclusively with the Jews. As Josephus says Apollonius
did not, like Apion, heap up his accusations in one place,
but calumniated the Jews in many passages and throughout
the work now in one manner now in another (*contra Apion.*
ii. 14: τὴν κατηγορίαν ὁ Ἀπολλώνιος οὐκ ἀθρόαν ὥσπερ
ὁ Ἀπίων ἔταξεν, ἀλλὰ σποράδην καὶ διὰ πάσης τῆς
συγγραφῆς . . . λοιδορεῖ), hence it must be supposed that
the work was *not* a purely polemical one, but that, in connection with statements concerning the Jews, it contained
much polemical invective. This is also thoroughly confirmed
by the fact, that the fragment in Alexander Polyhistor
(Euseb. *Praep. evang.* ix. 19) is occupied in a purely objective
manner with the history of Abraham. It follows from the
allusions of Josephus, that the history of the exodus from
Egypt was also treated of (*contra Apion.* ii. 2), and that the
work " contained unjust and untrue reports concerning our
legislator Moses and our laws " (ii. 14). In the latter respect
we learn also that Apollonius reproached the Jews with
" not worshipping the same gods as others " (ii. 7), with having
no fellowship with those who believed differently (ii. 36), and
with being therefore ἄθεοι and μισάνθρωποι, also as at one
time cowardly, at another fanatic, as the most incapable among
barbarians, and as having furnished nothing towards general
culture (ii. 14). Josephus on his part repays Apollonius in

---

[39] Comp. 1 Macc. xv. 16–24 and Div. ii. vol. ii. p. 221. The Carian
towns of Myndos, Halicarnassus and Cnidus and the neighbouring islands
of Cos and Rhodes are presupposed (1 Macc. xv. 16–24 and elsewhere) to
be abodes of the Jews. On Halicarnassus, comp. also Div. ii. vol. ii. p. 258
(Joseph. *Antt.* xiv. 10. 23).

his own coin, reproaching him with gross want of sense,
arrogance and immoral conduct (ii. 36, 37).

Comp. on Apollonius in general: C. Müller, *Fragm. hist.
graec.* iii. 208 sq.    Creuzer, *Theol. Stud. u. Krit.* 1853, p. 83 sq.
Teuffel in Pauly's *Real-Enc.* 1. 2 (2nd ed.), p. 1318.    J. G.
Müller, *Des Flavius Josephus Schrift gegen den Apion* (1877), p.
230.    Riese, "Molon oder Apollonius Molon?" (*Rheinisches
Museum*, vol. xxxiv. Jahrg. 1879, pp. 627–630).

3. *Lysimachus* (comp. Josephus, *contra Apion.* i. 34–35).
The fragment which Josephus, *ibid.*, gives from the work of a
certain Lysimachus relates to the departure of the Jews from
Egypt, and narrates concerning it similar fables, but still
more absurd than those told by Manetho.    The few occasional
notices which Josephus elsewhere (*contra Apion.* ii. 2, twice,
and ii. 14) gives, refer to the same fact.    According to *contra
Apion.* ii. 2: Ἀπίων . . . τὸν αὐτὸν Λυσιμάχῳ σχεδιάσας,
he seems to have been Apion's predecessor.    From the tenor
of the fragment it may be assumed that he was an Egyptian.
According to Cosmas Indicopleustes, the work from which the
fragment is taken is said to have been a "History of Egypt."[40]
Since however Cosmas evidently derives his information only
from Josephus, and erroneously reckons Apollonius Molon
among the Αἰγυπτιακὰ συγγραψάμενοι, and nothing else is
known of the Αἰγυπτιακά of Lysimachus, the matter must
be left uncertain.    Two works, Θηβαϊκὰ παράδοξα and
Νίστοι (returns, *reversiones, i.e.* of Greek heroes from Troy),
of an author named Lysimachus are frequently cited elsewhere in ancient literature.    As the author of the Νόστοι
seems to have been an Alexandrian and to have lived in the
first century before Christ, he is probably identical with this
Lysimachus.

[40] Cosmas Indicopleustes, *Topograph. christ.* lib. xii. (by Gallandi,
*Biblioth. Patr.* xi. 572): Οἱ δὲ τὰ Αἰγυπτιακὰ συγγραψάμενοι, τουτέστι
Μανεθὼν καὶ Χαιρημὼν καὶ Ἀπολλώνιος ὁ Μολῶν καὶ Λυσίμαχος καὶ Ἀπίων
ὁ γραμματικὸς, μέμνηνται Μωϋσέως καὶ τῆς ἐξόδου τῶν υἱῶν Ἰσραὴλ τῆς ἐξ
Αἰγύπτου.

The fragments of Lysimachus (both those from Josephus and those of the Θηβαϊκὰ παράδοξα and the Νόστοι) are collected in C. Müller, *Fragm. historicorum Graecorum*, iii. 334–342. The fragments of the Θηβ. παράδ. are also in Westermann, Παραδοξογράφοι (Brunsvigae 1839), p. xxx. sq., 164 sq. Comp. in general: Westermann in Pauly's *Real-Enc.* iv. 1311. Stiehle, "Die Nosten des Lysimachos" (*Philologus*, vol. iv. 1849, pp. 99–110; v. 1850, p. 382 sq.). J. G. Müller, *Des Flavius Josephus Scrhift gegen den Apion*, p. 208.

4. *Chaeremon* (comp. Josephus, *contra Apion.* i. 32–33). The fragment from Chaeremon also refers to the departure of the Jews from Egypt, and is with respect to its contents nearer to the narrative of Manetho than Lysimachus is. Josephus in this case expressly says, that the fragment was taken from the Αἰγυπτιακὴ ἱστορία of Chaeremon (*contra Apion.* i. 32) This Chaeremon is also elsewhere known as an author on Egyptian matters. In the letter of Porphyrius to the Egyptian Anebon, from which Eusebius, *Praep. evang.* iii. 4 and v. 10, gives extracts, two portions which relate to the Egyptian mythology and theology are cited from Chaeremon. In the second (Euseb. v. 10. 5, ed. Gaisford) Porphyrius designates Chaeremon as ἱερογραμματεύς. In the work of Porphyrius, which has come down to us, *De abstinentia*, iv. 6–8, a detailed description of the life of Egyptian priests is given from Chaeremon, which Porphyry introduces with the words: "*Chaeremon the Stoic, in treating of the Egyptian priests,* who, as he says, are esteemed philosophers among the Egyptians, relates, that they chose the sanctuaries as the place for philosophizing (Τὰ γοῦν κατὰ τοὺς Αἰγυπτίους ἱερέας Χαιρήμων ὁ Στωικὸς ἀφηγούμενος, οὓς καὶ φιλοσόφους ὑπειλῆφθαί φησι παρ' Αἰγυπτίοις, ἐξηγεῖται ὡς τόπον μὲν ἐξελέξαντο ἐμφιλοσοφῆσαι τὰ ἱερά). . . . Despising every other occupation and human pursuit, they devote their whole life to the contemplation of things divine," etc.[41] At the end

[41] The description does not refer to all Egyptian priests, but, as is declared at the conclusion (iv. 8), only to the *élite* among them, the προφῆται, ἱεροστολισταί, ἱερογραμματεῖς and ὡρολόγοι. Hieronymus, *adv. Jovinian.* ii. 13, borrows the description from Porphyrius (Vallarsi, ii. 342 sq.).

of this account Porphyrius calls Chaeremon a truth-loving, trustworthy and intelligent Stoic philosopher (iv. 8, *fin.*: ἀνδρὸς φιλαλήθους τε καὶ ἀκριβοῦς ἔν τε τοῖς Στωικοῖς πραγματικώτατα φιλοσοφήσαντος). All these portions may well have stood in an " Egyptian History." From it are also derived the communications from Chaeremon in a treatise of Psellus published by Sathas (1877). The same Chaeremon also wrote a work which is taken up in explaining the hieroglyphics (διδάγματα τῶν ἱερῶν γραμμάτων). From this the Byzantine Tzetzes has given extracts in his historical work (v. 403 in Müller, *Fragm.* iii. 499) and in his commentary on the *Iliad* (ed. Gottfr. Hermann, 1812, pp. 123 and 146). Tzetzes also designates Chaeremon as ἱερογραμματεύς and says, that according to Chaeremon's view " the φυσικὸς λόγος concerning the gods, their physical signification is allegorically exhibited in the hieroglyphics " (Zeller). This also characterizes Chaeremon as a Stoic. Hence there can be no doubt that he is identical with our ἱερογραμματεύς, who in a few other citations (*e.g.* in Origen's *contra Celsum*, l. 59. Euseb. *Hist. eccl.* vi. 19. 8) is simply called Στωικός. He is on this account a very remarkable personage for his age : *an Egyptian priest and at the same time a Stoic philosopher.* Since he was, according to Suidas, the instructor of Nero (Suidas' *Lex. s.v.* Ἀλέξανδρος Αἰγαῖος), and also the instructor and predecessor of Dionysius of Alexandria, who lived from Nero to Trajan (Suidas' *Lex. s.v. Διονύσιος Ἀλεξανδρεύς*), he must have lived towards the middle of the first century after Christ. He was, according to Suidas, the predecessor of Dionysius in the office of *librarian at Alexandria.* He cannot, by reason of the chronology stated, be identical with the Chaeremon who is mentioned by Strabo (xvii. 1. 29, p. 806) as a contemporary of Aelius Gallus. Besides the latter has been described as a man, who made himself ridiculous by his ostentation and ignorance, which are certainly not characteristics of a philosopher.

The fragments of Chaeremon are collected in C. Müller, *Frag. hist. graec.* iii. 495–499. To these are to be added: (1) the extracts given in Tzetzes, *Draconis Stratonicensis liber de metris poeticis et Joannis Tzetzae exegesis in Homeri Iliadem*, 1st ed. Godofr. Hermannus, Lips. 1812, pp. 123 and 146 ; and (2) those in the treatise of Psellus, published by Sathas (*Bulletin de correspondance hellénique*, vol. i. 1877, pp. 121–133, 194–208, 309–314). Comp. in general: Bähr in Pauly's *Real-Enc.* ii. 298 sq. Birch, "On the lost book of Chaeremon on Hieroglyphics" (*Transactions of the Royal Society of Literature*, second series, vol. iii. 1850, pp. 385–396). Bernays, *Theophrastos' Schrift über die Frömmigkeit* (1866), pp. 21 sq., 150 sq. Zeller, "Die Hieroglyphiker Chäremon und Horapollo" (*Hermes*, vol. xi. 1876, pp. 430–433). Nicolai, *Griechische Literaturgesch.* 2nd ed. ii. 559, 561, 677, 690, iii. 383. J. G. Müller, *Des Flavius Josephus Schrift gegen den Apion* (1877), p. 203 sqq.

5. *Apion* (comp. Josephus, *contra Apion.* ii. 1–13). Apion the grammarian, who was distinguished among all the opponents of the Jews for his special malevolence, and was therefore treated with special harshness by Josephus, was a contemporary and fellow-countryman of Chaeremon. His full name was Ἀπίων ὁ Πλειστονίκης.[42] According to Suidas, Πλειστονίκης was the name of his father (*Lex. s.v.* Ἀπίων ὁ Πλειστονίκου), which he afterwards took as a surname. When Julius Africanus (in Euseb. *Praep. evang.* x. 10. 16, ed. Gaisford; and in Syncellus, ed. Dindorf, i. 120 and 281) and after him the pseudo-Justinian, *Cohortatio ad Graecos*, c. 9, call the name of the father Ποσειδώνιος, this is certainly but a corruption of Πλειστονίκης. According to Josephus (*contra Apion.* ii. 3), Apion was born in the oasis of Egypt, and hence was not, as he gave himself out to be, a native of Alexandria. He afterwards however received the rights of Alexandrian citizenship (Jos. *l.c.*), and acquired some fame in Alexandria as a grammarian. He taught temporarily in Rome also in the

---

[42] Clemens Alex. *Strom.* i. 21. 101 (= Euseb. *Praep. evang.* x. 12. 2): Ἀπίων τοίνυν ὁ γραμματικὸς ὁ Πλειστονίκης ἐπικληθείς. Clem. Rom. *Homil.* iv. 6 : Ἀππίωνα τὸν Πλειστονίκην ἄνδρα Ἀλεξανδρέα, γραμματικὸν τὴν ἐπιστήμην. Plinius, *Hist. Nat.* xxxvii. 5. 75: Apion cognominatus Plistonices. Gellius, *Noct. Att.* v. 14 : Apion qui Plistonices appellatus est. *Ibid.* vi. 8 : Ἀπίων, Graecus homo, qui Πλειστονίκης est appellatus.

time of Tiberius and Claudius (Suidas, *Lex. s.v.* '*Απίων*). In the reign of Caligula he travelled through Greece as an itinerant orator delivering lectures on Homer (Seneca, *epist.* 88). It was also under Caligula, that, on the occasion of the sanguinary conflict of the Alexandrians with the Jews, he came to Rome as the ambassador of the former (Joseph. *Antt.* xviii. 8. 1). According to Josephus (*contra Apion.* ii. 3), his death was caused by ulcers in the genitals, against which circumcision was of no avail. He is described as having been ridiculously vain. Tiberius called him *cymbalum mundi.* He himself said, without embarrassment, that those to whom he addressed a work became thereby immortal,[43] and congratulated Alexandria on having such a citizen as he was (Joseph. *c. Apion.* ii. 12).

The works of Apion were manifold. The best known seem to have been his works on Homer (*Commentaries and a Dictionary*). We are here only concerned with his Egyptian History (*Αἰγυπτιακά*), which according to Tatian comprised five books, of which Josephus cites the third, Tatian and his successors the fourth, and Gellius the fifth book.[44] *This Egyptian History evidently contained all those attacks upon the Jews to which the reply of Josephus refers* (*c. Apion.* ii. 1–3). Josephus says, at the beginning of his discussion, that it was not easy to go through the discourse (τὸν λόγον) of Apion, because he brought forth all in the greatest disorder. But that about three points might be distinguished: (1) the fables

---

[43] Plinius, *Hist. Nat. praef.* § 25 : Apion quidam grammaticus (hic quem Tiberius Caesar cymbalum mundi vocabat, cum propriae famae tympanum potius videri posset) immortalitate donari a se scripsit ad quos aliqua conponebat.

[44] Joseph. *c. Apion.* ii. 2 : φησὶ γὰρ ἐν τῇ τρίτῃ τῶν Αἰγυπτιακῶν. Tatian, *Oratio ad Graecos,* c. 38 (= Euseb. *Praep. ev.* x. 11. 14): 'Απίων ὁ γραμματικός, ἀνὴρ δοκιμώτατος, ἐν τῇ τετάρτῃ τῶν Αἰγυπτιακῶν (πέντε δέ εἰσιν αὐτῷ γραφαί) κ.τ.λ. In agreement herewith Clemens Alex. *Strom.* i. 21. 101 = Euseb. *Praep. evang.* x. 12. 2. Julius Africanus in Euseb. *Praep. evang.* x. 10. 16, and in Syncell. ed. Dindorf, i. 120 and 281. Pseudo-Justin. *Cohortat. ad Graec.* c. 9. Gellius, *Noct. Att.* v. 14 : Apion . . . in libro Aegyptiacorum quinto scripsit.

concerning the departure of the Jews from Egypt, (2) the
malicious assertions concerning the Alexandrian Jews, and
(3) the accusations in respect of worship and legal customs.
Of the latter, Josephus says, that they are mixed up with the
accusations of the first two categories (ἐπὶ τούτοις μέμικται,
ii. 1, *fin.*). Thus it appears that a single λόγος of Apion, containing all these accusations, and divided by Josephus for the
sake of order into three categories, was in question. Josephus,
after entering successively into all three categories (*c. Apion.*
ii. 2–3 relates to the first, ii. 4–6 to the second, ii. 7–13 to the
third), leaves Apion and begins to give a positive delineation
of the Mosaic legislation. At its commencement he once
more touches incidentally upon Apion, and says of him that
he has heaped his indictments all together (ii. 14 : τὴν
κατηγορίαν . . . ἀθρόαν . . . ἔταξεν), in distinction from
Apollonius Molon, whose polemic pervades his whole work.
There can therefore be no doubt that the polemic of Josephus
refers to only *one* work of Apion's, and indeed to only one
section of a larger work. This work was, as Josephus
expressly says in the beginning of his discussion (ii. 2), the
Egyptian History. In it Apion apparently took occasion, in
narrating the departure of the Jews from Egypt, to give a
hostile description of them, in like manner as Tacitus does in
his Histories (*Hist.* v. 1–12). When consequently Clemens
Alexandrinus and later Church authors mention a special
work of Apion, κατὰ 'Ιουδαίων, this rests only upon a mistaken
inference from the information of Josephus. It is just the
silence of Josephus which proves that no such work ever
existed. That these Church authors also had no actual
acquaintance with it, is made evident by a more accurate
comparison of the text. For Clemens Alexandrinus, in the
passage where he mentions it, is in fact only copying from
Tatian, who on his part is only quoting Apion's Egyptian
History. And all subsequent writers, who pretend to know
anything of a work of Apion κατὰ 'Ιουδαίων, obtain their
information from either Clement or Josephus.

Tatian, *Oratio ad Graecos*, c. 38 (= Euseb. *Praep. evang.*
x. 11. 14, ed. Gaisford): Μετὰ δὲ τοῦτον Ἀπίων ὁ γραμματικός, ἀνὴρ
δοκιμώτατος, ἐν τῇ τετάρτῃ τῶν Αἰγυπτιακῶν (πέντε δέ εἰσιν αὐτῷ γραφαί)
πολλὰ μὲν καὶ ἄλλα, φησὶ δὲ ὅτι· Κατέσκαψε τὴν Αὔαριν Ἄμωσις κατὰ
τὸν Ἀργεῖον γενόμενος Ἴναχον, ὡς ἐν τοῖς Χρόνοις ἀνέγραψεν ὁ Μενδήσιος
Πτολεμαῖος.

Clemens Alex. *Strom.* i. 21. 101 (= Euseb. *Praep. evang.* x.
12. 2, ed. Gaisford): Ἀπίων τοίνυν ὁ γραμματικὸς ὁ Πλειστονίκης
ἐπικληθεὶς ἐν τῇ τετάρτῃ τῶν Αἰγυπτιακῶν ἱστοριῶν, καίτοι φιλαπεχ-
θημόνως πρὸς Ἑβραίους διακείμενος, ἅτε Αἰγύπτιος τὸ γένος, ὡς καὶ
κατὰ Ἰουδαίων συνπάξασθαι βιβλίον, Ἀμώσιος τοῦ Αἰγυπτίων
βασιλέως μεμνημένος καὶ τῶν κατ᾽ αὐτὸν πράξεων μάρτυρα παρατίθεται
Πτολεμαῖον τὸν Μενδήσιον, καὶ τὰ τῆς λέξεως αὐτοῦ ὧδε ἔχει· "Κατέσκαψε
δὲ τὴν κ.τ.λ." (here follows verbally the same quotation as in
Tatian, whom Clemens had just before expressly quoted).

Julius Africanus in Euseb. *Praep. evang.* x. 10. 16, and in
Syncell. ed. Dindorf, i. 120 and 281: Ἀπίων δὲ ὁ Ποσειδωνίου,
περιεργότατος γραμματικῶν, ἐν τῇ κατὰ Ἰουδαίων βίβλῳ καὶ ἐν τῇ
τετάρτῃ τῶν ἱστοριῶν φησί, κατὰ, Ἴναχον Ἄργους βασιλέα, Ἀμώσιος
Αἰγυπτίων βασιλεύοντος, ἀποστῆναι Ἰουδαίους, ὧν ἡγεῖσθαι Μωσέα.

Pseudo-Justin. *Cohortatio ad Graec.* c. 9: Οὕτω γὰρ Πολέμων
τε ἐν τῇ πρώτῃ τῶν Ἑλληνικῶν ἱστοριῶν μέμνηται καὶ Ἀπίων ὁ Ποσειδωνίου
ἐν τῇ κατὰ Ἰουδαίων βίβλῳ καὶ ἐν τῇ τετάρτῃ τῶν ἱστοριῶν,
λέγων κατὰ Ἴναχον Ἄργους βασιλέα Ἀμώσιδος Αἰγυπτίων βασιλεύοντος
ἀποστῆναι Ἰουδαίους, ὧν ἡγεῖσθαι Μωσέα. Καὶ Πτολεμαῖος δὲ ὁ Μενδήσιος, τὰ Αἰγυπτίων ἱστοριῶν, ἅπασι τούτοις συντρέχει.

The mention of Apion's supposed work κατὰ Ἰουδαίων was
first introduced in this connection by means of Clement. But
Clement only says that Apion wrote such a work; for the rest
he simply quotes, as Tatian does, Apion's Egyptian History as
his authority for the statement that Amosis reigned in the time
of Inachus. Julius Africanus, on the contrary, now ventures
to assert, on the foundation of the passage of Clement, that this
statement was found in both the supposed works of Apion, and
at the same time drags in Moses also, who is not even spoken
of in the passage quoted from Apion. Finally the author of
the *Cohortatio* again copies only from Julius Africanus. This
latter fact I have, I think, proved in Brieger's *Zeitschrift für
Kirchengesch.* ii. (1878) pp. 319–331. Comp. also Donaldson,
*History of Christian Literature*, ii. 96 sqq. Harnack, *Texte und
Untersuchungen*, vol. i. Nos. 1, 2, 1882, p. 157. Neumann, *Theol.
Literaturzeitung*, 1883, p. 582. Renan, *Marc-Aurèle*, 1882, p. 107,
note. The dependence of the *Cohortatio* upon the text to which
Julius Africanus had access is at any rate indubitable. Hence
Gutschmid, starting from the mistaken assumption that the
*Cohortatio* was more ancient than Julius Africanus, supposed
that both had a common source (*Jahrbb. für class. Philologie*,

1860, pp. 703–708). Some moderns also acquiesce in this view, more through faith in Gutschmid than on sufficient grounds. So Völter, *Zeitschr. für wissensch. Theol.* 1883, p. 180 sqq. Dräseke, *Zeitschr. für Kirchengesch.* vol. vii. p. 257 sqq. Eusebius, *Hist. eccl.* iii. 9. 4, in enumerating the works of Josephus, says that his work, *Ueber das hohe Alter der Juden* (i.e. *contra Apion.*), was written "against Apion the grammarian," who had then composed a λόγος against the Jews (πρὸς Ἀπίωνα τὸν γραμματικὸν κατὰ Ἰουδαίων τηνικάδε συντάξαντα λόγον). Evidently this is only inferred from Josephus. The same applies also to Hieronymus, *De viris illustr.* c. 13 (*Opp.* ed. Vallarsi, ii. 851): adversum Appionem grammaticum Alexandrinum, qui sub Caligula legatus missus ex parte gentilium contra Philonem etiam librum, vituperationem gentis Judicae continentem, scripserat. The account of Eusebius, which Jerome, as his custom is, copies, is here only enlarged by the combination that Apion's book was directed *against Philo*. This combination is founded on Joseph. *Antt.* xviii. 8. 1. From the Greek translation of Jerome (Sophronius) again arise the statements in Suidas, *Lex. s.v.* Ἰώσσηπος. When it is at last said in the *Clementine Homilies*, that Apion wrote πολλὰ βιβλία against the Jews, this statement must of course not be taken seriously.

Comp. on Apion in general: Burigny, "Mémoire sur Apion" (*Mémoires de l'Academie des Inscriptions et Belles-Lettres*, ancient series, vol. xxxviii. 1777, pp. 171–178). Lehrs, "Quid Apio Homero praestiterit" (*Quaestiones Epicae*, 1837, pp. 1–34). Cruice, *De Flavii Josephi in auctoribus contra Apionem offerendis fide et auctoritate* (Paris 1844), p. 9. Schliemann, *Die Clementinen* (1844), p. 111 sqq. C. Müller, *Fragm. hist. graec.* iii. 506–516. Volkmann in Pauly's *Real-Enc.* i. 1 (2nd ed.), p. 1243 sq. Creuzer, *Theol. Stud. und Krit.* 1853, p. 80 sq. Paret, *Des Flavius Josephus Werke übersetzt*, 7 vols. (1856), pp. 741–745. Hausrath, *Neutestamentliche Zeitgeschichte*, 2nd ed. ii. 187–195. Nicolai, *Griech. Literaturgesch.* 2nd ed. ii. 345–347. J. G. Müller, *Des Fl. Josephus Schrift gegen den Apion* (1877), pp. 14–17. Lightfoot, art. "Apion" in Smith and Wace, *Dictionary of Christian Biography*, i. 128–130.

6. The literary opponents of the Jews hitherto mentioned have been here treated of more thoroughly, because the polemic of Josephus is directed chiefly against them. An exhaustive enumeration of all the Greek and Roman authors, who from the beginning of the second century after Christ expressed themselves in a hostile manner against the Jews, would furnish a list of distinguished names. Almost all the

authors who have to speak of the Jews at all do so in a
hostile manner. Among pre-Christian *Greek* authors Josephus
chiefly names the distinguished historian and philosopher
Posidonius as an adversary of the Jews (*c. Apion.* ii. 7). In his
great historical work (see on it Div. i. vol. i. § 3) he probably
somewhere seized the opportunity of giving a polemical
excursus against the Jews, and afterwards many subsequent
writers, as Diodorus (xxxiv. 1) and Trogus Pompeius, who comes
down to us through the extract of Justin (xxxvi. 2, 3),[45] drew
either directly or indirectly from his much read work. The
works too of Nikarchus (Müller, *Fragm.* iii. 335) and Damo-
kritus (Müller, *Fragm.* iv. 377), which are scarcely known by
name, were also polemical. Of *Roman* historians, besides
Trogus Pompeius already mentioned, prominence must be
given to Tacitus, whose description of the Jews (*Hist.* v. 2 sqq.)
is dictated by the most profound contempt. The Roman
satirists Horace, Juvenal, and Martial have also notably made
the Jews the butt of their wit.

## 2. *Apologetics.*

Jewish Apologetic followed a twofold way of defence,
a direct and an indirect one, against the many attacks which
Judaism had to undergo. A large portion of the historic and
philosophic literature of Hellenistic Judaism is of an indirectly
apologetic character; it seeks to show that the Jewish nation
need in no respect shrink from a comparison with other nations.
But this was not thought enough; the attempt was also sometimes made to refute point after point in a systematic manner
the accusations raised against the Jews. Two of such syste-
matically apologetic works are known to us, one (that of Philo)
only by a short fragment, the other (that of Josephus) in the
complete text. (1) Eusebius gives in the *Praep. evang.* viii. 11

---

[45] Comp. on Posidonius as the source of subsequent writers the article of
J. G. Müller, *Stud. u. Kritik.* 1843, p. 893 sqq., and his commentary on
Joseph. *c. Apion.* (1877) pp. 214 sqq. and 258 sq.

the description of the Essenes from Philo's ἀπολογία ὑπὲρ Ἰουδαίων. From this however we can form no idea of its whole design. The work of Philo περὶ Ἰουδαίων, mentioned in Euseb. *Hist. eccl.* ii. 18. 6, is certainly identical with it. (2) The work of Josephus, to be mentioned in this connection, is known to us by the title of *contra Apion.* This title, which did not originate with Josephus himself, gives an erroneous idea of its contents. For it is by no means occupied with Apion alone, but undertakes a comprehensive and systematic defence of the Jewish people against all the accusations raised against them (further particulars, Div. i. vol. i. § 3).

In endeavouring in what follows to give a sketch of *the main substance of the indictment and defence*, we must chiefly restrict ourselves to the material afforded by Josephus, his work being the only one handed down to us, which both contains a survey of the points of accusation and furnishes a view of the method of apologetic demonstration. The *disposition* of the Graeco-Roman world towards the Jews has been already described (Div. ii. vol. ii. p. 291). Here only the actual accusations and the Jewish answer to them will be brought forward.

1. Extensive and learned matter is furnished by Josephus in the first section (i. 1–23) to prove, that *the Jewish nation was not inferior in point of antiquity to other cultured nations.* He says, that to maintain, that it is of recent origin because the Greek historians say nothing of it, is foolish, even if the assumption were correct. For even the silence of all the Greek historians would prove nothing against the early existence of the nation, since the Jews, as dwelling in an inland country, might easily remain unknown to the Greeks. In truth however *the Jewish nation was already known in very ancient times by the best historians of he Egyptians, Phoenicians, Chaldaeans* (Manetho, Dios, Menander, Berosus, and others), *nay even by Greek historians themselves.* The zeal which Josephus exhibits, and the large amount of matter he brings forward, show how important this point was in his

eyes. The assertion of modern origin was equivalent to the assertion of historical insignificance. A nation, which had but recently appeared upon the stage of history, had of course also no importance in history. It received its culture from the more ancient nations. But this was to strike at the roots of Jewish honour, and hence the Jewish apologist regarded it as his first duty thoroughly to repel such an insult.[46]

2. While the Greeks in general were satisfied with denying the high antiquity of the Jewish nation, the Alexandrians related very unfair things concerning the *origin of the Jews*. The quintessence of their fictions was, that the Jews were leprous Egyptians, who succeeded in a very dishonourable manner in forming themselves into a separate nation, in leaving Egypt and settling in Palestine.[47] Josephus felt himself master of the situation in opposing these fables. With dignified superiority he pointed out to the Alexandrians the absurdity and the internal discrepancy of their assertions (i. 24–35, ii. 1–3).

3. With the imputation of recentness of origin was connected the assertion, that the Jews had *done nothing for culture*. Apollonius Molon said, that they were the most incapable of barbarians and had therefore contributed no useful invention to general culture (*contra Apion*. ii. 14: ἀφνεστάτους εἶναι τῶν βαρβάρων καὶ διὰ τοῦτο μηδὲν εἰς τὸν βίον εὕρημα συμβεβλῆσθαι μόνους). Apion said, that they had produced no eminent men, such as inventors of arts or men distinguished for wisdom (*contra Apion*. ii. 12: θαυμαστοὺς ἄνδρας οὐ παρεσχήκαμεν, οἷον τεχνῶν τινῶν εὑρετὰς ἢ σοφίᾳ διαφέροντας). These reproaches were encountered with the older Jewish

---

[46] On the motive for the proof of antiquity, see *contra Apion*. ii. 15. It is well known, that Christian apologists also lay great stress upon it. See Tatian, c. xxxi. 36–41. Theophilus, *ad Autol*. iii. 20 sqq. Clemens Alexandrinus, *Strom*. i. 21. 101–147. Tertullian, *Apolog*. 19. Pseudo-Justin, *Cohort. ad Graec*. c. 9. Eusebius, *Praep. evang*. x. 9 sqq. And more in Semisch, *Justin*, i. 134.

[47] So with much variation of detail: Manetho (*contra Apion*. i. 26), Lysimachus (i. 34), Chäremon (i. 32), Apion (ii. 2). Also Justin, xxxvi. 2, and Tacitus, *Hist*. v. 3. Comp. also Div. ii. vol. ii. p. 250.

legend, that *the Jews were on the contrary the originators of all culture.* According to Eupolemus, Moses was the first sage, the inventor of alphabetic writing (see above, p. 203). According to Artapanus, Abraham instructed the Egyptians in astrology, Joseph undertook the improved cultivation of the land, and Moses introduced culture of every kind (p. 206). The philosopher Aristobulus already declares Moses to be the father of Greek philosophy, and that Pythagoras, Socrates, Plato, and the rest all derived their philosophy from him (p. 240 sq.). The same assertion is repeated by Philo, and Josephus takes just the same tone though making no use in his Apology of the legends of Eupolemus and Artapanus.   He lays the chief stress upon proving besides the high antiquity, the wisdom and excellence of the Mosaic legislation.

4. The special accusations against Judaism were above all in respect of its *religious worship*, which was always connected with the refusal to acknowledge any other worship as legitimate.   This last was in the era of heathenism a thing unheard of.   " To live and let live " was the motto in the province of religion.   The most opposite kinds of religious worship were readily tolerated, if only the adherents of one cultus would hold others legitimate.   Especially was it taken for granted as a thing self-evident, that the citizens of the same town should, besides any private worship of their own, participate in honouring the gods of the town.   What an abnormity then must it have been felt, that the Jews should entirely reject every kind of worship except their own, and absolutely refuse to take part in any other!   From the standpoint of Hellenism this was *synonymous with Atheism.*   If they are citizens, why do they not worship the gods of the city?   This accusation of ἀθεότης, of contempt for the gods, recurs in almost all adversaries of the Jews, from Apollonius Molon and Posidonius to Pliny and Tacitus;[48] and from it

---

[48] Apion in Joseph. *contra Apion.* ii. 6 : quomodo ergo, inquit, si sunt cives, eosdem deos, quos Alexandrini, non colunt?   Posidonius and Apollonius Molon, *ibid.* ii. 7 : accusant quidem nos, quare nos eosdem deos

certainly arose in great part the conflicts of municipalities
with the Jews, especially in the towns where they possessed
rights of citizenship. It was easy in theory but difficult in
practice, for apologetic to hold its ground in presence of this
accusation. With an educated reader it was not very difficult
to make manifest the advantages of the monotheistic and
spiritual view of the nature of God, especially as Greek
philosophy offered an abundance of thoughts, which came in
this respect to the aid of Jewish apologists. In this sense
does Josephus proceed, simply exhibiting the Jewish idea of
God in its superiority (*contra Apion.* ii. 22). In practice
however the masses were not to be influenced by such considerations. For the reproach still adhered to the Jews, that
they absolutely rejected what others regarded as the worship
of God. Hence the chief weapon of Jewish apologetic upon
this point was a vigorous attack. When the Jews were
reproached for despising the gods, they showed on their part
what kind of gods they were, whom others honoured; weak
images of wood, stone, silver, or gold, the work of men's
hands, or animals of every kind, or at best beings, who were
affected with manifold human weaknesses. The Jews might
well feel themselves superior to the worshippers of such
gods (comp. *e.g.* pseudo-Aristeas in Havercamp's *Josephus*, ii.
2. 116. *Sap. Salomonis*, c. 13–15. *The Epistle of Jeremiah*,
Joseph. *contra Apion.* ii. 33–35, and especially the *Sibyllines*).

Of less practical importance than the charge of ἀθεότης
were certain ridiculous fables which were related concerning
the Jewish worship; that they paid divine honours to an *ass's
head*, and that they annually *sacrificed a Greek* and fed upon
his entrails (see above, § 31, notes 239, 240, 250). Such
fables were indeed believed only in small circles, and Josephus
very easily proves their absurdity (*contra Apion.* ii. 7–9).

5. Of greater weight, on the other hand, was another

cum aliis non colimus. Apollonius Molon, *ibid.* ii. 14: ὡς ἀθίους . . .
λοιδορεῖ. Plinius, *H. N.* xiii. 4. 46: gens contumelia numinum insignis.
Tacitus, *Hist.* v. 5: contemnere deos.

point connected with the ἀθεότης of the Jews, viz. their refusal of *the worship of the emperor.* Subsequently to Augustus all the provinces emulated each other in the practice of this cult (see Div. ii. vol. i. p. 16 sq.). Zeal for this was the standard of a loyal and Rome-loving disposition, its entire rejection was synonymous with not showing due respect to the authorities. Such was at least the view of the Hellenistic population, who, according to the customs of the Hellenistic period, freely offered their worship to the emperor. The Jews were in a favourable position in this respect, inasmuch as the emperors of the first centuries, with the sole exception of Caligula, did not directly demand this worship. Nor, apart from the short episode under Caligula, was it ever required of the Jews, whose mode of worship received legal protection, together with the legal recognition of their communities from Caesar onwards (see above, Div. ii. vol. ii. p. 265). For the adversaries of the Jews, however, it was always a welcome point of attack, that they proved themselves bad citizens by their refusal of worship to the emperor.[49] Jewish apologists could, in answer to this charge, appeal to the fact, that a sacrifice was daily offered for the emperor in the temple at Jerusalem (Joseph. *c. Apion.* ii. 6, *fin.; Bell. Jud.* ii. 10. 4; comp. Div. ii. vol. i. p. 302), and that on special occasions even hecatombs were offered for the Roman emperor (Philo, *Leg. ad Caj.* § 45, Mang. ii. 598). Thus, in fact, was a certain equivalent furnished for that worship of the emperor which was impossible to Jews. Josephus, besides, does not neglect pointing on every occasion to the favour which the Jews enjoyed both from the Ptolemies and from Caesar (*c. Apion.* ii. 4, 5; *Antt.* xiv. 10, xvi. 6). This surely would have been impossible unless they had been loyal citizens!

6. With this religious isolation was connected a certain amount of *social isolation.* Judaism expressly repudiated the

---

[49] Apion in Joseph. *c. Apion.* ii. 6, *med.:* derogare nobis Apion voluit, quia imperatorum non statuamus imagines. Tacitus, *Hist.* v. 5 : non regibus haec adulatio, non Caesaribus honor.

idea, now more and more making its way in Hellenism, that
all men are brethren, and therefore equal before God.    It saw
in the unbeliever only the sinner, who has incurred the judgment of God, and referred the fatherly love of God only to
the seed of Abraham, on which account only the children of
Abraham are brethren to each other.    If this particularism
was not held in its full rigour by philosophic and Hellenistic
Judaism in general, it gained on the other hand a support
from the view, that the heathen as such were unclean, that
in the interest of Levitical purity intercourse with them was
as far as possible to be avoided, and from the anxiety with
which contact with everything that stood in any kind of relation
to idolatry was abhorred (comp. Div. ii. vol. i. pp. 51–56).
*If, then, the Jew was already directed in theory to regard the
non-Jew as only an " alien," it was also impossible to him in
practice, if he desired to observe the law, to live in any close social
intercourse with the heathen.*    This theoretical and practical
$\dot{\alpha}\mu\iota\xi\acute{\iota}\alpha$, which was in opposition to the entire tendency of the
Hellenistic period, was constantly and very specially made a
reproach against the Jews.    To the Greeks and Romans, who
were unacquainted with its deeper motives, it appeared only
as *a want of humanity, of true philanthropy, nay as criminal
misanthropy.*    And it may indeed not infrequently have really
manifested itself in such forms.[50]    The process adopted in this
respect by apologetic writers was on the one hand chiefly that

---

[50] The councillors of Antiochus Sidetes already pointed to the $\dot{\alpha}\mu\iota\xi\acute{\iota}\alpha$ of
the Jews (Joseph. *Antt.* xiii. 8. 3, and Diodor. xxxiv. 1, probably after
Posidonius).   Justinus, xxxvi. 2. 15: caverunt, ne cum peregrinis con-
viverent.   Apollonius Molon in Joseph. *c. Apion.* ii. 14: ὡς . . . μισαν-
θρώπους λοιδορεῖ.   *Ibid.* ii. 36: ὁ Μόλων Ἀπολλώνιος ἡμῶν κατηγόρησεν ὅτι
μὴ παραδεχόμεθα τοὺς ἄλλαις προκατειλημμένους δόξαις περὶ θεοῦ, μηδὲ
κοινωνεῖν ἐθέλομεν τοῖς καθ' ἑτέραν συνήθειαν βίου ζῆν προαιρουμένοις.   Lysimachus asserted (Joseph. *c. Apion.* i. 34), that Moses had directed the Jews:
μήτε ἀνθρώπων τινὶ εὐνοήσειν, etc.   According to Apion (Joseph. *c. Apion.*
ii. 8), the Jews were accustomed, at the annual sacrifice of a Greek, to
swear, ut inimicitias contra Graecos haberent, or, as it is said, ii. 10: μεδενὶ
εὐνοήσειν ἀλλοφύλῳ μάλιστα δὲ Ἕλλησιν   Tacit. *Hist.* v. 5: adversus omnes
alios hostile odium: separati epulis, discreti cubilibus . . . alienarum concubita
abstinent.   Juvenal, *Sat.* xiv. 103–104 (see Div. ii. vol. ii. p. 295).

of pointing to the humane appointments of the law, especially
with regard to strangers (Joseph. *c. Apion.* ii. 28–29), and on
the other that of showing, how the ancient laws of other
States went much farther in the exclusion of strangers than
the Mosaic law did (*c. Apion.* ii. 36–37).

7. The peculiarities of the Jews *already mentioned,* viz. their
ἀθεότης and their ἀμιξία, are those which *came forward the
most prominently in public life.* It was on this account that
the Jews appeared to be the enemies of such public regula-
tions and institutions as had then been formed, nay as the
opponents of all other human intercourse. Hence it is on
these points that attacks are most seriously directed. Other
peculiarities gave occasion rather to derision and contempt
than to actual accusations. Among these were (*a*) *circumcision,* (*b*) *abstinence from swine's flesh,* and (*c*) the *observance
of the Sabbath.*[51] Even the most malicious of their other
opponents did not venture upon the reproach of that special
immorality to which Tacitus alludes.[52] Apologetic writers
oppose to the derision shown towards these several peculiarities an *ideal picture of the entire Mosaic code.* As Philo by
his idealistic representation of the Mosaic legislation (see above,
p. 219 sq.) already gave an indirect apology for it, so also
does Josephus endeavour, by a connected and positive statement, to show, that the precepts of the Mosaic law are in
every respect the purest and most ideal (*c. Apion.* ii. 22–30).
In doing this he does not enter into these objectionable
points, but contents himself with referring his opponent, the
Egyptian Apion, to the fact, that the Egyptian priests also
were circumcised and abstained from swine's flesh (*Ap.* ii. 13).
To show the value and excellency of the law, he points out in
general its high antiquity (ii. 15), the blameless character of

[51] *Circumcision:* Apion in Joseph. *c. Apion.* ii. 13, *init.* Horace, *Sat.*
i. 9. 69 sq. *Swine's flesh:* Apion in Joseph. *c. Apion.* ii. 13, *init.* Juvenal,
*Sat.* vi. 160, xiv. 98. *Observance of the Sabbath:* Juvenal, *Sat.* xiv. 105–106.
Tacit. *Hist.* v. 4.

[52] Tacit. *Hist.* v. 5: projectissima ad libidinem gens . . . inter se nihil
illicitum.

Moses the lawgiver, and also the fact that this law really fulfilled its object, being known and obeyed by all, which astonishing result arose from its being not only taught but practised (ii. 16–19). Finally, Josephus brings forward the circumstance, that no Jew is ever unfaithful to his law, which is again a proof of its excellence (ii. 31–32, 38). The deficiencies found in this treatise, inasmuch as it does not further enter into those points which were objected to by the heathen, are abundantly compensated for by Philo, who in his special delineation of the Mosaic law treats all these points very thoroughly, and everywhere proves their reasonableness.[53]

### VII. JEWISH PROPAGANDA UNDER A HEATHEN MASK.

At the close of our survey, we have still to discuss a class of literary productions highly characteristic of Hellenistic Judaism, viz. *Jewish works under a heathen mask.* The works which belong to this category, differ greatly so far as their literary form is concerned, but have all the common feature of appearing under the name of some heathen authority, whether of a mythological authority, as the sibyl, or of persons eminent in history, as Hecataeus and Aristeas. The very choice of this pseudonymic form shows, that *all these works were calculated for heathen readers, and designed for the propagation of Judaism among the heathen.* For only with heathen readers were such names a standard authority, and only on their account could this form have been chosen by Jewish authors. Hence the tendency, which is peculiar to a large portion of the Graeco-Jewish literature in general, viz. the tendency to influence non-Jewish readers, here obtains significant expression. In one respect or another its intention was to carry on

---

[53] On *Circumcision: de circumcisione = Opp.* ed. Mang. ii. 210–212. *Sabbath observance: de septenario,* § 6–7 = Mang. ii. 281–284. *Prohibition of unclean animals: de concupiscentia,* § 4–9 = Mang. ii. 352–355. On the observance of the Sabbath, compare also Aristobulus in Euseb. *Praep. evang.* xiii. 12. 9–16, on unclean animals, pseudo-Aristeas in Havercamp's *Josephus,* ii. 2. 117.

among the heathen a propaganda for Judaism. The special
design however certainly differed in different cases. The Sibyllines desire to effect a propaganda properly so called. They
set forth directly before the heathen world the folly of idolatry
and the depravity of its moral conduct; they threaten punishment and ruin in case of impenitence, and promise reward
and eternal happiness in case of conversion, and they thus
seek to win adherents to the Jewish faith in the midst of the
heathen world. An effect however of quite a different kind
is aimed at in other works of this category; their purpose is
not so much to propagate the faith as the honour and credit
of the Jews. Thus, pseudo-Aristeas *e.g.* seeks, in his whole
narrative of the translation of the Jewish law into Greek, to
show what a high opinion was entertained by the learned
Ptolemy II. of this law and of Jewish wisdom in general,
and with what great honour he treated Jewish scholars. A
directly missionary purpose does not come forward in this
author; he cares more *to create a favourable disposition* towards
Judaism and the Jewish law. And thus throughout this
category, now one, now the other purpose comes more into
the foreground—at one time that of winning believers, at
another, that of creating a favourable impression. Still in one
way or the other and in the wider meaning all subserve the
propagation of Judaism. And since they all make choice of a
heathen mask for this purpose, they all belong, however much
they may differ otherwise in form and contents, to one
category.

We begin our discussion with the Sibylline oracles, not
because these are the oldest works of this class, but because
they are the most important both with respect to extent and
actual effect.

### 1. *The Sibyllines.*

The sibyl was in heathen antiquity " the semi-divine
prophetess of the orders and counsels of the gods concerning

the fate of cities and kingdoms" (Lücke).[54] She was distinguished from the official priestly order of prophets by representing a free and non-official prophetic power, being indeed
first of all a personification of the Deity as revealing itself
in nature. She is represented as a nymph dwelling by
streams and grottoes. The most ancient authors speak only
of a sibyl; so Heraclitus, who is the first to mention one at
all (in Plutarch, de Pythiae oraculis, c. 6); so also Euripides,
Aristophanes, Plato.[55] The fact, that her voice was said to
have been perceived in different places, then led to the supposition, that she wandered from place to place.[56] At last
this was not found sufficient, and different sibyls said to dwell
in different places were distinguished. Their number is very
differently stated. There are learned combinations, which
have been made now in one manner, now in another.[57] The
statement of Pausanias (Descr. Graec. x. 12), who distinguishes
four sibyls, is worthy of notice. These are: (1) The Hero-
phile who came from Marpessus in the region of Troy, prophesied in various parts of Asia Minor and Greece and was
falsely stated by the Erythraeans to have been an Erythraean;
(2) a more ancient one, probably the Libyan (Maass, p. 7),
but whose abode, in consequence of a gap in the text of
Pausanias, cannot be determined; (3) the Cumanian; and (4)
the Hebrew, who is also called the Babylonian or Egyptian.

---

[54] The most important material concerning the sibyls was already collected by Opsopöus in his edition of the Orac. Sibyll. pp. 56–143. For
more recent authorities, comp. especially: Klausen, Aeneas und die Penaten
(1839), pp. 203–312. Lücke, Einleitung in die Offenbarung des Johannes
(2nd ed.), p. 81 sqq. Alexandre in his 1st ed. vol. ii. (1856) pp. 1–101.
Scheiffele, art. "Sibyllae," in Pauly's Real-Enc. vi. 1147–1153. Pape-
Benseler, Wörterb. der griech. Eigennamen, s.v. Σίβυλλα. Marquardt,
Römische Staatsverwaltung, vol. iii. (1878) p. 336 sqq. Bouché-Leclercq,
Histoire de la divination, vol. ii. ; Les sacerdoces divinatoires; devins,
chresmologues, Sibylles ; Oracles des dieux, Paris 1879. Maass, De Sibyl-
larum indicibus, Diss. Gryphiswald 1879.

[55] Maass, De Sibyllarum indicibus, p. 1.

[56] E.g. Pausanias, Descr. Graec. x. 12.

[57] On the numerous calculations, see especially Maass, De Sibyllarum
indicibus, 1879.

It seems as if Pausanias purposed thus to state the four chief kinds of sibyl: the Libyan as the most ancient, that of Greek, Asia Minor, the Roman and the Oriental. He expressly designates the latter as the most recent. It is highly probable, that the information relating to this subject is already a deposite of the Jewish sibyl fiction.[58]    Among other computations, the most noted is that of Varro, who names ten sibyls.[59]    In the Roman period the most famous were the Erythraean (from Erythraea on the Ionian coast, opposite the island of Chios) and the Cumanian (in Lower Italy).

*Written records* of supposed Sibylline oracles were here and there in circulation; but such remains of them as have come down to us through occasional quotations in authors such as Plutarch, Pausanias and others, are brief and scanty, and furnish no distinct notion of them.[60]    In Asia Minor

[58] The words of Pausanias are as follows (*Descr. Graec.* x. 12. 9): Ἐπετράφη δὲ καὶ ὕστερον τῆς Δημοῦς [but there lived later than Demo] παρὰ Ἑβραίοις τοῖς ὑπὲρ τῆς Παλαιστίνης γυνὴ χρησμολόγος, ὄνομα δὲ αὐτῇ Σάββη. Βηρώσσου δὲ εἶναι πατρὸς καὶ Ἐρυμάνθης μητρός φασι Σάββην· οἱ δὲ αὐτὴν Βαβυλωνίαν, ἕτεροι δὲ Σίβυλλαν καλοῦσιν Αἰγυπτίαν. — Alexander Polyhistor being the first among Greek authors known to us, who quotes the Jewish sibyl (see below), we may perhaps conclude, that Pausanias derived his statements from Alexander (see Maass, pp. 12-22). From a similar source come also the statements concerning Σαμβήθη in Suidas, *Lex. s.v.* Σίβυλλα (Σίβυλλα Χαλδαία ἡ καὶ πρὸς τινῶν Ἑβραία ὀνομαζομένη, ἡ καὶ Περσίς, ἡ κυρίῳ ὀνόματι καλουμένη Σαμβήθη κ.τ.λ.), and in the anonymous catalogues allied to Suidas, which mention Σαμβήθη (Maass, *De Sibyll. indic.* pp. 38, 42, 44). The designation of the sibyl as a daughter of Berosus is found also in pseudo-Justin, *Cohort. ad Graec.* c. 37. The Jewish sibyl identifies herself with the Erythraean, but says that she came from Babylon (*Sib.* iii. 808 sqq.). Clemens Alex. *Protrept.* vi. 70–71, calls her προφῆτις Ἑβραίων. Comp. in general, Alexandre, ii. 82–87.

[59] Varro in Lactantius, *Div. Instit.* i. 6: primam fuisse de Persis . . . secundam Libycam . . . tertiam Delphida . . quartam Cimmeriam in Italia . . . quintam Erythraeam . . sextam Samiam . . septimam Cumanam . . . octavam Hellesponticam in agro Troiano natam vico Marmesso circa oppidum Gergitium . . . nonam Phrygiam . . decimam Tiburtem. See other computations, *e.g.* in Clem. Alex. *Strom.* i. 21. 108 and 132; Suidas, *Lex. s.v.* Σίβυλλα and others.

[60] See the collection in Alexandre's 1st ed. of the *Orac. Sibyll.* vol. ii. (1856) pp. 118–129. Some already in Opsopöus, in his edit. of the *Orac. Sibyll.* p. 414 sqq.

and Greece these pieces circulated only in private possession, without being publicly supervised or officially used. But their credit and influence must not be on that account slightly estimated.[61] They attained quite a different importance in Rome, where they arrived by way of Cumae from Asia Minor.[62] King Tarquin Superbus is said to have obtained a collection of Sibylline oracles, which were preserved in the temple of Jupiter Capitolinus.[63] These having perished in the conflagration of the Capitol, B.C. 83, the Senate, at the instigation of the consul C. Curio, sent an embassy, B.C. 76, to Asia Minor, which again made in Erythraea and other places a collection of about a thousand verses, which was again deposited in the Capitol.[64] The collection was afterwards occasionally enlarged and expurgated, and was in existence in the fourth century after Christ. Besides this official collection, Sibylline verses in private possession were also circulated, but these, by reason of the misuse made of them, were frequently confiscated and destroyed by the authorities. The official collection was kept secret, and only consulted on important occasions, chiefly to ascertain what expiations were required on the occurrence of public misfortunes.

This Sibyllism was from its very nature specially adapted for being turned to account in the interest of religious propaganda. The oracles, being of apocryphal origin, in private possession, and circulating without control, might be completed and added to at pleasure. What had been done in this respect by Greek hands might as easily be undertaken by Jewish. Besides the oracles, like the mysterious in general,

---

[61] See on the Sibylline oracles among the Greeks, Alexandre as above, ii. 102–147.

[62] See on the Sibylline oracles among the Romans, Opsopöus, pp. 462–496. Fabricius-Harles, *Biblioth. graec.* i. 248–257. Alexandre in his 1st ed. ii. 148–253. Marquardt, *Römische Staatsverwaltung*, vol. iii. (1878) p. 336 sqq. Huidekoper, *Judaism at Rome* (New York 1876), pp. 395–459.

[63] Dionys. Halicarn. iv. 62.

[64] Lactant. i. 6. 14 (comp. i. 6. 11). Tacit. *Annal.* vi. 12. Dionys. Halic. iv. 62.

enjoyed a high reputation among religiously disposed minds. It might then be hoped that entrance to extensive circles would be obtained under this form. Hence it was a happy hit when *Jewish propaganda took possession of this form to turn it to account for its own purposes.* As far as can be ascertained, it was in the second century before Christ that an extensive Sibylline oracle of Jewish origin was first put in circulation from Alexandria. The result seems to have been favourable, for imitators soon arose, at first among the Jews and subsequently among the Christians. For Christians were in this respect also the apt scholars of Hellenistic Judaism. They not only made willing use of the Jewish Sibylline oracles, and highly esteemed them, but also copiously increased what they found extant. Production in this department continued down to later imperial times, and it is just to the tradition of the Christian Church that we are indebted for the possession of the older Jewish Sibylline oracles also.

The first edition of the Judaeo-Christian Sibyllines (Basle 1545) which have come down to us was prepared by Xystus Betuleius after an Augsburg, now a Munich manuscript, and comprised *eight books.* The later editions show the same number down to and including that printed in Gallandi's *Bibliotheca patrum* (vol. i. Venice 1788). Angelo Mai was the first to publish from a Milan manuscript a *fourteenth* book (1817), and afterwards from two Vatican manuscript books *eleven to fourteen* (1828). All are combined in the modern editions of Alexandre (1st ed. in 2 vols. 1841–1856, 2nd ed. 1 vol. 1869) and Friedlieb (1852).

The form of these Judaeo-Christian Sibylline oracles is the same as that of the ancient heathen ones. The Jewish and Christian authors respectively make the ancient Sibyl speak to heathen nations in Greek hexameters, and in the language of Homer. The contents subserve throughout the purposes of religious propaganda. The Sibyl prophesies the fate of the world from the beginning to the times of the author, for the purpose of then uniting with it both threats and promises for the immediate future ; she rebukes the heathen nations for the sinfulness of their idolatry and blasphemy, and exhorts them to repent while yet there is time, for that fearful judgments will fall upon the impenitent.

The collection *as we have it is a chaotic wilderness,* to sift and arrange which will ever baffle the most acute criticism. For unfortunately it is not the case, that each book forms of itself an original whole, but that even the single books are some of them arbitrary aggregates of single fragments. The curse of pseudonymous authorship seems to have prevailed very specially over these oracles. Every reader and writer allowed himself to complete what existed after his own pleasure, and to arrange the scattered papers now in one, now in an opposite manner. Evidently much was at first circulated in detached portions, and the collection of these afterwards made by some admirer was a very accidental one. Hence duplicates of many portions are found in different places. And the manuscripts which have come down to us exhibit great discrepancies in the arrangement.[64a]

Such being the nature of the whole, it is not possible always to distinguish with certainty between *Jewish* and *Christian* matter. The oldest portions are at all events Jewish, worked up perhaps with single small heathen oracles. The main body of the later books is certainly Christian. But neither the one nor the other appears in large and closely connected masses. As a rule we have always but small portions quite loosely strung together, and often without any connection. Hence it is only with respect to single and comparatively small portions that we can pass a certain judgment, as to whether they are Jewish or Christian. Much is of so neutral a character, that it may just as well have proceeded from one side as from the other. *The following portions may with some probability be distinguished as Jewish.*

[64a] The preface of the compiler of our present collection is still preserved (Friedlieb, Appendix, pp. ii.–vii. Alexandre's 1st ed. i. 2–13, 2nd ed. pp. 14–21). Alexandre thinks he can place it in the sixth century after Christ (1st ed. ii. 421–435, 2nd ed. p. xxxvi. sqq ).

1. The most ancient and certainly Jewish portions are in any case contained in the *third book*. All critics since Bleek concur in this opinion. Views, however, differ widely as to any nearer determination, whether of the date of composition or of the extent of the Jewish portions. According to Bleek, Book iii. 97–807 (according to another computation, iii. 35–746) is the work of an Alexandrian Jew of the time of the Maccabees (170–160 B.C.), and contains also a working up of older Jewish fictions (97–161, 433–488 [= 35–99, 371–426]), and later Christian interpolations (350–380 [= 289–318]). The majority of Bleek's successors regard the whole as Jewish. Gfrörer, Lücke, and Friedlieb concur with Bleek with regard to the date of composition. Hilgenfeld, on the ground of an ingenious exposition of the difficult section iii. 388–400, places the whole (iii. 97–817) about 140 B.C., and is followed herein by Reuss, Badt, and Wittichen. Zündel also accepted his exposition of iii. 388–400, but kept to Bleek's view of the earlier date of composition. Ewald went a little farther forward than Hilgenfeld, by placing the composition of Book iii. 97–828 at about 124 B.C. But while all hitherto mentioned agree in assuming a Jewish authorship, Alexandre ascribes only the portions iii. 97–294, 489–817, to an Alexandrian Jew of about 168 B.C., and the intermediate portion, 295–488, on the contrary to a Christian writer. Larocque, while going still farther in the division, agrees with Alexandre in regarding the bulk of Book iii. 97–294, 489–828 as written about 168 B.C., but admits also later interpolations in the last section, and considers the sections iii. 1–96 and 295–488 as "subordinate collections of heterogeneous pieces," of which only certain individual portions belong to the author of the two first-named large portions. Delaunay also esteems the portions iii. 97–294 and 489–817 not as single productions, but as aggregates of separate unconnected oracles of different periods, ranging from about the beginning to the middle of the second century B.C.

For the purpose of forming a judgment we will first give

*a survey of the contents*, with the omission of the section
iii. 1–96, which certainly does not belong to what follows.
The rest is clearly divided by means of the recent additions
in vers. 295 and 498 into three groups (97–294, 295–488,
489–828). The beginning of *the first group* is wanting. It
commences abruptly by recalling the building of the Tower
of Babel and the Confusion of Tongues as the causes of the
dispersion of mankind in all lands (97–100). When the
whole earth was peopled, the sovereignty over it was divided
between Chronos, Titan, and Japetos. All three at first ruled
peacefully near each other, but a quarrel arose between
Chronos and Titan, which was only settled for a time by an
assembly of the gods (or as the Jewish author expresses it,
by an assembly of the βασιλεῖς), and resulted in the contest between the Chronides and Titans, and the destruction
of both these races. After their annihilation arose successively the kingdoms of the Egyptians, Persians, Medes,
Ethiopians, Assyrians, Babylonians, Macedonians, then again
of the Egyptians, and lastly of the Romans (110–161). Now
first does the Sibyl begin to prophesy; in the first place
the prosperity of the Solomonian kingdom, then the Graeco-
Macedonian, lastly the many-headed (πολύκρανος) kingdom
of the Romans. After the seventh king of Egypt of the
Hellenic race, the people of God again attain to sovereignty
and will be to all mortals a leader of life (162–195). The
judgment of God will fall upon all the kingdoms of the
world, from the Titans and Chronides onwards. Even the
pious men of Solomon's kingdom will be visited by misfortune.
Here the author takes occasion to give a sketch of the
Jewish people, their reverence for God, and the main points
of their history from their departure from Egypt down to
Cyrus (196–294). The *second group* is almost entirely taken
up with announcements of judgments and calamities: Against
Babylon (295–313), against Egypt (314–318), against Gog
and Magog (319–322), against Libya (323–333). After
the signs which forebode calamity have been stated, there

follow proclamations of woe to single towns and countries, concluding with the promise of a universal condition of Messianic prosperity and peace in Asia and Europe (341–380). Then follow oracles concerning Antiochus Epiphanes and his successors (381–400), concerning Phrygia, Troy (interspersed with polemic against Homer), Lycia, Cyprus, Italy, and other countries, towns and islands (401–488). The *third group* begins with oracles concerning Phoenicia, Crete, Thrace, Gog and Magog, the Hellenes (489–572); it then points to the people of Israel, who cleave to the law of God, and do not devote themselves to idolatry and unnatural crimes (573 – 600). Hereupon follows a second prophecy of judgment upon the sinful world terminating in promises (601–623), and an exhortation to conversion, with a description of the ruin which will come upon the ungodly world, and especially upon Hellas (624–651). The promise of the Messianic King, a prophecy of judgment, and a detailed description of Messianic prosperity, interspersed with exhortations to Hellas to cease from their presumption, and references to omens of the last judgment, form the conclusion (652–807). The Sibyl says in the epilogue, that she came from Babylon, but was wrongly regarded by the Greeks as a native of Erythraea (808–817), also that she was a daughter of Noah, and had been with him in the ark at the time of the Deluge (818–828).[65]

This survey of the contents shows, that in any case we have not to deal with a single composition. In the second group especially, the different portions are entirely unconnected with each other. Hence it is in any case *a collection of separate oracles*. Nevertheless it is at least possible, that the greater number of them are the work of one author. For there is not sufficient support for accepting either a heathen

---

[65] Bleek denies the authorship of the whole epilogue to the composer of the rest. With respect to the first half (808–817) there is no valid ground for such denial. It might rather be doubted whether the first and second halves belong to each other. See Hilgenfeld, *Apokal.* pp. 78–80.

or a Christian origin of the pieces. The mythological portion at the beginning, which kindly makes the heathen
gods guiltless human kings of antiquity, may very well have
been written by a Jew, nay this kind of intermixture of
Greek and Jewish legends just corresponds with the character
of Hellenistic Judaism. There exists however no reason for
supposing that it contains Christian elements, since instead
of υἱὸν θεοῖο in ver. 775 the correct reading is probably
νηὸν θεοῖο (see vol. ii. p. 139). The circumstance that the
time of the seventh Ptolemy is referred to in all three
groups (vers. 191–193, 316–318, 608–610) speaks for their
virtual connection. Hence the inference attained with respect
to the date of composition of the separate portions may with
a certain amount of probability be extended to the whole.

For determining the *date of composition*, the following
limits exist. The author is acquainted with the Book of
Daniel (vers. 388–400), and the expeditions of Antiochus
Epiphanes to Egypt (vers. 611–615). On the other hand
Rome is still a republic (ver. 176: πολύκρανος). But the
most accurate limit is furnished by the threefold recur-
rence of the assurance, that the end will appear under the
seventh king of Egypt of Hellenic race (vers. 191–193,
316–318, 608–610). Hence the author wrote under
Ptolemy VII. Physcon, who at first reigned together with his
brother Ptolemy VI. Philometor (170–164 B.C.), was then
banished from Egypt, but attained after his brother's death
to the sole sovereignty (145–117 B.C.). When Zundel
thinks, that because the king is called βασιλεὺς νέος (ver.
608), only the years from 170–164 B.C. can be thought of,
since Ptolemy Physcon could by no means be any longer
called young after the year 145, it must be answered, that
νέος means not only "young," but "new." The proper
sovereignty however of Ptolemy Physcon did not begin till
the year 145. And that the author intended just this period
of sole sovereignty is already in and by itself probable; for
he would have designated the joint government of the two

brothers as the sixth kingship. This too is confirmed by
the plain allusions to the destruction of Carthage and Corinth
(vers. 484 sq., 487 sq.), both which cities were, as is well
known, destroyed in the year 146 before Christ. The
section vers. 388–400 also leads, according to the ingenious,
but not indeed quite certain explanation of Hilgenfeld, to
the same period (*Apokalyptik*, p. 69 sq. ; *Zeitschr.* 1860, p.
314 sqq., 1871, p. 35). Here Antiochus Epiphanes is first
referred to, and his overthrow then prophesied: "He will
himself destroy their race, through whose race his race also
will be destroyed. He has a single root, which also the man-
slayer (Ares) will eradicate out of ten horns. But he will
plant another shoot beside it. He will eradicate the warlike
progenitor of a royal race. And he himself is exterminated
by the sons. And then will a horn planted near rule." [66]
The race which Antiochus Epiphanes will destroy is that
of his brother Seleucus IV. The sole root of Antiochus
Epiphanes, viz. his son Antiochus V. Eupator, is murdered by
Demetrius I., son of Seleucus IV., or, as the author expresses
it, he is eradicated out of ten horns, *i.e.* as the last of
ten kings. The shoot, which the god of war plants near, is
Alexander Balas. He will exterminate the warlike progenitor
of a royal race, viz. Demetrius I. But he will be himself
destroyed by Demetrius II. and Antiochus VII. Sidetes, sons
of Balas. And then will the upstart Trypho rule (146–
139 B.C.). According to this explanation of Hilgenfeld, our
author would have written about 140 B.C. And to this we
must in any case adhere, even if the details of the explanation should not be all correct.[67] Traces of a later time can

---

[66] Vers. 394–400 : ʽΩν δή περ γενεὴν αὐτὸς θέλει ἐξαπολέσσαι,
  ᾽Εκ τῶν δὴ γενεῆς κείνου γένος ἐξαπολεῖται·
  ῾Ρίζαν ἴαν γε διδοὺς, ἣν καὶ κόψει βροτολοιγὸς
  ᾽Εκ δέκα δὴ κεράτων, παρὰ δὲ φυτὸν ἄλλο φυτεύσει.
  Κόψει πορφυρέης γενεῆς γενετῆρα μαχητὴν,
  Καὐτὸς ἀφ᾽ υἱῶν, ὧν ἐς ὁμόφρονα αἴσιον ἄρρης,
  Φθεῖται· καὶ τότε δὴ παραφυόμενον κέρας ἄρξει.
The words ὧν ἐς ὁμόφρονα αἴσιον ἄρρης are certainly corrupt.

[67] Two things only are suspicious: (1) The subject of κόψει, ver. 398,

scarcely be found. For the western nation, which according to vers. 324, 328 sq. is to take part in the destruction of the temple, is not the Roman, but according to Ezek. xxxviii. 5 the Libyan (so Lücke, Hilgenfeld). Only vers. 464–470 seem to turn upon later Roman times, and to be an insertion (Hilgenfeld, *Apokal.* p. 72 ; *Zeitschr.* 1871, p. 35 sq.).

The conclusion arrived at is also confirmed by *external testimony.* For according to the information of Euseb. *Chron.* ed. Schoene, i. 23 = Syncell. ed. Dindorf, i. 81 = Cyrill. *adv. Julian.* ed. Spanh. p. 9, the prophecy of the Sibyl concerning the building of the Tower of Babel and the conflict between the Chronides and Titans which followed it, was already expressly quoted under the name of the Sibyl (Σίβυλλα δέ φησιν, etc.) by Alexander Polyhistor, and therefore in the first half of the first century before Christ, in his Χαλδαϊκά.[68] Such are also found, especially from the third book,[69] among the oldest patristic quotations.

2. To the oldest Jewish Sibylline oracles undoubtedly belong also the two extensive fragments (together eighty-four verses) communicated by Theophilus, *ad Autol.* ii. 36. Single verses from them are also quoted by other Fathers.[70] These are not found in our manuscripts. In the editions they are generally printed at the head of the whole collection, because

seems to be not φυτὸν ἄλλο, but the god of war, and αὐτός, ver. 399, not to go upon φυτὸν ἄλλο, but upon γενετήρ. (2) Alexander Balas was not over- thrown by Demetrius II. and Antiochus VII., but by the former and his father- in-law Ptolemy VI. Philometor (1 Macc. xi. 1–19 ; Joseph. *Antt.* xiii. 4. 5–8).

[68] The quotation in Josephus is taken from Alexander Polyhistor without mention of his name (*Antt.* i. 4. 3=Euseb. *Praep. evang.* ix. 15). See Bleek, i. 148–152. Freudenthal, *Alex. Polyh.* p. 25, note. The statements too concerning the building of the Tower of Babel in Abydenus (Euseb. *Chron.* i. 34 and *Praep. evang.* ix. 14. Syncell. i. 81 sq. Cyrill. p. 9).

[69] Athenagoras, *Suppl.* c. 30. Theophilus, *ad Autol.* ii. 31. Tertullian, *ad nationes,* ii. 12. Clemens Alex. *Protrept.* vi. 70, vii. 74. Pseudo- Justin. *Cohort. ad Graec.* c. 16.

[70] Gnostic fragment in Hippolyt. *Philosophum.* v. 16. Clemens Alex. *Protrept.* ii. 27 ; *Protr.* vi. 71=*Strom.* v. 14. 108 ; *Protr.* viii. 77 = *Strom.* v. 14. 115 ; *Strom.* iii. 3. 14. Pseudo-Justin. *Cohort. ad Graec.* c. 16. Lactantius, i. 6. 15–16, 7. 13, 8. 3 ; ii. 11. 18 (?), 12. 19 ; iv. 6. 5. *Id. de ira dei,* c. 22. 7.

Theophilus says that they stood at the beginning of the
Sibyl's prophecy (ἐν ἀρχῇ τῆς προφητείας αὐτῆς). But the
present first and second books being very recent and placed
quite by accident at the beginning of the collection, and the
third book being certainly the oldest part, it may be assumed
beforehand that these pieces formed *the introduction to our
third book*. This supposition, probable in itself, becomes
a certainty through the fact, that Lactantius, among his
numerous citations, calls only such portions as are found in
the Theophilus fragments and in our third book, prophecies
of the Erythraean Sibyl, nay evidently quotes both as parts
of one book.[71] The contents of these verses may be called the
special programme of all Jewish Sibyllism: they contain an
energetic direction to the only true God and as energetic
a polemic against idolatry. From no portion can the tendency
of Jewish Sibyllism be better perceived than from this proem.

3. Section iii. 36—92 (according to another computation:
vers. 36—62 of the intermediate section between Books ii. and
iii. and Book iv. 1–30), now standing at the beginning of the
third book, is also a Jewish fragment of the prae-Christian
period. Bleek already perceived, that this fragment proceeded
from an Alexandrian Jew of the time of the first triumvirate

---

[71] Comp. Bleek, i. 160–166. Lactantius distinguishes the different books
as different Sibyls. When after quoting from one book he makes a quotation from another, he says: *alia Sibylla dicit*. Among his somewhere
about fifty quotations, extending over Books iii. to viii. of our collection,
only those from the proem preserved in Theophilus and from the third
book, are entitled prophecies of the Erythraean Sibyl. From the proem:
Lact. i. 6. 13–16, 8. 3; ii. 12. 19; iv. 6. 5. From the third book: Lact.
ii. 16. 1 (=*Sib*. iii. 228, 229, ed. Friedlieb); iv. 6. 5 (=*Sib*. iii. 774); iv.
15. 29 (=*Sib*. iii. 814–817); vii. 19. 9 (=*Sib*. iii. 618); vii. 20. 1–2
(=*Sib*. iii. 741, 742); vii. 24. 12 (=*Sib*. iii. 787–793). The passage, Lact.
iv. 6. 5, is however the most instructive: Sibylla Erythraea in carminis sui
principio, quod a summo Deo exorsa est, filium Dei ducem et imperatorem
omnium his versibus praedicat: παντοτρόφον κτίστην ὅστις γλυκὺ πνεῦμα
ἅπασι ‖ κάτθετο, χ̓ ἡγητῆρα θεῶν πάντων ἐποίησε (=*proem*, vers. 5–6). Et
rursus in fine ejusdem carminis: αὐτὸν ἔδωκε θεὸς πιστοῖς ἀνδράσσι γεραίρειν
(=*Sib*. iii. 774, ed. Friedlieb). Et alia Sibylla praecipit hunc oportere
cognosci: αὐτὸν σὸν γίνωσκε θεὸν, θεοῦ υἱὸν ἐόντα (=*Sib*. viii. 329). Here
then it is plainly said, that the proem belongs to our third book.

(40–30 B.C.), and he has justly found general acquiescence.
So Gfrörer, Lücke, Friedlieb, Hilgenfeld (*Apokal.* p. 241),
Reuss, Larocque (at least for vers. 26–52) and Wittichen.
Only Badt (pp. 54–61) goes as far as 25 B.C., thinking,
according to a suggestion made by Frankel, that the Σεβασ-
τηνοί of ver. 63 must mean inhabitants of Sebaste-Samaria.
Alexandre and Ewald indeed ascribe the oracle to a Christian
author of the time of the Antonines (Alexandre), or even of
about A.D. 300 (Ewald). Bleek's view is however the best
founded. The piece begins with a cry of woe to the wicked
race, which is full of all crimes. With this is combined the
prophecy, that when Rome rules over Egypt also, then will
begin the judgment and the rule of the Messianic King.
Even this definition of time: " when Rome rules over Egypt
*also* " (ver. 46: Αὐτὰρ ἐπεὶ ῾Ρώμη καὶ Αἰγύπτου βασιλεύσει),
points to a period when the rule of Rome over Egypt was
something new, therefore to the time of Antony, soon after
40 B.C. The date becomes perfectly clear by the allusion to the
triumvirate of Antony, Octavius, and Lepidus (ver. 52: Τρεῖς
῾Ρώμην οἰκτρῇ μοίρῃ καταδηλήσονται), and by the mention of
the widow, under whose hands the world finds itself being
governed by her and obeying her in all things, *i.e.* Cleopatra (vers.
75–80). Hence the oracle was written between 40 and 30 B.C.
To go farther down is inadmissible, the end being expected
during the lifetime of Cleopatra. The mention of the Σεβασ-
τηνοί (ver. 63), on account of which Badt would place the oracle
as late as 25 B.C., may safely be laid to the account of a later
interpolator. It is probable, as Bleek and Lücke suppose, that
the bracketed words in vers. 60–63 should be expunged,—

> ῞Ηξει γὰρ, ὁπόταν θείου διαβήσεται ὀδμὴ
> Πᾶσιν ἐν ἀνθρώποισιν, [Ἀτὰρ τὰ ἕκαστ᾽ ἀγορεύσω,
> ῞Οσσαις ἐν πόλεσιν μέροπες κακότητα φέρουσιν,
> Ἐκ δὲ Σεβαστηνῶν ἥξει] Βελίαρ μετόπισθεν.

4. Opinions are more divided concerning the *fourth book*
than with regard to the passages hitherto treated of. The

majority of older critics regard it as Christian. Friedlieb,
Ewald, Hilgenfeld (*Zeitschr.* 1871, pp. 44–50) and especially
Badt (1878) admit a Jewish author and place its composition about A.D. 80.[72] This view must be allowed to pass as
correct. For there is nothing at all specifically Christian in
the book. The Sibyl, who at the commencement calls herself
the prophetess of the true God, proclaims by His commission manifold calamities through war, earthquakes and other
natural events to the cities, countries, and peoples of Asia
and Europe. Unless they repent, God will destroy the whole
world by fire and will then raise men from the dead and sit
in judgment, sending the ungodly to Tartarus and bestowing a
new life on earth upon the godly. There is nothing in these
particulars to recall the Christian sphere of thought, although
it would hardly be possible to a Christian author to avoid
mentioning Christ, when writing on eschatology. Nor are
there any grounds for supposing the author to have been an
Essene (so Ewald and Hilgenfeld). For the polemic against
animal sacrifices (ver. 29) is only directed against heathen
sacrifices ; and the baptism to which the heathen are summoned
is merely Jewish proselyte baptism (comp. Div. ii. vol. ii. p. 323).
For determining the date of composition it is decisive, that
the destruction of Jerusalem (vers. 115–127) and the eruption
of Vesuvius of A.D. 79 (vers. 130–136) are presupposed.
The author also believes with many of his contemporaries in
Nero's flight across the Euphrates and his impending return
(vers. 117–124, 137–139). Consequently the oracle must have
been composed about A.D. 80 or not much later, and more
probably in Asia Minor (so *e.g.* Lightfoot and Badt) than in
Palestine (so Freudenthal). The patristic quotations from this
book begin with Justin.[73] It is also noteworthy that two

---

[72] So too Lightfoot (*St. Paul's Epistles to the Colossians and to Philemon*,
2nd ed. 1876, p. 96 sq.) and Freudenthal (*Alex. Polyhistor*, pp. 129, 195).
Comp. also my account of the work of Badt in the *Theol. Litztg.* 1878, p.
358. Dechent again gives his decision for the Christian authorship, *Zeitschr.
für Kirchengesch.* ii. 491–496.

[73] Justin. *Apol.* i. 20 (refers to *Sib.* iv. 172–177). Clemens Alex. *Protrept.*

verses included in it (97-98) are already mentioned by Strabo,
p. 536, as oracular sayings.

5. Very divergent are the decisions of critics concerning
the *fifth book*. Bleek distinguishes the following portions as
Jewish:—(*a*) vers. 260–285, 481–531, written about the
middle of the second century before Christ, by an Alexandrian
Jew; (*b*) vers. 286–332 by a Jew of Asia Minor soon after
A.D. 20 ; (*c*) perhaps also vers. 342–433 by a Jewish author
about A.D. 70. While Lücke entirely, and Gfrörer at least
partly, agree with Bleek, Friedlieb ascribes the whole fifth book
to a Jew of the beginning of Hadrian's reign, and Badt to a
Jew of about A.D. 130 ; Ewald, Hilgenfeld (*Zeitschr.* 1871, pp.
37–44) and Hildebrandt regard at least Book v. 52–531 as
the work of a Jew of about A.D. 80 (Ewald) or a few years
earlier (Hilgenfeld, Hildebrandt) ; while Alexandre, Reuss and
Dechent (*Zeitschr. f. Kirchengesch.* ii. 497 sqq.) attribute
the book to a Christian Jew. It seems to me a vain
effort to attempt to settle in detail the origin and date of
composition of the pieces combined in this book. For it is
palpable, that we have here no compact whole, but a loose
conglomerate of heterogeneous portions. *The greater number
are certainly of Jewish origin;* for the sections, in which
Jewish interests and views are brought more or less plainly
forward, run through the whole book (comp. especially vers.
260–285, 328–332, 344–360, 397–413, 414–433, 492–
511). On the other hand the remarkable passage vers. 256–
259, in which " the excellent man coming from heaven who
spreads out his hands on the fruit-bearing tree " (Jesus) is
identified with Joshua (Jesus the son of Nave) is certainly
Christian.[74] Thus Jewish and Christian pieces are at all

---

iv. 50 and 62; *Paedag.* ii. 10. 99, iii. 3. 15; *Constit. apostol.* v. 7. Pseudo-
Justin. *Cohort.* c. 16. Lactant. vii. 23.4. *Id. de ira dei,* c. 23 (three passages).

[74] *Sib.* vers. 256–259 :—

Εἷς δέ τις ἔσσεται αὖθις ἀπ' αἰθέρος ἔξοχος ἀνήρ,
Οὗ παλάμας ἥπλωσεν ἐπὶ ξύλον πολύκαρπον
Ἑβραίων ὁ ἄριστος, ὃς ἠέλιόν ποτε στῆσεν,
Φωνήσας ῥήσει τε καλῇ καὶ χίλεσιν ἀγνοῖς.

events combined in this book. The summing up of the discrepant elements under the common term "Judaeo-Christian" is as unhappy an expedient as it is *e.g.* in the Testaments of the Twelve Patriarchs. When however the mixture of Jewish and Christian pieces in this fifth book is acknowledged, it cannot in many instances, where religion is a matter of indifference, be determined to which side they belong. So much only is certain, that the Jewish element preponderates. With such characteristics it is also impossible to determine the respective *dates of composition.* In the Jewish pieces the destruction of the temple at Jerusalem (397–413) and apparently the destruction also of the Onias-temple in Egypt (so far as vers. 492–511 refer to this) are lamented. These pieces and consequently the main body of the book might then have been written in the first century after Christ. On the other hand, the chronological oracle at the beginning (vers. 1–51) certainly leads as far as to the time of Hadrian. Quotations are first found in Clemens Alexandrinus.[75]

6. Of the remaining books, vi. vii. and viii. are generally and correctly esteemed to be of Christian authorship.[76] The origin on the other hand of Books i.–ii. and xi.–xiv. is doubtful. Most investigators regard these also as Christian. Lücke, Friedlieb and Dechent on the contrary ascribe Book xi. and Friedlieb Book xiv. also to a Jewish author. Dechent attempts, as Friedlieb also partly does, to point out in Books i. and ii. Jewish pieces of greater extent. How difficult it is to find sure footing in this respect is proved by the circumstance, that Lücke in a later section of his work (*Einl. die Offenb. des Joh.* p. 269 sqq.) retracted his view concerning Book xi. and ascribed it to a Christian author.[77] This eleventh book is

---

[75] Clem. Alex. *Protrept.* iv. 50 ; *Paedag.* ii. 10. 99.

[76] The eighth book (viii. 217–250) contains the famous acrostic upon Ἰησοῦς Χριστὸς θεοῦ υἱὸς σωτήρ σταυρός, which is also given in Constantine's *Oratio ad sanct. coet.* (= Euseb. *Vita Const.* v.) c. 18.

[77] So also Bleek in his notice of Lücke's book (*Stud. u. Krit.* 1854, p. 976). According to this the statement in Dechent (*Dissert.* p. 49), that Bleek's view concerning Book xi. "was not known," must be corrected.

really not worth contesting. It is a religiously colourless versified history of Egypt down to the beginning of the Roman supremacy, and may just as well be Jewish as Christian. Nor is it very different with the other pieces. The portions separated by Dechent from Books i. and ii. *may* in fact be Jewish, but they may just as well be Christian, and their entire lack of attestation by the Fathers of the first three centuries rather speaks for a later, *i.e.* a Christian origin.[78]

The most ancient author who quotes a Jewish Sibylline book (and indeed *Sib.* iii. 97 sqq. ed. Friedlieb) is Alexander Polyhistor about 80–40 B.C. See the passage from his Χαλδαϊκά in Euseb. *Chron.* ed. Schoene, i. 23 = Syncell. ed. Dindorf, i. 81 = Cyrill. *adv. Julian.* ed. Spanh. p. 9. The almost verbally identical passage in Josephus, *Antt.* i. 4. 3 (= Euseb. *Praep. evang.* ix. 15), is copied from Alexander Polyhistor without mention of his name. Comp. p. 282 above.

On the use of the Sibyllines by the Fathers, see Vervorst, *De carminibus Sibyllinis apud sanctos Patres disceptatio*, Paris 1844. Besançon, *De l'emploi que les Pères de l'église ont fait des oracles sibyllins*, Montauban 1851. Alexandre's 1st ed. vol. ii. (1856) pp. 254–311. A collection of the most ancient quotations is also given in Harnack's *Patres apostol.*, note on Hermas, *Vis.* ii. 4. A thorough discussion of the numerous citations in Lactantius is given by Struve, *Fragmenta librorum Sibyllinorum quae apud Lactantium reperiuntur*, Regiom. 1817. A manuscript collection by the Scotchman Sedulius (ninth century) of the quotations in Lactantius is printed in Montfaucon's *Paleogr. gr.* lib. iii. cap. vii. pp. 243–247, and from this in Gallandi's *Biblioth. patr.* i. 400–406, comp. his *proleg.* p. lxxxi.

Whether Clemens Romanus has quoted the Sibyllines is doubtful. For it is said in the pseudo-Justinian *Quaestt. et responss. ad orthodoxos*, quaest. 74 (*Corp. apolog.* ed. Otto, 3rd ed. vol. v. p. 108): εἰ τῆς παρούσης καταστάσεως τὸ τέλος ἐστὶν ἡ διὰ τοῦ πυρὸς κρίσις τῶν ἀσεβῶν, καθά φασιν αἱ γραφαὶ προφητῶν τε καὶ ἀπο-στόλων, ἔτι δὲ καὶ τῆς Σιβύλλης, καθώς φησιν ὁ μακάριος Κλήμης ἐν τῇ πρὸς Κορινθίους ἐπιστολῇ. The Sibyl not being mentioned in the received text of the Clementine Epistles, the καθώς must

---

[78] The oldest testimony which Dechent (*Dissert.* p. 37) can point out, is found in Constantine's *Oratio ad sanct. coet.* (=Euseb. *Vita Const.* v.) c. 18: ἡ τοίνυν Ἐρυθραία Σίβυλλα Φάσκουσα ἑαυτὴν ἔτη γενεᾷ, μετὰ τὸν κατακλυσμόν, γενέσθαι. Comp. *Sib.* i. 283 sqq.

probably be taken as parallel to the καθά, and thus the words ἔτι δὲ καὶ τῆς Σιβύλλης are not the words of Clement but of the pseudo-Justin. Comp. Harnack's 2nd ed. of the Clementine Epistles, Proleg. p. xl. ; Otto in his note on the passage is of the contrary opinion. Hermas, *Vis.* ii. 4, mentions only the Sibyl and not the Sibylline books. Quotations from the latter are on the other hand given in the *Predicatio Petri et Pauli* in Clemens Alex. *Strom.* vi. 5. 42–43 (see also Lücke, *Einl. in die Offenb. Joh.* p. 238; Hilgenfeld, *Nov. Test. extra canon. rec.* fasc. iv. 2nd ed. pp. 57, 63 sq.). Gnostics in Hippolyt. *Philosophum.* v. 16. Justin. *Apol.* i. 20. Athenagoras, *Suppl.* c. 30. Theophilus, *ad Autol.* ii. 3. 31, 36. Tertullian, *ad nationes*, ii. 12. Pseudo-Melito, *Apol.* c. 4 (in Otto, *Corp. apolog.* vol. ix. pp. 425, 463 sq.). Pseudo-Justin. *Cohortat. ad Graec.* c. 16, 37–38. Const. *Apost.* v. 7. Constantini *Oratio ad sanct. coet.* ( = Euseb. *Vita Const.* v.) c. 18–19. Quotations abound most in Clemens Alex. and Lactantius.

Clemens Alexandrinus quotes: (1) The prooemium : *Protrept.* ii. 27. *Protr.* vi. 71 = *Strom.* v. 14. 108. *Protr.* viii. 77 = *Strom.* v. 14. 115. *Strom.* iii. 3. 14. (2) The third book: *Protr.* vi. 70, vii. 74. (3) The fourth book: *Protrept.* iv. 50 and 62. *Paedag.* ii. 10. 99, iii. 3. 15. (4) The fifth book: *Protrept.* iv. 50. *Paedag.* ii. 10. 99. Comp. also *Strom.* i. 21. 108, 132. *It is seen from these statistics that just the three books which on internal grounds we esteem* (or at least their greater part) *to be Jewish, and these only, were known to Clement.* Other patristic quotations too down to Clement refer to these books alone. They thus evidently form the most ancient Jewish body of Sibylline oracles.

Lactantius quotes about fifty passages from our Sibyllines, most frequently from Book viii., next to this from Book iii., only sometimes from Books iv. v. vi. and vii., from the rest not at all. See the material in Struve and Alexandre. Hence it seems, that he was acquainted with only Books iii. to viii. of our present collection. He must however have had in them somewhat which is lacking in our MSS.; for apart from the passages from the *prooemium*, which indeed is only preserved to us by Theophilus, other quotations are also found in Lactantius, which cannot be pointed out in our texts, Lact. vii. 19. 2, viii. 24. 2. The verses too cited by Lactantius, ii. 11. 18, and very probably belonging to the prooemium, are not contained in Theophilus. Lactantius expresses himself in general on the books known to him as follows: *Inst.* 1, 6 (after an enumeration of the *ten* Sibyls), Harum omnium Sibyllarum carmina et feruntur et habentur praeterquam Cymaeae, cujus libri a Romanis occuluntur nec eos ab ullo nisi a quindecimviris inspectos habent.

Et sunt singularum singuli libri, qui quia Sibyllae nomine inscribuntur, unius esse creduntur; suntque confusi, nec discerni ac suum cuique adsignari potest, nisi Erythraeae, quae et nomen suum verum carmini inseruit, et Erythraeam se nominat, ubi praelocuta est, quum esset orta Babylone.

Celsus also testifies to the credit of the Sibyllines among Christians (Orig. *c. Celsus*, vi. 61, vii. 53, 56). Celsus, however, already *charges the Christians with having forged the oracles*, nor were such charges subsequently wanting. Comp. the allusions in Constantine's *Oratio ad sanct. coet.* (= Euseb. *Vita Const.* v.) c. 19. 1. Lactant. *Inst.* iv. 15. 26. Augustine, *de civ. Dei*, xviii. 46.

On the credit and use of the Sibyllines in the *Middle Ages*, see Alexandre's 1st ed. ii. 287–311. Lücken, "Die sibyllinischen Weissagungen, ihr Ursprung und ihr Zusammenhang mit den afterprophetischen Darstellungen christlicher Zeit" (*Katholische Studien*, No. V.), Würzb. 1875. Vogt, "Ueber Sibyllenweissagung" (*Beiträge zur Gesch. der deutschen Sprache und Literatur*, edited by Paul and Braune, vol. iv. 1877, pp. 48–100). Bang, *Voluspá und die sibyllinischen Orakel*, translated from the Danish, Wien 1880.

On the *manuscripts*, see Friedlieb, *De codicibus Sibyllinorum manuscriptis in usum criticum nondum adhibitis commentatio*, Vratislav. 1847. Friedlieb's edition, Introd. p. lxxii. sqq. and App. pp. ix.–xii. Alexandre's 1st ed. vol. i. p. xliii. sqq.; his 2nd ed. pp. xxxviii.–xlii. Volkmann, *Lectiones Sibyllinae*, Pyritz 1861. Bernhardy, *Grundriss der griech. Literatur*, ii. 1 (3rd ed. 1867), p. 452 sq.

On the *editions*, see Gallandi, *Biblioth. patr.* i. p. 81. Fabricius, *Biblioth. graec.* ed. Harles, i. 257–261. Bleek, i. p. 123 sq. Alexandre's 1st ed. vol. i. pp. xxx.–xliii. The first edition superintended by Xystus Betuleius, according to an Augsburg now a Munich manuscript, was brought out by Oporinus in Basle 1545. The same with a Latin translation by Seb. Castalio (which first appeared separately in 1546), Basle 1555. The most esteemed among the older editions is that of Opsopöus, Paris 1599 (repeated in 1607; the account by the bibliographers of a supposed edition of 1589 rests upon a mistake). The edition of Gallaeus, Amsterdam 1689, is less esteemed. The Sibyllines have appeared besides in various collections, *e.g.* in Gallandi's *Bibliotheca veterum patrum*, vol. i. (Venetiis 1788) pp. 333–410; comp. Proleg. pp. lxxvi.–lxxxii. *All these editions contain only the first eight books.* The fourteenth book was first published from a Milan manuscript by Angelo Mai (*Sibyllae liber* xiv. *editore et interprete Angelo Maio*, Mediolan. 1817); and afterwards Books xi. to xiv. from two

Vatican manuscripts by the same (*Scriptorum veterum nova collectio* ed. *ab Angelo Maio*, vol. iii. 3, 1828, pp. 202–215). Everything hithcrto known is combined in the editions of Alexandre (*Oracula Sibyllina, curante C. Alexandre*, 2 vols. Paris 1841–1856. *Editio altera ex priore ampliore contracta, integra tamen et passim aucta, multisque locis retractata*, Paris 1869 [the copious Excursi of the first edition are omitted in this second one]) and of Friedlieb (*Die sibyllinischen Weissagungen vollständig gesammelt, nach neuer Handschriften-Vergleichung, mit kritischen Commentare und metrischer deutscher Uebersetzung*, Leipzig 1852). A Latin translation is added to most editions, a German one to that of Friedlieb. A French one has been commenced by Bouché Leclercq (*Revue de l'histoire des religions*, vol. vii. 1883, pp. 236–248; vol. viii. 1883, pp. 619–634, etc.).

*Contributions to textual criticism :* Volkmann, *De oraculis Sibyllinis dissertatio, supplementum editionis a Friedliebio exhibitae*, Lips. 1853. The same, *Specimen novae Sibyllinorum editionis*, Lips. 1854 (containing the first book). A discussion of Alexandre's edition in the *Philologus*, vol. xv. 1860, p. 317 sqq. The same, *Lectiones Sibyllinae*, Pyritz 1861. X., "Zur Textkritik der sibyllin. Bücher" (*Zeitschr. für wissensch. Theol.* 1861, pp. 437–439). Meineke, "Zu den sibyllinischen Büchern" (*Philologus*, vol. xxviii. 1869, pp. 577–598). Ludwich, "Zu den sibyllinischen Orakeln" (*Neue Jahrbb. für Philol. und Pädagogik*, vol. cxvii. 1878, pp. 240–245). Nauck, "Kritische Bemerkungen " (*Mélanges gréco-romains tirés du bulletin de l'académie impériale des sciences de St. Pétersbourg*, vol. ii. 1859–1866, p. 484 sq.; iii. 1869–1874, pp. 278–282; iv. 1875–1880, pp. 155–157, 630–642). Rzach, "Zur Kritik der Sibyllinischen Weissagungen" (*Wiener Studien*, vol. iv. 1882, pp. 121–129). More in Engelmann's *Biblioth. script. class.* ed. Preuss.

Lists of *the literature on the Sibyllines* in general are given in Fabricius, *Biblioth. graec.* ed. Harles, i. 227–290. Bleek, i. 129–141. Reuss, *Gesch. der heil. Schriften Neuen Testaments*, § 274. Alexandre's 1st ed. ii. 2. 71–82, also 2nd ed. p. 418 sq. Engelmann, *Bibliotheca scriptorum classicorum* (8th ed. revised by Preuss), Div. i. 1880, p. 528 sq. The first to investigate the collection according to correct critical principles was: Bleek, "Ueber die Entstehung und Zusammensetzung der uns in 8 Büchern erhaltenen Sammlung Sibyllinischer Orakel" (*Theologische Zeitschrift*, edited by Schleiermacher, de Wette and Lücke, No. 1, 1819, pp. 120–246 ; No. 2, 1820, pp. 172–239). Comp. also his notice of Lücke's *Einl.* in the *Stud. und Krit.* 1854, pp. 972–979. Gfrörer, *Philo*, vol. ii. 1831, pp. 121–173. Lücke, *Versuch einer vollständigen Einleitung in die*

*Offenbarung des Johannes* (2nd ed. 1852), pp. 66–89, 248–274.
Friedlieb's Introd. to his edition (1852). Alexandre's 1st ed.
ii. 312–439; 2nd ed. p. 21 sqq. Hilgenfeld, *Die jüdische
Apokalyptik in ihrer geschichtlichen Entwickelung* (1857), pp.
51–90. The same, *Zeitschr. für wissenchaftl. Theologie*, vol. iii.
1860, pp. 313–319; xiv. 1871, pp. 30–50. Ewald, "Abhandlung über Entstehung Inhalt und Werth der Sibyllischen
Bucher" (*Transactions of the Göttinger Gesellsch. der Wissensch.*
vol. viii. 1858–1859, hist.-philol. Class. pp. 43–152, also
separately). Frankel, "Alexandrinische Messiashoffnungen"
(*Monatsschr. für Gesch. und Wissensch. des Judenth.* 1859, pp.
241–261, 285–308, 321–330, 359–364). Volkmann in the
"Philologus," vol. xv. 1860, pp. 317–327. Bernhardy, *Grundriss
der griechischen Literatur*, ii. 1 (3rd ed. 1867), pp. 441–453.
Reuss, art. "Sibyllen," in Herzog's *Real-Enc.* 1st ed. xiv. 1861,
pp. 315–329 (2nd ed. xiv. 1884, pp. 179–191). The same,
*Gesch. der heil. Schriften Alten Testaments*, 1881, § 489, 490, 537.
Zündel, *Kritische Untersuchungen über die Abfassungszeit des
Buches Daniel*, 1861, pp. 140–172. Langen, *Das Judenthum in
Palästina zur Zeit Christi*, 1866, pp. 169–174. Badt, *De
oraculis Sibyllinis a Judaeis compositis*, Bresl. 1869. The same,
*Ursprung, Inhalt und Text des vierten Buches der sibyllinischen
Orakel*, Breslau 1878. Larocque, "Sur la date du troisième
livre des Oracles sibyllins" (*Revue archéologique*, new series,
vol. xx. 1869, pp. 261–270). Wittichen, *Die Idee des Reiches
Gottes*, 1872, pp. 134–144, 160 sq. Dechent, *Ueber das erste,
zweite und elfte Buch der sibyllinischen Weissagungen*, Frankf.
1873. The same, "Charakter und Geschichte der altchrist-
lichen Sibyllenschriften" (*Zeitschr. für Kirchengesch.* vol. ii.
1878, pp. 481–509). Hildebrandt, "Das römische Antichris-
tenthum zur Zeit der Offenbarung Johannis und des fünften
sibyllinischen Buches" (*Zeitschr. f. wissensch. Theol.* 1874, pp.
57–95). Delaunay, *Moines et Sibylles dans l'antiquité judeo-
grecque*, Paris 1874. Renan, *Journal des Savants*, 1874, pp.
796–809. Delitzsch, "Versuchte Lösung eines sibyllischen
Räthsels" [on i. 137–146], *Zeitschr. für luth. Theol.* 1877,
pp. 216–218. *The Edinburgh Review*, No. 299, July 1877,
pp. 31–67. Drummond, *The Jewish Messiah*, 1877, pp. 10–17.
Nicolai, *Griechische Literaturgeschichte*, vol. iii. 1878, pp. 335–
338.


## 2. *Hystaspes.*

Ammianus Marcellinus (xxiii. 6. 32–33) relates of Hystaspes
the Mede, the father of King Darius, that during his sojourn

among the Indian Brahmins, he learned from them " the laws
of the motions of the world and stars and *pure religious
customs*" (purosque sacrorum ritus), and then imparted some
of these to the native Magi, who handed them down to posterity. A Greek work under the name of this Hystaspes, who
was thus regarded by antiquity as an authority in religious
matters, was known to the Fathers, by whom the following
indications concerning it are given. According to Justin, the
future destruction of the world by fire was therein predicted.
In the *Praedicatio Petri et Pauli* cited by Clemens Alex. it is
asserted, that Hystaspes plainly referred to the Son of God,
and to the conflict of Messiah and his people with many
kings, and to his stedfastness ($\dot{v}\pi o\mu o\nu\dot{\eta}$) and glorious appearing ($\pi a\rho o\nu\sigma\iota a$). Lastly, according to Lactantius the destruction of the Roman Empire was foretold in it, and also that in
the tribulation of the last times, the pious and believing
would pray to Zeus for assistance, and that Zeus would hear
them and destroy the ungodly. Lactantius finds fault here
only with the circumstance, that what God will do is
ascribed to Zeus, and at the same time laments, that in consequence of the deceit of the daemons, *nothing* is here said of
the sending of the Son of God. From these notices it is
evident, that the work was of an apocalyptic and eschatological tenor. Since Lactantius expressly says, that the
sending of the Son of God to judge the world is *not* mentioned in it, we must regard it as rather Jewish than Christian.
The choice too of Zeus as the name of God, corresponding
more with the literary usages of Hellenistic Judaism than
with those of Christianity, speaks for its Jewish origin.
What the author also of the *Praedicatio Petri et Pauli* says
concerning the appearance of the Messiah prophesied of in
Scripture, does not go beyond the framework of Jewish
expectation. The apparent contradiction between his statement and that of Lactantius may be explained by remem-
bering, that Lactantius only misses the co-operation of the
Messiah at the day of judgment. Yet it may be also possible

that the author of the *Praedicatio Petri et Pauli* had an interpolated copy before him. The limits of the date of composition are fixed by the appearance on the one side of the Roman
Empire as the power hostile to God, on the other by Justin's
acquaintance with the work.

Justin. *Apol.* i. 20: Καὶ Σίβυλλα δὲ καὶ Ὑστάσπης γενήσεσθαι
τῶν φθαρτῶν ἀνάλωσιν διὰ πυρὸς ἔφασαν. Comp. also c. 44.

*Praedicatio Petri et Pauli* in Clemens Alex. *Strom.* vi. 5.
42–43 (comp. Lucke, *Einl. in die Offenb. Joh.* p. 238; Hilgenfeld,
*Nov. Test. extra canonem rec.* fasc. iv. 2nd ed. pp. 57, 63 sq.):
Λάβετε καὶ τὰς Ἑλληνικὰς βίβλους, ἐπίγνωτε Σίβυλλαν, ὡς δηλοῖ ἕνα
θεὸν καὶ τὰ μέλλοντα ἔσεσθαι, καὶ τὸν Ὑστάσπην λαβόντες ἀνάγνωτε, καὶ
εὑρήσετε πολλῷ τηλαυγέστερον καὶ σαφέστερον γεγραμμένον τὸν υἱὸν τοῦ
θεοῦ, καὶ καθὼς παράταξιν ποιήσουσι τῷ Χριστῷ πολλοὶ βασιλεῖς μισοῦντες
αὐτὸν καὶ τοὺς φοροῦντας τὸ ὄνομα αὐτοῦ καὶ τοὺς πιστοὺς αὐτοῦ καὶ τὴν
ὑπομονὴν καὶ τὴν παρουσίαν αὐτοῦ.

Lactantius, *Inst.* vii. 15. 19: Hystaspes quoque, qui fuit
Medorum rex antiquissimus . . . admirabile somnium sub
interpretatione vaticinantis pueri ad memoriam posteris tra-
didit, *sublatum iri ex orbe imperium nomenque Romanum,* multo
ante praefatus, quam illa Troiana gens conderetur. *Ibid.* vii.
18. 2–3: Hystaspes enim, quem superius nominavi, descripta
iniquitate saeculi hujus extremi, pios ac fideles a nocentibus
segregatos ait cum fletu et gemitu extensuros esse ad coelum
manus et imploraturos fidem Jovis; Jovem respecturum ad
terram et auditurum voces hominum atque impios extincturum.
Quae omnia vera sunt, praeter unum, quod Jovem dixit illa
facturum, quae Deus faciet. Sed et illud non sine daemonum
fraude subtractum est, missum iri a patre tunc filium Dei, qui
deletis omnibus malis pios liberet.

Comp. in general: Walch, "De Hystaspe" (*Commentationes
societatis scientt.* Gotting. vol. ii. 1780). Fabricius - Harles,
*Biblioth. graec.* i. 108 sq. A. G. Hoffmann in Ersch and
Gruber's *Allgem. Encykl.* § 2, vol. xiii. 1836, p. 71 sq. Lücke.
*Einl. in die Offenbarung des Johannes,* 2nd ed. pp. 237–240.
Otto's *Anmerkung zu Justin* as above (in his edition of the
*Corpus apologet.*).

### 3  Forged Verses of Greek Poets.

Both Jewish and Christian apologists repeatedly appeal to
the most eminent *Greek poets* to prove, that the more intelligent
among the Greeks held correct views concerning the nature

of God, His unity, spirituality and supramundane character.
Many such quotations, especially in Clemens Alexandrinus,
are really taken from the genuine works of these poets, and
have been skilfully selected and explained by the apologists.[79]
But among these genuine quotations are also to be found not
a few which have been palpably forged in the interest of
either Jewish or Christian apologetic. The works where such
forged verses have been discovered are chiefly the following:
1. Aristobulus in Eusebius, *Praeparatio evangelica*, xiii. 12.
2. Clemens Alexandrinus, *Strom.* v. 14; also given in Euseb.
*Praep. evang.* xiii. 13; comp. also *Protrept.* vii. 74. 3. The
pseudo - Justinian *Cohortatio ad Graecos*, c. 15 and 18.
4. The pseudo-Justinian work, *De monarchia*, c. 2–4 (the two
latter in Otto's *Corpus apologetarum christian.* vol. iii.). The
authors to whom the verses are ascribed, are: the great tragic
poets Aeschylus, Sophocles, Euripides; the writers of comedies,
Philemon, Menander, Diphilus; a large fragment is ascribed
to Orpheus; and certain verses on the Sabbath to Hesiod,
Homer and Linus (or Callimachus).

In forming a judgment concerning *the origin of these pieces*
the following considerations are of importance. Almost all
the portions, which come under notice, are found both in
Clemens Al. *Str.* v. 14. 113–133 (=Eus. *Pr.* xiii. 13. 40–
62, ed. Gaisford), and in the pseudo-Justinian work, *De
monarchia*, c. 2–4. Aristobulus and the *Cohortatio ad Graecos*
have only single verses and such as are found in the others
also. Both in Clement and in the work *De monarchia* however, the suspicious portions stand pretty thick together; in
the *De monarchia* indeed almost without other accessories. It
is thus clear that either one made use of the other or that

---

[79] So *e.g.* the celebrated commencement of the *Phaenomena* of Aratus
(third century B.C.): Ἐκ Διὸς ἀρχώμεσθα, τὸν οὐδέποτ᾽ ἄνδρες ἐῶσιν ἄρρητον,
etc., from which is derived the saying quoted, Acts xvii. 28: τοῦ γὰρ καὶ
γένος ἐσμέν. The Jewish philosopher Aristobulus (in Euseb. *Praep. evang.*
xiii. 12. 6, ed. Gaisford) already quotes this verse; also Theophilus, *ad
Autol.* ii. 8. Clemens Alex. *Strom.* v. 14. 101=Euseb. *Praep. evang.* xiii.
13. 26.

both drew from a common source. A strict observation shows
however that the former supposition cannot be accepted.
For though the pieces quoted are almost all identical, they
are more completely and accurately given now by one now
by another.[80]   It is then indubitable that both *drew from a
common source*, in which all the suspected pieces were probably
found together.   What this source was moreover we are
directly told by Clement: it was the *work of the pseudo-
Hecataeus on Abraham*.   For Clement introduces the first of
the suspected quotations, a supposed portion of Sophocles,
with the words (*Strom.* v. 14. 113 = Eus. *Pr.* xiii. 13. 40, ed.
Gaisford): ʽΟ μὲν Σοφοκλῆς, ὥς φησιν ʽΕκαταῖος ὁ τὰς
ἱστορίας συνταξάμενος ἐν τῷ κατ᾽ ῎Αβραμον καὶ τοὺς Αἰγυπτίους, ἄντικρυς ἐπὶ τῆς σκηνῆς ἐκβοᾷ.   Böckh already showed
that he on the whole correctly perceived the state of matters
by ascribing all the quotations from the scenic poets (tragic
and comic) to the pseudo-Hecataeus.   Hence it was no
advance when Nauck, *e.g.* (in his edition of the *Fragm. tragic.*),
and Otto (in his notes in the *Corp. apologet.*) again spoke of
Christian forgeries, for the work of the pseudo-Hecataeus is
certainly Jewish.   The verdict of Böckh must however be
also extended to the large portion from Orpheus and to the
verses of Hesiod, Homer and Linus on the Sabbath, which

---

[80] *De monarchia*, c. 3, *e.g.* comp. with Clemens Alex. *Strom.* v. 14. 121–122
(=Euseb. *Praep. ev.* xiii. 13. 47–48), is instructive.  First a portion from
Sophocles is given in *De monarchia* (ἔσται γάρ, ἔσται, etc.).   Then Clement
has the same portion but divided into two halves; and the second half is
introduced by the formula : καὶ μετ᾽ ὀλίγα αὖθις ἐπιφέρει.   *Undoubtedly
Clement is here the more original.*   The author of *De monarchia* joined
together the two pieces which are not directly connected.   A contrary
relation takes place in the next following, but in Clement preceding, piece :
οἴει σὺ τοὺς θανόντας, of which Clement ascribes the whole to Diphilus,
while the author of *De monarchia* ascribes the first and longer half to
Philemon, the second and shorter to Euripides.   In the latter ascription he
is correct, for it contains a few genuine verses of Euripides, which are
completed by spurious ones (see Dindorf's note in his edition of
Clement).   *Here then the work " De monarchia " preserves the original;
Clement by an oversight ascribing the two unconnected pieces to one
author.*

are already cited by Aristobulus (in Euseb. xiii. 12) and the
forgery of which is therefore set by many, *e.g.* Valckenaer,
and also Böckh to the credit of Aristobulus. The Orphean
piece is also found both in Clem. Alex. *Strom.* v. 14. 123 sqq.
(= Euseb. xiii. 13. 50 sqq.) and in the work *De monarchia*,
c. 2, in the midst of the forged verses of the tragic and comic
poets. And the testimonies of Hesiod and Homer concerning
the Sabbath stand at least near in Clement (*Strom.* v. 14. 107
= Euseb. xiii. 13. 34), and in juxtaposition, along with the
Orphean piece, certainly in Aristobulus. It is hence very probable that these forgeries also belong to the pseudo-Hecataeus.

If our conjecture is correct, these forgeries belong to the
*third century before Christ;* for such is the date of the pseudo-
Hecataeus (see next paragraph). It seems that numerous
passages from Greek poets were collected in his work, as
testimonies to the true belief in God, that among them many
were certainly genuine, but that these not seeming sufficiently
powerful to the author he enhanced and completed them by
verses of his own making. The work was certainly in the
hands of Clemens Alex. and the author of *De monarchia* in
the original.

Comp. in general : Valckenaer, *Diatribe de Aristobulo Judaeo*
(Lugd. Bat. 1806), pp. 1–16, 73–125. Böckh, *Graecae tragoe-
diae principum, Aeschyli Sophoclis Euripidis, num ea quae
supersunt et genuina omnia sint et forma primitiva servata, an
eorum familiis aliquid debeat ex iis tribui* (Heidelb. 1808),
pp. 146–164 (treats especially on the Jewish forgeries).
Gfrörer, *Philo,* ii. 74 sqq. (on the Orphean verses). Dähne,
*Geschichtliche Darstellung der jüdisch-alexandrinischen Religions-
Philosophie,* ii. 89–94, 225–228. Meineke, *Menandri et Phile-
monis reliquiae,* Berol. 1823. The same, *Fragmenta comicorum
Graecorum,* vol. iv. Berol. 1841 (among others the Fragments
of Philemon, Menander, Diphilus). Nauck, *Tragicorum Graecorum fragmenta,* Lips. 1856. Cobet in Λόγιος Ἑρμῆς ἐκδ. ὑπὸ
Κόντου, vol. i. (Leyden 1866) pp. 176, 454, 459–463, 524.
Dindorf's notes on the passages in question in his edition of
*Clem. Alex.* Otto's notes on the passages in question in his
edition of the *Corpus apologet. christ.* vol. iii. Herzfeld, *Gesch.
des Volkes Jisrael,* iii. 566–568 (on the verses quoted by

Aristobulus). Freudenthal, *Alexander Polyhistor*, pp. 166–169.
Huidekoper, *Judaism at Rome* (New York 1876), pp. 336–342.
The several portions are (according to their order in the
pseudo-Justinian work *De monarchia*) as follows :—

1. Twelve verses of Aeschylus (Χώριζε θνητῶν τὸν θεόν) on the
elevation of God above every creature, *De monarchia*, c. 2 (Otto's
*Corpus apologetarum*, 3rd ed. vol. iii. p. 130); Clemens Alex.
*Strom.* v. 14. 131 = Euseb. *Praep. ev.* xiii. 13. 60, ed. Gaisford.
Böckh, p. 150 sq. Nauck, *Tragicorum Graec. fragm.* p. 100.

2. Nine verses of Sophocles (Εἷς ταῖς ἀληθείαισιν) on the unity
of God, who made heaven and earth, and on the folly of idolatry,
*De monarchia*, c. 2 (Otto's *Corpus apolog.* 3rd ed. vol. iii. p. 132);
Clemens Alex. *Strom.* v. 14. 113 = Euseb. *Praep. evang.* xiii.
13. 40, ed. Gaisford ; Clem. *Protrept.* vii. 74; Pseudo-Justin.
*Cohort. ad. Graec.* c. 18 ; Cyrill. Alex. *adv. Julian.* ed. Spanh.
p. 32 ; Theodoret, *Graecarum affectionum curatio*, c. vii. *s. fin.*
(*Opp.* ed. Schulze, iv. 896); Malalas, ed. Bonnens. p. 40 sq.,
Cedrenus, ed. Bonnens. i. 82. The two first verses are also in
Athenagoras, *Suppl.* c. 5. Böckh, p. 148 sq. Nauck, *Trag.
Graec. Fragm.* p. 284 sq. Müller, *Fragm. hist. graec.* ii. 196.
Dindorf's note to Clem. *Strom.* v. 14. 113.

3. Two verses, ascribed in *De monarchia*, c. 2, to the comic
poet Philemon, but in Clemens Alex. *Protrept.* vi. 68 to
Euripides (Θεὸν δὲ ποῖον), treat of God as one who sees everything,
but is himself unseen. On their spuriousness, see Meineke,
*Fragmenta comicorum Graec.* iv. 67 sq. Nauck, *Trag. Graec.
Frag.* p. 552. Otto, *Corp. Apologet.* 3rd ed. vol. iii. p. 132,
note 21. Dindorf's note to Clem. *Protr. l.c.*

4. A long piece attributed to Orpheus is extant in two
different recensions, which materially differ from each other.
The shortest is that in the two pseudo-Justinian works, *de
monarchia*, and *Cohort. ad graec.* c. 15. The text is identical in
both, only that in *De monarchia* the two introductory verses are
omitted. The *Cohortatio* also gives the text with an abbreviation
in the midst (Cyrill. Alex. *adv. Julian.* ed. Spanheim, p. 26).
The contents of the piece (one-and-twenty verses in the *Cohort.*)
turn upon the thought, that there is but one God who made
and still governs all things, who is enthroned in supramundane
glory in heaven, invisible, yet everywhere present. If further
proof of the Jewish origin of these verses were needed, it is
clearly found in the thought, borrowed from Isa. lxvi. 1, that
heaven is God's throne and earth His footstool—

Οὗτος γὰρ χάλκειον ἐπ' οὐρανὸν ἐστήρικται
Χρυσέῳ ἐνὶ θρόνῳ, γαίης δ' ἐπὶ ποσσὶ βέβηκε.[81]

---

[81] The same verses run according to Clem. Alex. *Strom.* v. 14. 124 =

It is worthy of remark, that the author lays stress on the notion, that evil too is sent by God—

Οὗτος δ' ἐξ ἀγαθοῖο κακὸν θνητοῖσι δίδωσι
Καὶ πόλεμον κρυόεντα καὶ ἄλγεα δακρυόεντα.

The whole instruction is addressed to Musaeus the son of Orpheus (to the latter according to *Cohort.* c. 15). According to *Monarchia*, c. 2, it is contained in the "Testament of Orpheus" in which, repenting of his former teaching of 360 gods, he proclaimed the one true God (μαρτυρήσει δέ μοι καὶ Ὀρφεύς, ὁ παρεισαγαγὼν τοὺς τριακοσίους ἐξήκοντα θεούς, ἐν τῷ Διαθῆκαι ἐπιγραφομένῳ βιβλίῳ, ὁπότε μετανοῶν ἐπὶ τούτῳ φαίνεται ἐξ ὧν γράφει). Comp. also *Cohort.* c. 15 and 36, and especially in Theophilus, *ad Autol.* iii. 2: τί γὰρ ὠφέλησεν . . . Ὀρφέα οἱ τριακόσιοι ἐξήκοντα πέντε θεοί, οὓς αὐτὸς ἐπὶ τέλει τοῦ βίου ἀθετεῖ, ἐν ταῖς Διαθήκαις αὐτοῦ λέγων ἕνα εἶναι θεόν.

(*b*) A longer recension of the same Orphean fragment is given by Aristobulus in Euseb. *Praep. evang.* xiii. 12. 5. At its commencement it coincides on the whole with the before-named recension, but adds considerably more towards the close, especially a reference to the Chaldaean (Abraham), who alone attained to the true knowledge of God. The passage, according to which God is also the inflicter of evil, is here corrected into its opposite—

Αὐτὸς δ' ἐξ ἀγαθῶν θνητοῖς κακὸν οὐκ ἐπιτέλλει
Ἀνθρώποις· αὐτῷ δὲ χάρις καὶ μῖσος ὀπηδεῖ,
Καὶ πόλεμος καὶ λοιμὸς ἰδ' ἄλγεα δακρυόεντα.

Aristobulus names as the source the poems of Orpheus κατὰ τὸν ἱερὸν λόγον (Euseb. *Praep.* xiii. 12. 4: ἔτι δὲ καὶ Ὀρφεὺς ἐν ποιήμασι τῶν κατὰ τὸν Ἱερὸν Λόγον αὐτῷ λεγομένων οὕτως ἐκτίθεται).

(*c*) The quotations in Clemens Alex. *Protrept.* vii. 74; *Strom.* v. 12. 78, and especially *Strom.* v. 14. 123–127 = Euseb. *Praep. evang.* xiii. 13. 50–54, ed. Gaisford, represent a third recension. Theodoret, *Graecarum affectionum curatio*, ii. (*Opp.* ed. Schulze, iv. 735 sq.)[82] again draws from Clement. Clement gives the

Euseb. *Praep. ev.* xiii. 13. 51 (and almost exactly so according to Aristobulus in Euseb. *Praep.* xiii. 12. 5)—

Αὐτὸς δ' αὖ μέγαν αὖτις ἐπ' οὐρανὸν ἐστήρικται
Χρυσέῳ εἰνὶ θρόνῳ, γαίῃ δ' ὑπὸ ποσσὶ βέβηκεν.

Clement already notices the agreement with Isa. lxvi. 1.

[82] Since it can be proved that Theodoret elsewhere borrows such quotations from Clement, there can be no doubt that his text is in the main a combination of Clem. *Strom.* v. 12. 78 and v. 14. 124. Only the first three verses in Theodoret agree in part more with Aristobulus than with Clem. *Protr.* vii. 74.

text only piecemeal, and broken up into separate quotations. But taking all these together, it is clearly seen, that not only the whole portion, given by Aristobulus, but also considerably more was in his hands. Much as he agrees in the main with Aristobulus (especially in having the passage concerning the Chaldee), this only on the other hand makes the coincidences in many details with the pseudo-Justinian works the more striking. Clement also has in particular the passage concerning the infliction of evil by God in its original form, like the pseudo-Justinian works (*Strom.* v. 14. 126 = Euseb. *Praep.* xiii. 13. 53). On the work of Orpheus, from which the passage is taken, Clement agrees with the others in saying, that Orpheus, "after teaching the orgies and the theology of idols, made a *recantation* conformable with truth by singing, though late, the truly holy doctrine" (*Protrept.* vii. 74: 'Ορφεὺς, μετὰ τὴν τῶν ὀλίων ἱεροφαντίαν καὶ τῶν εἰδώλων τὴν θεολογίαν, παλινῳδίαν ἀληθείας εἰσάγει, τὸν ἱερὸν ὄντως ὀψέ ποτε ὅμως δ' οὖν ᾄδων λόγον).

On the relation of the three recensions to each other Lobeck (*Aglaophamus*, i. 438 sqq.) has brought forward the view, that the recension of the Justinian works is the oldest, that of Clemens a more recent and that of Aristobulus the most recent, the latter being of a date subsequent to Clemens Alexandrinus (i. 448: Clementis certe temporibus posteriorem). There is however no constraining reason for the last notion. We have ourselves acknowledged, that the text of Aristobulus is in *one* point secondary in comparison with the other two. That is not however saying, that it is so in every respect. It may be regarded as certain, that none of the three recensions is *directly* the source of the others. Nor can the short portion in the Justinian works be the archetype, for it is evidently only a fragment from a larger copy, probably with abbreviations in the text. The three recensions will thus fall back upon a common source, which has afterwards been subjected to manifold variations. And this source may very well have been the *pseudo-Hecataeus*. In any case this Orphean passage is one of the boldest forgeries ever attempted. It is *a supposed legacy of Orpheus to his son Musaeus, in which, having arrived at the close of his life, he expressly recalls all his other poems, which are dedicated to polytheistic doctrines and proclaims the alone true God.* According to Suidas (*Lex. s.v.* 'Ορφεὺς) there were ἱεροὺς λόγους ἐν ῥαψωδίαις κδ' of Orpheus. This legacy, to speak with Clement, was to be his *true* ἱερὸς λόγος. Comp. on this Jewish piece: Gottfr. Hermann, *Orphica*, pp. 447–453 (the text). Valckenaer, *De Aristobulo*, pp. 11–16. 73–85. Lobeck, *Aglaophamus*, i. 438–465 (the most thorough investigation). Gfrörer, *Philo*, ii. 74 sqq. Dähne, *Geschichtliche Darstellung der jüd.-alex. Religionsphilo-*

*sophie*, ii. 89–94, 225–228. Abel, *Orphica*, pp. 144–148 (the text). On Orpheus and the Orphean literature in general: Fabricius, *Biblioth. graec.* ed. Harles, i. 140–181. Gottfr. Hermann, *Orphica*, Lips. 1805 (collection of the text and fragments). Lobeck, *Aglaophamus sive de theologiae mysticae Graecorum causis*, 2 vols. Regim. Pr. 1829 (chief work). Klausen, art. "Orpheus," in Ersch and Gruber's *Allgem. Encyclopädie*, § 3, vol. vi. 1835, pp. 9–42. Preller, art. "Orpheus," in Pauly's *Real-Enc.* v. 992–1004. Bernhardy, *Grundriss der griech. Literatur*, ii. 1, 3rd ed. 1867, pp. 408–441. Nicolai, *Griech. Literaturgesch.* i. 445–447, iii. 330–335. Abel, *Orphica*, Lips. 1885 (texts and fragments). Still more literature in Engelmann's *Biblioth. script. class.* ed. Preuss.

5. The next Jewish piece quoted in *De monarchia* is eleven verses of Sophocles on the future destruction of the world by fire, and the different lots of the righteous and unrighteous (Ἔσται γάρ, ἔσται κεῖνος αἰώνων χρόνος), *De monarchia*, c. 3 (Otto's *Corp. apol.* iii. 136). In Clemens Alex. *Strom.* v. 14, 121–122 = Euseb. *Pr.* xiii. 13. 48, the same verses are cited as words of the τραγῳδία without naming Sophocles. In Clemens they are also divided into halves by the remark, καὶ μετ᾽ ὀλίγα αὖθις ἐπιφέρει, while pseudo-Justin combines the two halves into a whole. Clement does not give the verses on the different lots of the righteous and unrighteous in this connection, but in the preceding fragment, which he quotes from Diphilus, where they are more suitable (*Strom.* v. 14. 121 = Euseb. *Praep.* viii. 13. 47). Böckh, p. 149 sq. Nauck, *Tragicorum Graec. fragm.* p. 285 sq.

6. Ten verses of the comic poet Philemon on the certain punishment of even hidden sins by the all-knowing and just God (Οἴει σὺ τοὺς θανόντας), and ten verses of Euripides on the same theme (Ἄφθονον βίου μῆκος), *De monarchia*, c. 3 (Otto's *Corp. apolog.* iii. 136–140). Part of the Euripidean verses is genuine, the rest spurious (see Dindorf's note to Clemens and Nauck). In Clemens Alex. *Strom.* v. 14. 121 = Euseb. *Praep.* xiii. 13. 47, both pieces are attributed to the comic poet Diphilus. Theodoret, *Graec. affect. curatio*, c. vi. (*Opp.* ed. Schulze, iv. 854 sq.), also gives the text of Clemens in the extract. Valckenaer, *De Aristobulo*, pp. 1–8. Böckh, pp. 158–160. Meineke, *Fragm. comicorum Graec.* iv. 67. Nauck, *Tragic. Graec. fragm.* p. 496 sq.

7. Twenty-four verses of Philemon on the theme that a moral life is more needful and of more value than sacrifice (Εἴ τις δὲ θυσίαν προσφέρων), *De monarchia*, c. 4 (Otto's *Corp. apol.* iii. 140 sq.). In Clemens Alex. *Strom.* v. 14. 119–120 = Euseb. *Praep. ev.* xiii. 13. 45–46, the same verses are attributed to Menander. Böckh, p. 157 sq., thinks that the piece is based upon single genuine verses.

8. Among the other pieces cited from scenic poets in *De monarchia* and in Clement there are also a few more suspicious verses, which are introduced in *De monarchia*, c. 5 (Otto's *Corp. apol.* iii. 150 sq.), by the formula Μένανδρος ἐν Διφίλῳ. In Clemens, *Strom.* v. 14. 133 = Euseb. *Praep. ev.* xiii. 13. 62, they are ascribed to Diphilus. They summon to the worship of the one true God. Comp. Meineke, *Fragm. com. Graec.* iv. 429 sq. Perhaps too the verses of Sophocles in Clem. *Strom.* v. 14. 111 = Euseb. *Praep.* xiii. 13. 38, in which Zeus is represented in a very unflattering light, are also spurious. Comp. Nauck, *Tragic. Graec. fragm.* p. 285. Dindorf's note to Clemens.

9. Lastly, in this connection must be noticed the verses on the Sabbath, to which Aristobulus and Clement appeal, Aristobulus in Euseb. *Praep. ev.* xiii. 12. 13–16. Clem. Alex. *Strom.* v. 14. 87 = Euseb. *Praep. ev.* xiii. 13. 34. They are—(*a*) two verses of Hesiod ; (*b*) three verses of Homer ; (*c*) five verses of Linus, for whom Clement erroneously has Callimachus. The verses are a mixture of genuine and spurious. The divergences in the text between Clement and Aristobulus are but unimportant. Comp. Valckenaer, *De Aristobulo*, pp. 8, 10, 89–125. Herzfeld, *Gesch. des Volkes Jisrael*, iii. 568. Schneider, *Callimachea*, vol. ii. Lips. 1873, p. 412 sq.


### 4. *Hecataeus.*


Hecataeus of Abdera (not to be confounded with the far more ancient geographer Hecataeus of Miletus about 500 B.C.) was according to Josephus a contemporary of Alexander the Great and of Ptolemy Lagos (Joseph. *c. Apion.* 22 : Ἑκαταῖος δὲ ὁ ᾽Αβδηρίτης, ἀνὴρ φιλόσοφος ἅμα καὶ περὶ τὰς πράξεις ἱκανώτατος, Ἀλεξάνδρῳ τῷ βασιλεῖ συνακμάσας καὶ Πτολεμαίῳ τῷ Λάγου συγγενόμενος). This statement is also confirmed by other testimony. According to Diogenes, *Laert.* ix. 69, Hecataeus was a hearer of the philosopher Pyrrho, a contemporary of Alexander. According to Diodor. Sic. i. 46, he made, in the time of Ptolemy Lagos, a journey to Thebes. He was a philosopher and historian, and seems to have lived chiefly at the court of Ptolemy. A work on the Hyperboreans (Müller, *Fr.* 1–6), a History of Egypt (Müller, *Fr.* 7–13), and in Suidas' *Lex. s.v.* Ἑκαταῖος, a work, περὶ τῆς ποιήσεως

'Ομήρου καὶ 'Ησιόδου, of which no other trace is found, are mentioned as his writings.

Under the name of this Hecataeus of Abdera there existed a book "*on the Jews*," or, as it is also entitled, "*on Abraham*," concerning which we have the following testimonies:—
(1) Pseudo-Aristeas quotes Hecataeus as authority for the notion that profane Greek authors do not mention the Jewish law just because the doctrine held forth in it is a sacred one (Aristeas, ed. Mor. Schmidt in Merx' *Archiv.* i. 259 = Havercamp's *Josephus*, ii. 2. 107 · διὸ πόρρω γεγόνασιν οἵ τε συγγραφεῖς καὶ ποιηταὶ καὶ τὸ τῶν ἱστορικῶν πλῆθος τῆς ἐπιμνήσεως τῶν προειρημένων βιβλίων, καὶ τῶν κατ' αὐτὰ πεπολιτευμένων καὶ πολιτευομένων ἀνδρῶν, διὰ τὸ ἁγνήν τινα καὶ σεμνὴν εἶναι τὴν ἐν αὐτοῖς θεωρίαν, ὥς φησιν Ἑκαταῖος ὁ Ἀβδηρίτης. See the passage also in Euseb. *Praep. ev.* viii. 3. 3, and more freely rendered in Joseph. *Antt.* xii. 2. 3). (2) Josephus says that Hecataeus not only incidentally alluded to the Jews, but also wrote a book concerning them (*contra Apion.* i. 22: οὐ παρέργως, ἀλλὰ περὶ αὐτῶν Ἰουδαίων συγγέγραφε βιβλίον; comp. i. 23: βιβλίον ἔγραψε περὶ ἡμῶν). He then gives in the same passage (*contra Apion.* i. 22 = Bekker's ed. vol. vi. pp. 202, 1–205, 22) long extracts from this work concerning the relations between the Jews and Ptolemy Lagos, their fidelity to the law, the organization of their priesthood, and the arrangement of their temple; lastly, a passage is given at the close in which Hecataeus relates an anecdote of which he was himself a witness at the Red Sea: a Jewish knight and archer, who belonged to the expeditionary corps, shot a bird dead, whose flight the augur was anxiously observing, and then derided those who were angry for their awe concerning a bird who did not even foreknow its own fate. Eusebius (*Praep. ev.* ix. 4) also gives single pieces from these extracts of Josephus. From the same source Josephus (*contra Apion.* ii. 4) gives the information that Alexander the Great bestowed upon the Jews the country of Samaria as a district exempt from taxation as a reward for their fidelity. While

according to all this there can be no doubt, that the book
treated on the Jews in general, Josephus tells us in another
passage, that Hecataeus not only mentions Abraham, but also
wrote a book concerning him (*Antt.* i. 7. 2 = Euseb. *Praep. ev.*
ix. 16 : μνημονεύει δὲ τοῦ πατρὸς ἡμῶν ᾿Αβράμου Βηρωσσός
. . . ᾿Εκαταῖος δὲ καὶ τοῦ μνησθῆναι πλέον τι πεποίηκε·
βιβλίον γὰρ περὶ αὐτοῦ συνταξάμενος κατέλιπε).    Is
this identical with the work on the Jews ?  To the decision
of this question the two following pieces of testimony mainly
contribute.    (3) According to Clemens Alexandrinus, the
spurious verses of Sophocles were contained in the work of
Hecataeus *on Abraham and others* (Clem. Al. *Strom.* v. 14. 113
= Euseb. *Praep. ev.* xiii. 40 : ὁ μὲν Σοφοκλῆς, ὥς φησιν ᾿Εκα-
ταῖος ὁ τὰς ἱστορίας συνταξάμενος ἐν τῷ κατ᾽ ῎Αβραμον
καὶ τοὺς Αἰγυπτίους, ἄντικρυς ἐπὶ τῆς σκηνῆς ἐκβοᾷ).
(4) Origen says that Hecataeus in his work *on the Jews* was so
strong a partisan for the Jewish people, that Herennius Philo
(beginning of the second century after Christ)[83] at first doubted,
in his work on the Jews, whether the work was indeed the
production of Hecataeus the historian, but afterwards said
that, if it were his, Hecataeus had been carried away by
Jewish powers of persuasion, and had embraced their doctrines
(Orig. *contra Cels.* i. 15 : καὶ ᾿Εκαταίου δὲ τοῦ ἱστορικοῦ
φέρεται περὶ ᾿Ιουδαίων βιβλίον, ἐν ᾧ προστίθεται μᾶλλόν
πως ὡς σοφῷ τῷ ἔθνει ἐπὶ τοσοῦτον, ὡς καὶ ᾿Ερέννιον Φίλωνα
ἐν τῷ περὶ ᾿Ιουδαίων συγγράμματι πρῶτον μὲν ἀμφιβάλλειν,
εἰ τοῦ ἱστορικοῦ ἐστι τὸ σύγγραμμα· δεύτερον δὲ λέγειν, ὅτι,
εἴπερ ἐστὶν αὐτοῦ, εἰκὸς αὐτὸν συνηρπάσθαι ἀπὸ τῆς παρὰ
᾿Ιουδαίοις πιθανότητος καὶ συγκατατεθεῖσθαι αὐτῶν τῷ λόγῳ).
According to these testimonies of Clement and Origen, there
can be no doubt that the work "*on the Jews*" was as much
forged by a Jew as that "*on Abraham.*"   We cannot therefore
conclude,—as according to the extracts in Josephus we might
feel inclined,—that the work on the Jews is genuine, and

---

[83] On Herennius Philo or Philo Byblius, see Müller, *Fragm. hist. Graec.*
560 sqq.

that on Abraham spurious. The two are on the contrary very probably identical, and the different titles to be explained by the circumstance that the work was indeed entitled περὶ Ἀβράμου, but dealt in fact περὶ Ἰουδαίων.

Certain however as is, especially according to the information of Origen, the spuriousness of the work " on the Jews," it is still probable that it is founded *on genuine portions of Hecataeus.* In the extracts of Josephus we already get a partial impression of genuineness. To this is to be added, that Diodorus Siculus gives a long portion from Hecataeus on the Jews, their origin, religious rites, political constitution, manners and customs, which from its whole tenor is certainly not derived from the pseudo-Jewish Hecataeus, but from the real Hecataeus, and indeed not as Diodorus mistakenly states from Hecataeus of Miletus, but from Hecataeus of Abdera.[84] It is thus probable, that the latter in his Egyptian history went into details concerning the Jews, and that the Jewish counterfeiter thence derived a portion of his material.

The scanty fragments are not sufficient to give us a clear idea of the design of the whole work. Since it dealt in the first instance with Abraham, it is probable that the life and acts of that patriarch served as the point of departure for a general description and glorification of Judaism. In this the honourable history of the Jews (*e.g.* the favour shown them by Alexander the Great and Ptolemy Lagos), as well as the purity of their religious ideas, were referred to. In the description of the latter, the forged verses of the Greek poets would be inserted, for the purpose of proving that the nobler Greeks also were quite in harmony with the views of Judaism (see the preceding section). The work seems to have been tolerably extensive and to have contained much genuine as well as spurious material from the Greek poets. It thus became a mine for subsequent Jewish and Christian apologists.

---

[84] The passage of Diodorus here in question (from Book xl. of his larger work) has been preserved by Photius, *Biblioth. cod.* 244. See the wording also in Müller, *Fragm. hist. Graec.* ii. 391–393.

*Its date of composition* may be approximately determined. It is already cited by pseudo - Aristeas, who flourished not later than about 200 B.C. (see the next section). Thus pseudo-Hecataeus would have lived in the third century before Christ.

The fragments of both the real and the spurious Hecataeus of Abdera are collected in Müller, *Fragmenta historicorum Graecorum,* ii. 384–396. Comp. in general: Hecataei Abderitae, *philosophi et historici Eclogae sive fragmenta integri olim libri de historia et antiquitatibus sacris veterum Ebraeorum graece et latine cum notis Jos. Scaligeri et commentario perpetuo P. Zornii,* Altona 1730. Eichhorn's *Allg. Bibliothek der bibl. Literatur,* v. 1793, pp. 431–443. Creuzer, *Historicorum graec. antiquiss. fragm.* (Heidelb. 1806) pp. 28–38. Kanngiesser in Ersch and Gruber's *Allgem. Encykl.* sec. ii. vol. v. (1829) p. 38 sq. Dähne, *Geschichtliche Darstellung der jüd.-alex. Religionsphilosophie,* ii. 216–219. Cruice, *De Flavii Josephi in auctoribus contra Apionem afferendis fide et auctoritate* (Paris 1844), pp. 64–75. Vaillant, *De historicis, qui ante Josephum Judaicas res scripsere* (Paris 1851), pp. 59–71. Müller, *Fragm. hist. Graec. l.c.* Creuzer, *Theol. Stud. und Krit.* 1853, pp. 70–72. Klein, *Jahrbb. für class. Philol.* vol. lxxxvii. 1863, p. 532. Ewald, *Gesch. des Volkes Israel,* ii. 131 sqq., iv. 320 sq. Freudenthal, *Alexander Polyhistor,* pp. 165 sq., 178. J. G. Müller, *Des Flavius Josephus Schrift gegen den Apion* (1877), p. 170 sqq.

## 5. *Aristeas.*

The celebrated Epistle of Aristeas to Philocrates on the translation of the Jewish law into Greek also belongs to the class of writings under consideration. The legend related forms only the external frame of the statement. The whole is in truth *a panegyric upon Jewish law, Jewish wisdom and the Jewish name in general from the mouth of a heathen.* The two individuals Aristeas and Philocrates are not known to history. Aristeas in the narrative gives himself out as an official of King Ptolemy II. Philadelphus, and as held in high esteem by that monarch (ed. Mor. Schmidt in Merx' *Archiv,* i. 261. 13–14 and 262. 8–10 = Havercamp's *Josephus,* ii.

2. 108). Philocrates was his brother (Merx' *Archiv*, i. 254.
10, 275. 20-21 = Havercamp's *Josephus*, ii. 2. 104, 115),
an earnest-minded man, eager for knowledge and desiring to
appropriate all the means of culture which the age afforded. It
is self-evident that both were not Jews (Aristeas says of the
Jews, 255. 34–256. 2 : τὸν γὰρ πάντων ἐπόπτην καὶ κτίστην
θεὸν οὗτοι σέβονται, ὃν καὶ πάντες, ἡμεῖς δὲ μάλιστα προσο-
νομάζοντες ἑτέρως Ζῆνα καὶ Δία). Aristeas then relates to
his brother Philocrates—and indeed as one who was both an
eye-witness and assistant—the manner in which the translation of the Jewish law into Greek took place. The librarian
Demetrius Phalereus called the attention of King Ptolemy II.
Philadelphus (for it is he who is intended, p. 255. 6 and
17) to the fact that the law of the Jews was yet lacking in
his great library, and that its translation into Greek was
desirable for the sake of its incorporation in the royal collection of books. The king obeyed this suggestion and presently
sent Andreas, the captain of his body-guard, and Aristeas to
Jerusalem, to Eleazar the Jewish high priest with rich
presents, and with the request that he would send him
experienced men capable of undertaking this difficult task.
Eleazar was ready to fulfil the king's desire and sent him
seventy-two Jewish scholars, six from each of the twelve
tribes. Aristeas then gives a full description of the splendid
presents sent on the occasion by Ptolemy to Eleazar, also a
description of the town of Jerusalem, of the Jewish temple,
the Jewish worship, nay, of the land, all which he had himself seen on the occasion of this embassy. The whole
description has evidently the tendency of glorifying the
Jewish people, with their excellent institutions and luxuriant
prosperity. With the same purpose does Aristeas then
communicate the purport of a conversation, he had carried
on with the high priest Eleazar concerning the Jewish
law. Aristeas was, by reason of this conversation, so much
persuaded of the excellency of the Jewish law, that he held
it necessary to explain to his brother Philocrates " its holi-

ness and its naturalness (reasonableness) " (283. 12–13 : τὴν σεμνότητα καὶ φυσικὴν διάνοιαν τοῦ νόμου προῆγμαι διασαφῆσαί σοι). Especially are the folly of idolatry and the reasonableness of the Jewish laws of purity thoroughly treated of. When the Jewish scholars arrived at Alexandria, they were received with distinguished honours by the king and were for seven days invited day after day to the royal table. During these repasts the king continually addressed to the Jewish scholars in turn a multitude of questions on the most important matters of politics, ethics, philosophy and prudence, which they answered so excellently, that the king was full of admiration for the wisdom of these Jews. Aristeas himself too, who was present at these repasts, could not contain himself for astonishment at the enormous wisdom of these men, who answered off-hand the most difficult questions, which with others usually require long consideration. After these festivities a splendid dwelling upon the island of Pharos, far from the tumult of the city, was allotted to the seventy-two interpreters, where they zealously set to work. Every day a portion of the translation was despatched in such wise, that by a comparison of what each had independently written, a harmonious common text was settled (306. 22–23 : οἱ δ' ἐπετέλουν ἕκαστα σύμφωνα ποιοῦντες πρὸς ἑαυτοὺς ταῖς ἀντιβολαῖς). The whole was in this manner completed in seventy-two days. When it was finished, the translation was first read to the assembled Jews, who acknowledged its accuracy with expressions of the highest praise. Then it was also read to the king, who " was much astonished at the intelligence of the lawgiver " (308. 8–9 : λίαν ἐξεθαύμασε τὴν τοῦ νομοθέτου διάνοιαν), and commanded, that the books should be carefully preserved in his library. Lastly the seventy-two interpreters were dismissed to Judea, and rich presents for themselves and the high priest bestowed upon them.

This survey of the contents shows, that *the object of the narrative is by no means that of relating the history in the abstract, but the history so far as it shows, what esteem and admiration were felt for the Jewish law and for Judaism in general by even heathen authorities, such as King Ptolemy and his ambassador Aristeas.* For the tendency of the whole culminates in the circumstance, that praise was accorded to the Jewish law by *heathen* lips. The whole is therefore in the first place intended for *heathen* readers. They are to be shown what interest the learned Ptolemy, the promoter of science, felt in the Jewish law, and with what admiration his highly placed official Aristeas spoke of it and of Judaism in general to his brother Philocrates. When then it is also remarked at the close, that the accuracy of the translation was acknowledged by the Jews also, this is not for the purpose of commending the translation to Jews, who might still oppose it, but to testify to the heathen, that they had in the present translation an accurate version of the genuine Jewish law, and it is *they*, the heathen, who are thus invited to read it.

No consensus concerning *the date* of this book has been arrived at by critics. It seems however tolerably certain to me, that it originated not later than about 200 years before Christ. The legend, that it was Demetrius Phalereus who suggested the whole undertaking to Ptolemy Philadelphus is unhistorical, not only in its details, but in the main point; for Demetrius Phalereus in the time of Ptolemy Philadelphus no longer lived at court at Alexandria (see above, p. 161). When then the Jewish philosopher Aristobulus designates just Demetrius Phalereus as the originator of the undertaking (in Euseb. *Praep. evang.* xiii. 12. 2, see the passage above, p. 160), it is very probable that the book in question was already in his hands. Now Aristobulus lived in the time of Ptolemy Philometor, about 170—150 B.C., and the result thus obtained is supported on internal grounds also. The period when the Jewish people were leading a peaceful and pros-perous existence under the conduct of their high priest and in a relation of very slight dependence upon Egypt, *i.e. the*

*period before the conquest of Palestine by the Seleucidae,* evidently
forms the background of the narrative. There is nowhere any
allusion to the complications and difficulties which begin with
the Seleucidian conquest. The Jewish people and their high
priest appear as almost politically independent. At all events
it is to a time of peace and prosperity that we are transferred.
Especially is it worthy of remark, that *the fortress of Jerusalem
is in the possession of the Jews* (Merx' *Archiv,* i. 272. 10 to
273. 4 = Havercamp's *Josephus,* ii. 2. 113). Whether this
stood on the same spot as the one subsequently erected by
Antiochus Epiphanes (1 Macc. i. 33) or not, the author is in
any case acquainted with only the one in the possession of the
Jews. The fortress however erected by Antiochus remained
in the possession of the Seleucidae till the time of the high
priest Simon (142–141 B.C., 1 Macc. xiii. 49–52). Of this
fact the author has evidently as yet no knowledge, and as little
of the subsequent princely position of the high priest; to him
the high priest is simply the high priest, and not also prince or
indeed king. In every respect then it is the circumstances of
the Ptolemaic age that are presupposed. If the author has
only artificially reproduced them, this is done with a certainty
and a refinement which cannot be assumed in the case of
a pseudonymous author living after it. Hence the opinion,
that the book originated not later than 200 B.C., is justified.[85]

The legend of this book has been willingly accepted and
frequently related by Jews and Christians. The first who
betrays an acquaintance with it is Aristobulus in Euseb. *Praep.
evang.* xiii. 12. 2. The next is Philo, *Vita Mosis,* lib. ii. § 5–7

[85] It may also be mentioned, that Mendelssohn (*Jenaer Literaturzeitung,*
1875, No. 23) places the composition in the first half of the first century
before Christ, because it is said of the Jewish land that it had "good
harbours" (λιμένας εὐκαίρους), viz. Ascalon, Joppa, Gaza, Ptolemais (Merx'
*Archiv,* 272. 23 sqq.=Havercamp's *Josephus,* ii. 2. 114). This presupposed
the union of these seaport towns with the Jewish land by Alexander
Jannaeus. But Ascalon and Ptolemais were never united at all to the
Jewish district, not even by Alexander Jannaeus. Hence the inference is
inconclusive. The notion of Grätz, that pseudo-Aristeas wrote under
Tiberius (*Monatsschr. für Gesch. und Wissensch. des Judenthums,* 1876, pp.
289 sqq., 337 sqq.), is worth as much as many others of this scholar's fancies.

(ed. Mangey, ii. 138–141). Josephus reproduces, *Antt.* xii. 2, a great portion of this composition almost verbally. Comp. also *Antt. proem.* 3, *contra Apion.* ii. 4, *fin.* In rabbinic literature also are found some echoes, though quite confused ones, of this legend. See Lightfoot, *Opp.* ed. Roterod. ii. 934 sqq. Frankel, *Vorstudien zu der Septuaginta* (1851), p. 25 sqq. Berliner, *Targum Onkelos* (1884), ii. 76 sqq.

*The passages of the Fathers and Byzantines* are most conveniently found collected (with full verbal correctness) in Gallandi, *Bibliotheca veterum patrum*, vol. ii. (Venetiis 1788) pp. 805–824. The legend is here reproduced with various modifications, especially the two following:—1. That the interpreters translated independently of each other and yet verbally coincided (the exact opposite of which is found in Aristeas, viz. that agreement was only obtained by comparison). 2. That not only the law but the entire Holy Scriptures were translated by the seventy-two (in Aristeas only the former is dealt with). See on the various forms of the legend: Eichhorn's *Repertorium für bibl. und morgenländ. Literatur*, i. (1777) p. 266 sqq., xiv. (1784) p. 39 sqq. The passages given in Gallandi are the following: Justin. *Apol.* i. 31. *Dial. c. Tryph.* c. 71. Pseudo-Justin. *Cohortatio ad Graec.* c. 13. Irenaeus, *adv. haer.* iii. 21. 2 (Greek in Euseb. *Hist. eccl.* v. 8. 11 sqq.). Clemens Alex. *Strom.* i. 22. 148 sq. Tertullian. *Apologet.* c. 18. Anatolius in Euseb. *Hist. eccl.* vii. 32. 16. Eusebius gives in his *Praeparatio evangelica*, viii. 2–5 and 9, large portions of the book of Aristeas verbatim; comp. also viii. 1. 8, ix. 38. *Chronic.* ed. Schoene, ii. 118 sq. (*ad ann. Abrah.* 1736). Cyrill. *Hieros. cateches.* iv. 34. Hilarius, *Pictav. prolog. ad librum psalmorum.* The same, *tractat. in psalmum* ii., *tractat. in psalmum* cxviii. Epiphanius, *De mensuris et ponderibus*, § 3, 6, 9–11 (fully and specially). Hieronymus, *Praefat. in version. Genes.* (*Opp.* ed. Vallarsi, ix. 3 sq.). The same, *Praefat. in librum quaestion. hebraic.* (Vallarsi, iii. 303). Augustinus, *De civitate dei*, xviii. 42–43. Chrysostomus, *Orat.* i. *adversus Judaeos.* The same, *homil.* iv. *in Genes.* Theodoret, "praefat. in psalmos." Pseudo-Athanasii *Synopsis scripturae sacrae*, c. 77. Cosmas Indicopleustes, *Topograph. christ.* lib. xii. Joannes Malala, *Chronogr.* lib. viii. ed. Dindorf, p. 196. *Chronicon paschale*, ed. Dindorf, i. 326. Georgius Syncellus, ed. Dindorf, i. 516–518. Georgius Cedrenus, ed. Bekker, i. 289 sq. Joannes Zonaras, *Annal.* iv. 16 (after Joseph. *Antt.* xii. 2). The five last-named are contained in the Bonn *Corpus scriptorum historiae Byzantinae.*

On the manuscripts of this book of Aristeas, comp. Moriz Schmidt in Merx' *Archiv für wissenschaftliche Erforschung des alten Testamentes*, i. 244 sqq.; and especially Lumbroso,

*Recherches sur l'économie politique de l'Egypte sous les Lagides*
(Turin 1870), p. 351 sqq. The latter specifies seven other manu-
scripts besides the two Parisian ones compared by Moriz Schmidt.
On the *editions* (and translations), see Fabricius, *Biblioth.
graec.* ed. Harles, iii. 660 sqq. Rosenmüller, *Handbuch für die
Literatur der bibl. Kritik und Exegese*, vol. ii. (1798) p. 344 sqq.
Moriz Schmidt's above-named work, p. 241 sqq. Lumbroso's
above-named work, p. 359 sqq. The *editio princeps* of the
Greek text was issued by Oporinus in Basle 1561. The book
has since been often reprinted in Havercamp's edition of
*Josephus* and elsewhere (ii. 2, pp. 103–132), and in Gallandi's
*Bibliotheca patrum* (ii. 773–804). Much however remains to
be done for the establishment of a critical text. Moriz Schmidt
has taken a first step towards it by his edition in Merx' *Archiv
für wissenschaftl. Erforschung des alten Testamentes*, vol. i.
(1869) pp. 241–312, for which two Parisian manuscripts were
compared.

The older literature on Aristeas is specified by Rosenmüller
as above, ii. 387–411; also in Fürst, *Biblioth. Jud.* i. 51–53.
Comp. especially : Hody, *Contra historiam Aristeae de LXX.
interpretibus dissertatio*, Oxon. 1685. The same, *De bibliorum
textibus originalibus, versionibus Graecis et Latina vulgata*, Oxon.
1705 (in this larger work the earlier dissertation is reprinted
and enriched with notes). Van Dale, *Dissertatio super Aristea
de LXX. interpretibus*, Amstelaed. 1705. Rosenmüller, *Handbuch für die Literatur der bibl. Kritik und Exegese*, vol. ii.
(1798) pp. 358–386. Gfrörer, *Philo*, ii. 61–71. Dähne,
*Geschichtliche Darstellung der jüdisch-alexandr. Rel.-Philosophie*,
ii. 205–215. Zunz, *Die gottesdienstl. Vorträge der Juden*, p. 125.
Herzfeld, *Gesch. des Volkes Jisrael*, i. 263 sq., iii. 545–547.
Frankel, *Monatsschr. für Gesch. und Wissensch. des Judenth.*
1858, pp. 237–250, 281–298. Ewald, *Gesch. des Volkes Israel*,
iv. 322 sqq. Hitzig, *Gesch. des Volkes Israel*, p. 338 sqq.
Nöldeke, *Die alttestamentliche Literatur* (1868), pp. 109–116.
Cobet in Λόγιος Ἑρμῆς ἐκδ. ὑπὸ Κόντου, vol. i. (Leyden 1866)
pp. 171 sqq., 177–181. Kurz, *Aristeae epistula ad Philocratem*,
Bern 1872 (comp. *Literar. Centralbl.* 1873, No. 4). Freudenthal,
*Alexander Polyhistor*, pp. 110–112, 124 sq., 141–143, 149 sq.,
162–165, 203 sq. Grätz, "Die Abfassungszeit des Pseudo-
Aristeas" (*Monatsschr. für Gesch. und Wissensch. des Judenth.*
1876, pp. 289 sqq., 337 sqq.). Papageorgios, *Ueber den Aristeas-
brief*, München 1880 (comp. Hilgenfeld's *Zeitschr. für wissensch.
Theol.* 1881, p. 380 sq.). Reuss, *Gesch. der heil. Schriften Alten
Testaments* (1881), § 515. The introductions to the Old Testa-
ment of Jahn, Eichhorn, Bertholdt, Herbst, Scholz, Hävernick,
De Wette-Schrader, Bleek, Keil, Reusch, Kaulen.

## 6. *Phocylides.*

Phocylides of Miletus, the old composer of apothegms, lived (according to the statements in Suidas, *Lex. s.v. Φωκυλίδης,* and Euseb. *Chron. ad Olymp.* 60, ed. Schoene, ii. 98) in the sixth century before Christ. Few of his genuine sayings have been preserved. He must however have been held as an authority in the department of moral poetry. For in the Hellenistic period a didactic poem (ποίημα νουθετικόν) was interpolated in his work by a Jew (or Christian ?) giving in 230 hexameters moral instruction of the most diversified kind. Having frequently been used as a school-book in the Byzantine period, it has been preserved in many manuscripts and often printed since the sixteenth century. The contents of these verses are almost exclusively ethical. It is but occasionally that we find the one true God and the future retribution also referred to. The moral doctrines, which the author inculcates, extend to the most various departments of practical life, some-what in the manner of Jesus the son of Sirach. *In their details however they coincide most closely with the Old Testament, especially with the Pentateuch,* echoes of which are heard throughout in the precepts on civil relations (property, marriage, pauperism, etc.). Even such special precepts are found here as that which enjoins, that when a bird's nest is taken, only the young ones must be kept, but the mother let fly (Deut. xxii. 6, 7 = Phocylides, vers. 84–85), or that the flesh of animals killed by beasts of prey may not be eaten (Deut. xiv. 21; Ex. xxii. 30 = Phocylides, vers. 139, 147–148). There can thus be no doubt, that the author was either a Jew or a Christian. The former is the prevailing opinion since the fundamental investigation of Bernays; Harnack has recently advocated the latter.[86] Both

---

[86] In the notice of Bernays' "Gesammelten Abhandlungen" in the *Theol. Literaturzeitung,* 1885, p. 160. Harnack chiefly relies upon ver. 104, where it is said of the risen, that they "afterwards become gods" (ὀπίσω δὲ θεοὶ τελέθονται). This is certainly a specifically Christian view, which Bernays gets rid of by changing θεοί into νέοι.

views have their difficulties. For there is nothing in the work either specifically Jewish or specifically Christian. The author designedly ignores the Jewish ceremonial law, and even the Sabbatic command, which is more striking here than in the Sibyllines, because the author in other respects enters into the details of the Mosaic law. On the other side there is no kind of reference to Christ, nor above all to any religious interposition for salvation. It is just bare morality which is here preached. Hence a *certain* decision as to the Jewish or Christian origin of the poem is scarcely possible. The scale against the Christian origin of the poem seems to me especially turned by the fact, that the author's moral teaching coincides only with the Old Testament and not with the moral legislation of Christ, as we have it in the synoptists. Of the latter there is in this poem, as far as I can see, no certain traces. And this is scarcely conceivable in a Christian author, who means to preach morality. If at the same time there are still single expressions or propositions in the poem, which betray a Christian hand (like θεοί, ver. 104), they must be set to the account of the Christian tradition, and how freely this dealt with the text is shown us by the portion, which by some chance or other got into the collection of the Sibyllines (*Sibyll.* ii. 56—148 = Phocylides, 5—79). The text as there presented diverges pretty much from that elsewhere handed down and plainly shows the hand of a Christian reviser.

If then this poem is of Jewish origin, it is of especial interest just through its lack of anything specifically Jewish. The design of the author is first of all to labour only for Jewish morality. He has not even the courage to speak strongly against idolatry. The two fundamental religious notions of Judaism, the unity of God and the future retribution, are indeed to be found in him also, and he indirectly advocates them. But he does it in so reticent a manner as to make it evident that morality occupies the first place in his regards. His Judaism is even paler than that of Philo.

For the *date of composition* no other limits can be laid

down than those which are given for Judaeo-Hellenistic
literature in general. It could not have appeared later than
the first century after Christ, and in all probability considerably earlier. It might seem strange that it is not cited by
Christian apologists, by a Clement or a Eusebius, who use so
much else of this kind.[87] But the strangeness disappears as
soon as we consider the object for which such quotations are
made, viz. in the first place to produce heathen testimony to
the *religious* ideas of Christianity, to the notions of the unity
of God and the future retribution, and these were not expressed
in Phocylides as forcibly as could be desired.

The most careful monograph on this poem is Bernays, *Ueber
das Phokylideische Gedicht, ein Beitrag zur hellenistischen
Litteratur*, Breslau 1856 (reprinted in Bernays, *Gesammelte
Abhandlungen*, published by Usener, 1885, vol. i. pp. 191–261).
The text of the poem with critical apparatus is best given in
Bergk, *Poetae lyrici Graeci*, vol. ii. (3rd ed. 1866) pp. 450–475
(the same, pp. 445–449, also the fragment of the genuine
Phocylides). Bernays as above gives the text according to his
own recension. On the older editions, especially in the collections of gnomic writers, see Schier in his separate edition, Lips.
1751. Fabricius-Harles, *Biblioth. Graec.* i. 704–749. Eckermann, art. "Phokylides," in Ersch and Gruber's *Allgem. Encyklopädie*, § 3, vol. xxiv. (1848) p. 485. Fürst, *Biblioth. Judaica*,
iii. 96 sqq. The separate edition: Phocylidis, etc., *carmina cum
selectis adnotationibus aliquot doct. virorum Graece et Latine, nunc
denuo ad editiones praestantissimas rec. Schier*, Lips. 1751, must
be brought forward. A German translation is given by Nickel,
*Phokylides Mahngedicht in metrischer Uebersetzung*, Mainz 1833.
Comp. in general: Wachler, *De Pseudo-Phocylide*, Rinteln
1788. Rohde, *De veterum poetarum sapientia gnomica,
Hebraeorum imprimis et Graecorum*, Havn. 1800. Bleek,
*Theol. Zeitschr.*, edited by Schleiermacher, de Wette and Lücke,
i. 1819, p. 185 (in the article on the Sibyllines). Dähne,
*Geschichtl. Darstellung der jüd.-alex. Religionsphilosophie*, ii.
222 sq. Eckermann, art. "Phokylides," in Ersch and Gruber's
*Allg. Encyklop.* § 3, vol. xxiv. (1848) pp. 482–485. Teuffel in
Pauly's *Real-Enc.* v. 1551. Alexandre's 1st ed. of the *Oracula
Sibyllina*, ii. 401–409. Bernhardy, *Grundriss der griechischen*

---

[87] The first traces of its being used are found in Stobaeus and in certain
classic scholia. See Bernhardy, *Grundriss der griechischen Litteratur*, ii. 1
(3rd ed. 1867), p. 520.

*Litteratur*, ii. 1 (3rd ed. 1867), pp. 517–523. Ewald, *Gesch. des Volkes Israel*, vi. 405, 412. Freudenthal, *Die Flavius Josephus beigelegte Schrift über die Herrschaft der Vernunft* (1869), p. 161 sqq. Leop. Schmidt's notice of Bernays' work in the *Jahrbb. für class. Philol.* vol. lxxv. (1857) pp. 510–519. Goram, "De Pseudo-Phocylide" (*Philologus*, vol. xiv. 1859, pp. 91–112). Hart, "Die Pseudophokylideia und Theognis im codex Venetus Marcianus 522" (*Jahrbb. für class. Philol.* vol. xcvii. 1868, pp. 331–336). Bergk, "Kritische Beiträge zu dem sog. Phokylides" (*Philologus*, vol. xli. 1882, pp. 577–601). Sitzler, "Zu den griechischen Elegikern" (*Jahrbb. für class. Philol.* vol. cxxix. 1884, p. 48 sqq.). Phocylides, *Poem of Admonition*, with introd. and commentaries by Feuling, trans. by Goodwin, Andover, Mass. 1879. Still more literature in Fürst, *Biblioth. Judaica*, iii. 96 sqq.; and in Engelmann's *Bibliotheca scriptorum classicorum*, ed. Preuss.


### 7. *Smaller Pieces perhaps of Jewish Origin under Heathen Names.*


1. *Letters of Heraclitus ?*—Epistolography was a favourite kind of literature in the later times of antiquity. The letters of eminent rhetoricians and philosophers were collected as a means of general culture. Letters were composed and also feigned under the names of famous persons, and generally for the purpose of furnishing entertaining and instructive reading. To the numerous species of the latter kind belong also nine supposed letters of Heraclitus, to which Bernays has devoted very thorough research. In two of them, the fourth and seventh, he thinks he can recognise the hand of "a believer in Scripture," and indeed in such wise, that the fourth is merely interpolated, but the seventh entirely composed by such an one. In fact the austere polemic against the worship of images in the fourth letter sounds quite Jewish or Christian, as does also the stern morality preached in the seventh, in which especially the partaking of "live" flesh, *i.e.* flesh with the blood, is denounced (τὰ ζῶντα κατεσθίετε; comp. on the Jewish and Christian prohibition, Acts xv. 29, and Div. ii. vol. ii. p. 318). It must however, as Bernays himself

acknowledges, remain a question, whether this "believer in the Scriptures" was a Jew or a Christian.

Bernays, *Die heraklitischen Briefe, ein Beitrag zur philosophischen und religionsgeschichtlichen Litteratur* (Berlin 1869), pp. 26 sqq., 72 sqq., 110 sq. Bernays gives also the text of the letters with a German translation. The latest edition of the *Epistolographi* in general is Hercher, *Epistolographi Graeci recensuit*, etc., Paris, Didot, 1873. A separate edition of the letters of Heraclitus: Westermann, *Heracliti epist. quae feruntur*, Lips. 1857 (*Universitäts-progr.*). Comp. on the entire epistolographic literature, Fabricius-Harles, *Biblioth. graec.* i. 166–703. Nicolai, *Griechische Literaturgeschichte*, 2nd ed. ii. 2 (1877), p. 502 sqq.

2. *A letter of Diogenes?*—Among the fifty-one supposed letters of Diogenes, Bernays thinks that one, the twenty-eighth, may be referred to the same source as the seventh of Heraclitus. In fact it contains a similar moral sermon to the latter.

Bernays, *Lucian und die Kyniker* (Berlin 1879), pp. 96–98. See the text in all the editions of the *Epistolographi*, *e.g.* in Hercher, *Epistolographi Graeci*, pp. 241–243.

3. *Hermippus?*—Hermippus Callimachius, who lived under Ptolemy III. and IV., and therefore in the second half of the third century before Christ, composed a large number of biographies of eminent persons. Among the pieces of information thence obtained, two arrest our attention. According to Origen, *contra Cels.* i. 15, it was said in the first book " on the lawgivers," that Pythagoras derived his philosophy from the Jews (Δέγεται δὲ καὶ "Ερμιππον ἐν τῷ πρώτῳ περὶ νομοθετῶν ἱστορηκέναι, Πυθαγόραν τὴν ἑαυτοῦ φιλοσοφίαν ἀπὸ ᾿Ιουδαίων εἰς "Ελληνας ἀγαγεῖν). According to Josephus, *contra Apion.* i. 22, a similar remark was contained in the first book " on Pythagoras." The notice of Josephus is however much more particular and accurate than that of Origen. For according to Josephus, Hermippus relates, that Pythagoras taught " not to go over a place where an ass had sunk on his

knees, to abstain from turbid water and to avoid all slander and blasphemy," and on this Hermippus then remarked : " Pythagoras did and taught these things, imitating and adopting the opinions of the Jews and Thracians " (ταῦτα δ' ἔπραττε καὶ ἔλεγε τὰς Ἰουδαίων καὶ Θρακῶν δόξας μιμούμενος καὶ μεταφέρων εἰς ἑαυτόν). *Thus Hermippus did not denote the philosophy of Pythagoras as a whole, but only those special doctrines as borrowed from the Jews.* For the words which follow in Josephus: λέγεται γὰρ ὡς ἀληθῶς ὁ ἀνὴρ ἐκεῖνος πολλὰ τῶν παρὰ Ἰουδαίοις νομίμων εἰς τὴν αὐτοῦ μετενεγκεῖν φιλοσοφίαν, are no longer the words of Hermippus but of Josephus. In the reference of Josephus, the words of Hermippus contain nothing which he might not actually have written. It is otherwise with the reference of Origen. If this had been accurate we should have had to conclude, that a Jew had interpolated the work of Hermippus. But Origen himself intimates, that he had not seen the work of Hermippus; he says only: " Hermippus *is said* to have declared." It is most probable, that he is here relying solely on the passage of Josephus, which he reproduces but incorrectly. Thus we have here *not a Jewish forgery* but only an inaccurate reference of Origen to authenticate.

C. Müller, *Fragm. hist. graec.* iii. 35–54, has admitted both passages among genuine fragments of Hermippus (*Fr.* 2 and 21). Comp. for and against their genuineness: Dähne, *Geschichtl. Darstellung der jüd.-alex. Religionsphilosophie,* ii. 219 sq. Kellner, *De fragmentis Manethonianis* (1859), p. 42. Hilgenfeld, *Einl. in das N. T.* p. 168, note. Freudenthal, *Alex. Polyh.* pp. 178, 192. J. G. Müller, *Des Flavius Josephus Schrift gegen den Apion* (1877), p. 161 sqq.

4. *Numenius?*—The Pythagorean and Platonist Numenius (towards the end of the second century after Christ) as the genuine precursor of Neo-Platonism was acquainted with and after his fashion made use of the Jewish Scriptures, nay of Jewish tradition (*e.g.* concerning Jannes and Jambres, see above, p. 149). Origen bears decided testimony to this, when he says, *contra Cels.* iv. 51, that he knows that Numenius

quotes " in many passages of his works sayings of Moses and
the prophets, and convincingly explains them in an allegorical
manner, as *e.g.* in the so-called Epops, in the books on numbers and in those on space " (ἐγὼ δ' οἶδα καὶ Νουμήνιον . . .
πολλαχοῦ τῶν συγγραμμάτων αὐτοῦ ἐκτιθέμενον τὰ Μωϋσέως
καὶ τῶν προφητῶν καὶ οὐκ ἀπιθάνως αὐτὰ τροπολογοῦντα,
ὥσπερ ἐν τῷ καλουμένῳ "Εποπι καὶ ἐν τοῖς " περὶ ἀριθμῶν "
καὶ ἐν τοῖς " περὶ τόπου "). Comp. also Orig. *c. Cels.* i. 15 ;
Zeller, *Philos. d. Griechen*, iii. 2. 217 sq. We have no reason
to mistrust this testimony. It is not however credible, that
Numenius should have used just this expression: τί γάρ
ἐστι Πλάτων ἢ Μωυσῆς ἀττικίζων, which Clemens Alex. and
others attribute to him.[88] If it really stood in a work
of Numenius, it would certainly have to be laid to the
account of a Jewish editor. We see however the real state of
affairs from Eusebius, who only says, that this saying is
ascribed to Numenius, viz. by oral tradition.[89] The saying
then is *not a Jewish forgery*, but only an exaggeration due to
oral tradition of the real view of Numenius.

Comp. on this question : Freudenthal, *Alex. Polyhistor*, p. 173,
note. On Numenius in general : Zeller, *Die Philosophie der
Griechen*, iii. 2 (3rd ed. 1881), pp. 216–223.

5. *Hermes Trismegistus ?*—The god Hermes, and that as Trismegistus, was first represented as an author by the Egyptians.
According to Clem. Alex. *Strom.* vi. 4. 37, there were forty-two
books of Hermes, thirty-six of which contained the entire philosophy of the Egyptians, the other six were devoted to medicine.
Tertullian, *de anima*, c. 2 and 33, is already acquainted with
books of Mercurius Aegyptius, which taught a Platonizing
psychology. From the latter circumstance it is seen, that
the later Platonists especially had already taken posses-

---

[88] Clem. Alex. *Strom.* i. 22. 150. Hesychius Miles. in Müller, *Fragm.
hist. graec.* iv. 171. Suidas, *Lex. s.v.* Νουμήνιος.

[89] Euseb. *Praep. ev.* xi. 10. 14, ed. Gaisford : Εἰκότως δῆτα εἰς αὐτὸν
ἐκεῖνο τὸ λόγιον περιφέρεται, δι' οὗ φάναι μνημονεύεται, τί γάρ ἐστι Πλάτων ἢ
Μωυσῆς ἀττικίζων;

sion of this pseudonym. Thus then the works of Hermes, which have come down to us, are of Neo-Platonic origin. They are first cited by Lactantius, and were probably of the third century after Christ. Their position with respect to the heathen popular religions is a thoroughly positive one. " Just the defence of national and particularly of Egyptian religion is one of their chief objects " (Zeller, iii. 2. 234 sq.). But all the pieces are not the work of one author, nor are they even all of heathen origin. *Neither can the co-operation of Jewish hands in the production of this literature be proved.* On the contrary, what is not of heathen seems to be of Christian origin (c. 1 and 13 of the so-called Poemander).

Comp. on this whole literature : Fabricius-Harles, *Biblioth. graec.* i. 46–94. Bähr in Pauly's *Real-Enc.* iii. 1209–1214. Ueberweg, *Grundriss der Gesch. der Philosophie,* i. (4th ed. 1871) p. 256. Erdmann, *Grundriss der Gesch. der Philos.* 3rd ed. 1878, vol. i. pp. 179–182. Zeller, *Die Philosophie der Griechen,* iii. 2 (3rd ed. 1881), pp. 224–235. Erdmann and Zeller did not enter into a thorough description of the Hermes works till the more recent editions of their works as cited above.

# § 34. PHILO THE JEWISH PHILOSOPHER.

## I. THE LIFE AND WRITINGS OF PHILO.

### *The Literature.*[1]

Mangey's edition of the works of Philo, the Prolegomena and especially the notes prefixed to the several works.

Fabricius, *Bibliotheca graeca*, ed. Harles, vol. iv. (1795) pp. 721–750.

Scheffer, *Quaestionum Philonianarum part. I. sive de ingenio moribusque Judaeorum per Ptolemaeorum saecula*, Marburgi 1829. Idem, *De usu Philonis in interpretatione Novi Testamenti*, Marburgi 1831.

Gfrörer, *Philo und die alexandrinische Theosophie*, vol. i. (1831) pp. 1–113.

Creuzer, " Zur Kritik der Schriften des Juden Philo" (*Theol. Stud. und Krit.* 1832, pp. 3–43).

Dähne, " Einige Bemerkungen über die Schriften des Juden Philo" (*Theol. Stud. und Krit.* 1833, pp. 984–1040). Idem, art. "Philon" in Ersch and Gruber's *Allg. Encyklopädie*, § 3, vol. xxiii. (1847) pp. 435–454.

Grossman, *De Philonis Judaei operum continua serie et ordine chronologico Comment.* Pts. i. ii. Lips. 1841–1842.

Steinhart, art. " Philo" in Pauly's *Real-Enc. der class. Alterthumswissensch.* vol. v. (1848) p. 1499 sq.

J. G. Müller, art. "Philo" in Herzog's *Real-Enc.* 1st ed. xi. (1859) pp. 578–603. Idem, *Ueber die Texteskritik der Schriften des Juden Philo*, Basel 1839 (printed in J. G. Müller, *Des Juden Philo Buch von der Weltschöpfung*, 1841, pp. 17–45).

Ewald, *Gesch. des Volkes Israel*, 3rd ed. vol. vi. (1868) pp. 257–312.

Ueberweg, *Grundriss der Gesch. der Philosophie*, 4th ed. i. (1871) pp. 240–249.

---

[1] The literature here named refers only to Philo as an author in general. For the literature on Philo's doctrine, see No. II. below. For the literature on his several works, see in the places where they are treated of. Still more literature is given in: Fabricius, *Biblioth. graec.* ed. Harles, iv. 721 sqq. Fürst, *Biblioth. Judaica*, iii. 87–94. Engelmann, *Bibliotheca scriptorum classicorum* (8th ed. revised by Preuss), vol. i. 1880, pp. 546–548.

Hausrath, *Neutestamentliche Zeitgesch.* 2nd ed. vol. ii. (1875) pp. 131–182.

Delaunay, *Philon d' Alexandrie, écrits historiques, influence luttes et persécutions des juifs dans le monde romain,* 2nd ed. Paris 1870.

Treitel, *De Philonis Judaei sermone,* Bresl. 1872 (30 pp.).

Siegfried, *Die hebräischen Worterklärungen des Philo und die Spuren ihrer Einwirkung auf die Kirchenväter* (37 pp. gr. 4), 1863.   Idem, " Philonische Studien " (Merx's *Archiv für Erforschung des A. T.* ii. 2, 1872, pp. 143–163).   Idem, " Philo und der überlieferte Text der LXX." (*Zeitschr. für wissenschaftl. Theol.* 1873, pp. 217 sqq., 411 sqq., 522 sqq.). Idem, *Zur Kritik der Schriften Philo's* (Ebendas. 1874, p. 562 sqq.)

Siegfried, *Philo von Alexandria als Ausleger des Alten Testaments an sich selbst und nach seinem geschichtlichen Einfluss betrachtet.  Nebst Untersuchungen über die Gräcität Philo's,* Jena 1875.

Nicolai, *Griechische Literaturgeschichte,* 2nd ed. ii. 2 (1877), pp. 653–659.

Grätz, *Gesch. der Juden,* vol. iii. (3rd ed. 1878) pp. 678–683.

Bernh. Ritter, *Philo und die Halacha, eine vergleichende Studie,* Leipzig 1879.

Reuss, *Geschichte der heil. Schriften Alten Testaments* (1881), § 566–568.

Hamburger, *Real-Enc. für Bibel und Talmud,* vol. ii. (1883) arts. " Philo " and " Religionsphilosophie."

Zöckler, art. " Philo " in Herzog's *Real-Enc.* 2nd ed. xi. (1883) pp. 636–649.

Among Jewish Hellenists none other, besides Josephus, takes so eminent a position as Philo the Alexandrian.   Even by reason of the extent of his works, which have been handed down, he is one of the most important *to us.*   Of no other can we form even approximately, so clear a picture of his thoughts, and literary and philosophic labours.   But he is also in himself evidently the most illustrious among all those, who strove to unite Jewish belief with Hellenic culture, to be the means of imparting to Jews the cultivation of the Greeks, and to Greeks the religious knowledge of the Jews.   No other Jewish Hellenist was so fully saturated with the wisdom of the Greeks; no other enjoyed equal consideration in history.   This is testified by the immense influence which he exercised upon after times and above all upon Christian theology the inheritor of the Judaeo-Hellenistic.[2]

---

[2] On the consideration enjoyed by Philo in antiquity, comp. especially Euseb. *Hist. eccl.* ii. 4. 3 : πλείστοις ἀνὴρ οὐ μόνον τῶν ἡμετέρων ἀλλὰ καὶ τῶν ἀπὸ τῆς ἔξωθεν ὁρμωμένων παιδείας ἐπισημότατος.

We have but a few scanty notices concerning his life. The assertion of Jerome, that he was of priestly race,[3] has no support from older sources, nor does Eusebius know anything of it. According to Josephus[4] he was a brother of the Alabarch Alexander, and consequently a member of one of the most aristocratic families of Alexandrian Jews.[5] The sole event in his life, which can be chronologically fixed, is his participation in the embassy to Caligula in A.D. 40, of which he has himself furnished an account in the work *De Legatione ad Cajum*. As he was then of advanced age[6] he may have been born about the year 20–10 B.C. The Christian legend, that he met St. Peter at Rome in the reign of Claudius, is of no historical value.[7]

Much has been lost of Philo's numerous works. But thanks to his being a favourite with the Fathers and Christian theologians the bulk of them has been preserved. Of the collective editions that of Mangey is, notwithstanding its deficiencies, the most valuable.[8] Among recent contributions

---

[3] *De viris illustribus*, c. 11 (*Opp.* ed. Vallarsi, ii. 847): Philo Judaeus, natione Alexandrinus, *de genere sacerdotum*.

[4] *Antt.* xviii. 8. 1.

[5] Ewald (*Gesch.* vi. 259) and Zeller (*Philos. der Griechen*, 3rd ed. iii. 2. 339) have of late incorrectly rejected the statement of Josephus and declared Philo to have been the uncle of Alexander, because a nephew of Philo named Alexander is mentioned in the work published by Aucher, *De ratione animalium*, pp. 123 sq., 161 (in the 8th vol. of Ritter's edition). But it is nowhere said in it that this Alexander was the Alabarch.

[6] He designates himself (*Legat. ad Cajum*, § 28, ed. Mangey, ii. 572) as Φρονεῖν τι δοκῶν περιττότερον καὶ δι᾽ ἡλικίαν καὶ τὴν ἄλλην παιδείαν. In the beginning of his work composed shortly after (§ 1, Mang. ii. 572) he calls himself γέρων.

[7] Euseb. *Hist. eccl.* ii. 17. 1. Hieronymus, *De viris illustr.* c. 11 (*Opp.* ed. Vallarsi, ii. 847). Photius, *Bibliotheca cod.* 105. Suidas, *Lex. s.v.* Φίλων (verbally according to the Greek translation of Jerome).

[8] On the editions of Philo's works (or of separate parts) and of the translations, comp. Fabricius-Harles, *Biblioth. gr.* iv. 746–750. S. F. W. Hoffmann, *Lexicon bibliogr.* vol. iii. p. 231 sqq. Fürst, *Biblioth. Judaica*, iii. 87–92. Graesse, *Trésor de livres rares et précieux*, vol. v. (1864) pp. 269–271. The *editio princeps* is: Φίλωνος Ἰουδαίου εἰς τα του Μωσέως κοσμοποιητικα, ιστορικα, νομοθετικα. Του αυτου μονοβιβλα. *Philonis Judaei in libros Mosis de mundi opificio, historicos, de legibus. Ejusdem libri singulares.*

the works of Philo preserved only in Armenian, published by
Aucher, are by far the most important.[9] Greek portions of
greater or less extent were given by Mai,[10] Grossmann,[11] and

*Ex bibliotheca regio*, Parisiis, ex officina Adriana Turnebi, 1552 fol.
Several publications of Höschel at first contributed to the completion of this
very imperfect edition (Francof. 1587, Augustae Vindel. 1614). Collective editions appeared also at Geneva 1613 fol., Paris 1640 fol., Frankfort
1691 fol. (the Frankfort edition is only a reprint of the Parisian with
identical paging). The edition of Mangey, 2 vols. London 1742 fol., marks
an important advance. It is the first which is based upon a more extensive comparison of the manuscripts and is also more complete than
any former one. The edition of Pfeiffer, vols. i.–v. Erlangen 1785–1792,
2nd ed. 1820, remained unfinished (it contains only what stands in Mangey
vols. i. and ii. 1–40). On the deficiencies in the editions of Mangey and
Pfeiffer, see Creuzer, *Stud. und Krit.* 1832, pp. 5–17. J. G. Müller, *Ueber
die Texteskritik der Schriften des Juden Philo*, Basel 1839, p. 5 sqq. (printed
in J. G. Müller, *Des Juden Philo Buch von der Weltschöpfung*, 1841,
p. 18 sqq.).

[9] They appeared in two vols. under separate titles : (1) *Philonis Judaei
sermones tres hactenus inediti*, i. et ii. *de providentia et* iii. *de animalibus, ex
Armino versione etc. nunc primum in Latium* [sic] fideliter translati per Jo.
Bapt. Aucher, Venetiis 1822. (2) *Philonis Judaei paralipomena Armena,
libri videlicet quatuor in Genesin, libri duo in Exodum, sermo unus de
Sampsone, alter de Jona, tertius de tribus angelis Abraamo apparentibus,
opera hactenus inedita ex Armena versione etc. nunc primum in Latium* fideliter translata per Jo. Bapt. Aucher, Venetiis 1826.

[10] The works here in question are: (1) *Philo et Virgilii interpretes.* In
it *Philonis Judaei de cophini festo et de colendis parentibus cum brevi scripto
de Jona*, editore ac interprete Angelo Maio, Mediolan. 1818. (2) *Classicorum auctorum e Vaticanis codicibus editorum*, vol. iv. curante Angelo
Maio, Romae 1831 (contains: pp. 402–407, *Philonis de cophini festo;* pp.
408–429, *Philonis de honorandis parentibus;* pp. 430–441, *Philonus ex
opere in Exodum selectae questiones*). (3) *Scriptorum veterum nova collectio
e Vaticanis codicibus*, edita ab Angelo Maio, vol. vii. Romae 1833 (contains,
Pt. I. pp. 74–109, specimens from a Florilegium of Leontius and Johannes
with numerous smaller fragments of Philo). (4) *Philonis Judaei, Por-
phyrii philosophi, Eusebii Pamphili opera inedita.* In it: *Philonis Judaei
de virtute ejusque partibus*, ed. Ang. Maius, Mediolan. 1816 (this work, which
in the Milan manuscript used by Mai bears the name of Philo, is in other
manuscripts attributed to Gemistus Pletho, and was long printed under his
name, as Mai himself subsequently remarked). See *Leipziger Literaturzeitung*, 1818, No. 276.

[11] Grossmann, *Anecdoton Graecum Philonis Judaei de Cherubinis Exod.
xxv. 18*, Lips. 1856 (this supposed *Anecdoton* from the *cod. Vat.* n. 379
was already printed in the year 1831 in Mai, *Classicorum auctorum*, vol. iv.
p. 430–441. Tischendorf indeed knew nothing of it in 1868, comp. his
*Philonea*, p. xix. sq.).

Tischendorf.[12] Pitra has communicated material of various kinds from manuscripts.[12a] In the more recent hand editions these publications have been at least partially turned to account.[13] A satisfactory collective edition is however as yet wanting. That planned long since by Grossmann has not been carried into execution.[14] For a new edition, a careful investigation also of the material offered by the as yet un-

---

[12] Tischendorf, *Anecdota sacra et profana* (2nd ed. Lips. 1861), pp. 171–174. But especially Tischendorf, *Philonea, inedita altera, altera nunc demum recte ex vetere scriptura eruta*, Lips. 1868. Holwerda in the *Verslagen en Mededeelingen der koninkl. Akademie van Wetenschappen, Afdeeling Letterkunde, tweede reeks derde deel*, Amsterdam 1873, pp. 271–288, gives emendations of Tischendorf's text. Idem, *Derde reeks eerste deel*, 1884, pp. 274–286.

[12a] Pitra, *Analecta sacra spicilegio Solesmensi parata*, vol. ii. (1884) pp. xxii. sq., 304–334. Pitra here gives: (1) Philo-fragments from the Florilegium of the *codex Coislinianus* 276 (pp. 304–310). (2) Philo-fragments from various Vatican MSS. (pp. 310–314). (3) A list of the Philo-manuscripts in the Vatican Library, together with a list of the several works of Philo contained in these manuscripts (pp. 314–319). (4) Information concerning various ancient and modern Latin translations of Philo (pp. 319–334).

[13] The hand edition of Richter (8 vols. Lips. 1828–1830) contains besides the text of Mangey the two publications of Aucher and those of Mai of the year 1818. The same texts are also in the Tauchnitz stereotype edition (8 vols. Lips. 1851–1853). On recent editions of separate works of Philo (*De opificio mundi*, by J. G. Müller, *De incorruptibilitate mundi*, by Bernays), see below at the proper places. I may also mention that a number of Philo's writings translated into German will be found in the *Bibliothek der griechischen und römischen Schriftsteller über Judenthum und Juden in neuen Uebertragungen und Sammlungen*, vol. i. Leipzig 1865 [vol. ii. contains *Josephus*], vol. iii. 1870, vol. iv. 1872.

[14] Grossmann publicly expressed his intention so long ago as 1829 (*Quaestiones Philoneae*, i. p. 7). Afterwards Tischendorf in particular collected materials for him, comp. *Anecdota sacra et profana*, p. 171: Quam Grossmannus longissimo ex tempore novam operum scriptoris istius gravissimi editionem praeparat, ea ex collationibus meis codicum fere triginta ubique terrarum dispersorum non modo apparatum habebit locupletissimum et textum prioribus editionibus multo correctiorem, verum etiam aucta erit ineditis nonnullis quae in Italia reperire mihi contigit. On the *manuscripts* of Philo, comp. the Prolegomena in Mangey's edition, Fabricius-Harles, *Biblioth. gr.* iv. 743–746. Tischendorf, *Philonea*, pp. vii.–xx. Some notices in Mai, *Nova patrum bibliotheca*, vi. 2, p. 67, note. A list of the Vatican manuscripts in Pitra, *Analecta sacra*, ii. p. 314, and at pp. 316–319, accurate information as to the manuscripts in which each separate work of Philo is contained.

printed Florilegia (collections of extracts from the Fathers and more ancient authors) would be necessary.[15]

A tolerably complete catalogue of Philo's works is already given by Eusebius in his Ecclesiastical History.[16] Unfortunately however it is in such disorder as to afford no foothold for the correct classification of the works. In this respect we are almost exclusively referred to the contents

[15] The best known among the extant printed Christian Florilegia are those of Maximus Confessor, Johannes Damascenus and Antonius Melissa. In all three Philo is frequently quoted (see the indexes in Fabricius-Harles, *Biblioth. gr.* ix. pp. 663, 731, 756). To the same category belong also the Florilegium of Leontius and Johannes in Mai, *Script. vet. nova collectio,* vii. 1. 74–109. Mangey has collected from Johannes Damascenus (*Sacra parallela*) and Antonius Melissa all those passages which are derived from lost works of Philo (*Philonis opp.* ii. 648–660, 670–674). But what Mangey here gives under the name of Johannes Damascenus really comes from two different collections. For Lequien gives in his edition of Johannes Damascenus first (ii. 274–730) the complete text of the *Sacra parallela,* but then also (ii. 730–790) a selection of passages from another and considerably divergent recension of the *sacra parallela,* which is also attributed to Johannes Damascenus. The latter (in a *codex Rupefucaldinus* of the Jesuit College, Paris) seems to me however exactly identical with the so-called *Johannes Monachus ineditus,* extracts of which from lost works of Philo are given by Mangey himself after the supposed extracts from Johannes Damascenus (*Philonis opp.* ii. 660–670). For both manuscripts belong to the Jesuit College at Paris and have exactly the same superscription (Lequien, ii. 274 sq., 731 ; Mangey, i. p. xviii. sq. and ii. 660). Seeing the importance of the so-called *Johannes Monachus ineditus* in the criticism of Philo, the matter deserved a more accurate investigation. Pitra (*Analecta sacra,* ii. 304–310) has given various fragments from Philo from a third recension of the *Sacra parallela* in the cod. *Coislinianus* 276. *Many similar collections of extracts moreover exist in manuscript, which have not as yet been turned to any account with respect to Philo.* See Fabricius-Harles, *Bibl. gr.* ix. 720 sq., 758 sq. Comp. on this literature in general: Fabricius-Harles, ix. 635–759. Nicolai, *Griech. Literaturgesch.* vol. iii. 1878, pp. 309–318. Wachsmuth, *Studien zu den griechischen Florilegien,* Berlin 1882. Zahn, *Forschungen zur Geschichte des neutestamentl. Kanons,* Pt. iii. (1884) pp. 7–10.

[16] Euseb. *Hist. eccl.* ii. 18. The statements of Jerome, *De viris illustr.* c. 11 (*Opp.* ed. Vallarsi, ii. 847 sq.), rest entirely upon this catalogue of Eusebius. Again the catalogue in Suidas (*Lex. s.v.* Φίλων) is copied with only a few additions of his own from the Greek translation of Jerome. Photius, *Bibliotheca cod.* 103, 104, 105 on the other hand gives somewhat that is independent. Comp. in general *the testimonia veterum* in Mangey, i. pp. xxi.–xxix. The long fragments from different works of Philo in the *Praep. evang.* of Eusebius are also especially valuable.

of the works themselves, a careful consideration of which evidently shows, that they by no means form so unconnected a mass, as appears from the titles in the editions. The great majority are on the contrary only sub-divisions of some few large works. And indeed, as especially Ewald has correctly perceived, *three chief works on the Pentateuch* may be distinguished, which alone embrace more than three-quarters of what has come down to us as Philo's.[17]

I. The *Ζητήματα καὶ λύσεις, Quaestiones et solutiones*, which first became more widely known through the publications of Aucher from the Armenian, are a comparatively brief *catechetical explanation of the Pentateuch in the form of questions and answers*. It is not easy to ascertain how far they extended. In the time of Eusebius, they were extant for only Genesis and Exodus (*H. E.* ii. 18. 1 and 5) and such other traces as may be regarded as certain extend only to these two books.[18] The explanation of Genesis comprised probably *six books*, at all events only so much can be certainly pointed out from the quotations.[19] The explanation of *Exodus* comprised, according to the testimony of Eusebius (*H. E.* ii. 18. 5) and Jerome, *five books*.

---

[17] More or less valuable contributions to the correct classification of Philo's works have been furnished by Mangey, Fabricius, Gfrörer, Dähne, Grossmann, Ewald and Siegfried in the above-named works and articles (Siegfried in the *Zeitschr. für wissenschaftl. Theol.* 1874, p. 562 sqq.). The arbitrarily got up surveys of J. G. Müller and Zöckler are on the contrary useless. Steinhart and Hamburger are also inaccurate. Hausrath, ii. 152–154, does the most for confusion.

[18] Grossmann (*De Phil. Jud. operum continua serie*, i. p. 25) and Ewald (*Gesch.* vi. 294 sq.) suppose, that the work extended to the three last books of the Pentateuch also. In Mai, *Script. vet. nova collectio*, vii. 1, p. 104ᵃ, is indeed found a fragment ἐκ τῶν ἐν τῷ λευιτικῷ ζητημάτων. But sometimes errors occur in these quotation formulae also.

[19] Three fragments ἐκ τοῦ ϛ´ τῶν ἐν γενέσει ζητημάτων (Mai, *Script. vet. nova collectio*, vii. 1, pp. 100ᵇ, 106ᵇ, 108ᵇ,) occur in the Florilegium of Leontius and Johannes. In Le Quien's edition of Johannes Damascenus, ii. 362, note, it is remarked, that a fragment there given is introduced in the *cod. Rupefucaldinus* (see above, note 15) by the formula ἐκ τοῦ ϛ´ τῶν αὐτῶν (scil. τῶν ἐν γενέσει ζητουμένων). All other known quotations refer to Books i.–v. Only once in Mai, *Script. vet. nov. coll.* vii. 1. 99ᵇ, is found ἐκ τοῦ θ´ τῶν ἐν γενέσει ζητημάτων, where however E must certainly be read for Θ.

Of these are preserved (1) in the *Armenian* tongue about the
half of these eleven books, viz. four on Genesis (incomplete)
and two on Exodus (also imperfect);[20] and (2) a large fragment (comprising about half of the fourth book on Genesis) in
an old *Latin* translation, which was repeatedly printed in the
beginning of the sixteenth century, but entirely ignored by
the publishers of the Greek works.[21] Lastly (3) in *Greek*
numerous small fragments still awaiting collection.[22]    By the

---

[20] Published in Armenian and Latin by Aucher, 1826 (see above,
note 9). After this in Latin also in Richter, *Philonis opp.* 6 and 7 vols.,
and in the Tauchnitz stereotype edition (also in 6 and 7 vols.). On the
gaps, comp. Dähne, *Stud. und Krit.* 1833, p. 1038.

[21] *Philonis Judaei centum et duae quaestiones et totidem responsiones super
Genesim*, Paris 1520, fol. (Fabricius-Harles, iv. 746).    The Giessen
University library possesses: *Philonis Judaei Alexandrini, libri anti-
quitatum, quaestionum et solutionum in Genesin, de Essaeis, de nominibus
Hebraicis, de mundo*, Basileae 1527, fol. (in which, pp. 61–83: Philonis
Judaei quaestionum et solutionum in Genesin liber).    There are also
impressions of 1538 and 1550 (Fabricius, *l.c.*).    Aucher, pp. 362–443 (under
the Armenio-Latin text), and Richter, vii. 212–261, follow the impression
of 1538.    Manuscripts also of this Latin text are still known, two Vaticans
(Vatican 488 and Urbin 61) and one Laurentianus; see thereon Pitra,
*Analecta sacra*, ii. 298 sq., 314, 332.    On the age and character of the
translation, Pitra, *Analecta*, ii. 298 sq., 319 sqq.

[22] Of *Greek fragments* are known: (1) A small piece: ἐκ τοῦ πρώτου τῶν
Φίλωνος Ζητημάτων καὶ λύσεων, on Genesis in Eusebius, *Praep. evang.*
vii. 13.    (2) The fragment *De Cherubinis* on Exodus, published by Mai,
Grossmann and Tischendorf (Mai, *Classicorum auctorum*, vol. iv.
pp. 430–441; Grossmann, *Anecdoton*, etc. 1856; Tischendorf, *Philonea*,
pp. 144–153).    (3) Numerous small fragments from Johannes Damascenus,
*Johannes Monachus ineditus*, Antonius Melissa and the Catena of the cod.
Paris, Reg. n. 1825, in Mangey, *Philonis opp.* ii. 648–680.    Of these
certainly it is only the fragments in the *codex Rupefucaldinus* and in
*Johannes Monachus ineditus*, Mang. ii. 653–670 (both probably identical, see
above, note 15), that are expressly traced to the ζητήματα καὶ λύσεις.    But
many others, especially those in the Catena, come from it.    (4) About thirty
to forty small fragments in the Florilegium of Leontius and Johannes, in
Mai, *Script. vet. nova collectio*, vii. 1. 96–109.    (5) A portion also of the small
fragments edited by Tischendorf (*Anecdota sacra et profana*, pp. 171–174;
*Philonea*, pp. 152–155) are probably derived from this work.    (6) Six small
fragments in the Florilegium of the *codex Coislinianus* in Pitra, *Analecta
sacra*, ii. 307 sq.    Various other fragments from Vatican manuscripts also
in Pitra, *Analecta*, ii. 310–314 (a portion at least of these fragments must
certainly be included).    (7) A more accurate investigation of the Florilegia,

help of the Armenian text it is now settled, that many
passages have been taken almost verbally from this work,
without mention of Philo's name, by the Fathers and especially
by Ambrose.[23] The composition of these *Quaestiones et
solutiones* is in some parts of earlier in other of later date,
than that of the large allegorical commentary, as is shown by
the allusions to each other in both works.[24]

II. While this shorter explanation in a catechetical form
was intended for more extensive circles, Philo's special and
chief scientific work is his *large allegorical commentary on
Genesis*, Νόμων ἱερῶν ἀλληγορίαι (such is the title given it in
Euseb. *Hist. eccl.* ii. 18. 1, and Photius, *Bibliotheca cod.* 103.
Comp. also Origen, *Comment. in Matth.* vol. xvii. c. 17 ; *contra
Celsum*, iv. 51).[25] These two works frequently approximate
each other as to their contents. For in the *Quaestiones et
solutiones* also, the deeper allegorical signification is given
as well as the literal meaning. In the great allegorical
commentary on the contrary, the allegorical interpretation
exclusively prevails. The deeper allegorical sense of the
sacred letter is settled in extensive and prolix discussion,
which by reason of the copious adducting of parallel passages
often seems to wander from the text. Thus the entire
exegetic method, with its dragging in of the most hetero-

especially of those not as yet edited (see note 15), would furnish considerable gain in the matter of small fragments.

[23] Numerous passages from Ambrose are reprinted in Aucher under the
Armenio-Latin text. Comp. on the use of Philo by Ambrose generally :
Siegfried, *Philo*, pp. 371–391. Förster, *Ambrosius Bischof von Mailand*
(1884), pp. 102–112.

[24] Ewald (*Gesch.* vi. 294) regards the *Quaestiones et solutiones* as older
than the large allegorical commentary. Dähne (*Stud. und Krit.* 1833,
p. 1037) considers it more recent. For a more minute discussion, see
Grossmann, *De Phil. Jud. operum continua serie*, ii. pp. 14–17.

[25] In the quotations in the Florilegia ἀλληγορία is always in the singular,
*e.g.* in *Johannes Monachus ineditus* ἐκ τοῦ α΄ τῆς νόμων ἱερῶν ἀλληγορίας, ἐκ
τοῦ δ΄ τῆς νόμων ἱερῶν ἀλληγορίας (both in Mangey, ii. 668). So too in the
Florilegium of the *codex Coislinianus* (Pitra, *Analecta sacra*), ii. 306, and
in that of Leontius and Johannes (Mai, *Script. vet. nov. coll.* vii. 1, pp. 95b,
96a, 98b, 99b, 100a, 102a, 105a, 107a, 107b).

geneous passages in elucidation of the idea supposed to exist
in the text, forcibly recalls the method of Rabbinical Midrash.
This allegorical interpretation however has with all its
arbitrariness, its rules and laws, the allegorical meaning as
once settled for certain persons, objects and events being
afterwards adhered to with tolerable consistency. Especially
is it *a fundamental thought*, from which the exposition is
everywhere deduced, *that the history of mankind as related in
Genesis is in reality nothing else than a system of psychology
and ethic.* The different individuals, who here make their
appearance, denote the different states of soul (τρόποι τῆς
ψυχῆς) which occur among men. To analyse these in their
variety and their relations both to each other and to the Deity
and the world of sense, and thence to deduce moral doctrines, is
the special aim of this great allegorical commentary. Thus
we perceive at the same time, that Philo's chief interest is
*not*—as might from the whole plan of his system be supposed
—speculative theology for its own sake, but on the contrary
psychology and ethic. To judge from his ultimate purpose he
is not a speculative theologian, but a psychologist and moralist
(comp. note 183).

The commentary at first follows the text of Genesis verse
by verse. Afterwards single sections are selected, and some
of them so fully treated, as to grow into regular monographs.
Thus *e.g.* Philo takes occasion from the history of Noah to
write two books on drunkenness (περὶ μέθης), which he does
with such thoroughness, that a collection of the opinions of
other philosophers on this subject filled the first of these lost
books (Mangey, i. 357).

The work, as we have it, begins at Gen. ii. 1: *Καὶ
ἐτελέσθησαν οἱ οὐρανοὶ καὶ ἡ γῆ.* The creation of the world
is therefore not treated of. For the composition, *De opificio
mundi*, which precedes it in our editions, is a work of an
entirely different character, being no allegorical commentary
on the history of the creation, but a statement of that history
itself. Nor does the first book of the *Legum allegoriae* by

any means join on to the work *De opificio mundi;* for the
former begins at Gen. ii. 1, while in *De opif. mundi,* the
creation of *man* also, according to Gen. ii., is already dealt
with.   Hence—as Gfrörer rightly asserts in answer to Dähne
—the allegorical commentary cannot be combined with *De
opif. mundi* as though the two were but parts of the same
work.   At most may the question be raised, whether Philo
did not also write an allegorical commentary on Gen. i.
This is however improbable.   For the allegorical commentary proposes to treat of the history of *mankind,* and this does
not begin till Gen. ii. 1.   Nor need the abrupt commencement
of *Leg. alleg.* i. seem strange, since this manner of starting
at once with the text to be expounded, quite corresponds
with the method of Rabbinical Midrash.   The later books too
of Philo's own commentary begin in fact in the same abrupt
manner.   In our manuscripts and editions only the first
books bear the title belonging to the whole work, Νόμων
ἱερῶν ἀλληγορίαι.   All the later books have special titles,
a circumstance which gives the appearance of their being
independent works.   In truth however *all that is contained
in Mangey's first vol.*—viz. the works which here follow—
belongs to the book in question (with the sole exception of
*De opificio mundi*).

1. Νόμων ἱερῶν ἀλληγορίαι πρῶται τῶν μετὰ τὴν ἑξαήμερον.
*Legum allegoriarum liber* i. (Mangey, i. 43–65).   On Gen.
ii. 1–17.—Νόμων ἱερῶν ἀλληγορίαι δεύτεραι τῶν μετὰ τὴν
ἑξαήμερον.   *Legum allegoriarum liber* ii. (Mangey, i. 66–86).
On Gen. ii. 18–iii. 1ᵃ. — Νόμων ἱερῶν ἀλληγορίαι τρίται
τῶν μετὰ τὴν ἑξαήμερον.   *Legum allegoriarum liber* iii.
(Mangey, i. 87–137).   On Gen. iii. 8ᵇ–19.—The titles here
given of the first three books, as customary in the editions
since Mangey,[26] require an important correction.   Even the
different extent of Books i. and ii. leads us to conjecture, that
they may properly be but *one* book.   In fact Mangey remarks

[26] I do not give the Latin titles exactly according to Mangey, but as
they are usually quoted.

at the commencement of the third book (i. 87, note): in
omnibus codicibus opusculum hoc inscribitur ἀλληγορία
δευτέρα. Thus we have in fact but two books. There is
however a gap between the two, the commentary on Gen. iii.
1ᵇ–8ᵃ being absent. The commentary too on Gen. iii. 20–23
is wanting, for the following book begins with Gen. iii. 24.
As Philo in these first books follows the text step by step, it
must be assumed, that each of the two pieces was worked up
into a book by itself, and this is even certain with respect to
the second.[27]    Hence the original condition was very probably as follows: Book i. on Gen. ii. 1–3, 1ᵃ, Book ii. on Gen.
iii. 1ᵇ–3, 8ᵃ, Book iii. on Gen. iii. 8ᵇ–19, Book iv. on Gen. iii.
20–23. With this coincides the fact, that in the so-called
*Johannes Monachus ineditus,* the commentary on Gen. iii.
8ᵇ–19 is indeed more often quoted as τὸ γ´ τῆς τῶν νόμων
ἱερῶν ἀλληγορίας (Mangey, i. 87, note). When on the other
hand the same book is entitled in the MSS. ἀλληγορία
δευτέρα, this must certainly be explained as showing that the
actual second book was already missing in the archetype of
these manuscripts.

2. *Περὶ τῶν Χερουβὶμ καὶ τῆς φλογίνης ῥομφαίας καὶ τοῦ
κτισθέντος πρώτου ἐξ ἀνθρώπου Κάϊν.*    De Cherubim et
flammeo gladio (Mangey, i. 138–162). On Gen. iii. 24 and
iv. 1.    From this point onwards the several books have been
handed down no longer under the general title νόμων ἱερῶν
ἀλληγορίαι, but under special titles. According to our conjecture as above, this book would be the *fifth,* unless it
formed the *fourth* together with the commentary on Gen. iii
20–23.

3. *Περὶ ὧν ἱερουργοῦσιν Ἄβελ τε καὶ Κάϊν.*    De sacrificiis
Abelis et Caini (Mangey, i. 163–190). On Gen. iv. 2–4. In
the *codex Vaticanus* the title runs: Περὶ γενέσεως Ἄβελ καὶ

---

[27] The remark in *De sacrificiis Abelis et Caini,* § 12, *fin.* (i. 171, Mang.):
τί δέ ἐστι τὸ τὴν γῆν ἐργάζεσθαι, διὰ τῶν προτέρων βίβλων ἐδηλώσαμεν, can
refer only to the missing commentary on Gen. iii. 23. Comp. Dähne,
*Stud. und Krit.* 1863, p. 1015. Grossmann indeed (i. p. 22) thinks it
relates to the book *De agricultura,* which was certainly a later composition.

ὧν αὐτὸς καὶ ὁ ἀδελφὸς αὐτοῦ Κάϊν ἱερουργοῦσιν. Frequently quoted in *Johannes Monachus ineditus* with the formula *Ἐκ τοῦ περὶ γενέσεως "Αβελ* (see Mangey, i. 163, note). Also in the Florilegium of the *codex Coislinianus*.[27a] The missing commentary on Gen. iv. 5–7 would have formed either the conclusion of this book, or a separate book.

4. *Περὶ τοῦ τὸ χεῖρον τῷ κρείττονι φιλεῖν ἐπιτίθεσθαι. Quod deterius potiori insidiari soleat* (Mangey, i. 191–225). On Gen. iv. 8–15. The book is already quoted by Origen under this special title (*Comm. in Matth.* vol. xv. c. 3). Eusebius mistakenly quotes under the same title several passages belonging to *De confusione linguarum* (*Praep. Ev.* xi. 15). In the Florilegium of Leontius and Johannes several passages are cited from our book with the formula *ἐκ τοῦ ζ καὶ η τῆς νόμων ἱερῶν ἀλληγορίας*.[28] Also in *Johannes Monachus ineditus* (Mangey, i. 191, note). The unusual formula *ἐκ τοῦ ζ καὶ η* must surely mean, that the seventh book was according to another computation also called the eighth (*ἐκ τοῦ ζ τοῦ καὶ η* would thus be the more accurate).[29] This book then is according to the usual numbering *the seventh*, but was, in consequence of *De opificio mundi* being placed first, also called the eighth.

5. *Περὶ τῶν τοῦ δοκησισόφου Κάϊν ἐγγόνων καὶ ὡς μετανάστης γίνεται. De posteritate Caini sibi visi sapientis et quo pacto sedem mutat* (Mangey, i. 226–261). On Gen. iv. 16–25. This book was first published by Mangey from the *cod. Vat.* 381. Much more correctly from the same manuscript by

---

[27a] Pitra, *Analecta sacra*, ii. 308 sq.

[28] The following passages are cited with this formula: 1. Κυρίως οὔτε ἐπὶ χρημάτων ἢ κτημάτων περιουσίᾳ οὔτε ἐπὶ δόξης λαμπρότητι κ.τ.λ. Mai, *Script. vet. nov. coll.* vii. 1, p. 96a = Mangey, i. 217, *med.* 2. Ἐν ᾗ μὲν ψυχῇ τὸ ἐκτὸς αἰσθητὸν ὡς μέγιστον ἀγαθῶν τετίμηται, ἐν ταύτῃ λόγος ἀστεῖος οὐχ εὑρίσκεται κ.τ.λ. Mai, *Script. vet. nov. coll.* vii. 1, p. 107a = Mangey, i. 192, *init.* The same formula is also found 3. *Script. vet. nov. coll.* vii. 1, p. 102a (where of course ζ καὶ η must be read for ζ καὶ ιγ) ; and 4. The same, p. 107b. The former passage is in the beginning of *De posteritate Caini* (Mang. i. 228) ; I have not succeeded in discovering the latter.

[29] Comp. Dähne, *Stud. und Kritik.* 1833, p. 1015.

Tischendorf, *Philonea*, pp. 84–143. Holwerda gave emendations in 1884 (see note 12 above). This book is in like manner as the former quoted with the formula ἐκ τοῦ η καὶ θ τῆς νόμων ἱερῶν ἀλληγορίας in Leontius and Johannes,[30] in the Florilegium of the *codex Coislinianus*,[30a] and in *Johannes Monachus ineditus* (Mangey, i. 226, note).

Of these books none is mentioned by its special title in the catalogue of Eusebius, *Hist. eccl.* ii. 18, while all that follow are quoted under these titles, evidently because Eusebius considers the former to be included and the latter not included in the joint title νόμων ἱερῶν ἀλληγορίαι. To this must be added, that in the Florilegia also, the quotations under the general title extend exactly thus far. *It is therefore highly probable, that Philo issued the following books only under the special titles.*[31] Nay, it is also evident why this was done, viz. *because from this point onwards the uninterrupted text was no longer commented on, but only selected passages.* The exegetic method is however quite the same in the following books.

6. Περὶ γιγάντων. *De gigantibus* (Mangey, i. 262–272). On Gen. vi. 1–4.—῞Οτι ἄτρεπτον τὸ θεῖον. *Quod deus sit immutabilis* (Mangey, i. 272–299). On Gen. vi. 4–12. These two paragraphs, which are in our editions separated, form together but *one* book. Hence Johannes Monachus ineditus cites passages from the latter paragraph with the formula ἐκ τοῦ περὶ γιγάντων (Mangey, i. 262, note, 272, note).

---

[30] Two passages : 1. Παιδείας σύμβολον ἡ ῥάβδος· ἄνευ γὰρ τοῦ δυσωπῆναι (*sic*) καὶ περὶ ἐνίων ἐπιπληχθῆναι, νουθεσίαν ἐνδέξασθαι καὶ σωφρονισμόν, ἀμήχανον κ.τ.λ. Mai, *Script. vet. nov. coll.* vii. 1, p. 99[b] = Mangey, i. 243. —2. Πέφυκεν ὁ ἄφρων ἐπὶ μηδενὸς ἑστάναι παγίως καὶ ἐνερίσθαι δόγματος· ἄλλοτε γοῦν ἀλλοῖα δοξάζει . . . Καί ἐστιν αὐτῷ πᾶσα ἡ ζωὴ κρεμαμένη βάσιν ἀκράδαντον οὐκ ἔχουσα κ.τ.λ. Mai, *Script. vet. nov. coll.* vii. 1, p. 100=Mangey, i. 230–231.

[30a] Pitra, *Analecta sacra*, vol. ii. (1884) p. 306. The two passages here given by Pitra are in Mangey, i. 230 above and 253 (*de posteritate Caini*, § 6 and 43).

[31] In answer to Dähne, *Stud. und Kritik.* 1833, pp. 1019–1024. Ersch and Grüber's *Enc.*, art. "Philo," p. 442.

Euseb. *H. E.* ii. 18. 4 : περὶ γιγάντων ἢ [elsewhere καὶ] περὶ τοῦ μὴ τρέπεσθαι τὸ θεῖον.

7. Περὶ γεωργίας. *De agricultura* (Mangey, i. 300–328). On Gen. ix. 20ᵃ.—Περὶ φυτουργίας Νῶε τὸ δεύτερον. *De plantatione Noe* (Mangey, i. 329–356). On Gen. ix. 20ᵇ. The common title of these two books is properly περὶ γεωργίας. Comp. Euseb. *H. E.* ii. 18. 2 : περὶ γεωργίας δύο. Hieronymus, *De vir. illustr.* 11 : de agricultura duo. Euseb. *Praep. Evang.* vii. 13. 3 (ed. Gaisford) : ἐν τῷ περὶ γεωργίας προτέρῳ. *Ibid.* vii. 13. 4 : ἐν τῷ δευτέρῳ.

8. Περὶ μέθης. *De ebrietate* (Mangey, i. 357–391). On Gen. ix. 21. From the beginning of this book it is evident that another book preceded it, in which τὰ τοῖς ἄλλοις φιλοσόφοις εἰρημένα περὶ μέθης were stated. This first book is lost, but was still extant in the time of Eusebius, Euseb. *H. E.* ii. 18. 2 : περὶ μέθης τοσαῦτα (viz. two). Hieronymus, *vir. illustr.* 11 : de ebrietate duo. They seem to have been in the hands of Johannes Monachus ineditus in the reverse order. For what he quotes with the formula ἐκ τοῦ περὶ μέθης αʹ, is found in that which has come down to us; while what he cites with the formula ἐκ τοῦ περὶ μέθης δευτέρου λόγου, is *not* found in it (Mangey, i. 357, note).

9. Περὶ τοῦ ἐξένηψε Νῶε. *De sobrietate* (Mangey, i. 392–403). On Gen. ix. 24.—In the best manuscripts (*Vaticanus and Mediceus*) the title runs : περὶ ὧν ἀνανήψας ὁ νοῦς εὔχεται καὶ καταρᾶται (Mangey, i. 392, note). Almost exactly the same, Euseb. *H. E.* ii. 18. 2 : περὶ ὧν νήψας ὁ νοῦς εὔχεται καὶ καταρᾶται. Hieronymus, *vir. illustr.* 11 : de his quae sensu precamur et detestamur.

10. Περὶ συγχύσεως διαλέκτων. *De confusione linguarum* (Mangey, i. 404–435). On Gen. xi. 1–9.—The same title also in Euseb. *H. E.* ii. 18. 2. In the *Praep. evang.* xi. 15, Eusebius quotes several passages from it with the mistaken statement, that they are from : Περὶ τοῦ τὸ χεῖρον τῷ κρείττονι φιλεῖν ἐπιτίθεσθαι.

11. Περὶ ἀποικίας. *De migratione Abrahami* (Mangey, i.

436–472).  On Gen. xii. 1–6. — The same title also in
Eusebius, *H. E.* ii. 18. 4.

12. Περὶ τοῦ τίς ὁ τῶν θείων πραγμάτων κληρονόμος.
*Quis rerum divinarum haeres sit* (Mangey, i. 437–518).    On
Gen. xv. 1–18.—Euseb. *H. E.* ii. 18. 2: περὶ τοῦ τίς ὁ τῶν
θείων ἐστὶ κληρονόμος ἢ περὶ τῆς εἰς τὰ ἴσα καὶ ἐναντία
τομῆς.  Hieronymus, *vir. illustr.* 11, makes from this double
title the two works: *De haerede divinarum rerum liber unus,
De divisione aequalium et contrariorum liber.*    Suidas, *Lex.
s.v.* Φίλων,[31a] also follows him.    Johannes Monachus ineditus
quotes this book with the formula ἐκ τοῦ τίς ὁ τῶν θείων
κληρονόμος (Mangey, i. 473, note).    When he likewise quotes
it with the formula ἐκ τοῦ περὶ κοσμοποιίας (Mangey, *l.c.*),
we must not conclude from this, that the latter was a general
title, which was applied to this book as well as others,[32] for
we have here simply an error in quotation.    In the commencement of this book a former composition is referred to in the
words: Ἐν μὲν τῇ πρὸ ταύτης βίβλῳ περὶ μισθῶν ὡς ἐνῆν
ἐπ᾽ ἀκριβείας διεξήλθομεν.  This composition is not lost as
Mangey supposed (see his note on the passage), but is the
book περὶ ἀποικίας, which in fact treats περὶ μισθῶν.[33]   We
see at the same time, that Gen. xiii.–xiv. was not commented
on by Philo.

13. Περὶ τῆς εἰς τὰ προπαιδεύματα συνόδου.    *De congressu
quaerendae eruditionis causa* (Mangey, i. 519–545).    On Gen.
xvi. 1–6.—In Eusebius, *H. E.* ii. 18. 2, the title runs: περὶ
τῆς πρὸς τὰ παιδεύματα συνόδου.  But the προπαιδεύματα,
which has come down in the Philo-manuscripts is preferable,
for the fact, that Abraham cohabited with Hagar, before he
had issue by Sarah, means according to Philo, that we must
become acquainted with propaideutic knowledge before we
can rise to the higher wisdom and obtain its fruit, namely,

---

[31a] Comp. also Grossmann, i. p. 24, on the fact of the two titles belonging
to the same book.
[32] Mangey, i. 473, note.  Comp. Dähne, *Stud. und Krit.* 1833, p. 1000 sqq.
[33] Dähne, 1018 sq.  Grossmann, i. p. 22.

virtue. Comp. also Philo's own allusion in the beginning of
the following book (*de profugis*): Εἰρηκότες ἐν τῷ προτέρῳ τὰ
πρέποντα περὶ τῶν προπαιδευμάτων καὶ περὶ κακώσεως κ.τ.λ.

14. Περὶ φυγάδων. *De profugis* (Mangey, i. 546–577).
On Gen. xvi. 6–14.—Euseb. *H. E.* ii. 18. 2: περὶ φυγῆς καὶ
εὑρέσεως.[34] And exactly so Johannes Monachus ineditus: ἐκ
τοῦ περὶ φυγῆς καὶ εὑρέσεως (Mangey, i. 546, note). This is
without doubt the correct title. For the work deals with the
flight and refinding of Hagar.

15. Περὶ τῶν μετονομαζομένων καὶ ὧν ἕνεκα μετονομά-
ζονται. *De mutatione nominum* (Mangey, i. 578–619). On
Gen. xvii. 1–22.—The same title in Euseb. *H. E.* ii. 18. 3.
Johannes Monachus ineditus quotes under this title much
that is not found in this book, nor in any of the preserved
works of Philo (Mangey, i. 578, note). In this book Philo
alludes to a lost work: Τὸν δὲ περὶ διαθηκῶν σύμπαντα
λόγον ἐν δυσὶν ἀναγέγραφα πράξεσι, which was no longer
extant in the time of Eusebius (comp. *H. E.* ii. 18. 3).[34a]

16. Περὶ τοῦ θεοπέμπτους εἶναι τοὺς ὀνείρους. *De somniis*,
lib. i. (Mangey, i. 620–658). On Gen. xxviii. 12 sqq. and
xxxi. 11 sqq. (the two dreams of Jacob).—Lib. ii. of the same
work (Mangey, i. 659–699). On Gen. xxxvii. and xl. 41
(the dreams of Joseph and of Pharaoh's chief butler and
baker).—According to Euseb. *H. E.* ii. 18. 4 and Hieronymus,
*vir. illustr.* 11, Philo wrote *five books* on dreams. Thus three
are lost. Those that have come down to us seem, to judge
from their openings, to be the second and third. In any case
our first was preceded by another, which probably treated on
the dream of Abimelech,[35] Gen. xx. 3. Origenes, *contra Celsum*,

[34] The text of Eusebius was here very early corrupted. Jerome (*de
natura et inventione*) already read φυγῆς instead of φύσεως. By continued
corruption there then arose in Nicephorus the double title: ὁ περὶ Φυγῆς καὶ
αἱρέσεως· ἔτι τε ὁ περὶ Φύσεως καὶ εὑρέσεως, which monstrosity has been
even admitted into the text of Eusebius by his recent editors.

[34a] The allusion in the *Quaest. et solut. in Exodum*, ed. Aucher, p. 493,
certainly relates to the same work. Comp. Grossmann, i. p. 25.

[35] Gfrörer, i. 43. Dähne, 1025. Grossmann, i. 25

vi. 21, *fin.*, already mentions the paragraph on Jacob's ladder,
Gen. xxviii. 12 (contained in the first of the preserved books).

III. The third chief group of Philo's works on the Pentateuch is a *Delineation of the Mosaic Legislation for non-Jews.*
In this whole group indeed, the allegorical explanation is still
occasionally employed. In the main however we have here
actual historical delineations, a systematic statement of the
great legislative work of Moses, the contents, excellence and
importance of which, the author desires to make evident to
non-Jewish readers, and indeed to as large a circle of them as
possible. For the delineation is more a popular one, while the
large allegorical commentary is an esoteric, and according to
Philo's notions a strictly scientific work. The contents of the
several compositions forming this group differ indeed considerably, and are apparently independent of each other. Their
connection however, and consequently the composition of the
whole work, cannot, according to Philo's own intimations, be
doubtful. As to plan it is divided into *three parts.* (*a*) The
beginning and as it were the introduction to the whole
is formed by a description of the creation of the world
(κοσμοποιΐα), which is placed first by Moses for the purpose of showing, that his legislation and its precepts are in
conformity with the will of nature (πρὸς τὸ βούλημα τῆς
φύσεως), and that consequently he who obeys it is truly a
citizen of the world (κοσμοπολίτης) (*de mundi opif.* § 1).
This introduction is next followed by (*b*) *biographies of virtuous
men.* These are, as it were, the living, unwritten laws (ἔμψυχοι
καὶ λογικοὶ νόμοι de Abrahamo, § 1, νόμοι ἄγραφοι de decalogo,
§ 1), which represent, in distinction from the written and
specific commands, universal moral norms (τοὺς καθολικω-
τέρους καὶ ὡσὰν ἀρχετύπους νόμους de Abrahamo, § 1).
Lastly, the third part embraces (*c*) *the delineation of the
legislation proper,* which is divided into two parts: (1) that of
the ten chief commandments of the law, and (2) that of the
special laws belonging to each of these ten commandments.
Then follow by way of appendix a few treatises on certain

cardinal virtues, and on the rewards of the good and the punishments of the wicked. This survey of the contents shows at
once, that it was Philo's intention to place before his readers a
clear description of the entire contents of the Pentateuch, which
should be in essential matters complete. His view however is
in this respect the genuinely Jewish one, that these entire contents fall under the notion of the νόμος. The work begins with:

1. Περὶ τῆς Μωϋσέως κοσμοποιΐας. *De mundi opificio*
(Mangey, i. 1–42).—It was customary to place this work at
the head of Philo's works, before the first book of the *Legum
allegoriae.* And this position has been resolutely defended,
especially by Dähne.[36] Gfrörer on the other hand already
convincingly showed, that the book *de Abrahamo* must be
immediately joined to *de mundi opificio.*[37] He has only erred
in the matter of declaring this whole group of writings older
than the allegorical commentary (p. 33 sq.). It was easy to
show in reply, that this popular delineation of the Mosaic
legislation is on the contrary more recent than the bulk of
the allegorical commentary.[38] On the other hand there is
nothing to prevent our relegating the work *de mundi opificio*
also, to the more recent group. We have already shown,
p. 331 above, that it is *not* connected with the allegorical
commentary. On the contrary the beginning of the work
*de mundi opificio* makes it quite evident that it was to form
the introduction to the delineation of the legislation, and it
is equally plain, that the composition *de Abrahamo* directly
follows it. Comp. *de Abrahamo,* § 1 : ʽΟν μὲν οὖν τρόπον ἡ
κοσμοποιΐα διατέτακται, διὰ τῆς προτέρας συντάξεως,
ὡς οἷόν τε ἦν, ἠκριβώσαμεν. To refer this intimation to the
whole series of the allegorical commentaries is, both by
reason of the expression κοσμοποιΐα and of the singular διὰ

---

[36] Dähne, *Stud. und Krit.* 1833, p. 1000 sqq. Ersch and Gruber's
*Encyklop.* art. "Philon," p. 441. Comp. also Grossmann, ii. p. 6. J. G.
Müller, *Des Juden Philo Buch von der Weltschöpfung,* pp. 13, 15 sqq. The
same in Herzog's *Real-Enc.* 1st ed. xi. 581.

[37] Gfrörer, i. pp. 8–10.

[38] See especially Grossmann, ii. pp. 13, 14.

τῆς προτέρας συντάξεως, quite impossible. — But however
certain all this is, the matter is not thus as yet settled. For
on the other hand it is just as certain, that the composition
*de mundi opificio* was subsequently placed at the head of the
allegorical commentaries to compensate for the missing commentary on Gen. i. Only thus can it be explained that
Eusebius, *Praep. evang.* viii. 13, quotes a passage from this
composition with the formula (viii. 12, *fin.* ed. Gaisford): ἀπὸ
τοῦ πρώτου τῶν εἰς τὸν νόμον).[39] It is just this which
explains the transposition of this treatise into the catalogue of
Eusebius, *Hist. eccl.* ii. 18 (it was in his eyes comprised in
the νόμων ἱερῶν ἀλληγορίαι), and also the peculiar form of
citation: ἐκ τοῦ ζ καὶ η [resp. ἐκ τοῦ η καὶ θ] τῆς νόμων ἱερῶν
ἀλληγορίας, mentioned p. 333 above.—There still remains the
question, whether this *supplementary* insertion of the *Legum
allegoriae* between *de mundi opificio* and *de Abrahamo*
originated with Philo himself? This is especially the view
of Siegfried.[40] It seems to me however, that the reasons
brought forward are not conclusive.[41] J. G. Müller has lately

---

[39] Another quotation from this treatise is introduced in the *Praep. evang.*
with the formula (xi. 23, *fin.* Gaisf.): λέγει δ᾽ οὖν ὁ Ἑβραῖος Φίλων τὰ
πάτρια διερμηνεύων αὐτοῖς ῥήμασιν.

[40] *Zeitschr. für wissenschaftl. Theol.* 1874, p. 562 sqq.

[41] For this arrangement of Philo's writings ((1) Creation of the world,
(2) Allegorical commentary, (3) Legislation) the following two passages
have, since Dähne, been cited as conclusive: 1. *Vita Mosis*, ed. Mang.
ii. 141, where it is said of the Holy Scriptures, which Moses composed: τὸ
μὲν ἱστορικὸν μέρος, τὸ δὲ περὶ τὰς προστάξεις καὶ ἀπαγορεύσεις, ὑπὲρ οὗ
δεύτερον λέξομεν, τὸ πρότερον τῇ τάξει πρότερον ἀκριβώσαντες.
Ἔστιν οὖν τοῦ ἱστορικοῦ τὸ μὲν περὶ τῆς τοῦ κόσμου γενέσεως, τὸ δὲ γενεα-
λογικόν· τοῦ δὲ γενεαλογικοῦ τὸ μὲν περὶ κολάσεως ἀσεβῶν, τὸ δ᾽ αὖ περὶ τιμῆς
δικαίων. Philo here divides the contents of the Mosaic writings into only
two chief groups, the *historical* and the *legislative*. When he then says,
that he would treat of the latter after having already minutely treated of the
former, it follows first only, that the delineation of the Mosaic legislation was
later than the allegorical commentary (to which the expression with respect
to the ἱστορικὸν μέρος probably refers; for the βίοι σοφῶν, which treat only of
the good, not of both good and bad, cannot by any means be intended).
When he next goes on to again divide the historical portion more particularly into two sections: (1) περὶ τῆς τοῦ κόσμου γενέσεως, (2) τὸ γενεα-
λογικόν, we may certainly infer, that the composition of *de mundi opificio*

brought out a separate edition of this composition with a commentary.[42]

2. Βίος σοφοῦ τοῦ κατὰ διδασκαλίαν τελειωθέντος ἢ περὶ τόμων ἀγράφων [α'], ὅ ἐστι περὶ 'Αβραάμ. De Abrahamo (Mangey, ii. 1–40).—With this composition commences the group of the νόμοι ἄγραφοι, i.e. the βίοι σοφῶν (de decalogo, § 1), the biographies of virtuous men, who exhibit by their exemplary behaviour the universal types of morality. Of such types there are twice three, viz. (1) Enos, Enoch, Noah; (2) Abraham, Isaac, Jacob. Enos represents ἐλπίς, Enoch μετάνοια καὶ βελτίωσις, Noah δικαιοσύνη (de Abrahamo, § 2, 3, 5). The second triad is more exalted: Abraham is the symbol of διδασκαλικὴ ἀρετή (virtue acquired by learning), Isaac of φυσικὴ ἀρετή (innate virtue), Jacob of ἀσκητικὴ ἀρετή (virtue attained by practice), see de Abrahamo, § 11; de Josepho, § 1 (Zeller, iii. 2. 411). The first three are only briefly dwelt on. The greater part of this composition is occupied with Abraham.—In Eusebius, H. E. ii. 18. 4, the title runs: βίου [read βίος] σοφοῦ τοῦ κατὰ δικαιοσύνην τελειωθέντος ἢ [περὶ] νόμων ἀγράφων. Δικαιοσύνην, instead of the διδασκαλίαν furnished by the Philo manuscripts, is here certainly incorrect. For Abraham is the type of διδασκαλικὴ ἀρετή. The number α' must be inserted after ἀγράφων, this book being only the first of the unwritten laws.

must be placed before that of the *vita Mosis*, which is also probable on other grounds (see note 82 below). *At all events there is in the passage no intimation as to what was the actual order of Philo's own works.* 2. This is also the case with the second passage, de praemiis et poenis, ed. Mang. ii. 408 sq. Philo here divides the revelations (λόγια) imparted by means of Moses into three categories (ἰδέαι), viz. (1) τὴν περὶ κοσμοποιΐας, (2) τὸ ἱστορικὸν μέρος, i.e. the ἀναγραφὴ πονηρῶν καὶ σπουδαίων βίων, and (3) τὸ νομοθετικὸν μέρος. Of all this he had, so far as time allowed, treated in his former writings. This indication too can with respect to the ἱστορικὸν μέρος refer only to the allegorical commentary. I cannot however discern in it any intimation as to the actual order of Philo's own works, since only the order of the contents of the Pentateuch is given, and it is said, that all this was treated of in Philo's earlier writings.

[42] J. G. Müller, *Des Juden Philo Buch von der Weltschöpfung, herausgegeben und erklärt*, Berlin 1841.

3. Βίος πολιτικὸς ὅπερ ἐστὶ περὶ Ἰωσήφ. De Josepho (Mangey, ii. 41–79).—After the life of Abraham we next expect the biographies of Isaac and Jacob. That Philo wrote these is made certain by the opening of de Josepho. They seem however to have been very soon lost, since not a trace of them is anywhere preserved. The beginning of de Josepho makes it also certain, that this composition follows here, which is strange, since we might have expected that the number of typical βίοι was exhausted with the triad Abraham, Isaac and Jacob. Joseph however is made to succeed them, because the examples of Abraham, Isaac and Jacob refer only to the ideal cosmopolitan state of the world, not to the empiric world with its various constitutions. The life of Joseph is therefore said to show, " how the wise man has to move in actually existing political life." [43]—In the editions the title is βίος πολιτικοῦ, the manuscripts have βίος πολιτικός (Mangey, ii. 41, note. Pitra, Analecta, ii. 317). Euseb. H. E. ii. 18. 6 : ὁ πολιτικός. Photius, Biblioth. cod. 103 : περὶ βίου πολιτικοῦ. Suidas, Lex. s.v. Ἀβραάμ· Φίλων ἐν τῷ τοῦ πολιτικοῦ βίῳ (Suidas in the article Φίλων, following the Greek translator of Jerome, writes περὶ ἀγωγῆς βίου).

4. Περὶ τῶν δέκα λογίων ἃ κεφάλαια νόμων εἰσί. De decalogo (Mangey, ii. 180–209).—After the life of Joseph is generally inserted the life of Moses, which certainly would, according to its literary character, be in place in this group. It is however nowhere intimated that this composition, which comes forward quite independently, is organically connected with the entire work now under discussion. Nay it would be an interruption in it. For in it Moses as a lawgiver stands alone, he is thus no universally valid type of moral conduct, nor is he depicted as such.—Hence the composition de decalogo with which the representation of the legislation proper (τῶν ἀναγραφέντων νόμων, de decal. § 1) begins, reciting indeed first of all the ten commandments, given by God Himself without the intervention of Moses, must necessarily follow

[43] Siegfried, Zeitschr. für wissenschaftl. Theologie, 1874, p. 565 sq.

the life of Joseph.—The title of this composition vacillates very
much in the manuscripts (Mangey, ii. 180, note). The usual
form περὶ τῶν δέκα λογίων, resting on the *cod. Augustanus,*
is confirmed by Euseb. *H. E.* ii. 18. 5. Jerome, in consequence of a careless abbreviation in the text of Eusebius,
has *de tabernaculo et decalogo libri quattuor.*

5. Περὶ τῶν ἀναφερομένων ἐν εἴδει νόμων εἰς τὰ συντείνοντα κεφάλαια τῶν δέκα λόγων α′ β′ γ′ δ′. *On the special
laws referring to the respective heads of the ten sayings.*
Such is the title according to Euseb. *H. E.* ii. 18. 5 of the
work *de specialibus legibus;* and with this agree the Philo-
manuscripts with the sole exception, that instead of εἰς τὰ
συντείνοντα κεφάλαια τῶν δέκα λόγων its special contents are
stated for each of the four books (*e.g.* εἰς τρία γένη τῶν δέκα
λόγων, τὸ τρίτον, τὸ τέταρτον, τὸ πέμπτον κ.τ.λ.). In this work
Philo makes a very laudable attempt to reduce the special Mosaic
laws to a systematic arrangement, according to the ten rubrics
of the decalogue. Thus he states in connection with the first
and second commandments (the worship of God) the entire
legislation concerning the priesthood and sacrifices, in connection with the fourth (the sanctification of the Sabbath) all
the laws concerning festivals, in connection with the seventh
(the prohibition of adultery) the marriage laws, in connection
with the remaining three the entire civil and criminal law.
Herein, notwithstanding the brevity of statement, we frequently recognise an agreement with the Palestinian Halachah.
Philo indeed has no professional acquaintance with it, on
which account we also meet with many divergences there-
from.[44] According to the testimony of Eusebius, *H. E.* ii. 18. 5,
the whole work comprised *four books,* which have, it seems,
been preserved entire, though needing to be restored, from the
mangling they have undergone in the manuscripts.

(*a*) Book I.: περὶ τῶν ἀναφερομένων ἐν εἴδει νόμων εἰς β′
κεφάλαια τῶν δέκα λογίων τό τε μὴ νομίζειν ἔξω ἑνὸς θεοῦ

---

[44] On Philo's relation to the Halachah, comp. the careful investigation of
Bernh. Ritter, *Philo und die Halacha, eine vergleichende Studie,* Leipzig 1879.

ἐτέρους αὐτοκρατεῖς καὶ τὸ μὴ χειρότμητα θεὸν πλαστεῖν. This title, which is missing in the editions, stands in the *cod. Mediceus* at the head of the treatise *de circumcisione* (Mangey, ii. 210, note). But even without this external evidence, the commencement of the said treatise would of itself prove, that this first book begins with it. The whole book comprises the following pieces : *de circumcisione* (Mangey, ii. 210–212), *de monarchia* (Mangey, ii. 213–222),[45] *de monarchia*, lib. ii. (Mangey, ii. 222–232), *de praemiis sacerdotum* (ii. 232–237), *de victimis* (ii. 237–250),[46] *de sacrificantibus* or *de victimas offerentibus* (ii. 251–264), *de mercede meretricis non accipienda in sacrarium* (ii. 264–269).[47]

(*b*) Book II. : περὶ τῶν ἀναφερομένων ἐν εἴδει νόμων εἰς τρία γένη τῶν δέκα λόγων, τὸ τρίτον, τὸ τέταρτον, τὸ πέμπτον, τὸ περὶ εὐορκίας καὶ σεβασμοῦ τῆς ἱερᾶς ἑβδομάδος καὶ γονέων τιμῆς.[48] Under this title the editions give first only a small portion (Mangey, ii. 270–277), and then add as a separate portion the treatise *de septenario* (Mangey, ii. 227–298), which of course belongs to this book. The text of *de septenario* is however incomplete in Mangey, and the treatise which we expect, *de colendis parentibus*, is entirely missing. The greater portion of this missing treatise was already given by Mai (*De cophini festo et de colendis parentibus*, Mediolan. 1818, also in *Classicor. auctor.* vol. iv. 402–429) ; but the complete text of this book was first given by Tischendorf, *Philonea*, pp. 1–83.[49]

(*c*) Book III. : περὶ τῶν ἀναφερομένων ἐν εἴδει νόμων εἰς δύο γένη τῶν δέκα λόγων, τὸ ἕκτον καὶ τὸ ἕβδομον, τὸ κατὰ μοίχων καὶ παντὸς ἀκολάστου καὶ τὸ κατὰ ἀνδροφόνων καὶ πάσης βίας (Mangey, ii. 299–334).—According to Mangey, ii. 299, note, Philo here shows a knowledge of Roman law.

---

[45] The beginning is also in Euseb. *Praep. ev.* xiii. 18. 12 sqq. ed. Gaisford.

[46] This piece is mentioned Euseb. *H. E.* ii. 18. 5, as a separate composition : περὶ τῶν εἰς τὰς ἱερουργίας ζώων καὶ τίνα τὰ τῶν θυσιῶν εἴδη.

[47] On where this piece belongs, see especially Gfrörer, i. 12 sq.

[48] The title according to Tischendorf, *Philonea*, p. 1.

[49] Emendations to the text of Tischendorf were given by Holwerda, 1873. See note 12 above.

(d) Book IV.: περὶ τῶν ἀναφερομένων ἐν εἴδει νόμων εἰς τρία
γένη τῶν δέκα λογίων, τὸ ή καὶ τὸ θ' καὶ ί, τὸ περὶ τοῦ μὴ
ἐπικλέπτειν καὶ ψευδομαρτυρεῖν καὶ μὴ ἐπιθυμεῖν καὶ τῶν ἐς
ἕκαστον ἀναφερομένων· καὶ περὶ δικαιοσύνης, ἣ πᾶσι τοῖς
λογίοις ἐφαρμόζει, ὅ ἐστι τῆς συντάξεως (Mangey, ii. 335–
358).—This book was first published by Mangey from the
cod. Bodleianus, 3400. Some kind of word (such as τέλος) or
the number δ' is missing at the close of the title. In the
editions the last sections also appear under the special titles:
de judice (ii. 344–348) and de concupiscentia (ii. 348–358).
That they are also integral portions of this book cannot, considering their contents, be doubtful.—To the same book too
belongs as an appendix, the treatise περὶ δικαιοσύνης, de
justitia (Mangey, ii. 358–374), which again is in the editions
wrongly divided into two sections: de justitia (ii. 358–361)
and de creatione principum (ii. 361–374). The latter section
does not deal exclusively with the appointment of authorities,
but is simply a continuation of the treatise de justitia. This
whole treatise is closely connected with the fourth book de
specialibus legibus, nay forms part of it, as is intimated by the
closing words of the latter (Mang. ii. 358: νυνὶ δὲ περὶ τῆς
. . . δικαιοσύνης λεκτέον) and especially by the title of the
whole book, in which it is expressly stated, that it also treats
περὶ δικαιοσύνης, ἣ πᾶσι τοῖς λογίοις ἐφαρμόζει (Mangey, ii.
335).[50]

6. Περὶ τριῶν ἀρετῶν ἤτοι περὶ ἀνδρείας καὶ φιλανθρωπίας
καὶ μετανοίας. De fortitudine (Mangey, ii. 375–383), de
caritate (ii. 383–405), de poenitentia (ii. 405–407).—The
treatise de justitia, the continuation of which is here given, is
referred to in the commencement of this book (περὶ δικαιοσύνης καὶ τῶν κατ' αὐτὴν ὅσα καίρια πρότερον εἰπών, μέτειμι

---

[50] In Mangey λογίκοις is printed. I suppose this, a printer's error, is for
λογίοις. At all events the latter must be the reading. For the thought is,
that justice, like the other cardinal virtues, is realized, not by the practice
of any one of the commandments, but by the practice of all the ten (it is
τοῖς δέκα λογίοις ἐφαρμόττουσα, as it is said at the close of de concupiscentia
(Mang. ii. 358).

τὸ ἑξῆς ἐπ᾿ ἀνδρίαν). This book then also belongs to the
appendix of the work *de specialibus legibus,* and it was only
an external reason (viz. that of making the two books nearly
equal in extent) which occasioned Philo to combine a portion
of this appendix with the fourth book itself, and to give the
rest as a separate book.[51]  The title of this book is found, as
given by Mangey in *cod. Bodleianus* (Mang. ii. 375, note).
Confirmed by Euseb. *H. E.* ii. 18. 2 : περὶ τῶν τριῶν ἀρετῶν,
ἃς σὺν ἄλλαις ἀνέγραψε Μωϋσῆς.  Hieronymus, *vir. illustr.*
11 : *de tribus virtutibus liber unus.*  Two manuscripts, the
*Mediceus* and *Lincolniensis,* have on the other hand : περὶ
ἀρετῶν ἤτοι περὶ ἀνδρείας καὶ εὐσεβείας καὶ φιλανθρωπίας
καὶ μετανοίας.  It seems to speak in favour of this title, that
the treatise *de caritate* begins with the words (Mang. ii. 383) :
τὴν δὲ εὐσεβείας συγγενεστάτην καὶ ἀδελφὴν καὶ δίδυμον
ὄντως ἑξῆς ἐπισκεπτέον, φιλανθρωπίαν, as though a treatise
*de pietate* were missing between *de fortitudine* and *de caritate.*
Still the words do not necessarily require this meaning.  On
the contrary the title of the *Med.* and *Lincoln.* seems to have
arisen from this incorrect meaning.[52]—According to Gfrörer
and Dähne only the treatise *de fortitudine* is in place here,
and the two others (*de caritate* and *de poenitentia*) must be
entirely separated from it and added as an appendix to the

---

[51] That such external reasons were of authority in the literary activity of
the ancients is shown especially by Birt (*Das antike Buchwesen in seinem
Verhältniss zur Litteratur,* 1882).—In Philo it is observable almost throughout, that his books occupy about thirty to forty pages in Mangey's edition.

[52] The predicate τὴν εὐσεβείας συγγενεστάτην is said to serve only to
characterize the high value of the φιλανθρωπία (it is directly related to
εὐσέβεια, the source of all virtues).—According to the close of *de concupiscentia* (Mang. ii. 358), Philo had already on a former occasion spoken on
εὐσέβεια and some other cardinal virtues (περὶ μὲν οὖν τῆς ἡγεμονίδος τῶν
ἀρετῶν εὐσεβείας καὶ ὁσιότητος, ἔτι δὲ καὶ Φρονήσεως καὶ σωφροσύνης εἴρηται
πρότερον).  It is probable that this does not mean a separate lost book, but
certain sections in the books that have come down to us.  See Grossmann,
i. pp. 22–24.—We see moreover that the Stoic enumeration of four cardinal
virtues, which Philo elsewhere adopts (*Leg. alleg.* i. 56, Mang. : φρόνησις,
σωφροσύνη, ἀνδρία, δικαιοσύνη ; comp. Zeller, 3rd ed. iii. 2. 403), is here also
the basis, though not strictly adhered to.

*Vita Mosis.*[53] The sole foundation however for this view
is the bare fact, that in the beginning of *de caritate* the *Vita
Mosis* is cited. This is certainly too weak an argument to
oppose to the testimony of the manuscripts to the connection of these three treatises with each other. Their contents
on the contrary show, that the treatises here placed together,
belong to the work *de specialibus legibus. Those Mosaic laws also
are here placed together which belong, not to the rubrics of the ten
commandments, but to the rubric of certain cardinal virtues,*
which latter indeed are only actually realized by the practice
of the Decalogue in its entirety (compare the close of *de
concupiscentia*, ii. 358, Mangey).[54]

7. Περὶ ἄθλων καὶ ἐπιτιμίων. *De praemiis et poenis*
(Mangey, ii. 408 – 428).— Περὶ ἀρῶν. *De execrationibus*
(Mangey, ii. 429–437). — These two pieces so inaptly
separated from each other form in reality but *one* book.
Comp. Euseb. *H. E.* ii. 18. 5 : περὶ τῶν προκειμένων ἐν τῷ
νόμῳ τοῖς μὲν ἀγαθοῖς ἄθλων, τοῖς δὲ πονηροῖς ἐπιτιμίων καὶ
ἀρῶν.—In the beginning of this composition Philo says, that
having in his former works treated of the three main
categories of the Mosaic revelations (the κοσμοποιΐα, the
ἱστορικόν and the νομοθετικὸν μέρος), he now purposed to
pass to the rewards appointed for the good, and the penalties
destined for the wicked. Hence this writing is later than
the works of Philo hitherto discussed and joins on as a sort
of epilogue to the delineation of the Mosaic legislation.—On
the treatise *de nobilitate*, which Mangey combines with this
composition, see below, No. IV. 7.

IV. Besides these three large works on the Pentateuch,

---

[53] Gfrörer, i. 17–25. Dähne, *Stud. und Krit.* 1833, pp. 1033–1036.
Ersch and Grüber, art. "Philon," p. 443.

[54] Gfrörer certainly asserts (i. 20) that the treatise *de caritate* "is not
written in so didactic and analytic a manner as the compositions *de fortitudine* and *de justitia*, but historically and with constant reference to the
life of Moses." In truth however the *de caritate*, being a summary of all
such Mosaic laws as fall under the rubric of φιλανθρωπία (comp. the survey
of its contents in Richter's ed. v. 181), properly belongs to the work *de
specialibus legibus.*

Philo wrote several separate compositions, of which the following have been preserved, some entire, some in fragments.

1. Περὶ βίου Μωσέως.[55] *Vita Mosis*, lib. i. (Mangey, ii. 80–133), lib. ii. (Mangey, ii. 134–144), lib. iii. (Mangey, ii. 145–179).—The division into three books is already found in the manuscripts, but is certainly a false one, as is proved by the following quotation by Philo himself, *de caritate*, § 1 (Mangey, ii. 383 sq.): δεδήλωται πρότερον ἐν δυσὶ συντάξεσιν, ἃς ἀνέγραψα περὶ τοῦ βίου Μωϋσέως.[56] Our books i. and ii. are in fact but one book, as even their extent serves to show. The work is already quoted by Clemens Alexandrinus, *Strom.* i. 23. 153: ᾗ φησι Φίλων ἐν τῷ Μωνσέως βίῳ. Comp. also *Strom.* ii. 19. 100. Hence it is the more remarkable, that it should be absent from the catalogue of Eusebius. In its place appears (*H. E.* ii. 18. 5) a work περὶ τῆς σκηνῆς. Now as the tabernacle is fully described in the *Vita Mosis*, the treatise περὶ τῆς σκηνῆς is certainly a portion of the *Vita Mosis*;[57] probably however the text of Eusebius is imperfect. The date of composition of this work was according to Mangey, ii. 141 (see the passage, note 41 above), probably antecedent to that of the large work on the Mosaic legislation; but probably subsequent to *de mundi opificio* (see below, note 82), and thus, to speak more precisely, between *de mundi opif.* and *de Abrahamo*. We have already seen (p. 342 sq.), that it is no integral element of the delineation of the Mosaic legislation, though certainly connected with it by its entire literary character. *For as in the larger work the Mosaic legislation, so in this the*

---

[55] Mangey gives the title in the following form: Περὶ βίου Μοσέως (*sic!*) ὅπερ ἐστὶ περὶ θεολογίας καὶ προφητείας. The addition is a very inappropriate one, since the work treats first (Book i.) of Moses as a ruler, and afterwards (Book ii.) of Moses as lawgiver, priest and prophet.

[56] The reading τρισί adopted by Mangey and his followers instead of δυσί is found in only *one* manuscript, *cod. Paris*, Reg. 2251 (Mangey, ii. 80, note, 383, note). Comp. also Dähne, *Stud. und Krit.* 1833, p. 1031 sq. Ewald, vi. 300.

[57] So also Grossmann, i. p. 24.

*life and acts of the legislator himself are portrayed for heathen
readers.*

2. Περὶ τοῦ πάντα σπουδαῖον εἶναι ἐλεύθερον. *Quod omnis
probus liber* (Mangey, ii. 445–470).—This work is properly
only one half of a larger one, which worked out the thought
suggested in the title in its two opposite aspects, Euseb.
*H. E.* ii. 18. 6 : περὶ τοῦ δοῦλον εἶναι πάντα φαῦλον,
ᾧ ἑξῆς ἐστιν ὁ περὶ τοῦ πάντα σπουδαῖον ἐλεύθερον εἶναι.
Philo himself alludes to the first and missing half in the
opening of the second and preserved half. A long portion of
the latter (on the Essenes) is given in Euseb. *Praep. evang.*
viii. 12. The *genuineness* of the work has not been un-
assailed. The circumstance that the description of the
Essenes differs in a few subordinate points from that given
by Philo himself in another work (*Apologia pro Judaeis* in
Euseb. *Praep. evang.* viii. 11), has especially given rise to
suspicion. Its genuineness is however, according to the
thorough investigations of Lucius, surpassingly probable.
The work may, it is conjectured, belong to Philo's earliest
period and may not give the description of the Essenes
according to his own inspection.[58]

3. Εἰς Φλάκκον. *Adversus Flaccum* (Mangey, ii. 517–
544).—Περὶ ἀρετῶν καὶ πρεσβείας πρὸς Γάιον. *De legatione
ad Cajum* (Mangey, ii. 545–600).—In these two books Philo
relates the persecutions which the Jews had to endure,
especially at Alexandria, in the time of Caligula. The narrative
is so detailed and graphic, that it could be written only by
one who had himself participated in a prominent manner in
the events. This circumstance makes these two books an
authority of the first rank, not only for the history of the
Jews of those days, but also for the history of Caligula. It
cannot be perceived from the statements in Mangey, how the

---

[58] Lucius, *Der Essenismus* (1881), pp. 13–23. Hilgenfeld also esteems
this work genuine, but on the contrary regards the *Apologia pro Judaei*
as spurious (*Zeitschrift für wissensch. Theol.* 1882, pp. 275–278. *Ketzer-
geschichte des Urchristenthums*, 1884, pp. 87 sq., 105–116).

titles run in the best manuscripts.    On the title Φίλωνος εἰς
Φλάκκον he only remarks (ii. 517): similiter codex Mediceus,
in reliquis vero manuscriptis scribitur Φίλωνος Ἑβραίου
ἱστορία ὠφέλιμος καὶ πάνυ βίῳ χρήσιμος.    Τὰ κατὰ τὸν
Φλάκκον [sic: therefore not τοῦ Φλάκκου] ἤτοι περὶ προνοίας.[58a]
Still more indefinite are Mangey's statements concerning the
title of the second composition (ii. 545): in nonnullis codicibus
sic legitur: ἱστορία χρήσιμος καὶ πάνυ ὠφέλιμος περὶ τῶν
κατὰ τὸν Γάϊον καὶ τῆς αἰτίας τῆς πρὸς ἅπαν τὸ Ἰουδαίων
ἔθνος ἀπεχθείας αὐτοῦ.    According to the statements of Pitra
(Analecta sacra, ii. 318 sq.) the titles usual in the printed text
Εἰς Φλάκκον and Περὶ ἀρετῶν καὶ πρεσβείας πρὸς Γάϊον appear
to be also those which prevail in the manuscripts.    In Photius,
Bibliotheca cod. 105 (ed. Bekker), it is said: Ἀνεγνώσθη δὲ
αὐτοῦ καὶ λόγος οὗ ἡ ἐπιγραφὴ " Γάϊος ψεγόμενος " καὶ
" Φλάκκος ἢ Φλάκκων ψεγόμενος," ἐν οἷς λόγοις κ.τ.λ.
(therefore two λόγοι).    So too Eusebius in the Chronicle.[59]
Comp. also Johannes Monachus ineditus (Mangey, ii. 517):
ἐκ τῶν κατὰ Φλάκκου.    On the titles mentioned by Eusebius
in the Ecclesiastical History see farther on.    Only the two
books which have come down to us seem to have been extant
in the time of Photius.    But the beginning of the first and
the close of the second show, that they are only portions of a
larger whole.    For the book adversus Flaccum begins (ii. 517):
Δεύτερος μετὰ Σηιανὸν Φλάκκος Ἀουίλλιος διαδέχεται
τὴν κατὰ τῶν Ἰουδαίων ἐπιβουλήν.    Thus this book was
preceded by another, in which the persecutions inflicted on
the Jews by Sejanus were narrated.    The book de legatione

---

[58a] The title κατὰ Φλάκκον also in the codex Coislinianus is in Pitra,
Analecta sacra, ii. 310.

[59] Euseb. Chron. ed. Schoene, ii. 150–151.    The text runs : (a) according
to Jerome (l.c. p. 151, note k): Refert Filo in eo libro qui Flaccus
inscribitur ; (b) according to the Armenian (p. 150, note q) : Philon in eo
libro, quem ipse ad Flacum scripsit, refert ; (c) according to Syncellus (ed.
Dindorf, i. 626) : Φίλων ἱστορεῖ ἐν τῷ ἐπιγεγραμμένῳ λόγῳ Φλάκκῳ (the title
ad Flacum in the Armenian translation arose from a mistaken understanding
of this dative Φλάκκῳ.    Thus a comparison of Jerome and the Armenian
shows, that the correct text of Eusebius is preserved in Syncellus).

*ad Cajum* moreover ends with the words: Εἴρηται μὲν οὖν κεφαλαιωδέστερον ἡ αἰτία τῆς πρὸς ἅπαν τὸ Ἰουδαίων ἔθνος ἀπεχθείας Γαΐου· λεκτέον δὲ καὶ τὴν παλινῳδίαν [πρὸς Γαΐον].⁶⁰ Hence another book must have followed, in which Philo related the παλινῳδία, *i.e.* the turn for the better in the fate of the Jews by the death of Caligula and the edict of toleration of Claudius. Now we know also from a notice in the *Chronicle* of Eusebius, that the persecutions under Sejanus were related in the *second book* of this entire work.⁶¹ Consequently we should reckon not less than *five books* for the whole. And this is confirmed by the decided statement in the *Ecclesiastical History* of Eusebius, ii. 5. 1: καὶ δὴ τὰ κατὰ Γάιον οὗτος Ἰουδαίοις συμβάντα πέντε βιβλίοις παραδίδωσι. The brief survey too, given by Eusebius of the contents of this work, agrees exactly with these results. For he says, that Philo here relates, how in the time of Tiberius Sejanus made great exertions in Rome to destroy the whole nation, and that in Judaea Pilate caused great commotion among the Jews, because he desired to undertake something with respect to the temple, which was contrary to their institutions.⁶² After the death however of Tiberius, Caius, who then came to the throne, behaved indeed with the greatest arrogance to all, but inflicted most injury on the

⁶⁰ The words πρὸς Γάιον are according to Mangey missing in the manuscripts, and must therefore certainly be expunged.

⁶¹ Euseb. *Chron.* ed. Schoene, ii. 150–151, and indeed: (*a*) according to Jerome (*l.c.* p. 151, note *b*): Seianus praefectus Tiberii, qui aput eum plurimum poterat, instantissime cohortatur, ut gentem Judaeorum deleat. Filo meminit *in libro legationis secundo.* (*b*) According to the Armenian (p. 150): Seianus Tiberii procurator, qui intimus erat consiliarius regis, universim gentem Judaeorum deperdendam exposcebat. Meminit autem hujus Philon *in secunda relatione.* (*c*) According to Syncellus (ed. Dindorf, i. 621): Σηιανὸς ἔπαρχος Τιβερίου Καίσαρος περὶ τελείας ἀπωλείας τοῦ ἔθνους τῶν Ἰουδαίων πολλὰ συνεβούλευε τῷ Καίσαρι, ὡς Φίλων Ἰουδαῖος ἐξ Ἀλεξανδρείας διάγων ἱστορεῖ ἐν τῇ δευτέρᾳ τῆς περὶ αὐτοῦ πρεσβείας.

⁶² *II. E.* ii. 5. 7: Πρῶτον δὴ οὖν κατὰ Τιβέριον ἐπὶ μὲν τῆς Ῥωμαίων πόλεως ἱστορεῖ Σηιανὸν ... ἄρδην τὸ πᾶν ἔθνος ἀπολέσθαι σπουδὴν εἰσηγηοχέναι, ἐπὶ δὲ τῆς Ἰουδαίας Πιλᾶτον ... περὶ τὸ ἐν Ἱεροσολύμοις ἔτι τότε συνεστὼς ἱερὸν ἐπιχειρήσαντά τι παρὰ τὸ Ἰουδαίοις ἐξὸν τὰ μέγιστα αὐτοὺς ἀναταράξαι.

whole Jewish nation.[63]      What is here said respecting Sejanus
and Pilate cannot refer to some occasional declarations in the
books preserved to us.   For these treat only of the time of
Caligula.   The oppressions however of Sejanus and Pilate
must, according to the above intimations of Eusebius, have
been related in a separate paragraph, before the events under
Caligula.   From all that has been said the following must
consequently have been the *arrangement of the whole work*.
Book i. contained, it may be presumed, a general introduction.
Book ii. related the oppressions in the reign of Tiberius, by
Sejanus in Rome and by Pilate in Judaea.   Among the former
must undoubtedly be placed the important measure of A.D. 19,
by which all Jews were banished from Rome.[64]      Among the
attempts of Pilate "to undertake something with respect to
the *temple* contrary to Jewish institutions," the setting up of
consecrated shields in the palace of Herod, mentioned in the
letter of Agrippa,[65] communicated by Philo, cannot at all
events be intended; we must rather regard them as the facts
recorded by Josephus, viz. that Pilate caused the soldiers to
march into Jerusalem with the imperial ensigns and employed
the temple-treasure in building an aqueduct.[66]   That the
former act was also related by Philo is expressly testified by
Eusebius.[67]   Book iii. is the preserved composition *adversus
Flaccum*, which relates the persecution of the Alexandrinian

---

[63] *H. E.* ii. 6. 1 : Μετὰ δὲ τὴν Τιβερίου τελευτὴν Γάϊον τὴν ἀρχὴν παρει-
ληφότα . . . πάντων μάλιστα τὸ πᾶν 'Ιουδαίων ἔθνος οὐ σμικρὰ κατα-
βλάψαι.

[64] Tacitus, *Annal.* ii. 85.   Sueton. *Tiber.* 36.   Joseph. *Antt.* xviii. 3. 5.
Comp. also Philo, *Legat. ad Cajum*, § 24 (Mang. ii. 569).

[65] Philo, *Legat. ad Cajum*, § 38 (Mang. ii. 589 sq.).

[66] Joseph. *Antt.* xviii. 3. 1–2.   *Bell. Jud.* ii. 9. 2–4.   Comp. Euseb.
*H. E.* ii. 6.

[67] Euseb. *Demonstratio evangelica*, viii. p. 403 : Αὐτὰ δὴ ταῦτα καὶ ὁ
Φίλων συμμαρτυρεῖ, τὰς σημαίας φάσκων τὰς βασιλικὰς τὸν Πιλάτον νύκτωρ
ἐν τῷ ἱερῷ ἀναθεῖναι.   A confusion with Josephus cannot exist, since
Eusebius just before in the same passage quotes Josephus also as authority
for the same fact.—It must also be remembered, that the setting up of the
statue took place according to Philo in the *temple, i.e.* the temple forecourt
(which indeed Eusebius erroneously gives as also the account of Josephus).

Jews arising from the initiative of the populace of that city
in the commencement of Caligula's reign. It had as yet
nothing to do with the setting up of the statue of the emperor
in the Jewish synagogue, nor with any edict of Caligula. In
Book iv., on the contrary, *i.e.* in the *Legatio ad Cajum*, which
is preserved, are depicted the sufferings inflicted on the Jews
in consequence of the edict of Caligula, that Divine honours
should everywhere be paid him. Lastly, the lost Book v.
treated of the παλινῳδία in the sense stated above.

The statements of Eusebius give rise also to some difficulties
with regard to the *title of the entire work*. According to the
passage from the *Chronicle* quoted above (note 61), the whole
work seems to have been designated ἡ πρεσβεία. And
Eusebius says also, when giving the contents of the whole
work, that all this is written ἐν ᾗ συνέγραψε πρεσβείᾳ (*H. E.*
ii. 5. 6). This title is therefore possible, because Philo's
account of the embassy to Caligula, of which he was the
leader, forms in fact the kernel of the whole. The several
books might then have had their special titles, such as Φλάκκος
or the like (see above, p. 350). Now Eusebius says further,
towards the conclusion of his summary of the contents, that
Philo had related a thousand other sufferings, which befell the
Jews at Alexandria ἐν δευτέρῳ συγγράμματι ᾧ ἐπέγραψε
"περὶ ἀρετῶν" (*H. E.* ii. 6. 3). From this it appears to
result, that Philo had treated of these events in two works,
the title of one being ἡ πρεσβεία, of the other περὶ ἀρετῶν.
This inference is however precluded not only by its
improbability, but by the circumstance, that Eusebius in his
chief catalogue of Philo's writings, *H. E.* ii. 18, only mentions
the latter title. He says, that Philo ironically gave to his
work on the ungodly deeds of Caius the title περὶ ἀρετῶν
(*H. E.* ii. 18. 8). No other work referring to these events is
mentioned, though the catalogue is in other respects a very
complete one. We are thus, I think, constrained to admit,
that the δευτέρῳ is the gloss of a transcriber, who could not
make the different titles in ii. 5. 6 and ii. 6. 3 harmonize,

and that in fact both titles refer to one and the same work.

A special interest has always been attached to this work by reason of its importance as an historical authority. It has been repeatedly published separately,[68] translated into modern languages[69] and made the subject of historical research.[70] The dispute of its genuineness by Grätz scarcely deserves mention.[71] This book must not be confounded with the book *de tribus virtutibus* (see above, p. 345), nor with that published by Mai, *de virtute ejusque partibus* (see above, note 10).

4. Περὶ προνοίας. *De providentia.*—The title in Euseb. *H. E.* ii. 18. 6 ; *Praep. evang.* vii. 20 *fin.*, viii. 13 *fin.* The work is only preserved in Armenian, and has been published by Aucher with a Latin translation.[72] Two Greek fragments, a smaller and a very large one in Euseb. *Praep. evang.* vii. 21

---

[68] *Philonis Judaei lib. de virtutibus s. de legatione ad Cajum imp. graece cura,* S. F. N. Mori, Lips. 1781. Dahl, *Chrestomathia Philoniana,* 2 vols. 1800–1802. On a Paris edition of 1626 comp. Fabricius–Harles, iv. 741. Fürst, *Biblioth. Judaica,* iii. 89.

[69] *Die Gesandtschaft an den Cajus, aus dem Griechischen des Philo,* translated by Jo. Frid. Eckhard, Leipzig 1783. *Philo Judaeus, om Judarnas förföljelse under Flaccus och Legationen till Cajus Caligula, etc., öfversättn. med noter och anmerkn.,* by J. Berggren, Söderköping 1853. *Philon d'Alexandrie, écrits historiques, influence, luttes et persécutions des juifs dans le monde romain,* by F. Delaunay, 2nd ed. Paris 1870 (gives a translation of *contra Flaccum* and *Leg. ad Caj.*). On an older French translation of d'Andilly, see Fabric.-Harles, iv. 749. On an English one, Fürst, *Bibl. Jud.* iii. 91. An English translation by Yonge of Philo's entire works appeared in 4 vols. London 1854–55.

[70] Comp. above, § 17ᵉ, and the literature there mentioned. Fabricius-Harles, *Biblioth. graec.* iv. 740 sq., and the works and articles there mentioned of Boecler, Tillemont, Ernesti and especially Jo. Christ. Gottleber, *Animadversiones historicae et philologico-criticae ad Philonis legationem ad Cajum,* 4 pts. Meissen 1773–74. Dähne in Ersch and Gruber, art. "Philon," pp. 439–440. Bloch, *Die Quellen des Flavius Josephus* (1879), pp. 117–123.

[71] Grätz, *Gesch. der Juden,* 2nd ed. iii. 487–492, abridged in the 3rd ed. iii. 681. Comp. also *Monaatsschr. für Gesch. und Wissensch. des Judenth.* 1877, pp. 97 sqq., 145 sqq.

[72] Aucher, *Philonis Judaei sermones tres,* etc. (1822) pp. 1–121. Also in Latin in Richter's hand edition (8th small vol.), and in the Tauchnitz edition (8th small vol.).

and viii. 14. The Armenian text comprises *two books*. Of
these however, the first, though on the whole genuine, has at
all events been preserved in only an abbreviated and in some
parts a touched up form.[73] Eusebius seems to have been
acquainted with only the second, at least both fragments
belong to this book, and are introduced by Eusebius with the
formula ἐν τῷ (*Sing*.) περὶ προνοίας.[74] In the *Ecclesiastical
History* the reading fluctuates between τὸ περὶ προνοίας and
τὰ περὶ προνοίας. There are quotations also in Johannes
Damascenus and Johannes Monachus ineditus.[75]

5. Ἀλέξανδρος ἢ περὶ τοῦ λόγον ἔχειν τὰ ἄλογα ζῶα (this
title in Euseb. *H. E.* ii. 18. 6). *De Alexandro et quod
propriam rationem muta animalia habeant* (so Jerome, *de viris
illustr.* c. 11).[76]—This work too is preserved only in Armenian,
and has been published by Aucher.[77] Two short Greek fragments are found in the Florilegium of Leontius and Johannes.[78]
The book belongs to Philo's later works, the embassy to Rome
being already contemplated, p. 152 (ed. Aucher).

6. Ὑποθετικά.—Our knowledge of this work rests solely
on the fragments in Euseb. *Praep. evang.* viii. 6–7, which are
introdu. ed by Eusebius with the words (viii. 5, *fin.*): Φίλωνος

---

[73] Comp. Diels, *Doxographi Graeci* (1879), pp. 1–4. Zeller, *Die
Philosophie der Griechen*, iii. 2 (3rd ed. 1881), p. 340.

[74] The first fragment (vii. 21) is from the middle of the second book
(Aucher, pp. 80–82) ; the second (viii. 14) consists of several large portions
extending throughout the second book, and forming a selection from it
(Aucher, pp. 44–121). The two small fragments, published by Höschel
(1614), and taken by him from the Ἰωνιά of Michael apostolius (see
Fabricius-Harles, v. 110 sq., ix. 758, xi. 189 sqq. Nicolai, *Griech. Litgesch.*
iii. 316 sqq.), are perhaps also derived from Eusebius. See the fragments
in the Frankfort ed. p. 1197 sq. ; and Euseb. *Praep. evang.* ed. Gaisford,
viii. 14. 2–7 and 39–41.

[75] See Mangey, ii. 634, note x.

[76] Some editions and manuscripts of Jerome have *De Alexandro dicente
quod*, etc.

[77] Aucher, *Philonis Judaei sermones tres*, etc. (1822) pp. 123–172. And
following him Richter (8th small vol.) and the Tauchnitz edition (8th
small vol.).

[78] Mai, *Script. vet. nov. coll.* vii. 1, p. 99ᵇ (below) : ἐκ τοῦ περὶ τῶν ἀλόγων
ζῷων. *Ibid.* p. 100ᵃ (above) : ἐκ τοῦ αὐτοῦ.

. . . ἀπὸ τοῦ πρώτου συγγράμματος ὧν ἐπέγραψεν Ὑποθετι-
κῶν, ἔνθα τὸν ὑπὲρ Ἰουδαίων ὡς πρὸς κατηγόρους αὐτῶν
ποιούμενος λόγον ταῦτά φησιν.    The title does not signify
" suppositions concerning the Jews,"[79] but, as Bernays has
pointed out, " counsels, recommendations."    For Ὑποθετικοὶ
λόγοι are such dissertations as contain moral counsels or
recommendations, in contradistinction to theoretical investigations of ethic questions.    Philo, as the preserved fragments
already show, has devoted the main point of his work to
the discussion of such Jewish precepts as he could *recommend* to the obedience of a non-Jewish circle of readers,
to whom the work is unmistakeably directed.[80]    As the
work pursues apologetic aims, we might be inclined to
regard it as identical with the *Apologia pro Judaeis* to be
forthwith mentioned, but that Eusebius distinguishes the two
by different titles.

7. Περὶ Ἰουδαίων.—This title in Euseb. *H. E.* ii. 18. 6.
Ἡ ὑπὲρ Ἰουδαίων ἀπολογία, from which Eusebius (*Praep.
evang.* viii. 11) borrows the description of the Essenes, is certainly
identical with this work.    The conjecture of Dähne, that the
piece *de nobilitate* (Mangey, ii. 437–444) also belongs to this
work is not improbable.[81]    It treats of true nobility *i.e.* of the
wisdom and virtue, of which the Jewish nation also was not
devoid, and is therefore a very suitable element in an apology
for the Jews.    The genuineness of the ἀπολογία has been
recently disputed by Hilgenfeld (see above, note 58).

V. The last-named works are only known to us by fragments, but the following books, most of which have been
already mentioned in this survey, are *entirely lost*.    (1) Of
the *Quaestiones et solutiones,* two books on Genesis and more

---

[79] So Ewald, vi. 304.   Comp. also Grossmann, i. p. 16.

[80] Bernays, "Philon's Hypothetika und die Verwünschungen des Buzyges
in Athen" (*Monatsberichte der Berliner Akademie*, 1876, pp. 589–609;
reprinted in Bernays, *Gesammelte Abhandlungen*, 1885, i. 262–282. Comp.
especially p. 599).

[81] Dähne, *Stud. und Krit.* 1833, pp. 990, 1037.   In the article " Philon "
in Ersch and Grüber, p. 440, Dähne again expresses this conjecture.

than three on Exodus (see above, p. 327). (2) Two books of
the *Legum allegoriae* (see above, p. 332). (3) The first book
περὶ μέθης (see p. 335). (4) Both the books περὶ διαθηκῶν
(see p. 337). (5) Three of the five books *de somniis* (see
p. 337). (6) The two biographies of Isaac and Jacob (see p.
342). (7) The work περὶ τοῦ δοῦλον εἶναι πάντα φαῦλον
(see p. 349). (8) The first, second and fifth books of the
work on the persecutions of the Jews under Caligula (see
p. 350). (9) A work περὶ ἀριθμῶν, to which Philo refers in
the *Vita Mosis* and elsewhere.[82] (10) A dialogue between Isaac
and Ishmael on the difference between true wisdom and sophisti-
cism, of which it is not indeed certain, whether Philo wrote or
only intended to write it.[83] (11) According to a remark in
*Quod omnis probus liber*, Philo intended to write a disquisi-
tion "On the government of the wise."[84] We do not know
whether this intention was carried out. (12) In the Florilegium of Leontius and Johannes a small piece is cited ἐκ τῶν
περὶ τοῦ ἱεροῦ.[85] Can a work known to us under some other
name be intended?

VI. The following supposed works of Philo are now pretty
generally regarded as spurious:—

1. Περὶ βίου θεωρητικοῦ ἢ ἱκετῶον ἀρετῶν. *De vita contemplativa* (Mangey, ii. 471–486).—Eusebius twice cites the

---

[82] *Vita Mosis*, lib. iii. § 11 (Mang. ii. 152): ἔχει δὲ καὶ τὰς ἄλλας ἀμυθήτους ἀρετὰς ἡ τετράς, ὧν τὰς πλείστας ἠκριβώσαμεν ἐν τῇ περὶ ἀριθμῶν
πραγματείᾳ.—*Quaest. et solut. in Genes.* ed. Aucher, p. 331: jam dictum
fuit in libro, in quo de numeris actum est. Comp. the same, pp. 224, 359.
Grossmann, i. p. 24. In the work *de opificio mundi* Philo refers to a
dissertation on the number four *as one yet to be written*, p. 11, Mang.:
πολλαῖς δὲ καὶ ἄλλαις κέχρηται δυνάμεσι ἡ τετρὰς ἃς ἀκριβέστερον καὶ ἐν τῷ
περὶ αὐτῆς ἰδίῳ λόγῳ προσυποδεικτέον. If this is identical with the work
περὶ ἀριθμῶν, it would follow, that the *Vita Mosis* was a later work than *de
opificio mundi*. Comp. Grossmann, ii. p. 6.

[83] *De sobrietate*, § 2 (Mang. i. 394 above): Σοφίαν μὲν γὰρ Ἰσαάκ,
σοφιστείαν δὲ Ἰσμαὴλ κεκλήρωται, ὡς, ἐπειδὰν ἑκάτερον χαρακτηρίζωμεν, ἔν
τισι διαλόγοις ἐπιδείκνυμεν. Comp. Grossmann, i. p. 25.

[84] *Quod omnis probus liber*, § 3 (Mang. ii. 448): Ἀλλ' ὁ μὲν περὶ τῆς
ἀρχῆς τοῦ σοφοῦ λόγος εἰς καιρὸν ἐπιτηδειότερον ὑπερκείσθω. Comp. Grossmann, i. p. 25.

[85] Mai, *Script. vet. nov. coll.* vii. 1, p. 103a.

title in the following form (*H. E.* ii. 17. 3 and ii. 18. 7):
περὶ βίου θεωρητικοῦ ἢ ἱκετῶν. The ἀρετῶν added at the
end must therefore be expunged. Eusebius, *H. E.* ii. 17, gives
full information concerning the contents, comp. also ii. 16. 2.
This composition has, since the time of Eusebius, enjoyed
special approbation in the Christian Church, Christian monks
being almost universally recognised in the "Therapeutae"
here described and glorified.[86] The likeness is indeed surprising; but for that very reason the suspicion is also well
founded, that the author's design was under the mask of
Philo to recommend Christian monachism. But apart from
this there are other suspicious elements, by reason of which
even such critics as do not regard the Therapeutae as representing a Christian, but as a Jewish ideal of life, have
denied the authorship of Philo.[87] Upon the ground of the
identification of the Therapeutae with Christian monks,
Lucius, after the precedent of Grätz and Jost,[88] has declared
this composition spurious.[89] It is by his thorough and
methodical investigation that the spuriousness of its authorship has been definitely decided.[90]

---

[86] Photius, *Bibliotheca cod.* 104 forms an exception: Ἀνεγνώσθησαν
δὲ καὶ τῶν παρὰ Ἰουδαίοις Φιλοσοφησάντων τήν τε θεωρητικὴν καὶ τὴν
πρακτικὴν Φιλοσοφίαν βίοι ὧν μὲν Ἐσσηνοὶ οἱ δὲ θεραπευταὶ ἐκαλοῦντο κ.τ.λ.
Epiphanius, *Haer.* 29. 5, quotes this composition with the formula ἐν τῇ περὶ
Ἰεσσαίων αὐτοῦ ἐπιγραφομένη βίβλῳ, but is nevertheless of opinion that it
treats of *Christians.* Compare the *testimonia veterum* before Mangey's
edition and the literature in Fabricius-Harles, iv. 738 sq. Of this older
literature must be specially mentioned Montfaucon's French translation,
furnished with valuable notes, *Le livre de Philon de la vie contemplative*
etc., *traduit sur l'original grec, avec des observations, ou l'on fait voir, que
les Therapeutes, dont il parle, etoient Chrestiens,* Paris 1709. The texts of
an old and of a more recent Latin version are given by Pitra, *Analecta
sacra,* ii. 322–331.

[87] Especially Nicolas, *Revue de Théologie,* Strasbourg 1868, p. 25 sqq.,
and Kuenen, *De godsdienst van Israël,* ii. 440–444. Also Weingarten,
art. "Mönchtum," in Herzog's *Real-Enc.* 2nd ed. 761–764.

[88] Grätz, *Gesch. der Juden,* 2nd ed. iii. 463 sqq. Jost, *Gesch. des
Judenthums und seiner Secten,* i. 214, note 2.

[89] Lucius, *Die Therapeuten und ihre Stellung in der Geschichte der Askese, eine
kritische Untersuchung der Schrift de vita contemplativa,* Strassburg 1879.

[90] Comp. also my notice of Lucius in the *Theol. Literaturzeitung,* 1880,

2. Περὶ ἀφθαρσίας κόσμου.   De incorruptibilitate mundi
(Mangey, ii. 487–516).—This composition is regarded as
genuine by Grossmann and Dähne.[91]  But even the transmission of the manuscripts and the external testimony are
unfavourable to its genuineness,[92] which since the investigations of Bernays has been generally given up.  Bernays has
also especially shown, that the traditional text has fallen into
disorder through the transposition of the pages.[93]  He has
published the text in Greek and German according to the
order restored by himself,[94] and furnished it with a commentary.[95]  Bücheler gives emendations of Bernays' text.[96]
Zeller attempts to show that the composition has been
touched up.[97]

3. Περὶ κόσμου.   De mundo (Mangey, ii. 601–624).—The
spuriousness of this work has long been acknowledged.[98]  It

pp. 111–118.  Hilgenfeld, *Zeitschr. für wissenschaftl. Theol.* 1880, pp. 423–
440.  Zeller, *Die Philosophie der Griechen,* iii. 2 (3rd ed. 1881), p. 307.  For
its genuineness also Delaunay, *Revue archéologique,* new series, vol. xxii.
(1870–71) pp. 268–282, xxvi. (1873) pp. 12–22.  The same, *Moines et
sibylles dans l'antiquité judéo-grecque* 1874, pp. 11–51.  Bestmann, *Gesch.
der christlichen Sitte,* vol. i. (1880) p. 133 sqq.

[91] Grossmann, i. p. 21.  Dähne in Ersch and Gruber, art. "Philon," p.
441.

[92] Mangey remarks of this composition (ii. 487, note) : deest in maxima
parte codicum, nec recensetur in indiculis Eusebii Hieronymi Photii et
Suidae.

[93] Bernays, "Ueber die Herstellung des Zusammenhanges in der unter
Philo's Namen gehenden Schrift περὶ ἀφθαρσίας κόσμου durch Blätterver-
setzung" (*Monatsberichte der Berliner Akademie,* 1863, pp. 34–40 ; reprinted
in Bernays, *Gesammelte Abhandlungen,* 1885, i. 283–290).

[94] Bernays, "Die unter Philon's Werken stehende Schrift über die
Unzerstörbarkeit des Weltalls nach ihrer ursprünglichen Anordnung wieder-
hergestellt und ins Deutsche übertragen" (*Transactions of the Berlin
Academy,* 1876, *phil.-hist. class,* pp. 209–278).  Also separately.

[95] Bernays, "Ueber die unter Philon's Werken stehende Schrift über
die Unzerstörbarkeit des Weltalls" (*Transactions of the Berlin Academy,*
1882, *phil.-hist. class,* Tr. iii. p. 82).  Also separately.  The commentary has
been published by Usener as a posthumous work of Bernays.

[96] Bücheler, *Philonea (Rhein. Museum,* vol. xxxii. 1877, pp. 433–444).

[97] Zeller, *Der pseudophilonische Bericht über Theophrast* (Hermes, vol.
xv. 1880, pp. 137–146).

[98] Wilh. Budäus, who translated it into Latin (1526), already acknowledged

is a collection of extracts from other works of Philo, especially
from the composition *de incorruptibilitate mundi*.[99]

4. *De Sampsone* (Aucher, *Paralipomena Armena*, 1826, pp.
549–577).—*De Jona* (Aucher, pp. 578–611).—A general
agreement prevails as to the spuriousness of these two
discourses, which are published in Armenian and Latin by
Aucher.[100]

5. *Interpretatio Hebraicorum nominum.* Origen, *Comment.
in Joann.* vol. ii. c. 27 (*Opp.* ed. Lommatzsch, i. 150), mentions
an apparently anonymous work on this subject: εὕρομεν
τοίνυν ἐν τῇ ἑρμηνείᾳ τῶν ὀνομάτων. Eusebius says, that it
is ascribed to Philo, but the manner in which he speaks of it
plainly shows, that he was only acquainted with the work as
an anonymous one, *H. E.* ii. 18. 7: καὶ τῶν ἐν νόμῳ δὲ καὶ
προφήταις Ἑβραϊκῶν ὀνομάτων αἱ ἑρμηνεῖαι τοῦ αὐτοῦ σπουδαὶ
εἶναι λέγονται. Jerome says, that according to the testimony
of Origen, Philo was the author. Hence he evidently saw
the work only in an anonymous copy. He himself desired to
translate it into Latin, but found the text so barbarized, that
he considered it necessary to undertake an entirely new
work.[101]   In the preface he expresses himself concerning the
history of these Onomastica as follows: Philo, vir disertissimus
Judaeorum, Origenis quoque testimonio conprobatur edidisse
librum hebraicorum nominum eorumque etymologias juxta
ordinem litterarum e latere copulasse. Qui cum vulgo
habeatur a Graecis et bibliothecas orbis inpleverit, studii
mihi fuit in latinam eum linguam vertere. Verum tam

its spuriousness. Comp. also Mangey, ii. 601, note. Fabricius-Harles,
iv. 742. Grossmann, i. p. 21. Dähne in Ersch and Grüber, art. "Philon."

[99] See the parallels pointed out in Grossmann, i. p. 28.

[100] The text is also given in Richter's and the Tauchnitz editions. Comp.
generally: Dähne, *Stud. und Krit.* 1833, pp. 987–989. Freudenthal, *Die
Flavius Josephus beigelegte Schrift über die Herrschaft der Vernunft*
(Fourth Book of Maccabees), 1869, pp. 9–12, 141–147. Grossmann, i. p.
21, does not express himself quite decidedly on the question of genuineness.

[101] This Onomasticon of Jerome (*liber interpetationis hebraicorum
nominum*) is in Vallarsi's edition of Jerome's works, vol. iii. 1–120,
and in Lagarde, *Onomastica sacra* (1870), pp. 1–81.

dissona inter se exemplaria repperi et sic confusum ordinem, ut tacere melius judicaverim quam reprehensione quid dignum scribere. Itaque . . . . singula per ordinem scripturarum volumina percucurri et vetus aedificium nova cura instaurans fecisse me reor quod a Graecis quoque adpetendum sit. . . . Ac ne forte consummato aedificio quasi extrema deesset manus, novi testamenti verba et nomina interpretatus sum, imitari volens ex parte Origenem, quem post apostolos ecclesiarum magistrum nemo nisi inperitus negat. Inter cetera enim ingeni sui praeclara monimenta etiam in hoc laboravit, ut quod Philo quasi Judaeus omiserat hic ut christianus inpleret. According to this account of Jerome *it must certainly be admitted, that Origen already considered Philo to be the author.* But the work being anonymous his testimony is not sufficient, and the question of authorship cannot be decided on internal grounds, because the work is no longer extant in its most ancient form.[102] A tolerably copious list of Philonean etymologies may be collected from those works of Philo which have been preserved.[103]

6. On a Latin work *de biblicis antiquitatibus,* ascribed to Philo, see Fabricius-Harles, iv. 743, and especially Pitra, *Analecta sacra,* ii. 298 sq., 319–322. The pseudo-Philonian *Breviarum temporum,* a forgery of Annius of Viterbo (Fabricius-Harles, *l.c.*), must not be confounded with this. On the treatise *de virtute ejusque partibus,* published by Mai under Philo's name, see above, note 10.

---

[102] For various Greek and Latin Onomastica of scriptural names, see Vallarsi, *Hieronymi Opp.* iii. 537 sqq., and Lagarde, *Onomastica sacra,* p. 161 sqq. The work *de nominibus Hebraicis* (see above, note 21), printed under Philo's name in the Basle collection of certain works of Philo, is simply the Onomasticon of Jerome. Comp. on this whole literature, Fabricius-Harles, *Bibliotheca graeca,* iv. 742 sq., vi. 199 sqq., vii. 226 sq.

[103] Such collections are found in Vallarsi, *Hieronymi Opp.* iii. 731–744, and in Siegfried, *Philonische Studien* (Merx' *Archiv,* ii. 2. 143–163).

## II. THE DOCTRINE OF PHILO.

*The Literature.*[104]

Stahl, " Versuch eines systematischen Entwurfs des Lehrbegriffs Philo's von Alexandrien" (Eichhorn's *Allgemeine Bibliothek der biblischen Litteratur*, vol. iv. paragraph 5, 1793, pp. 765–890).

Grossmann, *Questiones Philoneae.* I. *De theologiae Philonis fontibus et auctoritate quaestionis primae particula prima.* II. *De* λόγῳ *Philonis. Quaestio altera.* Lips. 1829.

Gfrörer, *Philo und die alexandrinische Theosophie* (also under the title *Kritische Geschichte des Urchristenthums*), 2 vols. Stuttgard 1831.

Dähne, *Geschichtliche Darstellung der jüdisch - alexandrinischen Religions- Philosophie*, 2 vols. Halle 1834. Comp. also his art. "Philon" in Ersch and Gruber's *Encyklopädie*.

Ritter, *Geschichte der Philosophi*, vol. iv. (1834), pp. 418–492.

Georgii, " Ueber die neuesten Gegensätze in Auffassung der Alexandri- nischen Religionsphilosophie, insbesondere des Jüdischen Alexan- drinismus" (*Zeitschr. für die histor. Theol.* 1839, No. 3, pp. 3–98, No. 4, pp. 3–98).

Lücke, *Commentar über das Evang. des Johannes*, vol. i. (3rd ed. 1840) p. 272 sqq.

Keferstein, *Philo's Lehre von den göttlichen Mittelwesen, zugleich eine kurze Darstellung der Grundzüge des philonischen Systems*, Leipzig 1846.

Bucher, *Philonische Studien*, Tübingen 1848.

Niedner, *De subsistentia* τῷ θείῳ λόγῳ *apud Philonem tributa quaestionis*, Parts i. ii. Lips. 1848, 1849 (also in the *Zeitsch. für die histor. Theol.* 1849).

Lutterbeck, *Die neutestamentlichen Lehrbegriffe*, vol. i. (1852) pp. 418–446.

Dorner, *Entwickelungsgesch. der Lehre von der Person Christi*, vol. i. pp. 21–57.

Wolff, *Die philonische Philosophie in ihren Hauptmomenten dargestellt*, 2nd ed. 1858.

Joel, " Ueber einige geschichtliche Beziehungen des philonischen Systems " (*Monatsschr. für Gesch. und Wissensch. des Judenth.* 1863, pp. 19–31).

---

[104] For the older literature see Fabricius-Harles, iv. 721–727. Comp. also Freudenthal, "Zur Geschichte der Anschauungen über die jüdisch- hellenistische Religionsphilosophie" (*Monatsschr. für Gesch. und Wissensch. des Judenth.* 1869, pp. 399–421).

Frankel, "Zur Ethik des jüdisch - alexandrinischen Philosophen Philo"
(*Monatsschr. für Gesch. und Wissensch. des Judenth.* 1867, pp. 241–252,
281–297).

Keim, *Gesch. Jesu*, i. 208–225.

Lipsius, art. "Alexandrinische Religionsphilosophie," in Schenkel's *Bibellex.* i. 85–99.

Zeller, *Die Philosophie der Griechen in ihrer geschichtlichen Entwicklung*,
Part iii. Div. 2 (3rd ed. 1881), pp. 338–418.

Heinze, *Die Lehre vom Logos in der griechischen Philosophie* (1872), pp.
204–297.

Stein, *Sieben Bücher zur Geschichte des Platonismus*, Part iii. (1875) pp.
3–17.

Soulier, *La doctrine du Logos chez Philon d'Alexandrie*, Turin 1876 (comp.
*Theol. Litztg.* 1877, 101).

Réville, *Le Logos d'après Philon d'Alexandrie*, Genève 1877 (see Bursian's
*Philol. Jahresber.* xxi. 35 sq.).   The same, *La doctrine du Logos dans
le quatrième évangile et dans les oeuvres de Philon*, Paris 1881.

Nicolas, "Etudes sur Philon d'Alexandrie" (*Revue de l'histoire des
religions*, vol. v. 1882, pp. 318–339 ; vol. vii. 1883, pp. 145–164 ; vol.
viii. 1883, pp. 468–488, 582–602, 756–772).

Comp. also the works and articles mentioned above, p. 321 sq., of Steinhart, J. G. Müller, Ewald, Ueberweg, Hausrath, Siegfried, Hamburger,
Zöckler.

The survey already given of Philo's works is sufficient to
show the many-sidedness of his culture and of his literary
efforts.   That which applies to the representatives of Judaeo-
Hellenism in general, viz. that they combined in themselves
both *Jewish and Hellenic* culture, is pre-eminently true of
him.   It must be admitted, that *Greek philosophy* comes the
most prominently into the foreground.[105]   He was a man
saturated with every means of culture afforded in his age
by the schools of the Greeks.   His diction was formed by
the Greek classical authors; and especially " may the influence of Plato's works upon Philo in even a lexical and
phraseological respect be called very considerable." [106]   He
was intimately acquainted with the great Greek poets Homer,

---

[105] Comp. on this and especially on Philo's linguistic culture, Siegfried,
*Philo von Alexandria*, pp. 31–141.   Also Zeller, iii. 2. 343 sqq.

[106] Siegfried, *Philo*, p. 32.

Euripides and others, whom he occasionally quotes.[107]   But
it is the philosophers whom he most highly esteems.   He
calls Plato "the great;"[108] Parmenides, Empedocles, Zeno,
Cleanthes are in his eyes divine men and form a sacred
society.[109]   But it is his own view of the world and of life,
which shows more than aught else how highly he esteemed
the Greek philosophers.   It agrees in the most essential
points with the great teachers of the Greeks.   Nay, Philo has
so profoundly absorbed their doctrines and so peculiarly
worked them up into a new whole, as himself to belong to
the series of Greek philosophers.   His system may on the
whole be entitled an eclectic one, Platonic, Stoic, and Neo-
Pythagorean doctrines being the most prominent.   Just in
proportion as now one now the other was embraced, has he
been designated at one time a *Platonist,* at another a *Pythagorean.*[110]   He might just as correctly be called a Stoic, for the
influence of Stoicism was at least as strong upon him as that
of Platonism or Neo-Pythagoreanism.[111]

Notwithstanding however this profound appropriation of

[107] A list of Greek classics quoted by Philo is given by Grossmann,
*Quaestiones Philoneae,* i. p. 5.   Siegfried, *Philo,* p. 137 sqq.

[108] *De providentia,* ii. 42, p. 77, ed. Aucher (Richter, 8th small vol.).
Comp. also *Quod omnis probus liber,* ii. 447, Mangey (Richter, 5th small
vol.), where, according to the *cod. Mediceus* (one of the best manuscripts),
τὸν ἱερώτατον Πλάτωνα is the reading instead of τὸν λιγυρώτατον Πλάτωνα.

[109] *De providentia,* ii. 48, p. 79, ed. Aucher (Richter, 8th small vol.):
Parmenides, Empedocles, Zeno, Cleanthes aliique divi homines ac velut
verus quidam proprieque sacer coetus.   Comp. *Quod omnis probus liber,* ii.
444, Mang. (Richter, 5th small vol.): τὸν τῶν Πυθαγορείων ἱερώτατον θίασον.

[110] A Platonist in the well-known proverb: ἢ Πλάτων φιλωνίζει ἢ Φίλων
πλατωνίζει (Hieronymus, *vir. illustr.* c. 11.   Suidas, *Lex. s.v.* Φίλων.
Photius, *Bibliotheca cod.* 105).   Clemens Alex. calls him a Pythagorean,
and that in the two passages in which he is characterizing his philosophical
tendency, *Strom.* i. 15. 72: διὰ πολλῶν ὁ Πυθαγόρειος ὑποδείκνυσι Φίλων.
*Strom.* ii. 19, 100: ὥς φησιν ὁ Πυθαγόρειος Φίλων.   Eusebius brings
forward both his Platonism and his Pythagoreanism, *H. E.* ii. 4. 3: μάλιστα
τὴν κατὰ Πλάτωνα καὶ Πυθαγόραν ἐζηλωκὼς ἀγωγήν.

[111] Zeller and Heinze in particular have pointed out the strong influence
of Stoicism.   Stein in opposition to them seeks to lay more stress on
Platonism.   But comp. Heinze, *Theol. Litztg.* 1877, 112 (in the discussion
on Stein's *Geschichte des Platonismus*).

Greek philosophy, Philo remained *a Jew:* and the wisdom of
the Greeks did not make him unfaithful to the religion of his
fathers. Nor must his *Jewish education* be depreciated in
presence of the philosophical culture, which certainly appears
the more prominent.[112] He was *not indeed fluent* in the
*Hebrew tongue,* and he read the Old Testament exclusively
in the Greek translation. Still he had a respectable knowledge of Hebrew, as is shown by his numerous etymologies,
which indeed often appear absurd to us, but are in truth not
worse than those of the Palestinian Rabbis.[113] He had
indeed no accurate knowledge of the Palestinian Halachah.
But that he had a general acquaintance with it is proved, not
only by a single decided intimation,[114] but especially by his
whole work *de specialibus legibus.*[115] In the *Haggadic interpretation of Scripture* he was quite a master. For the whole
of his allegorical commentary is with respect to form nothing
else than a transference of the method of the Palestinian
Midrash to the region of Hellenism. It is just by this means
that Philo gains the possibility of showing, that his philosophical doctrine already exists in the Old Testament. Many
close approximations are also found with respect to substance,
though these are much slighter than the agreement in
method.[116] For his legendary embellishment of the life of
Moses, Philo expressly appeals to the tradition of the πρεσ-
βύτεροι, who "always combined oral tradition with what was
read aloud." [117]

[112] Comp. Siegfried, pp. 142–159.

[113] Comp. the collections of Vallarsi and Siegfried named above (note
103).

[114] Euseb. *Praep. evang.* viii. 7. 6 (from the first book of the *Hypothetica*).
Philo having here given by way of example a series of commands, says
there are also μυρία ἄλλα ἐπὶ τούτοις, ὅσα καὶ ἐπὶ ἀγράφων ἐθῶν καὶ νομίμων,
κἄν τοῖς νομίμοις αὐτοῖς.

[115] See above, p. 343, and Ritter's work, *Philo und die Halacha,* 1879,
there named; also Siegfried, p. 145.

[116] Comp. Siegfried, p. 145 sqq. Also much in Frankel, *Ueber den
Einfluss der palästinischen Exegese auf die alexandrinische Hermeneutik*
(1851), especially pp. 190–200.

[117] *Vita Mosis,* lib. i. § 1 (Mang. ii. 81): 'Αλλ' ἔγωγε . . . τὰ περὶ τὸν

Philo has nowhere given a systematic statement of his
system. He has at most developed single points, such as
the doctrine of the creation of the world with some degree
of connection. As a rule he gives the ideas he has worked
out, in conjunction with the text of the Old Testament. This
is consistent with the *formal principle* of his whole theology,
viz. the assumption of the absolute authority of the Mosaic
law. The Thorah of Moses is to him, as to every Jew, the
supreme, nay the sole and absolutely decisive authority : a
perfect revelation of Divine wisdom. Every word written in
Holy Scripture by Moses is a divine declaration.[118] Hence no
word in it is without definite meaning.[119] The Scriptures also
of the other prophets in conjunction with those of Moses
contain Divine revelations. For all the prophets are God's
interpreters, who makes use of them as instruments for the
revelation of the Divine will.[120] With this formal principle

---

ἄνδρα μηνύσω, μαθὼν αὐτὰ καὶ ἐκ βίβλων τῶν ἱερῶν . . . καὶ παρά τινων
ἀπὸ τοῦ ἔθνους πρεσβυτέρων. Τὰ γὰρ λεγόμενα τοῖς ἀναγινωσκομένοις ἀεὶ
συνῦφαινον.

[118] *Vita Mosis,* ii. 163, ed. Mangey (Richter, 4th small vol.) : Οὐκ ἀγνοῶ
μὲν οὖν, ὡς πάντα εἰσὶ χρησμοὶ ὅσα ἐν ταῖς ἱεραῖς βίβλοις ἀναγέγραπται χρησ-
θέντες δι' αὐτοῦ (*scil.* Μωϋσέως).

[119] In *De profugis,* i. 554, Mangey (Richter, 3rd small vol.), we are told
of Philo, that the expression θανάτῳ θανατοῦσθαι instead of the simple
θανατοῦσθαι, Ex. xxi. 12, disquieted him, because he well knew, ὅτι περιττὸν
ὄνομα οὐδὲν τίθησιν.—For other examples see *De Cherubim,* i. 149, Mangey
(Richter, 1st small vol.). *De agricultura Noe,* i. 300, Mangey (Richter, 2nd
small vol.).

[120] The extent of Philo's *Canon* cannot be defined as to details. It is
quite certain, that the Thorah of Moses has in his view quite a different
importance to the rest of Holy Scripture. But the latter also, *i.e.* the most
important of the Nebiim and Kethubim, are quoted by him as prophetic
and sacred writings. For further particulars see Gfrörer, i. 46 sqq. On
the inspiration of the prophets see *De monarchia,* ii. 222, Mang. (Richter, 4th
small vol.) : προφήτης θεοφόρητος θεσπιεῖ καὶ προφητεύσει, λέγων μὲν οἰκεῖον
οὐδὲν· οὐδὲ γάρ, εἰ λέγει, δύναται καταλαβεῖν ὅγε κατεχόμενος ὄντως καὶ
ἐνθουσιῶν. Ὅσα δὲ ἐνηχεῖται, διελεύσεται καθάπερ ὑποβάλλοντος ἑτέρου.
Ἑρμηνεῖς γάρ εἰσιν οἱ προφῆται θεοῦ καταχρωμένου τοῖς ἐκείνων ὀργάνοις πρὸς
δήλωσιν ὧν ἂν ἐθελήσῃ. Comp. also *De specialibus legibus,* ii. 343, Mangey
(Richter, 5th small vol.). *Quis rerum divinarum heres.* i. 511, Mangey
(Richter, 3rd small vol.). For more on Philo's doctrine of inspiration see
Gfrörer. i. 54–68.

of the absolute authority of Holy Scripture and especially of
the Mosaic law, is connected the further assumption that all
true wisdom was actually contained just in this source of all
knowledge.   In other words, Philo deduces formally from the
Old Testament all those philosophical doctrines which he had
in fact appropriated from the Greek philosophers. Not in
Plato, Pythagoras and Zeno, but above all in the writings of
Moses, is to be found the deepest and most perfect instruction
concerning things divine and human.   In them was already
comprised all that was good and true, which the Greek philosophers subsequently taught.   Thus Moses is the true teacher
of mankind, and it is from him—as Philo, like Aristobulus, presupposes—that the Greek philosophers derived their wisdom.[121]

The scientific means by which it was possible for Philo to
adhere to and carry out these assumptions is *allegorical interpretation*.[122]   This was no invention of Philo, but one which
had already been perfected and wielded by others.[123]   Hence
it was for him a quite self - evident process, which he
nowhere thought it necessary to justify, although he occasionally extols its value and declares it indispensable.   By the
help of this process he was able to read out of the primitive
history of Genesis those profound philosophical theories,
especially in the department of Psychology and Ethic, which
really grew up in the soil of Greek philosophy.   The most
external occurrences of scriptural history become in his hands
mines of instruction concerning the supreme problems of
human existence.

Only by means of this method could the *double mission* be
in fact fulfilled which Philo saw allotted to him.   He thus
became to his Jewish co-religionists, with whom he shared
the presupposition of the Divine authority of the Mosaic

---

[121] So Heraclitus (*Leg. allegor.* i. 65, Mang., Richter, 1st small vol.   *Quis
rerum divinarum heres.* i. 503, Mang., Richter, 3rd small vol.).   Zeno (*Quod
omnis probus liber*, ii. 454, Mang., Richter, 5th small vol.).

[122] Comp. Gfrörer, i. 68–113.   Zeller, iii. 2. 346–352 ; and especially
Siegfried, *Philo*, pp. 160–197.

[123] Zeller, iii. 2. 265 sq.

law, the medium of the philosophic culture of the Greeks;
showing them, that Moses had taught just what appeared
to him true and valuable in Greek philosophy.   On the other
hand he proved to the Greeks by the same means, that
all the knowledge and intuition, for which they so highly
esteemed their own philosophers, were already to be found in
the writings of Moses.   It was not they but Moses, who was
both the best of lawgivers and the first and greatest of
philosophers.   These two tendencies are, it may be plainly
perceived, the mainsprings of Philo's extensive literary
activity.   Being himself both *Jew* and *Greek* he desired to
act upon both, to make the Jews Greeks and the Greeks
Jews.   His religious assumptions are in the first place those
of Judaism with its belief in revelation.   But these religious
assumptions underwent a powerful and peculiar modification
by the elements which he derived from the Greek philosophy.
And as he combined both in himself, he desired to set up a
propaganda on both sides.

No strictly completed *system of Philo* can in truth be
spoken of.   The elements, of which his view of the world
is compounded, are too heterogeneous to form a strictly
completed unity.   Nevertheless his several views exhibit a
connected whole, whose members mutually condition one
another.   In the following attempt to give a brief sketch of
this whole, we shall leave out of consideration his specifically
Jewish assumptions and confine ourselves to his philosophical
views.   The characteristic feature of his standpoint is just
this, that his philosophy, *i.e.* his entire view of the world,
may be completely stated without the necessity of mentioning any Jewish, particularistic notions. *His Judaism virtually
consists in the formal claim, that the Jewish people are by
reason of the Mosaic revelation in possession of the highest
religious knowledge—one might almost say of the true religious
illumination.   In a material respect Greek views have gained
the upper hand.* For even his theology is only so far Jewish
as to insist on monotheism and on the worship of God apart

from images.  In this however it stands in opposition only
to the polytheism of the heathen *religions*, but not to the idea
of God of Greek *philosophy*, which on the contrary Philo
very closely follows.  Thus his Judaism is already very
powerfully modified.  Moreover the specifically Jewish, *i.e.*
the particularistic notions are embraced by him in a form
which is tantamount to their denial.  It is just this which
makes it possible, entirely to disregard them in a sketch of his
view of the world.[124]—The following survey follows chiefly
the excellent exposition of Zeller, certainly the best we now
have.

1. *The Doctrine of God.*[125]  The fundamental thought from
which Philo starts, is that of the dualism of God and the
world.  God alone is good and perfect, the finite as such is
imperfect.  All determinations, which are adapted to finite
existence, are therefore to be denied of God.  He is eternal,
unchangeable, simple, free, self-sufficing.[126]  He is not only

---

[124] With regard to detail the following remarks may suffice.  Philo
firmly adheres to the *obligation of the Mosaic law*.  But only because it is in
his eyes the most perfect, just and reasonable, because its moral demands
are always the purest, its social institutions the best and most humane, its
religious ceremonies the most consistent with the Divine intelligence.  In
this sense it is that he exhibits it in his work *de specialibus legibus*.  He also
adheres to the *prerogative of the Jewish people:* the Jews are the privileged
people of God (Gfrörer, i. 486 sq.  Dähne, i. 428 sq.).  But they owe
their privileges to their own and their forefathers' virtues.  God makes no
distinction between men as such.  Hence too the *Messianic promise, i.e.*
the promise of earthly prosperity, to which also Philo adheres (see § 29),
applies not to Israel according to the flesh, but to all who are converted
from idolatry to the only true God (see especially *de execrationibus*, § 8,
Mang. ii. 435).  We see that Jewish particularism is here everywhere
in course of dissolution.  Judaism is on the contrary the best religion just
because it is cosmopolitan (comp. below, note 179).

[125] Comp. Gfrörer, i. 113 sqq.  Dähne, i. 114 sqq.  Zeller, iii. 2, pp.
353–360.

[126] *Eternal*, ἀΐδιος, *De mundi opificio*, i. 3, Mang. (Richter, small vol 5) ;
*De caritate*, ii. 386, Mang. (Richter, small vol. 5), and elsewhere.  *Unchangeable*, ἄτρεπτος, *De Cherubim*, i. 142, Mang. (Richter, small vol. 1) ; *Legum
allegoriae*, i. 53, Mang. (Richter, small vol. 1), and the whole work *Quod
deus sit immutabilis*, i. 272 sqq., Mang. (Richter, small vol. 2).—*Simple*,
ἁπλοῦς, *Legum allegor.* i. 66, Mang. (Richter, small vol. 1).—*Free, De*

free from human faults, but exalted above all human virtues,
He is better than the good and the beautiful.[127]   Nay, since
every determination would be a limitation, He is devoid of
qualities ἄποιος, without a ποιότης,[128] and thus His nature is
undefinable.   We can only say that He is, not what He is.[129]—
It is true that together with these purely negative definitions,
which advance almost to an absence of attributes, is found also
a series of positive assertions on the nature of God, by which
assertions of the former kind are again abolished.   This contradiction however is not to be wondered at.   For the object
of this assertion of an absence of attributes is merely to
remove all limitation, all imperfection from God.   And
therefore Philo makes no difficulty in placing beside it the
other assertion: that *all perfection is combined* in God and
derived from Him, He fills and comprises everything.[130]   All

*somniis*, i. 692, Mang. (Richter, small vol. 3). — *Self-sufficing*, χρῄζων
οὐδενὸς τὸ παράπαν, ἑαυτῷ ἱκανός, αὐταρκέστατος ἑαυτῷ, *Legum allegor.*
i. 66, Mang. (Richter, small vol. 1); *De mutatione nominum*, i. 582, Mang.
(Richter, small vol. 3); *De fortitudine*, ii. 377, Mang. (Richter, small
vol. 5).

[127] *De mundi opificio*, i. 2, Mang. (Richter, small vol. 1): ὁ τῶν ὅλων νοῦς
—εἰλικρινέστατος καὶ ἀκραιφνέστατος, κρείττων τε ἢ ἀρετὴ καὶ κρείττων ἢ
ἐπιστήμη καὶ κρείττων ἢ αὐτὸ τὸ ἀγαθὸν καὶ αὐτὸ τὸ καλόν.

[128] *Legum allegoriae*, i. 50, Mang. (Richter, small vol. 1): ἄποιος—ὁ
θεός.—*Ibid.* i. 53: ὁ γὰρ ἢ ποιότητα οἰόμενος ἔχειν τὸν θεὸν ἢ μὴ ἕνα εἶναι
ἢ μὴ ἀγέννητον καὶ ἄφθαρτον ἢ μὴ ἄτρεπτον, ἑαυτὸν ἀδικεῖ οὐ θεόν.—*Quod deus
sit immutabilis*, i. 281, Mang. (Richter, small vol. 2): God must be withdrawn from all determination (quality) (ἐκβιβάζειν—πάσης ποιότητος).

[129] *Vita Mosis*, ii. 92, Mang. (Richter, small vol. 4): Ὁ δὲ· Τὸ μὲν
πρῶτον λέγε, φησίν, αὐτοῖς· Ἐγώ εἰμι ὁ ὤν, ἵνα μαθόντες διαφορὰν ὄντος τε καὶ
μὴ ὄντος προσαναδιδαχθῶσιν, ὡς οὐδὲν ὄνομα ἐπ' ἐμοῦ τὸ παράπαν κυριο-
λογεῖται, ᾧ μόνῳ πρόσεστι τὸ εἶναι.— *Quod deus sit immutabilis*, i. 282,
Mang. (Richter, small vol. 2): ὁ δ' ἄρα οὐδὲ τῷ νῷ καταληπτός, ὅτι μὴ
κατὰ τὸ εἶναι μόνον.  Ὕπαρξις γάρ ἐσθ' ὁ καταλαμβάνομεν αὐτοῦ, τὸ δὲ
χωρὶς ὑπάρξεως οὐδέν.—*De mutatione nominum*, i. 580, Mang. (Richter, small
vol. 3).—*De somniis*, i. 655, Mang. (Richter, small vol. 3).

[130] *Legum allegoriae*, i. 52, Mang. (Richter, small vol. 1): τὰ μὲν ἄλλα
ἐπιδεῆ καὶ ἔρημα καὶ κενὰ ὄντα πληρῶν καὶ περιέχων, αὐτὸς δὲ ὑπ' οὐδενὸς
ἄλλου περιεχόμενος, ἅτε εἰς καὶ τὸ πᾶν αὐτὸς ὤν.—*Ibid.* i. 88, Mang.:
Πάντα γὰρ πεπλήρωκεν ὁ θεός, καὶ διὰ πάντων διελήλυθεν, καὶ κενὸν οὐδὲ
ἔρημον ἀπολέλοιπεν ἑαυτοῦ.—*Ibid.* i. 97, Mang.—*De confusione linguarum*,
i. 425 Mang. (Richter, small vol. 2).—*De migratione Abrahami*, i. 466,

perfection in the creature is derived solely and only from Him.[131]

2. *The Intermediate Beings.*[132] God, as the absolutely Perfect, cannot enter into direct contact with matter. All contact therewith would defile Him.[133] An acting therefore of God upon the world and in the world is according to Philo only possible through the intervention of intermediate causes, of interposing powers who establish an intercourse between God and the world. For the more precise definition of these intermediate beings, four notions, suited to this purpose, offered themselves to Philo; two belonging to the philosophical, two to the religious region. These were the *Platonic* doctrine of *ideas*, the *Stoic* doctrine of active *causes*, the *Jewish* doctrine of *angels*, and the *Greek* doctrine of *daemons*. All these elements, but chiefly the Stoic doctrine of powers, were used by Philo in constructing his peculiar doctrine of intermediate beings. Before the creation of this world of the senses, he teaches, God created the spiritual types of all things.[134] These types or ideas must however be conceived of as active causes, as powers which bring disordered matter into order.[135] It is by means of these spiritual powers

Mang. (Richter, small vol. 2).—*De somniis*, i. 630, Mang. (Richter, small vol. 3).—Gfrörer, i. 123 sqq.—Dähne, i. 282 sqq.

[131] *Legum alleg.* i. 44, Mang. (Richter, small vol. 1): Παύεται γὰρ οὐδέποτε ποιῶν ὁ θεός, ἀλλ᾽ ὥσπερ ἴδιον τὸ καίειν πυρός, καὶ χιόνος τὸ ψύχειν, οὕτω καὶ θεοῦ τὸ ποιεῖν· καὶ πολύ γε μᾶλλον, ὅσῳ καὶ τοῖς ἄλλοις ἅπασιν ἀρχὴ τοῦ δρᾶν ἐστίν.

[132] Comp. Gfrörer, i. 143 sqq. Dähne, i. 161 sqq., 202 sqq. Zeller, iii. 2, pp. 360-370. Keferstein's above-named *Monograph*.

[133] *De victimas offerentibus*, ii. 261, Mang. (Richter, small vol. 4): Ἐξ ἐκείνης γὰρ [τῆς ὕλης] πάντ᾽ ἐγέννησεν ὁ θεός, οὐκ ἐφαπτόμενος αὐτός· οὐ γὰρ ἦν θέμις ἀπείρου καὶ πεφυρμένης ὕλης ψαύειν τὸν ἴδμονα καὶ μακάριον.

[134] *De mundi opificio*, i. 4, Mang. (Richter, small vol. 1): Προλαβὼν γὰρ ὁ θεὸς ἅτε θεός, ὅτι μίμημα καλὸν οὐκ ἄν ποτε γένοιτο καλοῦ δίχα παραδείγματος, οὐδέ τι τῶν αἰσθητῶν ἀνυπαίτιον, ὃ μὴ πρὸς ἀρχέτυπον καὶ νοητὴν ἰδέαν ἀπεικονίσθη, βουληθεὶς τὸν ὁρατὸν τουτονὶ κόσμον δημιουργῆσαι, προεξετύπου τὸν νοητόν, ἵνα χρώμενος ἀσωμάτῳ καὶ θεοειδεστάτῳ παραδείγματι, τὸν σωματικὸν τοῦτον ἀπεργάσηται, πρεσβυτέρου νεώτερον ἀπεικόνισμα, τοσαῦτα περιέξοντα αἰσθητὰ γένη, ὅσαπερ ἐν ἐκείνῳ νοητά. Comp. the work *De mundi opificio*.

[135] *De victimas offerentibus*, ii. 261, Mang. (Richter, small vol. 4): ταῖς

that God acts in the world. They are His ministers and vicegerents, the ambassadors and mediums between God and things finite,[136] the λόγοι or partial powers of the universal reason.[137] By Moses they are called angels, by the Greeks daemons.[138] If according to this they appear to be conceived of as independent hypostases, nay as personal beings, other assertions again forbid us to take them for decidedly such. It is expressly said, that they exist only in the Divine thought.[139] They are designated as the infinite powers of the infinite God,[140] and thus regarded as an inseparable portion of the Divine existence. But it would again be a mistake, on the ground of these assertions to deny definitely the personification of the λόγοι or δυνάμεις. The truth is just this, that Philo conceived of them *both as independent hypostases and as immanent determinations of the Divine existence.* And it is an apt remark of Zeller's, that this contradiction is necessarily required by the premisses of Philo's system. "He combines both definitions without observing their contradiction, nay he

ἀσωμάτοις δυνάμεσιν, ὧν ἔτυμον ὄνομα αἱ ἰδέαι, κατεχρήσατο πρὸς τὸ γένος ἕκαστον τὴν ἁρμόττουσαν λαβεῖν μορφήν.—*De monarchia,* ii. 218 sq., Mang. (Richter, small vol. 4).

[136] *De Abrahamo,* ii. 17 sq., Mang. (Richter, small vol. 4): ἱεραὶ καὶ θεῖαι φύσεις, ὑποδιάκονοι καὶ ὕπαρχοι τοῦ πρώτου θεοῦ.—*De somniis,* i. 642, Mang. (Richter, small vol. 3).

[137] *Legum alleg.* i. 122, Mang. (Richter, small vol. 1): τοὺς ἀγγέλους καὶ λόγους αὐτοῦ.—*De somniis,* i. 631, Mang. (Richter, 3): τοὺς ἑαυτοῦ λόγους ἐπικουρίας ἕνεκα τῶν φιλαρέτων ἀποστέλλει.—*Ibid.* i. 640: ψυχαὶ δέ εἰσιν ἀθάνατοι οἱ λόγοι οὗτοι.—On the identity of the λόγοι with the ideas see Heinze, *Lehre vom Logos,* p. 220.

[138] *De somniis,* i. 638, Mang. (Richter, 3): ἀθανάτοις λόγοις, οὓς καλεῖν ἔθος ἀγγέλους.—*Ibid.* i. 642: ταύτας (viz. pure souls) δαίμονας μὲν οἱ ἄλλοι φιλόσοφοι, ὁ δὲ ἱερὸς λόγος ἀγγέλους εἴωθε καλεῖν.—*De gigantibus,* i. 263, Mang. (Richter, 2): Οὓς ἄλλοι φιλόσοφοι δαίμονας, ἀγγέλους Μωϋσῆς εἴωθεν ὀνομάζειν· ψυχαὶ δέ εἰσι κατὰ τὸν ἀέρα πετόμεναι.

[139] *De mundi opificio,* i. 4, Mang. (Richter, 1): As the ideal city, whose plan the artist sketches, exists only in his mind, τὸν αὐτὸν τρόπον οὐδὲ ὁ ἐκ τῶν ἰδεῶν κόσμος ἄλλον ἂν ἔχοι τόπον ἢ τὸν θεῖον λόγον τὸν ταῦτα διακοσμήσαντα.—*Ibid.* i. 5, Mang.: Εἰ δέ τις ἐθελήσεις γυμνοτέροις χρήσασθαι τοῖς ὀνόμασιν, οὐδὲν ἂν ἕτερον εἴποι τὸν νοητὸν εἶναι κόσμον, ἢ θεοῦ λόγον ἤδη κοσμοποιοῦντος.

[140] *De sacrificiis Abelis et Caini,* i. 173, Mang. (Richter, 1): ἀπερίγραφος γὰρ ὁ θεός, ἀπερίγραφοι καὶ αἱ δυνάμεις αὐτοῦ.

is unable to observe it, because otherwise the intermediary
rôle assigned to the Divine powers would be forfeited, even
that double nature, by reason of which they are on the one
hand to be identical with God, that a participation in the
Deity may by their means be possible to the finite, and on
the other hand different from Him, that the Deity, notwithstanding this participation, may remain apart from all contact
with the world." [141]

With this ambiguous view of the nature of the δυνάμεις,
the question as to their origin must also necessarily remain
undecided. It is true that Philo frequently expresses himself
in an emanistic sense. But yet he never distinctly formulates
the doctrine of emanation.[142] The number of the δυνάμεις is
in itself unlimited.[143] Yet Philo sometimes gives calculations,
when comprising the individual powers under certain notions of
species.[144] He mostly distinguishes two supreme powers : *goodness* and *might*,[145] which again are combined and reconciled by
the Divine *Logos*, which, so far as it is reckoned among the
powers at all, is the chief of all, the root from which the rest
proceed, the most universal intermediary between God and the
world, that in which are comprised all the operations of God.[146]

---

[141] *Philosophie der Griechen*, iii. 2, p. 365.

[142] Comp. Zeller, pp. 366–369.—*Emanistic, e.g. De profugis*, i. 575,
Mang. (Richter, 3) : God is ἡ πρεσβυτάτη πηγή. Καὶ μήποτ᾽ εἰκότως.
Τὸν γὰρ σύμπαντα τοῦτον κόσμον ὤμβρησε.—Also *De somniis*, i. 688, Mang.
(Richter, 3).

[143] *De sacrificiis Abelis et Caini*, i. 173, Mang. (Richter, 1) : ἀπερίγραφοι
αἱ δυνάμεις.—*De confusione linguarum*, i. 431, Mang. (Richter, 2) : Εἷς ὢν
ὁ θεὸς ἀμυθήτους περὶ αὐτὸν ἔχει δυνάμεις.

[144] In *de profugis*, i. 560, Mang. (Richter, 3), he counts in all *six*, viz.
besides the θεῖος λόγος the five following : ἡ ποιητική, ἡ βασιλική, ἡ ἵλεως,
ἡ νομοθετική, . . . (the last is wanting).

[145] Ἀγαθότης and ἀρχή (*De Cherubim*, i. 144, Mang., Richter, 1 ; *De
sacrificiis Abelis et Caini*, i. 173, Mang., Richter, 1), εὐεργεσία and
ἡγεμονία, or ἡ χαριστική and ἡ βασιλική (both *de somniis*, i. 645, Mang.,
Richter, 3), ἡ εὐεργέτις and ἡ κολαστήριος (*de victimas offerentibus*, ii.
258, Mang., Richter, 4), also ἡ ποιητική and ἡ βασιλική (because God
created the world in consequence of His goodness, so *de Abrahamo*, ii. 19,
Mang., Richter, 4. *Vita Mosis*, ii. 150, Mang., Richter, 4).

[146] *De profugis*, i. 560, Mang. (Richter, 3). *Quaest. in Exod.* ii. 68,
p. 514 sq. (Richter, 7). Contrary to Zeller, who attempts to understand

3. *The Logos.*[147]  " By the Logos Philo understands *the power of God or the active Divine intelligence in general ;* he designates it as the idea which comprises all other ideas, the power which comprises all powers in itself, as the entirety of the supersensuous world or of the Divine powers."[148]  It is neither uncreated nor created after the manner of finite things.[149]  It is the vicegerent and ambassador of God ;[150] the angel or archangel which delivers to us the revelations of God ;[151] the instrument by which God made the world.[152]  The Logos is thus identified with the creative word of God.[153]  But not only is it the mediator for the relations of God to the world, but also for the relations of the world to God.  The Logos is the High Priest, who makes intercession for the world to God.[154]  But notwithstanding this apparently undoubted personification of the Logos, what has been said above of the Divine powers in general applies here also.  " The definitions, which, according to the presuppositions of our thought, would

certain passages as saying, that the Logos is to be conceived of not as the root, but as the product or result of the two supreme powers (p. 370) ; see Heinze, *Die Lehre vom Logos,* p. 248 sqq.

[147] Comp. Gfrörer, i. 168–326.  Dähne, i. 202 sqq.  Zeller, iii. 2, pp. 370–386, and the above-named *Monographs,* especially those of Heinze and Soulier.

[148] Zeller, iii. 2, p. 371.

[149] *Quis rerum divinarum heres.* i. 501 sq., Mang. (Richter, 3): οὔτε ἀγέννητος ὡς ὁ θεὸς ὤν, οὔτε γεννητὸς ὡς ὑμεῖς, ἀλλὰ μέσος τῶν ἄκρων, ἀμφοτέροις ὁμηρεύων.

[150] *Quis rer. div. her. l.c.:* πρεσβευτὴς τοῦ ἡγεμόνος πρὸς τὸ ὑπήκοον.

[151] *Leg. allegor.* l. 122, Mang. (Richter, 1) : τὸν ἄγγελον, ὅς ἐστι λόγος. —*De confusione linguarum,* i. 427, Mang. (Richter, 2) : τὸν πρωτόγονον αὐτοῦ λόγον, τὸν ἄγγελον πρεσβύτατον, ὡς ἀρχάγγελον πολυώνυμον ὑπάρχοντα. —*De somniis,* i. 656, Mang. (Richter, 3).—*Quis rer. div. her.* i. 501, *fin.* (Richter, 3).—*Quaest. in Exod.* ii. 13, p. 476 (Richter, 7).

[152] *Leg. allegor.* i. 106, Mang. *fin.* (Richter, 1) : Σκιὰ θεοῦ δὲ ὁ λόγος αὐτοῦ ἐστίν, ᾧ καθάπερ ὀργάνῳ προσχρησάμενος ἐκοσμοποίει.—*De Cherubim,* i. 162, Mang. (Richter, 1) : Εὑρήσεις γὰρ αἴτιον μὲν αὐτοῦ [τοῦ κόσμου] τὸν θεόν, ὑφ' οὗ γέγονεν ὕλην δὲ τὰ τέσσαρα στοιχεῖα, ἐξ ὧν συνεκράθη· ὄργανον δὲ λόγον θεοῦ, δι' οὗ κατεσκευάσθη· τῆς δὲ κατασκευῆς αἰτίαν τὴν ἀγαθότητα τοῦ δημιουργοῦ.

[153] *Leg. alleg.* i. 47, Mang. (Richter, 1).  *De sacrif. Abel. et Cain.* i. 165, Mang. (Richter, 1).  Heinze, *Die Lehre vom Logos,* p. 230.

[154] *De gigantibus,* i. 269, Mang. *fin.* (Richter, 2): ὁ ἀρχιερεὺς λόγος ἐνδια-

require the personality of the Logos, are crossed in Philo by
such as make it impossible, and the peculiarity of his mode
of conception consists in his not perceiving the contradiction
involved in making the idea of the Logos oscillate obscurely
between personal and impersonal being. This peculiarity is
equally misunderstood, when Philo's Logos is regarded absolutely
as a person separate from God, and when on the contrary it is
supposed that it only denotes God under a definite relation,
according to the aspect of His activity. According to Philo's
opinion the Logos is both, but for this very reason neither
one nor the other exclusively; and he does not perceive, that
it is impossible to combine these definitions into one notion."[155]
"But Philo cannot dispense with these definitions. With
him the Logos, like all the Divine powers, is only necessary,
because the supreme God Himself can enter into no direct
contact with the finite; it must stand between the two and
be the medium of their mutual relation; and how can it be
this unless it were different from both, if it were only a
certain Divine property? In this case we should have again
that direct action of God upon finite things, which Philo
declares inadmissible. On the other hand the Logos must
now indeed be again identical with each of the opposites
which it was to reconcile, it must likewise be a property
of God as a power operative in the world. Philo could not
without contradiction succeed in combining the two."[156]

Philo was, as it seems, the first to postulate, under the
name of the Logos, such an intermediate being between God

τρίβειν ἀεὶ καὶ σχολάζειν ἐν τοῖς ἁγίοις δώμασι δυνάμενος.—De migratione
Abrahami, i. 452, Mang. (Richter, 2): τὸν ἀρχιερέα λόγον.—De profugis,
i. 562, Mang. (Richter, 3): λέγομεν γάρ, τὸν ἀρχιερέα οὐκ ἄνθρωπον, ἀλλα
λόγον θεῖον εἶναι, πάντων οὐχ ἑκουσίων μόνον, ἀλλὰ καὶ ἀκουσίων ἀδικημάτων
ἀμέτοχον.—Quis rer. div. her. i. 501, Mang. fin. (Richter, 3): Ὁ δ' αὐτός
ἱκέτης μέν ἐστι τοῦ θνητοῦ κηραίνοντος ἀεὶ πρὸς τὸ ἄφθαρτον.—Vita Mosis,
ii. 155, Mang. (Richter, 4): Ἀναγκαῖον γὰρ ἦν τὸν ἱερωμένον τῷ τοῦ κόσμου
πατρὶ παρακλήτῳ χρῆσθαι τελειοτάτῳ τὴν ἀρετὴν υἱῷ, πρός τε ἀμνηστείαν
ἁμαρτημάτων καὶ χορηγίαν ἀφθονωτάτων ἀγαθῶν.

[155] Zeller, iii. 2, p. 378.
[156] Zeller, iii. 2, p. 380 sq.

and the world.[157]   Points of contact for his doctrine lay in
both Jewish theology and Greek philosophy.   In the former
it was chiefly the doctrine of the *wisdom* of God, and in the
second place, that of the *Spirit* and the *Word* of God, which
Philo took up.   From the Platonic philosophy it was the
doctrine of ideas and of the soul of the world, which he
utilized for his purpose.   But it is the Stoic doctrine of the
Deity as the active reason of the world, which is the nearest
to his.   " We need only to strip off from this Stoic doctrine
of the Logos, its pantheistic element, by distinguishing the
Logos from the Deity, and its materialistic element by distinguishing it from organized matter, to have the Philonean
Logos complete." [158]

4. *The creation and preservation of the world.*[159]   All existence cannot however, the intermediate beings notwithstanding,
be traced back to God.   For the evil, the imperfect can in no
wise, not even indirectly, have its cause in God.[160]   It originates from a second principle, from matter (ὕλη, or stoically
οὐσία).   This is the formless, lifeless, unmoved, unordered
mass devoid of properties, from which God, by means of the
Logos and the divine powers, formed the world.[161]   For only

[157] In the Wisdom of Solomon the Divine word is certainly once personified as elsewhere wisdom is.   But this is merely a poetical personification, not an actual hypostatification.   The author applies the term
*Wisdom* of God to represent the notion of an intermediary hypostasis, so
far as he entertains it.   Comp. also Grimm on the passage.   In the
Targums the "word of God" (Memra) certainly plays a *rôle* similar to
that of the Logos in Philo.   But these were very probably already under
his influence.

[158] Zeller, iii. 2, p. 385.

[159] Comp. Gfrörer, i. 327 sqq.   Dähne, i. 170 sqq., 246 sqq.   Zeller, iii. 2,
pp. 386–393.

[160] Comp. Zeller, iii. 3, p. 386, note 1.

[161] *De mundi opificio*, i. 5, Mang. (Richter, 1): Matter is ἐξ ἑαυτῆς
ἄτακτος, ἄποιος, ἄψυχος, ἑτεροποιότητος, ἀναρμοστίας, ἀσυμφωνίας μεστή.—
*Quis rerum divinarum heres.* i. 492, Mang. *fin.* (Richter, 3): τήν τε ἄμορφον
καὶ ἄποιον τῶν ὅλων οὐσίαν.—*De profugis*, i. 547, Mang. (Richter, 3): τὴν
ἄποιον καὶ ἀνείδεον καὶ ἀσχημάτιστον οὐσίαν. — *Ibid.:* ἡ ἄποιος ὕλη.—*De
victimas offerentibus*, ii. 261, Mang. (Richter, 4): ἄμορφος ὕλη. — *Ibid.:*
ἀπείρου καὶ πεφυρμένης ὕλης. — *De creatione principum*, ii. 367, Mang.

a forming of the world and not creation in its proper sense
is spoken of in Philo, since the origin of matter is not in God,
but it is placed as a second principle beside Him. And the
preservation of the world as well as its formation is effected
by means of the Logos and the Divine powers. Nay the
former is in truth but a continuation of the latter; and what
we call the laws of nature are but the totality of the regular
Divine operations.[162]

5. *Anthropology.*[163] It is in anthropology, where Philo
chiefly follows the Platonic doctrine, that the dualistic basis
of his system comes most strongly to light. Philo here starts
from the assumption, that the entire atmosphere is filled with
souls. Of these it is the angels or demons dwelling in
its higher parts who are the mediums of God's intercourse
with the world.[164] Those on the contrary who remain nearer
to the earth, are attracted by sense and descend into mortal
bodies.[165] Consequently the soul of man is nothing else than
one of those Divine powers, of those emanations of Deity,
which in their original state are called angels or daemons. It
is only the life-sustaining, sensitive soul that originates by
generation, and indeed from the aeriform elements of the seed;
reason on the contrary enters into man from without.[166] The

(Richter, 5): Μηνύει δ' ἡ τοῦ κόσμου γένεσίς τε καὶ διοίκησις. Τὰ γὰρ μὴ
ὄντα ἐκάλεσεν εἰς τὸ εἶναι, τάξιν ἐξ ἀταξίας, καὶ ἐξ ἀποίων ποιότητας, καὶ ἐξ
ἀνομοίων ὁμοιότητας, καὶ ἐξ ἑτεροτήτων ταυτότητας, καὶ ἐξ ἀκοινωνήτων καὶ
ἀναρμόστων κοινωνίας καὶ ἁρμονίας, καὶ ἐκ μὲν ἀνισότητος ἰσότητα, ἐκ δὲ
σκότους φῶς ἐργασάμενος. Ἀεὶ γάρ ἐστιν ἐπιμελὲς αὐτῷ καὶ ταῖς εὐεργέτισιν
αὐτοῦ δυνάμεσι τὸ πλημμελὲς τῆς χείρονος οὐσίας μεταποιεῖν καὶ μεθαρμόζεσθαι
πρὸς τὴν ἀμείνω.

[162] Comp. Zeller, iii. 2, p. 389 sq.

[163] Comp. Gfrörer, i. 373-415. Dähne, i. 288-340. Zeller, iii. 2, pp.
393-402.

[164] *De somniis*, i. 642, Mang. (Richter, 3).

[165] *De gigantibus*, i. 263 sq., Mang. (Richter, 2).

[166] *De mundi opificio*, i. 15, Mang. (Richter, 1): Ἡ δὲ [ἡ κίνησις] οἷα
τεχνίτης, ἢ κυριώτερον εἰπεῖν, ἀνεπίληπτος τέχνη, ζωοπλαστεῖ τὴν μὲν ὑγρὰν
οὐσίαν εἰς τὰ τοῦ σώματος μέλη καὶ μέρη διανέμουσα, τὴν δὲ πνευματικὴν εἰς
τὰς τῆς ψυχῆς δυνάμεις, τήν τε θρεπτικὴν καὶ τὴν αἰσθητικήν. Τὴν γὰρ τοῦ
λογισμοῦ τανῦν ὑπερθετέον, διὰ τοὺς φάσκοντας θύραθεν αὐτὸν
ἐπεισιέναι, θεῖον καὶ ἀΐδιον ὄντα.

human πνεῦμα is thus an emanation of Deity : God breathed
*His* spirit into man.[167]—The body as the animal part of man
is the source of all evil, it is the prison to which the spirit is
banished,[168] the corpse which the soul drags about with it,[169]
the coffin or the grave, from which it will first awake to true
life.[170] Sense as such being evil, sin is innate in man.[171] No
one can keep himself free from it, even if he were to live
but a day.[172]

6. *Ethic.*[173] According to these anthropologic assumptions
it is self-evident, that the chief principle of ethic is the *utmost
possible renunciation of sensuousness,* the extirpation of desire and
of the passions. Hence among philosophical systems, the Stoic
must be most of all congenial to Philo in the matter of ethic.
It is this that he chiefly embraces, not only in its fundamental
thought of the mortification of the senses, but also in single
statements, as in the doctrine of the four cardinal virtues [174] and
of the four passions.[175] Like the Stoics he teaches, that there

---

[167] *Quod deterius potiori insidiatur,* i. 206 sq., Mang. (Richter, 1).—*De
mundi opificio,* i. 32, Mang. (Richter, 1).—*De specialibus legibus,* ii. 356,
Mang. (Richter, 5).—*Quis rerum divinarum heres.* i. 480 sq., 498 sq., Mang.
(Richter, 3).

[168] Δεσμωτήριον, *De ebrietate,* i. 372, *fin.,* Mang. (Richter, 2). *Leg.
allegor.* i. 95, *sub. fin.,* Mang. (Richter, 1). *De migratione Abrahami,* i. 437,
*sub fin.,* Mang. (Richter, 2).

[169] Νεκρὸν σῶμα, *Leg. allegor.* i. 100 sq., Mang. (Richter, 1). *De
gigantibus,* i. 264, med. Mang. (Richter, 2). Τὸν ψυχῆς ἔγγιστα οἶκον, ὅν
ἀπὸ γενέσεως ἄχρι τελευτῆς, ἄχθος τοσοῦτον, οὐκ ἀποτίθεται νεκροφοροῦσα,
*De Agricultura Noe,* i. 305, Mang. (Richter, 2).

[170] Λάρναξ ἢ σορός, *De migratione Abrahami,* i. 438, *sub fin.,* Mang.
(Richter, 2).—σῆμα, *Leg. allegor.* i. 65, *sub fin.,* Mang. (Richter, 1).

[171] *Vita Mosis,* ii. 157, Mang. (Richter, 4): παντὶ γεννητῷ καὶ ἂν
σπουδαῖον ᾖ, παρ' ὅσον ἦλθεν εἰς γένεσιν, συμφυὲς τὸ ἁμαρτάνον ἐστίν.

[172] *De mutatione nominum,* i. 585, Mang. (Richter, 3): Τίς γὰρ, ὡς ὁ
Ἰὼβ φησι, καθαρὸς ἀπὸ ῥύπου, καὶ ἂν μία ἡμέρα ἐστὶν ἡ ζωή (Job xiv.
4 sq.).

[173] Comp. Gfrörer, i. 415 sqq. Dähne, i. 341–423. Zeller, iii. 2, pp.
402–416. Frankel in the above-cited article. Kähler, *Das Gewissen,* i. 1
(1878), p. 171 sqq.

[174] Φρόνησις, σωφροσύνη, ἀνδρία, δικαιοσύνη, *Leg. allegor.* i. 56, Mang.
(Richter, 1), and frequently.

[175] *Leg. allegor.* i. 111, *sub fin.,* Mang. (Richter, 1).

is only one good, morality;[176] like them he requires freedom
from all passions,[177] and the greatest possible simplicity of
life;[178] like them he also is a cosmopolitan.[179] But with all
this affinity Philo's ethic still essentially differs from the Stoic.
The Stoics refer man to his own strength; according to
Philo, man, as a sensuous being, is incapable of liberating
himself from sensuousness: for this he needs the help of God.
It is God who plants and promotes the virtues in the soul
of man. Only he, who honours Him and yields himself to
His influence, can attain to perfection.[180] True morality is,
as Plato teaches, the imitation of the Deity.[181] In this
religious basis of ethic Philo is very decidedly distinguished
from the Stoics. Political activity, and practical morality in
general, have a value only so far as they are a necessary
medium for contending against evil.[182] But knowledge also
must subserve this one object, and hence ethic is the most
important part of philosophy.[183] Nevertheless the purity of

[176] Μόνον εἶναι τὸ καλὸν ἀγαθόν, De posteritate Caini, i. 251, init., Mang.
(Richter, 2).

[177] Leg. allegor. i. 100, Mang. (Richter, 1): Ὁ δὲ ὄφις, ἡ ἡδονὴ, ἐξ ἑαυτῆς
ἐστὶ μοχθηρά. Διὰ τοῦτο ἐν μὲν σπουδαίῳ οὐχ εὑρίσκεται τὸ παράπαν, μόνος δὲ
αὐτῆς ὁ Φαῦλος ἀπολαύει.—Ibid. i. 113, init.: Μωϋσῆς δὲ ὅλον τὸν θυμὸν
ἐκτέμνειν καὶ ἀποκόπτειν οἴεται δεῖν τῆς ψυχῆς, οὐ μετριοπάθειαν, ἀλλὰ
συνόλως ἀπάθειαν ἀγαπῶν.

[178] De somniis, i. 639–665, Mang. (Richter, 3).—Leg. allegor. i. 115,
Mang. (Richter, 1).—Quod deterius potiori insidiatur, i. 198, init., Mang.
(Richter, 1).

[179] See Zeller, iii. 2, p. 404.

[180] Leg. allegor. i. 53, init., Mang. (Richter, 1): πρέπει τῷ θεῷ Φυτεύειν καὶ
οἰκοδομεῖν ἐν ψυχῇ τὰς ἀρετάς.—Ibid. i. 60: Ὅταν ἐκβῇ ὁ νοῦς ἑαυτοῦ καὶ
ἑαυτὸν ἀνενέγκῃ θεῷ, ὥσπερ ὁ γέλως Ἰσαάκ, τηνικαῦτα ὁμολογίαν τὴν πρὸς τὸν
ὄντα ποιεῖται. Ἕως δὲ αὐτὸν ὑποτίθηται ὡς αἴτιόν τινος, μακρὰν ἀφέστηκε τοῦ
παραχωρεῖν θεῷ καὶ ὁμολογεῖν αὐτῷ. Καὶ γὰρ αὐτὸ τοῦτο τὸ ἐξομολογεῖσθαι
νοητέον, ὅτι ἔργον ἐστὶν οὐχὶ τῆς ψυχῆς, ἀλλὰ τοῦ Φαίνοντος αὐτῇ θεοῦ τὸ
εὐχάριστον.—Ibid. i. 131: αὐτὸς γὰρ [ὁ κύριος] πατήρ ἐστι τῆς τελείας Φύσεως,
σπείρων ἐν ταῖς ψυχαῖς καὶ γεννῶν τὸ εὐδαιμονεῖν.

[181] De mundi opificio, i. 35, init., Mang. (Richter, 1).—De decalogo, ii.
193, init., Mang. (Richter, 4)—De caritate, ii. 404, init., Mang. (Richter,
5).—De migratione Abrahami, i. 456, med. 463, Mang. (Richter, 2).

[182] See Zeller, iii. 2, p. 406 sq.

[183] De mutatione nominum, i. 589, Mang. (Richter, 3): Καθάπερ δένδρων

life attained by such self-knowledge is not the ultimate and
supreme object of human development.   On the contrary the
origin of man being transcendental, the object of his development is likewise transcendental.   As it was by falling away
from God that he was entangled in this life of sense, so must
he struggle up from it to the direct *vision of God.*   This
object is attainable even in this earthly life.   For the truly
wise and virtuous man is lifted above and out of himself, and
in such ecstasy beholds and recognises Deity itself.   His own
consciousness sinks and disappears in the Divine light ; and
the Spirit of God dwells in him and stirs him like the strings
of a musical instrument.[184]   He, who has in this way attained
to the vision of the Divine, has reached the highest degree of
earthly happiness.   Beyond it lies only complete deliverance
from this body, that return of the soul to its original incor-
poreal condition, which is bestowed on those who have kept
themselves free from attachment to this sensuous body.[185]

---

οὐδὲν ὄφελος, εἰ μὴ καρπῶν οἰστικὰ γένοιτο, τὸν αὐτὸν δὲ τρόπον οὐδὲν Φυσιο-
λογίας, εἰ μὴ μέλλοι κτῆσιν ἀρετῆς ἐνεγκεῖν κ.τ.λ.—*De agricultura Noe,* i.
302, Mang. (Richter, 2).   In both passages Philo compares physics to the
plants and trees ; logic to the hedges and fences ; ethic to the fruits.   He
praises the Essenes for exclusively occupying themselves with ethic (*Quod
omnis probus liber,* ii. 458, Mang.).

[184] Philo thus addresses the soul in *Quis rerum divinarum heres.* i. 482,
Mang. (Richter, 3): σαυτὴν ἀπόδραθι καὶ ἔκστηθι σεαυτῆς, καθάπερ οἱ κορυβαν-
τιῶντες καὶ κατεχόμενοι, βακχευθεῖσα καὶ θεαφορηθεῖσα κατά τινα προφητικὸν
ἐπιθειασμόν.   Ἐνθουσιώσης γὰρ καὶ οὐκ ἔτι οὔσης ἐν ἑαυτῇ διανοίας, ἀλλ' ἔρωτ
οὐρανίῳ σεσοβημένης καὶ ἐκμεμηνυίας κ.τ.λ.   *Quis rerum divinarum heres.* i.
508 sqq., Mang. (Richter, 3), especially i. 511 (where Philo dilates at
length upon the ecstatic state).

[185] *De Abrahamo,* ii. 37, Mang. (Richter, 4): Wisdom teaches, τὸν
θάνατον νομίζειν μὴ σβέσιν ψυχῆς, ἀλλὰ χωρισμὸν καὶ διάζευξιν ἀπὸ σώματος,
ὅθεν ἦλθεν ἀπιούσης.   Ἦλθε δὲ, ὡς ἐν τῇ κοσμοποιίᾳ δεδήλωται, παρὰ θεοῦ.—
*Leg. allegor.* i. 65 (Richter, 1): Εὖ καὶ ὁ Ἡράκλειτος κατὰ τοῦτο Μωϋσέως
ἀκολουθήσας τῷ δόγματι· Φησὶ γὰρ· " Ζῶμεν τὸν ἐκείνων θάνατον, τεθνήκαμεν
δὲ τὸν ἐκείνων βίον," ὡς νῦν μὲν, ὅτε ἐνζῶμεν, τεθνηκυίας τῆς ψυχῆς, καὶ ὡς ἂν
ἐν σήματι τῷ σώματι ἐντετυμβευμένης· εἰ δὲ ἀποθάνοιμεν, τῆς ψυχῆς ζώσης τὸν
ἴδιον βίον, καὶ ἀπηλλαγμένης κακοῦ καὶ νεκροῦ τοῦ συνθέτου σώματος.   For
those who have not freed themselves from sense, Philo has to accept, after
the occurrence of natural death, a transition to another body, that is a
*transmigration of souls.*   See Zeller, iii. 2. 397

Philo's influence upon the two circles, which he had chiefly in view, viz. Judaism and heathenism, was impaired by the fact, that from his time onward Jewish Hellenism in general gradually lost in importance. On the one hand, the Pharisaic tendency gained strength in the Dispersion also, on the other Hellenistic Judaism was, in respect of its influence upon heathen circles, repressed, nay altogether dissolved by Christianity, which was now in its prime. Hence Judaeo-Hellenistic philosophy had gradually to give place to its stronger rival in both regions. Its influence was nevertheless still considerable. Jewish Rabbis and heathen neo-Platonists were more or less affected by it. Its strongest and most enduring influence was however exercised, in a direction which still lay outside Philo's horizon, upon the development of Christian dogma. The New Testament already shows unmistakeable traces of Philonean wisdom; and almost all the Greek Fathers of the first century, the apologists as well as the Alexandrians, the Gnostics as well as their adversaries, and even the great Greek theologians of subsequent centuries have, some more some less, either directly or indirectly, consciously or unconsciously drawn from Philo. But to follow out these traces lies beyond the province of this work.[186]

[186] Compare on the history of Philo's influence, Siegfried, *Philo*, pp. 273–399.

# LIST OF ABBREVIATIONS

| | |
|---|---|
| AJSL | American Journal of Semitic Languages |
| ATR | Anglican Theological Review |
| BS | Biblische Studien |
| BZ | Biblische Zeitschrift |
| CBQ | Catholic Biblical Quarterly |
| HTR | Harvard Theological Review |
| HZ | Historische Zeitschrift |
| JAOS | Journal of the American Oriental Society |
| JBL | Journal of Biblical Literature |
| JJS | Journal of Jewish Studies |
| JTS | Journal of Theological Studies |
| JQR | Jewish Quarterly Review |
| MGWJ | Monatsschrift für Geschichte und Wissenschaft des Judentums |
| NT | Novum Testamentum |
| OLZ | Orientalistische Literaturzeitung |
| PAAJR | Proceedings of the American Academy for Jewish Research |
| RB | Revue biblique |
| REJ | Revue des études juives |
| RHR | Revue de l'Histoire des Religions |
| RQ | Revue de Qumrân |
| RR | Review of Religion |
| TSK | Theologische Studien und Kritiken |
| VD | Verbum Domini |
| ZAW | Zeitschrift für alttestamentliche Wissenschaft |
| ZNW | Zeitschrift für neutestamentliche Wissenschaft |

# SELECTED BIBLIOGRAPHY

(1900–1970)

This list covers an introduction to the period and the various apocryphal works in the order of Schürer's presentation. Titles mentioned in the Introduction are not repeated here. Attention is called to Ralph Marcus' "Selected Bibliography (1920–1945) of the Jews in the Hellenistic-Roman Period" in the *Proceedings of the American Academy for Jewish Research,* XVI (1946–47). A general bibliography of Philo is given in E. R. Goodenough and H. L. Goodhart, *The Politics of Philo Judaeus* (New Haven, 1938); a selected bibliography in *The Essential Philo,* ed. Nahum N. Glatzer (New York, 1971); see also Earle Hilgert, *Philo Studies 1963–1970: A Bibliography,* in *Studia Philonica,* vol. I. On Josephus, see H. Schreckenberg, *Bibliographie zu Flavius Josephus* (Leiden, 1968). See also Louis Feldman, *Studies in Judaica: Scholarship on Philo and Josephus (1937–1962)* (New York, n.d.). On Qumran: William S. Lasor, *Bibliography of the Dead Sea Scrolls, 1948–1957* (Pasadena, Calif., 1958). On the Septuagint: Otto Eissfeldt, *The Old Testament: An Introduction* (New York and Evanston, 1965), pp. 701–15, 783 f.

INTRODUCTION

Baldensperger, W. *Die messianisch-apokalyptischen Hoffnungen des Judentums.* Strassburg, 1903.
Bevan, Edwyn R. "Hellenistic Judaism." In *The Legacy of Israel,* ed. E. R. Bevan and Charles Singer. Oxford, 1927.
Bloch, Joshua. *On the Apocalyptic in Judaism (JQR* Monograph Series, II). Philadelphia, 1952.

Bousset, W., and Gressmann, H. *Die Religion des Judentums im neutestamentlichen Zeitalter.* Tübingen, 1926.

Burkitt, F. C. *Jewish and Christian Apocalypses.* London, 1914.

Fiedler, M. J. *"Dikaiosune* in der diaspora-jüdischen und inter-testamentarischen Literatur," *Journal for the Study of Judaism,* I (1970).

Forster, A. Haire. "Propaganda Analysis Applied to Alexandrian-Jewish Apologetic." In *The Study of the Bible Today and Tomorrow,* ed. H. R. Willoughby. Chicago, 1947.

Gaster, Moses. *Studies and Texts in Folklore, Magic, Medieval Romance, Hebrew Apocrypha, etc.* 3 vols. London, 1925–28.

Ginzberg, Louis. *Legends of the Jews.* 7 vols. Philadelphia, 1909–38.

Goodenough, E. R. *Jewish Symbols in the Greco-Roman Period.* 8 vols. New York, 1953–68.

Goodspeed, E. J. *The Apocrypha: An American Translation.* Chicago, 1938.

———. *The Story of the Apocrypha.* Chicago, 1939.

Hadas, M. *Hellenistic Culture: Fusion and Diffusion.* New York, 1959.

Herford, R. T. *Talmud and Apocrypha.* London, 1933.

Hurwitz, Siegmund. *Die Gestalt des sterbenden Messias.* Zurich, 1958.

Laqueur, R. "Griechische Urkunden in der jüdisch-hellenistischen Literatur," *HZ,* CXXXVI (1927).

Lieberman, S. "How Much Greek in Jewish Palestine?" In *Biblical and Other Studies,* ed. A. Altmann (Philip W. Lown Institute of Advanced Judaic Studies, Brandeis University, Studies and Texts, I). Cambridge, Mass., 1963.

Moore, George Foot. *Judaism in the First Centuries of the Christian Era.* 2 vols. New York, 1971.

Oesterley, W. O. E. *Introduction to the Books of the Apocrypha.* New York and London, 1935; new ed., 1953.

Rankin, O. S. *Israel's Wisdom Literature.* Edinburgh, 1936; New York, 1969.

Rostovtzeff, M. *The Social and Economic History of the Hellenistic World.* 3 vols. Oxford, 1941.

Rowley, H. H. *The Relevance of the Apocalyptic.* London, 1944.

Stählin, Otto. "Die hellenistisch-jüdische Literatur." In *Geschichte der griechischen Literatur,* ed. Christ-Schmid, 6th ed., vol. II, pt. 1. Munich, 1920.

Stein, E. *Alttestamentliche Bibelkritik in der spät-hellenistischen Literatur.* Lemberg, 1935.

Täubler, Eugen. *Imperium Romanum.* Leipzig, 1913.

Wendland, P. *Die hellenistisch-römische Kultur in ihren Beziehungen zu Judentum und Christentum.* Tübingen, 1912.

Zeitlin, S. "Jewish Apocryphal Literature," *JQR*, XL (1949–50).


## THE MACCABEES

Abel, F. M. *Les Livres des Maccabées.* Paris, 1949.

Avi-Yonah, M. "The Battles in the Books of the Maccabees." In *Hans Lewy Memorial Volume* (in Hebrew). Jerusalem, 1949.

Maas, Max. "Die Maccabäer als christliche Heilige," *MGWJ*, XLIV (1900).

Marcus, R. "The Name Makkabaios." In *Joshua Starr Memorial Volume.* New York, 1953.

Schunk, K. D. *Die Quellen des I. und II. Makkabäerbuches.* Halle, 1954.

Stein, S. "The Liturgy of Hanukkah and the First Two Books of Maccabees," *JJS*, V (1954).


## THE FIRST BOOK OF MACCABEES

Bévenoth, H. "Prolegomena to the Maccabees," *Bibliotheca Sacra*, LXXXI (1924).

Dancy, J. C. *A Commentary on I Maccabees.* Oxford, 1954.

Farmer, W. R. *Maccabees, Zealots, and Josephus: An Inquiry into Jewish Nationalism in the Greco-Roman Period.* New York, 1956.

Fischel, H. A. *The First Book of Maccabees.* New York, 1948.

Heinemann, Isaak. "Wer veranlasste den Glaubenszwang der Makkabäerzeit?" *MGWJ*, XLVI (1938).

Momigliano, A. *Prime lines di storia della tradizione maccabaica.* Rome, 1930.

Niese, B. *Kritik der beiden Makkabäerbücher.* Berlin, 1900.

Salamina, L. *I Maccabei.* Turin, 1933.

Schwabe, M., and Melamed, E. Z. "Zum Texte der Seronepisode im I Macc. und bei Josephus," *MGWJ*, LXXII (1928).

Torrey, C. C. "Three Troublesome Proper Names in First Maccabees," *JBL*, LIII (1934).

Zeitlin, S. "The Tobias Family and the Hasmoneans," *PAAJR*, IV (1932–33).

## THE PSALMS OF SOLOMON

Aberbach, M. "The Historical Allusions of Chapters IV, XI and XIII of the Psalms of Solomon," *JQR*, XLI (1950–51).

Begrich, J. "Der Text der Psalmen Salomos," *ZNW*, XXXVIII (1939).

Dölger, F. "Zum 2ten Salomonischen Psalm," *Antike und Christentum*, I (1929).

Harris, J. R., and Mingana, A. *The Odes and Psalms of Solomon.* 2 vols. Manchester, England, 1916–20.

Jensen, Ludin. *Die spätjüdische Psalmendichtung.* Oslo, 1937.

O'Dell, Jerry. "The Religious Background of the Psalms of Solomon," *RQ*, III (1961–62).

## JESUS THE SON OF SIRACH

Baumgartner, W. "Die literarischen Gattungen in der Weisheit des Jesus Sirach," *ZAW*, XXXIV (1914).

Büchler, A. "Ben Sira's Conception of Sin and Atonement," *JQR*, XIII (1922–23) and XIV (1923–24).

Caspary, W. "Der Schriftgelehrte besingt seine Stellung: Sir. 51," *ZNW*, XXVIII (1929).

Driver, G. R. "Hebrew Notes on the Wisdom of Jesus ben Sirach," *JBL*, LIII (1934).

Ginsberg, H. L. "The Original Hebrew of Ben Sira XII, 10–14," *JBL*, LXXIV (1955).

Jacob, Edmond. "L'histoire d'Israël vue par Ben Sira." In *André Robert Festschrift.* Paris, 1957.

Lehmann, M. R. "Ben Sira and the Qumran Literature," *RQ*, III (1961–62).

Lévi, Israel. *The Hebrew Text of the Book of Ecclesiasticus* (Semitic Study Series, III). Leiden, 1904.

———. "Chapitre III de Ben Sira." In *Albert Harkavy Festschrift.* St. Petersburg, 1908.

Liebermann, S. "Ben Sira à la lumière de Yerouchalmi," *REJ*, CXCI–CXCII (1934).

Marcus, Joseph. "A Fifth Manuscript of Ben Sira," *JQR*, XXI (1930).

——. *The Newly Discovered Original Hebrew of Ben Sira* (Ecclus. 32:16–34). Philadelphia, 1931.

Margoliouth, D. "The Date of Ben Sira." In *Gaster Festschrift.* London, 1936.

Nöldeke, T. "Bemerkungen zum hebräischen Ben Sira," *ZAW,* XX (1900).

Power, A. D. *Ecclesiasticus or the Wisdom of Jesus Son of Sira.* London, 1939.

Rivkin, E. "Ben Sira and the Non-Existence of the Synagogue." In *Abba Hillel Silver Festschrift.* New York, 1963.

Schirmann, J. "A New Leaf from the Hebrew 'Ecclesiasticus' (Ben Sira)" (in Hebrew), *Tarbiz,* XXVII (1958–59).

Segal, M. H. *The Book of Wisdom of Ben Sira* (in Hebrew). Jerusalem, 1933.

——. "The Evolution of the Hebrew Text of Ben Sira," *JQR,* XXV (1934).

——. "The Fifth Ms. of Ben Sira," *Tarbiz,* II (1930–31).

Skehan, Patrick W. "Sirach 40:11–17," *CBQ,* XXX (1968).

Smend, Rudolf. *Die Weisheit des Jesus Sirach. Erklärt.* Berlin, 1906.

——. *Griechisch-syrisch-hebräischer Index zur Weisheit des Jesus Sirach.* Berlin, 1907.

Snaith, J. G. "Biblical Quotations in the Hebrew of Ecclesiasticus," *JTS,* XVIII (1967).

Taylor, W. R. *The Originality of the Hebrew Text of Ben Sira in the Light of Vocabulary and the Versions.* Toronto, 1910.

Torrey, C. C. "The Hebrew of the Geniza Sirach." In *Alexander Marx Jubilee Volume,* English Section. New York, 1950.

Winter, P. "Ben Sira and the Teaching of 'Two Ways,'" *VT,* V (1955).

Yadin, Y. "The Ben Sira Scroll Found at Masada" (in Hebrew). In *Sukenik Memorial Volume.* Jerusalem, 1967.

THE BOOK OF JUDITH

Büchler, A. "The Position of the Woman in the Book of Judith" (in Hebrew). In *Blau Festschrift.* Budapest, 1926.

Chajes, H. P. "Sefer Yehudit." In *Albert Harkavy Festschrift.* St. Petersburg, 1908.

Churgin, Pinchas. "The Book of Judith" (in Hebrew), *Horeb*, I (1934).

Haag, Ernst. *Studien zum Buch Judith*. Trier, 1963.

Meyer, Carl. "Zur Entstehungsgeschichte des Buches Judith," *Biblica*, III (1922).

Skehan, Patrick W. "The Hand of Judith," *CBQ*, XXV (1963).

Zimmermann, F. "Aids for the Recovery of the Hebrew Original of Judith," *JBL*, LVII (1938).


THE BOOK OF TOBIT

Abrahams, Israel. "Tobit Drama in the Sixteenth Century." In *Judaica: Hermann Cohen Festschrift*. Berlin, 1912.

Haupt, Paul. "Asmodeus," *JBL*, XL (1921).

Joüon, P. "Quelques hébraismes de Codex Sinaiticus de Tobie," *Biblica*, XIV (1933).

Müller, J. *Beiträge zur Kritik des Buches Tobit* (*ZAW*, Beihefte XIII). Giessen, 1908.

Priero, G. *Il Libro di Tobia: testi e introduzioni*. Como, 1924.

Simonsen, D. J. "Tobit-Aphorismen." In *David Kaufmann Gedenkbuch*. Breslau, 1900.

Torrey, C. C. "Nineveh in the Book of Tobit," *JBL*, XLI (1922).


THE BOOK OF ENOCH

Black, Matthew. "The Eschatology of the Similitudes of Enoch," *JTS*, N.S. III (1952).

Bonwetsch, G. N. *Die Bücher der Geheimnisse Henochs* (Texte und Untersuchungen, XLIV, 2). Leipzig, 1922.

Caplan, C. "The Pharisaic Character and Date of the Book of Enoch," *ATR*, XII (1930).

———. "The Angel of Peace, Uriel, Metatron (I Enoch 40:8), *ATR*, XIII (1931).

———. "The Original Language of Enoch," *Horeb*, II (1935–36).

Charles, R. H. *The Ethiopic Version of the Book of Enoch*. Oxford, 1906.

———. "The Date and Place of Writing of the Slavonic Enoch," *JTS*, XXII (1921).

Dix, G. H. "The Enochic Pentateuch," *JTS*, XXVII (1925).

Grelot, P. "La géographie mythique d'Hénoch et ses sources orientales," *RB*, LXV (1958).

———. "L'eschatologie des Esséniens et le livre d'Hénoch," *RQ*, I (1958–59).

Gry, Léon, "Mystique, gnostique juive et chrétienne en finale des paraboles d'Hénoch," *Muséon*, LII (1939).

Jansen, H. L. *Die Henochgestalt: eine vergleichende religionsgeschichtliche Untersuchung.* Oslo, 1939.

Messel, N. *Der Menschensohn in den Bilderreden des Henoch* (*ZAW*, Beihefte XXXV). Giessen, 1922.

Muilenberg, James. "The Son of Man in Daniel and the Ethiopic Apocalypse of Enoch," *JBL*, LXXIX (1960).

Pedersen, P. "Zur Erklärung der eschatologischen Visionen Henochs," *Islamica*, II (1926).

Rubinstein, Arie. "Observations on the Slavonic Book of Enoch," *JJS*, XIII (1962).

Schmidt, N. "The Two Recensions of Slavonic Enoch," *JAOS*, XLI (1921).

Sjöberg, Erik. *Der Menschensohn im äthiopischen Henochbuch.* Lund, 1946.

Stier, F. "Zur Komposition und Literaturkritik der Bilderreden des äthiopischen Henoch." In *Enno Littmann Festschrift.* Leiden, 1935.

Zimmermann, F. "The Bilingual Character of I Enoch," *JBL*, LX (1941).

Zuntz, G. "The Greek Text of Enoch 102:1–3," *JBL*, LXIII (1944).

———. "Enoch and the Last Judgment (102:1–3)," *JTS*, XLV (1944).

THE ASSUMPTIO MOSIS

Kuhn, Gottfried. "Zur Assumptio Mosis," *ZAW*, XLIII (1925).

Lattey, Cuthbert. "The Messianic Expectation in 'The Assumption of Moses,'" *CBQ*, IV (1942).

Rowley, H. H. "The Figure of 'Taxo' in the Assumption of Moses," *JBL*, LXIV (1945).

Wacholder, Ben Zion. *Nicolaus of Damascus* (University of California Publications in History, LXXV). Berkeley, 1962.

Zeitlin, S. "The Assumption of Moses and the Revolt of Bar Kokba," *JQR*, XXXVIII (1947–48).

## THE APOCALYPSE OF BARUCH

Gry, Léon. "La date de la fin des temps selon les révélations du Pseudo-Philon et de Baruch," *RB*, XLVIII (1939).

Sigwalt, C. "Die Chronologie der syrischen Baruchapokalypse," *BZ*, IX (1911).

Vallisolato, X. "Christologia in Apocalypsi Baruch syriaca," *VD*, XI (1931).

Zimmermann, F. "Textual Observations on the Apocalypse of Baruch," *JTS*, XL (1939).

———. "Translation and Mistranslation in the Apocalypse of Baruch." In *A. A. Neuman Festschrift*. Leiden, 1962.

## THE FOURTH BOOK OF EZRA

Blake, R. P. "The Georgian Text of 4 Esdras," *HTR*, XIX (1926).

Bloch, Joshua. "Was there a Greek Version of the Apocalypse of Ezra?" *JQR*, XLVI (1955–56).

Gry, Léon. *Les dires prophétiques d'Esdras*. 2 vols. Paris, 1938.

———. "La 'mort du Messie' en IV Esdras." In *Mémorial Lagrange*. Paris, 1940.

Kaminka, Armand. "Beiträge zur Erklärung der Esra-Apokalypse," *MGWJ*, LXXVI–LXXVII (1932–33).

———. *The Visions of Assir Shealtiel, King of Judah* (in Hebrew). Tel Aviv, 1936.

Metzger, Bruce M. "The Lost Section of II Esdras (=IV Ezra)," *JBL*, LXXVI (1957).

Montefiore, C. G. *IV Ezra: A Study in the Development of Universalism*. London, 1929.

Mundle, W. "Das religiöse Problem des IVten Esrabuches," *ZAW*, XLVII (1929).

Oesterley, W. O. E. *II Esdras: The Ezra Apocalypse*. London, 1933.

Pelaia, B. M. "Eschatalogia messianica IV libri Esdrae," *VD*, XI (1931).

Simonsen, D. "Ein Midrasch in IV. Buch Esra." In *Israel Lewy Festschrift*. Breslau, 1911.

Stone, Michael. "Some Remarks on the Textual Criticism of IV Ezra," *HTR*, LX (1967).

———. "The Concept of the Messiah in IV Ezra." In *Goodenough Memorial Volume*. Leiden, 1968.

Torrey, C. C. "A Revised View of First Esdras." In *Louis Ginzberg Jubilee Volume*, English Section. New York, 1945.

———. "The Messiah Son of Ephraim," *JBL*, LXVI (1947).

Zeitlin, S. "The Ben Sira Scroll from Masada," *JQR*, LVI (1966).

Zimmermann, F. "Underlying Documents of IV Ezra," *JQR*, LI (1960–61).


THE TESTAMENT OF ABRAHAM

Box, G. H. *The Testament of Abraham.* London, 1927.

Macurdy, G. H. "Platonic Orphism in the Testament of Abraham," *JBL*, LXI (1942).

Piatelli, Elio. "Il testamento di Abramo." In *Artum Memorial Volume*. Rome, 1966.

Riessler, P. "Das Testament Abrahams," *Theologische Quartalschrift*, CVI (1925).


THE TESTAMENTS OF THE TWELVE PATRIARCHS

Bickerman, E. "The Date of the Testaments of the Twelve Patriarchs," *JBL*, LXIX (1950).

Bousset, W. "Die Testamente der 12 Patriarchen," *ZNW*, I (1900).

De Jonge, M. *The Testaments of the Twelve Patriarchs.* Assen, 1953.

———. "Christian Influence in the Testaments of the Twelve Patriarchs," *NT*, IV (1960). See also *NT*, V (1962).

Eppel, R. *Le piétisme juif dans les Testaments des douze Patriarches.* Paris, 1930.

Hunkin, J. W. "The Testaments of the Twelve Patriarchs," *JTS*, XVI (1915).

Munich, P. A. "The Spirits in the Testaments of the Twelve Patriarchs," *Acta Orientalia*, Leiden, XIII (1935).

Perles, F. "Zur Erklärung von Testament Naphtali 2:8 ff.," *OLZ*, XXX (1927).

Rabin, Chaim. "The 'Teacher of Righteousness' in the 'Testaments of the Twelve Patriarchs'?" *JJS*, III (1952).

Segal, M. H. "The Descent of the Messianic King in the Testament of the Twelve Patriarchs" (in Hebrew), *Tarbiz*, XXI (1949–50).

Turdeanu, L. "Les Testaments des douze Patriarches en slave," *Journal for the Study of Judaism*, I (1970).


THE BOOK OF JUBILEES

Baumgarten, J. M. "The Calendar of the Book of Jubilees and the Bible" (in Hebrew), *Tarbiz*, XXXII (1962–63).

Büchler, A. "Studies in the Book of Jubilees." In *Israel Lévi Festschrift* (*REJ*, LXXXII). Paris, 1926.

———. "Traces des idées et des coutumes hellénistiques dans le Livre des Jubilés," *REJ*, LXXXIX (1930).

Finkelstein, Louis. "The Book of Jubilees and the Rabbinic Halaka," *HTR*, XVI (1932).

———. "The Date of the Book of Jubilees," *HTR*, XXXVI (1943).

Klein, S. "Palästinisches im Jubiläenbuch," *Zeitschrift des deutschen Palästinavereins*, LVII (1934).

Levi della Vida, G. "Una traccia del libro dei Guibilee nella letteratura arabica musulmana," *Orientalia*, I (1932).

Morgenstern, Julian. "The Calendar of the Book of Jubilees, its Origin and its Character," *VT*, V (1955).

Rowley, H. H., and Zeitlin, S. "Criteria for the Dating of Jubilees," *JQR*, XXXVI (1945–46).

Zeitlin, S. *The Book of Jubilees: Its Character and Significance.* Philadelphia, 1939.

———. "The Book of 'Jubilees' and the Pentateuch," *JQR*, XLVIII (1957–58).

———. "The Beginning of the Day in the Calendar of Jubilees," *JBL*, LXXVIII (1959).


ASCENSIO ISAIAE

Burch, V. "The Literary Unity of the *Ascensio Isaiae*," *JTS*, XX (1919).

———. "Material for the Interpretation of the Ascensio Isaiae," *JTS*, XXI (1920).

Charles, R. H. *The Ascension of Isaiah.* London, 1900.

Flusser, David. "The Apocryphal Book of Ascensio Isaiae and the Dead Sea Sect," *Israel Exploration Journal*, III (1953).

Lacau, P. "Fragments de l'Ascension d'Isaïe en copte." In *Mélanges L. Th. Lefort.* Louvain, 1946.

THE THIRD BOOK OF EZRA

Bayer, P. *Das dritte Buch Esdras und sein Verhältnis zu den Büchern Esra-Nehemia (BS,* XVI, 1). Freiburg, 1911.
Tedesche, Sidney. *A Critical Edition of I Esdras.* New Haven, 1928 (Dissertation, Yale University).
Torrey, C. C. *Ezra Studies.* Chicago, 1910.
―――. "A Revised View of First Esdras." In *Louis Ginzberg Jubilee Volume,* English Section. New York, 1945.
Walde, B. *Die Esdrasbücher der Septuaginta (BS,* XVIII, 4). Freiburg, 1913.

THE SECOND BOOK OF MACCABEES

Bickerman, E. "Ein jüdischer Festbrief vom Jahre 124 v. Chr," *ZNW,* XXXII (1933).
Finkelstein, L. "The Family of the High Priest Menelaus," *HTR,* XXXVI (1943).
Katz, Peter. "The Text of 2 Maccabees Reconsidered," *ZNW,* LI (1960).
Kraeling, C. H. "The Jewish Community at Antioch," *JBL,* LI (1932).
Laqueur, R. *Kritische Untersuchungen zum zweiten Makkabäerbuche.* Strassburg, 1904.
Tcherikover, V. "The Documents in the Second Book of Maccabees" (in Hebrew), *Tarbiz,* I (1930).
Torrey, C. C. "The Letter Prefixed to Second Maccabees," *JAOS,* LX (1940).

THE THIRD BOOK OF MACCABEES

Baars, W. "Eine neue griechische Handschrift des 3. Makkabäerbuches," *VT,* XIII (1963).
Cohen, Jakob. *Judaica et Aegyptiaca: de Maccabaeorum libro III, quaestiones historicae.* Groningen, 1941.
Hadas, M. "III Maccabees and the Tradition of Patriotic Romance," *Chronique d'Égypte,* XLVII, 1949.
―――. "III Maccabees and Greek Romance," *RR,* XIII (1949).

————, trans. *The Third and Fourth Books of Maccabees*. New York, 1953.

Loewe, R. "A Jewish Counterpart to the Acts of the Alexandrians," *JJS*, XII (1961).

Tcherikover, V. "The Third Book of Maccabees as a Historical Source of the Augustan Period" (in Hebrew), *Zion*, X (1945).

Tracy, S. "Aristeas and III Maccabees." In *Yale Classical Studies*, I. New Haven, 1928.

Willrich, H. "Der historische Kern des III. Makkabäerbuches," *Hermes*, XXXIX (1904).


THE WISDOM OF SOLOMON

Cohn, J. "Weltschöpfung in der Sapienz." In *Jakob Guttmann Festschrift*. Leipzig, 1915.

Feldmann, F. *Die Weisheit Salomos*. Bonn, 1926.

Fichtner, J. *Die Weisheit Salomos*. Tübingen, 1937.

————. "Die Stellung der Sapientia Salomonis in der Literatur- und Geistesgeschichte ihrer Zeit," *ZNW*, XXXVI (1938).

Grelot, P. "L'eschatologie de la Sagesse et les apocalypses juives." In *Mémorial Gelin*, 1961.

Heinemann, I. "Die griechische Quelle der 'Weisheit Salomos.'" In *Jahresbericht des jüdisch-theologischen Seminars für das Jahr 1920*. Breslau, 1921.

Kuhn, G. "Beiträge zur Erklärung der Weisheit," *ZNW*, XXVIII (1929).

————. "Exegetische und textkritische Anmerkungen zum Buche der Weisheit," *TSK*, CIII (1931).

Lange, Stella. "The Wisdom of Solomon and Plato," *JBL*, LV (1936).

Macdonald, D. B. *The Hebrew Philosophical Genius*. Princeton, 1936.

Marx, A. "An Aramaic Fragment of the Wisdom of Solomon," *JBL*, XL (1921).

Purinton, Carl. *Translation Greek in the Wisdom of Solomon*. New Haven, 1928 (Dissertation, Yale University); *JBL*, XLVII (1928).

Reese, James M. "Plan and Structure in the Book of Wisdom," *CBQ*, XXVII (1965).

Reider, J. *The Book of Wisdom*. New York, 1957.

Romaniuk, C. "Le traducteur grec du livre de Jésus Ben Sira n'est-il pas l'auteur du livre de la Sagesse?" *Revista Biblica,* XV (1967) ; see G. Scarpat, *ibid.,* and Romaniuk's answer, *ibid.*

Schütz, R. *Les idées eschatologiques du livre de la Sagesse.* Paris, 1935.

Skehan, Patrick W. *The Literary Relationship between the Book of Wisdom and the Protocanonical Wisdom Books of the O.T.* Washington, D.C., 1938.

————. "Notes on the Latin Text of the Book of Wisdom," *CBQ,* IV (1942).

Speiser, E. A. "The Hebrew Origin of the First Part of the Book of Wisdom," *JQR,* XIV (1923–24).

Weinfeld, M. "Deuteronomy and Wisdom" (in Hebrew). In *Y. Kaufmann Jubilee Volume.* Jerusalem, 1961.

Wright, A. G. "Numerical Patterns in the Book of Wisdom," *CBQ,* XXIX (1967).

————. "The Structure of the Book of Wisdom," *Biblica,* XLVIII (1967).

THE FOURTH BOOK OF MACCABEES

Bickerman, E. "The Date of Fourth Maccabees." In *Louis Ginzberg Memorial Volume,* English Section. New York, 1945.

Dörrie, H. *Passio SS. Machabaeorum: die antike lateinische Uebersetzung des IV Makkabäerbuches.* Göttingen, 1938.

Gutman, Yehoshua. "The Story of the Mother and Her Seven Sons in the Second and the Fourth Maccabees" (in Hebrew). In *Hans Lewy Memorial Volume.* Jerusalem, 1949.

Heinemann, I. "Das IV. Makkabäerbuch." In *Realenzyklopädie der klassischen Altertumswissenschaft,* XIV, ed. Pauly-Kroll.

Zeitlin, S. "The Legend of the Ten Martyrs and Its Apocalyptic Origin," *JQR,* XXXVI (1945–46).

THE SIBYLLINES

Kerényi, K. "Das persische Millennium im Mahabharata, bei der Sibylle und Vergil," *Klio,* XXIX (1936).

Kocsis, E. "Ost-West Gegensatz in den jüdischen Sibyllinen," *NT,* V (1962).

Kugler, F. X. *Sibyllinischer Sternkampf und Phaeton.* Münster, 1927.

Kurfess, A. "Horaz und Vergil und die jüdische Sibylle," *Pastor Bonus,* XLV (1934).

Rowley, H. H. "The Interpretation and Date of Sibylline Oracles III, 388–400," *ZAW,* XLIV (1926).

ARISTEAS

Bickerman, E. "Zur Datierung des Pseudo-Aristeas," *ZNW,* XXIX (1930).

———. "Notes sur la chancellerie des Lagides," *Revue Internationale des Droits de l'Antiquité,* IX (1962).

Gooding, D. W. "Aristeas and the Septuagint Origins: A Review of Recent Studies," *VT,* XIII (1963).

Gutman, Yehoshua. "The Letter of Aristeas" (in Hebrew), *Ha-Goren,* X (1928).

Jellicoe, S. "Aristeas, Philo and the Septuagint Vorlage," *JTS,* XII (1961).

———. "St. Luke and the Letter of Aristeas," *JBL,* LXXX (1961).

Meecham, H. D. *The Oldest Version of the Bible: "Aristeas" on its Traditional Origin, etc.* London, 1932.

———. *The Letter of Aristeas: A Linguistic Study.* Manchester, England, 1935.

Momigliano, A. "Per la data e la caratteristica della lettera di Aristea," *Aegyptus,* XII (1932).

Staehlin, G. "Josephus und der Aristeasbrief," *TSK,* CII (1930).

Stein, M. "The Author of the Letter of Aristeas as an Apologist of Judaism" (in Hebrew), *Zion,* I (1936).

Tcherikover, V. "The Ideology of the Letter of Aristeas," *HTR,* LI (1958).

Thackeray, H. St. John, trans. *The Letter of Aristeas.* London, 1917.

Wendland, P. "Observationes criticae in Aristeae epistulam." In *Johannes Vahlen Festschrift.* Berlin, 1900.

# INDEX